The City of Zloczow
(Zolochiv, Ukraine)

Translation of
Sefer kehilat Zloczow

Original Book Edited by: Baruch Karu (Krupnik)

Originally published in Tel Aviv 1967

JewishGen
מרכז עולמי לגנאלוגיה יהודית
The Global Home for Jewish Genealogy

A Publication of JewishGen, INC
Edmond J. Safra Plaza, 36 Battery Place, New York, NY 10280
646.494.5972 | info@JewishGen.org | www.jewishgen.org

MUSEUM OF JEWISH HERITAGE
A LIVING MEMORIAL TO THE HOLOCAUST

The City of Zloczow (Zolochiv, Ukraine)
Translation of *Sefer kehilat Zloczow*

Copyright © 2022 by JewishGen, INC All rights reserved.
First Printing: October 2022, Tishrei 5783

Editor of Original Yizkor Book: Baruch Karu (Krupnik)
Project Coordinator: Moshe Kuten
Cover Design: Rachel Kolokoff Hopper
Layout and Name Indexing: Jonathan Wind
Hebrew Translations: Moshe Kuten
Photo Extraction: Stefanie Holzman

Printed in the United States of America by Lightning Source, Inc.

Library of Congress Control Number (LCCN): 2022944853

ISBN: 978-1-954176-56-0 (hard cover: 426 pages, alk. paper)

About JewishGen.org

JewishGen, an affiliate of the Museum of Jewish Heritage - A Living Memorial to the Holocaust, serves as the global home for Jewish genealogy.

Featuring unparalleled access to 30+ million records, it offers unique search tools, along with opportunities for researchers to connect with others who share similar interests. Award winning resources such as the Family Finder, Discussion Groups, and ViewMate, are relied upon by thousands each day.

In addition, JewishGen's extensive informational, educational and historical offerings, such as the Jewish Communities Database, Yizkor Book translations, InfoFiles, Family Tree of the Jewish People, and KehilaLinks, provide critical insights, first-hand accounts, and context about Jewish communal and familial life throughout the world.

Offered as a free resource, JewishGen.org has facilitated thousands of family connections and success stories, and is currently engaged in an intensive expansion effort that will bring many more records, tools, and resources to its collections.

Please visit https://www.jewishgen.org/ to learn more.

Executive Director: Avraham Groll

About the JewishGen Yizkor Book Project

Yizkor Books (Memorial Books) were traditionally written to memorialize the names of departed family and martyrs during holiday services in the synagogue (a practice that still exists in many synagogues today).

Over the centuries, as a result of countless persecutions and horrific atrocities committed against the Jews, Yizkor Books (Sefer Zikaron in Hebrew) were expanded to include more historical information, such as biographical sketches of famous personalities and descriptions of daily town life.

Following the Holocaust, the idea of remembrance and learning took on an urgent and crucial importance. Survivors of the Holocaust sought out other surviving residents of their former towns to memorialize and document the names and way of life of those who were ruthlessly murdered by the Nazis. These remembrances were documented in Yizkor Books, hundreds of which were published in the first decades after the Holocaust.

Most of these books were published privately, or through landsmanshaftn (social organizations comprised of members originating from the same European town or region) that still existed, and were often distributed free of charge. Sadly, the languages used to document these crucial histories and links to our past, Yiddish and Hebrew, are no longer commonly understood by a significant percentage of Jews today. As a result, JewishGen has undertaken the sacred responsibility of translating these books into English so that the culture and way of life of these communities will be preserved and transmitted to future generations.

In 1986, a group of farsighted JewishGenners started a project to pool their efforts together in groups based upon their ancestors from each town and donate money to get the Yizkor books of their ancestral towns translated into English. As the translated material became available, it was made accessible for free at www.JewishGen.org/Yizkor. Hardcover copies can be purchased by visiting https://www.jewishgen.org/Yizkor/ybip.html (see below).

It is our hope that the translation of these books into English (and other languages) will assist the countless Jewish family researchers who are so desperately seeking to forge a connection with their heritage.

Director of JewishGen Yizkor Book Project: Lance Ackerfeld

About JewishGen Press

JewishGen Press (formerly the Yizkor Books-in-Print Project) is the publishing division of JewishGen.org, and provides a venue for the publication of non-fiction books pertaining to Jewish genealogy, history, culture, and heritage.

In addition to the Yizkor Book category, publications in the Other Non-Fiction category include Shoah memoirs and research, genealogical research, collections of genealogical and historical materials, biographies, diaries and letters, studies of Jewish experience and cultural life in the past, academic theses, and other books of interest to the Jewish community.

Please visit https://www.jewishgen.org/Yizkor/ybip.html to learn more.

Director of JewishGen Press: Joel Alpert
Managing Editor - Jessica Feinstein
Publications Manager - Susan Rosin

Notes to the Reader

The images in the original book were reproduced from photographs from the time of the first edition. These reproductions were already of poor quality, being pre-war and at least 30 or more years old. As a result the images in the book are not very good and the best achievable.

A reader can view the original scans of the book on the websites listed below.

The original book can be seen online at the Yiddish Book Center website:

https://www.yiddishbookcenter.org/collections/yizkor-books/yzk-nybc314130/boneh-eli-ezer-lask-i-m-sefer-kehilat-zlots-ov

or

at the New York Public Library Digital Collections website:

https://digitalcollections.nypl.org/items/28c6dfd0-232c-0133-3191-58d385a7b928

To obtain a list of Shoah victims from Zloczow (Zolochiv, Ukraine), the reader should access the Yad Vashem web site listed below; one can also search for specific family names using family name option. These lists are continually updated by Yad Vashem, so it is worthwhile to periodically search these lists.

There is more valuable information (including the Pages of Testimony, etc.) available on this website: https://yvng.yadvashem.org/

A list of all books available from JewishGen Press along with prices is available at: https://www.jewishgen.org/Yizkor/ybip.html

Photo Credits

Front Cover Illustration:
A picture from Zloczow of the painter Schorr. [Columns 475-476].

Back Cover Poem: *A Mourning Poem about the Destruction of Zloczow* by Yekhiel Imber. [Columns 239-240].

Back Cover Photos:

Top left: *A public soup kitchen for children.* [Columns 37-38].
Top right: *Dr. Hirshhorn and his family.* [Column 470].
Bottom left: *R' Khaim Moshe Zilbershitz.* [Columns 433-434].
Bottom right: *A group of girls in Zloczow.* [Columns 27-28].

Front and Back Cover Background Photo: *Wildflowers* by Rachel Kolokoff Hopper

Geopolitical Information

Zolochiv, Ukraine is located at 49°48' N 24°54' E and 253 miles W of Kyyiv

	Town	District	Province	Country
Before WWI (c. 1900):	Złoczów	Złoczów	Galicia	Austrian Empire
Between the wars (c. 1930):	Złoczów	Złoczów	Tarnopol	Poland
After WWII (c. 1950):	Zolochev			Soviet Union
Today (c. 2000):	Zolochiv			Ukraine

Alternate Names for the Town:

Zolochiv [Ukr], Złoczów [Pol], Zlotshev [Yid], Zolochev [Rus], Solotschiw [Ger], Zlochev, Zlochuv, Zlotchev, Zolociv

Nearby Jewish Communities:

Sasiv 5 miles NNE

Bilyi Kamin 8 miles NNW

Skvaryava 8 miles NW

Holohory 9 miles WSW

Olesko 12 miles N

Pomoryany 12 miles S

Dunayev 13 miles SSW

Yezezhanka 13 miles SE

Zboriv 14 miles SE

Sokolivka 16 miles N

Busk 17 miles NW

Hlyniany 17 miles W

Peremyshlyany 18 miles WSW

Narayiv 19 miles SSW

Pidkamin 21 miles ENE

Zaliztsi 21 miles E

Brody 23 miles NNE

Ozerna 23 miles ESE

Svirzh 23 miles WSW

Toporiv 23 miles NNW

Berezhany 24 miles S

Mykolayiv 25 miles W

Stratin 25 miles SSW

Stanislavchyk 25 miles N

Didyliv 25 miles WNW

Sokolya 26 miles NW

Kozliv 27 miles SE

Novyy Oleksinets 27 miles E

Kozova 28 miles SSE

Radyvyliv 28 miles NE

Novyy Yarychiv 28 miles WNW

Borshchovychi 29 miles W

Lopatyn 29 miles N

Bobrka 29 miles WSW

Rohatyn 29 miles SSW

Zvenyhorod 29 miles W

Kukeziv 30 miles WNW

Novi Strilyshcha 30 miles SW

Pochayev 30 miles ENE

Dmytriv 30 miles NNW

Jewish Population: 4,046 (in 1890), 5,744 (in 1921)

Map of Ukraine with **Zolochiv** indicated

Table of Contents

Chapter D: Personalities and People in Zloczow

The City of Zloczow
(Zolochiv, Ukraine)

49°48' / 24°54'

Translation of
Sefer kehilat Zloczow

Edited by: Baruch Karu (Krupnik)

Published in Tel Aviv 1967

*****

Acknowledgments

Project Coordinator: Moshe Kutten

Our sincere appreciation to Genia Hollander for typing up the English text to facilitate its addition to this project and to Stefanie Holzman for extracting the pictures from the original book, enabling their addition to the project.

This is a translation from: *Sefer kehilat Zloczow* (The city of Zloczow),
ed. Baruch Karu (Krupnik), Zloczow Society, Published in Tel Aviv 1967 (748 cols, HE)

*****

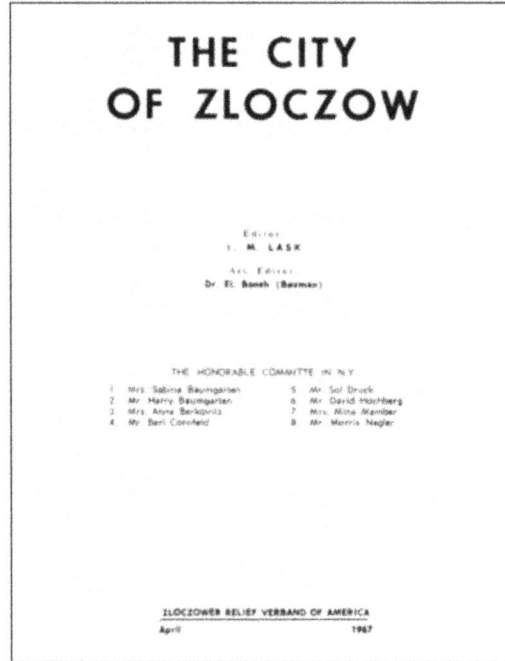

Zloczow's Community Book

[blank]

Zloczow's [Zolochiv] Community Book

Editor:
Barukh Karu

Ass. Editor:
Dr. Eliezer Boneh (Bauman)

Members of the Editorial Committee:
D. Shlomo Altman, Member of the Knesset Dr. Yaakov Katz, Ben–Tzion Tzverdling, Moshe Reizer, Mordekhai Deutsch

Idit Publishing – The Organization of Zloczow's Expatriates

1967 5727

[Columns 7-8]

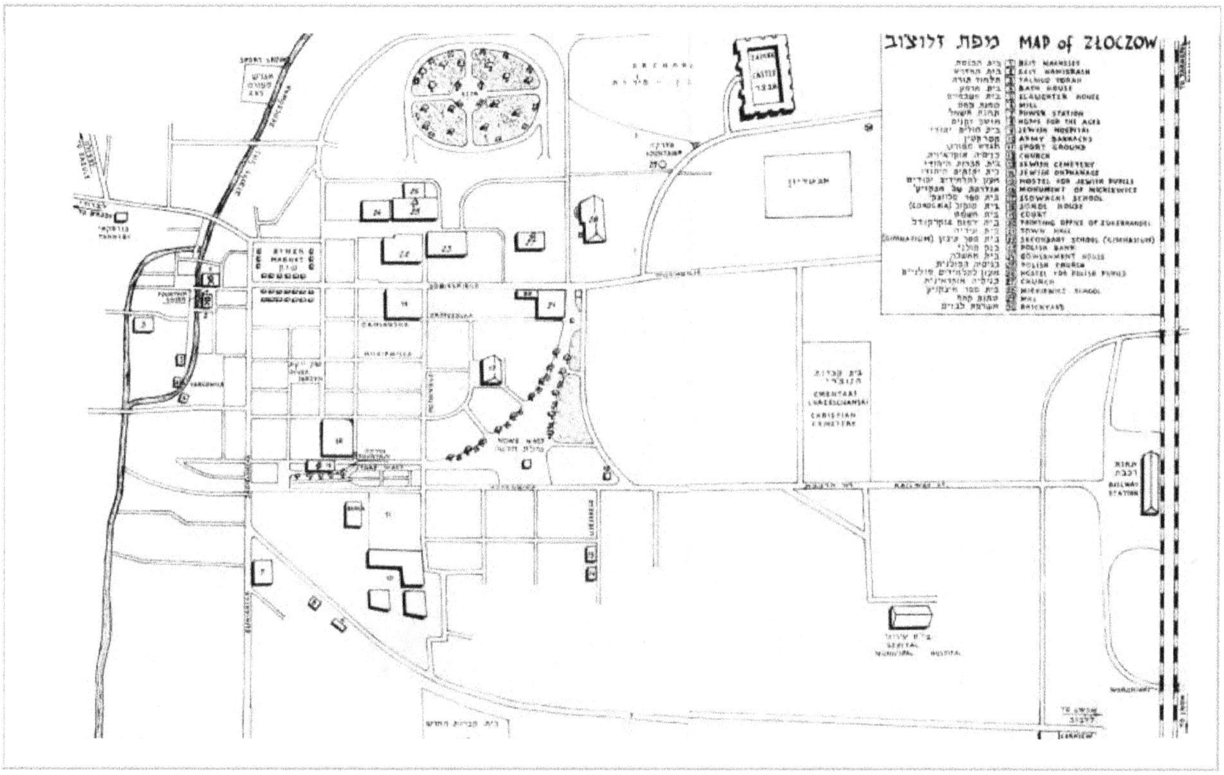

[Columns 9-10]

The Committee Members of the Organization of Zloczow's Expatriates in Israel 1967

1. Dr. Sh. Altman

2. Dr. E. Boneh

3. Sh. Buchach

4. Engineer Sh. Bar-Am

5. Mr. E. Davidson

6. Mr. M. Hokhman

7. Mr. Y. Weis

8. Mr. Y. Kahana

9. Member of the Knesset Y. Katz

10. Mrs. A Laks

11. Mr. K. Lans

12. Mr. M. Merder

13. Mrs. S. Noisberg (Ofer)

14. Mr. Y, Fenster

15. Mr. B Tzverdling

16. Mr. A. Ron

17. Mr. M. Reiser

[Columns 13-14]

Introduction

Note: The Hebrew version is a short version of Dr. Boneh's Introduction on column 11 of the English section

Eulogy for the victims of the Nazis, at the memorial for Zloczow natives, Israel, 1964

[Columns 15-16]

Gathering of Zloczow Natives, 1964

[Columns 17-18]

The presidential desk during a gathering in Israel, 1964

Chapter A

The City of Zloczow [Zolochiv] and its History

Translated by Moshe Kutten

[Columns 23-24]

[blank]

[Columns 25-26]

Dr. Nathan Michael Gelber, one of the greatest historians of Polish Jewry, was born in the city of Lviv [Lvov], and was descended from a family of scholars. His historical research was first published in the monthly magazine of the Zionist academic youth "Moriah". His scientific work was conducted along two routes: Research of the history of Jewish communities in Poland and the history of the Zionist idea. We received the sorrowful news about the passing of Dr. Gelber before the book was published.

* * *

The History of the City

by N. Gelber

Chapter 1 – The City

The oldest settlements in the district of Zloczow [Zolochiv] are Zborivv [Zborov] and Olesko. [The Polish King] Casimir the Great conquered these settlements from the Ruthenians and handed them over to Vladislav Opolchik, who was appointed the governor of Reisyn [Red Russia and Eastern Galitsia]. The area did not experience peace for a long time. Lithuania and Poland waged wars there. In 1431 the army of [Polish King] Jagiello conquered it from [Lithuanian Grand Duke] Svidrigiello. Jan Sienianski, who excelled in that war, was awarded a lease of Olesko and its environs, which included Zloczow.

As part of that award, which was granted by King Wladyslaw Warneñczyk in 1441, Jan Sienianski was allowed to establish cities and towns according to the "Magdenburgian Law" [An urban law, developed in the German town of Magdeburg, which became a basis for new city constitutions in Central and Eastern Europe].

The fortress of Zloczow was built during that lease along with 97 villages which were leased to a flag carrier by the name of Jarzhi Strumilen. However, due to conflicts with the former lease owner, the king handed over Zloczow, in 1443, to Michael of Buchach, who committed to settling in Zloczow.

Its geographic situation – on the road leading to the city of Lviv contributed greatly to the economic development of Zloczow. The people who traveled on that road were always stopping at Zloczow. The local people demanded that the travelers pay a customs tax, although they were not entitled to collect it. The city prosecutor of Lviv, Mikolai Gerzimalah, brought this issue before the court, which issued a ruling prohibiting the collection of the customs tax.

A group of lawyers in Zloczow

[Columns 27-28]

A group of girls in Zloczow

Zloczow is mentioned as a private city with a customs station where municipal taxes were collected as early as 1494.

The city suffered from Tatar invasions from the start. The invasions took place in 1512, 1514, 1519, and 1524. In 1523, Stanislaw Sienianski received a Magdenburg Law permit from King Zygmunt and authorization for holding a market every Saturday and two annual fairs.

As mentioned above, Zloczow was declared a city toward the end of the 15th century. However, official approval of the city's special status was only received in 1527.

The city's owner, Stanislaw Sienianski, quarreled with the church because of a private matter. He was living in adultery with a foreigner – Dorota of Sandomierz and the archbishop of Dunajow excommunicated him from the church in 1528. This was probably why, in 1532, Stanislaw Sienianski sold Zloczow and its citadel to the new owner – Jedrzej Gorka. Gorka leased Zloczow to Zborovski for 70,000 gold bullions.

Jedrzej Gorka exempted the city dwellers from paying any taxes following the destruction caused by the enemy invasion in 1537. However, they were burdened with the improvement of the city's fortifications. Jedrzej was named "the city's restorer" as he did much for the city's rehabilitation caused by the wars and invasions.

In 1553, King Zygmunt August allowed the city to hold a third annual fair.

In 1592, upon the death of Stanislav, the last member of the Gorka family, Zloczow was inherited by Barbara Charnkovska, the sister of Lukasz Gorka. Following quarrels with Zborovski, Barbara's sons sold Zloczow along with 18 villages to Marek Sobieski, the fraternal grandfather of King Sobieski.

The city was significantly developed during the ownership period of the Marek Sobieski family. However, the good days did not last. The Cossacks attacked the city in 1649, burnt it, and slaughtered most of its residents.

Following the victory by the Poles [over the Ukrainian Cossacks], in the Battle of Berestechko, a pandemic erupted in Zloczow, which resulted in the death of numerous people. In 1650, a recommendation was forwarded to the Sejm representatives to exempt Zloczow from paying taxes.

Zloczow also suffered from the war with the Ottomans during 1666 – 1667 and later in 1675 and 1678.

Jakub Sobieski took care of the defense needs of the city and its development. During his time, essential industrial plants such as sawmills, brick kilns, marble quarries, and glass kilns were built in the city. A paper factory and a wine and liquor brewery were established, and orchards were planted in Sasiv [Sasov]

Armenians, headed by Daniel Dzarogovitch (1686 – 1687) settled in Zloczow during the reign of King Sobieski. They established their own community, headed by a leader who had judicial authority. The Armenians were exempted from paying any taxes or duties for 20 years. They built their own church, which existed until 1800. During that year, the last Armenian priest, Bazilo Daminovitz, passed away.

The German tourist, Olrikh Vardom who toured Poland during the years 1678 – 1680, arrived at Zloczow on 24 July 1671 and found it beautiful.

The French – Dalreikh wrote in 1867: "The city was built, almost entirely, with wooden houses and was well populated, particularly by Jews."

Since the city was built almost entirely from wood, it is no surprise that it suffered greatly from fires during 1671 – 1672. However, the city managed to recover after every fire.

Swedes invaded the city in 1702.

[Columns 29-30]

Later on, Moscow's armies passed through the city. They burdened the city with fines and taxes and confiscated jewelry and monies. That led to an economic collapse. It was so severe that the city was largely uninhabited during the first half of the 18th century. The roads around the city were in just a poor state, and travelers avoided them altogether. There were only 269 houses in the city during the second half of the 18th century. Among them were 139 large houses of gentiles, 70 large houses of Jews, and the rest were small houses of both gentiles and Jews.

The "Piarists" came to Zloczow in 1731 on the initiative of Jakub Sobieski, and in 1742, they established an elementary school in the city.

Jakub Sobieski's grandmother –princess Maria Karolina de Bouillon, purchased the city and villages in 1740. [She, in turn, sold everything (in the form of a donation.) to Prince Michal Casimir Radziwill, the grandson of Katarzyna Sobieska, Jana´s sister].

Prince Radziwill tried to revive the trade in the city. He made efforts to direct the trade to the roads connecting the city to the cities of Ternopil [Tarnopol] and Brody. However, he was forced to give up the idea and declare bankruptcy due to the many debts, which he was burdened with.

Zloczow, which came under the ownership of Princess Sapieha, remained in private hands and was subjected to the rule of its owners until the 19th century, however, it did enjoy a certain autonomy in judiciary and management matters. Its residents, including the Jews, had to pay property taxes (for houses and land) to the city's owners and to perform tasks associated with the construction of roads and bridges and the erection of fences.

Residents who worked in agriculture were forced to provide agricultural services and pay taxes related to various crops.

Artisans were organized in guilds, with the Czechs and the Armenians organized in their own separate guilds.

The guilds were strictly vigilant about guarding the rights of the artisans. Their main interest was to maintain a monopoly on marketing their products in the city and the surrounding area. The rights they received in that regard guaranteed the ability to market their products in a circle of 2 miles around the city. The guilds who enjoyed such rights were mainly the shoemakers and the weavers. Residents of the city suburbs cultivated beekeeping. They also developed fish farming, which was directed only toward the wholesale trade.

With the Austrian conquest and the establishment of the district office, Zloczow experienced a significant transformation. The "Magdenburg Law" was entirely voided.

In 1789, a general school was established in the city, where the teaching language was German [1]. The number of allowed annual fairs was increased to four with a duration of up to eight days each.

In 1786, the municipality requested to approve of its city charter from the days of the Polish regime. The authorities ignored these requests and continued to manage the city affairs, including the selection of the mayor and establishment of the various offices, according to Austrian laws. In 1805, the election law was made void and the regime appointed the mayors.

Among all of these mayors, Mayor Eiechmuller stood out as a person who did the most for the improvement of the city and its buildings. In 1842 he lobbied to establish a high school. It was established in 1873, initially only containing four classes. In 1881, it was completed and contained all of its classes.

In 1866, a city law was enacted, and Zloczow was allowed to elect its city management. There were 650 brick houses in 1867, and the population reached 6000.

The industry in Zloczow experienced substantial development during the Austrian regime. At the neighboring village of Kotkorz, the residents were involved in the production of silk belts. Factories for producing gunpowder and paper were also established there. Factories for wax and candles and an iron casting plant were established in the village of Kavarovtza.

During the Austrian regime, when the anti-church policy of Emperor Joseph was enacted, the buildings of the Piarists and the Reformed Church monasteries, built by Michael Radziwill in the year 1750, were confiscated and converted to army barracks. The regime did not touch the Basilian (Greek–Catholic) monastery which was built by Jan Sobieski in 1665.

Toward the end of the 18th century, The Ruthenians asked the Austrian authorities to give them the ruined Piarist church, as their own Ruthenian church was too small. According to an agreement signed between the Poles and the Ruthenians, the Poles handed over their church to the Ruthenians for the Piarist Church, which became the main Catholic church.

The Austrian authorities took care to improve the health situation. A hospital for the poor already existed, but there was neither a specialist physician nor a pharmacy. In 1788, the authorities transferred the Dominican pharmacy of Podkamen to Zloczow. A district specialist physician and a paramedic and a midwife were nominated

[Column 31]

A group of the "Zionist Youth", 1938

Due to Radziwill's bankruptcy, a public auction of Zloczow and its villages was held in 1801. It was sold to Count Lukasz Komarnitzki, an arrogant Polish nobleman character who was an appellate counselor in Lviv. He renovated the castle abut sold it afterward.

When in 1873 In 1873, the walls of the castle were about to be torn down, the government bought it (under the initiative of the high court president Pozhniak) and turned it into a prison and the site of the offices of the court.

In 1810, following the Austrian–French war, 10 villages (containing 668 homes, 983 families, and 4012 people) were separated from the Zloczow district and annexed by Russia.

Starting in 1867, the city changed owners. After Komarnitzki came Frankovski and Lind, and following them the estates were purchased by Halberthal, Weinberg and the last one – Seltzer.

A new chapter in the development of the city began in 1870 with the opening of the railroad between Lviv and Brody with a side branch of Zloczow–Ternopol–Podbolitzki. The trade and the industry began to flourish.

By 1918, Zloczow was the home of the district government, the district court, the district assembly, the district education assembly, and the headquarters of the 80th battalion and the gendarme. Except for the high school, the city had a general school for boys, established by the district government and maintained by Radziwill and later on by Princess Sapieha. Starting in 1853, the city also had a general school for girls. Among other institutions, we should mention the clinic established by Jan Sobieski in 1636 and the Hospital established in 1847.

Until 1848, the teaching language in school was German. After that Polish. The Ruthenian language was taught compulsorily.

[Column 32]

Chapter 2 - The Jewish Community During the Polish Regime

According to tradition, the oldest gravestones in the cemetery were from the 16th century. The first Jews resided in the city in the 15th century, before an organized community was in place. There were no Jews in the neighboring towns either– Mykolaiv, Pomorzany, and Sasiv [Sasov], until 1628.

One of the first Jews in Zloczow was Israel, son of Yosef Zlotsovsky, whose name points to his origin [Zlots'ov is the Yiddish spelling of Zloczow]. He also lived in Lviv [Lvov]. He was also called Idelis after his mother Idela. His main business was being a lender and a lessee. In 1595, he leased for two years from Samuel and Alexander Zborovski all the estates in Zloczow, all the pools in Bialokomin, Sasiv, Gologory [Holohory], and Zloczow, the custom stations located in the fairs and roads, as well as the mills, workshops, breweries of beer, wine and liquor, and the tavern. All of that for 4000 golden bullions, paid upfront. He was one of the known tycoons in the area. He lent one of Lviv's residents, by the name of Shimon Spas, 300 golden bullions, and another resident by the name of Jerzy Tzartorisky, 7000 golden bullions. These were huge sums in those days.

Most of his businesses were in Zloczow, but he resided mainly in Lviv, where he served as a *parnas* [one of the Jewish community leaders]. His house was located opposite the house of Mordekhai Izkovitz. His daughter Bella was married to Joshua Ben Alexander Falk, the author of the book "Meir Einayim" [Enlightening].

[Columns 33-34]

In 1596, robbers attacked his leased pools in Zloczow and its surrounding, took out the fish from the pools, and sold them to Lviv's merchants. Israel sued [the owner] Zborovski in court, demanding retributions. He won the case and was allowed to confiscate the village of Tiltzitzi.

In the meantime, the number of Jews in Zloczow, who established themselves economically, continued to grow.

The geographic location of the city - on the road leading from Lviv to Iasi and from there to Turkey on one side, and to Volyn and Lithuania on the other, attracted Jews who believed that they would be able to secure themselves economically in Zloczow. Merchants and travelers, who came from Lithuanian and Volyn's cities – Lutsk, Ostroh, and Kremenets, on the way to the salt mines in Reisyn, passed through Zloczow.

Zloczow's merchants, many Jews among them, accompanied the trade convoys from Lviv on their way to Skalat, Trembowla [Terebovlia], and from there through Kamianets-Podilskyi to Turkey.

Zloczow's natives in a gathering in 1964, Israel

The fairs in Zloczow contributed significantly to the economic development of the city. Through the fairs, the city acquired fame throughout Poland and abroad.

Zloczow suffered from many invasions in the 17th century, which also harmed the Jews significantly. However, over time they managed to recover and slowly rehabilitate themselves.

Following the devastation and destruction of the city, Zloczow's Jews received a "Letter of Rights" in 1654, which was renewed in 1681 by King Sobieski.

The letter opened with a statement stating: "The city's owners are interested in having people from any class. People should not only live in peace with each other but also enjoy economically and sound standard of living, above a certain minimum level".

The previous "Letter of Rights" awarded the Jews of Zloczow the right to establish themselves in the city and bring their family members and friends. The Jews were allowed to build a synagogue, cemetery, meat stores, and ritual bath on their plots. They were allowed to trade in all things except for church goods. That included furs, bonnets, shoes, and cattle leather. Jews were also allowed to sell all sorts of alcoholic drinks. The home of the rabbi, cantor, and caretaker, as well as the hospital, were exempt from taxes and other obligations imposed by the [owner's] palace and municipality. The community leaders [*parnasim*] also benefited from that exemption. Trials among the Jews were litigated by the rabbinic court. Trials between Jews and gentiles were litigated at the municipal court. Appeals were handled by the representatives of the [owner] palace. The Jews were also allowed to appeal to the city owners. In cases when an imprisonment punishment had to be administered, it had to be done at the palace's jail rather than the municipal jail. In many cases, judgments in a form of fines were paid to Christian churches. A Jew found guilty of adultery with a gentile woman was forced to pay a fine of 50 grzywna's (one grzywna was worth about 200 grams of silver). The Jews, like all other city residents, had obligations toward the city's and palace's owners. However, they were exempt from any service obligation during the Sabbaths and holidays.

[Columns 35-36]

A youth group in Zloczow

The "Letter of Rights' was approved on 29 November 1681 by King Jan Sobieski, the owner of the city, with specific instructions to his subjects to fulfill it in its entirety.

Organizationally, Zloczow [Jewish community] was similar to other Jewish communities in Poland. The leaders [*parnasim*] and the rabbi were elected by the community.

The Jews residing in the 59 neighboring villages were subjects of the Zloczow's congregation (Zloczow itself was located in Lviv province). These Jews paid a poll tax and the rest of the fees imposed on the Jews, including the congregation's taxes.

These Jews, whose numbers were between 4 to 17 people per isolated village, worked as tavern barmen and other occupations.

On 20 November 1684, Jan Sobieski awarded the Jews, in a special document, the right of every congregation to elect their own officials according to rules and customs in other communities.

This "Letter of Rights" was issued due to complaints made by the congregation about the appointment of Shlomo Ben-Mordekhai (Mordkovitz) as a congregation's elder for life by the palace bureau.

The appointment of Shlomo Ben-Mordekhai to the position of the congregation's head for life was done against the decision by the Council of Four Lands from 1582 (5343) that said: "When it comes to appointments of a Jewish rabbi, leaders, elders or other officials, then it would be carried out with the agreement of the leaders, elders and the congregations based on the Jewish Torah. It is forbidden for a Jew to accept an appointment from the king, ministers, or governors. This would violate the oath sworn at the Giving of the Torah on Mount Sinai.

That prohibition was renewed at the 1670 (5781) session of the Council of the Four Lands. It was accompanied by a warning that a severe boycott would be imposed on "anybody who would accept an appointment through the authorities."

Following the lobbying by the congregation, King Jan Sobieski annulled the appointment of Shlomo Ben Mordekhai, as part of the "Letter of Rights" mentioned above, as it went against the community customs. The King approved the right of the community to publicly elect its leaders as was customary in all other communities.

The elders [*parnasim*] were entrusted to develop the congregation's budget, manage the financial affairs and represent the community before the municipal authorities and the palace. The elders regulated the "right to possess" permit, which was required for any Jew who wanted to work in a certain occupation. The elders were also the ones who received the money from loans awarded to the congregation. They were entrusted with the selection and appointment of the rabbi, religious judges, caretakers and administrators, and the clerical administration of the community. They elected the candidates to the congregation's institutions as well the representatives to the province and state autonomous Jewish institutions. Besides the elders, the community's leadership included three to five city aldermen, most of whom were past elders. Their main task was to serve as advisors to the elders. Like in any other Jewish community, Zloczow had a council of the community's representatives, also named "People Called Upon by the Congregation", or "*Gabbais*" [congregation administrators], who numbered four or five.

Three to five *parnasim* served as heads of the community. The role of the community's top leader would have passed monthly from one *parnas* to the other.

[Columns 37-38]

A public soup kitchen for children

That leader was called "The *Parnas* of the Month". The role would be passed quarterly rather than monthly, very rarely. "The monthly "*parnasim*" had to swear an oath to the palace. The appointment had to be approved by the city owner. The gentiles called the "*parnas*" - "the "Mayor of the Jews".

Zloczow's Jewish community was organized based on the structure of the Jewish community of Zholkova [Zholkiew], which was also owned by the Sobieski family we can assume that Zloczow's community had a "Rules Committee" that was tasked with the task of examining the old rules, from time to time, so that they could be corrected and updated.

That committee also nominated the "Guardians of the Rules", whose role was to guard that the rules were being followed and act upon any violation. Members of the committees served as *gabbai's* [administrators] for some specific tasks of the community affairs: supervision of the synagogues, religious schools, burial society (*Khevereh Kadisha*), elderly homes, hospital, ritual baths, charity affairs, bride charity (*Hakhnasat Kala*), ritual objects, an administrator for affairs related to Eretz Israel, market affairs, and Kosher affairs. The community elected its leaders in an election that was held annually and attended by the rabbi. The caretaker would place notes with the name of every person who paid the poll tax into the ballot box. After that, he would arbitrarily pull out nine notes one by one. The people, whose names were withdrawn, were called the arbitrators. They, in turn, elected five from among themselves who would select the elders, aldermen, appraisers, judges, *gabbai's*, and the community leaders.

Besides the above-mentioned leaders, there was also an administrative apparatus whose members received salaries: The rabbi, who was also the head of the rabbinical court, the rabbinical judges, community writer, caretakers, tax collectors, lobbyists, and the community physician.

The community also oversaw the activity of charities and organizations for religious affairs and Torah education. The committee also supervised other secondary organizations - the artisans' guilds organized according to the various occupations: tailors, furriers, butchers, barbers and paramedics, goldsmiths, cable makers, bartenders, and merchants. The nominees and special administrators were responsible for approving the regulations and supervising the activities of these guilds and organizations.

The community had a budget of revenues and expenses.

The sources for the revenues included the direct membership tax, which was collected based on the declaration of one's property. Other sources were the indirect taxes (called "*Kropka*") from the sale of Kosher meat, wine, grape skin mead, food items, goods, crafts materials, and license fees.

The community funded the synagogues, cemetery, butcheries, a ritual bath, a poor house, a hospital, a physician, and paramedics. The expenses were mainly covered by the Kosher meat tax.

The first synagogue in Zloczow was a wooden building. It was burnt in the 1727 fire along with 8 inns.

The palace, which wanted to help the fire victims, agreed to provide from its own forests, they needed wood for rebuilding. I also extended an offer for a loan of 1000 golden bullions with annual payments.

The Jews also suffered from damages caused by fires in 1754 and 1761.

Like other Jewish communities, the palace's owner imposed special taxes on Zloczow's Jewish community. The community was also obligated to pay a special tax upon the appointment of a new rabbi. The city rabbi also served the neighboring community of Sasiv.

[Similar to other communities] conflicts rosed during the 18th century between the community's leadership and the people who opposed the regime of the elders [*Parnasim*].

[Columns 39-40]

Complaints increased particularly robustly in 1703 against the elder Aharon because he did not submit reports about the management of the financial affairs of the community.

These complaints had probably reached the owner of the city, Alexander Sobieski. He declared that he wanted to intensify his supervision over all of his subjects to prevent the rich from dominating the poor. On January 1st, 1704, Jan Sobieski issued a special instruction. He announced that the people were allowed "to directly elect separate representatives who would manage the cashbox and the financial affairs". He stated that they would be obliged to provide a detailed report to the entire community.

It would be logical to assume that in Zloczow like in Zholkova, also owned by the Sobieski family, the community leaders were obligated to elect a wise and dependable person of understanding, in consultation with some wise and science-oriented people. That person would supervise the collection of the revenues and approve all expenses and bills. He should be a trustworthy person who could be trusted to handle cash and even pawn money collected by the collectors. He would not be controlled by any leader, even by the "Monthly *Parnas*", regardless of the reason. He would be entrusted to record all collections. The "Monthly *Parnas*" would be obliged to provide him with receipts for all the expenses incurred by the rabbi, the head of the rabbinical court, and the leaders".

Zloczow's community was part of the provincial community organization of the Lviv province along with eight other communities, those of Lviv, Brody, Buchach, Tysmienica, Zholkova, Bohorodczany, Rohatyn, and Lesko [Linsk]. Lviv head of the rabbinical court was also the state's rabbi and the rabbi of the entire state of Reisyn.

According to the available documentation, Zloczow's representative participated in the [provincial community organization] committee meeting in the city of Kulikyv [Kulikov] in 1720. It is unknown whether Zloczow 's representatives participated in earlier meetings such as the meeting in 1709, those in Burshtyn [Burstein] in 1714, Novi Strilyshcha [Stelusk?] in 1705, and Burka in 1723. Documents of the committee assembled in Kulikyv on 11 Tamuz 5484 (1724) were signed by "Ya'akov Avraham of Zloczow".

Lipman - the son of Yaakov Avraham BaRa" Z (acronym of the son of Reb Avraham Zolkver) was the son-in-law of the Rabbi Shmuel Kahana of Dubno.

In 1726, the provincial committee assembled in Zloczow to decide upon the dispersion of the Poll tax. It was said to be assembled with "a full forum in Zloczow.

In 1732, Avraham from Zloczow, the head of the Jewish community of Reisyn, along with 9 other leaders from 9 different countries, signed on the dispersion of the poll taxes in the country [Poland].

A meeting of the "Four States Council", led by physician Dr. Yitzkhak Khazak, took place in Zloczow in 1728.

The structure of the state committee was determined in the statute of the state committee's meeting in Ruzhany from 1740. The state committee would consist of 13 members. The statute also detailed the order by which they would be seated during discussions. However, no representative from Zloczow was mentioned among the committee members. The thirteen members were: 5 elders from Zholkova, 4 from Lviv, and 4 from Brody. There was also no representative from Zloczow in the state committee, which gathered in Bobrka in 1753. In that meeting, 15 representatives participated: 4 elders from Lviv, 4 from Zholkova, 3 from Tysmenitsa, 1 from Stryy, 1 from Lyskiv, and 1 from Yavoriv.

Ulrich Vardom described the city as follows:

"Zloczow has long suburban streets, seeded by wooden houses between the hill and the lake (on its northeast side). The city, with its wooden houses, is built nicely around its central square, populated mainly by Jews, whose masses spread over the entire area of Podolia and Reisyn. A castle is standing on a tall hill, is fortified well by earth embankments and stone fortresses, and is surrounded by a moat. The city and the castle are owned by the great Hetman and the kingdom's chieftain Jan Sobieski".

The "Letter of Rights" issued in 1654 did not only allow Jews the right to settle in the city but also encouraged them to attract their relatives to the city. Their city neighbors protested against the Jew's unrestricted freedom of dwelling and tried to act against the broadening of that right with all the means available to them. In 1727 the municipality issued a decree that if a Jew had bought a house, and a short time later, a gentile desired to buy the same house, the Jew had to give up on the purchase. The Jews were allowed to build a new house, provided that no gentile wanted to build on the same lot within 58 weeks. Despite these limitations, many houses remained empty in the city, The municipality was indifferent to the growth in the Jewish population following the fire, even though the municipality announced that Jews were allowed to purchase houses, the owner of the city forbade the gentile residents to sell lots to the Jews by threatening that the lots would be confiscated by the palace. Despite the prohibition, the number of Jewish residents in the city center continued to grow. Toward the end of the 18th century, most houses in the city center were owned by Jews.

Like in the cities of Zholkova and Brody, the Jews in Zloczow participated in the municipal elections during the 18th century. They were present during the election of the magistrate and mayor but were absent when the elected officials took an oath.

[Columns 41-42]

In the official documents, the Jews were called "the city residents and its citizens".

In 1687 – Dolriech, who visited Zloczow stated that – "the number of Jews in the city was significant".

According to the "Letter of Rights" from 1754, Zloczow's Jews were allowed to get involved in any trade (including the sale of [alcoholic] beverages), except for trading in Christian ritual items and goods originating from theft or murder.

Especially emphasized was the retail trade in fur hats and leathers. That trade violated the "Letter of Rights" given to the shoemakers' guild in 1599, in which "the Jews were only allowed to purchase leathers on wholesale, during fairs, and not on retail". That "Letter of Rights stated that "the entire inventory of a person who would violate that rule would be confiscated and handed over to the palace".

The gentile furriers were not enthusiastic about the furs' trading freedom awarded to the Jewish furriers and used every opportunity to limit that right to purchasing only furs of lambs and foxes.

A critical economic area for the Jews was the taverns and inns and the sale of brandy. The Jews were not allowed to distill brandy on Sundays and Catholic holidays. The palace issued instructions on whether the Jews could sell alcoholic beverages on credit to rich people or poor.

The alcohol distillery industry grew more and more in Zloczow during the reign of Sobieski.

Besides the alcohol distillery industry, a sawmill, brick kiln, glass kiln, and marble quarry were established in Zloczow. A paper factory existed in Sasiv. The part Jews played in the operations of those plants was unknown.

A limited number of Jews worked in support of the city's owners. That involvement included the leasing of the municipal revenues, such as customs and certain taxes as well as the utilization of estates, forests, and more.

A few rich Jewish wholesale traders gained fame during the Sobieski period: Moshe Turtzin, Moshe Postin, and Shmuel Ben-Ber (Berowitz) from Zloczow, to name a few. The latter leased the beverages' tax throughout the entire Lviv province, according to a lease signed on 14 December 1633, encompassing Zloczow, Zboriv [Zborov], Yerzyna[?], Markopil [Markopola], Hologory [Golohory], Bilyi Kamin [Bialokamin], Pomorezhny [Pomoryany], Dunayov [Dunayiv], Zalosce [Zaliztsi], Olesko, Pirliov[?] and Sasov [Sasiv].

The Jewish industrialists, Yitzkhak Bianioshovitz, and Ya'akov Ben-Shlomo operated industrial plants based on franchising licenses they obtained from Alexander and Yaakov, the sons of [Jan] Sobieski. Especially noted were the glass foundries in the villages around Zloczow and the activities associated with the forest resources for manufacturing and trade.

Most of the trade in agricultural products was concentrated in the hands of Jews during the 18th century, especially the export of grains sent to Dantzig [Gdansk]. Estate owners in the surrounding areas, even the small ones, grew tobacco, which brought them significant profits. The tobacco trade was concentrated in the hands of Jews. The tobacco grower would receive credit and even cash advances from the Jewish merchants. That trade expanded significantly until the Austrian conquest when a monopoly was established on the tobacco trade.

The Jews would buy wholesale agricultural products from the city's owners, large estate owners, and nobles, owners of the small estates. Most estate owners leased whole farms with their workshops, mills, and alcohol distilleries to the Jews.

During the days of the Polish Republic, many nobles (often up to 150 in the area around Zloczow), who resided in villages cultivated small plots of land mostly leased from estate owners. They sold their harvests to Jewish merchants and tavern operators. The city's owner, Prince Radziwill, who was in a difficult financial situation, leased his villages in exchange for loans from Jews. It is worthwhile to note that agriculture was more developed around Zloczow than in other provinces of Reisyn. Therefore, its products were in high demand in the markets.

In the large estates, the wood industry was also promoted. Its products were diversified and included windows sills, roofs, wood coal, potash, and asphalt. Economically, the mills and paper industries, which were integrated with the Jewish trade, were particularly important. The fabric industry also captured a significant part of the breadth of the Jewish trade.

An important [economic] area in Zloczow was the growing and fattening of cattle. Fattened oxen were sent from Zloczow to Prussia, Shelzia [Silesia], and Austria. The wholesale part of that trade was concentrated in the hands of the Armenians. However, the Jewish traders, who bought the oxen directly from the farmers, occupied a noteworthy part. The bristle trade was also partially held by the Jews.

Beekeeping, the products of which included honey and beeswax, was cultivated efficiently in large numbers of Zloczow's villages. The trade of these products was held entirely by Jews, who sold the harvest to wholesalers in Brody as well as Lesser Poland [a historical region of southern Poland].

Another important economic area occupied by Jews was the crafts. According to the regulations of the various artisan guilds, particularly those of the tailors, bakers, furriers, and butchers, enacted during the reign of [King] Jan [Sobieski] III.

[Columns 43-44]

The old cemetery and the army barracks building

The guilds accepted Jews into their ranks to increase the guilds' revenues.

Instead of compulsory participation in praying in the Catholic church, the Jewish members of these guilds had to deliver a liter of beeswax during the main Catholic holidays.

As craftsmen, the Jews who were members of the artisan guilds would receive a certificate that certified them as artisans. As a privilege of the tailors and furriers awarded by King Sobieski, the Jews were specifically mentioned as "Jewish members awarded the title of artisan". However, due to their absence from the prayers at the church, they were obligated to donate a liter of beeswax on every holiday.

Favorable conditions for the development of trade in the city were created as a result of the permit to hold market days in Zloczow every Tuesday. That permit was issued in addition to the annual fairs (according to the "Letter of Rights" from 1523). Another contributing factor was the exemption of Zloczow's residents from paying the internal custom tax of the kingdom. The right of tax exemption was awarded on March 12, 1633, to be part of the original "Letter of Rights" (from February 4, 1532) on behalf of King Vladislav IV.

Merchants brought all of their goods, and numerous shoppers, who came from surrounding areas, flocked to annual fairs. One of the fairs was held two weeks after Easter and the second was on the 21st of October. Each fair lasted three days. The farmers also brought their products to the city during the fairs.

During the period of the ownership of the city by the Gorka family, a third annual fair and a second weekly market day, on Monday, were added to the "Letter of Rights" of King Zygmunt August issued on August 8, 1553.

Following the disastrous years of the Kozaks and Swedes' Wars, King Jan [Sobieski] III, awarded the city, on February 22, 1667, the right to hold a fair that lasted four weeks (to encourage recovery and economic recuperation).

In 1719, when the city's economic condition worsened more and more, [the noble] Jacob Sobieski decided to increase the number of annual fairs. That situation lasted until the end of the 18th century. During the Austrian conquest, Emperor [Franz] Joseph II awarded the city the right to hold four annual fairs, each lasting eight days, during December, Mars, May, and October.

The economic situation of the Jewish traders, particularly the retail merchants, worsened as a result of the competition from the artisan guilds, who did their best to sell their products during the fairs and also in the surrounding areas, where they were allowed to sell, at a distance farther away than 2 miles. The artisans, who were supported by the city's owners, forced the merchants to pay a special tax [on imported goods] to discourage imported goods from coming to the fairs.

As mentioned above, the part played by the Jews in the wholesale trade was substantial, within the country and abroad. That included the export of grains, wood, honey, and dried fruits. They used roads leading to Walachia [Romania], Moldova, and Turkey. Among the Jewish wholesalers in the 16th century, Moshe Tortzin was very well known.

Jews used to lease from the municipality the collection of taxes and other fees, such as market fees, fair fees and rent (for the shops at the city hall), public bath fees, weights and measures fees, fish ponds fees, asphalt production fees, and candles tax. These were all significant sources of revenue for the city. These revenues grew from one year to another, and the municipality preferred to lease them rather than manage them. Because Jews managed the collection of most taxes and fees resulted in many complaints and grievances by the city residents against the Jews as if they had taken over all of the city revenues, which reached 400 – 600 golden bullions annually. The city used these revenues to cover its expenses of drying the swamps, street cleaning, deepening the embankments, and mending the fences and the fortifications.

[Columns 45-46]

As city residents, the Jews had to participate in paying for the expenses of repairing the roads, bridges, and fences. Jews had to participate in activities related to the defense of the city, like other residents, when it was attacked by enemies. For that reason, they had to keep weapons and ammunition in their homes.

Difficult years of bloody events and destruction befallen the city at the beginning of the 18th century.

The fires in 1724 and 1754, the [Polish] confederations and the intra-country fights, the Swedes invasions, and the passing of the Russian and Austrian armies through the city caused tremendous destruction. The entire population suffered, including the Jews.

In 1716, a poll tax of 350 golden bullions was imposed on the Jews.

The city had been abandoned between 1733 and 1740 due to the invasions by the Swedes and other armies. As a result, all limitations on purchasing houses and plots imposed on the Jews were annulled. The municipality announced that the Jews were only allowed to purchase a house that the gentiles did not want. Most of the houses in the city center were transferred to the hands of the Jews (until then, the Jewish center was at the Tatars' mill). The ritual bath, rabbi's house, and synagogue were also located in the city center. In 1782, the center of the town consisted only of Jews, except one gentile.

There were 169 big gentile houses, 70 large Jewish houses, and 60 small houses of both gentiles and Jews in the city in 1782.

According to the "Letter of Rights", Zloczow's Jews could attend and participate in the election of the municipal senate, the mayor, and other city leaders. However, the Jews had to leave the election hall during the swearing of the elected officials.

According to the census held in Zloczow in 1765, there were 1150 Jews, including 62 children aged one year or younger. There were 618 Jews in the 59 surrounding villages, including 40 children aged one year or younger. Altogether, the community and its branches contained 1758 people, including 102 children aged one year or younger. The community paid a poll tax of 3312 golden bullions for 1656 Jews.

In Zloczow, the children aged one-year-old or younger were 5.6% of the Jewish population. In comparison, the percentage in Zloczow, also located in Lviv's province, was 11.1.

In 1767, the Zloczow's Jewish community was requested to pay off its debt [to the kingdom], like other Jewish communities in Reisyn, according to a notice letter of the committee established to eliminate the debts of the Jewish communities. The debts were accumulated due to payment delays, which also resulted in interest accumulation and fines.

We only have just a few pieces of evidence, or more like hints, that there were several "believers" in Zloczow during the periods of Shabtai Tzvi and Ya'akov Frank. However, there is no doubt that their numbers were small. These "believers" kept tight connections with the people of the sect and waited for the appropriate moment for when they could come out publicly. In Zloczow, there was one operative by the name of Fishel who along with Itzik Kadeiner and his brother-in-law, Meir Kaminer from Zloczow, were among the leaders of the sect in Poland. A story was told about him by the sect people that was confirmed by Rabbi Ya'akov Emden (Known by his acronym - Ya'avetz). That operative came to the rabbi of his own will and confessed his sins, which were not known publicly. He claimed he knew that he had violated the commandments of the Torah and came to ask for forgiveness. The rabbis thought he should be treated as *Ba'al Tshuva* [penitent], since he confessed his sins voluntarily and because he agreed to become a religiously observant person again. However, soon after his confession, he sinned again. He drank a liquor made of grain at the synagogue during Passover and sinned in many other ways. When he was caught, he was asked: "Why did you confess if you have intended to sin again?" He responded that he wanted to suffer an insult on his honor the way ShabtaiZevi suffered for his people.

His brother-in-law, Moshe-Meir Kaminer from Zloczow, used to travel from one city to another in Poland and Germany and preach in favor of Sabbateanism. A branch of the sect was established in Zloczow under the influence and help of his brother-in-law Fishel, who later joined the sect of Yaakov Frank.

We know from the testimony by Nathan Ben Levi in Brody's Kloiz on 12 Nisan 5513 (25 April 1753) that Feibish from Zloczow and Itzik-Meir Zlotsover from Buchach committed "abominations and lewd acts". They also quoted from dubious writings such as Rabbi Jonathan Eibshitz's book "Ve'avo Hayom El Ha'ain" [literally - "And I Will Come Today to the Eye"].

Except for the aforementioned testimonies, we do not have any accurate details about the Frankists in Zloczow.

We note that nobody from Zloczow was among those Frankists who converted to Christianity after the Lviv debate in 1759. That is proof that even those few believers of Ya'akov Frank in Zloczow did not follow him to the end of the road when he abandoned Judaism.

[Column 47]

During the second half of the 18th century, the popularity of the Hasidic movement in Zloczow grew so much that the Jewish community extended an invitation to one of the movement's leaders in Galitsia – Rebbe [Hasidic Rabbi] Yekhiel Mikhel, the son of Rabbi Yitzkhak of Drohobitz, to become a "Magid" [preacher] in the city. Yekhiel Mikhel was a student of the BESHT [Rabbi Israel Ben-Eliezer, Ba'al Shem Tov] and was one of the ten "loafers" in the "*Beit Hamidrash*" of the rich man and the famous philanthrope during that period – R' Yozefa Ostra. Yekhiel Mikhel was born in Brody. He was an enthusiastic follower of the Hasidic movement from his youth. The BESHT said about him:

"He was given a tiny soul from heaven, as small as anyone can get in that generation, and he elevated it to the level of the soul of the holy *Tannai* sage Rabbi Shimon Ben Yokhai". Later on, Mikhel became one of the renowned disciples of the BESHT. After the death of the BESHT, Yekhiel Mikhel went to Mezritch and studied Hasidism from the Great Magid Rebbe Ber of Mezritch. He was a member of the circle of the Magid's disciples along with Rebbe Levi Yitzkhak from Berditchev, Rebbe Nakhum Tzernovler, Rebbe Zeev Walkh of Zhytomyr, Rebbe Elimelekh of Lizhensk, Rebbe Aharon Karliner and Rebbe Mendil of Vitebsk.

The Hasidim considered Rebbe Mikehl to be one of Hasidism's greats. In 5546 (1785/6), Rebbe Khaike of Amdor said about him to his students, that "the man Mikhel from Zloczow is the reincarnation of the prophet Habakkuk", a phrase that invoked mockery against him among the "Mitnagdim" [the people who opposed Hasidism].

It was known that the BESHT urged Rebbe Mikhel, during his youth, to accept a position of a rabbi in one of the Jewish communities, but Rebbe Mikhel refused to do so.

When Rebbe Mikhel returned to Brody, he used to pray in a special Hasidic "minyan", which was named "Hasidim of the Shtibel" [Shtibel – Hasidic house of prayer].

In 1781, Yekhiel Mikhel witnessed the burning of the books of the author of "Toldot Ya'akov Yosef" [literally – the Chronicles of Ya'akov Yosef, written by Rebbe Ya'akov Yosef of Pollonye, one of the first and most known of BESHT's students] in front of his house in Brody. He suffered tremendously during the period of the persecution of Hasidism in Brody, particularly by Rabbi Yekhezkel Landau, the author of the book "Noda BeYehuda" [literally – "Known among the Jews"]. Things got so bad that Rabbi Pinchas Horowitz asked Rabbi [Yosef] from Poznan to ask his father-in-law Rabbi Yekhezkel Landau to "please do not cause sorrow to the holy Teacher and Rabbi Yekhiel Mikhel of Zloczow". Due to the persecutions in Brody, Rabbi Yekhiel Mikhel accepted the invitation extended to him by the Jewish community of Zloczow to become a Magid there.

Rabbe Yekhiel Mikhel was among those salient people who spread Hasidism in Eastern Galitsia and was an effective teacher of Hasidic customs.

A collection of some of his sermons was published in the Hasidism primary book: Likutei Yekarim" [literally 'Precious Collections"]. He captivated the hearts of his listeners from the masses with his sermons that contained a polemic undertone. The "Mitnagdim" mocked him and told all sorts of derogatory stories about him.

[Column 48]

The students of Rebbe Yekhiel Mikhel included the head of Nezkizh [Nesukhoyezhe] rabbinical court, Rabbi Mordkehi [Shapiro] who was earlier a rabbi in Leshniv, near Brody, Rabbi Yaakov Yitzkhak Horwitz [Wagschal] of Lantzut, Rabbi Meshulam Feibish Helir from Zbarazh, Rabbi Yitzkah Izik HaKohen, head of the rabbinical court of Kartz, Rabbi Khaim of Tzernovitz [Chernivtsi] (the author of "Be'er [Ma'im] Khaim"), and Aharon Leib, the son of Rabbi Meir of Peremyshliany.

The five sons of Rebbe Yekhiel Mikhel – Yosef of Yampol, Mordekhai of Kremenetz, Yitzkhak of Radyvyliv, Moshe of Zvohil, and Ze'ev Wolf of Zbarazh spread the strongholds of Hasidism throughout Galitsia and Ukraine.

Rebbe Yekhiel Mikhel left Zloczow, at the end of his life, and became a "*maggid*" at the Jewish congregation of Yampol in Podolia, where he passed away close to year 5552 (1792).

Chapter 3

Zloczow Rabbis and the Situation in the City

Translated by Moshe Kutten

The following were from among the first famed rabbis in Zloczow:

Rabbi Eliezer, also called the "The Famous *Gaon* from Zloczow", was the father of Rabbi Yekhiel Mikhel, who was the head of a yeshiva and the author of the book "Shivrei Lukhot" [literally - The Fragments the Tablets]. The book contains sermons about the weekly Torah readings and kabbalistic commentary on several Talmud sections (published [posthumously] in Lublin in 1680). Rabbi Mikhel was murdered in the Pogrom of Nemerov [also known as the Cossack Riots] on 20 Nisan 5408]1648] along with 6000 other Jewish martyrs who were murdered in the riots. His son-in-law - Rabbi Yehudah of Potok, was a well-known rabbi of his generation.

Rabbi Moshe Elkhanan Heilperin served as a rabbi after him (during 1690 – 1710). He was the son-in-law of the leader of the province of Lviv, Gershon Nathan, the son of Zloczow's tax collector - Betsalel. His son, Nathan Heilperin, was the son-in-law of the author of the book "Pnei Yehoshua" [Rabbi Jacob Joshua Falk] and the brother-in-law of Rabbi David, the son of "Hakhakham Tzvi" [literally – Tzvi the Sage by Rabbi Tzvi Hirsch Ashkenazi]. Rabbi Heilperin was taken from Zloczow to be the rabbi of Szharogrod.

Rabbi Meir, the son of [Rebbe] Shmuel Shmelki Horowitz, served as the city rabbi during 1701-1718. Before serving in Zloczow, he served as the Rabbi of Bolechiv [Bolechow]. In 1696 he was invited to serve as a rabbi in Tykocin, where he died in 1743. He was the father of Rabbi Ya'akov Yukel Horowitz, the head of the rabbinical court in Glowgo.

After him (probably at the beginning of the 18th century) served Rabbi Eliezer, the son of Zekharya Mendel, the head of the rabbinical court in Belz city and the country. He served as the rabbi in Komarno. His realm included the holy community of Zloczow. He was the father of Lviv's Rabbi, Moshe Khaim, the rival of Rabbi Ya'akov Yehoshua (author of the book "Pnie Yehoshua"). The latter was nominated to the rabbinic position with the help of his rich father-in-law. He was also supported by governor Jablonowsky.

[Columns 49-50]

Rabbi Moshe, the son of Rabbi Elazar Rokeakh, the author of the book "Ma'asei Rokeakh" was the rabbi in Zloczow and Zbarazh until 1740. He settled in Zloczow in that year with his second wife, the daughter of Rabbi Tzvi Ashkenazi of Lviv. He died in Brodyon 2 Kislev 5514 (1753). He had a son, Rabbi Shmuel Shmelki, the rabbi of the tailors in Brody from his first wife, the daughter of Frankfurt's head of the rabbinical court, Rabbi Naftali. He was the grandfather of Rabbi Shalom Rokeakh, the head of the rabbinical court in Belz, and the founder of the Hasidic *Admors* [great rebbes] dynasty of Belz.

During the same period, a famous scholar and one of Galitsia's most eminent people of the period lived in Zloczow – Rabbi Arye Leibush Kantchuger, the great-grandson of Rabbi Zekharya from Krakow.

He was born in 1698 in the Galitsia town of Kantchuga. He excelled in his talents and piety from his youth. He did not eat meat during the week and was immersed in cold water daily. According to Rabbi Yehoshua, the author of the book "Pnei Yehoshua", "he was the greatest scholar of the Mishnah and Jewish law in his generation".

He was nominated at a young age to be the rabbi in Kantchuga and later was elected as the rabbi in Hrubieszow but stayed there for only a short time. He settled in Zloczow, as a private person, in 1728. He taught Torah and ordained many students.

A group of women beggars

He refused to accept an offer to become a rabbi in Dubno and preferred to live in Zloczow. He made a living by working as a teacher until his passing in 1786. His innovations about the Mishnah were published after his death (Lviv, 5631 - 1871) in the book - "Ateret Zkenim" [literally – The Crown of the Elders]. His son, Rabbi Meir, was a rabbi in Roman, and the other son - Rabbi Yekhiel Mikhel, in Lukiv [Matsiv]. After the city of Lukiv was burnt, Rabbi Yekhiel Mikhel transferred to Zloczow.

The community's rabbi during the second half of the 18th century was Rabbi Yisaskhar Berish, the author of the book "Bat Eini" [literally - The Apple of my Eye]. The book contained new interpretations of the Gemara [with Rashi commentaries] and the Nidah tractate. The book was published in Dubno in 1798, along with his book "Mevaser Tzedek" [literally - The Herald of Justice] about the Torah, published after his death by his son Yehuda Leib and his grandson R' Efraim Fishel. He lost his eyesight at the end of his life[2]. He immigrated to Eretz Israel in 1793/4 and died there in 1798.

In a letter written by the Hasidim of Tveria [Tiberias] in the month of Shvat 1795 to their fellow Hasidim in Russia, they announced the following: "Great scholars and luminaries had arrived at our Holy Land. The honorable *Gaon* Rabbi of the holy community of Shepetovka, and the *Gaon* Rabbi of the holy community of Zloczow, Yehuda Leib and his grandson Efraim Fishel".

After him, the person who served as the rabbi, for a short period, was the author of the book "Pnie Yehoshua" and later, the son-in-law of Rabbi Yissaskhar Berish, Rabbi Avraham, the son of Gedalia. He was the student of Rabbi Shmelki HaLevi Horwitz, the head of the rabbinical court of Nikolsburg. He was also one of the students of the *Maggid* of Mezritch [Rabbi Dov Berish, the son of Avraham], and Rabbi Yekhiel Mikhel of Zloczow. He was the son-in-law of Rabbi Pinkhas HaLevi Horwitz, the author of the book "Hafla'a" [literally – Turning into a Miracle. It is also an acronym of his name]. After the death of his first wife, he married a second wife, the daughter of Rabbi Yisaskhar Berish. He authored the book - "Orakh LeKhaim" [literally – A Way of Life] about the Torah. He was beloved by the people of his community because of his virtues and his charity work.

After him, Rabbi Khaim Wolf Katz served as the rabbi of the city for a short time. Later, he moved to Brody and managed the financial affairs of Polish nobles and the shoemakers' guild.

According to the "Jewish Statute" from 7 May 1789, every district could nominate a single rabbi (the district rabbi) and for the rest of the places, only teachers and cantors were allowed to serve. Similar to the heads of the communities, rabbis were elected for three years.

[Columns 51-52]

The place of residence of the District Rabbi was the district city. Since Zloczow was located in the Brody district, the District Rabbi resided in Brody. However, the Zloczow community was allowed to have a rabbinical court headed by a rabbi, according to the spirit of the [Empress] Maria Teressa's "Jewish Statute". The authority of the rabbi spanned religious, judicial, property, and financial matters. One could appeal before the state court in Lviv, which was under the authority of the state rabbi. The court consisted of five additional judges. However, based on decrees from 25 August 1783 and 23 May 1784, the Jewish judicial system was annulled and the rabbinical courts were abolished.

The first district rabbi was Rabbi Meir Kristianpoler, which served during 1785 – 1815. He was the son of Rabbi Tzvi Hirsch, the son of Rabbi Moshe of Bialokamin, and later the head of the rabbinical court in Lviv. Rabbi Meir was one of the students of the Country Rabbi of Moravia, Rabbi Shmuel Shmelki Horwitz. He also served as a rabbi in Chervonohrad [Kristynopol] and Brody.

Following him, the district rabbi was Rabbi Arye Leib Teomim. When the latter fell ill, the grandson of Rabbi Yekhezkel Landau was nominated in 1829. Following him, the son of Rabbi Meir Kristianpoler, Rabbi Yekhiel Mikhel, served until 1863.

The district rabbi supervised the religious affairs, managed the vital records' ledgers, oversaw the use of the serving staff, supervised the cantors and caretakers, declared a shun according to the instructions from the authorities, and satiated people handling political affairs.

During his reign as the Zloczow district rabbi, Rabbi Kristianpoler received a salary of 450 Florin and as a Rabbi in Brody – 900 Florin.

The religious teachers in the various locations received the salaries or made a living as follows:

Busk – 31 Florin, Toporov – contributions and donations only, Bialokomin – 104 Florin, Hlynjany – an apartment and exemption from taxes only, Kaminka – 312 Florin, Shchurovychi – a monopoly in the casting of candles, Shetshmiltza [?] – no salary, Olesko – no salary (contributions and donations), Podkamen – 52 Florin, Pomoryani [Pomorzhany] – no salary, Radekhiv [Radzhiakhov], Uzlovoye [Kholojow]. Ozerna [Yazhirna] – made a living only from tuition, Stoyaniv [Stoyanov] – 10 Florin, Zaliztsi [Zalozhtse]– donations, only, Zboriv [Zborov] – 312 Florin and Zloczow – arbitration fees.

During the beginning of the Austrian conquest, Zloczow played a major role in both domestic and foreign trade. All the cargo of goods that originated in Volyn and Podolia passed through Zloczow. It passed on the road that spitted at Zloczow to two branches: the northern branch, leading to Brody and Radyvyliv [Radzivilov, and the eastern branch leading toward Ternopil and Lutsk. Goods from Vienna, Lviv, and Krakow were also transported to Volyn, Podolia, and the other aforementioned cities and countries. Goods sent from Russia to Brody passed through that road, particularly after the opening of the port in Odessa.

Since all of that trade was concentrated in the hands of Brody's Jews, they used the assistance of Zloczow's Jews for all associated services such as transportation, loading, and unloading.

Until the construction of the railroad, many of Zloczow 's Jews worked in freight and transportation.

Despite all of that, the Jews experienced difficulties in adapting to the new conditions. These conditions were very different from those that existed in Poland.

At the beginning of the Austrian conquest, the community was organized based on Empress Maria Teressa's "Jewish Statute", issued on 16 July 1776, the "Jewish Statute" issued by [Emperor] Joseph II on 27 May 1785, and the "Edict of Tolerance" on 7 May 1789. The latter was a regulation that attempted to find a permanent arrangement of the Jewish affairs in the entire area of Galitsia.

A committee ("*Kahal*" or assembly) consisted of elected elders who headed the community. However, they had limited authority, and they also had to obey and yield to any demand of the district authorities. The community was responsible for all the government taxes imposed on the Jews and for completing the quota of army recruits. According to the "Jewish Statute" from 1776, the community committee consisted of six members, and according to the Statue of [Emperor] Joseph II – three members. However, in Brody and Lviv, the community committees consisted of 7 members, as the Jewish populations in these cities were sizable. Members were elected to serve for three years. Heads of households were allowed to actively participate in the election if they paid the tax on Shabbat Candles for at least seven candles during the preceding year. Reputable heads of families residing in Zloczow, were awarded the right to passively participate in the election if they fulfilled the following conditions: 1) They paid the tax on at least ten Shabbat candles in the preceding year 2) They could read and write in German. Besides the leaders, the community elected the heads of *Khevra Kadishah* [the burial society], superiors of the synagogues and hospitals, and the bookkeepers.

The administrative organization of the community consisted of the community secretary (*Sofer* or writer), community caretaker, cantors, synagogue caretakers, slaughterers, and undertakers. The rabbi, who was elected by the community voters for three years, was responsible for all the religious matters. According to the Statute from 1785, the position of the community rabbi was eliminated and replaced by regular teachers, teachers of religious subjects, and cantors. However, every district had its own rabbi.

[Columns 53-54]

Zloczow, as the district city, was where the rabbi resided. A unique right was awarded to the city of Brody. Its rabbi was independent of the district rabbi, although the latter, who resided in Zloczow, retained all of the judicial rights. That situation was maintained until the annulment of the Jewish Judicial system and the rabbinical courts. That was done based on the decrees by the central authorities in Vienna on 25 August 1783 and 23 May 1784.

According to the "Jewish Statute" on 7 May 1789, the leaders of the community received salaries from the community tax revenues. That was why so many people pursued the positions of the leaders of the community. They also chased after the honor associated with these positions. That was true even from the days of Jewish autonomy in Poland. In Zloczow, as in other places, there were no elections where there was no opposition. The opposition challenged the legitimacy of the elected officials and blamed them for illegally imposing taxes. That was the case since the main burden was imposed on the unwealthy classes, while the elite and their relatives were nearly exempt from paying any tax. Conflicts and quarrels broke out from time to time. The case of David Lezerovitz (Ben-Eliezer) was well known. His tax book was taken away from him, which led to his removal from the community. He turned to Vienna to complain and requested that the tax book would be given back to him. Vienna responded that he must first appeal to the governor's office. On April 1793, he was notified that his request had been denied.

That was not the only case when the heads of the community attempted to get rid of "undesirable elements" and people who were fans of the opposition.

In 1774, the authorities increased the poll tax from 30 Kreuzers to one Gulden. This tax was also mentioned in the "Jewish Statue" from 1776, as a Tolerance Tax (*Taleh Rantzsteir - Toleranzsteuer*) of 4 Gulden per family. Each family has also levied an income tax of 4 Gulden.

However, a property-based marriage fee was considered as part of that tax. The tax quota was levied on individual Jewish communities, and every community divided the total among its members.

In 1784, Emperor Joseph II canceled the income and property tax and replaced them with the following taxes:

1. A national household tax of one Gulden per family.

2. The marriage fee was replaced by a marriage tax on three brackets:

1. Artisans and employees paid one Ducat for the first son, 6 for the second, and 12 for the third. If the income exceeded 100 Guldens, the tax was doubled.
2. Public service workers paid 12 Ducats for the first son and 24 for the second.
3. All merchants and people working in related fields with income not exceeding 400 Guldens paid 20, 40, and 80 Ducats respectively.
4. Jewish farmers and people who worked in agriculture were exempt from paying these taxes.
5. Kosher meat Tax – according to the type of meat.

In 1789, people who were working in agriculture were also exempt from paying the Tolerance Tax. According to the "Jewish Statute" of Joseph II (1789), additional fees were imposed:

1. A fee for a new synagogue or a new cemetery – a one-time fee of 2000 Gulden and an annual tax of 100 Gulden.
2. A "Minyan" fee of 50 Gulden annually.

In 1797, the poll tax was canceled and was replaced by a tax on candles. Additional taxes were levied:

1. To ensure that the Kosher Meat and the candle taxes were sufficient to reach the desired allotment, a supplement tax was levied – to take care of any shortfall.
2. Special tax, the alternative to the income tax imposed on the gentiles. All Jews who paid candle tax were levied that tax as well

People who were exempt from that tax were:

1. People who work in agriculture
2. Military personnel and their wives
3. Widows of military men
4. Bachelors and bachelorettes who live with their parents, guardians, relatives, and friends
5. Trade assistants, apprentices, servants, housekeepers, bachelors, or widowers

Besides these taxes, the Jews paid a tax on storage and a tax on plots, and obviously, they also paid a tax for their community.

Many quarrels erupted upon the establishment of the [Kosher] meat tax, which carried significant profits. In actuality, this was the monopoly of the tax lessee, who had the authority to raise the Kosher meat tax and void the slaughtering permit of many butchers as he saw fit. Using that authority, the butchers, who colluded with the lessee were able to increase the meat price, infuriating the masses, particularly to poor, who were agitated by the boycotted butchers.

On the other hand, the rest of the taxes, which were also leased, were collected vigorously, often with the help of military horsemen and policemen, who confiscated furniture and other household items and did not even shy away from blackmailing. These oppressions intensified with the imposition of the tax on candles.

[Columns 55-56]

A couple of demented people

The [tax] lessees were often the elders-leaders of the community, so the anger of the population would be directed at them.

Gregory Bartholomeus served as a magister for Jewish affairs on behalf of the authorities. His annual salary was 350 Florins. Besides him, an additional magister, employed daily, was hired with a salary of 150 Florins.

Disagreements about the [Kosher] meat tax also rose between the community and the tax lease management in Lviv.

Following a request by the Sasiv community, which was affiliated with the Zloczow community, it was disassociated in 1785 from Zloczow in matters associated with the meat tax. That meant a loss of revenues for the meat tax lessee in Zloczow. Zloczow community, which was interested in keeping Sasiv under its authority, appealed to Lviv. In March of that year, Lviv advised Zloczow that they would need to contact the appropriate authority in that matter. We could not find any documentation of whether the disagreement was ever resolved.

The meat tax lessees during that period were Kalman and Funkelstein. Aharon Horowitz complained against them in 1785, claiming that he had the leasing license, and requested compensation. After losing his court case, Mr. Horowitz appealed to the Justice Ministry in Vienna. However, the matter was transferred to the governor, and, in the end, the governor ruled against him.

In 1798, Khaim Kahana and Eliezer Landau secured the lease of the meat tax in Zloczow. A person by the name of Shlomo Oxsenhass appealed on behalf of the butchers in the city. They claimed that the lessees were interfering with their work. The appeal was also transferred from Vienna to the governor.

During wars, Galitsian Jews were required to purchase emergency bonds, besides the regular taxes. That happened during 1794 – 1799.

In 1798, the district authorities were supposed to collect the war bond from the Jews. For some reason, the bond was not collected from Zloczow's Jews. When the governor in Lviv heard about it, he imposed a monetary fine upon the district minister in Zloczow and confiscated his salary.

A worsening in the tax collection situation occurred in 1784. A decree was issued that any Jew lagging in paying the taxes would be proclaimed a beggar who may be subject to expulsion from Galitsia. Many censuses followed that decree, which caused a horrendous situation and fear of being exposed as a "*Yuden Bootle*" [Jewish loafer] or as somebody who was married fictitiously (to subvert poll tax law). There were always people, gentile or Jewish, ready to tell the authorities about tax evasion by a "*Yuden Bootle*" and particularly about fictitious marriage. One would get an award for such information. One such informer – Berl Ya'akov from Podkamen, cast fear onto the Jews of Zloczow and its neighboring area. He asked the authorities for protection since "his enemies were threatening him due to his devotion to the state treasury". Indeed, embittered people attacked him more than once, and they bit him harshly more than once. They were also some gentile officials who snitched on Jews for a fee. A post office manager in Zboriv, Anton Retel, was known to have requested a "reporting fee" for his reports about fictitious marriages of Jews in Zboriv and its environs. A special investigating committee was established based on the information provided by that official.

In 1782, a class committee proposed to remove the Jews from all leases (*Arendas*). The central government in Vienna took advantage of that proposal and issued a decree in the spirit of the proposal.

The district minister of Zloczow, Von Tanhauzer, opposed that arbitrary ruling claiming that the estate owners would not be able to find Christian lessees who would be sufficiently skilled to replace the Jews. However, Tanhauzer's opposition was in vain.

The Jews were deported from many villages in the district of Zloczow. The representatives of the Zloczow community turned immediately to the authorities and asked to keep the tavern owners and bartenders in their places.

[Columns 57-58]

Their request reached the emperor in Vienna on 8 February 1787. The Jews supported their request by the fact that, as part of the privileges they received during the Polish republic, they were awarded the right to serve brandy, wine, and other alcoholic beverages. In 1789, the heads of the community requested again for the privileges to be re-approved. They considered these privileges the legal basis for sustaining all the occupations associated with serving alcoholic beverages. The Jews hoped that the privilege would be recertified and that the authorities would refrain from deporting the tavern owners and bartenders from the villages and possibly eradicate them in the city. Their hope did not materialize.

Besides the worry about the tavern owners, who were forced to abandon their occupation, other concerns and troubles rested on the shoulders of the community leaders.

During the first years of the Austrian regime, the community leaders lobbied to obtain new approval for Jewish privileges.

As early as 1778, the Zloczow Jewish community requested, in a special appeal to the Governor in Lviv, through the local authorities, to approve the privileges that the Jews received from the Polish King Jan Sobieski III. However, the governor was not in a hurry to resolve the matter. He reported to Vienna about the request to approve Zloczow's community privileges, which consisted of rules about the relations between the Jews, the city, and its owners, only in October 1782. In the end, the central government ruled that the privileges could remain in the future without any recertification. Even before the appeal mentioned above, the community requested to forbid the municipality from imposing unreasonable taxes. They also petitioned to act against the malicious duty of hosting military personnel, which resulted in substantial expenses for the Jewish population.

Vienna responded with a reprimand. They told the community that they must first turn to the local authorities with any of their complaints. They can turn to the governor only when the local authorities did not resolve the matter. Only upon the rejection by the governor could the community turn to Vienna.

That was how Zloczow's Jewish community learned about the nature of the Austrian bureaucracy and its operation!

The debts that rested upon the community, from as early as the days of the Polish regime, also caused problems. The rulings of the committee for the elimination of the Jewish debts imposed all sorts of obligations on Galitsia's communities, including the one in Zloczow. These debts were accumulated from the days of the Polish Republic. In 1788, the Jews of Zloczow were obligated to pay all of their debts in five years.

At the beginning of 1785, Zlozow's community with the community of Pomoryany turned once more to the authorities. They appealed to certify their privileges from the Polish period. However, their request failed again. The governor passed Vienna's response on 10 June, which stated that approval could not be provided at that time.

Several fires broke out in the city during 1755 – 1780. However, the authorities prohibited Jews to rebuild their houses. Appeals submitted to the authority were delayed for over one year until the Jews finally got the needed approval.

We learned about the Jewish population of the Zloczow district from a census held in 1788. However, we could not find details about the number of Jews in the city itself.

According to that census, there were 14 Jewish communities affiliated with the city community, consisting of 5324 Jewish families: among them were - 5111 men, 5151 women, 2095 boys, and 1857 girls (the children above the age of twelve). These families had 1544 male housekeepers and 1544 female housekeepers. There were 190 poor males and 735 poor females. Altogether 12,867 people. The total number of men in the community was 11,571 and women 26,185. Of the 5324 families, there were 4487- first-level taxpayers' households, 379 – second-level, 371 – third-level, and 87 poor households.

In 1790, the district had 5185 Jewish families, who were obligated to pay 20,740 Florin of Tolerance Tax and 5185 Florin of additional tax - a total of 25, 925 Florin. In actuality, only 4885 Florin of the Tolerance Tax and 1221 Florin of the "additional tax" (together 6106 Florin) were paid. 19,818 Florin were registered as a debt.

In 1791, the total number of Jewish families was 5029, and the number of people was 23,960, 11,751 men, and 12,209 women. Of the 5029 during that year, 4150 were first-level taxpayers, 539 – were second-layer, 201 – were third-layer, and 130 were considered poor families.

Compared to 1788, the number of Jews decreased by 2225 people, and the number of first, second, and third-level taxpayers decreased by 348 (from 5237 to 4889). The number of poor families increased from 87 in 1788 to 130 in 1791 (an increase of 43 families).

The economic situation of Zloczow's Jews improved at the beginning of the Austrian regime, albite not in all the classes. During those years, the property value of the Jews increased. The Jews preferred to invest their money in houses and plots, particularly in the city center.

The famed scholar, Professor Belkhazar Hakeh, who toured throughout Galitsia between 1790 and 1796 wrote: "The Jews in Zloczow, have the upper hand. They reside in houses with large plots, while the Christian population is crowding in small alleys".

[Columns 59-60]

Most of the Jews were occupied in commerce. Toward the end of the 18th century and in the first half of the 19th century, the trade of Podolia and Volyn regions, and the trade of Ternopil and Brody, passed through Zloczow. The vast majority of that trade was in the hand of Jews. Brody [Jewish] traders employed Jews by commission or brokerage or in transportation in Zloczow, which served as a critical transfer stop for the free trade city of Brody.

In the city of Zloczow itself, virtually all the stores were in the hands of Jews. They imported all the goods needed in the city. Artisans, particularly shoemakers, tailors, and bakers, worked mainly for Jewish merchants. Zloczow and its neighboring areas were an important center for weavers of fabric, nets, and sails. Jews brought these products to Gdansk [Dantzig] in loads of 1000 packages, 25 Arshins [1 Arshin = 28 inches] each. The owners of large and medium-sized estates around Zloczow, Pomoryani, and Holohory used to lease their villages to Jews and sell them their agricultural products: grains, honey, wax, fruits, cattle, brandy, flour, and wood products. Local Jews were given priority. The grain trade brought substantial profits. During the Polish days, the traders earned 1 Florin for every Koretz [1 Koretz = 128 liters]. The price of a Koretz of grain for an intermediary trader was 4 florins

In the city of Zloczow itself, virtually all the stores were in the hands of Jews. They imported all the goods needed for the city. Artisans, particularly shoemakers, tailors, and bakers, worked mainly for Jewish merchants. Zloczow and its neighboring areas were an important center for weavers of fabric, nets, and sails. Jews brought these products to Gdansk [Dantzig] in loads of 1000 packages, 25 Arshins [1 Arshin = 28 inches] each.

With the Austrian conquest, various factories began to sprout in the district of Zloczow. For example, a plant with an annual production that reached 15,000 leathers was built near Kotkorz. A person by the name of Fridreikh Hershel planted large areas of hops that yielded 30 – 40 Kanters [1 Kanter = about 300 kg.]. A paper factory, owned by a person named Bini, was established in Busk.

A vital trade field, the horse trade, was concentrated at the hand of Jews. Zloczow's traders would buy horses in Russia and eastern Galitsia, in collaboration with traders from Brody, Chortkiv, Pidhaytsi, and Kosova, and sell them in Silesia, Prussia, and Austria. They also provided horses to the Austrian military.

In 1791, a massive fire broke out in Zloczow, which destroyed almost the entire city, including the Jewish houses and particularly their stores in the city center. Construction of stone houses and stone stores commenced following the fire.

The commerce incurred a substantial loss and suffering upon the third partition of Poland when a border pass with Russia was established in Brody. As a result of probationary economic tendencies, high customs were imposed at the border. In particular, Zloczow's traders, who were dependent on the traders in Brody, suffered from that situation. A considerable upturn for the better occurred at the beginning of the 19th century. That was especially felt during 1806 – 1812 due to the blockade Napoleon imposed on all of Europe's ports.

* * *

The education of Jewish in Zloczow was carried out, like in all Galitsia, in traditional educational institutions.

Unlike the Polish authorities, which were not interested in educating Jewish children and did not make any effort to accomplish it, the Austrian authorities, while handling the general education in Galitsia, did try to take care of the education of Jewish children.

The authorities allowed the traditional education institutions, the supervision of which was assigned to the state chief rabbi, to continue to operate. However, as part of the regulations, the authorities set a framework, curriculum, teachers' obligations, and a timeline for tests, for these institutions. The Jews did not receive these changes enthusiastically and that led the authorities to change their mind. After the abolishment of the state community organization in 1782, Jewish children were allowed to study in the general state elementary schools.

On 27 May 1785, the authorities requested that Jewish communities establish schools of general studies. When nothing was done about it, stern orders were issued. According to these orders, the Jewish communities were responsible to ensure that every youth under the age of 13 would study in general education schools. Even the *melamed* assistants had to attend a school of general education studies.

The Jews did not pay attention to these stern orders since they felt that attending general studies school would lead the youth to assimilation.

With the issuance of the Jewish Rights document ("*Yuden Patent*") by Emperor Joseph II in 1789, its role was to change the lifestyle of Galitsia's Jews, a sharp turn in the government's attitude toward Jewish education.

In clauses 11-14 of the "*Yuden Patent*" the Jews were obliged to establish a German school of general studies in every community "to correct the Jews through education". The "*Yuden Patent*" document stated that no Jew would be allowed to get married without a graduation certificate from a school of general studies or from studying privately at home. A teacher seminar was established in Lviv to prepare an appropriate teaching workforce.

[Columns 61-62]

A student and assistant of Moshe Mendelson – Hertz Homberg (1749 – 1841), was nominated as the head of the Jewish education system in the entire Galitsian in 1787.

In 1788, 48 [Jewish] schools of general studies were established in Galitsia (including in Zloczow).

Most of these schools were for boys. Only in Brody and Lviv, girls' schools were also established. A special fund of 259,028 Guldens was established for that system. Jewish heads of households were forced to finance it.

As mentioned, the school of general studies in Zloczow was established in 1788, where the teacher was Yaakov Frenkel. He received a salary of 200 Guldens. However, the Jews did not cooperate and refused to send their children to school. Neither gentle lobbying nor threats of punishments and fines helped. The aspiration of Joseph II did not find an echo or support among the Jewish masses. There was no other choice left for the government in Vienna but to abolish the Jewish school network and the [teacher] seminar. That was done according to the decree by Emperor Frantz I, on 26 June 1806. The teachers were paid meager compensation. They dispersed and went each their own way.

* * *

As known, Emperor Joseph II aspired to transfer some of Galitsia's Jews to agriculture as part of his "Corrections of the Jews" policy.

This matter was discussed among the circles of the government in Vienna as early as 1774. These discussions were held under the influence of the Physiocratic Theory. There was also the need to compensate the Jews for the loss of their livelihood as lessees of taverns. One way to do so would be to employ them in agriculture.

Jews who would settle and dedicate themselves to work in agriculture were promised to receive a reduction of 50%, and later, a total exemption from the Tolerance Tax.

Thousands of families were left without a way to make a living following the Jewish Regulations from 1785. In his decree from 16 August 1785, Emperor Joseph II ordered to begin with the immediate settlement of 1400 Jewish families, from throughout Galitsia, in agricultural settlements. The district of Zloczow was obligated to fulfill a quota of 228 families, including 12 families from Zloczow city itself. By the end of 1793, the following communities managed to reach their quotas: Leshniv – 7 families, Olesko – 5, Bialokomin -9, Podkamen – 7, Kamika – 8, Zalitsi – 10, Holohory – 6, Zloczow – 12, Pomoryany – 6, Vitkam[?] – 8, Busk – 7, Zboriv – 8, altogether 113 families. The quota for Brody was - 128, which was reached by 1803.

The execution of that decree progressed very slowly, which the authorities did not like. Sambir [Sambor], Zhokova [Zalkiew], Stryj, Rzeszów [Raysha], Tarnov, Mishelnitza[?], Buchnia Gobi Suntz[?], Zalischyky, and Chernivtsi [Tzernovitz], managed to fill their quota as early as 1792. The governor in Lviv notified Vienna of that progress in a special report. In a directive from Vienna on July 1792, the authorities commended and thanked the officials in the aforementioned districts for properly executing the instructions and timely fulfilling the quota.

An instruction to reprimand the district authorities of Ternopil [Ternopol], Zamosc [Zamoshetz], Ivano-Frankivsk [Stanislavov], and Zloczow, was included in the same directive, and they were sternly ordered to execute the mission.

By the end of 1803, 288 Jewish families settled on 104 plots. These families included: 258 men, 251 women, 146 boys, and 132 girls under the age of 18. The settlers received 29 houses, 258 barns and cowsheds, 461 horses, 389 oxen, and 412 cows.

The Jewish communities located in the area of the settlements were forced to cover the settlement budget in their area. Between 25 to 40 families were required to cover the expenses incurred in settling one family, which amounted to 250 Gulden.

All the farmers who had settled in the district of Zloczow before the end of 1793 were surveyed in 1822. Only families whose settlement was financed by the communities were inspected. The authorities treated the settlers very strictly. They were investigated as to whether they were suitable to work in agriculture, physically and mentally. The settlers were not allowed to employ workers to cultivate their fields and work in other occupations.

Anybody who did not perform his job appropriately was deported from the village. That was how the Jewish farmer by the name of Moshe Shliter had to leave the village of Salvia on July 1823 by the ruling of the district office. That village was where some of the farmers from Zloczow had probably settled. The reason given for the ruling was that the Jewish farmer did not fulfill the essential conditions of a Jewish agriculturalist – he did not work in his fields by himself and also worked in a forbidden occupation. The ruling of the district office was approved by Galitsia's governor's office. Shliter submitted an appeal to the palace bureau in Vienna, which discussed the matter in its meeting on 19 October 1826. The bureau approved the district office's ruling.

Author's Notes:

1. Starting in October 1848 and on, the teaching language was Polish.
2. He ordered to call the book "Bat Eini" [The Apple of My Eye] since it is identical to his name – Yisaskhar Dov in gematria (542). That name was also a hint about his blindness.

[Columns 63-64]

Chapter 4

The 19th century

The Jews found themselves in dire economic distress at the end of the 19th century without any hope that their situation would improve. During the first decade of the 19th century, the tax burden imposed by the authorities on the tax lessees and the Jewish population increased. The lags in tax payments also grew. Without considering the dire situation of the Jews, the finance ministry requested to equate the importance of paying off the debts accumulated from the Tolerance Tax to the debts accrued from the 1794 – 1798 war bonds. That resulted in an amount of 98,193 Florins, which was levied on all of the Jewish communities. Zloczow's war bonds obligation was 2,041 Florins, but the community only paid 1,711 Florins. The authorities added the difference to the debt from the Tolerance Tax of 1,290 Florins. All of the Jewish communities appealed to Emperor Frantz [Joseph I].

The cemetery in Zloczow

In its meeting, held on October 5, 1803, the finance ministry decided to force Zloczow's Jewish community to pay its debt in ten years. That debt included a war bonds debt of 330 Florins and a Tolerance Tax debt of 1.290 Florin. Despite that compromise, the Jewish community was unable to adhere to that order. The debts accumulated from the kosher meat tax and the tax on candles grew because the taxes during the later years of 1810 – 1812 increased. The Jews were also obligated to pay for state bonds imposed during the same period.

The taxes on kosher meat and Shabbat candles oppressed not only the lower classes but also the wealthy. Neither could afford to buy meat. For example, the cost of a litra [327.6 gram = 12 Oz.] of meat for a Christian customer was 6 kreutzers. The cost of a Litra of kosher meat was 20 kreutzers. However, that was not the actual price paid at the counter because the tax lessees raised the price even higher since they did not have any competition. The kosher meat tax was a monopoly. The situation with the Shabbat candles tax was even worse. The lessees treated the Jews with horrendous cruelty. The Jews consider them "torturous devils" and "money suckers".

The Jews were subjected to injustice with other taxes, both in terms of the allotment and collection.

In 1811 – 1819, the Jews in Zloczow complained about the tax assessors who were elected by the community to assess the supplemental tax (which was based on property and income). The Jews claimed that the assessors worked in collaboration with the leaders of the community. They also complained about the fact that the assessors had total control over the properties of the debtors. Their judgment was considered final, and they were the sole authority that assessed the taxes. Even the authorities could not intervene in the assessors' decisions. Among the various direct state taxes imposed on Jews during those days were the following:

a. Tax on plots of land
b. Building tax
c. Personal tax
d. Income tax

The Jews had to also pay a supplemental tax to cover the deficits from the taxes on kosher meat and candles.

These issues resulted in extortions, ongoing disputes, quarrels, and increased resentment in the community. It also led to the formation of permanent opposition. The multitude of appeals motivated the authorities in 1826 to propose eliminating the supplemental tax for that year. The government in Vienna approved that proposal. They realized that Jews paid as much as five times more income tax than Christian taxpayers (who paid only one florin and 17.5 kreutzers).

In 1805, the central government planned to establish a new updated Jewish Statute.

[Columns 65-66]

In doing so, they relied upon memorandums and notes issued to describe the status and influence of the Jews on the non–Jewish population. They also relied upon the social–economic activities of the Jews from the point of view of the state policy.

Schmidt, the Zloczow District's minister, delivered a detailed report, on 14 August 1806, with notes about "the Jews of Galitsia in light of the new Jewish Statute."

In his opinion, an in-depth discussion about the Jewish problem was required. Following a general description of the population situation in the District of Zloczow, he emphasized that the Jewish residents were pious but insincere, immoral, and had drinking tendencies. He claimed that the estate owners were after large profits from their leased taverns, so they encouraged those tendencies.

He claimed that it would be erroneous to blame the Jews for the poor condition of their population. Although he painted the Jews as greedy and selfish, he stated that one needed to consider the conditions which made them a harmful factor in both cities and villages.

He mentioned that in the cities they needed to compete with Christian merchants and artisans. He considered their communities to be the reason for the Jewish problem. He claimed that the Jews' close communities strengthened their seclusion and coalescence as a nation. In a separate chapter, he wrote about Jewish commerce, which suffered from a lack of capital, which in turn, led to the need to seek high–interest loans. He also stated that a small group of Jews exploited the situation by offering loans with an exorbitant rate of interest. That group of people was taking advantage of any circumstance to increase their wealth and was getting richer at the expense of the borrowers.

In his report, Schmidt stated that court cases and feuds were common among Galitsia's Jews. He claimed that the Jews feuded in their private and public life. There were numerous disputes and controversies in every Jewish community. The oppression by the lessees of the candle and kosher meat taxes resulted in snitches and malicious informing. According to Schmidt, a Jewish family paid on average 28 Florins per year [in taxes].

Schmidt considered the tax burden to be one of the main reasons for the fact that Jews were immoral and for the fact that they resisted the authorities.

In a special review section Schmidt offered several concrete proposals to improve the situation, which should be used as a basis for the new Jewish Statue:

    a.   Elimination of the Jews' influence on the general population and limiting their proliferation.
    b.   Eliminating the [Jewish] national sentiment
    c.   Changing the occupations of the Jews and transferring them to farming and crafts.

For turning the Jews into contributing agents, he proposed the following:

- Force them to get rid of the Jewish attire,
- establish schools,
- forbid the youth from studying the Talmud before graduating from elementary school,

• and eliminate the Jewish community organizations because they were responsible for instilling the national spirit!

He proclaimed that the Jewish communities were superfluous. He suggested handing over the tasks of the community and the rabbinate to the municipalities. He stated that Jews must be immediately recruited to the military as the only way for them to adapt themselves and become regular citizens. He suggested that the military was one of the best educational institutions.

He further suggested establishing workplaces and to place there anybody who loathes working.

District ministers from other Galitsia provinces sent similar memorandums.

Papers were piling up at the office of Galitsia's governor and the offices of the central government, with various plans to convert the Jews into loyal and contributing citizens of the country. However, the issue of the renewal of the Jewish Statute was removed from the agenda and postponed for a few years.

Instead of corrections and improvements to the situation, which were extensively discussed and written about, the tax burden continued to grow more and more.

One of the components of that burden was the issue of military lodging, particularly during the years 1810 – 1811. Zloczow community submitted a complaint, in 1811, about the fact that the Jewish homes were assessed higher than their actual value so that the authorities could impose higher military lodging fees. The community appealed again in the same year about the tax assessment. They claimed that the assessment was unjustified and did not reflect the actual situation.

The authorities raised the tax quota significantly during the 1820s. Like other Jewish communities, the Zloczow community submitted a request to lower taxes in light of the economic downturn. The community particularly emphasized the cruel behavior of the lessees of the kosher meat and candle taxes. The governor adopted a conciliatory position at that time since he was very well aware of the deteriorating economic situation of the Jewish masses. He offered to give up on the supplemental tax but stated that to successfully collect the taxes, the community must correct the unrealistic ratio between the levies and the income of the tax debtors. Considering the grievance of the Jewish population – as demonstrated by the appeals, the governor did not shy away from taking another step and offered to eliminate the candle, supplemental, and special taxes. However, Vienna did not even wish to entertain that proposal. Vienna's response was unmistakably negative. Vienna blamed the lessees–collectors for the situation and suggested handing over the collection to the local authorities.

[Columns 67-68]

However, before the authorities made any decision, they asked the district ministers for their opinion.
Zloczow District minister, together with the district ministers of Ivano–Frankivsk [Stanislavov], Przemysl [Pshemishel], and Lviv, accepted Vienna's offer. However, in the end, nothing came out of that, and the tax system was not revised.
In A census of Galitsia's Jews that took place in 1810, 361 families were counted in the city of Zloczow. Among them, there were 674 men and 764 women, and a total of 1438 people.
6209 Jewish families were counted in the District of Zloczow in that census, 11864 men, 12,896 women, and a total of 24,760 people.
That constituted a significant increase compared to the year 1788.
Nine years later, in 1879, 6658 families were counted, among them 288 agricultural families.
It is worthwhile to note that the number of Jewish families in the District of Zloczow compared to the 1810 census, increased by 449 families in 7 years.
204,817 Christians and 30,134 Jews were counted in the District of Zloczow in the census conducted in 1826.
In 1827, out of a total; of 327,612 residents [in the Zloczow District], 31,936 were Jewish. That constituted an increase of 1802 [Jewish] people.

The censuses provide several additional details, although somewhat limited, about the occupations of the Jews during the 1820s

1820 there were the following merchants]:

a. 3073 Jewish retailers in the whole of Galitsia. 284 were in the district of Zloczow.
b. In 1824 there were 80 Jewish street vendors and peddlers in the District of Zloczow.
c. 101 Jewish wood dealers in the District of Zloczow.

In 1820 there were 1842 Jewish merchants of all kinds in the District of Zloczow, among them, 708 were in Brody alone. 30 Jewish merchants owned their firms in the District of Zloczow (63 in Brody alone).

In 1820, there were the following Jewish artisans:

1. Out of a total of 2015 Jewish alcoholic beverages distillers in the whole of Galitsia, 305 were in the District of Zloczow.
2. Out of 1358 tailors in the entire Galitsia, 190 were in the District of Zloczow.
3. Out of a total of 77 salesmen in Galitsia, 12 were in Zloczow District.
4. Out of a total of 8 pillow makers in Galitsia, 3 were in Zloczow District.
5. Out of 7194 artisans in the entire Galitsia, 989 were in Zloczow District (among them, 393 in Brody). One–third of the total number of artisans were distillers of alcoholic beverages, and another third included tailors, shoemakers, furriers, and cable weavers.

At the beginning of the 19th century, several new industries began to develop: fabrics, silk belts, paper, gunpowder, wax, candles, tanning, starch, and even iron casting plants (in the villages of Sialtze, Bonkova, and Ostafloptze). The plants existed for only a short time. The reasons for this were the lack of capital and shortages of raw materials and skilled workforce. Most of the plants were established with the support of the government and capital invested by outside people. The trade for the products of these plants was mostly concentrated in the hands of Zloczow's Jews.

In the first half of the 18th century, prominent families, who colluded with the tax lessees, ruled the Jewish community of Zloczow. They held on to that power for decades, despite the Jewish Statute of Emperor Franz] Joseph that dictated an election every three years. Somehow, the powerful always found an appropriate excuse to influence the district authorities not to follow the clauses of the Statute.

In 1821, the issue of the traditional Jewish attire occupied the attention of Galitsia's Jews. According to clause no. 47 in Franz Joseph's Jewish Statute, Galitsia's Jews had to abandon their traditional attire, which distinguished them from the rest of the population. Rabbis were the only ones exempted from obeying that rule. The Jews did not follow and did not even lift a finger to obey that decree. In light of that overt resistance, the authorities had no other choice but to abort the rule implementation.

During the period 1816 – 1821, the central government worked on preparing a new Jewish statute. They conspired to ban, as a law, the traditional attire of the Jews. Galitsia's governor, Baron Joseph von Hauer, recommended including a specific ban on Jewish attire in the statute.

Somehow, the Jewish public of Galitsia found out about these plots, which awoke a resistance movement among the masses. The Jewish community of Stryj was the first community to go against the governor's demand. All other Jewish communities of Galitsia followed the Stryj community's initiative and submitted a letter– request to Vienna demanding to allow the Jews to keep their attire. Zloczow community, who joined that request, sent a petition on its own as well. The merchants and the furriers submitted a memorandum highlighting the economic damage that a ban on Jewish attire would cause to the various Jewish and non–Jewish occupations.. The Jewish intellectuals, except a group from Brody, joined the protest. In a special memorandum, a group of Jewish intellectuals from Brody explained their consent to Baron von Hauer's proposal.

[Columns 69-70]

A group of "Kadima" [Forward] members

They claimed that the change in the Jewish attire would accelerate the Europeanization process among Galitsia's Jews.

The Austrian merchants, the furriers, and the owners of textile and silk factories submitted a petition against the attire decree following a request by Galitsia's communities. An answer from Vienna arrived on April 1821. The government claimed that all of the explanations brought up by the Jewish communities against changing attire were invalid. As proof, they pointed at Moravia, where the expenses involved in abolishing the attire, did not cause any reduction in the collection of the meat–tax.

After all that, the governor's proposal was not approved, and the issue was postponed.

During the same years, the Hasidic movement in Zloczow and its surroundings gained so much popularity that the authorities became interested in its reach and influence on the Jewish population. The authorities paid attention mainly to the spread of Hasidism in the Zloczow District. In addition to the boycott against the Jewish intelligentsia that was announced in 1815 in Lviv, the authorities issued, with direct special instructions from Vienna, stringent commands to track after the Hasidim and their *Tzaddiks*.

Under the influence of the intelligentsia, the Jewish community leaders began to worry, in the 1830s and 1840s, about improvements in the political status of Galitsia's Jews. They also tried to lobby the authorities to eliminate the special taxes and reduce the tax burden.

In 1846, the District of Zloczow underwent a severe economic crisis due to uprising preparations by the revolutionary forces among the Poles in Eastern Galitsia. That was felt particularly in the provinces, Lviv, Ivano–Frankivsk [Stanislavov], Sambir [Sambor], and Zloczow.

In the District of Zloczow, the rebels planned to organize themselves in companies and platoons to attack Zloczow. However, these platoons had to disperse due to the resistance by the farmers (who were mainly Ruthenians) to the aspirations of the revolting Polish nobles. That situation caused significant interruptions in economic affairs, and the Jews were the people who suffer from that the most.

The leaders of all Jewish communities gathered in 1847 in Lviv, by the initiative by the Jewish community of Lviv, which was led by people with academic education. The gathering objective was to consult and discuss the state of the Jews. Representatives of the Zloczow's community attended the gathering. They attended the meeting even though the leaders were orthodox Jews who have not yet recognized the positive side of political activism. At that gathering, it was decided to submit a petition to the central government that would contain a description of the actual state of the Jews. That petition was submitted only on behalf of the large Jewish communities.

A hospital was established in Zloczow in the 1830s. It was maintained, for some time, through charitable contributions. However, the hospital was later neglected due to a lack of financial means. After the cholera pandemic and the spread of other diseases, which besieged the poor, the Jewish community leaders had decided to request the district authorities to add one Kreutzer to the price of a Litra of kosher meat, to support the hospital.

Vienna government agreed. On March 4, 1845, a ¼ Kreutzer was added to the price of kosher meat to pay for the maintenance of the Jewish hospital.

A district hospital for syphilis patients, under the management of the Jewish physician Moshe Rekhen, the municipal orthopedical, also operated from 1874.

On July 1, 1849, the physician reached an agreement with the municipality to operate that hospital as a general hospital for the broad population. The physician made all the arrangements, including adequate lighting. According to the agreement, the town paid the hospital, from the municipal treasury, an amount of 16 Kreutzers per day for every patient.

[Columns 71-72]

On 20 March 1853, the district bureau realized that the hospital did not address the needs of the city. They came to that conclusion based on the report submitted by the district physician, Dr. Carter. in 1853, Dr. Rekhen reached a new agreement with the city, under which the hospital was recognized as the official hospital of the city. Dr. Rekhen managed the hospital. After his death, his widow, Getzya Rekhen, managed the hospital together with Abraham Amper (under a confidential partnership with the orthopedic physician Dr. Max Deutsch). Since the financial situation of the hospital did not improve, the state committee contributed 3000 Florins for a new building more suitable for its purpose. A building committee consisting of representatives of the city residents was established. However, the committee was not active and did not achieve any progress. Only in 1872, did the district committee buy a dedicated building, where the city relocated the municipal hospital.

The events of 1848 did make a significant impression on Zloczow's Jews, as they did on the Jews of Lviv, Ivano–Frankivsk [Stanislavov], Zloczow, and Brody. Along with the rest of the Jewish communities in Galitsia, The Jews in the Zloczow district stopped paying the special taxes upon issuance of the new constitution in March 1848. They based it on clauses 25 and 27 of the constitution, which guaranteed freedom and equality in the payment of taxes.

However, the city authorities had a different opinion.

The communities in the District of Zloczow received explicit instruction from the district bureau. After receiving complaints from the lessees of the candle and kosher meat taxes, the authorities found it necessary to announce that the news about the discontinuance of these taxes was a false rumor. They stated that the Jewish community leadership must alert the Jewish residents and the residents of the neighboring villages to ensure that there would be no disruptions or stoppage of tax payments to the lessees.

Fearing the loss of their profits, the lessees acted behind the scenes and demanded that the authority take drastic measures. That had happened not just in Zloczow and Galitsia. Similar instructions were issued throughout the Austrian empire, which angered the Jews. They mobilized to fight the hypocritical policy of the government. They claimed that the government interpreted the spirit of freedom of religion, faith, and equality differently for the Jews.

The elections for the first parliament, which was supposed to decide upon the first constitution, were held in June 1848. Since the Jews in Zloczow were not allowed to elect their own representative to the parliament, they did not participate in any political activity like the Jews in Ivano–Frankivsk [Stanislavov], Brody, and Lviv.

The Greek–Catholic Gregory Levitzki (a Ruthenian) was elected as the representative in Zloczow. Little is known about the participation of the Jews in the election. No details are available about whether they went to the polling station or whom they had voted for. During the first session of the parliament, in 1848, an article was published in the [German Language weekly] magazine, "*Oesterreichishes Zentral Organ Fuer Glaubensfreiheit, Cultur, Gescchichte und Literatur der Juden*" [The Austrian Magazine for Jewish Faith, Culture, History, and Literature]. The article called for all the Jewish communities of Galitsia to submit a petition to the parliament. That petition should highlight their [dire] state of affairs and emphasize the limitations imposed on the Jewish population and the [heavy] tax burden, especially the candle and the kosher meat taxes. The article suggested that the communities present their demands for equal rights at the end of that petition.

That initiative was successful, and all the Jewish communities signed the petition. The leader of the Zloczow's community, Dov Bear Landau, signed it. The petition was given to the district's representative. A copy of the petition was sent to the Jewish representatives from Galitsia, Rabbi Dov Bearish Meizlish, the preacher Mannheimer, and Abraham Heilperin. A copy of the petition was also sent to the Polish representatives who were known to support the cause of equal rights for the Jews. It was also sent to the Jewish representatives from outside Galitsia, Dr. Adolf Fischhof, and Dr. Goldmark.

The Jewish members of the large communities, such as Brody, Lviv, and Zloczow, joyfully accepted the news that the Kremsier Parliament decided to abolish the special taxes imposed on the Jews. The representative from Brody, the Jewish Viennese preacher, Mannheimer, should receive the credit for the effort.

We could not find any acknowledgment of the news in the period's Jewish newspapers. They treated them indifferently without appreciating the fact that their faith was tied to them.

There were no signs that anything changed in the life of the Zloczow's Jews, even after 1848. The management of the community was in the hands of the Haredim who managed the community affairs in the spirit of the Jewish tradition without taking any steps to improve the state of the masses.

The influence of the few intellectuals in the city was minuscule. Therefore, it is no wonder that the community leaders treated apathetically the political actions taken by the representatives from the Jewish communities of Lviv, Ternopil [Tarnopol], Ivano–Frankivsk [Stanislavov], and Brody. These activities were taken to improve the political and social standing of Galitsia's Jews. It included the efforts made in 1853 to repeal the law, from 2 October 1853, that limited the ownership rights of the Jews, which was awarded in 1848. It also included the effort to rescind the 1803 law prohibiting employment by Jews of Christian wet–nurses, apprentices, and trainees.

[Columns 73-74]

That law was canceled in 1848 but renewed in 1853.

The Jews were allowed to purchase real–estate in 1860. It is worthwhile to note that, in contrast to other communities, where quite a few Jews submitted applications to buy lots, houses, estates, and plots of land, only two applications were submitted by Jews in Zloczow. The two were: a) The community leader, Herman Burstein indicated that he had served as the community leader for thirty years. He received the permit in 1862. b) Moshe Schwadron, who received the permit in 1864.

Commerce and industry bureaus were first established in Austria in 1850. Among them, one bureau was for Galitsia. It was located in Brody and represented the districts of Ternopil, Chertkiv [Chertkov], Berezhany, and Zloczow. Meir Kalir from Brody was elected as the president of that bureau.

The Austrian army barracks

According to the new organization of the court network in Galitsia, only 106 lawyers were allowed to serve in the courts. That number included 20 Jewish lawyers. Only one Jewish lawyer, Dr. Adolf Rekhen, was allowed to appear in Zloczow. The court in Zloczow was the district court.

No changes were made in the leadership of the Zloczow Jewish community. Dov Bear Landau held the leadership post from 1831 until 1850.

Later on, the post was held by Herman Burstein, who ruled with a strong arm until 1863. However, the *Maskilim* [generally educated people] managed to gradually capture the leadership of the community. The *Maskil* Neteh Schorr became the leader after Burstein. From then on, the Maskilim, one after the other, served as the leaders of the community: Neteh Schorr, Yehuda Finkelstein, Yosef Kuten. These *Maskilim* were fierce *Mitnagdim* [opponents to the Hasidim]. They did not hesitate to implement many plans against the will and wrath of the zealots. Fierce disputes often erupted between the Hasidim and the *Mitnagdim*.

In 1860, the community leaders discussed the possibility of establishing an elementary school similar to those in Ternopil, Lviv, Brody, and Bolekhiv [Bolekhov]. The community turned to the school in Bolekhiv, headed by Shlomo Rubin (1823 – 1910), to send the bylaws of their school to them. Bolekhiv management complied with the request. However, the leadership of the Zloczow's community did not progress beyond discussion and consultation. The masses, incited by the Hasidim, treated the idea with hostility and would have avoided sending their children to that school. Although going to school was compulsory by law, people always found ways to evade it.

In January 1866, the community leaders turned to establish a charity fund to help the poor.

A discussion was held at the rabbi's home, and a decision was made to collect the required capital. Yosef Zeev Shuger, Zalman Halberthal, Yaakov Shmuel Laks, and Shmuel Auerbach went from house to house soliciting contributions. [Following Genesis 44:12 – "He started with the eldest and finished with the youngest…"] – they started with the affluent and ended with the destitute. They "sweet-talked" people to commit to contributing weekly as much as they could afford [following Deuteronomy 16:17 "Every man shall give as he is able..."]. They succeeded to collect 40 Guldens weekly for the charity organization for the poor – "Lemish'an Lekehm".

The leaders of the Zloczow Jewish community, the *Maskilim*, Yehuda Funkelstein, and Yosef Kuten, were influenced by the spirit exhibited by the initiatives of the Lviv–based organization – "Shomer Israel" ["Guardian of Israel"]. That organization led to a substantial change in the political lives of Galitsia's Jews. The main objective of the organization was to structure the Jewish communities based on proper and updated bylaws. The organization's commission demanded that the Jewish communities go through a reorganization to modernize themselves. The "Shomer Israel" organization made efforts to stabilize the status of the Jewish communities by establishing uniform countrywide bylaws approved by the government and by unifying the communities into a single countrywide organization. The communities were requested to participate in the "Communities Day" event, organized by "Shomer Israel", which took place in Lviv on 18 – 20 June 1878. Zloczow's community was represented in that event by Shmuel Auerbach and Yosef Kuten. They took an active part in the discussions at the conference. Yosef Kuten was also elected as a member of a committee tasked with overseeing the execution of the conference's resolutions.

[Columns 75-76]

After "Communities Day," the *Haredim* started a stubborn war against any attempt of renewals in the communities and grouped themselves in an organization called "Makhzikei Ha'dat" ["Keepers of the Religion"], which was led by Rabbi Shimon Sofer of Krakow, and the Admo"r from Belz. The Jewish community of Zloczow protested against that organization's initiatives.

A substantial change occurred in the lives of Jews following the award of equal rights to them. On the other hand, the orthodox Jews were befuddled. They feared that freedom would be tied to compulsory service in the military, which would substantially harm the Jewish way of life and tradition.

Even the community's non–ultra-orthodox feared the freedom of attending general education schools and universities. They feared that the intellectuals would grow in numbers and would capture the power in the community.

The *Parnasim* [leaders] of the community in that period were: Shmuel Auerbach, Mordekhai Moiter, Eliezer Swartz, and Avraham Garfunkel.

Eliyahu Vashitz (the father of Dr. Efraim Vashitz) served as the community secretary and the vital records registrar from 1895.

Zloczow, together with Brody, voted for their representatives in Vienna by direct elections during the years of the Austrian Parliamentarianism (1873 – 1919).

Dr. Joachim Landau from Brody, who served in the parliament until 1879, was elected in the first direct elections in 1873. The Christian Hausner served after him. In 1885, the palace advisor Dr. Edward Sutor Freiheger von Frodrichstal was elected against the Jewish candidate, the manager of the train tracks, Karl Ludwig, who was supported by the Hasidim. The Christian Hausner served after him. The latter served until 1891. After him, the head of "Shomer Israel", Dr. Emil Bik (1845 – 1906), advanced his candidacy against Dr. Sutor, who was supported by the Rabbi from Belz, although he was non–Jewish. Dr. Bik won and joined the Polish faction. He served as the representative of Zloczow and Brody until his death in the summer of 1906. The main factors in that election were bribery, bargaining, and purchasing of votes.

A special election was held in 1906, after the death of Dr. Bik. At that time, the Zionists nominated a candidate – Adolf Shtand. Jewish physician from Zloczow – Dr. Yosef Guld, ran as the candidate of the assimilators. The latter was supported by his father–in–law, Yosef Guld, who was the leader of the Zloczow community. Dr. Guld was elected under the pressure exerted by the authorities and shameful coercion. Dr. Guld served in parliament until the spring of 1907.

* * *

Rabbi Khaim Burstein served as the city's rabbi from the middle of the 19th century until 1883. After him, Rabbi Yoel Ashkenazi, a decadent of Rabbi Tzvi Ashkenazi, the author of "Khakham Tzvi" ["The Wise Man Tzvi"] served as the city rabbi.

Zloczow's native, Rabbi Yeshayahu Zeev Rosenberg, served as the head of the rabbinical court from 1860. He was a prominent scholar and had exceptional virtues. He was the teacher of Rabbi Shalom Schwadron, the rabbi of Berezhany.

Rabbi Menakhem Mendel Meizel was nominated to serve as the head of the rabbinical court after the death of Rabbi Yeshayahu Zeev. He previously served in Bila Tserkva [Belaïa Tserkov], Ukraine, but, as an Austrian citizen, he could not secure a residence status there so he had to return to Zloczow to his father–in–law, Rabbi Moshe Schwadron. Rabbi Menakhem Mendel, a Sadgora's Hasid, arrived in Zloczow together with Rabbi Feivel Rohatyn. The latter was a "*Mitnaged*" [Someone who resisted the rise of Hassidism]. It was difficult for both of them to serve together.

Rabbi Feivel Rohatyn (1858 – 1910) was born in Lviv. He was the student of Rabbi Abner (a prominent scholar in Lviv) and also a student of Rabbi Yitzkhak Ettinger of Lviv. Rabbi Feivel was the son–in–law of the magnate, Moshe Griss, from Kulykiv [Kulykov]. Rabbi Feivel was ordained as a rabbi at the age of 16 by Rabbi Tzvi Orenstein, Rabbi Yitzkhak Ettinger, and Rabbi Yitzkhak Shmelkes. He served as the rabbi in Narayiv from 1878 – 1883. In 1883, he was elected as a rabbi in Zloczow. He devoted himself to general studies and prepared for a high school matriculation examination. In 1893, he successfully passed the final exams in Zloczow's high school and received the diploma, which greatly angered the Hasidim. He was accepted to the university in Lviv and studied philosophy. He received his university diploma in 1898. He later received a doctorate in philosophy after completing research about Ramba"m [Maimonides].

Despite his secular studies, he did not neglect his rabbinical work and studying the Torah. He published a religious law book by the name "Mishpat Mekhokek". Rabbi Rohatyn was the first orthodox rabbi who gave a speech in Polish at the synagogue during a public celebration.

Rabbi Feivel Rohatyn kept connections vigorously communicated in writing with Jewish scientists such as Prof. D. H. Miller, Dr. Gidman, and Salomon Buber. He was also involved in religious responsa communication with the greatest rabbis of his generation. He took an active role in Zloczow's public affairs, served in the municipality, and taught Talmud lessons. Despite his secular studies, he did not neglect his rabbinical work and studying the Torah.

In 1901, a fierce business conflict erupted between Rabbi Rohatyn and Zloczow's famed tycoon, Yosef Kuten. The authorities invited bidding on building an army barrack. Yosef Kuten was a professional contractor, and so was the rabbi.

[Column 77]

Rabbi Rohatyn's bid, which was probably cheaper, was accepted. The authorities nominated him to build the barrack. Kuten did not forgive Rabbi Rohatyn for that and joined with his opponents – the Hasidim. Rabbi Rohatyn was forced to leave the city because of conflict. Only after several years, in 1907, he returned and served as the rabbi until he died in 1910.

During Rabbi Rohatyn's period, Rabbi Menakhem Miller, a native of Terniv [Ternov], served as the head of the rabbinical court. As mentioned, he encountered resistance from the Hasidim, who considered him the assistant and supporter of Rabbi Rohatyn.

Chapter 5

Under the Austrian Conquest

When Austria annexed Reisyn, Zloczow was a ravaged and depleted city, lacked residential houses in proper conditions, and had a sparse population.

That was why the Austrians did not consider Zloczow to be a city. Officials reported the city residents to be considered in the middle between city residents and village dwellers.

The city's rehabilitation and development began with the appointment of Von Tannhauser to the position of district minister.

The district office resided in Brody. In 1783, the government discussed the possibility of transferring it to Zloczow. Brody's Jewish community requested to leave the office in Brody in consideration of the economic interests of the city. The authorities delayed the transfer until 1787. It is unknown whether the delay was caused because of due Brody's request. The Pole Bojakowski, who served as the district minister in Brody until 1782, was appointed district manager. He relocated to Zloczow in 1783.

The district office was transferred from Brody to Zloczow even though Zloczow was smaller than Brody in terms of its population and economic importance. The district officials were against the transfer. They claimed that Zloczow was too small and lacked the resources for hosting the offices. Only the office of the district minister remained in Brody.

A period of development began when Zloczow became a district city.

Tannhauser had to temporarily locate his office in Berezhany [Bzhezhani] due to the poor residential situation in Zloczow. When the appropriate conditions for maintaining offices developed, the office returned to Zloczow. The office organization consisted of the following: The district minister, 3–4 commissioners, a secretary, two clerks, 1–2 apprentices, and two messengers.

For a certain period, Zloczow had only one physician, one orthopedic, and one midwife. For a while, there was no pharmacy in the city. That situation lasted until the pharmacy of the Dominican Monastery moved to Zloczow from Podkamen.

Unlike other Austrian officials sent to Galitsia, Tannhauser was not a follower of the pan-German movement. He was non–partisan and treated the Poles with sympathy. Unlike other district ministers, his main activity was in the economic area. He objected to the oppressive approach to collecting taxes. The first governor [commissar] in Zloczow, Golbakh, held the same opinions as Tannhauser. The population considered the district ministers the symbol of the regime and the state government arm, serving the nobility, church, Jews, and peasants.

Tannhauser recognized that Zloczow's area was an important industrial center, particularly in the field of weaving. Indeed, many artisans were in the area – shoemakers, tailors, and bakers who sold their products to Jewish merchants.

Tannhauser lobbied the kingdom to provide financial assistance to the city's needy because he determined that the earnings were too low.

In particular, Tannhauser investigated the economic state of the estates. He realized that the medium and small estates were better positioned financially than the large ones, although their farms were still primitive. The large estate owners accumulated debts and had to lease their villages.

Due to the cessation of the ties with Gdansk [Dantzig], the wheat trade underwent a severe crisis. However, the situation gradually improved later as new markets were found. Due to that disconnection, the estate owners, who maintained wood potash kilns industries in their village, suffered. Tobacco cultivation, which brought substantial profits to the farmers and Jewish traders, received considerable attention in Zloczow. With the establishment of the state monopoly, tobacco cultivation ceased. The Jews leased the tobacco monopolies, which were established outside Zloczow and Galitsia. Cultivation of potatoes began in 1783 under encouragement from the authorities. Substantial progress was achieved in growing apples, planting fruit orchards, and raising cattle, particularly oxen. Armenian and Jewish wholesalers bought the oxen and exported them to Bohemia, Moravia, Silesia, and Austria.

City councils were established in Galitsian cities after the Galitsian Sejm passed the City Regulations Act in October 1868, following a debate on the issue during 1862 – 1868. Thirty members served in the Zloczow council.

[Columns 79-80]

Among them, 14 were Catholics (Poles), 3 were Greek Catholics (Ruthenians), and 13 were Jews.

The Jewish physician Dr. David Bilt was elected as the mayor at the end of the 19th century. Dr. Yosef Guld, the son–in–law of the Jewish community leader, Yosef Guld, served as a mayor during 1906 –1914.

The established families captured influential positions among the Jewish public in Zloczow and filled critical roles in the community, organizations, and overall social life. The Landau family ruled the community for many years. Dov Bear Landau was notably known. His name as the "*Regirend*" ["Ruler" in Yiddish], preceded him in Eastern Galitsia during the 1830s and 1840s of the 19th century.

Dov Bear Landau was an orthodox Jew and a Hasid. We should also mention Dvorah Landau from the Landau family. She was married to Moshe Schlager. He was a scholar, intellectual, and one of the famous contractors in Zloczow. The mother of Dvorah was Freida, the daughter of Rabbi Rubinstein of Zloczow. When she arrived in Zloczow after her wedding, she brought a special medicine for the eyes (Nux-Vasser), which she used to provide, free of charge, to eye patients. She was a known communal leader and was cherished by the poor and the needy.

Another established family was Auerbach. The head of the family, Shmuel Auerbach, was not only wealthy but a scholar and learned. His son-in-law was Meir Rapoport, the grandson of the rabbi of Lviv, Rabbi Khaim Rapoport. Rabbi Khaim was known for his participation in the debate with the Frankists. Meir Rapoport was an orthodox Jew but also a scholar. He knew a few classical languages and was knowledgeable in general literature.

Burstein, Weinberger, and Halberthal families, who were all related, were also among the established families. The family of Arye Winebarger was devout. He and his father-in-law, Halberthal, bought estates that used to belong to "Zloczow Developer" [Sobieski], along with their forests, fields, and the palace. Later on, they suddenly lost their fortune. Seltzer, the father-in-law of Dr. Itamar Eidelberg, bought the estates.

The son–in–law of Arye Weinberger, David Lvov, was also among the wealthy people in the city. He owned a store for agricultural machinery. The family of Yosef Kuten belonged to the affluent. He was not a native of the city. He came to Zloczow in 1818 from the town of Kuzyn in Volyn. He ran away to Brody to evade recruitment to the Russian army. He went to Zloczow to hand over a letter to the community leader from the rabbi of Kuzyn and stayed there.

His grandfather, Rabbi Azriel from Kuzyn, was a loyal student of the famous *Tzadik* Rabbi Leib Sara"s.

When he arrived at Zloczow, he was received by Rabbi Dov Bear Landau, who hosted him in his house and took care of his needs. Kuten continued with his Torah studies, and a short while later married Khava, the daughter of Rabbi Landau. His father-in-law opened a textile store for him.

Later on, he received the contract of providing food to the local jail on behalf of the court and supplying grocery items to the railroad officials. He gained fame as a contractor supplying food, wood, and gravel for road construction. He established queries for that purpose around Zloczow. He went from strength to strength and became the contractor for constructing buildings for the government. His profits increased more and more. When he became rich, he bought himself an estate.

Kuten was initiative and full of energy throughout his entire life. He fulfilled critical roles in the life of the Jewish community. He served as a community Parnas, and a deputy leader. He also served as the head of the community's committee and was its representative at the "Communities Day" held [in Lviv] in 1878. Kuten contributed substantially to Jewish organizations. His home was traditional, and he educated his son traditionally. He died in 1897.

His wife Khava, was a typical daughter of an affluent Jewish family in the 19th century. She cared for the city poor, providing them with woods and potatoes for the winter, and clothes for their children. She always hosted two high school students at home. She died in 1905.

Yosef and Khava Kuten had a son, Eliezer, and a daughter Rachel. The daughter married the lawyer Dr. Gross. The son, Eliezer, actively participated in the affairs of the Jewish community.

The national sentiment was already apparent within the affluent families of Moshe Schwadron, Avraham Yaakov Igel, Fishel Reis, Nakhman Gritz, and Zeev Yosefberg. The latter was the husband of Elka, a community activist and the granddaughter of the head of the rabbinical court, Rabbi Yeshayahu Rosenberg.

Against these families stood Yosef Guld, who was very wealthy, but character of a tough guy, who did not shy away from any means to achieve what he wanted.

One of the veteran families was Tzukerkendel. The patriarch of the family, Avi Tzukerkendel, was a lessee of alcoholic beverage distillers in 1797. One of his great-grandchildren, Wilhelm Tzukerkendel, opened a bookstore in 1870. A short time later, he founded a printing and a folk publishing business.

[Columns 81-82]

His business specialized in publishing Polish classic books and international translated literature based on the precedent set by Reklad publisher in Leipzig.

Tzukerkendel's business captured a respectable position in the Polish publishing industry. By 1914, it published more than a thousand books and many translations of Roman and Greek masterpieces.

Three "Talmud Torah" schools [religious schools], containing three hundred pupils and three teachers, were counted in the census, held by the authorities in 1869. There were also fifteen private "*Kheders*" [religious schools for preschoolers]. The census data does not mention the number of students in public schools.

The famed Viennese scholar and preacher, Rabbi Dr. Adolf Jellinek, had the initiative to establish a fund named after Barone Hirsch. The fund secured capital of 25 million Francs. It aimed at establishing vocational schools for Jewish youths in Galitsia and Bukovina. Twenty–one elementary and vocational schools were established by that fund in towns throughout Galitsia and Bukovina during 1891 – 1893. As many as 5000 boys and girls studied in these schools. Additionally, 3000 boys who studied in various organizations were supported by the fund.

The Jewish public soup Kitchen

The fund also supported the establishment of a Jewish elementary school in Zloczow.

The fund management in Lviv established a local committee in Zloczow, headed by Dr. David Bolt [to oversee the school]. Worlenger was nominated to manage the school. Mordekhai Dreyfus, Shmaryahu Imber, and Yitzkhak Margaliot served as teachers.

Since the central management of the fund in Lviv was at the hands of Jewish assimilation extremists, the Jewish studies in that school were neglected, against the regulations. That caused quarrels with the parents, who claimed that: "to educate gentiles, the general schools would suffice and there was no need for a school that carries the name of Barone Hirsch". Due to the firm position of the parents, the management was forced to establish special Hebrew courses. The teachers, Mordekhai Dreyfus, and Israel Meshir taught these courses. However, that by itself did not satisfy the leaders of the Jewish national intelligentsia in the city.

In 1905, the parents' association established a "general *Kheder*" [a school combining religious and general studies] under the management of the intellectual Israel Meshir. The association was headed by Shmuel Wildengur, Nathan Negelberg, Merdekhai Semel, Israel Wolfskoit, and Moshe Auerbach. Hundreds of children studied in the "general *Kheder*".

Meshir himself taught the Bible, Hebrew, grammar, and Jewish history. Jewish history was taught according to [historian Heinrich] Graetz (translated by [the Jewish scholar] Saul Pinkhas Rabinowitz). The *Kheder* encouraged people to establish a Jewish school. The idea materialized when Dr. Simkha Bunim came to live in Zloczow. Under his initiative, a committee supporting the concept of a Jewish school was formed. The committee members were: Dr. Hirschhorn and his wife – Sara, nee Tartakover, Dr. Gruber, and Dr. Groskopf.

[Columns 83-84]

The school – "Safa Brurah" ["Clear Language"] headed by Naftali Zigel, was established in the same year as a memorial for Rabbi Feivel Rohatyn.

In 1880, the number of Christian residents in the district of Zloczow reached 107,221, and the number of Jews – 19,208. Among them, 21,243 Christians (80.4%) resided in 10 cities and towns. 1,791 Jews (28%) lived in 131 villages.

In 1890, the number of Christian residents in the district of Zloczow reached 127,417, and the number of Jews – 20,947. Among them, 24,389 Christians (19.1%), and 15,834 Jews (75.6%), resided in 10 cities and towns. 2,225 Jews (29.8%) lived in 130 villages.

In 1900, the number of Christian residents in the district of Zloczow reached 140,622, and the number of Jews – 21,548. Among them, 27,358 Christians (19.5%), and 16,380 Jews (76%), resided in cities and towns. 1,927 Jews (26.4%) resided in 130 villages.

In 1921, the number of residents in the district of Zloczow was 107,079. The Jews numbered – 10,522. Among the Jewish residents, 7,476 (41.8%), resided in cities, 1,257 (19.2%) in other urban communities, and 1,819 (2.2%) in villages.

In the city of Zloczow itself there were:

In 1869 – 3200 Jews (44.7%)
In 1880 – 4,046 Jews (48.5%)
In 1890 – 5,086 Jews (50.3%)
In 1900 – 5,401 Jews (45.6%)
In 1910 – 5,243 Jews (39.6%)
In 1921 – 5,744 Jews (51.6%)

The actual number of Jews increased from 3,200 people in 1869 to 5,744 people in 1921. However, the Jewish population percentage decreased from 44.8% in 1869 to 39.6% in 1910. Only in 1921, did that number increase to 51.6%.

The following are the numbers of Christian residents:

	Poles	Ruthenians	Others
1880	2,219 (26.6%)	2,048 (24.5%)	34 (0.4%)
1890	2,190 (21.7%)	2,826 (27.9%)	11 (0.7%)
1900	3,302 (25.6%)	3,356 (28.4%)	53 (10.4%)
1910	3,946 (29.8%)	4,003 (30.3%)	42 (10.3%)

The Jewish property registered as real–estate in the deed office reached a total of 6,562 Hectares [1 Hectare = 2.471 acres or 10 Dunam] in 1869 (9.2%). That number reached 11,874 Hectares (17.8%) in 1902.

The number of Jewish real estate owners in 1869 was 13 out of a total number of owners of 101 (94 Christians and 4 public owners). In 1902 there were 22 Jewish owners out of 86 owners (56 Christian owners and 8 public owners).

The JCA ["Jewish Colonization Association"], established a credit union in January 1905. The objective was to ease the economic hardship of the retailers and artisans.

In 1906, the credit union included 338 members, 292 loans amounting to 75,230 Krones were issued, 59,493 Krones were paid on these loans, and 1,200 Krones of administrative expenses were incurred.

In 1907, there were 439 members. 327 loans totaling 101,610 Krones were issued. 83,356 Krones were paid on these loans, and 1,522 Krones of administrative expenses were incurred.

In 1908, there were 537 members, and 437 loans totaling 120,210 (?) Krones were issued, 114,889 Krones were paid on these loans, and 2,093 Krones of administrative expenses were incurred.

During the years 1906–1908, 1,342 loans totaling 353,262 Krones were issued, and until 12/13/1908, 284,822 were paid on these loans.

Besides the JCA credit union, there were 25 other credit unions in 1908. Among them, 9 were Christian and 16 Jewish. There were also 47 loan–associations based on Schultz's method. Among them, 17 were Christian, containing 30,768 members, and 30 were Jewish, consisting of 29,863 members. The total amount of the members' stocks in the Jewish associations reached 734,485 Krones in 1908. The reserve fund reached 167,375 Krones and the savings – 2,021,483 Krones. The total amount of loans issued reached 4,264,434 Krones while the administrative expenses reached 115,268 Krones

Among the Jewish community organizations devoted to the needs of the population was the hospital. The construction of the building was completed only in 1885 after numerous and hard efforts. It took a while since "many of the wealthy among us, kept their distance from the charity needs. Their love for their fortune caused them to be always aloof in any effort that was a useful and good endeavor. So they were hard-hearted in this case, and could not be trusted to support the needs of the people".

For those reasons, the inauguration of the hospital was delayed until December 1886. Representatives from the government and the officer corp and distinguished people from the Jewish and non–Jewish communities attended the inauguration.

[Column 85]

Rabbi Rohatyn gave a speech in German. After him, the government representative spoke. He praised the diligence of Jews. Dr. Stein, Dr. Shenkar, and Dr. Gross also delivered speeches.

Besides the hospital, there were other public-supported organizations: "Moshav Zkenim" [nursing home], "Talmud Torah" [Torah school for boys], and "*Khevre Kadisha*" [burial society]. However, they were in a miserable situation due to the apathy of the heads of the community. Only after World War I, did improvements in their state had begun.

To the list of public organizations, we should add "Yad Kharutzim" [Artisans organization] and "Ezrat Yisrael" [an organization to help the poor].

The number of academically educated intellectuals grew during the beginning of the 19th century.

The famous lawyers in the city were: Dr. Itamar Eidelberg, Dr. Meiblum, Dr. Yitzkhak Mitelman, Dr. Alter Bernhard, Dr. Groskopf, Dr. Menashe Epstein, Dr. Heinrikh Hirschhorn, Dr, Hesel, Dr. Louis Rotenberg, Dr. Halpern, and Dr. Lukah Anzelem.

The famous physicians were: Dr. Yosef Guld, Dr. Deutsch, Dr, Bendel Sigmund, Dr. Planer, Dr. Haan, Dr. Baradakh, and Dr. Mintz.

[Columns 85-86]

Chapter 6

Intellectuals and Authors

The Jewish Enlightenment Movement [*Haskalah* in Hebrew] was late in arriving in Zloczow, despite its proximity to the two Galitsian enlightenment centers, Brody and Ternopil. Although a few in the city were fans of the new movement, at the beginning of the 19th century, they were just a small minority. The Hasidism and the apathy of Zloczow people toward general studies delayed the process of enlightenment.

We have learned about the following case that occurred in the 1830s:

The book: "Bokhen *Tzadik*" ["Examine the Righteous"], by Yosef Perl, was published (in Prague) in 1838, without mentioning the name of the author. Similar to Perl's earlier book: "Megaleh Tmirin" ["Revealer of Secrets"] (Vienna, 1819), the book was written as an exchange of letters (between R' Moshe Umanir and Ovadia Ben Ptakhia). In that book, Perl mocked the Hasidim and criticized the failings of the Jewish society in Galitsia as a whole. He pointed out the need for changes by going back to nature – becoming workers of the land. The location of his story was Abdaro (Brody). Perl disliked Brody's rabbis, *maggids* [preachers], and Torah students on one side and the educated assimilators on the other. One enlightened person from Brody protested sharply against the author. In his critical article, he protested that the book's author was mimicking the book "Megaleh Tmirin" by Perl. He also criticized the author for daring to defame all the Jews in Galitsia, especially in Brody. The article's author suspected that the book's author belonged to the people who opposed the Enlightenment Movement. It took another article, authored by an enlightened intellectual in Zloczow, signed as W.L.K., to reveal that the author of "Bokhen *Tzadik*" was also Perl. That article had nothing but praise for the book.

The first enlightened people in Zloczow belonged to the generation of the Galitsia Enlightenment Movement's epigones. They appeared after the sun of movement had already set.

One of the first members of Zloczow's enlightened generation was the teacher and *melamed*, Barukh Stern. He was an educated researcher and a wise Torah student. He was admired by the Hasidim. He educated a generation of enlightened people in the city.

An established circle of enlightened people already existed in Zloczow in the 1860s – 1870s. Neteh Schorr, the head of the Jewish community, Yehuda Funkenstein, and Shlomo Auerbach belonged to that circle. They all acquired a general and Jewish education. Funkenstein's house contained a rich library of Hebrew, German and French books and served as the center for that camp. The enlightened people and youths of Zloczow who were thirsty for general education would gather there.

The organization, "Khevrat Khokhma Ve'Haskalah" ["Wisdom and Education Association"], was established in 1878. Zealous Hasidim destroyed their center a short while later. Unfortunately, the enlightened people failed to resurrect the association and its reading hall for several years. In the meantime, the whole generation of youths, graduates of general public schools and universities, became adults.

In 1885, the "Wisdom and Education Association" was revived by Itamar Eidelberg and Aharon Rapoport, who founded a Hebrew library with a reading hall filled with Hebrew magazines. The association leaned toward the movement of "Khibat Tzion" ["Love of Zion"]. Unfortunately, the association did not last long and disintegrated with time.

The most prominent figure among Zloczow's enlightened people, Yehuda Funkenstein (1820 – 1890), was a member of a renowned family in the city. One of his ancestors was a community leader at the beginning of the Austrian regime. He was a partner of Kalman in leasing the kosher tax and was embattled in fights with his competitors.

Yehuda Funkenstein – a staunch community character, received a general education. He was particularly hostile against ignorance and superstitious. He went against *Admo"rs* [a prominent Hasidic rebbe] and *tzadikim* [righteous and pious people] with a firmness, very reminiscent of the Ternopil Enlightenment Movement's pioneer – Yosef Perl. In Funkenstein's eyes, the latter symbolized the enlightened who stubbornly fought against the rebels who resisted the light.

[Columns 87-88]

Funkenstein did not shy away from any means in his fight with the *tzadikim*.

Rabbi Uri Ben Pinkhas of Strelisk was the founder of the Hasidic *Admo"r* dynasty. The story about what Funkenstein did to the Rabbi was well known.

Rabbi Uri was invited to stay with his Hasidic followers in Zloczow, whose numbers were substantial. Rabbi Uri accepted the invitation and came. What did Yehuda Funkenstein do? He used his courageous ties with the authorities to keep the Rabbi afar from the city on Friday night. With this deed, he imitated his mentor, Yosef Perl. In 1829, Perl led to the expulsion of the head of the Hasidic sect, Hirsh Eikhenstein (nicknamed "Hirsh Zydachover" [from Zhydachiv]). He prevented the Rebbe from visiting after the Rabbi was invited, by Zbarazh, the leader of the Jewish community to spend the Sabbath in the city.

Rabbi Uri Strelisker was forced to spend the Sabbath with his followers in a neighboring village.

Following that event, the Hasidim spread a false rumor that Funkenstein was going insane and that his family was struck by nerve disease.

The intellectual and educated Funkenstein was also an author, He published articles and essays in the [Jewish journal] "HaMaggid", under a pseudo name "Ivry" ["Israelite"].

As mentioned, the library of Funkenstein, which was filled with Hebrew, German and French books, served as a center where the Enlightened gathered for discussions and debates about literature matters and public issues.

He owned multiple businesses, and his condition was financially sound and integrated with the economic life of Eastern Galitsia.

His son–in–law, Mordekhai Muter, also belonged to Zoczow's Enlightened Camp. Mordekhai was born in 1840 in Berezhany. His mother was married (second marriage) to Simkha Bunim Eiger, the son of Rabbi Akiva Eiger of Poznan. Rabbi Akiva educated Mordekhai. After his marriage, Mordekhai became a banker in Zloczow. He was a learned and educated person. He lectured on Sabbaths about the weekly Torah reading in the "*Shulelekhel*" [the small synagogue], near the big synagogue. He published articles in Hebrew newspapers and was a public activist. He served continuously for several years as a member of the council of the Jewish community council. He also served as the leader of the community during the years 1908 – 1909.

A completely different character was Ben–Tzion Dreyfus (1843 – 1910), a native of Zloczow. He was an orthodox Jew and scholar. He was also a fan of general education and Hebrew literature from the Enlightenment period. He was one of the friends of the linguist Shulboim. He published articles about the Torah and wisdom. He also authored some language innovations in the [Hebrew magazine] "Ivry Anokhi" ["I am an Israelite"] and the magazine "Ha'Et" ["The Time"] edited by Shulboim.

His son, Ya'akov–Mordekhi (born in 1861), was also one of Zloczow's Enlightened. He published articles in Hebrew journals, including the story, "Doresh Tov Le'Amo" ["Advocating for the Interests of his People"]. He wrote the story against the background of the history of Jews in Switzerland. Ya'akov Mordekhai Dreyfus also served as a teacher in Zloczow's school named after Barone Hirsch.

Yosef Shalit[1] was also a member of the Enlightened camp. He was born in Zloczow in 1848. He received a traditional education from his father, who was a *melamed*. However, he was later "enlightened" and published articles in Hebrew newspapers "Ivry Anokhi" and "Ha'Maggid". Yosef Shalit left Zloczow in 1871 for Vienna, where he learned German. While making a living as a junior clerk at a bank, he continued to publish articles in Viennese newspapers.

Several years later, Yosef Shalit was appointed a senior clerk at the bank. In 1884 he left the bank and used his connections with the Austro–Hungarian finance minister Kalai to establish a private bank with a partner. The bank dealt mainly with the sales of stocks.

At the same time, a German newspaper in Hebrew letters, "Vinner Israellit", was published in Vienna under the editor, Weiss. The newspaper was established with the help of the Austrian prime minister Traaffe [Taaffe?]. The objective of the newspaper was to influence the Jews toward the conservative orientation of the government. After the death of Weiss, the newspaper was purchased by Ritter Von Stofle. Due to the substantial debt accumulated by the newspaper, Von Stofle sold it to Shalit. The latter published and edited the magazine until 1892. Shalit converted it into a Jewish magazine, which stood guard over the interests of the Jews in Austria, but not according to the spirit of assimilation. Shalit wrote most of the articles by himself. He joined the first Viennese association of the organization "Khibat Tzion" ["Love of Zion"], which advocated settlement in Eretz Israel. Later on, he joined Herzl's Zionist movement [3].

Neteh Schorr also belonged to an enlightened family. He was a pious man who acquired general education. Schorr was an admirer of Rabbi Shraga Rohatyn, a known activist within the Jewish public.

Israel Meshir, a friend of the Teller brothers, was the first enlightened who built a general-education school. Children were taught [Hebrew] grammar and the bible in that school. Meshir contributed substantially to the dissemination of enlightenment in the city with his knowledge and activities.

[Columns 89-90]

We should also count the two Teller brothers among the Enlightened as learners and spreaders. They were active in their native city for several years. We should also count the two Teller brothers among the enlightened as learners and spreaders. They were active in their native city for several years.

Another apprentice of Zloczow's enlightened people was the poet and author of [the Israeli anthem] "HaTikvah", Naftali Hertz Imber (1856 – 1910). He was born in Zloczow, on Hanukkah Sabbath 5617 (1856), to his father Ya'akov and his mother Hodah. His father, an orthodox Jew and "*Mitnaged*" [opposing Hasidism] educated him traditionally. Because his mother pampered him, he tended to be capricious. He knew the Bible by heart at the age of ten. At that age, he wrote a poem by the name "Beit Tefilati" ["My House of Prayer"], dedicated to the Prussia–Austria war and the constitution proclamation in Austria (1866). When the story about the song reached Zloczow's enlightened people (via his friend Wagner), they began taking an interest in him. They invited him to stay in their houses. He was especially drawn near the enlightened camp by Yehuda Funkelstein, Shmuel Auerbach, and Neteh Schorr (who was, then, the head of the community). Shmuel Auerbach's daughter taught him reading and writing, and Yehuda Funkelstein invited him to his library. He borrowed reading books from the library and advanced his knowledge in general subjects that way.

When the Hasidim found out about him, they started to harass him. Once, when he was asked by his friends and admirers to give a sermon at the big synagogue, the Hasidim mobilized their followers to prevent it. However, the enlightened people, headed by the community leaders, Neteh Schorr and Yehuda Funkelstein, begged him not to retreat. They encouraged him to give his sermon, despite the resistance of the Hasidim. A harsh feud nearly ensued, but Imber withdrew from delivering the sermon thanks to his mother's intervention.

In 1874, Imber wrote a Hebrew poem dedicated to Emperor Frantz Joseph on the centenary of the annexation of Bukovina by the Austrian Empire. Imber sent the poem to the emperor's court. In response, he received a thank–you letter and a cash gift of 25 Gulden. After receiving the prize from the court, Imber's acclaim rose. The enlightened continued to like him for his conversations and sayings.

After his father's death, the Hasidim increased their harassment and it became very difficult for him to stay in the city. For that reason and to ease the burden on his poor widowed mother, who was taking care of five orphans, he left Zloczow for Brody, and from there, to Lviv.

A new chapter in his life, which was not connected to his native city Zloczow, began. It would be worthwhile to shortly describe it:

In Brody, Imber met Avraham Kromkhel, Rabbi Nakhman Kromkhel's son, who was already a well-known author and researcher. He also met Yehoshua Heshil Schorr, the author of "Ha'Khalutz", and Yermiyahu Mozen, the author and grammar scholar. As mentioned, Imber later moved to Lviv from Brody. In Lviv, the preacher [Rabbi] Yissaskhar Ber Lunstein, drew him close, hosted him in his house, and hired teachers to teach him general studies.

When his mother found out that he was becoming assimilated, dressing in German clothes, she traveled to Lviv to save her son from the sin of secularism. After many persuasions by the rabbi, she agreed to leave her son with him. However, half a year later, she traveled to Lviv again and took her son back to Zloczow. Imber stayed only a short time in his mother's home. He left her and traveled to Vienna, where, in 1858, he was received by Emperor Franz Joseph for an interview for the third time. Again, Imber received a large cash prize from the emperor. He sent part of the money to his mother and used the rest to travel to Romania through Hungary and Serbia.

In the city of Iasi, Romania, he made a living by giving private lessons. In Iasi, he met Barone Moshe Walberg, the brother of Rabbi Walberg of Yaroslav. The Barone was an orthodox Jew and the author of the book: "Kakh Darka Shel HaTorah" ["That is the Way of the Torah"]. The Barone drew Imber close and hosted him in his house.

According to his own testimony, Imber wrote his song, "HaTikvah", in 1878, at Barone Waldberg's house. Several years later, when the first colonies in Eretz Israel were established, the song became the national anthem.

In 1879, he moved to Istanbul and made a living by selling haberdashery. In Istanbul, he met Sir Laurence Oliphant while offering him his merchandise. Sir Oliphant, who was an enthusiastic fan of "Khovevi–Zion" ["Lovers of Zion"], conducted negotiations with the Turkish government about allowing for a large settlement movement in Eretz Israel. Oliphant decided to settle in Haifa and offered Imber to be his secretary for Jewish affairs. Imber accepted the offer and traveled with Sir Oliphant to Israel. Oliphant and his wife became Imber's good friends and did not do anything without consulting with him.

Imber lived in Eretz Israel for five years and was very active in helping the new Jewish settlement movement. He felt rejuvenated himself. Like a "troubadour", he inspired the settlers, whom he called pioneers, with his national poems. He tried to instill courage, pride, and confidence in them. He also helped them in their fight with the officialdom of Barone Rothchild, who tyrannized them as they pleased.

Imber left Haifa (in 1884), due to a fight with Sir Oliphant, and moved to Jerusalem. Oliphant and his wife visited him and tried to appease him, but he refused to go back.

[Columns 91-92]

During that time, Imber published several secular songs and feuilletons, in the magazine "Khavatselet" ["Lili"] against the Christian mission, which was active among Jewish refugees from Russia who lived in Jerusalem.

After a short while, he returned to Oliphant's house in Haifa.

He prepared a collection of Hebrew songs for publication. It was published in 1886 (under the name "Barkai" ["Morning Star"]) with the help of Yekhiel Mikhel Pinnes, who wrote an introduction for the book.

He also began to publish songs in the magazine "HaTzvi" ["The Deer"] of Eliezer Ben Yehuda. However, since Imber supported the rabbis on the issue of the first "Shmita" [1889], a fight broke out between him and Ben Yehuda. Imber left the magazine "HaTzvi" and continued to publish his songs and articles in the periodical "Khavatzelet" ["Lili"] of Frumkin.

Imber left for Egypt for a short period before returning to Eretz Israel. After the death of Oliphant, he left Eretz Israel, and ended up in London after many wanderings in various countries. In London, he met the famous author, Israel Zangwill, who taught him English. In return, he taught Zangwill Hebrew. He mastered talking and writing English until he secured a permanent position as an author for a local Jewish–English newspaper. He also published Yiddish songs.

However, after a while the spirit of wandering awakened in him again. and he left for America in 1892. He lived pennilessly and in poverty until he became acquainted with Judge Meir Sulzberger from Philadelphia. The judge appreciated his talents and allocated him a decent monthly allowance. As a result, his economic situation improved.

In America, he published songs and articles in Hebrew, Yiddish, and English in various journals. His essays were written with abundant talent and excelled in their originality. For example, in his research article published in a medical journal, he proved that Professor Koch's therapeutic invention against tuberculosis was not new. He demonstrated that the medication was known from as early as the time of the Tanaim. His article about Jesus spurred a lot of clamor but bought him many enemies.

At the beginning of the 20th century, he prepared a new collection of his Hebrew songs by the name of "Barkai Khadash" ["The New Morning Star"]. The collection was published in Zloczow in 1903. A short time later, he published his third collection by the name "Barkai Shlishi" ["The Third Morning Star"], in New York. That collection contained an English translation.

In 1905, he translated part of the famous Persian poet Omar Khayyam's "quatrains" into Hebrew. He used an English version translated version by Fitzgerald.

Besides poems, songs, and articles, he published research articles about the history of the coin, ghetto music, mystery, and more.

He received a professor degree for his essays: "The Letters of Rabbi Akiva" (1896) and "Education in the Talmud", which the US government published at its expense. Later on, he published an English monthly magazine, in Boston, by the name of "Uriel" which dealt with the occult [Kabbalah].

In 1909 he fell sick with kidney disease [due to his chronic alcoholism] and died in New York, poor and impoverished, at 53.

Imber's entire life, activities, and certainly his poetry reflected a single ideal – Zionism. He was devoted to the idea of the revival of the Jewish people in their land in Eretz Israel until his last day.

The love of freedom fueled his dissatisfaction with all norms of society. That made him an eternal wanderer, tempestuous and eaten by yearning, who could not find his place in Eretz Israel or America.

A characteristic common thread in his life and his poetry had been the tendency to use somewhat intelligent rhetoric. However, he did contribute to Hebrew poetry quite a bit. He could be considered to be the first romantic poet of the new Hebrew literature.

His love for his nation and its land was throbbing throughout his poetry. It also reflected the longing of the nation for returning to Zion.

A short time before his death, he asked his friend, who visited him on his deathbed, to sing the "HaTikva". Imber was convinced that his "HaTikva" would not go down with him to his grave and that it would survive a long time after him. Before his death, he wrote his last song, in which he asked to "bring his bones to Eretz Israel, and bury him in his city – Jerusalem".

His last request was fulfilled upon the establishment of the state of Israel.

The Teller brothers, Israel Yehuda (born in December 1839) and Tzvi–Eliezer (Born on 18 July 1840), were also natives of Zloczow. They became two of the pioneers of the Enlightened movement in their native city. They received a traditional education at their Rozhin Hasidic home. However, the parents allowed them to study the Bible and Hebrew grammar, the German language, and generally applied sciences.

Israel spent several years at the court of the Admor of Sadigura although he had already distanced himself from Hasidism, and was already affected by the Enlightened movement. He kept in touch with the Enlightened in Sadhora [Sadigora]. When his ties with the Enlightened movement became known, he was defamed and not welcomed by Rebbe and his followers. He moved to Botosani in 1868 and worked as a teacher there. Later on, he worked as a teacher in Bakoi, and Focsani and in 1888 in Galatz, where he resided until his Aliya to Eretz Israel (in 1897).

[Column 93]

While in Romania, he joined the movement "Khovevei Tzion". He was one of the movement's first activities and among the people who initiated the congress in Focsani. That congress convened on 8 Kislev 5646 (30 December 1887). The temporary central committee of "Khovevei Tzion" in Romania was elected at that congress. Teller, who served as the deputy chair, published the congress's resolutions in the Hebrew newspapers "HaShakar" and "HaMaggid". In a special article, Teller called Jews in Romania to join "Khovevei Tzion". His call aimed at increasing the revenues of the organization. He urged the members to help in doing "the noble and inspiring holy work, none of which existed in the Jewish life for thousands of years since we arrived at the diaspora".

Teller also played a leading role in preparing for the large congress held in Focsani on 30–31st December 1882. He was the one who gave the opening and closing speeches in that congress.

His activities and education contributed substantially to the movement's support of the settlement in Eretz Israel. In 1886 he wanted to make Aliya together with the founder of the colony Zikhron Yaakov. However, "Kovevei Tzion" did not let him leave the movement, which was still in its beginning stages. They feared that without his activity, the movement would fall apart.

He was the driving force at the national conference of "Khovevie Tzion", which convened in Galatz on 7– 8 January 1895, and at the second conference. He also served as the secretary of the central committee of the organization.

He always stood on guard and invested substantial efforts to settle the conflicting views and personal feuds that broke out between the leaders, Dr. Karl Lippa and Shmuel Pinnles. He also published essays and reports about the happenings at "Khovevie Tzion" in Romania. At the conference itself, he brought up practical proposals to enhance the collection of contributions and amplify information dissemination among the Jewish public.

Israel Teller also devoted himself to his literacy work besides his public engagement and teaching work. He was a linguist and grammarian and published many linguistic pieces of research. His research concentrated on improving the Hebrew accent and the restoration of the grammar theory and corrections in vowel dotting. He advocated the abolition of the use of the "*dagesh forte*" [consonant–doubling] and the Hebrew grammatic law of "*begedkefet*" [non–emphatic consonants lenition], both of which complicate speech. He collected his linguistic research in a book, "Torat HaLashon" ["The Theory of the (Hebrew) Language"], published in Jerusalem in 5673 (1912). He published poems in newspapers and literary supplements and later, issued them in a collection called – "Higaion Lev" ["The Logic of the Heart"] in 5663 (1902). His other publications included: "Otzar Balum" ["A Treasure Trove"], Jaffa 5682 (1921), and "Binah Be'Toltdot Avoteinu" ["Wisdom in the History of Our Ancestors"], [Jaffa, 5676 (1915/6)]. He also published the book "Ben-Oni" issued in memory of his son Yehuda –a teacher in Rehovot that died at the young age of 24.

[Column 94]

Dr. Reuvan Schwager

The brother of Israel Teller, Tzvi–Eliezer, was a Hebrew teacher, in the Jewish school in Botosani, from 1866 to 1866. That school was established by the intellectual Hillel Kahana (1827 – 1908), a native of Galitsaia. Tzvi Eliezer was also active in public life.

During the 1860s, the situation of the Romanian Jews worsened. The conditions continued to deteriorate by the day due to the persecution by the regime. The Jewish public started to consider immigration. An argument emerged among Romanian Jews: Where to immigrate, America or Eretz Israel. The Hebrew author, Aharon Yehuda Leib Horwitz (AIL" H), was one of the principal supporters of immigrating to America. He made himself an example for others by moving to America in 1870. He worked there in the Hebrew newspaper "HaTsofe BeEretz Khadasha" ["The Observer in a New Land"]. He also authored the book "Romania and America" (Berlin, 1874).

The first group of 30 families immigrated to America in 1872. Another group of 500 families was organized in Botosani. The objective of the group was to work the land in America. Tzvi–Eliezer Teller, who published articles from Roamina in the magazine "Ha'Maggid", was one of the group's organizers. He and David Yeshayahu Silberbusch established the monthly magazine "HaOr" [The Light"] in Botosani, in 1872.

Following the pogroms in Russia in 1881, Tzvi Eliezer concluded that the flow of Russian refugees should not be directed to America, from one diaspora to another, but Eretz Israel, to settle it and revive the historical homeland.

[Columns 95-96]

Tzvi Eliezer Teller, who like his brother Israel was a rhymer, published the song "Shuvah Israel" ["Return, Jews"]. In that song, he came out against the trend of assimilation and the mockery of Jewish nationalism and Hebrew among the Enlightened.

Tzvi Eliezer Teller was nominated (in 1892) as a Hebrew teacher, when the schools funded by the fund of Barone de Hirsch, were established. He taught at the school in Boryslav. Immediately upon his arrival, he became active in public affairs. His first act was to establish a national association, "Bnei Tzion" with a library and a reading hall.

The management of the Barone Hirsch schools was at the hands of the assimilators. They tended to put obstacles to the teaching of the Hebrew language. That led to frequent quarrels between Teller and the management. However, he did not balk and continued to criticize the neglect of Hebrew studies. He continuously and sternly demanded to remedy the situation.

Tzvi Eliezer moved from Boryslav to the school in Pomoryani [Pomorzhani] and taught there until he died in 1920. When he lived in Romania, Tzvi Eliezer Teller published articles and songs in Hebrew journals. He was also interested in the political situation of the Jews in the Balkan. In his article: "Teudon Israel" (["Jewish Aspirations"] Brody, 5638 –1878), Tzvi Eliezer requested equal rights for the Jews of the Balkan. He published poems for various festivities and Jubilees, like the poem "Ben Porat Yosef" ["Beloved Son"] in honor of the visit to Galitsia by the crown prince Rudolph (Lviv 5642 – 1881/2). Other poems include "Masah to Galitsia" ["A Trip to Galitsia"], on the occasion of the trip to Galitsia by Rabbi Immanuel Vinitsiani [Secratary of Barone de Hirsch] (Drohobych, 5648 –1888), a collection of songs "Siftei Renanot" ["Lips of Songs"] (Drohobych, 5652 –1891/2), "Tziona", national and Zionist songs on the occasion of the fifth [Zionist] Congress in Basle (Drohobych, 5662, 1901), and the second collection of his songs "Hed HaAm" [The Echo of the People] (Drohobych 5673 – 1912/3)

The following are some of his stories: "Mistarim" ["Concealed"] (Drohobych, 5641 – 1880/1), "Nakhalat Avot" [Patrimony] (5655 – 1894/50), about the leader Khaim Shternbach from Boryslav, "Shlomim" (5665 – 1904/5), "Osher Shamur" ["Guarded Wealth"] (5667 – 1906/7), and "Ekharti Lavo" ["I Came Late"] (Lviv, 5668 – 1907/8). He was also the editor of the Jewish periodical "HaEitanim" ["The Forceful"].

Tzvi Eliezer translated to Hebrew the play "HaYehudim" ["The Jews"] by Lessing (Vienna, 5641 – 1880/1), and "Kesher Ben Nethania" ["A Plot by Nethania's Son"] by Ludwig Phillipson (Krakow,5648 – 1887/8). He wrote "Shem Olam" ["World Renown"], describing the life of the preacher from Lviv, Bernard Levinstein (Krakow, 5649 – 1888/9). As an author, Tzvi Eliezer Teller was a typical intellectual. He considered literature as a meaningful way of preaching and guidance.

Yitzkhak Maragliot, the son of Berl Broder Margaliot (the founder of "Brody Singers" 1815–1868), was the same age as Naftali Hertz Imber. He was born on 8th November 1855 in Podkamin, studied there in a Kherder, and later on in Brody. After the death of his father in Iasi, he moved to Zloczow with his mother. There he studied in the "Beit HaMidrash". A turning point in his life occurred when he was exposed to Enlightened books. He began to study German. In 1892 he became a teacher at the Jewish school in Sasov and later on in Zloczow. As an educator and teacher, he knew to attract the youth and influence them to become productive according to the national spirit.

He started to publish Hebrew songs from a young age in the periodical "Ivri Anoki" ["I'm an Israelite"]. Later on, he published feuilletons, stories, and songs, in Yiddish, under pseudo names such as Y"Sh [In Hebrew, acronym of fear of Heaven] and "Yam Tzioni" ["Zionist Sea"]. He published in the periodicals "Karmel" of Reuven Asher Broide, "Veker" ["The Spectator"] of Eliezer Rokeakh, and in the Yiddish daily newspapers.

In his stories, Margaliot described the Jewish folklore in Galitsia's Jewish shtetels during the latest years of the 19th century. In his articles, he preached productization, organization of craftsmen, and changes in the life of the Jewish people. He was a nationalist and Zionist.

When World War I broke, he ran away to Vienna, where he wrote romances, plays, and Hasidic stories, which were kept handwritten. His son, who lives in New York has them now.

In 1918, he returned to Zloczow and passed away there on 23rd December 1919.

Arye Leib Schwartz, a native of Zloczow was a completely different character. He published a collection of Hebrew songs translated into Yiddish called "Shirei Emunim" (Lviv, 1881, 100 pages) ["Songs of Faith"]. The publication received the approval of *tzadikim* and the leaders of the religious association of "Makhzikei HaDat" ["Keepers of the Religion"].

In his poetry, Schwartz, a zealous Hasid, highlighted the fight of the Galitsia's Enlightened against the Haredim. He attacked the seculars and the Enlightened who mock the pious. He warned against the influence of the assimilators and the Enlightened intellectuals, which could lead, in his opinion, to the collapse of Jewish life in Galitsia. He blamed them for creating a deep void between the old generation and the new. He especially poured out his wrath upon the religious youth, who read Enlightened books to learn Hebrew and thereby fall into the atheists' net. He referred to those who publish Hebrew songs only to spread their ideas. He directed his anger particularly against the poet and singer "Velvel'li Zbarazh'er ([Benjamin Wolf] Ahronkrantz [from Zbarazh]) whom he named "chief evil". He referred to him as someone whose pen was abounding with mockery and venom toward the pious. He also came out sharply against the boycott on Yiddish imposed by parents who pushed their children to learn Polish and German.

[Columns 97-98]

In the second part of his song collection "Shirei Emunim", Schwartz described the sorrowful state of the Jewish merchants.

Anshel Schorr, also a native of Zloczow (born in 1871), received traditional education at home. His father was a zealous Hasid and a *melamed* of the Mishnah and Halakha. However, Anshel studied Polish and German secretly. Anshel established the worker association "Shiloh" (power) at the end of the 1880s. He wrote the Yiddish play "May di shvueh bay der royter fon" ["May Oath to the Red Flad"] and showed it to the members of the group.

Anshel became an actor and joined the theater of Gimpel in Lviv. In 1890, the famous actor, Yaakov Adler, took him to America, where he first served as a prompter and lateras an actor. He returned to Zloczow because he missed his parents. In Zloczow, and joined a troupe of actors who performed in Galitsia and Romania. In 1900, he returned to America, where he wrote songs for operettas and plays. He toured the cities of America and Argentina. He died on 1 June 1942.

The following are additional authors and poets who were born in Zloczow:

1. Shmuel Yaakov Imber, son of Shmaryahu and the brother of Naftali Hertz, was one of the first modern Yiddish poets. Born in Sasov on 24 February 1889, he received a Jewish education at home. Shmuel Yaakov studied at a high school in Zloczow and Lviv. Later on, he attended the University of Lviv and obtained a doctorate in philosophy. In his youth, he published songs in Yiddish and Polish. In 1909, he published a collection of his songs: "Vos ikh zing un zag" ["What I sing and say"]. Two years later, he published the poem "Ester'ke". In 1914 he published a second song collection: "Royzenbleter" ["Rose Petals"]. Following his visit to Eretz Israel, he published "In Yudeshen Land" ["In the Jewish Land"] (Lviv 1912) and "Heym Lider" ["Songs from Home"] (1918). He edited and published the journal "Litearishe Flugshriftn" ["Literary Pamphlets"]. He also published in the Yiddish and Polish newspapers. During 1933

– 1938 he published two polemic books against racism and anti–Semitism, using satirical and witty language. He was killed by the Nazis in 1942.

2. Moshe Leib Halpern (1886 – 1932) was born in Zloczow and received a Jewish education. He was a student at the Jewish school in Zloczow. At the age of 12, he was sent to Vienna to learn the craft of sign painting. He was influenced by the modern German language there. When he returned, he began to write, in Yiddish, under the influence of Imber and Yaakov Memshal, He wrote for Lviv's daily– "Tagblet", and later on in the "Yiddeshe Arbeiter" ["The Jewish Worker"]. He immigrated to America in 1908 and participated in the periodicals: "Yiddishe Falk" ["Jewish People"], and "Yiddisher Kemper" ["The Jewish Fighter"]. He published literary anthologies together with Moshe Nadir. Moshe Leib was a representative of the "Yung Yiddish" (Young Yiddish) authors movement. He started as a satirist and humorist but went through a turning point upon the publication of his poem: "The Goldeneh Paveh" ["The Golden Peacock"], in which he demonstrated a philosophical skepticism.

3. Yaakov Mestel was born in Zloczow in 1884. He completed his studies at the teaching school in Lviv and became a teacher. In 1907 he moved to Vienna and studied drama, and during 1910 – 1914 he worked in the Yiddish theater there. During the years 1914 – 1918, he served as an officer in the Austrian military. He was injured on the front and was awarded a medal. In 1918 he immigrated to America and joined the theater of Morris Schwartz. He became active in Yiddish literature in 1903. He edited the periodical, "Yung Galitsisher Almanakh" ["Young Galitsia Almanac"] along with Dr. Tzvi Shpitzer. He also published the collections of songs, "Ferkhlomteh Shaah" ["Dreamt Hour"] (1909), "A Lebens Li'ed" ["A Life Song"] (1911), and "Dimyonot" ["Images"] (a dramatic trilogy). He also issued notes from the war: "Milkhama Natizen fon a Yidesheh Ofitzer" ["Notes from the War by a Jewish Officer"]. He wrote the following books: "Yiden in der Nieste Deutscher Literatur" ["Jews in the latest German Literature"] and "Yidesheh Ofitzern in der Estreikhisher Armey" [Jewish Officer in the Austrian Army"].

4. David Shrentzel was born in Zloczow in 1897 to pious parents. He served in the Austrian military, on the Italian front, during World War I. Upon his return from the war, he became one of the "Poalei Tzion" ["Workers of Zion"] organization activists. He took an active role in the organization's newspaper and also published a song collection: "Oisen Hartzen" ["Out of Mind"].

5. Moshe Pitznik was born in Zloczow in 1895 to his banker father. He published articles and feuilletons in Lviv's "Tagblat" and the "Yiddisher Arbeiter". During the Ukrainian regime in Eastern Galitsia, he published a weekly in Zloczow named "Folksblat" ["People's paper"]. He took interest in folklore and published several articles on the subject. He translated the "Odyssey" by Homer to Yiddish with a commentary. He also published two novels in ancient Yiddish "Sefer Reb Kalman Ani" ["A Book about the Poor Mr. Kalman"] and "Moshe Kabtzan" ["Moshe the Beggar"]. The subject of these books was the Enlightenment movement.

6. The famed Hebrew publicist and author, Dr. Avraham Schwadron–Sharon, was also a native Zloczow, a member of an old and honorable family in the city. He was born to his father Yitzkhak Schwadron on 12 Elul 5647 [should be 5638] (1883 – [should be 1888]) in the village of Bieniow near Zloczow. He was educated according to Jewish traditional–national spirit. Avraham excelled in his abilities as a child and was considered a prodigy.

[Column 99]

He arrived at "Yoreh De'ah" at the age of 6 – 7. Later on, he studied at the yeshiva of his uncle, Mordekhai Schwadron Ha'Kohen the Rabbi of Berezhany. He graduated from high school as an external student. Later, he studied chemistry at a university in Vienna. He was one of the founders of the student association "Ha'Tkhia" ["The Revival"] in Vienna. He started to collect handwritten notes of Jewish greats. The Chief Rabbi of Vienna, Dr. Mordekhai [Moritz] Giudemann, sent him a citation letter. In that letter, the rabbi praised Schwadron for his commentary on a Hebrew manuscript, which the rabbi had a problem deciphering in his book: "HaTorah and Khaim Be'Artzot Ha'Ma'arav, Be'Yemei Ha'Beina'im" ["The Torah and Life in the Western Countries During the Middle Ages"]. That citation encouraged Schwadron to start with his lifetime project, which later became the foundation for the national collection of autographs, portraits, and manuscripts of prominent Jews [The Rabbi's letter became the first document in his collection]. Schwadron invested several decades of effort and a substantial amount of money researching and purchasing the collection documents.

After he made Aliya to Eretz Israel in 192 Schwadron donated his entire valuable collection to the Israel National Library. The collection was established as a unified assemblage in memory of his parents, and he was nominated to manage it. By 1954, the collection grew to 17,000 autographs, portraits, and manuscripts of prominent Jews from as early as the 15th century.

He began to publish articles and essays, in German, about the fundamental problems, faced by the Zionist movement, when he was still a student. He expressed his opinions, which were extreme and free from any party affiliation, wittingly. He advocated "Cruel Zionism", which denounced the diaspora and demanded all the Jews leave their countries and make Aliya to Eretz Israel before they were forced to leave. He suggested expelling all the Arabs from Eretz Israel to Arab countries to avoid a potential future irritant for the Jewish state. He also advocated that the land would only be for the Jews.

In 1957, a short time before his death, he arranged all of his writings in two volumes.

The following are some of his major publications:
His chemistry research, which published by the Sciences Academy of Vienna in 1911

- "Miflatsei Ha'Galut Hanitzkhit" ["The Horrors of the Eternal Diaspora"] (5689 – 1928/9)
- Critique of the Foundations of "Brit Shalom" ["Covenant of Peace"] Ideology (5691 – 1930/1)
- "Avoda Yehudanit" ["Hebrew Labor"] (5691 – 1930/1)
- For Yiddish Speakers Anywhere (Against Yiddish) (5693 – 1932/3)
- "The Ideology of "Cruel Zionism"
- "Memories from the Cats' World"

[Column 100]

Dr. Avraham Sharon was also a musician. He composed the melodies for nine of poet Rachel's songs published in two pamphlets during the years, 5694 – 5696 (1933/4 – 1935/6).

Chapter 7

The Zionist Movement

In 1894, Zionism's publicity effort began in Zloczow. At an assembly that took place in August of that year, M. Ehrenpreis and Yehoshua Thon gave speeches, and a committee, which was tasked with preparations for Zionist activities, was established. Moshe Aharon Neiger, Yitzkhak Schwadron, and Avraham Yaakov Igel were nominated to head the committee. The first act of the committee was to establish a Zionist association by the name "Degel Yeshurun" [" The Jewish Flag"]. Despite the objections of the Haredim [ultra-orthodox Jews], the new association unified within its ranks the best of the progressive religious Jews.

The following is some information about the founders:

Moshe Aharon Neiger received basic traditional education at home. His father was a wise man who was knowledgeable about world affairs and had secular knowledge. In his youth, Moshe Aharon was known to be a diligent student who studied day and night. He knew Jewish literature thoroughly. He was also well-informed about the research books concerning the Middle Ages. Despite his piousness, he was one of the first to join the Zionist movement and devoted himself to public activism. Many Haredim followed him and joined "Degel Yeshurun". He moved to Tarnow, where, in 1906, he assembled the first conference of the "HaMizrakhi" [religious Zionist party].

Yitzkhak Schwadron, a known industrialist in Galitsia who owned a wine factory, was born in 1848 in Bereslavka [Yanovka]. Together with his brother, Rabbi Shalom Mordekhai (who later became one of Galitsia Torah greats and the rabbi in Barazhani), he received a traditional Jewish education at home. However, Yitzkhak also learned sciences and was one of the fans of the new Hebrew literature. Despite his piousness (he was a Hosiyatin's Hasid), he was among the first Zionist activists in his town and stood guard over the national ideology.

Schwadron was among the admirers of Dr. Herzl and sent him a gift of wine bottles from his factory. In his letter from February 2, 1889, Dr. Herzl thanked him for his generous gift, however, he noted not to be accustomed to these "spiritual" beverages. Schwadron was a representative in the eleventh Zionist Congress in Vienna and was the chairman of the "Bnei Tzion" ["Sons of Zion"] association.

[Columns 101-102]

The District Court in Zloczow

Shmaryahu Imber (1866 – 1950), the brother of Naftali Hertz and the father of Dr. Shmuel Yaakov Imber, served as a teacher for many years at the school named after Barone de Hirsch. He educated the youth in the spirit of Nationalism and Zionism. Together with Teller, Shmaryahu came out against the elimination of Hebrew in these schools. He was active in the Zionist movement during his entire time in Zloczow. After he escaped to Vienna in 1914, he continued his Zionist activity there. He made Aliya to Eretz Israel in 1933. He was among the founders and activists of "Brit HaRishonim" ["The Founders' Covenant"], an association of the Zionist founders. Shmaryahu published a selection of his brother's writings (Tel Aviv, 5689 – 1929). He also wrote articles and feuilletons in Hebrew and Yiddish.

The first Zionist ball, organized by "Degel Yeshurun" took place during the holiday of Sukkot 5655 [1894]. The Hebrew author Reuven Moshe Broides, Yitzkhak Schwadron, and Khaim Neiger gave speeches at the ball.

One of the initial activities of the Zionists was to wage a war against the management of Barone de Hirsch's school. That management had purposely neglected the teaching of the Hebrew language. In protest, Rabbi Feivel Rohatyn quit the school committee. The Zionist committee members, Grafein and Tzukerkendel, also resigned.

In that fight, the Zionists were helped by the teacher, Shmaryahu Imber, one of the first teachers in that school.

Moshe Aharon Neiger and Yitzkhak Schwadron were among the influential activists of the association. They devoted most of their time and effort to publicizing the idea of a national home for the Jews and encouraged support of the settlements in Eretz Israel.

The following people were among the founders and first activists of the association: Yitzkhak Butcher, Israel Yetzes, David Meir Shalit, Ben-Tzion Lehrer, Hirsh Rosenboim, and Avraham Yaakov Igel.

In 1898 the association had already 102 members. The association began to sell stocks of the "Jewish Colonial Trust" in 1899. About 400 stocks were sold In Zloczow.

In 1899, representatives of academic students from Zloczow participated in the academic conference in Galitsia. It took place in Lviv on 25-26 July. A resolution passed at the conference called for giving national rights to Jewish students.

Preparations for the Viennese Parliament (in four curiae) began in Galitsia in 1900. In the second curia, encompassing cities, an election of a Jewish representative for the district of Brody-Zloczow seemed feasible.

Adolf Shtand turned to Dr. Herzl on September 9, 1900, about that election, as he thought that Zionist should participate. He proposed that the Zionist executive committee publish a proclamation containing general principles in preparation for the election. He further proposed that Dr. Herzl, the leader of the Zionist movement, would issue a request for all Jews to adhere to those principles. However, the executive committee decided against it, and Galitsia's Jews did not participate in the election campaign. In Lviv, the Zionists supported the candidate, Ernest Breiter.

Initially, Dr. Shaul Refael Landau, who had quarreled with Herzl, arrived in Brody and Zloczow. He requested to become the Zionist candidate opposing the candidate from Zloczow, Dr. Emil Bik. He presented himself as the candidate on behalf of the organization "Yudisher Falks-Ferein" ["The Union of The Jewish People"] in Vienna. He told the president of the "Bnei Tzion" association that he received 15,000 Guldens from the Union for expenses associated with the election. He claimed by using that fund he would certainly be able to beat Dr. Bik. However, it became evident, pretty quickly, that he also presented himself as a Jewish national socialist before the Jewish socialists.

"Bnei Tzion" association, and Yitzkhak Schwadron himself, turned to the Zionist Executive committee in Vienna, in a confidential letter, to ask for instructions.

[Column 103-104]

Dr. Landau, who realized that he encountered a frosty reception, removed his candidacy. Dr. Emil Bik was elected in the Brody-Zloczow district.

Dr. Yaakov Grosskopf, who headed the organization "Ahavat Tzion" ["Love of Zion"], was active in the Zionist movement in the region during 1901 – 1904. During that time, the association of "Poalie Tzion" ["Workers of Zion"] had already existed. Its leader was Yaakov Rekht. A Zionist women association, "Ohel Leah" ["Leah's Tent"], headed by Sara Vashitz, was also established.

The association of "Tzeirei Tzion" ["Youths of Zion"] encompassed high school students. The association organized courses for learning the Hebrew language and Jewish history.

In 1911 four Zionist high school youth organizations contained 80 members.

In 1907, the union - "Bakhurei HaTalmud" ["Talmud Youths"], which served the religious students of Beit HaMidrash - "Hashakhar" ["The Dawn"] was established in Galitsia. A branch for that union, headed by Yosef Miller, was established in Zloczow. Yosef Miller also created a district committee for the entire district.

In 1910, a branch of "HaMizrkahi", headed by Nathan Schorr, was already active in the city. Two representatives of the branch, Binyamin Zusman and Tzvi Weitzman were elected to the central state committee. Their election took place during the founding conference of the "HaMizrkahi" party in Galitsia.

The Zionist movement waged a war against the assimilated during that period. The movement also raised the issue of national autonomy for the Jews with the government. The movement expanded throughout the entire Jewish population in Galitsia and helped to create an atmosphere of national pride among the Jews. It clearly demonstrated that the aspiration for independent national existence was alive and deep-rooted. A strong demand to recognize the Jews as a nation was issued at every gathering. The Jews of all Galitsia's cities, including Zloczow, signed a petition, requesting as much. The petition was submitted to the central government in Vienna.

That movement worried the assimilated people and the activists of the Jewish community, who hatefully tried to choke any Jewish national aspirations.

In their eagerness to weaken and suppress the Zionist movement, Dr. Bik and his colleagues did not shy away from drastic steps, which led to the closure of Zionist companies and even Hebrew schools by the authorities.

On February 7, 1906, the presidents of the Zionist associations in cities throughout Galitsia, including Zloczow, received an order to close all Zionist associations and their affiliated schools.

The Austrian Parliament representatives, Dr. Shtraukhel and Ernest Breiter turned to the interior minister. They protested against the ploys of the Galitsian authorities, which acted entirely against the constitution. The query was supported by representatives from various parties, except the Social Democrats.

In its political activities, the Zionist movement experienced even a more difficult struggle with the assimilated and the authorities following Dr. Bik's death, on July 23, 1906. His seat, representing Brody and Zloczow, was vacated upon his death. The Zionist Union was thereby allowed to withstand a test of its might in its first political fight.

The first [Zionist] rallies in Zloczow and speeches, which were filled with pure enthusiasm and national courage, invigorated the Jewish masses. The leaders of the Jewish community were stunned to see the robust cheers of the crowd. They realized that, for the first time, they were dealing with a popular movement, which had already stroke deep roots in the hearts of the masses. The Zionists in Brody and Zloczow selected their leader, Adolf Shtand, as their candidate. Against him, the assimilated elected Dr. Yosef Guld, positioning him as a national-Polish candidate. The physician, Dr. Guld, lacked any political experience and did not have any Jewish public standing. Even with the help of the authorities, the assimilated leaders could not suppress the enthusiasm that the masses exhibited toward the Zionist candidate. The Jews saw him as a symbol of their freedom from the traditional leadership of the Jewish community. Despite all of that, the Zionists failed.

Unprecedented and despicable coarse forgeries and deceptions helped Dr. Guld to receive most of the votes. He was elected to be the representative to the parliament.

Despite their failure, the Zionists passed their first political test successfully. They were the real winners. They inspired the Jews and instilled faith in the power of the Jewish nation in them.

The passing of the new election law in the Austrian Parliament, which granted all the citizens, the right to vote, resulted in a turning point in political life.

[Column 105-106]

The Zionists elected Adolf Shtand as their candidate Brody / Zloczow. The Assimilated elected Dr. Wahrlrand, a senior official in the treasury department of Galitsia. Dr. Wahrland was a wealthy man, but he had no political experience or recognition. Early on, he approached the Zionist Union with a promise to donate several thousand Krones to their campaign and to adopt the political policy of the Zionists. His condition for that support was that the public would only find out about that contribution after the election when he would not depend anymore on his Polish superiors. He wrote a letter with that offer to the Zionist, Dr. Tsiper. Obviously, his offer was rejected. He then turned to the assimilated. However, his letter to Dr. Tsiper was published, and as a result, he came out of this demoralized.

As many as 5876 people participated in the election in Brody-Zloczow. Dr. Wahrland received 1517 votes. The Jewish Social-Democrat, Dr. Heinrikh Lunherz-1244 votes and Shtand – 1493. Since no candidate received an absolute majority, the authorities called a special election between Shtand and Wahrland. In those elections, Adolf Shtand was elected with a large majority.

The election to the community was held after the election to the parliament. The following people were elected: Yosef Guld, Dr. Yitzkhak Mitelman (Zionist), Avish Garfunkel, Nakhman Gritz, Markus Sitter, Nathan Schorr, Leizer

Schwartz, Dr. Yaakov Groskopf (Zionist), Dr. Itamar Eidelberg (Zionist), Dr. Bermard Alter, Shaul Roller, and Lipa Maar. Yosef Guld was elected as the leader and Eliezer Kuten as his deputy (During the years 1913 – 1914, Dr. Yitzkhak Mitelman served as the deputy). The following people were elected to the community's central management team: Avish Garfunkel, Nakhman Gritz, and Markus Khoter [Sitter?].

The elected Zionist representative challenged the archaic regime of the assimilated. They demanded to modernize the community's orientation and character to address the needs and aspirations of the Jewish population.

Dr. Guld, who was elected as a mayor of the city, participated in a national referendum about the Jewish question, held in January 1911. The referendum was held by the state committee of the Galitsian Sejm. Only two Zionist representatives were invited to participate: Adolf Shtand and Avraham Kurkis.

However, Dr. Guld supported the assimilated position and warned the Poles not to support Hebrew schools. They wanted to prevent Zionism from spreading. The referendum resulted in some [positive?] resolutions. However, these resolutions stayed on paper and did bring any changes in the state of the Jews.

The election for the Austrian Parliament was held in the same year – 1911.

Ernest Breiter was elected in Zloczow but he gave up his seat since he was also elected in Lviv. Special elections were therefore held in Zloczow in November 1911. Henrik Rittses (1878 – 1931), who was supported by the Zionists was elected. Rittses served as a representative in the Austrian parliament until the collapse of the monarchy in 1918. He was a Jewish nationalist and stood guard to defend and advance Jewish interests. During World War I, he was among the people who organized assistance for the Jewish refugees from Galitsia.

In 1910, a branch of the Zionist bank "Unia Kredytowa" was established in Zloczow.

In the election to the municipality, which took place in 1912, three Zionists were elected: Dr. Eidelberg, Dr. Yaakov Grosskopf, and Dr. Landsberg.

During that period, the Zionists were active in all Jewish life affairs. The Zionist movement in the area was headed by Dr. Eidelberg, Dr. Hirschhorn, Dr. Feldman, and Dr. Groskopf.

The Zionist influence increased to such an extent that in December 1913, when the Zionists organized protest rallies against the relief society "Hilfsferein" policy against Hebrew in the Technion Institute in Haifa, the assimilated joined the protest movement in Zloczow. Dr. Guld participated in the protest rally in Zloczow on behalf of the assimilated people.

The Zionist organization played a crucial role in directing and defining the Jewish public life in the city before World War I.

The Zionist Union made preparations for another election campaign [when the war broke].

Author's Note:

1. Shalit was the father of Isidore Shalit, Herzl's private secretary, and Leon Shalit, a famed author who wrote in English and German and the one who translated John Galsworthy's writings.

[Columns 107-108]

Zloczow Chronicles

by Ron – Tzimmer

Translated by Moshe Kutten

Zloczow was located on the southeastern edge of Poland. Its beginning is shrouded in mystery. The princes that ruled that wide geographic area (which spanned the entire water basins of the Vistula, Dnieper, and Bog Rivers) during the 11th, 12th, and 13th centuries, were named the Princes of the Red Reisyn. Ancient convoys traveling from Baghdad passed through the Crimea Peninsula, Ukraine, and from there via the cities of Red Reisyn to Central Europe and farther north to the Baltic Sea. Zloczow was located on one of the crossroads, which led from Lviv toward the southeast. The road led to Iasi and the Moldavian and Wallachian regions and from there, to Istanbul [Constantinople]. That crossroad was a topographically and economically sensitive location because it was the starting point of a major trade route. From the beginning of the year 1241, the area served as a bridgehead for ceaseless wars between the Tatars on one side and the border residents – Poles and Ruthenians on the other side. The latter defended the forward positions of the Polish kingdom, which aspired to expand southeast. During the 14th and 15th centuries, conflicts erupted between the Polish kings and the princes of Reisyn and Lithuania. Later on, endless scrimmages between the Polish defenders on one side and the Kozaks and the Tatars on the other took place. In the 15th century, the latter surrendered to Turkey, the largest and mightiest empire in southeastern

Europe. The border defenders were devastated by the endless wars between the Ottoman Empire and Poland, which served as the "defense wall" for Christian Europe.

Polish kings, ministers, and noblemen, who were the owners of large fertile areas in that region, wished to settle these strategic outposts. They fortified these places, widened agricultural plots, and developed towns and cities to attract new settlers to the area.

That was the motive behind the establishment of the "key city" Zloczow. As early as the 15th century, a "key area" with an urban center and 75 villages surrounding it, was established, spreading northeast toward Brody and southeast toward Ternopil.

We should note that a fort was established in the area earlier. The fort changed hands during the frequent wars. In 1441 it became the property of the Sobieski family, along with the surrounding areas and villages.

The Polish King Wladyslaw of Varna, awarded noblemen like the Sobieski the right to establish towns and cities. As mentioned, Polish kings attracted settlers from Germany and Silesia to settle in destructed and desolated areas. He lured the settlers by awarding them autonomy and self–governance rights. These privileges were based on the Magdeburg Law (named after the city of Magdeburg in Eastern Germany).

A group of Students from Zloczow's High School

[Columns 109-110]

The Building of the School Named after Mitzkevitz

In 1523, the Polish King Sigismund awarded Zloczow the right to incorporate under the Magdeburg Constitution, as requested by its owner Stanislaw Sobieski. As a result, Zloczow was transformed from an enslaved city, lacking any human rights, to a free city. The residents were no longer required to pay harsh and endless fees imposed on towns and villages during the Middle Ages.

The city did not become a state city and remained in private hands. As such, its residents were still considered subjects (in many aspects) of its owners. These owners owned the city and the villages that surrounded it.

The "key area" of Zloczow city and its environs was immense. It was fertile and rich in forests, meadows, fish pools, pasture fields, and wheat fields, yielding abundant crops. Documents from the 16th and subsequent centuries contained praises for the bountiful fields, numerous hydraulically operated flour mills, quality of the honey and the wax, famed fish pools, wood–rich forests, and the alcoholic beverages distilleries.

During the 17th and 18th centuries, Zloczow gained fame as a city containing vintage fruit trees. They also grew vines in the area near the fort, which we will expand on below.

French tourists who visited Poland during the 17th century, and stopped by Zloczow, praised its gardens and vineyards. The city could have grown and become rich if not for the frequent battles with the Tatars, Kozaks, and Turks. Zloczow had all the necessary conditions. It was an economic center, located on a trade crossroad, in the center of a populated area seeded by many villages and towns that enjoyed high–quality agriculture.

Zloczow was a large market city where agricultural products from the surrounding villages were sold. Many artisans, organized in professional guilds, worked in it. The accelerated development of Zloczow began toward the end of the 16th century. It continued during the 17th century, particularly during the first half. The main factor that brought that development was the members of the Sobieski family. They were awarded Zloczow, with the entire area around it, in 1598 and held it for 180 years. One of the decedents, Jan III Sobieski, ascended to the throne. He fought and won the battle against the Turks in the Battle of Vienna [1683]. That family contributed tremendously to the city. They supported it and managed to attract many new settlers, including Jews, Armenians, and even the prisoners–of–war Tatars.

The King's father, Jakub Sobieski, King Jan himself (who reigned during 1661 – 1696), and two princes who did not ascend to the throne, loved the city immensely. They all lived in the Zloczow for many years and erected numerous buildings including, public institutions, churches, and synagogues. They fortified the city and took pride in it. They also renovated the fort. The fort, located on the top of a hill, towered over the city and commanded a view of the entire area. During the 17th century the fort, which was built long before Sobieski's period, gained renewed importance. It played a major role during the conquering campaigns of the Tatars, and their allies – the Kozaks.

During the 17th century, a moat was dug out around the fort. In 1634, the renovation of the fort itself was completed. The fort was fitted with protruded towers seen from afar, entrance gates on its four walls, which surrounded the fort from all directions, and dirt embankments in front of them. The initials J. S. of the fort's owner (Jacub Sobieski) were inscribed on one of the towers. The fort was equipped with an abundance of weapons, cannons, and a large inventory of military equipment.

Many of the city residents gathered at the fort when the city itself was robbed numerous times by the enemy. The 1860s and 1870s were the most disastrous. The entire country, including the border area of Zloczow and the neighboring towns, was robbed and destroyed.

[Columns 111-112]

Sokol Street in Zloczow

During the attacks, the residents escaped, and the fields were abandoned. With all of that, Zloczow suffered less than other cities, which luck strong fortifications. As an example, in 1661 the neighboring town of Zboriv [Zborov] was destroyed. The town's buildings burnt to the ground, and the residents were slaughtered.

Zloczow's residents had to, from time to time, repair the fort fortifications. They also had to supply construction stones and wood, transport various materials, and improve the access roads. Additionally, they had to replenish the inventories of food and equipment, re–dig the ditches, and reconstruct the bridges. One of the fort's buildings was transformed into a palace and served as a residence for the city's owners. It contained numerous rooms, nicely floored and furnished according to the best fashion of the period. There was also a luxurious tent, which was taken as war booty. It was an exquisite and delicate sample of a work of art from the east.

The Ethnic Composition: Poles, Ruthenians, Jews, Armenians, and Tatars

From ancient times, like in other cities in Reisyn, Ruthenians and Poles were residents in Zloczow. The Ruthenians who belonged to the Greek–Orthodox Church were the first. The poles settled there in the 14th century, from the time of Great Kazimir. Many were small Polish nobles, on the fringes of the aristocratic families. The Poles and Ruthenians served on the Municipal council. The officials that managed the affairs of the city were all nominated from among the council's members. These officials included the advisors, judges, and managers of the revenues, markets, and fairs,

Jews resided in Zloczow as early as the 16th century. Israel, son of Idela, who was called Idelis the Zloczowski [Zlotsovski] was a leading businessman. In 1695, he leased the entire "key area" of Zloczow. He also leased the collection of all passage fees, road fees, fair fees, fees associated with the distillation of alcoholic beverages, and even the supervision of all work performed by enslaved farmers. In 1697, the customs official that collected custom tax at one of the city gates was no other than the Jew, Yehuda (called Yehuda the Custom Tax Collector). According to surviving documentation, Zloczow resident, Shmuel Birobitz, was one of the leading custom tax collectors in the entire region. In the 17th century, there was already a substantial number of Jews in the city. They rebuilt houses that were destroyed or burnt during the numerous fires and wars.

The city was deserted several times, which led to an urgent need to resettle it and develop the craft and trade. In 1654, Zloczow's Jews were awarded a privilege that allowed them a free settlement. They were also encouraged to invite their relatives and friends to follow them. When, in 1724, the synagogue burnt down, the city owners provided the Jews with woods from forests they owned. The inheriting prince, Alexander Sobieski, had good relations with the Jews.

[Columns 113-114]

The Youth Movement "Ha'Hit'akhdut" ["The Federation"]

Like in other cities, the city officials and its owners, usually assisted the Jews. However, the urban Christian population tried to put obstacles in their way. Despite that, the Jewish artisans were members of professional guilds in the 18th century. Since the Jews developed the crafts and trade in Zloczow, over time they gained the right to participate in the mayoral election.

Armenian artisans and merchants settled in the city during the 1670s – 1680s. There were also Armenian communities in Lviv. In Zloczow, the Armenian community enjoyed special privileges, which allowed them judicial autonomy and the right to elect representatives for secular and religious institutions. They erected their own church, which was freed from any taxes for 20 years. They were also exempt from paying various other fees and the authorities assisted them in securing revenues. Their clergies, dignities, and leaders enjoyed various other privileges. The remnants of this community survived until the 20th century. One of the city's streets was named "The Armenians Street".

King Jan Sobieski took many Muslim Tatars as prisoners of war. He tried to settle them in his estate, particularly in the village of Voronyaki [Vronki], near Zloczow. According to a legend, 300 Tatars were slaughtered there. They were accused of treason against their patron– the king who gave them land. After causing fear among the residents of southern and eastern Poland for hundreds of years, the attempt to settle the Tatars ceased. Later on, when the Russians conquered the area from Nazi–Germany, they again settled many Tatars in the area to weaken the nationalistic Ukrainian movement. They also moved whole Ukrainian villages, along with their entire Ukrainian population, and moved them to distant Russia.

When the Austrian took over Zloczow and the entire Galitsia, Germans and Czechs arrived at Zloczow. The Austrian Emperor, Joseph II, and his heirs aspired into Germanize the area. They took advantage of the conflict between the Poles and the Ruthenians (who began to call themselves – Ukrainians). The Austrian officials slashed the rights of the [Polish] nobility. They tried to settle Germans in the villages and brought over German and Czech officials to establish proper order within the shaky Polish administration. The palace was transforming into a barrack, and at the end, a jail. Some of the Austrian administrators succeeded in their effort to improve the look of the city. The administrator, Ishnoller, was especially successful in doing so. He converted the old dirt embarkments into avenues and established a high school in the city, which opened in 1873. Construction of a railroad, which connected Zloczow, Brody, and Ternopil, commenced even earlier. The new railroad station, which was built outside of the city, contributed greatly to its development. However, the time when Brody and Zloczow served as the starting point for the massive trade that connected Vienna and the rest of Europe with Odessa and the Tzarist Russia had passed. Gone was the time of the big fairs, which were such an integral part of the trade during the 18th century and perhaps also the first half of the 19th century. Galitsia began to decline and sink into poverty, carrying Zloczow with it.

A unique, dramatic, and fascinating story surfaced when we researched the relations among the ethnic groups and various nations in Zloczow and Eastern Galitsia. Zloczow was located in a very sensitive corner from the point of view of the evolution of the relations between the Poles, who were the owners of the estates and the urban intelligentsia, and the Ukrainian Ruthenians. Most of the neighboring villages were populated by Ukrainians who were Geek–Orthodox. There were some exceptions (e.g. the village of Yetsin) where Polish settlers were brought over by the Polish nobility who controlled the Polish Sejm. The Polish aristocracy knew to take advantage of its weight in the Austrian Parliament in Vienna, where they served as the balance of power.

[Columns 115-116]

Zloczow's Representatives Welcome the Emperor Karl I

A fight commenced between the Poles and the Ruthenians starting at the beginning of the 19th century about positions, rights, and the language taught in schools. A similar fierce fight also took place in Zloczow. Zloczow's Jews, like Jews throughout Galitsia, were put in a difficult position. Some of them supported the Poles, the previous rulers who were culturally on a higher level. In Zloczow and Brody, the supporters of the Poles succeeded in electing the Jewish representatives, Bik and Guld, to the Austrian Parliament (they served during 1891 – 1907). The Ukrainians considered the tendencies of the Jews to support the Poles negatively and tried to develop their own political and economic institutions.

The Jews, who found themselves between the hammer and the anvil, were pushed aside from their economic positions. Notwithstanding, a robust Zionist movement developed in Zloczow from as early as the 1890s. Zionist institutions were established, which fought against the large and powerful Haredi camp. That camp boasted a long tradition, which began in the 18th century when a Hasidic nucleus was established. It was named after the famous *Maggid* Rabbi Yekhiel Mikhel.

Intense political unrest strengthened during the years 1907 – 1911. During those years, a heightened battle between the various political factions took place. The battle was associated with the election of Adolf Shtand, the president of the Galitsia Zionist movement, to the Austrian parliament. The central government in Austria dreaded the strengthening of Polish influence. Therefore, it often supported the Ukrainians against the Poles. On the other side, Tzarist Russia took advantage of the Polish–Ukrainian conflict to inflame hatred and pry open an old wound. That wound opened as a result of the unification of the Greek Orthodox Church with the Roman Catholic Church (also called the "Union of Brest"). The unification took place at the end of the 16th century. That wound in the Greek Catholic Church never healed. The Ukrainians [separated from the Greek Orthodox Church and] established the Moscophiles Church [Galitsian Russophile] in Eastern Galitsia.

However, both the Poles and Ukrainians considered the growth of the Jewish population unfavorably. They feared the "Judaization" of commerce in the cities of Eastern Galitsia. The rivalries got fiercer and fiercer. That was also reflected well in Zloczow. The city was a bustling and dynamic town and thus sensitive to all of the economic, national, and religious trends.

The Ukrainian propaganda took root in the years 1918/19. An independent Ukrainian republic, which embodied the entire area of Eastern Galitsia, was declared in November 1918. The Ukrainians obviously, took control of Zloczow. They considered Zloczow as an essential center of their administration. The investigation of a group of Poles by the Ukrainian authorities ended in harsh torture and tragic deaths of the group's members in April 1919. They were suspected of being members of the underground that was connected to the Polish enemy. Among those who were executed, were 17 years old students from the local high school.

In 1920, the Bolsheviks conquered Zloczow during the war between Soviet Russia and Poland, whose marshal Pilsudski tried to take Kyiv. The Russian rule lasted only one month. The Poles established themselves in Zloczow after winning a series of battles named "The Miracle on the Vistula". The area became an integral part of the new country of Poland. After that, the number of residents in Zloczow fluctuated. The events, which took place during the period 1914 – 1920, took their toll on the city. It suffered tremendously from the armies that fought in the surrounding areas during that period. The Poles did not fulfill the promise to provide autonomy to the Ukrainian settlements. The Poles' military carried out a punishment operation in the villages surrounding Zloczow. The authorities looked for spies, and people who resisted the regime. The cruel verdicts that followed, "calmed" the enthusiastic Ukrainians, who did not get used to the Polish rule of the region.

[Columns 117-118]

Zloczow until World War II

by Mordekhai Deutsch

Translated by Moshe Kutten

The Road Leading from Zloczow to Lviv

Upon leaving Zloczow, one encounters two cemeteries. On the left – the old cemetery and on the right – the new one. The old cemetery was deserted. Only a few gravestones remain standing. However, there are many fallen, buried, and broken gravestones.

The following words are etched on one of the gravestones that were left standing: "Here buried a groom and a bride, killed on the day of their marriage, by Khmelnytsky's murderers, damn them".

That happened during the so–called "Khmelnytskyi Uprising" when the famous Jews' foe assaulted Galitsia's cities, robbed and looted Jewish property, and murdered men, women, and children. On his way to Lviv, he passed through Zloczow, and here too, wreaked havoc on the Jews. That gravestone stands as a memorial and testimony to that big calamity. As customary, the Jews used to visit the cemetery on the 9th of Av. People visited the graves of their relatives. Then they visited the grave of the "*Tzadik*" – Rabbi Avraham Khaim son of Gedalyahu and his disciple the "*Maggid* from Mezritch" (a "grave–tent" [a mausoleum] – built by the community activists, surrounded the grave of the *Tzadik*). After leaving, on their way back home, they would also stop by the graves of the bride and groom martyrs in the old cemetery.

A stone fence was erected around the new cemetery. A house was also built for the tombstone carver who lived there with his family and guarded the place. However, there was no fence or a guard at the old cemetery. During World War I, when the Russian armies invaded the town, every empty lot served as an encampment. Since the old cemetery was adjacent to the barrack, the remaining standing gravestones were destroyed. Only after the war, when life returned to normal, our landsmen in the United States sent emissaries for reconstructing the public institutions in the city. A fence around the old cemetery was erected at that time.

The elders used to tell folklore stories about these two cemeteries and the road that separated them. They said that, in the beginning, there was only one cemetery. However, the Polish governor aspired to accelerate the development of the city. Around the city, there were villages with fields yielding plenty of crops. The villages also raised cattle.

A Group of Intellectuals in Zloczow

[Columns 119-120]

The Soup Kitchen Building, Named after Barukh

The governor found it necessary to construct a straight road to transport the crops and the cattle to Lviv. The governor claimed that the development was dependent on traders coming from afar to the city to purchase the crops and cattle and transfer them to Lviv. His advisors could not find any area to construct the road through other than the Jewish cemetery. The governors invited all the Jewish community leaders to him. He requested that they move their dead from the area planned for the new road. The leaders found themselves in a dilemma. They asked the governor to give them an extension of three days to consult with their rabbis and people. They claimed that they could not decide by themselves, since moving the dead was considered a sin of tarnishing the honor of the dead

When the request of the city's governor became known, the people turned to *Tzadik* Rabbi Mikheli. They pleaded with him to prevent the punishment they would receive by executing the evil decree. The holy *Tzadik* told them to turn to the water–carrier. They went to the water–carrier and told him that they were referred to him by the *Tzadik* Rabbi Mikheli. He answered humbly: "Why did the holy *Tzadik* send you to me? I am a simple Jew who does not even understand the meaning of your plea. Go and tell him that I cannot do anything for you regarding this difficult matter". However, they pleaded with him and emphasized again that the holy *Tzadik* sent them to him. He relented and told them: "Gentlemen, this is a cruel decree brought upon you from heaven. You Must get together, pray, and ask for forgiveness".

The leaders ordered to hold a day of fasting. They also sanctioned the public to gather at the great synagogue and pray and plead to the dead and encourage them to petition for their honor with G–d.

Three days later, as was agreed with the governor, workers came to uproot the tombstones marked by the road planners. However, they found out that there were no tombstones located on the planned route. When the news about the miracle was made known, the governor invited the leaders and asked them: "Who is the holy man who performed this miracle?" They told him the story about the water carrier who ordered them to pray and fast. They said that he was the one that should be credited for the miracle. The governor asked to meet with the water carrier. However, when the leaders went to look for him at his home, they did not find him. The water–carriers left town at night so that people would not recognize him as one of the 36 hidden righteous people. When the leaders told rabbi Mikheli about the water–carrier he told them: "One needs to know whom to call on to bring salvation"

The Fire

The event happened when I was a little child studying with the Melamed R' Yudal Mendel. One day, his wife came into the study room. With tears in her eyes, she yelled with a choked voice: "Fire. Fire!" A fire broke at the workshop of the cotton–balls artisan. He was the one that resided by Itah Weisman. R' Mendel's house was located a hundred and fifty meters from the fire. Therefore, they decided to send the children home. They brought me over to the bridge on Brodska Street and I walked home from there by myself. That fire left a strong impression on me. The event was etched in my memory despite my young age. I haven't slept throughout the night and watched the billows of smoke and columns of the blaze rising to heaven. The fire sent its tongue and ate one house after the other.

[Columns 121-122]

A Youth Group – "Bernstein Grupoeh"
["The Bernstein Group"]

A strong wind blew in a western direction, and indeed all the houses in that direction burnt to the ground. Panic gripped the people. They left their home and turned north and east. Some children got lost and searches were conducted to find them. The cries and wailing ascended to heaven. When daylight came, the children were found.

However, there were sick and handicapped people, at the hospital and in the handicapped–home, who could save themselves. They were burnt alive. The death of these poor people put the people in a depressed mood.

Stories about the Fire

That was not an ordinary fire. It looked like the work of evil angels, who came to take revenge following an event in the past. The story spread by a word of mouth. A young man committed suicide. When the relatives came to "*Khevere Kadishe*" [the burial society] to ask for a plot, Rabbi Eliezer Shwartz, who headed the burial society, sent them to the community Rabbi. The Rabbi instructed that a person who committed the suicide must be buried near the fence and not among the other graves. The parents and friends of the young man objected. They began digging the grave by themselves, despite protests by the people of "*Khevre Kaadishe*" and the city residents. The police probably helped the family and friends. The following day, men and women said that their deceased relatives came to them in their dreams and complained about the fact that a person who committed suicide was buried near them. They stated that this would bring calamity to the city. A short while later, a fire broke out. It blew from the same direction where the relatives of that man carried his bed. Years later, when anybody committed suicide, everybody agreed to bury that person in a grave near the cemetery fence.

Help from the Surrounding Area

When the Jews in the surrounding area heard about the disaster that had befallen our town, they brought carts loaded with bread and other foods. Thanks to them, the city did not go hungry. Almost all of the bakeries burnt down, and the fire broke down Friday night. Frydrykh's bakery, which was not burnt down, operated day and night to provide bread for the Sabbath. People lived outdoors, near their burnt houses, for weeks after the fire. However, when the first signs of winter appeared, everybody began to look for a place to live until they could rebuild their houses. The people whose home was not destroyed in the fire hosted the homeless. About forty people were living in our house, which was designed to accommodate only twelve. Nobody was looking to profit from the disaster that had befallen the city.

The Recovery

Zloczow's residents did not wait for outside help. Everybody began to take care of their house. The municipal institutions awarded tax discounts to people who rebuilt their houses, and the Mortgage Bank provided long–term loans to the owners of the newly rebuilt houses. People who owned a plot managed to build newer and more spacious houses. There was no shortage of contractors. The most famous ones were Avraham Mozlush, Ze'ev Yosefsberg, Berl Tzeiler, Moshe Waggen, and Leibush Fishman. The latter also owned a carpentry shop. There were also Jewish masons, like Herman "the builder" and Ekel "the builder". Some Jewish builders came from Russia. They defected from the Red Army. The builders Yosl Remenyuk and his friend Lev arrived in Zloczow through the border in Brody. They heard that there was plenty of work in the town that could earn good money. The Jews in Zloczow invested an abundance of effort and work until they rebuilt their city anew. The carpentry shops operated diligently, to build the houses. The tinsmiths, painters, and locksmiths did not rest either. Soon enough, the whole city began to take a new look. Two and three–level brick buildings replaced the old clay houses.

[Columns 123-124]

Participants in a Zionist seminar

King Franz Joseph's Birthday

During those days, Jews were not interested in politics. There were a few exceptional people who read newspapers and understood what was happing in the world. However, the masses considered them "Enlightened". The simple people believed in the grace of his majesty Franz Joseph the First. They gathered in the great synagogue every year for a festive assembly. The district officer, police, and other dignitaries were also invited. Gaon Rabbi Feivel Rohatyn gave a speech in German sermonizing about the welfare of the king and kingdom. Later on, the cantor and the chorus sang in honor of the king. The festive assembly left a good impression, so the Jews went home trusting that there is somebody in Vianna who cared for them.

"The Revised Kheder"

The person who initiated a fundamental revision in the Jewish education system was Shmuel Wildeniger, better known as Shmuel "Americaner". He was born in Kalwarya Zebrzydowska[?]. He was an energetic person who traveled to the USA as a young man. That was how he acquired his nickname. During his travel, he showed interest in education. He concluded that the [Jewish] education system must be revised. A committee of parents, who helped him in his work, was established. The committee consisted of the following people: Nathan Negelberg, Moshe Auerbach, Rekl Semel, and Israel Wolfshoit. The committee rented an entire floor from Lemel Mestul for use by the "Revised Kheder". Israel Meshir was nominated as the principal. He was an intelligent man, with a vast knowledge of the Bible, grammar, Israeli history, and Hebrew literature. Rabbi Meshir advocated a modern approach to teaching. The teaching material was written with chalk on a blackboard, a method that was similar to the one practiced in the state school at the time. Based on Rabbi Maeshir's recommendation, teachers of Gemara and Mishna were hired. The children studied the Bible and grammar in the "Revised Kherder". They also learned how to write in a neat style. Examiners from among the Jewish scholars and the city's intellectuals were invited to test the children every Shabbat. Rabbi Shlomo Belter tested the children about the Bible and RabbiFievel Rohatyn tested them about the Mishna. The latter was impressed greatly with the newly revised teaching system and supported the "Revised Kheder". We loved the principal, Rabbi Israel Meshir. When he taught about the prophet Isaiah, we felt that the prophet was talking out of his mouth. Hundreds of students studied in the "Revised Kheder". Among them, Professor Avraham Shalit, today at the University of Jerusalem, the author Moshe Leib Potashnik, the teacher Yaakov Zeltz who taught at the high school in Lviv, and physician Dr. Khaim Zelkai. B. Tz. Tzverdling, lawyer Avraham Shalit, Yitzkhak Negelberg, and Shmuel Korshen are some of Meshir's students who currently reside in Israel. Meshir taught his students to read Gratz's history books and the novels "Ahavat Zion" ["Love of Zion"], and "Ashmat Shomron" ["Guilt of Samaria"] by Avraham Mapu. These books aroused a longing for Eretz Israel. Meshir himself corresponded with the authors – the Teller brothers in Eretz Israel.

Zionism in our City

A Zionist association was established in our city, like in all other cities in Galitsia. The quiet life of the Jews in the city began to simmer. Echoes of Dreyfus's trial in France reached us.

[Columns 125-126]

The JNF [Keren Kayement Le'Israel] Committee in Zloczow – 1921

Distinguished people belonged to the Zionist association such as Rabbi Yitskhak Schwadron, the father of the author Dr. Avraham Sharon, Dr. Itamar Eidelberg, one of the famous lawyers in the city and the owner of many properties, Rabbi Avraham Yaakov Ogel, an enlightened person and scholar, contractor, and owner of some businesses, Mr. Israel Weis, an enlightened person and owner of properties, Mr. Yitskhak Buchacher, a building contractor, and Mr. Shmaryahu Imber, a teacher in Baron Hirsch's school, and the father of poet Shmuel Yaakov Imber (brother of the poet N. H. Imber author of "HaTikvah") who was killed by Hitler's murderous troops. These distinguished activists attracted younger people such as Dr. Groskopf, a young lawyer, Mr. Tzvi Rosenboim, an owner of a store and merchant of wines, Dr. Fishel Veshitz, Dr. Gustav Katz, Dr. Moshe Shwager, Wolf Rosen, and Moshe Rosen. Even the very young participate in bearing the burden of the Zionist workload. Among them were Yaakov Shmuel Vilig, Moshe Shwartz, and Yaakov Mizlis. Young Zionist lawyers from other cities came to our city. Among them, Dr. Tzvi Hirschhorn, Dr. David Verpel, and Dr. Simkha Bunim Feldman. The latter became a representative in the Polish Sejm after the establishment of an independent Poland. Simkha Bunim Feldman represented the "HaMizrkhai" party. He also served as the secretary of the Jewish caucus in the Polish Sejm.

Election for the Community's Committee

The time for the election for the community's committee arrived. Before the establishment of the Zionist movement, the election was conducted peacefully. The extreme religious and the assimilators did not shy away from working together. The assimilators did not get involved in Kosher affairs, and the religious extremists did not get involved in political affairs. However, when Zionism was established, its motto was "Conquering the Communities". A fight broke out between the Zionists and the assimilators. Two Zionists, Dr. Itamar Eidelberg and Dr, Groskopf were elected to the community's committee for the first time in the history of Zloczow. That was just the first step, as the two were in the minority.

A very sad story occurred in the city. There was a Jewish school, which was built from the fund established by Baron Hirsch. It was an elementary school in which the Polish language was taught. However, the teachers were all Jewish. The children came from impoverished homes where they spoke only Yiddish. The children did not suffer from any antisemitism, which allowed them to excel in their studies since the teachers could explain in Yiddish whatever was unclear in Polish. However, the district governor found it necessary to transform the school into a pure Polish state school. The municipality's council probably supported the idea. The community's committee discussed that proposal. Since the Zionists had only two representatives on the committee, it became apparent that their objection would not be fruitful. it was decided that the residents would express publicly their bitterness about the confiscating of Jewish property, particularly a school that was built from money contributed by the benevolent Barone Hirsch. However, two distinguished people supported the proposal. One of them was mayor Yosef Guld, the chairman of the community committee. The other was the person who was the trustee that managed the property of Baron Hirsch in Zloczow (the son–in–law of the mayor Yosef Guld).

[Columns 127-128]

In the end, the Jewish community committee decided to hand over the building to the municipality and transform it into a public municipal school. They received that resolution despite the objections of the Zionist members of the committee. When the committee members, with elder Yosef Guld among them, came out from that faithful meeting, they encountered an unexpected reception. Many residents and organized youths greeted them with shouts of contempt and with the ringing of bells, which were prepared in advance. The crowd's anger was so immense that the committee members had to look for a shelter to protect themselves.

The Elected Officials of the Community Committee

The election to the Austrian House of Representatives was held in 1908. Dr. Adolf Shtand, the chairman of the Eastern Galitsia Zionist movement, was selected as the Zionist candidate. Another [Jewish] candidate was Dr. Yosef Guld, the head of the council of Zloczow municipality. He ran as a candidate for the Polish party. The Poles knew that the chances of a Polish representative being elected were slim. The reason for that was that the Jews held the majority of the population of Zloczow and its surroundings. The Poles decided that it would be advantageous to nominate Dr. Guld as their candidate. There were additional reasons for the selection of Dr. Guld. The first reason was that he was a Jewish physician who would likely draw some Jewish voters. Secondly, the Jewish residents had to obey him being the chairman of the Jewish community committee. He was also supported by the district governor. The Zionists received no outside help. They had to fight, for the election of Adolf Shtand, by themselves. They invited guest speakers such as Dr. Gershon Tzofar from Lviv, Rabbi Gedalyahu Shmelkis from Przemysl [Pshemishel], and Israel Waldman from Ternopil.

The youth helped to carry the burden during the campaign. Many public gatherings took place. Members of the Ukrainian intelligentsia participated in one such outdoor gathering. During that election, the Zionists united with the Ukrainians against the Poles. The appearance of speaker, Dr. Hirschhorn, left an immense impression. Being a tall man, sporting a beautiful forelock, and speaking flawless Ukrainian poised to become advantageous during the election itself. Unfortunately for the city residents, Dr. Yosef Guld was elected to the Austrian parliament. He was elected due to fraudulent schemes by the assimilators and the Poles. Also, some greedy wealthy Jews helped in the election of Dr. Guld.

[Columns 129-130]

Members of the Self–Defense group During the Ukrainian Rule 1918 – 1919

Mr. Reitsis was elected in Zloczow to replace Dr. Guld during the following election to the Austrian parliament, which was held in 1911. He was elected not as a Zionist but as a nonaffiliated. He was very devoted to the city residents. He assisted the residents during World War I when he served as a representative in the Austrian parliament

The Declaration of World War I

On the nine of Av 5674 (1914), The Austrian government declared war against Serbia. The reason for that declaration was that the Crown Prince of the House of Hesburgh, Franz Ferdinand, was killed during a tour in Bosnia–Herzegovina. As known, that declarant caused World War I. General mobilization was announced, and hordes of soldiers flooded the city because Zloczow served as the camping ground of two infantry battalions and one cavalry battalion.

The Jews who were Austrian patriots, joined the military to fight for the Habsburg dynasty because Franz Joseph was considered the patron of the Jews. Not long after, a flow of refugees passed through Zloczow from the neighboring border cities: Brody, Pidkamin, Zaliztsi, and other settlements near the border, in which Jews resided. The Jews ran away as they feared the Russian army and the Kozaks, who were known to rob and murderers. In Zloczow Jews were sure, or just had an illusion, that the enemy would not reach the city's gates. Firstly, three well–armed battalions were camping in the city. Secondly because of the flood of the recruited people., and thirdly because Zloczow was surrounded by mountains with an old fort built during the Ottoman rule. The Jews decided that the Austrian army would place cannons on the top of the mountains and thus would be able to defend the city from the enemy. The Jews simply wished, naively, to live in peace. However, the bitter reality slapped them in their faces. It happened at noon on Friday. Almost everything was ready for Shabbat. Austrian soldiers, who ran away from the nearby front, entered the city hurriedly and yelled at people to run away in the face of the approaching enemy. The government offices in the city cleared. All of the government officials left town with the last train. Rumors spread that the enemy is approaching from all directions. None of the Austrian soldiers remained in the city. The fear that descended was horrible. Men packed a small package, loaded it on their shoulders, and went out with their family toward the neighboring city of Holohory. Whoever had a "vehicle" (a wagon and a horse), used it. However, most of the city's Jews walked on foot. A solar eclipse occurred on the way. People were depressed about the two events: leaving their houses and properties behind and the solar eclipse. Upon approaching Holohory they observed the [Austrian] Tirolian battalions and artillerymen with their cannons preparing for battle. The people of Holohory welcomed the refugees and hosted them in their homes. However, the congestion was horrible, and there was also a shortage of food. Such much so that some people returned home to Zloczow. However, most of the people remained in Holohory and waited for the victory. Two days passed without any shooting. However, an artillery battle began on the third day, causing the houses to rattle. Artillery shells landed, but miraculously no one got hurt. On the fifth day (Friday), the Russian army entered the city. Zloczow residents were allowed to return to their city. On their way home, they encountered fear and terror. Dead Austrian soldiers covered the side of the roads. Russian horsemen could be seen riding in the direction of Lviv.

[Columns 131-132]

The Drama Club named after Ansky

The Russians had probably buried their dead before to hide them from their soldiers. However, they left the Austrian dead to demonstrate their big win, as if they have not lost any casualties. The Russian military considered the Jews as enemies. Therefore, when they came back home after venturing between the two enemy militaries, they were happy to return safe and sound.

The Destruction of Galitsia

The [Russian] military brought carnage, destruction, and devastation to Galitsia cities, populated mostly by Jews. Our city was probably the only one in which a miracle happened. It happened thanks to one of the distinguished residents, a famous Jewish lawyer, Dr. Hirschhorn. Hirschhorn, who hosted a high–ranked Russian officer in his apartment, managed to refute the plot, for which people tried to blame the Jews. According to that plot, a few shots were directed at the Russian military from Rabbi David Lvov's house. Bad news, about Jews being murdered and houses being burnt, reached the city from the rest of the cities in the area.

The town Bilyi Kamin burnt to the ground. All of its Jewish residents escaped to Zloczow until the storm blew over. Even the Jews who lived in Zloczow's surroundings, including Jewish farmers, had to abandon their houses and properties and move to the city. The means for making a living evaporated. However, Jews with wagons loaded with merchandizes began to arrive from Russian cities close to the [old] border. In the meantime, the Russian Tzar, Nikolai, passed through Zloczow to witness his military victories. The city residents stood in line to cheer. He looked at them as being tired and weak. People wondered how he managed to instill fear in the numerous nations of Russia.

Refugees Arrive in the City

Jewish refugees from Tlumach and Tysmenytsia arrived one morning in the city. They presented a big problem for Zloczow's Jewish residents. The state of most of the residents was already atrocious. Many other refugees from the neighboring towns and villages had already arrived in the city, therefore a new wave presented an additional burden. However, the Jews found a solution to the problem quickly. Each family hosted new refugees. A committee was organized with members from among the city's distinguished residents. The committee consisted of Mr.

Yeshayahu Tenenbaum, Rabi Yaakov Negler, and some prominent women. A short time later, a soup kitchen was established, and refugees received a free lunch.

Zloczow is Ruled Again by the Austrians

A few months later, the Austrian army advanced, conquered Zloczow, and reached the Seret River. The Jewish residents were joyful. However, the joy did not last long. The news about the first recruits who died on the front reached the city. General mobilization of people between the ages of eighteen and fifty commenced. Among the casualties were: Munio Negler, Noiget, Schwadron, Aharon Weintraub, and others. Aharon Weintraub, the son of Mendel Weintraub (who was survived by his wife and a daughter), and others. Every day brought more bad news from the front about additional casualties, which depressed the city residents. In 1917, a revolution broke out in Russia. The war which followed, between Krensky and the Bolsheviks, weakened the Russian army. The attack by the Austro–German forces on Russia broke open the front on the Seret and advance into Ukraine's interior. However, Austria, which consisted of many nations, fell apart, and each nation got its part of Eastern Galitsia. A war [a sustained warlike conflict, that lasted from 1917 to 1921] erupted between the Poles and Ukrainians [which resulted in the establishment and development of a Ukrainian republic].   In the meantime, the Poles conducted a pogrom against the Jews in Lviv.

[Columns 133-134]

The Committee of the Organization "Tzeirei Tzion" (Youth of Zion)

The Ukrainian Regime (1917– 1918)

The Jews began to organize themselves under the Ukrainian regime. Judge Belterovich was elected as the city's mayor. His attitude toward the Jews was not too bad. The authorities opened the high school, in which the teaching language was Ukrainian. The school employed Jewish teachers. The youths who studied during the war in the capital Vienna came back to the city. They prepared the youths for immigration to Eretz Israel. Balfour Declaration was treated seriously. Every circle prepared their youths for abandoning the diaspora and building a national home in Eretz Israel. Mordekhai Imber was the organizing and guiding force behind that effort. Hundreds of boys and girls learned how to work the land and cultivate a garden. They studied Hebrew, Israeli history, and useful crafts. Dov Ofer recruited youths to the "HaShomer" ["The Guard"] Zionist movement. Numerous youths, from all levels, joined the movement. Torah students organized in the club, "Aviv" ["Spring"]. They also prepared themselves for Aliya to Eretz Israel. They studied Hebrew and useful crafts. The driving force in that club was Mr. Yekhiel Imber. Barukh Stertiner and Shtultzberg brothers were also members of that club. Dr. Schwadron organized and managed seminar courses. He was helped by Dr. David Verpel, Mordekhai Imber, Dr. Shalit, Mrs. Hirschhorn, Dr. Kalman Schweig, Moshe Schorr, and others. Moshe Kleinman taught Hebrew. Many students mastered the Hebrew language and acquired knowledge of the Bible, literature, and History in those courses. A Hebrew-speaking club, "Tarbut" ["Culture"] was established. The members of the club were: Dr. Simkha Bunim Feldman, lawyer Dr. Verpel, Dr. Avraham Schwadron, Mrs. Hischhorn (a descendant of the famous Galitsian Zionist family, Tartakover), a native of Brody, and the wife of Dr. Tzvi Hirschhorn, Mr. Mordekhai Imber, and Dr. Feivel Gruber. Then club members gathered every Shabbat for a discussion, lecture, or reading. Dr. Khaim Leider (Zalkai), who was a member of that club, gave lectures on various topics in fluent Hebrew. Another cultural club was organized under the initiative of Dr. Avraham Schwadron (Sharon). The members studied the books of the author, Akhad Ha'Am. Dr. Sharon had a substantial influence on the educated youths.

The war between the Poles and the Ukrainians separated us from the rest of the world. One could get to Europe only through Romania. However, the train's schedule was irregular, and passengers experienced many difficulties on the way there.

A Yiddish weekly magazine began to appear in the city under the initiative of the Zionist executive committee. Dr. Yekutiel Shuster, Moshe Schorr, and others served as editors. The magazine was published every Friday and included the news, political articles, feuilletons, and even information about life in Eretz Israel. The "Bund" people also published a Yiddish newspaper. However, after the publication of the weekly magazine, they ceased its publication.

Dreadful Days

The city experienced a few dreadful days when an internal conflict among companies of the Ukrainian military. One company shot the other within the city limits, and the battle continued outside of the city. The residents stayed at home, not daring to venture out. There were dead and wounded among the soldiers.

[Columns 135-136]

A few days later, when it was possible to go out of the house, people discovered the extent of the destruction in the city. The storefront windows were broken and the contents of the stores were robbed.

The Polish Regime

In the spring of 1918, the Poles received some equipment from France and they overpowered the Ukrainians. A few days later, the latter came back but retreated again. The Ukrainian front disintegrated without the ability to reestablish it. Fear descended upon the Jews. Firstly, because the Ukrainians retreated. Secondly – the fear of the Poles, who were known to abuse the Jews. There were stories about them cutting the beards with the skin of the faces. When the first Polish company came and discovered a city crowded with Jewish residents, their officer's first question was: "Did we conquer a Jewish City"? The Polish soldiers entered the Jewish homes and robbed anything they could put their hands on. Later on, when the civil regime was established, order returned. However, antisemitism raised its ugly head: All the Jewish officials were fired. A heavy tax load was imposed. The Jews realized that they did not have any defense against the Polish regime in power. The first "HaShomer" group made Aliya to Eretz Israel. Although horrible news about the murder of Dov Ofer at the hands of Arab perpetrators arrived from Eretz Israel, the youths banded together and continued to make Aliya. Among the people who made Aliya were: Mordekhai Bukhbinder, Lola Yosefsberg, Sara Negler, Dr. Yehoshua Yosefsberg, Yitzkhak Negelberg with his wife Dvorah Negelberg, Mordekhai Imber, and Dov Glazer and his family. The elderly such as Shmaryahu Imber, the family of Yehoshua Stertiner, and others also made Aliya.

*****

[Column 137]

The Kempa and Zlotsov'ka

by Dr. E. Boneh (Bauman)

Translated by Moshe Kutten

Two natural sites were important centers for the city's vibrant youths. One of the sites was the Kempa – that hill at the center of town, adorned with trees, lawns, and playgrounds. The second site was the small twisting river, named after the city's name – Zlotsov'ka [Zlotsov – the Yiddish pronunciation of Zloczow. Today it is called Zolochiv].

These two sites were teeming with hundreds of youths, during all days of the year. During the summer months, the youths spent their time on the hill playing various games or immersed themselves in the river. During the winter months, the hill and the river served as sites for ice skating. Boys and girls of every religion spent their energy there. They played, romped, and dreamt about their future, dreams that were shattered by the mundane reality of their adolescence.

Today, after twenty-five years, when I evoke my memories about these sites, I feel the pain of those best of the youth who fell victims to the Nazi beast. Thousands of youths fell victims to the Nazis' wild rampage, precisely at these sites, the Kempa and the Zlotsov'ka. They suffered tortures and lost their lives near these sites that served as sources for joy and youthful happiness.

The years that passed may have dimmed memories of the mind and the heart. Therefore, the description might not be complete. However, it is advantageous to bring up some of the things that made the Kempa and Zlotsov'ka such memorable places.

The Kempa

The Kempa was a small towering hill above the center of the city. That was not a steep and high hill. The height difference between the city plane and the top of the hill did not exceed 30 meters. Trails led to the hill from every direction in the city. However, climbing to the top did not require a lot of effort, even though the trails were not paved. The top of the Kempa was flat. The flattening earthworks on that hill transformed it into an ideal area for the young to spend their leisure time there.

[Column 138]

A double row of trees, separated by gaps of about 3 meters, was planted around the Kempa's summit, creating a promenade. The fresh odor and the shade given by the trees created a pleasant atmosphere. Most of the visitors to the promenade, which surrounded the Kempa like a ring, were students. They used to walk around and study their school material for the following day or prepare for a test. Tens of youths could be seen walking around the Kempa, holding their study books, memorizing the material while watching the treetops or the playgrounds. When the walkers would meet each other, they would stop and exchanged jokes and teases. Many would spend hours walking around.

Two parts of the Kempa area served as playgrounds. One served as a soccer field and the other as a place for riding bicycles. The third part was a lawn, where young children set. Smaller children tended to stay away from older children who sometimes played too recklessly. Benches were scattered around the last part, which was overflowing with greenery and flowers. Romantic and elderly couples could be spotted there.

Many boys brought their bicycles to perform acrobatic tricks or carry their girlfriends on the back seat. Most of the time, the boys carried thin girls to avoid blowing up the tires.

A Group of Bathers in the Zlotsov'ka

[Columns 139-140]

The Zlotsov'ka River

Another experience was climbing on trees and the games of hiding in the treetops. We once hid in a chestnut treetop and disappeared in the middle of a gym class. When the teacher realized that we were missing (most of the time, 3 or 4 students hid together) he would send other students to look for us. When they approached us, we welcomed them with a shower of chestnuts. The attacked had to search for cover behind the trunks of the adjacent trees. Any time any of them dared to reveal himself, he would be besieged by another shower of chestnuts, accompanied by roars of laughter.

The Kempa served as a center, not only during the days of the summer. When the winter came, the hill would be covered by blankets of snow, and its frozen trails became sledding tracks. The main trail, located near the co-ed state high school, was the eastern one. We used to gather there with our sport sleds, after school hours to sled down the slope. Since the trail was quite narrow, going around another sled presented a problem. The issue of overtaking another sled became a matter of honor and arrogance. A boy of the front sled considered it an insult when somebody tried to pass him from behind. Conflicts, fights, and brawls erupted often. At times, these fights became an expression of racial hatred when they erupted between the Jewish and the Polish or Ukrainian youths. At other times, the girls were the reason for the fights, as the girls tended to mock the losing boy or the one who could not overtake other sleds.

As described, the Kempa was a source of delight all year-round. Many of Zloczow's natives, who survived the Holocaust, carry that site in their hearts.

The Zlotsov'ka River

The other site that attracted the youth was the river. Perhaps that stream of water was not worthy of the title – river. It was not even noted on maps. However, the city youths valued it tremendously. We called it Zlotsov'ka-an endearment name derived from the name of our city. The depth of Zlotsov'ka did not reach two meters except for a few isolated places. Its width was only 4 to 6 meters. The only exception was the small dam, which was erected to allow for storing fish. At the dam, the width reached 10 – 12 meters.

The river flew from behind the Kempa. That formed a connection between the two sites. [During the summer], the youths, sweating from their sports games, rushed straight to the Zlotsov'ka from the Kempa. During the wintertime, when the river froze, the youths ice skated on it.

[Columns 141-142]

The Zlotsov'ka was the only place to learn how to swim since there were no natural lakes or swimming pools in Zloczow. Many of Zloczow's natives, scattered today around the world, still, likely remember their first swimming sessions in that small river of Zloczow. The Zlotsov'ka flew along its natural twisting and turning ravine, which the river carved for hundreds of years. Vast fields spread on both banks of the rivers. Trees and bushes, which served as a hiding place for changing clothes, chequered the area. There were no dressing rooms along the river, which presented a problem, particularly for the girls who had to go far to change into their bathing suits. Leaving the unguarded clothes at the riverbank was another problem. Often, a bather who came out of the river would not find his or her clothes where they left them. It was not a theft, but a practical joke, which caused a temporary embarrassment. Girls often cried and begged for help find their clothes, since they could not return home in their bathing suits.

There were sections of the river where the water was deep. These sections were safe only for skilled swimmers. Since there weren't that many, bathing in these places was more pleasant. One such place was located near the village of Yeniov, about a kilometer and a half from the Kempa. Near that village, the river carved out a small square-like pond. That location served as a place for water-ball games, diving and underwater swimming, and diving from the back of one's friends. We named the pond "Biyeniov'ka" after the village mentioned above.

Although the Zlotsov'ka was a meager and small river, it filled up during periods of heavy rains. The creek would fill up, overflow, and flood many adjacent fields. Once it happened that a wide area, a few kilometers wide, was flooded. Hundreds of Zloczow residents flocked to the scene to look at the "ocean". The depth of that "ocean" was only about 30 to 40 centimeters. However, it left an impression of an infinite sea. The "ocean" disappeared two days later, and the city was left with its small river.

[Columns 143-144]

Chapter B

Holocaust and Heroism in Zloczow

Translated by Moshe Kutten

[Columns 145-150]

[blank]

[Columns 151-152]

[Columns 153-178]

The Holocaust in its Occurrence

Note: The Hebrew version is a short version of the Dr. Altman's article ("Haunting Memories") on column 29 of the English section

[Column 161]

Arbeitsamt: Lemberg
Nebenstelle: Zloczow

Meldekarte für Juden

Nr. 91423

Der Jude / Die Jüdin Helbraun [illegible]
geboren am: 19. November 1901
in Sasow ledig, verh., gesch., verw
Wohnort: Zloczow
[illegible] Str. Nr.: 8a
Berufsgruppe u. Art: 21 f

ist auf Grund der Zweiten Durchführungsvorschrift zur Verordnung vom 26. Oktober 1939 über die Einführung des Arbeitszwanges für die jüdische Bevölkerung des Generalgouvernements vom 12. Dezember 1939 erfasst und steht dem Arbeitsamt zum Arbeitseinsatz zur Verfügung. Ein Auffangen auf der Strasse ist nicht statthaft.

(Lichtbild)

(Stempel d. Arbeitsamts)

(Unterschrift)

Kontrollmeldung am Montag | Mittwoch | Freitag
jeder Woche, soweit kein Arbeitsverhältnis besteht.

Staatsdruckerei Warschau — Nr. 4779-41.

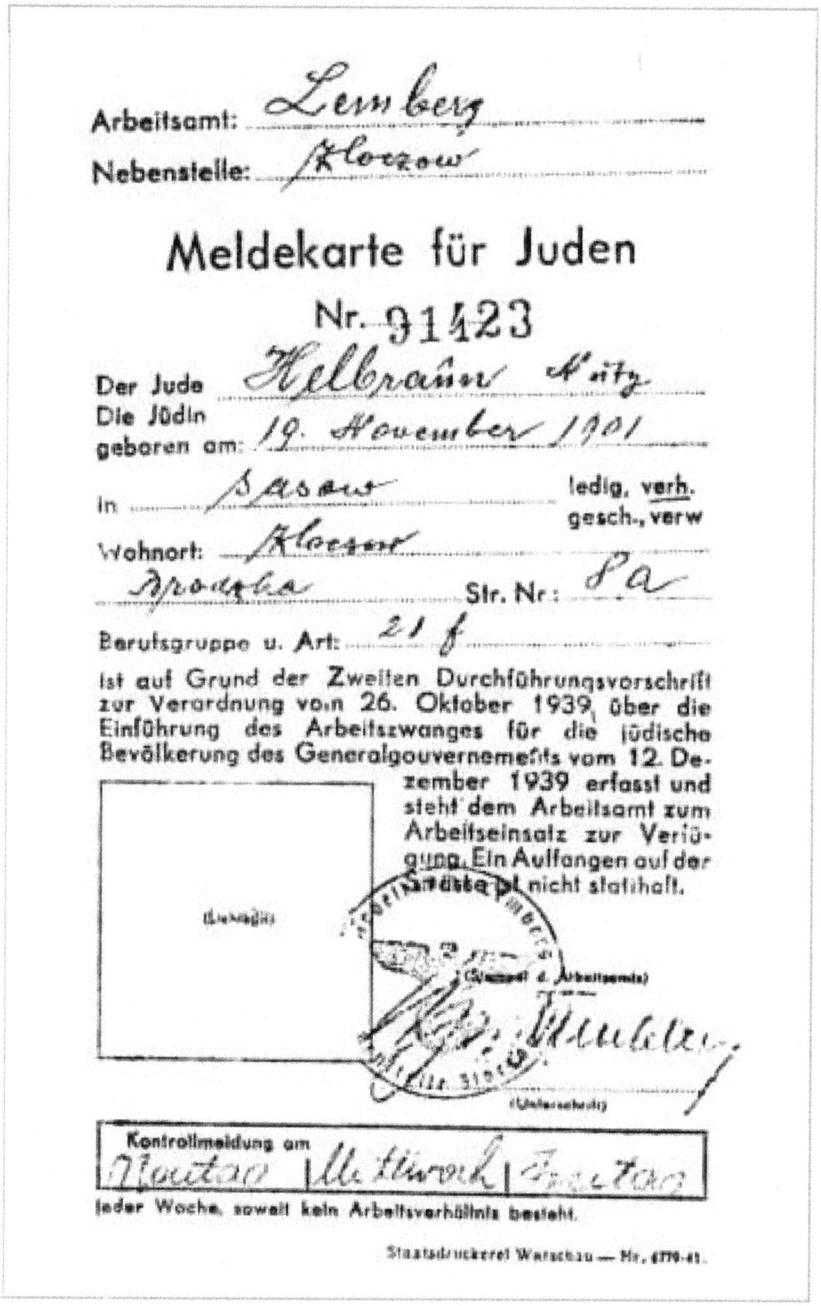

A Certificate for Reporting to Forced Labor during the Nazi regime in Zloczow

[Columns 165-166]

Mass Grave of Zloczow's Jewish Residents in 1943

[Columns 179-180]

Sections from "Chapters from Galitsia"

Edited by Israel Cohen and Prof. Dov Sadan

"Am Oved" Publishing, Tel Aviv 5716 (1956)

The wave of pogroms swelled during the summer and fall of 1941. In many cities, the first in line to be executed was the intelligentsia. The following are some examples: In Lviv, the Germans demanded a quota to come forward. In Ivano-Frankivsk [Stanislawow] 600 people were murdered in August. In Kolomyia, 200 physicians, lawyers, engineers, and clerks were executed. In Chortkiv, more than 300 victims were killed. Similar stories occurred in other places… (see page 429).

… In November 1941, [concentration] camps were established in Borki Wielkie, Jaktorow, Kamyanky, near Ternopil, Kosow Lacki, Winniki-Ostrov, and Korovitza. Jews from Zloczow were brought to the concentration camp established in Kozaki in January 1942 … (Page 431).

… The ghetto in Zloczow was sealed and surrounded by a barbwire fence in December 1942. Remnants of the Jewish populations from the neighboring towns: Olesko, Sasiv [Sasov], Bialy Kamien, Sokolovka, and other locations crowded in that ghetto. Altogether 9000 Jews resided in the ghetto … (Page 434).

German rounding operations [Aktsia's] took place in numerous locations: in Rava Ruska, Borislav (involving 5000 people), Drohobich (where most of the people were sent to Belzec, and those who were able to work were sent to Janowska camp), Chortkiv (where more than 3000 people were involved), Buchach (where approximately 1800 people were involved), and Zloczow (where 2700 people were involved in an Aktsia, which occurred on August 28) … (Page 437).

… Rounding operations (Aktisias) also took place in the following locations: in Brody (4500 people), Berezhany (approximately 6000 people), Ternopil (more than 2000 people), Zloczow (80 people were killed on the spot and 1000 were murdered in Belzec camp) … (Page 438).

… The murderous operations continued unabated. Bloody slaughtering has befallen upon the Jewish settlements: Horodenka (September-October – 6000 victims), Zloczow (2 – 3 November – 2500 victims) … (Page 438).

According to the report by Katzmann [the commander of the SS and Police in the District of Galitsia], 34,239 Jews were "deported" from the province of Galitsia until June 1943. According to the same report, Galitsia was declared "free of Jews", on 25 June 1943. Indeed, July 1943 was the final date by which the destruction of the last Jewish settlements in Galitsia was final. Three hundred artisans from Zloczow were executed in the Janowska camp and the survivors were killed in Yaktorov Forest. The last seventy of the Jewish workers were killed in Zhovkva … (Pages 440 – 441).

… The number of survivors in Zloczow – 74. Out of 2000 Jewish residents on Gliniani, only 25 survived.

… The poet Shmuel Yaakov Imber was murdered during the second bloody Aktsia in Zloczow … (page 443).

… Gravestones like those from the cemeteries in Lviv, Kolomyia, Gliniani, Zloczow, Ternopil, Rava-Ruska, and many other towns, were used to pave streets and roads. Only a few gravestones, which they could not uproot, remained standing. For example, the "grave-tent" of [Rabbi Avraham Khaim] the author of the book "Orakh Le'Khaim", and the gravestones of other *Tzadik's*) remained standing… (page 444).

… Some of the members of the Judenrat in Eastern Galitsia showed courage and refused to blindly serve as instruments in the hands of the German executioners. They were the scapegoats. The murderers poured their fearsome and cruel anger out on them. The first chairman of the Judenrat in Lviv, Dr. Yosef Parnas, paid with his life because he refused to surrender to the demands of the German executioners. Like him, the chairman of the Judenrat in Zloczow, Dr. Sigmund Meiblum, was shot because he refused to sign a document authored by the Germans. That document stated that an Aktsia had to take place because of a typhus epidemic that broke out in the ghetto. The Aktsia occurred on 2nd April 1943 … (Page 447).

… There were bunkers in the ghetto, like the Stersler's Bunker in Zloczow, where twenty-three Jews hid and survived until they were freed … (Page 448).

When the hiding bunkers in Ternopil (on Barone Hirsch Street) and Zloczow (at the home of V. Tzukerkendel) were discovered, the Jews were driven to stubbornly resist their oppressors. During an Aktsia in Kolomyia, on 17 September 1942, a young Jewish girl, Batya Singer, attacked a Ukrainian policeman. She was cruelly murdered on the spot.

… Jewish groups from Lviv arrived there [forest underground bunker] accompanied by a Jew who had a "good look" (Arian appearance).

[Columns 181-182]

Resistance groups were established in the ghettoes and camps in Toporiv, Zloczow, Kozaki, and Sasiv with the help of the organization of Brody warriors.

The Jewish warriors bombed the turpentine factory near the village of Sokolovka. Acts of sabotage took place in German military and industrial installations. According to Katzmann's Report, a search operation, was held in the forest on May 15, 1943. Gendarme brigades, Ukrainian police units, and six Wehrmach battalions participated in that operation. Thirty-three Jewish warriors (named "members of the gang" by the report) were killed … (page 450).

… Attempts to organize partisan groups in the area of Stryj and Zloczow, were only slightly successful. However, some of the rebellious Jewish were renowned. They were feared throughout the entire region due to their daring operations and courageous resistance … (page 452).

[Column 183]

The Loss of the City

by Shlomo Meir

Translations by Gloria Berkenstat Freund **and** Moshe Kutten

Note: this article was taken from the translation appearing
at https://www.jewishgen.org/Yizkor/Zolochiv/Zolochiv.html (translation of the publication *Der Untergang fun Zloczów*, except the introduction which only appeared in this Yizkor book.

Zloczow, located between Lviv and Ternopil, was one of the oldest Jewish settlements in Galitsia, Advanced social and cultural lives developed there over time. Jewish brew schools, libraries, drama clubs, and the rest of the public institutions contributed significantly to the cultural level of the Jewish population. The poets, Moshe Leib Halpern, Shmuel Yaakov Imber, Israel Ashendorf, Nakhum Bomze, Hirsch Fenster Arye Shrentzel, and others took their first steps in Zloczow.

Fourteen thousand Jews perished in Zloczow during the years of the Nazi regime. None of them was given a Jewish burial. In this article, I highlighted the important issues, provided some dates and statistics, and mentioned episodes. The latter are symptomatic, and reflect the lives, suffering, and scarifying of the fourteen thousand martyrs.

I

This Is How It Began

On the 15th of September 1939, the Jewish population of the city of Zloczow experienced a cruel day. The defeat of the Polish Army was unavoidable; with each hour, the Germans came closer to the city. Panic arose among the Jews. The Jewish young began to head for the eastern border utilizing every road, believing that there they would find a safe place where they would not be threatened by Hilterism. While the fear of the Germans and the trust of Russia were great, the number of refugees was greater. However, it was shown that with luck they had only suffered from fear. According to a special agreement, Russia occupied the eastern areas of Poland. The Jewish population breathed freely. The Soviet government saved it from Hitlerism. Although the Soviet regime brought by Russia did not please everyone, everyone related to the new regime with respect and it was regarded by all of the Jews as a redeemer, a protector from Hitlerism. The situation lasted for a scant two years. The war broke out between Germany and Russia. The Jewish population again found itself in danger. However, this time they were much calmer than they had been in 1939 because, if earlier they had thought little of the military power of Poland, for Jews the Soviet Army was a big deal and few doubted its power and its readiness to fight. Sadly, however, it was obvious immediately on the first day that "something" was not working. The Soviet civilian population secretly evacuated from the city, but the local population was not told anything. The Soviet representatives kept secret the situation in which they found themselves until the last moment and demanded that the population remain calm, not escape and not spread a feeling of panic. It was no secret anymore for anyone and also not for the Soviets that as soon as the Germans occupied the city the Jews would be in danger because the other nationalities were waiting impatiently for liberation from the Bolsheviks. No one found it necessary to evacuate or at least warn the local Jews. When a group of activists decided to leave the city on the 25th of June, they returned from outside Tarnapol. The assurance with which the Soviet government organs behaved led the population to believe that this was an exceptional strategy; it would not take long and the Germans would be driven out. Therefore, it was decided to remain in the city and wait out the critical days. There was bitter retribution for this mistake. On the 30th of June, the last Soviet military divisions left the city. The German air force bombed the city for the entire night. All of Lemberger Street stood in flames. The Germans were not concerned with any morality. Every house, regardless of whether it had a military connection or not, was besieged with bombs. There were no longer any hostile soldiers in the city and the bombing still did not cease. Approximately 40 Jews perished during the bombardment.

[Column 184]

Dr. Julek, a physician in the Forced Labor Camp in Latzki near Zloczow

The first German motorcycles entered Zloczow on the first of July at four o'clock in the morning. An automobile of wounded members of the Red Army stood at the marketplace. The automobile was damaged. The Germans poured benzene over it and burned it along with the wounded. This was the first terrible act with which they introduced themselves to the Zloczow population.

[Columns 185-186]

The "heroes," one like the other, young members of the *S.S.*, started to wildly go through the Jewish houses; they raped Jewish girls, murdered pregnant women, and robbed and plundered Jewish possessions.

The first victim who fell was the city [fool], known by the name "Jopak." He fell as a result of the first German bullet, not understanding that one could be killed for no reason and that it was necessary to hide.

A woman holding her child in her arms stood behind a closed door on Lemberger Street. The child cried. A German was passing by and noticed this; he murdered the mother and child with two shots. A neighbor, a pregnant woman, started to scream; she did not understand the gravity of the situation and tried to speak to his conscience. His answer was wild laughter and a shot in her stomach.

Many Jews paid with their lives for their naivety on the same day. No one could yet conceive of what the Germans were capable of. Someone looked out through a window, another stood at the door, and a third dared to go for water. Immediately, on the first day, the local Ukrainians appeared as loyal collaborators of the "victor." Rich and poor, the members of the intelligentsia, the worker and the peasant, all, without distinction, presented themselves for service with the Germans. They had long awaited such an auspicious opportunity; this was the fulfillment of their dreams. Their murderous and criminal instincts finally could be realized.

Under the protection of the Germans, they behaved freer in relation to the Jews. The peasants from the surrounding villages, incited by the intelligentsia, armed with weapons, and clubs and provided with sticks, went through the Jewish houses. They stole whatever there was: Jewelry, clothing, shoes, food – everything that had little value. The provincials, who did not know exactly where the Jews lived, were helped by the local Ukrainian neighbors. They knew about everything and in the majority of cases, they played the role of leader. The more sensible and refined tried to maintain "neutrality" where they lived. Therefore, the rampaging in the quarter was boundless. The Jews did not even try to defend their possessions; they were ready to give everything away in order to save their lives. The murderers went in groups. One group left and another one arrived. What people had saved from generations–long work was abandoned in one moment.

On the second day, that is Wednesday, the 2nd of July, the leaders of the nationalist–leaning Ukrainian intelligentsia gathered in the Ukrainian casino hall. A committee of 30 men was organized there to which belonged: the businessmen Antoniak, Mudry, Alyszkewicz, Dzwonnik; the lawyers Wanio, Jojko; the doctor Gilewicz; the teachers Symczyszyn, Sobolewa, the wife and daughter of the lawyer Wanio, the officials Lewicki, Krawczuk, the priest Mykietyn, Hupalowski, Pawlyszyn and so on.

The committee established as one of its first tasks to organize and carry out an anti–Jewish pogrom. This was supposed to be a political action by the Ukrainian nationalists and therefore had to take on a mass character both in perception and in results. Everything had to be "legally" justified. This legal justification, which made the pogrom accepted among the wide Ukrainian masses, quickly was found.

The Ukrainian nationalists immediately on the first day of the war organized sabotage against the Russian regime bureaus. The Russians answered with mass arrests; all of the arrestees were shot during the retreat. The execution was carried out at the city jail, which at that time was located in the castle and they also were buried there.

The Ukrainian committee issued a proclamation in which they made the Zlochzow Jews responsible for the death of their nationalists. This blood libel spread quickly and [caused the right conditions] for a pogrom. In the proclamation, the committee called upon all of the people to take revenge against the Jews for the spilled "innocent" blood. In addition to the proclamation, meetings were called at which representatives of the committee appeared with speeches. The daughter of the lawyer Wanio particularly distinguished herself on that day.

The Germans received the initiative by the Ukrainians with satisfaction, accepted their plan, and promised far–reaching aid in this area. The pogrom was set for the 3rd of July 1941.

II

The Pogrom

It was Thursday. Zloczow Jews, who endured the hardships of the first two days, consoled themselves with the hope that everything would be quiet and return to normal. They sat in the houses and waited for the agitated mood to be stilled. No one, or more likely, only a few knew what the enemies had in store.

On that day, at seven o'clock in the morning, the Ukrainian representatives adorned with yellow–blue bands on their arms, armed from their heads to their feet, began to go through Jewish houses. Some nicely and some severely lured the people out into the streets. The pretext was to go to work. Given that everyone was ready to work, many went out willingly. Jews had to bring their work tools with them from home. This calmed the people to a certain degree and they were filled with trust. However, the trust disappeared immediately after leaving the house. The wild horde lay in wait on the streets. They immediately took the Jews into their jurisdiction and drove them to the castle that was designated by the regime as the collection point. The demonstration that was encouraged by the committee found favorable soil. They came from the surrounding areas en masse.

It should be understood that everyone had a sack with him because the main purpose for everyone taking part was thievery. The young and the old took part in the "sacred" work.

[Column 187]

A mother identifies her child murdered by the Nazis in 1942

Ten–year old gentile boys chased old Jews and murderously beat them; adult Christians tortured innocent children and, in addition, laughed at them victoriously. The murderers had great satisfaction when an old, sick Jew or a pregnant woman fell into their hands. Whoever was caught at prayer was not permitted to put away his *talit* and *tefilin* [prayer shawl and phylacteries], but was driven in them through the streets. Compassion was an unfamiliar thing to the murderers. They used whatever they had for hitting [people]: with sticks, with iron bars and spades… Every innocent work instrument was a tool of murder in their hands. A large number of those Jews who were caught were not brought to the castle, which was the collection point, but simply were murdered on the way. They perished with the first blow if they were sick or weak; strong people had to endure great suffering. Their bodies were tortured systematically and they were condemned to a slow death.

It was said about the death of Hersh Tabak: Hersh Tabak was one of the healthy young people. He was tall, broadly built, and stood out because of his extraordinary physical power. The murderers dragged him away to the [non–Jewish] cemetery and there a certain chimney sweep, Serba, beat him all over his body and over the head with a monkey wrench until, bloodied, he fell down to the ground. He was tormented and stamped on with feet until he breathed out his soul. (Incidentally, it is worth mentioning that this murderer lives to this day and [enjoys] his freedom.) The Soviet government organs, to whom they turned after the liberation to punish him, did not consider it important and necessary.

Even crueler was the death of Dovid Lvov. When the murderers began to torture him, he did not try to ask for any mercy, but boldly shouted, *Shema Yisroel* ["Hear O Israel" – the central prayer of Judaism]. A German *S.S.* man, not able to bear his shouting, fired at him. Dovid Lvov, to everyone's astonishment, did not fall off his feet and *Shema Yisroel* again tore from his heart. The *S.S.* man delivered a second and third shot and these had no greater an effect than the first one. The soul did not want to leave the healthy body and Dovid L did not give up his belief and with his last strength called out *Shema Yisroel*. The *S.S.* man became confused. The patriarchal figure and the extraordinary power of the Jew frightened him and he withdrew. At that moment, a local Ukrainian pounced and split Dovid Lvov's head in two with a spade. The *Shema Yisroel* remained hanging in the air. One of the most pious Zloczow Jews was dead.

[Column 188]

It also is difficult to forget the terrible death of Kosower religious judge, Elenberg. He was praying, when he was pulled from the house, tied by his beard to a motorcycle and dragged through the streets until his body became a formless, bloody mass of flesh.

The cries of the tormented and murdered Jews filled the air. All who were still in their homes understood from the voices what was happening outside. It became clear to everyone who was not fooled into leaving the house that they needed somewhere to hide. However, this was difficult because the murderers searched everywhere up to 10 times.

Death threatened everywhere. A number of Jews had Christian friends and tried to hide with them. However, very few succeeded. The majority had to pay for their false illusions with their lives. Salek Parnes can serve as an example.

Salek Parnes had a Christian wife. It was shortly after the wedding. They loved each other. Despite all of these circumstances, right on the first day after the Germans entered their residence, she pointed to her husband, about whom it was difficult to recognize his racial background, and declared that he was a Jew. The Germans took him. He succeeded in escaping from them, but later he fell victim.

The fate of young Friedlander is also widely known. The Jewish workers from the Zloczow canned goods factory tore through a thousand dangers on that day in order to enter the factory. Since the factory was built and belonged to the Jew Oskar Robinson who had acquired a good reputation for his relationship with the workers without regard to background, the Jews believed that the Christian workers in the factory would help them during this difficult time. However, they were bitterly disappointed. They were allowed into the factory, welcomed with friendship and when the doors were closed behind them, the knives came out. [The daughter of] Friedlander, a young girl of 14, who was hiding with her father, was raped by the murderers and then bestially murdered; the father had to watch this with his own eyes. A number of Jewish workers successfully escaped from their "friends" and saved their lives. Among the above–mentioned murderers, those who particularly stood out are Malyk, Stryk, Szluz, Szczerban, and so on, who the entire time played the role of friends of the Jews and who even succeeded in becoming troublemakers for the Soviets.

It is characteristic that during the pogrom days all those who had presented themselves as friends of Jews were our greatest persecutors and bitterest enemies. It is enough to remember the sadly famous S. Wanio. She would spend time with Jews, was the choreographic leader at the Jewish Dramatic Club, "Ansky," and during the Hitler days, this S. Wanio was one of our greatest enemies. She gave speeches at meetings, traveled through villages, organized pogroms, and personally took part in them.

[Columns 189-190]

She beat and murdered dozens of Jews with her own hands. The well–known merchant, Antiniak, distinguished himself no less. He, who had traded with Jews for all the years, was friends with them and placed himself at the head of all anti–Jewish *aktsias* [actions, often deportations].

It turned out that all of our friends had forgotten us; in the best cases, they acted passively or acted as if they did not remember us.

However, during the first days, it was not easy for the Jews to free themselves of their inborn optimism and of their trust in the justice of their fellow men with different beliefs. The case of Dr. Eisen is typical. When the murderers brought him to the castle, he met a Ukrainian acquaintance by chance, who wanted to save him. He [the Ukrainian] told him [Dr. Eisen] to go home and bring a rope.

Dr. Eisen, in his naivety, did not understand the true intention of the Ukrainian and returned quickly with the rope.

There was a similar case with the fish merchant, Peysye Bloch, and several other Zloczow Jews. They paid with their lives for their naivety and trust.

It was no accident that immediately on the first day, the majority of Orthodox Jewry was annihilated. Their faith was so great and so strong that they did not even try to hide. They could not understand what the enemy was capable of. The older ones among them remembered the pogroms and various persecutions that they had lived through and, therefore, believed in modesty and in God's care.

Chana Opper, a …[1] Rabbi Feywl Rohatiner, a woman in her 60s, refused all opportunities proposed by her neighbor to hide. During the fervor of the pogrom, she sat alone in her house and recited Psalms. A band of murderers under the leadership of the house owner barged into the residence and forced her out to the collection point. She recited Psalms on the way there. Because of her age, the barbarians treated her particularly murderously.

After the liberation, that is three years later, when a Soviet Historical Commission opened the mass graves at the castle, among the first found was her body. It was apparent with what barbarism she was murdered. Only the ring that she wore on her finger allowed her to be identified.

Those who were saved from the castle told about a horrible and simultaneously wonderful scene that played out before their eyes: when the group, among whom were the religious judge B. Szapiro and his brothers, the ritual slaughterers and their families, the pious Jew Shlomo Tenenbaum (known as Maite's son Shlomo), was brought to the execution spot, his son Sholem, Dovid Lvov's son and other pious Jews began to sing aloud with ecstasy. Their ecstasy grew and their prayers were transformed into song. The murderers began to shoot into the wonderful group. One by one, they fell from the bullets; those who still were on their feet continued singing with their last strength. But, from minute to minute, it became quieter and weaker and when the last of them fell, a martyr, the singing ceased.

At the same time, the murderers did not forget that the defilement of houses of prayer also belonged to a pogrom. A group of Ukrainians under the leadership of the *S.S.* left in the direction of the houses of prayer. They shattered the doors, looted whatever had a practical value, and destroyed everything else. They gathered all of the sacred books and set them on fire.

They are few familiar with the heroic death of Chaim–Yoel Horn. Chaim–Yoel Horn was a simple man–of–the–people. He was the *shamash* [caretaker and assistant to the rabbi] of the large synagogue for all of his years and, like the majority of the *shamashim* a very poor man. He had a large family; however, his home was the synagogue. He was dedicated to it from very early until late at night. During the day of the pogrom, he could in no way decide to stay at home. He wanted to be where he usually was – in the synagogue. Not listening to the pleas from his wife and children, the old, broken Chaim–Yoel hurried through the city during the most intense time of the pogrom and reached the synagogue where the hangmen rampaged. It is difficult to understand what happened then. Chaim–Yoel saved a *sefer–Torah* [Torah scroll] from the flames and started to run away with it. The murderers watched with mockery and laughter and when he reached the small bridge that crossed the river, they shot after him. The bullets reached him and Chaim–Yoel fell into the water with the scroll. The water ejected the body of Chaim–Yoel Horn several days later. His hands held fast to the rescued *Sefer–Torah*.

At the same time, cruel scenes were played out at the castle. The gathered Jews were forced to dig up the pits where the Soviets had buried the Ukrainian nationalists. The corpses had to be removed by command and were photographed.

The pictures were printed later in all the newspapers with the headline: "The Victims of Jewish Terror."

It was a hot summer day. The sun burned without mercy. The dug-up dead smelled terrible. People vomited and fainted from the smell. The Germans and Ukrainians, holding handkerchiefs to their noses, did not trust themselves to go closer. Few could endure the work. The people fell like flies. The Ukrainian corpses that were removed from the pit were carried out of the area of the castle. Finding an opportunity, a small number of those gathered at the castle succeeded in sneaking out and running away. Few of those who ran away survived because the murderers lay in wait everywhere. When the pit was empty of the Ukrainian dead, an order came to fill it with Jews. In the rush, people were thrown in half alive. When the pit was full, the murderers threw in a few grenades and shot into it with dum–dum bullets.

The Jews had to count their own victims. One of the Germans, who it appeared was still new to the work and still had a spark of humanity in him, said to one of the Jews that they should count more (that is, they should be deceptive), it would be better. However, the Jews did not trust him and saw a new trick in this.

At three o'clock a German general arrived at the execution spot to learn about the number of victims; he considered the number sufficient and ordered that the slaughter end by four o'clock.

Those carrying out the pogrom still had authority for not quite another hour. They tried to make use of the time as much as they could. The general stood with a watch in his hand and counted the minutes. When four o'clock arrived, he ended the slaughter. At this time, he told the surviving Jews to run home "*schnell*" [fast]. The murderers shot after [the Jews]. They ran over each other in fear. There was a tumult. The majority were exhausted and could not run. Therefore, they paid with their lives. Only a small number were successful in saving themselves from this hell on this day.

[Columns 191-192]

It rained in the evening. Many who had fainted, but whom the murderers believed had died, were in the mass graves. The rain revived them and they [regained consciousness]. They waited until darkness fell and then with a great effort they came out from under the corpses with which they were covered. So as not to be noticed by anyone, they entered the river that flows not far from the castle and entered the city in the water.

The victims in the graves had hugged each other and pressed firmly against each other at the moment of their being shot.

One of those remaining alive could not leave the pit because a corpse held him so firmly by the foot that he could not free himself from the dead one's hand. Not wanting to be buried alive, he was forced to cut off the hand and he entered the city with the hand that was pulled after him all the way.

Those who returned from the castle had changed so much in just one day that it was hard to recognize them. They could not eat anything for a long time. What they had lived through on that day took away their sleep for a long time. Of them still alive today - A. Rosen, K. Sznap, and Wilner. – I spoke to the last one. It was difficult for him to describe in words what he had endured and it was even harder for me to write it down.

Three thousand five hundred Jews were murdered during the days of the pogrom. These were the most precious of Zloczow Jewry. The majority of them found their rest at the castle. The remaining lie spread over the entire city: at the marketplace, on the old ramparts, on Lemberger Street, at the sports place, in the courtyards of the Linsk [Hasidim], of Lipa–Mer, and many other places.

Everywhere that Jews lived, they were murdered and where they were murdered, they were buried.

The Germans declared on the second day after the pogrom that nothing would happen to whoever reported making order after the pogrom. Despite the fact that they had little trust in their promises, they went out so as to carry the few corpses that lay in the streets and to cover them with a little bit of dirt. (Understand that there could be no talk of burial according to Jewish law.)

The pogrom of the 3rd of July was the beginning of the downfall of Zloczow Jewry. Each of the 3,500 murdered Jews has his own story. One story is more terrible than the other and all of them together is an accusation against the "peaceful" Ukrainian citizens and their German teachers with whom we lived together for many generations.

III

Judenrat and the Contributions

A deathly pallor reigned over the city on the first day after the pogrom. They did not dare go out into the streets; they had fear of the bright sunshine. They sat in their houses and quietly mourned the victims of the pogrom. There was not one family in the city that had not been touched by the pogrom. Every Jew was a mourner. The grief was great and to this grief was added the fear of one's own fate. They did not know what the morning would bring and did not know with what it would end. Hooligans, who did whatever they felt like doing, still were threatening in the streets from time to time. There was fear of crossing the threshold to bring in water. There was no talk of providing food. This situation lasted for two weeks. The German administration that took over the city was not satisfied with the condition of the business. It had the task to exploit, as far as possible, the economic estates of the city and this could be done only with the help of the local population, of which the majority were Jews. The robbing of Jewish possessions by the Ukrainians also was against their interest. They had to reserve this for themselves so as to take it over legally at the appropriate moment. Therefore, placards in two languages were hung over the entire city that warned the population [against] further anti–Jewish pogroms and [against] robberies. These placards calmed the mood to a certain degree. They began to leave their houses, to take care of their daily bread.

The necessity to organize emerged, to create an administrative body that could represent and act in the name of the surviving Jews. Dr. Meiblum, the longtime vice mayor and chairman of the general Zionist organization, took upon himself this task. The [members] of the created committee, in addition to him, were Dr. Szotz and Dr. Zlatkes. Their first task was supposed to be to establish the exact number of the pogrom victims. Some optimists believed that the calamities had ended and that these events had to be preserved in writing so that people would not forget that a pogrom took place in the 20th century.

Dr. Zlatkes and Dr. Szotz went from house to house and everywhere recorded the exact number of victims. The work lasted for four weeks. At that time, the German city authorities called on all of the Jews to assemble at the market. The Jews, for whom the memory of the pogrom still was fresh, did not appear for the assembly. Only 25 Jews dared to do this. The purpose of the assembly was to inform the Jews how they were to behave, the symbols they had to wear, and so on. The Germans demanded that a *Judenrat* [Jewish council created by and beholden to the Germans] be created with which they could maintain contact. The already existing committee reported and promised to maintain contact with the Germans and to carry out all of their orders. The *Judenrat*, which was given a series of tasks, such as keeping order among the Jews, providing workers for the German firms, and so on, had to increase the number of its members. Many Jews, who were proposed for this post, refused.

Despite the fact that the tasks that the committee had to fulfill were still enveloped in a fog, some people foreswore its traitorous role. Among those who categorically refused and warned everyone else of the game into which they were being drawn was Dr. Tajchman.

In time the *Judenrat* was completed. Dr. M. Gruber, Dr. Prager, Dr. M. Rubin, Dr. Diwer, Dr. Hreczanik, Dr. Gerber, M. Cukerkandl, Jakier, O. Szmirer and Bernsztein joined. Dr. Glanz and L. Cwerling were unofficial members.

As soon as the members of the *Judenrat* were freed of work obligations, other children of influence sneaked in, often as assistants in this institution. It should be understood that only the intelligentsia benefitted from this "luck." "Jewish Social Aid" was organized under the direction of Dr. G. Kac, Dr. Kitaj, and Dr. Szwager. Their task was to organize aid for the needy and maintain contact with the camp Jews and their families. They even dreamed about making contact with the JOINT [Joint Distribution Committee], but understand that this was a clear case of Don Quixote... Dr. Kahane, Wajsztok, and Tauber also joined as assistants at the *Judenrat*. They were representatives of M. Cukerkandl and their work consisted of providing the Germans with the goods they wanted.

A Jewish militia was organized at the same time under the leadership of D. Landesberg. His representative was Steinwurcl. The task of the militia was to keep order among the Jews. It should be understood that one had to have patronage to become a member of the militia. However, not everyone benefitted from it. Many foresaw the shameful role that the militia would play and therefore did not want to be found in its ranks. That was said about a certain Gershon Spodek, who was a militia member during the first days but understood the role he would have to play and, therefore, immediately resigned from it. The same thing was done by L. Walfisz. The situation began to be relatively normal. The mood turned optimistic. Newspapers published in the large ghetto cities, like Warsaw, Lodz and Bialystok, reached Zloczow.

[Columns 193-194]

A certain F. Prager, who for the entire time had been a member of the militia in the Warsaw ghetto, returned from German captivity. It appeared that the ghettos everywhere were [part of a] system and one grew accustomed to them. The theater was created; newspapers were published; communal life was developed. The belief began that the German was not terrible and if things continued this way, they would survive somehow. The entire bitterness of the Jews was turned against the Ukrainians who persecuted the Jews in their daily life with their poisonous hate and with all means. It was enough that a Jew bought something from a peasant and it was noticed by a Ukrainian and a crowd would gather that divided the purchase (it was a lucky thing if the buyer succeeded in escaping with his life). Because of financial motives, the Ukrainians were interested in grabbing and handing over the Jewish "criminal" who succeeded in buying something from a peasant because everything [that had been bought] was given to them. This were part of the normal troubles that was called *gezunte tsores* [healthy troubles].

It did not take long for the Germans to make a new word popular in the Jewish neighborhoods: contributions [actually, ransoms or mandatory payments]. An order came "from above" that Jews must pay contributions. The *Judenrat* became responsible for providing the contributions. The amount of the contribution was kept secret from the mass of the people. It was said that it was a giant sum, about half a million *zlotys*. The *Judenrat* was the appraiser and the dunner. [It determined how much each Jew would pay and it collected that amount.] It [the *Judenrat*] took whatever it could. No amount was enough. The *Judenrat* was a tool of the Germans in the collection of contributions.

The German administration in the city grew larger from day to day. Every day new officials arrived. The *Judenrat* had to provide everyone with a place to live, services, and so on. It was taken from the Jews and given to the Germans. J. Tauber and Wajnsztok, who had large businesses before the war, knew exactly what each Jew had and, therefore, they were given this refined work. The nobles[2] were satisfied with their work, the Jews less so. Jewish furniture, bedding, and clothing migrated to the Germans and the Jews had to provide them for them. The wives of the rulers had other caprices every day and every caprice had to be accommodated.

At the beginning of November 1941, the first labor camp was organized 12 kilometers from Zloczow in Lackie Wielke. The administrator was the known murderer, *Hauptsturmfuhrer* [Nazi party rank equivalent to captain] Warzok. On the same morning, all of the streets were closed and manned by *S.S.* members. People were grabbed; they were packed into vehicles and they were taken to Lackie Wielke. No one knew what this meant; the methods with which they "recruited" the people did not indicate anything good. On the same day, 200 people were grabbed. Among those caught were found those who were employed in other German firms and those who stood in the service of the *Judenrat*. The *Judenrat* intervened for them. They made contact with the murderer Warzok and an exchange of a number of those "caught" was proposed to him. The negotiations were carried out by Lonek Cwerling. He succeeded in winning the trust of the Germans, who nominated him as the regular intermediary between him and the Jews. They asked Warzok that no more "recruiting" take place, but that he should communicate with the *Judenrat* and that it would provide as many people as would be needed. Warzok agreed to this proposal. In time, Lonek Cwerling, with his doggish nature, made himself beloved with Warzok, was an intimate of his, and even had a little influence over him. He could ransom whomever he wanted from the Lackie camp for a nice diamond or for another object. At first, he only used his influence "for the good of the people," but in time he understood that he could procure money through this. He became a dealer of people. He was responsible for who would be in the camp and who would be freed from it. He became the Jewish Warzok. Whoever could, tried to be on good terms with him; everyone else tried to encounter him less and less. Whoever did not please him was sent to Lackie immediately and Lackie sounded like a death sentence for every Jew.

The role he played during the war years was not a surprise for those who knew Lonek Cwerling from before the war. He belonged to the intelligentsia that had great aspirations and they had not succeeded in attaining the communal and material position of which they dreamed. A bankrupt and a defrauder, a *Moszke Polak* [a Jew who was obsequious to the Poles], and a card player. It was not difficult for people with such baggage to tumble down to the position of traitor to their people. Alas, it must be understood that among the traitors there also were people who were contented with their good reputation; however, they let themselves be drawn into the devilish plan and became assistants of the Germans. However, this was a small percentage. The majority of the traitors had assimilated earlier or were simply the type that society should have spit out long ago.

The second Jew, who sadly made himself well–known in the downfall of Zloczow Jewry, was Dr. Glanc. He was an advisor to the labor office. Who and where one had to work was dependent on him. It was in his power to free someone from work. However, as this insignificant person's greediness for money conquered every other human feeling, the old people and the sick had to go to work and the young and healthy would ransom themselves from the obligation to work. He was autocratic in the matter and no one would dare to offer him advice. He was the second individual after Cwerling.

In addition to these two, still, others distinguished themselves: Oyzer Szmirer, Dr. M. Gruber, Sztajnwurzl, D. Landesburg, and so on. Their names are covered in shame and will always be remembered for being in the ranks with the Germans and other murderers of Jews.

Mass hunger came to Zloczow Jewry immediately during the first months of 1942. I write "mass hunger" because just hunger was not unusual for the poor of Zloczow. The Jews had to endure a great deal to be able to provide themselves with a little food during the first months of Hitler's rule. Many families did not have anything with which to survive the day, but they still benefited from the compassion of the richer Jews. However, in time the supplies from the rich Jews grew smaller and they began to fear for their own fate. It was difficult to convince them to open their wallets. The Germans, who were occupied with breaking the morale of the Jews to make it easier to annihilate them physically later, increased their numbers. Money was raised to such a level, as people saw it as the only way to save themselves. The Germans freed people from the camps for money; they freed people from work for money; they gave people their lives for money; they provided the means to live for money. Money was a tool with which they murdered the Jewish conscience. They forgot all of the ethical and religious laws. Colossal antagonism arose between the hungry and the sated. One hid from the other. They ate behind closed doors so no one would see. However, in the atmosphere of self–centeredness, some people organized help for the hungry. To these belonged S. Safran, Ch. Zimand, B. Lifszic and others. However, their number was so small that in the created situation their help could only have a minimal effect.

The German defeat outside Moscow gave the Jews courage and hope. However, it did not have any effect on hunger. The self–centeredness increased. They calculated how long the road back from Moscow would take and if they would be able to survive during that time. They began to keep things for themselves and not give anything to another person. People became swollen from hunger. They went out and searched the pile of garbage. They ate whatever they could find. It was not rare to kill dogs and cats in order to avoid deadly hunger.

At that time, new camps arose in the Zloczow area. Kozaki, Yaktoruv, Plew, Zarvanitsa, Olesko, Sasov. They demanded workers. The *Judenrat* again received the order and again it began to trade in people.

[Columns 195-196]

The Ruins of the Synagogue "Yad Kharutzim" During the Holocaust

However, this time, the *Herrn* [Misters] Cwerling and Glanz had experience in their work and their appetites were so great, for what they did not want to say. They held to the principle: "If one eats pork let it pour out over the snout" and it ran over their snouts... The rich people brought them the most expensive gifts and poor people took their place in the camps. As the conditions in the new camps were no better than in Lackie, the majority of people did not last long there. Exhausted and hungry, they were not capable of work and the Germans did not need anyone that was incapable of work... Selections took place every day and hundreds of people were shot every day. Warzok was commandant of all of the camps in the Zloczow area and wherever he reigned, death reigned there.

The Jews had not yet washed their hands of the first contribution and they received a second one, larger than the first. The same procedure took place as with the first contribution. The *Judenrat* appraised, dunned, and threatened. The Jews sold their last [possessions] and paid. Everyone believed that obeying the Germans would quiet him. However, it became apparent that these were false hopes. The German worked according to a systematic plan and, alas, his purpose did not remain a secret. After the success of breaking the morale of Zloczow Jewry, he began the physical annihilation. The first step was the *aktsias* [actions, usually deportations].

IV

Aktsias – The Death of Sh. J. Imber

Rumors arrived that the Germans were organizing *aktsias* [actions, usually deportations]. No one knew exactly what they were. *Aktsia* is an innocent word and it can be understood to mean whatever one wishes. Optimists said that they were taking people to work in Russia – pessimists, that they were being taken to a death camp, where soap and other useful articles were being made from the people. They could not imagine the exact purpose of the *aktsias*, but it was clear to everyone that people were being taken away and that someone the Germans took away no longer returned. If the mass of people still had certain doubts about the matter, the *Judenrat* [Jewish council appointed by and beholden to the Germans] was well informed as to what kind of *aktsias* and to what they led. Such *aktsias* already had been carried out in surrounding cities and the Zloczow *Judenrat* knew very well about them. It also was clear that Zloczow would not be spared. However, some people convinced themselves that the Zloczow *Judenrat* was empowered to do a great deal and as a result [could] also block the edict. Moshe Cukerhandl was successful in befriending the heads of the Gestapo, bribing them, and delaying the *aktsia*. Understandably, this cost the Jews a great deal of money; however, this did not prevent the Germans from carrying out the aktsia a short time later.

On the 28th of August, the *Judenrat* received an order to present 2,700 souls. Panic arose among the population. They [the *Judenrat*] had to provide people from among them [the population] and give them into the hands of the hangmen. The *Judenrat*, which was ordered to carry out the *aktsia*, found itself in a repugnant situation. They had to decide: either work with the Gestapo at the *aktsia* or passively oppose it.

A small *shtetl* [town], Sasow, was located in the Zloczow area. When the Sasow *Judenrat* received an order to submit people, it warned the population and they escaped to the forest. When the Gestapo came, all of the houses were empty.

However, the Zloczow *Judenrat* lacked the courage to take such a step. They decided to cooperate at the *aktsia*. They convinced themselves that if the *Judenrat* took part, the *aktsia* would be carried out with compassion and they would have the opportunity to "fool" the Germans, that is, they would give away the inferior element of the city (the sick, the weak, the old) and save the young, the healthy and the intelligentsia. Time revealed how much of a false calculation this was. Those, who sincerely believed in the opportunity their action [would provide] did not understand their naivety, that is, if "A," one must also sooner or later say, "B." For the mass of people, the decision of the *Judenrat* was a knife in the back. They thought of it as treason and it was that.

On the 28th of August 1942, the Tarnopol Gestapo arrived in Zloczow. The Ukrainian militia from the entire area was mobilized. All of the streets where the Jews lived were closed and attacked. The *aktsia* began.

[Columns 197-198]

Discovery of a Mass Grave of Holocaust Victims

The Jews hid, some in an attic, some in a cellar and some in rooms. The murderers banged on closed doors everywhere. Since the murderers were no great heroes and since they were afraid to happen upon resistance on the part of the hidden, a representative of the *Judenrat* or of the Jewish militia had to accompany each group [of the murderers].

The Jews had to walk in front and open the Jewish houses and when this was of no help, they were given axes and they hacked open the doors. All of the *Judenrat* members took part in this shameful work. The only one who refused to [take part] was Dr. Majblum. The people were attacked without restraint during the *aktsia*. They tried to provide the designated quota as quickly as possible. (It should be said that one of those taking part in this *aktsia*, Dr. Gerber, still is alive and lives in Paris.) D. Landesberg, the commandant of the Jewish militia, promised Jewish children candy and thus induced them to go out to the street. B. Szapiro went to his woman friend, R. Rozenbaum; he knew that she had a small child. He did not leave until he found the child and he took it from the house. The chase for souls lasted two days. The victims were brought to the train station where they had to wait to kneel for the train wagons. They were not permitted to have any food or drink. During the wait for the train wagons, a number of those caught were freed due to their patronage. There also was no lack of cases of magnanimity, where people refused to be freed. Krancja Wajntraub was given the opportunity to leave the train wagon with the proviso that she must leave her child there. However, she decided to die with her child. There was a similar case of Etl Fodernacht, who did not want to leave her sick sister–in–law during the second *aktsia*.

Train wagons were provided on the third day. Two thousand seven hundred people were placed in the train wagons like cattle. So many people were pushed into each wagon, as many as could stand; there was no place to sit or to fall. There was no place for someone who fell ill. Those who died on the way had to stand hanging among the living. The transport went to Belzec near Rawa–Ruska. The newly installed crematoria waited at Belzec. Two thousand seven hundred hearts ceased to beat. Many tried to save themselves on the way by jumping out of the train. However, few of those who "jumped" were successful in saving their lives. A number of them fell under the wheels. Some were shot and some were given to the Germans by the peasants. It was said about Mekhl Trajber: he decided to take a chance with his wife and child. His wife jumped first; she fell down and did not move from the spot. He took his child on his back, tied it with a handkerchief and he jumped with the child. When night fell, he went to look for his wife. He found her in terrible condition, she did not recognize him; she had gone insane. With great effort, he succeeded in bringing her to the city. They all perished during the liquidation...[3] ...only ones who sprang from the train and survived until the liberation, were R. Szenker and her son.

The second *aktsia* took place eight weeks later, on the 2nd and 3rd of November 1942. This time the city had to provide 2,500 victims. The *Judenrat* provided them. Special emphasis was given to children during the second *aktsia*. The living children were packed into sacks and they were taken to the train in vehicles. The most precious Jew produced by Zloczow at that time, the poet Sh. Y. Imber,[4] perished during the second *aktsia*.

Sh. Y. Imber, the author of the book, *Asy Czystej Rasy* [*Aces of a Pure Race*], a publication of the journal *Oyg Oyf Oyg* [*Face to Face*], was born in Zloczow. In 1941 he was in Lemberg under the name Weiss and disappeared from there and settled in Gline, a small *shtetele* [town] where his mother–in–law's parents lived. He had to escape from there and he came to Zloczow. He hid with his brother–in–law, Dr. Hreczanik, in Zloczow. Dr. Hreczanik, who was the director of the Jewish hospital, arranged for him to work with him. In his free time, Sh. Y. Imber wrote a great deal and he strongly believed that he would survive the difficult times. He would read his new creations to personnel and to the sick and, in so doing, encourage them. However, he [his work] could not be confined to the hospital society. It reached the city, where the Jewish masses lived, where a word of consolation was needed. The second *aktsia* found Sh. Y. Imber in the city. It was too late for him to enter the hospital because all of the streets were besieged by the murderers. Sh. Y. Imber hid in a cellar with his friend whose guest he had just been. The cellar was discovered and Sh. Y. Imber emerged to share the fate of 2,500 Jews from Zloczow who were taken to Belzec on the 3rd of November 1942. After his death, his friends gathered all of his manuscripts, hoping to publish them at some time. However, alas, all of his friends perished and, along with them, the literary treasure of Sh. Y. Imber.

V

Ghetto

Immediately on the first day, when the Germans occupied the city, the Ukrainians turned to them with a request that the Jews be enclosed in a ghetto.

[Columns 199-200]

However, the Germans did not yet consider this as necessary. It was still too early to create a ghetto and they did not yet have any instructions for this. They limited themselves to creating special houses, in which only Jews were permitted to live. The Jews had to leave the houses in which the majority of residents were Christian. The Jews were not permitted to appear in recreation areas or in gardens. They were not supposed to cross the threshold from [areas] designated for Jews. All of this was too little for the Ukrainians. They besieged the regime organs with pleas to create a ghetto. They [the Germans] paid no attention to them [the Ukrainians] for as long as it was not an actual question. However, this did not last long and instructions arrived to create ghettos in all of Galicia. The Ukrainians were full of joy. However, the Jews still convinced themselves that they would get around the edict. They bribed one official after another and the Jews were left alone for a time.

On the 1ˢᵗ of December 1942, the ghetto was closed. All of the surviving Jews were driven from all of the surrounding *shtetlekh*, such as Olesk, Bialy–Kamen, Sokolawka and so on. About 9,000 Jews were taken. These Jews were quartered with up to eight to 10 souls in one room.

The area occupied by the ghetto was very small. The ghetto was fenced in with barbed wire and guarded by Ukrainian militiamen. There was the threat of death for crossing through the fence. However, there were many who risked their lives to obtain bread. The hunger, however, was greater than all of the orders. They risked their lives to obtain a bread or a few potatoes. It reached the point where they gave away their most expensive suit of clothes for a bread. The peasants knew to make use of the situation and to speculate on Jewish need. It was winter. There was no heating material in the ghetto. Hunger and cold was felt at every turn. In addition, the ghetto population had to endure great hardship from the members of the Gestapo and from their Ukrainian collaborators. Two members of the Gestapo, Zwillinger and Mury, particularly distinguished themselves. Their names already evoked feverish trembling from every Jew and from every Jewish child. They [the Germans] found their sadistic pleasure in the terrible torture of people and they particularly liked to beat naked women and children. As soon as they appeared in the ghetto street, the Jewish inhabitants hid in their residences and watched through their windows to see where they were going; everyone breathed with relief when they did not stop. Not everyone had the luck that Zwillinger and Mury would pass their house and not stop. My brother, Elye–Meir, said, "A Friday night is especially set in my memory; the *Shabbos* candles were burning on the table. News spread like a flash of light that Zwillinger was in the ghetto. This was enough for the *Shabbos* to be a sad one. We sat with fear in our hearts and waited for the joyful news that Zwillinger had left the ghetto. It was revealed that Zwillinger was visiting a certain woman, Gutfrajnd, who lay sick in the crisis stage of typhus with a temperature of 40°C 104-° F.]. Moans, screams reached us for an entire hour and then suddenly the voice stopped. We understood that the murderer had left the neighboring residence and I went to the sick woman. She lay naked on the ground; the window was open; the ground was wet from much water and the woman's small daughter stood crying and the blood ran from her. There were visible signs of beating on the body of the unlucky woman and her face seemed liked a bloody mask. When the woman was successfully revived, she said that Zwillinger carried out his beloved sadistic sport on her child and on her. He drove the sick woman out of bed, forced her to undress and to open the window; then she had to stand on a chair and the sadist poured ice–cold water over her for an hour and smacked her with a thick whip. He constantly warned her that if she stepped off the chair, he would inflict the same torture on her 11–year old daughter. The woman fainted after an hour and fell off the chair. However, this did not satisfy the sadist enough. When the mother lay on the ground, he carried out the same torture on the 11–year old child. When the mother came to and heard the crying of her child, she quickly stood up, took down the child and stood herself on the chair. When the woman fainted the second time, falling off the chair, Zwillinger finally left the room, convinced that the woman no longer was alive." (Told by E.M.)

Thus, the days and nights passed in eternal fear and in eternal trembling for their fate. Dozens of corpses were taken out of the ghetto each day. Among the corpses were the victims of German bestiality and victims of hunger. The corpses were the only ones who had the right to leave the ghetto. The boxes in which the wagon drivers took them were not searched because the Ukrainian militiamen were afraid of catching an illness. The wagon drivers used this fact that the boxes were not searched and smuggled potatoes and other produce into the ghetto in them [the boxes]. It was horrible. There was the threat of illness, but the people did not consider this. A typhus epidemic broke out in the ghetto.

VI

Typhus Epidemic

The typhus epidemic that broke out in the ghetto was not something new for the Jews. Only its scope was the greatest ever.

The first typhus epidemic broke out in the Lackie camp at the beginning of 1942. Three doctors worked in this camp: Dr. Julek, Dr. Holenderski, and Dr. Cigelman. They had an order from the camp managing committee not to permit the epidemic to spread. Warzog threatened that otherwise, he would set fire to the entire ghetto with all its inhabitants. However, the doctors were not given any means in addition to the order with which to be able to protect the camp from an epidemic. Hunger and dirt brought catastrophe. The typhus epidemic broke out. The epidemic immediately covered a wide area. The doctors were overtaken by panic. They trembled for the fate of the entire camp. Dr. Julek turned to the city hospital and to the *Judenrat* for help. He received an order to inform the camp managing committee about the epidemic. As the doctors Holenderski and Cigelman were already among the victims of the epidemic, it fell on Dr. Julek to go to the murderers with the notice. This was considered certain death. Dr. Holenderski asked Dr. Julek to hide and he, Dr. Holenderski, would take on the mission. He, who no longer had anyone, wanted to make the sacrifice for a man who still had a wife and a child. However, Dr. Julek did not agree with this. He said goodbye to his family and his acquaintances and went to the bandits to report about the epidemic. He had unexpected luck. Warzog, the murderer, had gone away and he was represented by someone who still possessed a spark of humanity.

[Columns 201-202]

He listened to the doctor in despair and promised him help in order to end the epidemic more quickly. (This person was certainly afraid that Warzog would hold him responsible for the epidemic and, therefore, he behaved well.) The sick were permitted to leave the camp. The sick were taken to the city where a large Jewish hospital was located. However, the hospital could not take in all of the sick, so two more houses were provided for this purpose. Dr. Julek, who alone remained at his post, worked day and night. His work was very difficult. The people in the camp saw the epidemic as the only way that would get them out of the accursed camp. Healthy people lay with the sick, infecting themselves and thus with great effort reached [their goal] of being taken out of the ghetto. This was a hazardous way because many died immediately after leaving the gates of the camp. However, this did not frighten anyone. It then was clear to Jews that they had nothing to lose. Thanks to the heroism of the medical personnel and, particularly of Dr. Julek, [and] thanks to the practical aid given by the *Judenrat* at that time the epidemic was fought successfully.

The typhus epidemic that broke out in the ghetto was worse. It spread at a rapid rate. The hospital immediately on the first day was overflowing with the sick. There was a lack of beds; [the sick] lay on the ground. There was a lack of space, so they lay in the corridors. The doctors Hreczanik, Julek, Reichard, Zwerdling, Szalit, Thun, Flaszner went from room to room and brought help to the needy. It was said about the doctors Julek and Reichard, that they would leave money for the patients to buy medicines. Berish Lifschutz, who worked in the apothecary outside the ghetto, helped in any way that he could to serve. He would take the most valuable and best medicines from the apothecary and give them to the ghetto. But this did not help much. It [the epidemic] led to the entire ghetto being transformed into one large hospital. There was no house skipped by the epidemic. The sick lay together with the healthy. It was difficult to protect a healthy child, who was located in one room with his sick mother, from coming in contact with her. The opposite was the same. One was a witness to the course of the illness; one was a witness to death and one could not help. The number of victims reached 500 souls. The doctors were powerless. However, they did not leave the ghetto and provided help until the epidemic reached them personally and they were forced to leave their posts. The Zloczow medical workers are inscribed in the history of our city in golden letters and we, the survivors, will always remember them with gratitude. They brought help to our sisters and brothers at the most tragic moments of their lives. They courageously fought the typhus epidemic, which was one of the great enemies of the ghetto Jews.

The only doctor who distinguished himself during that year and who survives to this day is Dr. Sh. Julek. He left for the forest and became active as a doctor in various partisan groups several weeks before the liquidation of the camps. Since the liberation, he has worked in the Deggendorf [displaced persons] camp as hospital director.

VII

Ghetto Liquidation

The typhus epidemic consumed a considerable number of victims and ceased. The ghetto residents looked at the future with anxiety. They felt as if in a cage and they waited for the inevitable to happen. Anyone who had the opportunity to live outside the ghetto was among the fortunate. The belief arose that was later confirmed that the workshops located outside the ghetto that were valued by the Germans would temporarily not suffer the fate of those in the ghetto. People began to ask to be taken into the workshops, even into the camps. The supervisors understood how to make use of the situation and, therefore, took advantage. The Jews in Gebeck's firm felt safest. Gebeck, himself a German, showed compassion to the Jews and would help them in any way he could. When the situation grew even more strained, Gebeck agreed that the workers from the Schweiger firm and their wives would be quartered with him in the camp and thus protected them from danger. Dovid Zimand, the Jewish supervisor of the camp, feeling that he would not be able to take any money from the above- mentioned workers, used his entire influence with the Germans to annul this [Gebeck's] decision. He succeeded. The people remained in the ghetto and later the majority of them paid with their lives. Lonek Cwerling, whose name requires no commentary, had the main word in all of the other workshops. Those who had money could count on his help. These events occurred a short time later. Shortly after the typhus epidemic, on the 2nd of April 1943, the last and most frightening chapter in the history of Zloczow Jewry occurred – the liquidation of the ghetto.

Engel, the well–known murderer and liquidator in the Galicia district, who was the representative of Katzman, the Lemberg and Tarnopol Gestapo [commander], came to the liquidation.

The ghetto was surrounded on the night of the 1st into the 2nd of April, as the Jews slept calmly, not sensing that danger was so near. Thus, the murderers made sure that no mouse could leave from there. All who were in the ghetto that night had to die. There were many from the camps and workshops who, by chance, were spending the night with their families in the ghetto and, therefore, they paid with their lives. In the morning the murderers accompanied by Jewish militia men went from house to house, drove the victims out of their beds and everyone, from young to old, was driven to the collection point which was located at the so called Green Market. The hunt was large. The victims were not given any time to dress. The mood of the masses on the 2nd of April was more apathetic, in contradiction to the panic that reigned during the pogrom and *aktsias* [deportations]. Few believed in the sweet promises of the Germans; they knew that this was the end – and yet they acted calmly…

The experiences of the last year so exhausted the people that they [no longer cared]. It was rare that someone started crying. Very few shouted. It was rare that someone asked for mercy. If they were afraid, it was not of death, but of the manner of death because no one could imagine what kind of death the Germans had thought up this time. The people stood for a long in the square and waited.

[Columns 203-204]

The murderers proposed to Dr. Majblum, the chairman of the *Judenrat*, the signing of a document that typhus was rampant at present in the ghetto, so the liquidation was necessary. Dr. Majblum refused to sign the document. Engel, the murderer, used every means: from sweet words and promises to threats and arguments with a riding crop. However, Dr. Majblum's decision was firm and he did not sign the document. Engel, seeing that [his plan] would not be carried out, murdered Dr. Majblum himself. (It must be remembered here that Dr. Majblum was the only [member] of the *Judenrat* who refused to take part in the *aktsias*.)

The marketplace was full of people. The Germans placed a basket into which the victims had to toss their money, watches, rings and other such items that they had with them. The Jewish militiamen saw to it that the order would be precisely carried out. The militiaman, Yosl Landau, was particularly brutal. He tore the rings from fingers with such brutality that blood began to flow from a number of victims. Trucks pulled up to the square. They began to load in the people. Up to 40 people on each truck. The trucks left in the direction of Yelekhovitse [Yelikhovichi]. The village of Yelekhovitse is four kilometers from Zloczow and is surrounded by forests. In the past it served as summer homes for the surrounding population.

The last way of the ghetto victims

During the month of April 1943 Yelekhovitse was the burial place for the Zloczow Jews. For two weeks the Russian prisoners dug three large pits in Yelekhovitse. The population saw them going to work every day with shovels. However, no one realized that they were going to dig graves for the remaining Jews. The trucks drove right up to the pits in Yelekhovitse. The victims were brought to the pits, forced to undress and enter the pits. They had to stand in rows, close behind each other and, when the pit was filled so that the victims no longer could move, machine guns began to shoot at their heads. No one observed whether or not everyone had been shot. Therefore, it is no surprise that many people were buried alive. The peasants from the village said that the earth over the graves moved for several days after the executions and blood spurted out.

[Columns 205-206]

The dirt surrounding the graves was dug around in order to lessen the pressure from within the ground. The trucks worked without a break. People were taken to Yelekhovitse; bloodied clothing returned from Yelekhovitse. People in the workshops could see those closest to them taken to their death and could not help in any way.

The only witnesses who were present at the terrible Yelekhovitse massacre and survived were the dentist, I. Halpern, and Laya Cwerling–Frenkel. Warzog made a "joke" of the former, who was the camp dentist in Sasow. He asked him to take part in each procedure that the victims went through and, at the last minute, gave him a gift of his life. Laya Cwerling–Frenkel courageously escaped naked from the pit. She ran right into the forest. They shot after her but with luck the bullets did not reach her. Peasants of her acquaintance clothed her and hid her until the liberation. Another girl also escaped – the Czortkower [from Chortkiv]. However, her fate is not known.

The liquidation lasted two days. However, the Germans did not succeed in exterminating all of the Jews during those two days. A large number hid in the attics and in the cellars. However, the murderers were persistent. They searched each house separately and not futilely. They found new hiding places every day. The people were gathered and when a large transport was gathered together, they were taken to Yelekhovitse. They would have to wait three or four days. They were not given even a drop of water during this time. The murderers did not make allowances for any disorder. Hilel Safran had the opportunity to watch his parents and his entire family struggling with hunger and waiting for death. His 10–year–old nephew, A. Szpicer, called to him in tears: "Uncle, a little water!" – and he could not help.

Among others murdered during the days of the liquidation was Hersh Guttman, the prose writer. He did not submit to the liquidation, but when he was caught hiding women and children, he was taken away to the Yelekhovitse execution spot with them.

When the number of Jews caught began to decrease, the Germans decided not to take them to Yelekhovitse anymore. They would take them to the market near a wall and shoot them naked in front of the still surviving Jews.

The last victims would be shot at the cemetery. They had to dig their own pits and lie down in them.

The ghetto was destroyed; 6,000 Jews were murdered; only a small handful of Jews remained alive in the workshops and in the camps.

VIII

The Last Struggle

All of the hopes and illusions of the survivors were liquidated along with the 6,000 Jews. No one wanted to rely any longer on the justice of the Germans. The idea was ripe for the creation of a partisan organization and to escape to the forest. Two groups were organized: one under the leadership of F. Nachimowicz and the second under the leadership of H. Safran. F. Nachimowicz was an artist. He labored in the workshops. After the liquidation, the clothing of the annihilated ghetto Jews was washed and ironed in the workshops. Valuable items and money were found in some of the clothing. Weapons were obtained with the found money. When everything was ready, Nachimowicz and a group of 30 people entered the forest. They dug a bunker in the forest and the group was supposed to focus on life in the bunker. The entire plan was naive and fantasy and the initiators lacked experience and knowledge of an organization. After eight days, a accidentlly knocked against the bunker. Sh. Frajman wanted to kill the peasant. Nachimowicz opposed this. He began a discussion with the peasant. The peasant, like all peasants, said that he was a friend of the Jews, praised the initiative of the group, and promised them help. Nachimowicz believed him and was very pleased that he had succeeded in meeting such a good Christian. They released the peasant, but in any case, they began to dig a new bunker. They did not have to wait long. The peasant went straight to the Gestapo. The site [of the bunker] was surrounded. There actually were few people in the bunker. The majority was busy building the new bunker. Shooting started. However, the small group was powerless against the overwhelming number of members of the Gestapo. Despite this, they defended themselves to the last man. The last was S. Frajman. The murderers had to pay dearly for their life. They succeeded in shooting him in the end and thus invaded the bunker. However, their surprise was great when they saw how few "partisans" they had fought against and that the leader, Nachimowicz, was not among the dead. Warzog, the *shturmfurer* [assault leader – a Nazi paramilitary rank], who himself went to the forest, left a note to Nachimowicz in the bunker in which he guaranteed his safety if he returned to the camp. Nachimowicz, who was a weak type, lost his courage and returned. Warzog kept his word and Nachimowicz was given his life. The group was liquidated. Nachimowicz was taken to Lemburg to the Janow camp during the liquidation of the Lackie camp. He fell into the hands of the Gestapo during an unsuccessful attempt to escape.

Warzog, who was the commandant of Janow at that time, took bitter revenge on him. He [Nachimowicz] was tied to a pole and wild dogs were set on him. The dogs tore him apart and ate him alive.

[Columns 207-208]

The second group, which was organized at the same time under the leadership of H. Safran had a wider and more serious membership. After the liquidation of the ghetto, engineer Hillel Safran had the idea to organize a partisan group. However, the situation was not yet ready enough and it was difficult to find people who would accept and be interested in the matter. Safran worked as an engineer at the German firm "Radebuele." His work allowed him to always move everywhere freely. After the liquidation of the ghetto, he decided to realize his idea at any price.

Bialystocki and Moskowicz, the Warsaw engineers who worked with him, approved of his plan and promised to help. Safran stayed in contact with individual people from all of the workshops and from the surrounding camps. The people's task consisted of gathering trustworthy and combative people around themselves. The work evolved. The idea was warmly accepted and had a particularly good appeal among the young. They undertook the acquisition of weapons and ammunition. F. Rozen, G. Spodek, and S. Grynberg received the task, sneaked into the armory, and removed ammunition from it. Old Soviet ammunition was located in the armory to which the Germans gave no significance and, therefore, had abandoned. However, it was difficult for a camp person to enter [the armory] because the armory was located far outside the city. However, the three young men did not consider any difficulties and risked their lives. Under the cover of the night, they sneaked into the armory and removed a considerable number of weapons, and grenades from it. They buried these objects in a forest not far from the armory. It remained for them to carry them into the city. H. Safran took this task upon himself because he could move around freely. Every day he went into the forest with his briefcase, dug up a few grenades and smuggled them into the city. Once he had the misfortune to meet Warzog, the *hauptsturmfuhrer* [Nazi paramilitary rank equivalent to captain]. He was accompanied by his beloved, the wife of a Czech engineer who had a good attitude toward Jews. Warzog immediately noticed that there were no papers in the briefcase, but something heavy. He stopped Safran and asked him what he was carrying in the bag. With luck, the woman noticed Safran's uncertain answer and decided to help him. She did not leave Warzog any time to discover the contents of the bag and quickly drew him away. Safran was saved. Izio Silber succeeded in making contact with a Christian who provided weapons for money. The weapons and ammunition were brought into the Radebeule building and hidden in clothing warehouses. Only a few people knew about this place. A committee of five people was created. Safran was at the head of the committee. A group of 50 men was organized that first had to take everything into the forest. New groups were supposed to be systematically organized. The fate of Nachimowicz's group became known in the middle [of the organizing]. This had a demoralizing effect and disrupted the plan. The people were controlled by despair and fearfulness. They gave up on this way out and they looked to save themselves with less risky means. However, Safran did not lose his courage and continued the work. He looked for contact with the Polish partisans. An officer with the Polish underground movement promised everything and betrayed Safran at the last minute. Safran made contact with the Ukrainian partisans. However, the people who were sent (two groups of six men) were attacked and murdered by them [the Ukrainian partisans].

It was decided that they would rely on their own strength to enter the forest. They chose the place and the date. Everything was prepared and exactly calculated. The auto that would take out the tools for the workers to the highway at 11 o'clock in the morning needed to take the weapons from the warehouse and take them to the forest that was near the highway. The driver was one of them [the group]. Everything was so well decided and planned that there could be no suspicion. A young man from Lemberg, who no one knew, worked in the block in which the warehouse was located. However, he did not have a good reputation and, therefore, the entire plan was kept secret from him. However, he had watched every step and it was clear that the man could cause harm. Safran was warned about him and, simultaneously, some people wanted to make this individual harmless. But Safran was against this. It was his opinion that the killing of a little German spy would arouse the watchfulness of the Germans and everything would be lost. This was a tragic error. This individual brought [information] about everyone to the Gestapo. The *S.S.* members unexpectedly organized a hunt for the committee members on the day on which the escape was supposed to take place. They succeeded in catching and arresting all five. The Gestapo demanded of the arrestees that they give a full list of their people. They refused. The murderers promised to give them their lives, but futilely, it did not help. They decided to die and not hand over anyone. They were locked in a cellar. Their comrades came to their aid. G. Horowicz succeeded in passing a tool to cut through the bars. However, Moshe Cukerkandl, the former *Judenrat* member mixed in and undid the entire plan. He always had great success in extracting Jews from the Gestapo and promised that he would save these people. He assured them that he already had negotiated with the murderers and they had promised to free them. It is difficult to ascertain whether Cukerkandl was the one fooled by the Gestapo or if he deceived the victims. However, on the other hand, the arrestees were not inclined to escape because they were afraid that their escape would move the murderers to take revenge against the remaining Jews. They did not want to be the cause of a new slaughter and, therefore, they convinced their comrades that they believed the German promise. The next day, the arrestees were taken to the marketplace to a wall that was soaked through with Jewish blood. Two engineers, Bialystocki and Moskowicz, broke loose and escaped. The *S.S.* members shot at them. Hilel Safran, the third one calmly went to the wall and stood next to it. The murderers ordered him to take off his clothes; as an answer, Safran threw himself on the *rottenfuhrer* [Nazi paramilitary rank, section leader] Sommer and threw him to the ground and, with a complete feeling of vengeful hate that had collected in him, began to strangle him. The struggle between the devouring murderer and the physically weak H. Safran took place in the blink of an eye and, when the latter succeeded in grabbing Sommer's revolver, a Ukrainian militia man shot H. Safran. H. Safran breathed out his soul. He left orphaned a wife and a small child.

The tragic death of the leader undid all the plans of the pugnacious Zloczow young. Only one way out remained: to save oneself with one's fists.

IX

The New Legend

A separate chapter in the history of the Zloczow Jews was the bunkers. The Jews saw in the bunkers the only possibility of saving themselves. However, the first bunkers were barely disguised and, therefore, easily discovered. Plans were worked out for underground bunkers. However, they required a great deal of work. In order for the bunker to be of value, it had to be deep and had to have a connection to the sewer system. Otherwise, there was no air and no water. The dirt that was turned out during the digging had to be taken out with pails and immediately concealed. The work had to be done at night because otherwise they could be observed. They guarded themselves even from the neighbors. During the liquidation, the Germans let in gas through the sewer pipes so that the Jews would have to leave their hiding places.

The bunker in W. Cukerhandl's house was one of the longest lasting. Despite the fact that it was not underground, it was well disguised and it was discovered only by chance. A Gestapo agent and his dog passed by; the dog smelled something and began tugging [the agent] toward the spot where the bunker was located. The Gestapo agent followed him. He understood that someone was hidden there. The Jews shot from the bunker and wounded the German. The commandant was alerted.

[Columns 209-210]

The militia arrived with machine guns. They surrounded the block; the machine guns were placed on the surrounding roofs. The Jews in the bunker decided to defend themselves. They had in their possession one weapon and a small amount of ammunition. The struggle was hopeless and yet they decided to carry on to the last cartridge. A large number of the besieged Jews had poison. They took the poison, not wanting to fall into the hands of the Germans. However, the doses were very small and the victims did not die, but struggled in terrible pain. They made an end to their suffering with the last remaining bullets. The survivors started a chase over attics and roofs and the Germans followed them. Only three people from the entire group successfully saved themselves from death: Merkac, Krautstick and Sigal; everyone else was murdered. The Germans also left a few dead during the struggle with the heroic group.

The largest bunker that held out until the liberation was the Sztrazler bunker, in which 22 people were saved. Wilo Freiman was found in the bunker in addition to the 22 survivors. Wilo Freiman was murdered in this bunker. Which of the 22 people and under what conditions the murder was carried out has not been cleared up to this day. A large number of Jews, who had money and acquaintances, hid with peasants. However, most of the peasants cheated the money from the Jews and then murdered them. A small percentage of the Zloczow Jews obtained Aryan documents and thus saved their lives.

Those who did not have any money and yet yearned for life went into the forest. Because of the anti–Semitic feelings of the Ukrainian partisans (the so called *Banderowces* [members of the Organization of Ukrainian Nationalists led by Stepan Bandera]), very few successfully survived. The majority were murdered in the forest or died of hunger.

The liquidation of all of the camps took place on the 23rd of August, 1942. The *aktsia* was carried out without delay, as brutally as all of the earlier *aktsias*. The liquidator was the well–known murderer of Jews, [Josef] Grzymek. He took the place of Warzog who at that time was nominated as the commandant of the Janow camp in Lemberg.

During this liquidation, a group of prisoners in the Lackie camp staged a resistance. However, the resistance was immediately broken by the overwhelming strength of the Germans.

The poet, Arie Szrenzel (author of the book of poems, *Der Kas* [*The Anger*]) was murdered on the 20th of Tammuz 5703 [23 July 1943]. Arie Szrenzel worked in the workshops. The heavy physical labor interrupted his literary activity. He perished during the liquidation of the camps.

A small group of well–qualified workers was taken to Lemberg to the Janow camp that was liquidated on the 20th of November 1943. The gifted painter and caricaturist, Mendl Reif (known from the satirical journal, *Szpilki* [*Pins*]), was among other Zloczow Jews in the Janow camp who perished.

The city was liberated from the German occupation on the 13th of July 1944. However, the liberation came too late for the Jews. In the city where Jewish culture had blossomed for many generations, in the city in which every street, every house, every stone had breathed with specific small town *yidishkayt* [Jewish way of life], in Zloczow, the Jewish city, there were no longer Jews.

The small handful of surviving Jews who, on the first days [after the liberation] found themselves drawn to Zloczow, "their Zloczow," were disappointed and immediately ran from there. It was no longer the city about which they had dreamed and for which they longed. The old houses of prayer were no longer there, nor were the Jews who would find consolation in them; the "An–ski" club with its literary evenings was no longer there, no Jewish library and there were no more readers of Jewish books. The Yiddish and Hebrew schools were no longer there and no children who needed them. The city was dead; Jewish Zloczow had disappeared.

What remained? The center of the city was burned out, empty brick buildings in the former ghetto. In the middle of the former cemetery, were several headstones of the Zloczow *tzadikim* [righteous ones], behind which was found the headstone of the great *Tzadik* and gifted man, Ohr Chaim.

The ghetto walls reminded one of death and ruin; the remaining headstones told of the power and the timelessness of Jewish culture and of Jewish spirit.

For those who were not in Zloczow after the Holocaust and for those who did not see the headstone, it echoes as only a distant legend; those who were there know that this is not a legend, but the truth.

The Germans obliterated the Zloczow cemetery. All of the headstones were removed and the earth was smoothed over. An *ohel* [structure built over the grave of a prominent person] stood in the middle of the cemetery and the grave and the headstone of the great Ohr Chaim were in the *ohel*. The surprise of the Germans was great when they noticed the stones with which the *ohel* had been constructed and the headstone did not surrender to the sharp iron. The Germans unsuccessfully used every means. The stones were only slightly damaged but they remained in place. They returned several times to this headstone, but each time they saw that the headstone would not move from its place. Ohr Chaim's headstone and those of other *tzadikim* remained standing.

The countless Zloczow legends were joined by one more and this was the last one. It is difficult to say what will happen to the few Jewish headstones on the extensive Zloczow field [cemetery] in a city where there no longer are any Jews. However, they will be a symbol to the survivors, which the remnant of Zloczow Jewry will never forget. The headstones will not be forgotten nor will thousands of Zloczow Jews who died with pride *al Kiddush haShem* [as martyrs, in the sanctification of God's name] and in sanctification of the [Jewish] people. Hilel Safran, Ch. J. Horn and hundreds of other simple men of the people who during the horrible years demonstrated [an ability] to rise above their personal interest, wrote themselves with golden letters into the history of the Jewish people

******

The names of the traitors and of all the timid people, who dealt with Jewish souls and handed them over to the devils, are covered with eternal shame.

Among the survivors are found people with doubtful reputations. The commandant of the ghetto militia, Steinwurcl, is alive; J. Landau, M. Alsztok, Karger, J. Chutiner, Halpern, W. Kirszen, Keller and Kin are alive. Shameful accusations are presented against many of those listed. It is not in my competence to judge how many of the accusations are correct and how far the responsibility of the accused reaches. It is a serious and complicated problem and it [must] be considered with the greatest impartiality.

It is the task of all of the people listed to stand before a Jewish communal tribunal. Only such a tribunal can have the right to condemn them or to rehabilitate them.

At the same time, it is particularly the task of all surviving Zloczow Jews to compel all of those who, out of compassion, do not want to place them before a tribunal to do so.

In Europe or in America, in Eretz–Yisroel or in Santa Domingo, wherever they are found, they need to be drawn to their responsibility. Whoever is innocent should be rehabilitated; the guilty need to be punished.

Translator's Footnotes:

1. In the source text, a piece of opaque tape has been placed over the words represented by the three dots and they cannot be read.
2. The author is using irony in his descriptions of "refined work" and "nobles" and so on.
3. The corner of page 21 is missing and part of the sentence is missing.
4. Shmuel Yakov Imber was the nephew of Naftali Herz Imber who wrote the lyrics to *Hatikvah* – now the national anthem of the State of Israel.

[Columns 211-212]

Two People from the Viklitski's Bunker

by Sionio Fenster

Translated by Moshe Kutten

A forced–labor camp was established at the beginning of Brodezka Street, where the wood warehouse of the Zilber family used to be. The official name of the camp was "Viklitski Plant for Construction and Demolition". The commander, Viklitski, was German– Austrian. He was always accompanied by a big dog. Viklitzki was known to be a harsh and cruel person who excelled in performing the act – "25 lashes on one's butt ". My aunt, Dvorka Merder, was an accountant in that plant. She also worked on other various tasks in the female workers' kitchen. Fate determined that I would be recruited to work in the same plant a short while later. We were sent to houses destructed by bombing and took out unbroken bricks, which were later transferred to the train station to be sent to Germany. When any kind of wood, such as roof support beams or foundation beams, were found, we transferred them, on our shoulders, to the plant's yard. After work, I returned home to my mother and my two sisters, Regina and Minah. I always tried to bring home some wood refuse and boards for heating. They waited for me impatiently at home with tearing eyes since that work was hard for me. It affected me greatly since I was unaccustomed to it. There was almost nothing to eat, but my mother always managed to get and keep something for me.

The situation was arduous as rumors about aktsias in various neighboring towns were always floating around. Since we lived in a bustling location, we decided to move to my grandmother's home, which was located at the edge of the city. The entire family concentrated there: my grandmother, aunt Zeltka, her husband, Yaakov Freed, my mother, and my two sisters. Our father, Izik, was taken away from us early on 7 March 1941, on the third day following the entrance of the Nazi invader to Zloczow. The food shortage forced us to collect potato peels, cook soup from them, and then fry them.

When the ghetto was established, we got a room with another family. However, I was later on transferred to the central concentration camp at the end of Jablonovska Street, which used to be an army barrack. We went to work in Viklitski camp in the morning and came back to sleep at night. In the beginning, I visited my family in the ghetto daily. However, when the ghetto was closed, I could not do that any longer. My aunt Dovrka obtained, once in a while, a special permit for a single visit. I managed to sneak into the ghetto through the barbwire fences, under the nose of the Ukrainian police that guarded the ghetto.

A big carpentry workshop, in which several carpentry artisans worked, was located in Viklitski camp. During one of the musters, artisans were asked to step forward. It was a difficult decision since anything out of the ordinary was suspicious. However, I instinctively stepped forward. I experienced panic when they asked me about my profession, but I answered that I was a carpenter. That was how I was sent to work in the carpentry shop. I had to carry large boards and clean the shop. Once in a while, I assisted in operating the lathe when the electricity was not working. Since my transfer to the carpentry shop, I went to work in the early hours of the morning and came back at ten at night. When was passing near the gates of the ghetto, my mother used to stand there, and wave her hand. She used to hold a package for me and tried to pass it over to me.

We heard about the extermination of the Jews in various places in the area from Jewish workers who had been transferred to the Zloczow's camp. We began to think about running away to the forests, in case the camp was to be liquidated or a selection occurred. We met with a group, which transferred weapons and ammunition [to the forest]. However, a short while later the Germans killed a part of the group located already in the forest. We established an action–group and decided to dig a bunker. We began the work shortly thereafter. The digging took place at the backside of the kitchen since it was close to the Zlotsovska River. Three youths worked there during the day, and six during the night. We took out the dirt in pails to the river bank. We reached a depth of about three meters and began to dig under the house toward the camp's yard. Later we decided to dig toward the river, a distance of about 10 meters. We transferred boards at night from the carpentry shop to support against a tunnel collapse. The work progressed in a complete secret. The rest of the inmates did not know about the existence of the bunker group. Every digger had to be replaced every few minutes, to replenish the air in his lungs. We enlarged the area under the kitchen into a small room. After considerable efforts, we managed to reach the lower opening of the house's chimney.

[Columns 213-214]

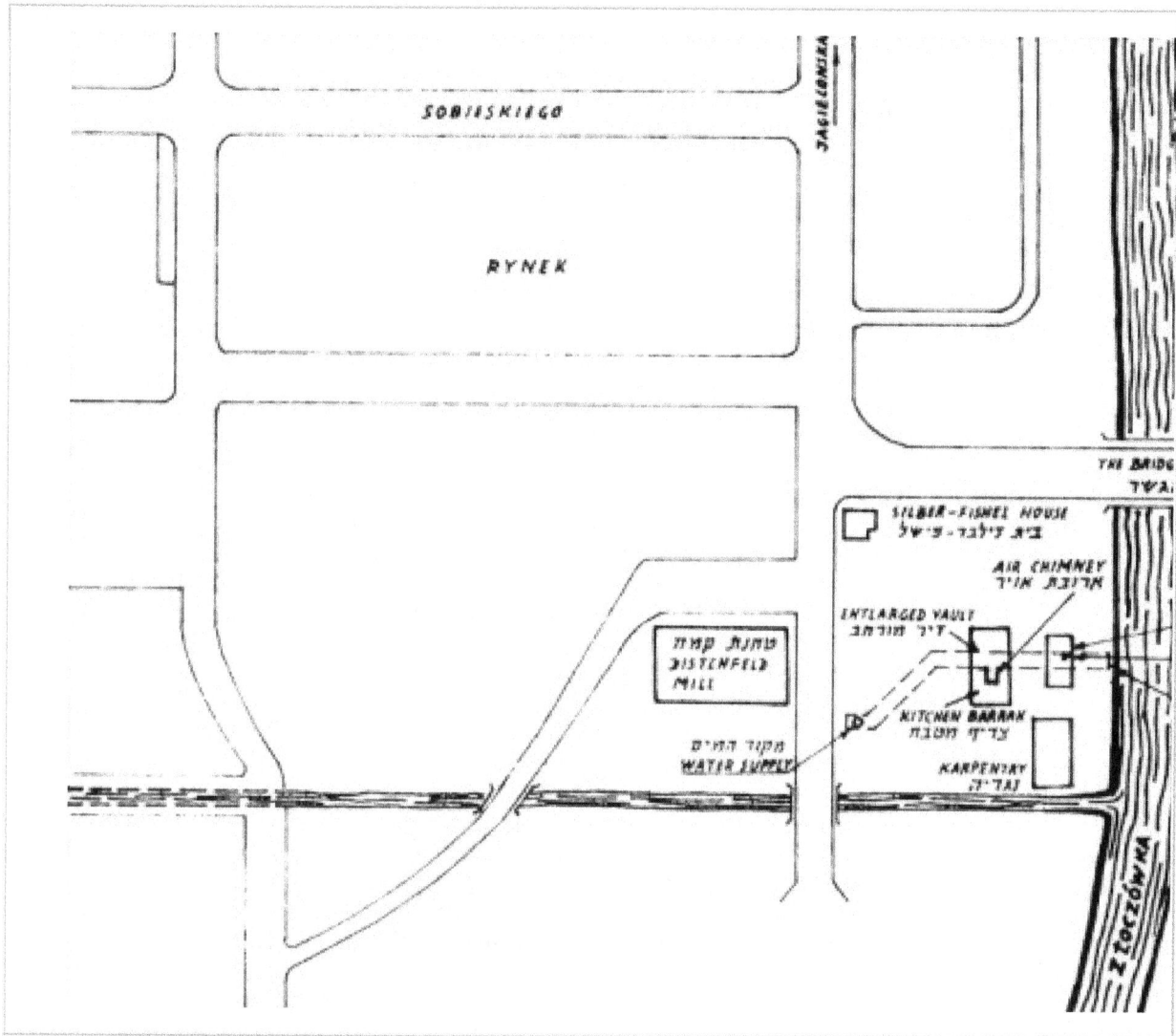

The plan for the Viklitski Bunker

The fact that we had to return, every night, to the concentration camp, for sleep caused a delay in our progress. However, there were always some youths who worked during the night.

A rumor reached us on 2nd April 1943 that the Germans were liquidating the ghetto in Zloczow. Several shots and movement of cars and German soldiers served as a verification for the rumor. They instructed us to continue with our work and not to pay attention to it. There was no way for us to get in touch with our families in the ghetto.

Close to noontime, we saw trucks loaded with people moving toward Brody. The convoy reached Yelykhovychi forest and there, everybody was murdered. I stood by the camps' fence and watched. I was hoping to see somebody from my family for the last time, among the people on the trucks. My wait was in vain. My entire family was exterminated then, except for my aunt Dvorka and myself. We were the only ones left. Our lives continued. We tried to accelerate the rate of our work at the bunker. In addition to the digging effort, we also began to accumulate food products. We managed to secure, from several sources, tin tubs. After a thorough cleaning, we put flour and groats in them and soldered them shut. According to our plan, the bunker was supposed to contain twenty to thirty people. Only a few of them knew about its construction and location. Fortunately, the digging progressed without any interruption but under constant fear.

One evening, on 22nd July 1943, I worked at the carpentry shop. Close to 10 pm, we planned to go back to the concentration camp. However, the electricity did not stop, as it usually did. We continued to work for at least an additional hour. Suddenly, a Ukrainian policeman came and instructed us to leave. We invited him to the dining hall and gave him vodka, but he insisted that we should go. We left on our way back to the camp at around 11:30 at night. The entire city was lighted but we did not suspect anything. After walking for about half an hour, we arrived at the end of Jeblonovska Street, about a hundred meters from the camps' gate. A sudden burst of gunfire interrupted the night's silence. We stopped. A single shot was heard and then again, bursts of shots from sub–machine–guns. The Ukrainian policeman said that this was probably an attack on the camp by the Partisans. We sent him to find out what was going on.

[Columns 215-216]

As he approached the gate of the camp he began to shout: "This is me, a Ukrainian policeman". But we did not hear anything after that, except a few occasional shots. We panicked for a short while but overcame quickly and began to retrace our steps. We walked through the lighted city's streets and saw the movement of cars. We arrived back at Viklitski's camp and discussed our way forward. Some people lowered themselves down into the bunker, although it was not ready yet to host "residents". We, the young ones, stayed above at the camp and hid in the carpentry shop's attic. In the morning, Christian workers arrived and told us about the liquidation of the concentration camp. At that point, we had no choice. We all gathered at the bunker entrance located in the horse stable. We proceeded to descend to the depths of the earth, into our bunker. We closed the entrance with dirt and manure and tried not to leave any traces. To our surprise, we discovered that the total number of our people was forty rather than twenty. We kept our cool and waited the whole day in the bunker. We tried to make a few initial arrangements. We did not have means and tools to cook, except two sacks of wood–coal. We made a samovar from two tin tubs, and instead of soldering them together, we used dough. That was how we began to cook. The samovar was placed under the chimney, in the small room, so most of the smoke rose through the chimney.

We formed a connection with a Polish engineer while still in the concentration camp. He was loyal and knew about the existence of the bunker. A few days later, he lowered a loaf of bread through the chimney, containing a letter to us. In the letter, he told us that people who wanted to work in Lviv's [forced–labor] camp could come out and get in touch with Viklitski. After some discussion, several artisans went out, and they were transferred to Lviv's camp. The others decided to stay. Since we did not have any water, we began to dig at the rear side of the bunker. We did reach water; however, it contained chemicals that caused damage to the digestive system. To combat that, we would hold the water in a pail for several hours and use only the upper layer for drinking and cooking. The quantities of food were meager. We received four to six loaves of bread through the chimney every few days. That was hardly sufficient compared to the number of people. The sanitary situation was also very difficult. We used a pail, which we emptied at the river bank through a small opening near the river. That opening also provided us with fresh air. We also took turns to guard against anybody approaching. During one of the mornings, the guard at the rear opening noticed a wolf–dog walking around; however, the dog did not come closer because of the foul smell. We began to suspect that something was wrong. Added to that suspicion was the fact that the engineer did not get in touch with us for several days.

One day, we heard a loud noise above us. We began to block the bunker, at the point just below the noise, trying to persuade the people who would be looking for us to think that the bunker had been abandoned. We immediately understood that the people above us are digging down to try to find the entrance. We worked quickly and managed to block the entire entry from the floor to the ceiling for a width of about 3 meters. When we were done, some men began to dig at the rear end of the bunker trying to reach the surface and escape. Unfortunately, we encountered heavy rocks. We tried to dig up in another location but had no luck either. In the meantime, we heard that people had already entered the bunker. We did not have any doubt that the end was near.

All of a sudden, a small opening broke through in our barrier. We heard a burst of shots followed by moans and shouts. From one burst of shots to another, Mrs. Gross yelled: "Stop shooting! We are coming out. We are not armed". Ukrainians began to hurry us up, shouting and pushing. All of a sudden, I recognized a Ukrainian, in the dark, who used to work with my father before the war. He directed a pocket flashlight toward me and said: "The son of Izik Fenster! What are you doing here?". I could not answer him. I just held his hand and the hand of my aunt Dvorka and followed him. We progressed toward the entrance, where I saw three Germans laying down at a machine–gun. I instinctively jumped backward and told him: "I will give you anything if you leave us alone!" He looked at my aunt and saw a necklace with a pendant. He just tore it out and went away. I backed away several more steps and found myself in the bunker's small room. I pulled my aunt Dvorka with me. We heard the Germans asking the Ukrainians whether everybody got out. They received a positive answer. The Germans proceeded to shoot at the wounded, then they finally left and silence descended on the bunker. A short while later, the Ukrainians returned. They looted everything they found, including the food tubs as well as the clothing and valuables of the murdered. That lasted for several hours. I began to discuss with aunt Dvorka how to escape.

All of a sudden just as we were ready to leave, I heard voices. I froze and could not move. A person asked in Yiddish:" Is there anybody there? We are Avraham and Sender.

[Columns 217-218]

These were two youths who worked with us on the construction of the bunker. During that faithful night, they stayed in the concentration camp, but they managed to escape. During the time we stayed at the bunker, about five weeks, they hid in various places. They came to hide in the bunker on the day, the Germans discover and liquidated it. We moved the wooden boards and left the bunker the same way we entered it. Together, we crossed the river and began our search for our future.

That is the story about the survival of two people out of the original forty that hid in Viklitski's Bunker. May the memory of all of those who perished be blessed.

*****

[Columns 219-220]

Beyond the Wall

by Nushka Altman

Translated by Moshe Kutten

The words "life beyond the wall" sounded so innocuous they could lead to the belief that the lives of those who managed to escape [from the ghetto], were heaven on earth.

Let me provide a short description of my hardships to prove that life beyond the wall was hell on earth.

After going through the horrors of the ghetto and three "aktsias", in which my father, mother, and younger brother were taken away from me, people tried to convince me to take advantage of my Arian appearance and move to one of Poland's big cities. At first, I resisted the idea of separating from my family; I did not dare to do so.

However, my husband insisted by claiming that splitting the family may provide better chances for survival.

The idea that if not all of us would survive, at least one of us would, sounded cruel and horrific. The thought that I would have to leave my only son, husband, and brother and go to an unknown and dangerous place drove me insane.

I finally gave up because of my health condition. I suffered from coughing attacks, which at times of excitement, intensified. It could have led to the discovery of our bunker.

After many trials and efforts, my husband managed to obtain original birth and Baptism certificates for me, carrying the name "Maria Rubchinska."

After consulting with our "savior-angel", Mr. Joseph Mayer, it was decided to find me a job with a high-ranked German official in Lviv. That official was anti-Nazi in his views.

I took comfort from the fact that I would not be far from my family, and perhaps I would be able to stay in touch with them through Mr. Mayer.

Unfortunately, fate decided otherwise. That official had already employed another young Jewish as a seamstress. However, thanks to an informant, not only did the official refuse to take me, but he also had the get rid of that seamstress. Mr. Mayer had to move her back to Zloczow.

We had to change our plans and look for another opportunity. Due to a strange coincidence, my father met a young Polish professional, at the office of Mr. Mayer, by the name of Kazhik. My husband left a good impression on him, so he was willing to take to the "other side" and employ a Jewish person (particularly a woman). That was before the satanic plan of Hitler to exterminate all the Jews became known. So my husband did not consider the offer by the young Pole seriously.

In 1943, when the plan to bring me to Lviv failed, my father met again with Mr. Kazhik, and he agreed to take someone who had a "proper appearance" and arrange for a safe location. Kazhik knew me and agreed to take me without hesitation. It was irresponsible to rely on a stranger but I took that desperate step, as I was in such a poor emotional state that I would not be able to describe it now. Following a dramatic separation scene, Mr. Mayer collected me at night, along with the other young women, and we went to his house. Depressed and fearful, I later traveled to Warsaw.

As it turned out later, Kazhik was a member of the fighting underground. He placed me in a village, near Warsaw, with a working family. I only stayed there for a month as the neighbors started to suspect me.

I was desperate and suicidal. My guardian, Kazhik, did not show up. I felt like a wounded and haunted animal, subject to the grace of destiny. In the end, Kazhik arrived and found another hideout for me in Warsaw with a widow. Her daughter-in-law, Batya, was also a member of the underground.

I was supposed to impersonate the wife of a former Polish officer who had been arrested by the Gestapo. It did not last long there either. A former resident, also Jewish, warned me about the widow's son who stayed temporarily in Lviv. She told me that he was a dangerous thug who used to "devour" Jews. He had a unique sense of uncovering them. His former wife, Batya, who separated from him, also warned me about him.

Indeed, trouble occurred shortly thereafter. Batya received the news that her [former] husband returned. At about the same time, another disaster occurred. During a ride on the tram, a thief stole my wallet with my money. Worse than that, he also took my certificates. During those days, thieves used to take valuables and hand over the certificates to the police. I feared that the police would find out that the certificates were forged and uncover my identity. Miserable and helpless, I did not know what to do. The only salvation was the run away as soon as possible. The question was: where?

[Columns 221-222]

My only choice was my friend Lina Baar, who lived with her little son in Milnowek [west of Warsaw]. Her brother moved her there from Zloczow at the beginning of 1942. They lived as Poles using Arian certificates.

Nervous and sick from fear I went to my friend, and she opened her arms and accepted me. We so lived with her until the liberation.

These were days of hardships and deprivation. Once and a while we received limited financial assistance from the "Joint" [JDC - The American Jewish Joint Distribution Committee]. The risk of getting that money was considerable because the imposters disguised themselves as contact agents ambushed the Jews, and handed them over to the police.

Fear followed us day and night. We became pale as dying people just by seeing a German. A knock on the door would cause a contraction of the heart or fainting. Some days we thought about leaving Milnowek and returning to Zloczow, to the bunker. Horrible and risky was the fear of meeting Ukrainian acquaintances from Zloczow, many of whom stayed in Warsaw. I did meet acquaintances from Zloczow. Fortunately, these were Poles who were honest and were happy to see me alive.

Mundek, one of the friends of my late brother, was happy to meet me. However, he warned me about his sister. She was known to be a "*Volksdeutsche*".

I can't describe my state of mind when I went to the police to receive a new identity card, without which one could not travel in the streets. Sitting the whole day at home was not advisable since it would have raised the suspicion of the neighbors.

Street kidnappings were daily events. There was not a day without informing about Jews. Extortionists extorted the last pennies from their victims and then handed them over to the Gestapo.

We waited for our salvation with our last drops of energy. The liberation seemed to be so close! The offensive by Red Army began, and at the same time, the Uprising in Ghetto Warsaw took place. But that was in vain. The Russians took over Praga but stopped at the Vistula River.

The Germans suppressed the revolt with blood and fire. Warsaw's residents escaped from their city in masses. Milnowek was filled with Warsaw's refugees, among them a few Jewish survivors. Fear and hunger strengthened. Kidnappings of men and women for forced labor in Germany began.

I also fell victim to one of the kidnapping operations and was incarcerated in the transit camp in Pruszkow [Proshkov]. Due to the kindness of a Polish physician, I was not transferred to Germany.

Our situation worsened from one day to another. However, our salvation finally arrived. The Red Army conquered Warsaw. We were free! However, we were not fully happy and joyful. The worry about the fate of my family consumed my whole being. I left Warsaw in March 1945, hungry and depleted, in search of my family.

Following three weeks of wandering, the Soviets captured me along with Ukrainian gangs. They refused to believe me that I was Jewish and was returning home. They suspected and accused me of spying. It took a miracle to escape the transfer to Siberia. I had finally arrived in Zloczow, or more correctly the "cemetery" of the former Zloczow.

After two years of separation, I found my family among the Holocaust survivors. We all looked like walking skeletons.

*****

[Columns 223-224]

A Bunch of Memories from the Holocaust

by Nakhum Ben-Meir (Pasternak)

Translated by Moshe Kutten

On 22nd June 1941, when Hitler attacked Soviet Russia, the Germans bombed all the cities and towns in Eastern Poland, which were under the Soviet regime. Our city, Zloczow, was also heavily bombed. Tens of Jews were killed in that bombardment.

It was an "Introduction" to the great massacre of the Jews that occurred later on.

On 1st July, at dawn, brutal German troops broke into the city. The large-scale pogrom, which lasted until Saturday, 5th July, began on the following day. About 5000 Jews perished in that horrible pogrom. Many of the victims were refugees, which arrived at the city from other places.

I was among a group of fifty people taken to be shot. The S. S. troops led us on the road leading to the Jewish hospital. The murderers stood opposite the hospital in two columns, waiting for their victims. We were ordered to pass in between the two columns. When we passed through, they hit us with sticks and stabbed us with their daggers. Later, they sprayed us with bursts of deadly bullets. A small group, me included, managed to escape. Hirsch Tzvardling (the son-in-law of Leibchi Peres), and two others whose names I do not remember, escaped with me. Herman Shprukh, Feivel Katz, and the son of Hirsch Tzvardling (son-in-law of Bluma, the baker) fell literally at my feet, wallowing in their blood.

The miller, Bocharski, saw me escaping and collected me to his home for the night. He returned me to my house at dawn. My wife hurried to our neighbors and begged them to hide me. A few minutes later, I heard loud knocks on the locked door. Wild yelling came out from the throats of the Ukrainians and the Germans. Fear and horror took hold of me, but I did not lose my senses. I kneeled and rolled myself under the bed. The door was busted open noisily, and the thugs came in. They went up to the kitchen and then the bedroom. They managed to turn over and demolish everything in the house in one minute.

They destroyed the cloth closet and scattered the bedding but miraculously did not discover me. The Germans left as quickly as they came.

I escaped death for the second time.

When the murderous frenzy subsided, the Germans ordered all Zloczow's surviving Jews to gather in the old market square. The Germans announced at that gathering that all the Jews, men, and women 12 years and older, must wear on their right arm a white band with a blue Star of David on it. Anybody found not wearing it would be shot on the spot. The Germans also announced that Jews were forbidden from being outside of their homes from 7 p.m. until 6 a.m. A Judenrat was established at that gathering. Dr. Meiblum was nominated to head it. Other members of the Judenrat were: Dr. Matyetyahu Gruber, Dr. Garber, Dr. Shaf, the Shmirer brothers (the wood merchants), Nunki Weinshtok, Leon Tzverdling, and several other people.

Several days later, I witnessed a courageous and proudful act, which I would never forget. R' Moshe Marder was walking innocently in the street when the manager of the Ukrainian chamber of commerce, Antoniak, was walking toward him. Antoniak stopped, stretched his arm toward R' Moshe, and said: "Are you still alive?" R' Moshe Marder answered: "I cannot touch a hand sullied with Jewish blood". He said that and then just passed by the gentile without turning his head.

Those who think that the Jewish Militia only performed tasks dictated by the Judenrat are mistaken.

One militiaman, who was assigned to guard over women and girls that were taken to the public bath, had a habit of breaking into the bath, while the bathers were still naked. Holding a stick in his hand, he would force them to hurry up, get dressed quickly, and get out. Outside, he would hit them with his stick and force them to sing.

There was also a story about a militiaman who saw Jews running away and hiding in bunkers and ditches. That happened on 2nd April, the day the ghetto in Zloczow was liquidated. He decided to act "courageously". He jumped into a sewer ditch and ordered the Jewish escapees to get out. When the Jews did not obey, he called some Germans and Ukrainians to help him. The Germans obliged enthusiastically, but instead of jumping into the ditch, they threw several hand grenades into the ditch.

And now, I would like to tell you some details about my own accounts.

When the ghetto was liquidated, I managed to hide my little girl, Rani-Rachel, in the camp's workshops (at the house of Sunny Ettinger). One day, the militiamen, Yankile Rutiner and Yaakov, and Itzik Halperin took me aside and told me that they know that I hid my daughter in the workshop.

[Columns 225-226]

Opening of Mass Graves on Hill of the Fort - "Zamek",
where Jews were Executed by the Nazis

The militiamen told me that they are not comfortable with that idea. However, they causally added that they would be willing to "negotiate" before they report about it. That was a definitive hint about a ransom. My anger boiled over, and I rejected their offer disgustedly. They did not wait long and reported about my secret immediately. The supervisor of the workshops came to me and demanded that I take my daughter immediately. I pleaded with him to wait until dark when I could find her a new hiding place with one of my Christian friends. He agreed. In the evening, when the militiamen saw me leaving the camp with my little daughter, they were satisfied. Two days later, at 2 a.m., my Christian acquaintance brought my daughter back. I quickly found another, more secure, location with one of my friends in Dzvynyach.

On Friday 20 Tamuz, 23 July 1943, the Germans, with the help of the Ukrainians and Valsov's soldiers, liquidated all of the forced-labor camps in our area from Viniki to Ternopil. Along with the forced-labor camps, they also liquidated all the workshops. About 100 Jews, including myself, were transferred to Janower camp in Lviv. The rest, about six hundred Jews who resided in the camp at Zloczow, were brought to Vokhtarov forests and were shot there.

There were about a thousand Jews in Lackie, about six hundred in Pluhow, and three hundred at Sasiv. In the Lackie there Jews from Zloczow, Lviv, Stanislawow (now Ivano-Frankivsk), Zholiv [?], and even Hungary.

Hidden away within a container, I kept a dose of poison. All those who survived the liquidation of the ghetto knew well that the Germans would not keep them alive for long. That became particularly evident in light of rumors that started to spread. They were about the defeat suffered by the invaders on all the fronts and their panic retreat. I have decided, ahead of time, not to let the murderers kill me. When I would feel that my end is near, I would preempt and commit suicide. I was not alone with that decision. Many even acted upon that decision. That happened to a group of women, my wife among them, who committed suicide with the poison doses they had kept, during the nights of the camps' liquidation.

I do not know why and from where my will to live came. It was immensely strong and it would not let go. I began to plan an escape from the Janower camp. My only goal was to reach Dzvynyach and see my little daughter, who just celebrated her ninth birthday.

When I went to work, I met an acquaintance who was a train conductor. At noon, the S.S. people would travel to the camp to eat lunch. Vlasov soldiers who guarded us during work-hours also stepped out to eat somewhere. The conductor agreed to execute my plan for 4000 Guldens. As we had agreed, he came to pick me up on 27 October 1943, between 1 - 2 pm, (when the policemen and the oppressors were out), and hid me in his house overnight. The following day early morning, he dressed me up in a conductor uniform, and we both traveled on the train from Podazamcho [?] station to Keniazshi [?]. From there, we continued our way on foot to the forests in Dzvynyach area. I returned the conductor uniform to the man and gave him the rest of the agreed-upon money. We said goodbye to each other, and we went on our separate ways.

I turned toward the house of Marchin Kozshak in Dzvynyach, where my daughter was staying. I was following signs etched in my memory.

[Columns 227-228]

Suddenly, as I was walking self-assuredly in the depth of the forest, three Germans appeared in front of me. They leveled a submachine gun toward me and yelled: "Juda, halt! Hands up!". Immediately, a thought flashed in my head - I should not show them that I was confused or panicked. With an apathetic motion, I responded in a typical Polish accent: "I am Polish". I was then ordered to go with the soldiers, but I pretended not to understand their order. They called a non-commissioned officer and told him: that they caught a Jew. The officer approached me and asked in a voice calmer than that of the soldiers: "You are a Jew, admit it". I explained to him that I am Polish who is going to work. To support my claim, I pulled out my work-tools - a hummer, plane, measuring tape… A soldier commented: "In my opinion, we need to bring him to the Hauptmann [Captain]". The non-commissioned officer responded by saying: "Why? There is no need. Don't you see that he is not Jewish? Jews would know German. This one does not understand or know anything. He is just a stupid Pole". He turned to me and called: "Go! We say go! Go to hell! Stupid Pole, marsh!... You go now! Next time bring documents! Did you understand?". I remained standing pretending not to understand. The officer caught me on my shoulder and shook me up. Then, they all disappeared and I resumed my journey.

Suddenly, I noticed a shadow approaching. It was the forester. I found myself in danger again, perhaps in greater than encountering the Germans. If he were one of my acquaintances (not all the friends and acquaintances were sincere), he probably would not hesitate and quickly deliver me to the murderers. Perhaps he would kill me himself to get the prize offered by the Germans.

When the forester saw me — he recognized me. Indeed, he was an old acquaintance. However, he invited me to sleep at his house. The following evening, he accompanied me and showed me the way to Marchin's house. I arrived there safely and found my daughter safe and sound.

More than few groups of Jews, from places such as Zloczow, Sasiv, Pidkamin, Brody, and Lviv found a shelter in the forests that surrounded Dzvynyach. These Jews used to come out of their hideouts at nightfall, go to the village, and beg for food. With Marchin's advice and help, I was able to join one of these groups. I would come to him once or twice a week to receive some food. I boiled water and roasted the few potatoes in the small bunker I dug for myself in the forest. At noon, I would eat a dish with a piece of bread, gifted to me by Marchin.

At the village, my daughter was considered a Christian girl, a member of Marchin's family. She was named Orka Kozshak. She went to the church every Sunday with the Kozshak family. She would say her prayer every morning and evening and crossed herself. Once, when I came to the village, I was told that the kettles-maker, Yenkili Ritvomatsov told about us in the house of the Valtis (village elder). He said that the father of the girl arrived at the village. He also said that I usually stayed with the refugees in the forest. One woman, who was in attendance at the Valtis's home, wondered: "The father of Orka? He is a Christian and can live with us freely!". The kettles-maker responded that Orka's father is Jewish and that her real name is not Orka but Rani Rachel. He added that Rani's father escaped from Janower's camp. In short, that Yenkili told everything about us.

That woman neighbor did not remain idle. She sent a note to the German company who patrolled the forests, probably the same Germans I had encountered earlier. She told them that a Jewish girl is being hosted at Kozshak's house. They visited Marchin, on the same day to catch and kill the girl. Miraculously, Rani was not home at the time. By chance, she was at Mrs. Bronia - Kozshak's mother, who resided in a house on the other side of the village. Obviously, I could not leave the girl in the village any longer. I hurried up and took my daughter to the forest.

A Ukrainian militia appeared in the area on the 23rd of December 1943. They conducted a manhunt of the Jews in the forests. During our escape to the depth of the forest, a bullet hit me in my right hand. However, thanks to the medical treatment I received from the partisans of Armia Ludowa (which were friendly to the Jews, unlike the partisans of the Home Army - *Armia Krajowa*), I got out of danger. These partisans came out of their hidings and quickly opened a heavy fire upon the militiamen. The Ukrainians, finding themselves under fire and surrounded, retreated and left the forest.

Haunted and injured, in tatters and barefoot, I wandered around, day and night, trying to save my only daughter. A few times, I lost the will to live, seeing my daughter suffering from hunger and fear. Our only food was the snow. We could not go back to the village. When the Germans found out that some of the farmers hid Jewish refugees, they angrily attacked all the area villages and burnt them. There wasn't any more a single location for long, as predators in the form of Germans and Ukrainians haunted us.

[Columns 229-230]

Nobody had any delusion about surviving that hell.

That situation lasted until April 1944.

On the 23rd of April, partisans from the battalion of General Kovpak appeared in the forest. When they found us, tens of men, women, and children, gripped with fear and hopelessness and famished from hunger. They gathered and transferred us to beyond the front-line, to the town of Pidkamin. The Russians had already occupied that town. From there, we were transferred to Pochaiv and later on Kremenets.

A new chapter of our wandering began. However, we were free of the fear of death.

I traveled with my daughter from Kremenets to Zloczow, Lviv, and Lublin. From there, we went to lower Silesia, where we stayed until 1948. Later on, we went to Paris and from there to Israel. We settled in Acre. In that town, I was able to raise my daughter, Rani Rachel until she got married. She awarded me with two granddaughters.

*****

[Columns 231-232]

The Rescue of Batish and Altman Families

by Jozef Mayer

Translated by Moshe Kutten

Mr. Jozef Mayer, a German, was in charge of supply and agriculture during the Nazi conquest. He helped the Jews in Zloczow a great deal.
After the war, he visited Israel and was honored with the title of "Righteous Among Nations" by Yad Vashem".

I was nominated by the "General Government" administration of [occupied] Poland as the person in charge of supply and agriculture. I arrived in Zloczow, Galitsia, which was the seat of the provincial government, in November 1941.

* * *

My role was to concentrate agricultural produce and its distribution. The role also included the supervision of various plants associated with the supply chain.

Initially, I rented a room in the house of a Ukrainian clergy. It took many weeks for the regime to provide me with a small apartment, which enabled me to bring my family from the "Reich". Before several weeks had passed, representatives of Jewish and Polish circles sought relations with me. Most of them were from the intelligentsia, who were still alive at that point. They realized, very quickly, that I was a different kind of German with different political views. The person who had especially sought to approach me was Dr. Altman. He came to me often with all sorts of requests and wishes. Obviously, I tried to help him, as much as possible under the conditions during that time. In most cases, I had to take extreme precautions because of the Gestapo people who ruled Zloczow. They had criticized me even before the war.

It was Dr. Altman who recommended Yosef Batish as an efficient, diligent, and loyal assistant.

Since I brought my family to Zloczow in January 1942, I was very thankful for his help. I found Batish, who was 28 years old at the time, to be honest, and pleasant, and I could trust him with my daughters, who were 9 and 11 years old. We developed a relationship that could only be developed within the framework of a nourishing family. Batish, an accountant, felt safe and secure among us, as he knew that our German family understood his feelings.

My daughters became attached to him. They are keeping in touch with "their Yosef", who now resides in Denver, Colorado, USA, until today. The separation from him was very hard for the family. As a Jew, he was not able to stay with us and had, in the summer of 1943, to leave us and go undercover.

I still remember how we had conferred about all sorts of subversive plans I especially remember how we managed to keep in touch. We promised each other that we would reconnect if we survive the war. Therefore, Batish kept my address [in Germany] with him.

A Group of Holocaust Survivors with their Savior - Jozef Mayer, a "Righteous among Nations"

[Column 233]

Josef Mayer a "Righteous Among Nations"

He connected and showed the first sign of life from Austria in 1946, using that address.

The Nazi views were foreign to my daughters, who grew up in a Christian-Catholic environment. Even the influence they received in school could not convince them otherwise. None of the teachers in school could change their minds.

On the other hand, they were intelligent enough not to raise any suspicion. My daughters did not see the Jew in Batish but the person -Yosef. From his side, Yosef protected them against external threats, while they were his loyal friends and advocators.

In the Zloczow area, the "Jewish Aktsia's" began in July 1942. One such "aktsia" was conducted in our area of the city in April 1943. During precarious days, Batish would not return home, as was his daily custom, but would stay with us and sleep in the kitchen.

During unexpected and sudden "aktsia's" numerous Jewish families found shelter in my apartment. To avoid discovery by friends or other Germans, who used to visit us, we hid our proteges in the cellar or adjacent rooms. My daughters took care of them and "their Yosef".

In July 1943, things got to the point that city of Zloczow was announced as being *"Judenfrei"* ["free of Jews"]. It meant that anybody was allowed to shoot a Jew on the spot if he or she happened to see one. Indeed, there were some incidents in the city when Jews were shot. We were obligated to protect our proteges. However, I realized that my family would have to return back to the "Reich" when the front would approach.

[Column 234]

The civil authorities would also have to leave.

It was necessary to find a secure location for our proteges. It had to be a safe location during the transition period and when the front would approach. We decided to look for a safe place in the village. Yosef Batish and his wife found a shelter with one of the farmers near Remidovitza [Remezivtsi ?], about 10 kilometers south of Zloczow. They were housed in a potato storage shack about 30 meters from the farmer's house. During the period between July 1943 and the liberation by the Soviet army in July 1944, they experienced horrific conditions.

Obviously, we continued to maintain a close connection, using strict precautions. Our communication was verbal through the farmer. That farmer provided me with a report about Batish's situation and I gave him food and medicines from me for the Batish family. In mid-March 1944, I evacuated from Zloczow with the rest of the civil regime. The women and children were evacuated to the "Reich", even earlier, in January 1944. From that point on, Batish and his wife remained without our assistance. That was the most arduous period for them. Before the evacuation, I sent Batish all sorts of necessities and food. I then returned to Krakow, and our connection was interrupted.

Only in 1946, did Batish let me know from Bad Gastein [Austria] that he survived.

I would have hosted Batish and his wife, who experienced long sufferings and deteriorating health, in our home. It would have been a better and healthier environment than Bad Gastein in Austria.

However, the rules of the occupation authorities were quite ridiculous. They did not allow, despite my great efforts, anybody coming from Austria. We managed to see each other twice, both times - illegally, near Berchtesgaden, before Batish and his wife immigrated to the USA.

I succeeded in saving another family from the hands of the oppressor – the Altman family. Dr. Altman was a lawyer. He lived with his wifea ten-year-old son, and brother-in-law in Zloczow. Dr. Altman was coming and going to my house without attracting any attention. He told me about what was happening in the city. In turn, I told him about any planned "aktsia" (as best as I could guess in advance). As time progressed, the state of the Jewish population deteriorated. Complete extermination was all but a certainty. We began to search for ways to rescue his family. We sat down for hours and discussed feasible (and unfeasible) solutions. First, we had to place Dr. Altman's wife in a safe place since being a woman would have made it difficult to do in some situations. In some aspects, the arrangement for Mrs. Altman was not very difficult since she was blond and had an Arian appearance. People would not have recognized her as Jewish in another location. On May 29, 1943, my Polish driver transported Mrs. Altman and another Jewish woman in my official car to Lviv, about 80 kilometers away.

Jews were forbidden to ride the train. Besides, Mrs. Altman was a known figure. People would have recognized her immediately at the Zloczow's train station. Therefore, we did not have any way other than risking travel in my official car.

From Lviv, Mrs. Altman traveled to Warsaw as an Arian woman equipped with a counterfeited passport. She then settled in Warsaw as an Arian, thereby situated in a reasonably safe location.

After a thorough review and consideration, Dr. Altman decided to initiate negotiations with a reliable Polish farmer. The latter resided in Yelkhovichy, about 2-3 kilometers from Zloczow. We decided to provide the farmer with a permit, issued by my office, to operate a roadside kiosk. We based that on the fact that his farm was suitable and located strategically on a busy crossroads junction.

The owner of the kiosk received food products monthly, based on a predetermined norm. Dr. Altman and his family benefited from these products. The farmer himself also benefited from these products and thereby was rewarded for his help and scarify. I was awarded the license. The idea behind that arrangement was to guarantee that Dr. Altman and his family would be provided with food products even if they would transfer me from Zloczow to another location.

Dr. Altman visited my apartment for the last time on July 14, 1943. Since he stayed by me beyond the curfew deadline, I accompanied him to his house. The farewell did not come easy for either of us.

We later received a confirmation to the fact that the timing for hiding Dr. Altman was appropriate. Sweeping "aktsia's", executed with extreme cruelty, took place after June 26. Finally, on July 22, the remnants of the Jews girded themselves and responded with a rain of bullets. Some of them barricaded themselves under the roof of the city hall and the adjacent houses.

On July 27 and 28, 1948, the shots heightened to the point that the German police suffered some casualties. The shooting finally ceased on July 29. In the meantime, I received several letters from Dr. Altman, without a signature, through the Polish farmer. Among other things, Dr. Altmen asked me to send him alcohol. I sent him several bottles. He did not use alcohol for drinking but for hygienic and medical needs. As described below, he and his family benefitted from them tremendously.

Unfortunately, I could not keep his letters since I was not safe from the Gestapo. I destroyed the letters upon reading them.

Dr. Altman asked me several times to visit him at his hideout. Since that mission carried substantial risk, I had initially hesitated to do so. Only after many appeals, I relented and promised to visit him on Sunday, August 8.

I related to him that I would come in the morning when the Polish farmer family would be in church. I traveled without any escort or a driver in my official car.

Upon arrival, I stopped the car in front of the farmer's house, raised the hood, and began to fiddle with the car cooling system as if I needed water for the car engine.

I entered the house where the farmer expected me. Whispering, he welcomed me, and without any delay, brought me to a separate room and asked me to sit down. He immediately disappeared and left me by myself. Tensed, I wrapped my hand around my ear as a funnel but did not hear even a faint sound.

With full expectations for what was about to happen, the door opened. Dr. Altman appeared, wearing a pajama and sleepers. I was shocked at his appearance. He held his hand out and we shook hands. After a short talk, Dr. Altman asked me to follow him. He wanted me to see the hideout with my own eyes and to witness the conditions under which he, his brother-in-law, and ten years old son endure. Dr. Altman went in front and we descended narrow wooden stairs. He opened the door and entered a cowshed where three cows lay down.

The cowshed measured 6 by 4 meters. Dr. Altman showed me a hole in the ground, located under the stall and measuring no more than 30 by 40 centimeters. That hole led to a bunker of 3 by 4 meters and a height of 1.5 meters. An adult could not stand erect in that bunker. The air was dense and it was completely dark. They had to survive in that cowshed until the liberation. Dr, Altman also showed me a rock, which the farmer used to seal the hole in case of danger. They used blankets in the bunker for seating and laying down only. There was also a pail that served as a toilet. We covered it with a piece of wood when the farmer handed over the food through the hole. Only at midnight, the family could get out of the bunker and breath the air in the cowshed. In the best case, they went out to breathe some fresh air in the yard, but only at midnight. Even then, maximal caution had to be exercised. Only then, the need for alcohol became clear to me. They needed it for washing to maintain minimal hygiene. The farmer was reliable. He did allow access for his family to the cowshed to prevent the possibility of discovery. The farmer exercised strict care of returning the rock every time Dr. Altman went through it.

[Columns 237-238]

Parting from Dr. Altman, who I saw for the last time, was very emotional. It was hard for me to grasp how people could survive under these conditions. It was only probably possible when people felt assured and immensely hopeful that they would survive.

The experience caused me a profound mental shock, particularly since I was forbidden to demonstrate any dissatisfaction with the circumstances.

* * *

I heard from Mr. Batish, whom I met in 1946, and for a second time in 1946, on the German-Austria border, that Dr. Altman survived and that he lives in the east. I hadn't been able to connect with him as yet. Perhaps this article would lead to a sign of life from him.

The description of the events was based on my memory. Despite the time that has passed, these memories have not fainted and remained clear in my mind. Experiences such as these are etched in one's memory for eternity.

Besides my memory, I used my journal, particularly for the dates, of key events. While I did keep a journal, it was not possible, for obvious reasons, to indicate the nature of the events except as outlines. Despite that, these outlines saved me as fairly accurate chronicles.

Finally, the question remains as to what reasons motivated me to risk myself and my family to help these ill-fated people.

Even during the period before the war, when I was still in my homeland, I was shocked by the injustice in many areas and the cruel oppression force of the National-Socialistic ideology.

The more I witnessed the cruelness of the S. S. and the civil administration, the more my desire to help the oppressed and the sufferers grew.

Despite Hitler's great victories, I was convinced that the day would come soon when justice would win over injustice. With my dedication to the oppressed, I was convinced that I provided the best service for my country. The world should know that another Germany existed. I also acted according to my religious belief. I would receive great satisfaction if the lines written here, contribute to the healing of the wounds that we caused to the Jewish people. I would be elated if I have sowed a seed for the sprouting of a mutual understanding.

A Women Organization Named After Leah Opel

[Columns 239-240]

A Mourning Poem
about the Destruction of Zloczow

by Yekhiel Imber (April 8th 1959)

Translated by Moshe Kutten

I cry over the deceit and ancient sin,
I cry over the brothers who sold their sibling to be a slave.
How could I not weep over thousands of brothers,
given away to die by evil people?

I cry over the thousand, and over the one,
I cry over a stricken nation in ancient times.
How could I not weep over my nation, when she is bleeding,
her people, sacrificed, and the fruits of their hard work, looted?

I cry over tortured mother and father,
and their bitter fate.
How could I not weep over what they saw with their own eyes:
their daughter is dishonored and their son is murdered?

I cry over the baby taken away from his mother's bosom,
and I cry over the infant, hacked to pieces against the wall.
How could I not weep when the cruel nation,
destroyed and annihilated us without leaving a remnant?

I cry over the city, a glorious community,
an oasis built and strengthened by generations.

How could I not weep when the silence is screaming:
"The city sits as a desolate weeping widow?" [Book of Lamentations]

I cry over her wealthy people and the poor,
over her culture and her writers and poets.
How could I not weep over those who were buried alive,
their heart still beating when they covered the pit?

I cry about the youths aspiring for salvation,
I cry over the generation yearning to be free.
I could I not weep when the calamity is so great,
the wound is mortal, with no medicine or cure?

I curse that nation, the criminal nation,
I curse its collaborators, skilled in murder.
Cursed is their land from yielding harvests,
Cursed is their land for eternity.

[Columns 241-242]

Chapter C

The Social Activities in Zloczow

[Columns 243-244]

[blank]

[Columns 245-246]

Zloczow's Rabbis and its Righteous People

by David Imber

Translated by Moshe Kutten

According to tradition, some of the Jewish greats and the Torah pillars served in Zloczow's rabbinates. Rabbi Elazar Rokeakh, Z"L, the author of the book "Maasei Rokeakh" is considered one of these greats. He became the Rabbi of Amsterdam (and was named after the city – Rabbi Elazar Amsterdammer).

Rabbi Mikhel from Zloczow

Rabbi Yekhiel Mikhel was born in Brody in 5486 (1726) to his father, Rabbi Yitzkhak of Drohobitz (R' Itzikle Drobitzer), and died in Yampol on Saturday, 25 Elul 5546, (1786).

According to the Hasidic tradition, he died during the "Third Meal", when he sat down with his followers – admirers, at the time of the Hasidic ecstasy, which took place, as usual, in the middle of the meal. They tried, in vain, to revive him.

In his youth, he was fortunate to study with the Besht [Ba'al Shem Tov]. The Besht pleaded with him to accept a rabbinical position, but he refused to do it. The Besht scolded him for that and said: "You have lost your world – this one and the next". However, R' Mikhel continued to refuse. The Besht told him joyfully later on: "You are blessed by G-d and your choice is also blessed. I was only trying you out, to see what was truly in your heart".

After the death of the Besht, Rabbi Mikhel became the student of Dov Ber, the great *Maggid* of Mezritch. In Brody R' Mikhel prayed in the special "Hasidic Minyan" (Hasidim Shtibel), where it was allowed to pray in the Sephardic style, using the Siddur [praying book] of the "Ha'Ari".

In year 5541 (1780/1), after the second boycott of the Hasidim, R' Mikhel witnessed the burning of the book "Toldot Yaakov Yosef" by Rabbi [Yaakov Yosef Katz] of Polonne. R' Mikhel himself also suffered from the persecution of the Hasidim. His friend, Rabbi Pinkhas Horowitz, had to intervene and asked not to sadden him and not dismiss his work since all of his intentions were in honor of G-d.

Rabbi Mikhel was nominated as a *Maggid* [preacher] in Zloczow and toward the end of his life in Yampol, Podolia, where he passed away. He was the type of a *Tzadik* [righteous] who taught Hasidism ways to others. He was considered one of the leaders of the new religious movement. He did not author any books; however, his sermons were included in one of the elemental Hasidic books, the compilation "Likutei Yekarim"["Precious Collections']. On the cover of the book, Rabbi Mikhel was referred to as *Maggid* Meisharim [Preacher of Righteousness] from the holy community of Yampol. In his sayings, we recognize some of the polemic sharpness of his friend, Rabbi Yaakov Yosef Hakohen, the author of "Toldot Yaakov Yosef" ["History of Yaakov Yosef"].

The Head of a Dynasty

R' Mikhel was the head of a dynasty of Admors [spiritual leaders in the Hasidic movement]. The Hasidim used to say that his five sons, Rebbe Yosef, Rebbe Mordekhai, Rebbe Yitzkhak, Rebbe Moshe, and Rebbe Wolf, represent the five books of the Torah. R' Wolf of Zbaraz was the most famous. He projected a unique sanctity resulting from his inner moral integrity. [Rabbi Menakhem Mendel Bodek], the author of "The Seder Hadorot Ha'Khadash" ["The New Book of Generations"] who lived in the same period, wrote about him: "His innocence, piousness, and love of people, could not be surmised".

[People used to tell the following story about him]: His wife once quarreled with her servant and decided to take her to court, to sue the servant for all the things she broke. R' Wolf put on his clothes and also went out to go to the court. The rebbetzin [the rabbi's wife] thought that her husband was going to argue her case in front of the rabbinical judges and told him: "You do not need to dishonor yourself in a financial suit? I would manage by myself". The *Tzadik* responded: "I am not going to argue your case in court. I am going to argue for your servant. She is an orphan. It is s a Mitzva to support her, as was said [Job 31:13]: if I have rejected the cause of my manservant or maidservant when they made a complaint against me... [what will I do when God rises to judge me?]".

Another story told about him: His followers sat down with him for the "Third Meal" of Shabbat. Another person came in, sat at the table, took a radish, cut it into small pieces, and chewed on it noisily. The Hasidim, who used to sit in silence and reverence around their rabbi, scolded that person: "You are a glutton. Why are you interfering with the thinking of our holy rabbi?" The person felt ashamed. The *Tzadik* sensed his embarrassment and said: "I wish to eat a radish. Please hand it to me to eat".

R' Wolf of Zabraz was also known for his modesty. One time, he traveled on a cart to a meal organized by one of his followers celebrating his son's circumcision. It was in the wintertime and it was freezing outside. In the middle of the meal, the rabbi remembered that the waggoneer stayed outside to guard the horses. He secretly went outside and told the waggoneer: "You go inside the house to warm up a bit. I will watch over the horses". The meal participants noticed R' Wolf's absence and went out to look for him. They found him standing by the horses, shaking from the cold.

[Columns 247-248]

Rabbi Meshulam Feibush Heller of Zabraz

Rabbi Feibush, son of Aharon Moshe, was the student of Rabbi Mikhel of Zloczow. He was fortunate to meet, in his youth, the great *Maggid,* R' Ber of Mezrich. However, he received his knowledge of the Torah from R' Mikhel. He participated in the authoring of the great compilation "Likutei Yekarim". The sermons of the Besht, *Maggid* Rabbi Ber of Mezrich, and Rabbi Mikhel were included in that compilation.

Rabbi Meshulam Feibush Heller died in 20 Kislev 5552 [16 December 1791], in Zabraz.

Rabbi Mordekhi of Niskiz Z"L

Rabbi Mordekhai [Shapira] of Niskiz was the second student of R' Mikhel of Zloczow. He was born in 5502 (1741/2) to his father, Rabbi Dov Ber (the secretary and writer of the "Council of Four Lands"). R" Mordekhai had four sons: R' Yosef, R' Yaakov Arye, and R' Yitzkhak, the author of "Toldot Yitzkahk"["The History of Yitzkhak"].

Among his students were R' Uri "Hasaraf" ["Angel of Fire"] from Sterlisk and R' Klonimus Kalman from Krakow, author of "Ma'or VaShemesh" ["Light and Sun"].

R' Mordekhai died in 8 Nisan 5560 [3 April 1800].

At the beginning of his career, R' Mordekhai served as rabbi in Leshniv, a town in the Brody district. A group of Hasidim was formed there. In 5550 (1789/90) he settled in Niskiz, near Kovel in Vohlyn. He gained fame there as a *Tzadik* and a "miracle -maker". He performed miracles on heaven and earth. He revived the dead, healed the sick, provide *Heiter Agunot*. Sick people from many nations came to seek his help. They lay down in their wagons parked in front of his apartment. He used to come out and give them his healing blessing.

Rabbi Mordekhai authored a smell pamphlet, which was later published as "Rishfei Esh" [Sparks of Fire].

The content of that pamphlet includes commentaries on the Bible and the sayings of the Besht.

Rabbi Yisaskhar Dov Ber Z"L

R' Yisaskhar Ber, son of R' Leibush, was the grandson of Gaon Rabbi Naftali of Frankfurt, author of "Smikhat Khakhamim" ["Certification for Sages"]. In Zloczow, R' Yisaskhar Ber served for many years. Toward the end of his life, he made Aliya to Eretz Israel but did not live there for long. He died in Av, 5570 (1810).

R' Yisaskhar Ber lived at the time of the Besht's students. One of these students was the great *Maggid* from Merzrich, Rabbi R' Ber. His time was also the period of the great Talmudic scholars who became Hasidic: – R' Shmuel Shmelki of Nikolsburg and his brother, R' Pinkhas, the author of the "Hafla'ah" ["Amazement"], ABD [the head of the rabbinical court] of Frankfurt.

R' Yisaskhar's book, "Bat Eini" ["The Apple of my Eye"], was printed after his death by his son, R' Yehudah Leib, his grandson, R' Efraim Fishel, and his son-in-law, R' Gershon ABD in Skalat. The book, which was published on a one-eighth of a sheet, was printed in Rashi's letters. The book contains 159 pages and has two parts:

   a.   New interpretations of the Talmud (pages 1 – 76)
   b.   Responsa (Pages 77 – 159)

The new interpretations were about the tractates: Pesakhim, Beitza, Rosh HaShanah, Yoma, Shabbat, Yevamot, Ketubot, Kiddushin, Gittin, Bava Kamma, Bava Metzia, Bava Batra, Shavuot, Zevakhim, Nidah, and others.

Some of the [questions] contain nine answers. Among the answers, there is one to the Famous Gaon Rabbi, ABD, and head of the Yeshiva in Lviv.

Another book - "Mevaser Tzedek" [Heralding Justice] by him was published in a large format using Rashi letters. The book contains 44 pages and its content includes new interpretations of the Torah. R' Yisaskhar's son, R' Yehuda Leibish, R' Yisaskhar's grandson, R' Efraim Fishel, and R' Yisaskhar's son-in-law, R' Gershon Margaliot ABD Skalat, published the book.

Rabbi Avraham Khaim, Z'L, Author of Orakh LaKhaim" [A Way of Life]

R' Avraham was born in Zhovkva to his father, Gedalyahu, who was the ABD there. R' Avraham Khaim was a student of *Tzadikim* R' Shmelkeh of Nikolsburg and R' Shmelk's brother, R' Pinkhas, the author of the "Hafla'ah", ABD of Frankfurt, Z"L.

The first wife of the author of "Orakh LeKhaim" was the daughter of R' Pinkhas. After ten years without a child, he divorced her. For his second marriage, he married the daughter of R' Yisaskhar, the author of "Bat Eini", who was a rabbi in Zloczow. When R' Yisaskhar made Aliya to Eretz Israel, R' Avraham took his position as the rabbi at Zloczow. He lived a long life (older than ninety). He died on 26 Tevet 5576 [1816. The date given in the article - 5508-1848 is an error]. He was buried in Zloczow, and the community built a mausoleum ("a tent") on his grave.

Besides his book "Orach LeKhaim" he authored three more books: [Pri Khaim] about "Pirkei Avot" tractate and [Pri Khaim] about the Haggadah of Passover. He also wrote about the judgments and interoperations of the Rambam.

The book "Orakh LeKhaim" was one of Hassidism's elemental books. The content was about the interpretations of the Torah through the ways of the Kabbalah and Hassidism. The book is divided according to the five books of the Torah. The book contains 199 pages divided according to the following: Genesis - 43 pages starting on page 9, Exodus - 59, Leviticus - 29, Numbers - 37, and Deuteronomy – 31. The title page, Haskamot [approbations], and the introductions are included in the first nine pages. All of the Hassidism's greats are mentioned in the book: The Besht is mentioned without a title and only with the honorific Z"L [of blessed memory] –

[Columns 249-250]

"I heard from the Besht, Z"L.

Maggid, Rabbi Dov Ber of Mezritch, is mentioned on almost every page. The author used the honorifics: "The Holy Rabbi", "The Great and Holy Rabbi", or other similar honorifics.

The author of "Bat Eini"- the rabbi of Zloczow, is called - The Gaon Hasid" Yisaskhar Ber Z"L.

R' Mkhel of Zlczow is mentioned with the statement - "I heard from the Holy Rabbi Yekihiel Mikhel, Z"L.

The author quoted R' Levi of Bedychiv - "I heard from Gaon Rabbi Levi Yitzkhak from Berdychiv".

Teachers and Students at the "Talmud Torah"

The author quoted "the Mal'akh" [the angel], R' Avraham, with the words: "I heard from the "Famous Hasid, Butzina Kadisha [holy candle], Rabbi Avraham, the son of the *Tzadik*, Butzina Kadisha, the rabbi of the entire diaspora, Dov Ber.

He quoted R' Shmelk Horowitz of Nikolsburg – "I heard from "the Admor, Gaon, Rabbi, The famous Hasid Shmuel Shmelik, ABD of the holy community of Nikolsburg".

The author quoted the RIMENDEL [Rabbi Menakhem Mendel] of Premishlan with the honorifics - "Butzina Kadisha Moh"ar [our Teacher the Rabbi] Menakhem Mendikh ZLL"HH [of blessed memory for the life in the next world] from the Promishlan community".

The author also mentioned the Greek philosopher Aristo, several times. He gave him the title "the Devilish Greek".

Rabbi Yoel Ashkenazi Z"L

R' Yoel was born to his father, R' Moshe David Ashkenazi, ABD in the community of Tolcsva, Hungary. The father authored two books: "Toldot Adam" ["History of Adam"] about the Mishna tractates and "Be'er Sheva" about the Torah. R' Moshe David made Aliya, toward the end of his life, and accepted a position of ABD in the holy city of Safed, where he was buried.

His son was a colorful figure. Besides his genius, and justness, which went beyond what was customary for rabbis in his days, he excelled in many other attributes. These attributes, typical of the Torah greats of his generation were: extraordinary innocence and frugality. One could get a good picture of his noble soul from his sayings and small talks. He also excelled in writing, which was all in the form of rhymes and poetry. That talent is evident in his book "Responsa by the R"Y [Rabbi Yoel] Ashkenazi". Usually, other authors did not use poetry in such books. However, the author could not free himself from his flair.

We do not have any knowledge about his childhood. During his youth, he studied with the Gaon Rabbi Yaakov of Lissa, the author of "Khavat Da'at" [an opinion] about Sidur Tefilah and the book "Yoreh De'ah" [by Rabbi Yaakov Ben Asher]. That was how he became the son-in-law of the Rabbi of Lissa.

R' Yoel left an extensive family whose descendants married *Tzadikim* and Torah greats.

His son, Asher Anshil, married the daughter of the first Admor of Olesk, R' Khanokh Henikh, Z"L, the author of "Lev Same'akh" ["Happy Heart"] about the Torah.

His son-in-law, R' Khanania Yom Tov Lipah Teitelbaum, was the ABD of Sighet, Hungary.

R' Yoel taught many students, who later became rabbis in Jewish communities. Among his great students was the Gaon Rabbi Mordekhai HaKohen Schwadron, Z"L, author of "Mishpat Shalom" [Justice of Peace], about "Khoshen Mishpat" [the fourth part of By Rabbi Yaakov Asher's book] and some questions about the Maharsham [Rabbi Sholom Mordechai Schwadron], the Rabbi of Berezhany.

R' Yoel died in 5643 (1882) and was buried at the cemetery of Zloczow.

His book "Responsa by R" Y Ashkenazi" is about Halakhah and answers to questions he received on matters of the Halakhah. The book was published in 5653 [1892/3] in Mukachevo [Muncatch], with the effort of the author's grandsons, R' Yisrael Ashkenazi and R' Tzvi Hirsch Ashkenazi.

[Columns 251-252]

The book is divided into two parts: Orakh Khaim and Yoreh De'ah. There are 34 answers in the first book. As indicated above, the style in the book is poetic. Most of the people who submitted questions were from among the author generation's rabbis but some questions came from people who were not rabbis, for example, Siman vav [six] was asked by Zalman Halberthal, the father-in-law of R' Leibel Weinberger.

At the beginning of the book, there is an endorsement by the author's son-in-law, the rabbi from Sighet, and an introduction by the author's son, R'Asher Anshil.

Meshamshim Ba'Kodesh [Servers in Holiness]

R' Itzik David Shapira, A"H [may peace be upon him], served as a cantor and caretaker at the large synagogue. Since he worked once as a Torah scribe, he was called R' Itzik David Sofer [writer, scribe]. He used to attend weddings and other festive occasions. However, he was also the one who sang the 'El Maleh Rakhamim" at funerals.

He once belonged to the Chortkiv's Hasidim. However, when he became a cantor-caretaker, he ceased going to Chertkov. His son, Hershel Shapira, HY" D, who knew all of the melodies and compositions of Cantor Wineman, directed the chorus.

The synagogue had three gabbais: The first, R' Yudel Mandel was older and short-built. He taught little boys. Most of our Jewish townspeople studied with him.

The second gabbai was R' Khaim Perlmutter, a carpenter and an owner of a furniture store.

The third gabbai, was R' Elkanah Fogelfenger. He did not have any children and devoted himself to public affairs. His wife was also active in many of the charity institutions in the city, such as the nursing home, orphanage, and the Jewish hospital.

The small Synagogues

Two small synagogues existed in the corridor of the large synagogue. One had its windows directed toward the river, and the other had windows directed toward the street. People who did not want to pray in the large synagogue, for various reasons, prayed in the first one. During weekdays, they prayed there Tefilat Hashkama and during Shabbat, in two minyans: the first at 6 a.m. and the second at 8:30 a.m. Artisans and owners of large wagons prayed in the second one. Wagon owners traveled to Lviv and other places to bring products. They prayed early at dawn so that they could leave earlier. During the evenings, Torah was taught, and on Shabbat – Pirkei Avot in these two synagogues. On Shabbat, they have a person who led the service.

The caretaker in the second synagogue was R' Yerukham. He was a maker of Atarah's for tallits. He used to sit down at the special machine and embroider after the service. During the market days on Mondays, he had a unique occupation. There was always somebody who did not say a "kaddish" prayer in his own town before leaving for the market. R' Yerukham would go to search for people for a minyan and would receive a fee for his service.

It was customary to arrange for a big "Melaveh Malkah" [Escorting the Queen] meal, on Saturday nights. Many guests and the poor attended. The preparation for the "Melaveh Malka" meal began as early as mid-week. People were asked to contribute khallahs, fish, and borscht. The gabbai and a few helpers served the food. After the meal, they used to sing melodies for Shabbat.R' Yehuda Tzvi Fisher, A"H, served as a *maggid* [preacher] in the synagogue.

Folklore in the *Kloiz* of Zhydachiv [Ziditshov]

The *hillula* [festive celebration in memory] of the Great *Maggid*, R' Ber of Mezrich, ZTZ"L [may the memory of the righteous be a blessing], was held annually on 19 Kislev. Large banquets were held, on 3rd Kheshvan, as part of the *hillula* of R' Yisrael of Ruzhyn, ZTZ"L.

The preparations for an *hillula* were intensive. They lighted candles in all of the twelve windows and every available corner. Shlomo Kremnitzer, HY"D, took care of that. At times, they constructed a *hillula* lantern made of pieces of paper of various colors and hung it in the middle of the kloiz after they assembled a powerful electric bulb in it.

The Hasidim gathered at the kloiz about an hour after the "ma'ariv" [evening] prayer. They set around tables covered with purely white tableclothes and drank "le'khaim" chanting: "May his virtue stand us, and all the Jewish people, in good stead". After that, R' Mikhel Glazer A"H (named "The Storyteller") would tell stories about the *tzadik*, in memory of whom the hillula was held. Later on, they served small khalahs and cooked fish and took another drink "le'khaim" accompanied by the chanting of "May his virtue...". At the end festivity, they all sang in harmony.

Simkhat Torah Night

The Hasidim from the Rozhyn Hassidic dynasty, who prayed in the kloiz used to gather on Shemini Atzeret [a holiday that follows Sukkot and coincides with the holiday of Simkhat Torah]. They gathered at 3 p.m. at the sukkah of the grandfather, R' Khaim Tzvi Friedman. They drank good quality honey-water brought by the young Hasidim. According to the adults, the young, who received the drink from various people in the city, would drink some on the way home. To cover the shortage, they would stop by the spring to add water. The Hasidim suspected as much but did not have any proof.

In the evening they would bless each other by saying: "As we are privileged to sit today in this sukkah, we will be privileged to, someday, sit in a sukkah covered by the skin of a whale". They concluded the evening by singing "The Next Year in Jerusalem" and getting into a circle of a jubilant Hasidic dance.

[Columns 253-254]

The Kloiz's Worshippers

R' Fishel Reiz, A"H, was a Torah learned person. He liked to study the book "Sifrenu" ["Our Book"] (Torah Interpretation). He was the son-in-law of the Gaon Rabbi Yeshayah Zeev Rosenberg, Z"L, a rabbinical judge in Zloczow. His son was R' Elkana Riez, HY"D, liked to study. He was the son of R' Hirshel Shternberg, A"H.

The second son of Fishel – R' Moshe HY" D, the gabbai of the kloiz of the Admor of Chortkiv, was a Torah learned person. He studied the Torah and was also knowledgeable in German literature. He was able to quote, by heart, whole chapters from Goethe and Schiller's works.

R' Fishel Reiz's son-in-law, R' Volf Yosefsberg, A"H, was an educated scholar with a good heart. He was one of Chortkiv Hasidism greats. R' Fishel's other son-in-law, R' Pinkhas Kanner, HY" D, was a scholar and a pious man. He was diligent in studying the Torah and in his work.

The Schorr family: R' Naftali Schorr, A"H, was a strict Jew but provided his sons with modern education. His brother, R' Yaakov Schorr, A"H, was smart and educated. He liked to read modern Hebrew literature, such as Akhad Ha'Am's "Al Parashat Drakhim" ["At a Crossroad"]. That book was considered "unkosher and forbidden" [among the "Hassidim"]. Later on, R' Yaakov moved to pray at the "Ezart Israel" synagogue. He was one of the "Ha'Mizrakhi"'s [religious Zionist movement] activists.

R' Gadil Pasternak was a scholar and a Belz Hasid. He liked to joke, even about Hassidic matters.

R' Moshe Tannenbaum, A"H, who originated from Chrzanów [Kshanov], in Western Galitsia, was a Sanz Hasid. He was a Torah learned person who claimed that, in his youth, he knew R' Halberstam, ZTZ"L, the Rabbi of Sanz. He liked to "calculate the end" [the time of the coming of the Messiah].

R" Khaim Zeiden, A"H, was smart and a scholar. He was one of Chortkiv Hasidim's greats.

R' Khaim Nagler, A"H, was a Torah learned person and a Chortkiv Hasid.

R' Shmuel Tilles, A"H, – prayed close to the heater. He never had an idle conversation.

R' Shmuel Auerbach, A"H, was a Melamed of children. He was a dear Jew.

Yaakov, son of Eliyahu, served as an assistant caretaker. He had a compelling biography. Yaakov originated in Chernivtsi [Tzernovits] where he studied in high school. He failed the exams, became depressed, and ran away to Zloczow. In the beginning, he was ashamed and did not leave the kloiz. People brought him chicken and soup for him to the kloiz. Later on, he got accustomed to his situation, and became a beggar and a caretaker. He made sure that the sink is always full of water. He swept the floor and performed other dirty chores. He was praying, covered with an unusually small Tefillin. For a snack – he made a small hole in the floor of the kloiz and put in it a small piece of bread. He washed his hand, lay down flat on the ground, blessed over food, and took the piece of bread out of the hole with his teeth. All of that was to fulfill the commandment of the blessing: "Hamotzi lekhem min ha'aretz" [literally - "Blessed are You… who brings forth bread from the earth"].

During "Yartzeit" [an anniversary day of a *Tzadik's* death], when he was called up to the Torah reading, people asked him what was his vow. He would answer: "fifty thousand pails of water". He slept in the kloiz behind the heater. Years later, he began to gorge himself and drink. He used to sit [and drink] at Mishkovitz's tavern, whose daughter he secretly loved.

He used to keep a picture of emperor Franz Jozef in his pocket, take it out often, and kiss it.

And now, to the rest of the list of Zhydachiv Kloiz worshippers:
R' Medil Reiz, A"H, – an ultra-orthodox Jew who prayed in the first minyan. He lived far from the kloiz but came in daily at dawn. He belonged to the Belz Hasidim. He also served as a gabbai for many years.

R' Meshulam Reiz, A"H, was a Torah learned person who devoted time to studying Torah. He was a respectable and friendly person.

R' Alter Deutsch, A"H, - was an old fashion Jew and a descendant of a family of rabbis. He was one of the most distinguished people in town. He had a wholesale business.

R' Yaakov Shwartz, A"H, was a scholar and intellectual. He knew German literature comprehensively. He also secretly read modern Hebrew literature. He was not one of the Hasidim and liked to argue with them. He brought up some innovative interpretations of the Torah, about the weekly portion, and excelled as a pleasant conversationalist. He possessed pleasant manners. R' Yaakov was the son-in-law of R' Nakhman Gritz, Z"L, one of the city honorable.

R' shalom Imber, HY" D, was pious and G-d fearing to the extreme. He was a Chertkiv's Hasid and one of the activists of "Agudat Israel" [An ultra-orthodox and Hasidic party]. He was one of the founders of the ultra-orthodox girls' school "Beit Yaakov". His sons made aliya to Eretz Israel. The first son, Avraham, was one of the "Hekhalutz" [The Pioneer] movement firsts. He settled in Eretz Israel as early as during the twenties. The second son, Barukh, was among the founders of the "Torah and Avoda" [Torah and Work] movement in Zloczow. He attracted many students to the movement. In Eretz Israel, he was among the organizers of the kibbutz "Avraham". He witnessed the destruction of Etzion Bloc [during the Israel Independence war of 1948]. Today he lives with his family in Jerusalem.

[Column 255]

Laying a cornerstone to the "Talmud Torah" [school]

R' Barukh Hirsh Imber, HY" D, was a pious person and a scholar. He would wake up early, go to the Zhydachiv Kloiz, and study Torah for several hours before he turned to his business. R' Barukh was one of Chertkiv's Hasidim, although he did not travel to see the Chertkiv Rabbi as often. In his [book] shop, he used to browse books between one shopper to another.

R' Leizer Bakhunt, HY" D.

Yitzkhak Garfunkel, HY" D, was the son R' Nakhum, HY" D.

R. Shalom Auerbach, A"H, the son-in-law of R' Yehoshua Zeiden, A"H. He was a fan of Chertkiv's Hasidim. He owned a cigarette and tobacco shop. During weekdays, he prayed at the "Ezrat Israel" synagogue.

R' Khaim Pardes, A"H, was a G-d fearing man and an enthusiastic Husiatyn Hasid. He liked to study the book "Toldot [Yaakov Yosef]", the classic book of the Hasidic literature pioneer R' Yaakov Yosef ben Tzvi HaKohen Katz of Polonne, the great student of the Besht, ZTZ"L.

R' Limelekh Rezen was a learned G-d fearing person and a follower of the Admor from Chertkiv. He served as a teacher in "Talmud Torah".

R' Shmuel Yitzkhak Imber, A"H, was a scholar. He was among the Chretkiv's Hasidim greats. He devoted most of his time to studying Torah.

[Column 256]

When R' Shmuel Yitzkhak became older and weak, he prayed in the minyan of Rabbi Leizer, Z"L [of blessed memory], close to his home.

R' Hirsh Halberthal, Z"L, was a scholar. He was one of the Belz Hasidim. He used to lead the prayer during Shabbat and holidays. His son, Zalman, was one of the activists of the movement "Tzeirei Agudat Israel" [The youths of Agudat Israel]. The other son was a scholar. He studied at the Zhydachiv Kloiz. The family survived the Holocaust and settled in Belgium.

The Small *Kloiz*

Near the Zhydachiv Kloiz, which was called in Yiddish "De Groiseh Kloiz" [the Large *Kloiz*], was another synagogue called "Das Kleineh Kleizel" [the "Small *Kloiz*"]. "House owners" with a slant toward Hasidism, prayed in that *kloiz*. Spiritually, they were under the influence of the people of the "Large *Kloiz*". For many years, the spiritual leader of the "Small *Kloiz*" was R' Itzik Friedman, A"H. He was partially educated. He was versed in religious philosophy. Such philosophy expressed in books like "Moreh Nevokhim" ["The Guide for the Perplexed"], "Akedat Yitzkhak" ["Binding of Isaac"], and *"Ba'al Ma'alah"* ["A Man of Virtues"]. The latter title is what people used to call somebody, like R' Itzik, who could read and lead the prayers, and somebody who could read the Torah.

During the High Holy Days, he always read the "Musaf Prayer", and on Shabbat, the Torah Chapter and the chapter from the tractate "Avot" preceded by "Midrash Shmuel".

A short-built Jew, R" Leizer Ekhoiz, A"H, served as the gabbai in the *kloiz*. I recall that during harsh winters, with minus thirty degrees outside, the gabbai used to come in at 3 a.m. to light the heater. People who came to study at 4:30 a.m. in the "Large K*loiz*" stopped by the "Small *Kloiz*" because it was illuminated and warm. When R' Leizer passed away, all the people, from large and the small *kloizes* came to his funeral.

R' Tzvi Hirsh, served as a gabbai after R' Leizer. He managed the *kloiz* forcefully, as he considered the position a big promotion for him. He originated in Sasiv, near Zloczow. He used to host a large banquet on 4 Shvat (on the day of the *Hillula* of the *Tzadik Admor*, Rabbi Moshe Leib of Sasiv). R' Tzvi claimed that he had previously experienced a miracle on that day.

The Small Kloiz's Worshippers

R' Avraham Tzverdling, A"H, was a wealthy Jew who was the owner of a large iron store.

His son-in-law, R' Yisrael Amrent, A"H, - educated and innovator. He was a scholar and reader of the Torah. He taught lessons about the Torah weekly chapters in the small synagogue.

[Columns 257-258]

His other son-in-law, R' Merkil Smal, A"H, was a pious and G-d fearing Jew. He owned an iron Store.

R' Merkil's son, R' Bentzion Tzverdling - an educated man, a scholar, and an activist who lives today in Haifa, Israel

R' Yisrael Wolfshoit, A"H, - an ultra-orthodox man. He loved music and used to entertain at the "Third Meal" held in the Small *Kloiz*, singing zmirot [religious songs].

His son, Mordekhai Deutsch, was a scholar and educated man. He was among the best students at Zhydachiv Kloiz. He was the student of Rabbi Shmuel Shapira, Z"L, who was a rabbinical judge and the ABD our city. He married the daughter of R' Henikh Tripp, A"H, from Ternopil, who was a scholar and one of the Husiyatin Hasidim's greats. R' Mordekhai settled in Israel and is managing a CREDIT UNION.

R' Yaakov Nagler A"H - a pious man, a tinsmith, and an owner of a store. He used to wake up early in the morning, pray the psalms, and study chapters of the Mishnah. He prayed in the first Minyan. He was an activist. He a member of the union, "Yad Kharutzim" [a union of craftsmen and academics], and of the bank owned by his union. He was fortunate to make Aliya to Ertz Israel and died there at an old age. However, his wife, Mrs. Tzila, who was very pleasant and educated, died in the diaspora.

R' Avraham Gutman, HY" D, - was a learned man, an activist in public affairs. He was a member of the steering committee of the "Agudat Israel" movement and the steering committee of the community. He provided religious and general education to his son. he made a living from his haberdashery store.

R' Gedalia Printz, A"H. He used to pray in a loud voice and tells stories and jokes. His son, Moshe, was a member of the "Hamizrakhi" movement.

R' Yosef Goldshtein, A"H, was a pious and G-d fearing man and a fan of the Rozhyn Hasidim.

R' Yosef Hollander, A"H, - was a pious man. He was reading from a Torah. He liked to tell stories.

Sterlisk-Stratyn Kloiz

Hasidic Scholars prayed in that kloiz. They prayed exceptionally enthusiastically.

Rabbi R' Yisrael Landau, Z"L - He prayed there regularly.

R' Betzalel Apter, Z"L, led the prayer there, during the High Holy Days. He immigrated to the U.S. but returned later on. The cantor was the son of R' Shlomo, R' Shalom Mendel, HY" D. He had an exceptionally pleasant voice, which people liked. He became the cantor in the large synagogue after the passing of R' Itzik David Shapira.

R' Avish[ai?] Tzipper, A"H, one of the Olesk Hasidim greats, served as a gabbai of that kloiz for many years. He used to wake up at two a.m. and go to the kloiz to pray "Tikun Khatzot" [of Midnight Rectification"]. He used to host many guests from among Olesk Hasidim and other guests.

When Stratyn Kloiz became an "Aguda [Association] of Beit Sterlisk-Stratyn" and was registered as such with the authorities. It then became the center of the movement of "Agudat Israel". Elections were held there for a steering committee and a chairman like in any other association.

Stratyn Kloiz was filled with a crowd of worshippers on Shabbats and weekdays. They excelled in charity activities.

Stratyn *Kloiz* Worshippers

R' Khaim Mikhel Aizen, A"H, was a scholar who devoted much of his time to studying the Torah. He was prominent Olesk Hasid, and among the regular examiners at "Talmud Torah" school and Yeshiva "Orakh Le'Kahim".

R' Avraham Yehoshua Varim, A"H, was a profound scholar. People called him R' Yehosha'l Batkover because he leased an estate in Batkiv [Batkov]. He used to study thoroughly. He also belonged to the regular examiners' group at "Talmud Torah". When the student saw him coming, they began to tremble from fear and began to look for excuses not to be tested by him.

R" Mikhel Glazer was from among the strictest testers. He had another custom: he used to ask a question and did not allow the tested student to answer it. He told the student:" I did not ask this question for you to answer, but for you to understand the question".

Students were happy to see Rabbi R' Shmuel Shapira, Z"L, because he was not as strict.

The students were even happier to see R' Yaakov Shwartz A"H. He used to review the Gemarah quickly and did not test on Rashi.

Other worshippers at the Stratyn Kloiz were:

R' Efraim Shapira, HY" D, was a follower of the Rabbi from Sasiv. He was a public activist.

R' Yehoshua Stertinner, A"H, was a scholar and an enthusiastic Hasid, follower of the Rabbis from Stratyn dynasty. He was fortunate to be able to make Aliya to Eretz Israel with his wife. He lived several years in Jerusalem. He taught Gemarah and Mishnah there. He died in Tel-Aviv and was buried in Jerusalem. He left sons and daughters in Israel.

R' Khaim Katz, A"H - a Torah learned person, was one of the eminent Stratyn Hasidim. He was one of the leaders of the "Agudat Israel" movement in Zloczow and one of the people who formed its image. He was a public activist and charity activist. He was a representative in the community steering committee and an activist for the school "Beit Yosef". He was fortunate to be able to make Aliya to Eretz Israel with his wife. He passed away in Haifa at an old age

[Column 259]

R' Khaim Katz

R' Levi Bukhoit - was a wealthy and respectable merchant, activist, and philanthropist. He was the son-in-law of R' Pinkhas Kener.

R' Elyakim Yeshaya Katz, A"H. He was a great learner. He was one of the Belz Hasidim who belonged to "Agudat Israel". He owned a leather factory.

R' Yisrael Kener, Z"L , was known to be clever and wise.

R' Uri Shapira, A"H, was a scholar. He was one of the Belz Hasidim who belonged to "Agudat Israel". On Shabbat, R' Uri prayed with R' Leizer, Z"L. He owned a leather store.

R' Shaul Raller, HY" D. He was an ultra-orthodox Jew who supported several institutions, especially the "Agudat Israel" movement, where he served as a chairman. He was a philanthropist. In 1910, following the death of Rabbi Feivil Rohatyn, Z"L, the city remained without a head of the rabbinical court. Several candidates competed over the position. The candidates came from the "Ha'Mizrakhi" Religious Zionist movement and "Agudat Israel" [Ultra-orthodox movement]. Some candidates were unaffiliated. A fierce battle developed between the Zionists and "Ha'Mizrakhi" on one side, and "Agudat Israel" on the other. As the chairman of "Agudat Israel", R' Shaul Raller was the fiercest opponent to "Ha'Mizrakhi's" rabbis. His opinion was the decisive one.

R' Elkana Katz was a remnant of the old generation who wanted to preserve public praying and Torah lessons. He was an Olesk Hasid. His son, Zvulun Katz, lives today in Tel Aviv.

R' Mordekhai Tzipor, HY" D, was a Torah learned man. He was one of the heads of "Agudat Israel", and the chairman of the association "Bikur Kholim", which helped many poor families.

R' Shmarya Imber, A"H, was a pious man and a Zionist. He liked to argue with anybody whose Zionist views were not as developed as his. He was blessed with "good hands" and used that talent to maintain the holy tools and assist in taking care of the needs of the public. When the water heater broke in the Mikveh [public ritual bath], they called R' Shmarya. He was fortunate to make Aliya with his wife and died at an old age.

[Column 260]

His son, Yekhiel, was considered to be one of the best among the youths of Stratyn Kloiz. He lives now in Israel and is known to be an educated person.

Rinteh Villig, HY" D, was a pious, clever, and moderate man. He was one of the influential leaders and advisors of "Agudat Israel". He was a representative of "Agudat Israel" in the community steering committee and the municipality. His son, Yaakov Villig, HY" D, was among the leaders of the Zionist movement and its representative at the municipal management team. He was known for his good nature.

R' Nakhman Helbron, A"H, was a slaughterer and an [Kosher] inspector. He was involved in society and welcomed everybody with a smile. His son R' Neteh and his son-in-law R' Frumer reside in Australia.

R' Leibeleh Vielkatch, A"H, was a learned dear Jew. He never raised his voice or was angry with anybody. He ran a kheder in his apartment and taught his student Talmud with interoperations.

R' Moshe Marder, A"H - used to interrupt his work to pray in a minyan.

Yosef Katz, A"H, was one of the Stratyn Kloiz caretakers He originated from a town in the Zboriv District. He did not stay as a guest at someone's home and cooked his meals in a pot. He washed his body, the pot, and his clothes in the spring next to the great synagogue.

R' Shlomo Mandel was a scholar and exceptionally pious. He used to dress in his Shabbat clothes early on Fridays, go out to the city, and walk from one store to the other to warn the owners to close in time before the commencement of the Sabbath. R' Shlomo was an enthusiastic follower of the Stratyn rabbis. On Friday night, he made sure to host the needy, even though he was not wealthy.

R' Arye Leib Berinstein, A"H, was an educated Jew who studied the Rambam daily. He liked to tell that he was among the firsts who read Kalman Schulman's [abbreviated translation of] "The Mysteries of Paris".

R' David Buterman – was the son-in-law of R' Shlomo Mitis.

R' Yosef Brandeis, A"H, was a Torah-learned man. He studied the "Yerushalmi" [Jerusalem Talmud]. He liked to tease people about their knowledge of "Piyyut Kasheh" [any dreadful poem]. His "hobby" was to play the "devil's advocate".

The Printz brothers – R' David and R' Moshe. They used to pray enthusiastically in Stratyn Hasidim's style.

R' Yaakov Belzer, A"H, was a slaughterer and inspector. He was one of the old-timers of Stratyn Hasidim. He used to host Admors in his home. His son R' Eliyahu A"H was a slaughterer and inspector as well. His other sons Hirsh Eliezer, HY"D was one of the principal supporters of Rabbi Yisrael Landau, Z"L.

R' Nakhum Garfunkel was one of the city's old-timers. He was an educated and clever person. He was a merchant of construction material.

[Columns 261-262]

R' Khaim and R' Moshe Shapira, the sons of R' Efraim, HY"D, were known for their tenderness and education.

"Ezrat Israel' Synagogue

Mordekhai Deutsch, A"H, invested all of his fortune and life to establish the synagogue. He was an innocent Jew who prepared his gravestone when he was still alive. The picture of the synagogue was etched on it.

The goal of "Ezrat Israel" was to help people in various areas. For example, they helped a sick person who could not afford to hire anybody, by sending somebody from "Ezrat". They would also provide teachers to teach "Mishnah', the book "Ein Yaakov", and other topics. Employees of the court, custom, and even homeowners prayed there.

R' Yehuda Tzvi Zeltz, A"H - served as "*Ba'al Musaf*" [The leader of the Musaf prayer] during the High Holy Days.

R' Matel Gruber, A"H - served as the cantor and gabbi, and "*Ba'al Shakharit*" [The leader of Shakharit prayer].

R' Velvel Shapira, A"H, who had an exceptionally good memory, served as the caretaker. He remembered the birthdays and other strange things about everyone.

The number of people who prayed at that synagogue multiplied when most of the members of the "HaMizrakhi" organization transferred to it. R' Yitzkhak Friedman, A"H, the chairman of the "HaMizrakhi" in the city, became the leader of the Musaf prayer, during the High Holy Days. R' Mikhel Kuhan and Moshe Tiekhman A"H became the synagogue's gabbaim.

The Worshippers of "Ezrat Israel" Synagogue

Dr. Werpel, A"H - one of the heads and trailblazers of the Zionist movement. He was a leading activist and the chairman of the "Ivria" club (a Hebrew drama club).

R' Avraham Kreger, A"H, and his sons, R' Nakhum Kreger, A"H, and R' Yaakov Kreger, A"H. R' Yaakov was a champion of charity. His wife, Mrs. Rivka, A"H, was an activist who acted for the benefit of the orphanage. R' Yaakov was fortunate to make Aliya to Eretz Israel with his wife Frida may she live long. He died at an old age.

R' Yitzkhak Ruten, A"H - one of the "HaMizrakhi" movement's leaders and speakers.

R' Leibush Fiering, A"H - was a public activist and was influential in matters related to public affairs.

R' Aizik Menkes, A"H - the son of R' Leib Berinstein, moderate, knowledgeable but did not involve himself in politics.

R' Aizik Menkes, A"H - a pious man who taught sections of the Mishnah to the public [the name Izik Menkes appears twice in the original article].

R' Ginsberg, A"H, worked in the court. He loved to listen to leaders of Hasidic prayers.

R' Khaim Leib Klahr, HY"D – was from among the activists of the "HaMizrakhi" movement. He was one of the people who selected the head of the rabbinical court.

R' Meir Leibush Drumer, A"H – an educated Jew. He was from among the people who established the 'HaMizrakhi" movement in Zloczow. He prayed in Kloiz Stratyn on weekdays.

Dr. Shekhtel was a quiet man who did not involve himself in politics.

R' Menashe Groskopf, A"H, used to work in the forests. When he got old, he became an inspector of bills, which he listed in his notebook. He lived in the house of R' Yaakov Aharonfries, A"H, opposite of the "Ezrat" synagogue. He liked to tell stories about Hasidim.

The "Yad Kharutzim" Organization

"Yad Kharutizim" ["Assiduous Hand"] was an organization of craftsmen whose management was elected democratically. People with free professions were also members of the organization. For example, the engineer Berl, A"H, served as the organization's chairman for many years.

"Yad Kharutzim" was located in a large building. The first floor contained a synagogue, ornated with beautiful pictures. A large hall for weddings and balls was located on the second floor. Many balls were held there to raise funds for the nursing home, orphanage, soup kitchen, and other charities. The "Hand" owned a bank, which provided loans at low interest to whoever needed a loan, including non-members.

"Yad Kharutizim" Worshippers

R' Yaakov Rekht, from among the founders of the "Yad" and its chairman for many years. He was active in his community. He frequently participated in activities related to public needs and expressed his views in public. He lives today in the U.S.

R' Leon Nadel, A"H, was a master tailor and a shop owner.

R' Yisrael was one of the leaders of the "Yad". He was one of the few whose occupation was to saw Hasidim clothing, such as capotes, razubelka's [?], etc...

R' Wolf Rezen, A"H, was a master tailor and an owner of a tailor's shop.

R' Zalman Lifshitz was an exceptional tailor. He employed many assistants.

[Column 263]

R' Yitzkhak Schwadron

R' Daniel Zvierhoif, A"H, was an ultra-orthodox craftsman. He actively participates in public activities.

R' Hirshel Landau, A"H, was a craftsman of women's clothing. One of the dedicated people of the synagogue and a public affairs activist.

The Synagogue Near the Polskikh [Polish Church?]

The synagogue was called the "Cadet Minyan" because veterans probably once prayed in it. That synagogue served anybody who, for one treason or the other, left their previous synagogue. It also served people who liked to lead the prayer or read the Torah. Everyone was accepted with open arms, and the members tried their best to fulfill newcomers' wishes. R' David Tzeidel, A"H, served as the gabbai in the synagogue.

The Worshippers at the Synagogue Near the Polskikh

R' Shmuel Pesil, HY" D, - a pious man, wealthy and involved with the public. One of the activists of the "Talmud Torah". He gave his son a Torah education. He used to lead the prayer. He used to pray in the minyan of R' Leizer. His son, Mordekhai Pesil, was a scholar and educated. One of the best students in kloiz Zydochyv. Mordekhai resides in Israel today. His second son, R' Leiba'le Pesil, HY" D, was a scholar who became a teacher. He was a thinker with refined views and a good soul.

R' Shmuel's son-in-law, R' Moshe Eliezer, A"H, the son of R' Mendel Riez, was a person with a delicate soul and good manners. He died at a young age.

[Column 264]

The second son-in-law of R' Shmuel, Mr. Segal, HY" D, was a Torah educated and one of the prominent members of the "HaMizrakhi" movement.

The Synagogue of Rabbi R' Yisrael'tzi, HY" D

The synagogue was called – "the synagogue near the water". The people who prayed there were the followers of R' Barukh, his son-in-law "der Rabbi Burekh'l" and the followers of the Admor R' Nakhum ZTz"l, of Bilyi Kamin, whom R' Yisrael'tzi was the grandson of. The latter was a scholar who traveled to Chortkiv. He was a fan of the Kloiz of Zhydachiv and Stratyn. On weekdays, when he did not have a minyan, he came to the kloiz and talk to the youths about Torah matters and Hasidic phrases.

Once, a sad incident occurred once to the minyan of R' Yisrael'tzi. On one Friday night, a candle was left burning at the amud [prayer leader podium], near the holy ark. Two Torah books burned in the fire that erupted. On Sunday, a funeral for the Torah books took place, and they were buried in the cemetery.

R' Shalom Toiv[?] Z"L from Sasiv, who came especially for the funeral, gave a eulogy that left a deep impression on people. He gave his eulogy outdoors at the square of the large synagogue. He blamed people who are not diligent about keeping Kosher and about the purity of the family.

The Synagogue of Rabbi R' Eliezer Wugschal Z"L

Various people prayed at that synagogue - homeowners as well as Hasidim. The latter came because R' Eliezer was the grandson of Belz and Olesk *Tzadikim*. He would lead the prayer himself during the High Holy Days. He had a nice appearance and a pleasant voice. He was known to have a kind demeanor and friendly attitude. The synagogue contained a section for women, where the wives of Zhydachiv Kloiz Hasidim prayed. I recall that my grandmother, Mrs. Drezil, my mother, and all of my aunts from my father and mother's families, prayed there during the High Holy Days. Rabbi Eliezer's wife continued to hold the *minyan* after the rabbi passed away.

R' Eliezer's son made Aliya to Eretz Israel and lived in Jerusalem with his wife. They both passed away during the same period. Another son of R' Eliezer, R' Yekhiel, lived for several years in Argentina, later made aliya tom Eretz Israel.

Another son, R' Shalom, who made Aliya many years ago, lives in Jerusalem.

The Worshippers at the Synagogue of Rabbi Eliezer Z"L

R' Aharon Arat, HY" D, a Torah educated person, was a member of "Agudat Israel". He was a moderate who served in the community management team. He often served as a conflict mediator.

[Columns 265-266]

His son, Nakhum Arat, HY" D, was one of the best youths of Kloiz Stratyn. He was Torah educated and from among the activists of "Tzeirei Agudat Israel" [The youth of "Agudat Israel"].

R' Leibish Tietil, HY" D, was a lawyer and Torah educated. He was one of Belz Hasidim.

His son, R' Yitzkhak Tietil, HY" D, was Torah educated and enlightened. He woke up early in the morning to go to the Stratyn Kloiz to study. As a member of "Tzeirei Agudat Israel", he was one of the activists in the cultural and religious area. For a long time, he lectured the "Daf Yomi" [Daily Talmud chapter], for all the members.

R' Yaakov Kahana, A"H, the patriarch of the Kahana family, currently residing in Israel. That honorable person was a Startyn Hasid.

The *Minyan* Of R' Menakhem Mendil Miller, Z"L

R' Miller originated in Tarnów [Ternov], in Western Galicia, a city of scholars and writers. He was a prominent scholar who loved the longwinded debate and the in-depth study customary in Western Galicia. His followers prayed in his *minyan*. There was also a "women's section". Women whose husbands prayed in other synagogues also prayed there.

R' Menakhem Mendil belonged to Sanz Hasidim. When he talked about the Admor R' Khaim [Halberstam of Sanz], he became ecstatic.

The Institution and the *Minyan* of the "Nursing Home"

That was an institution where older people, who had to leave their homes for various reasons, found a roof above their heads. In their loneliness, they found a shelter filled with love, something that they needed the most. The building was distanced somewhat from the center of town and was surrounded by a tree garden. There were marriages between the instruction's residents. The community established the institution, but there was also the need for donations and charity balls to keep it going. The institution's residents prayed in the synagogue there, but city residents were often invited to solicit donations.

The Minyan of R' Yisrael Landau, Z"L

R' Yisrael Landau a radiant and colorful figure. He was a descendant of the family of R' Gaon Yekhezkel Landau, ZTz "L, the ABD of Prague, and the author of the responsa books "Noda b'Yehuda" ["Known in Judah"] and "Kamah v'Tninah". R' Yekhezkel was the grandson of [Rabbi Elazar Segal Landau] the author of "Yad ha'Melekh". He originated in Brody. He lived many years in Kyiv as a wealthy man. However, after the war, when his financial situation was not as bright, he settled in Zloczow and served as a rabbinical judge. He was very knowledgeable about the Torah and was G-d fearing man. He was a Sterlisk-Stratyn Hasid. He prayed with great intensity and a pleasant voice according to the Startyn Hasidic style, During the High Holy Days, he led the praying. I still recall him praying "Nishmat Kol Khai" prayers and how he managed to move people by singing "ve'Kol ha'Levavot…" ["All hearts shall fear You, and all innermost feelings and thoughts shall sing praises to Your name"].

For many years, R' Yisrael prayed in Kloiz Stratyn. However, in his old age, when lost his vision, he prayed at home.

One of his great supporters was R' Shaul Raler HY" D, who gave the Rabbi a spacious apartment in his big house located on the main street, Ternopoler Shtraseh, and also supported him significantly. R' Yisrael authored a book by the name "Nefesh Khaya" ["Living Soul"] in memory of his daughter, Khaya, A"H. His son, Dr. Landau, A"H, was an ultra-orthodox Jew. He had a noble soul with a heart for charity, suited for such a family.

"The Association of the Coffin Bearers"

The objective of this association was to handle all burial matters.

I recall that an epidemic erupted in Zloczow, which caused many deaths. R' Leib Shreiber, from among the best youths of Kloiz Zydochyv who resided for many years in America, returned to the city at the same period. Upon his return, he established the "Association of the Coffin Bearer". He, himself, was the association's chairman. A nice two-stories house was built for the association not long after that. A glorious synagogue was located on the first floor, and on the second – a large wedding hall. Some people wondered: "What does a wedding hall have to do with such an association?" The association people responded:" We bury on the first floor, and wed on the second"

The management team was elected democratically, an election, which was preceded by a turbulent campaign.

———

[Columns 267-268]

Zloczow's Poets

By Ron Tzimmer

Translated by Moshe Kutten

Eastern Galitsia was always the land of struggle and unrest. The cultures western and eastern cultures met there. The land served as the background for a scene of the momentous culture clash between the Russian-Benzathine world and the Western Catholic world.

Various nations settled in Eastern Galitsia: Poles, Ukrainians, Tatars, Jews, and settlers from Germany and Czechoslovakia. These nations battled each other about the ruling religion, the language, and the regime.

The major currents of Judaism- Hasidism, Enlightenment, and Zionism, plowed deeply in Galtisia.

Hasidism grew on Eastern Galitsia's border while Brody, Ternopil, Lviv, and Zhovkva [Zholkiv] became the centers of the Enlightenment movement. And so, the youths who live in a compressed atmosphere in those cities and towns absorbed the yearning for changes and a different world. As poverty advanced more and more, the big immigration wave swelled.

During the 19th century, rich Jewish literature thrived. The Jewish authors wrote in German, Hebrew, Yiddish, and Polish. The enlightened people mocked the Yiddish language but needed it to spread their ideas. The Yiddish development accelerated, yielding outstanding results. And so, the Jewish folklore songs and Jewish humor together with the sarcastic political writings and philosophical and religious thinking flourished.

In Zloczow, the mystic atmosphere, deep religious feelings, and the aspiration for progress all lived side by side.

Naphtali Hertz Imber embodied the character of that period. Born in [Zloczow] in 1856, he lived through the entire spectrum of Jewish fate of that time. A wanderer throughout his entire life he experienced poverty and suffering. He went from yearning for Zion to being a pioneer and a settler in Eretz Israel. He witnessed the doings of the pioneers of the BILU movement, which founded the colonies of Rishon Le'Tzion and Zikhron Yaakov. They aroused enthusiasm and warm feelings in him. He sang the songs of the awakening homeland and its beloved children. He became the troubadour-poet of the First Aliya movement. In his poetry, the memories of the nation's past were carried on the wings of dreams about a shining future.

> Hear, oh my brothers in the lands of exile,
> The voice of one of our visionaries,
> [Who declares] that only with the very last Jew,
> Only then is the end of our hope!
>
> To my homeland, I sing, hastening the future,
> to me people I chant, astonish their hearts.

Jerusalem is in my thoughts and depths of my heart
to Zion-Zion my harp is dedicated!

In my vision, I see - the End of Days,
when my people will rise and endure.
It will round a herd, harrow furrows,
and wonder no more among other nations!

The last verse of the poem **"After the Destruction"**:

And one oath they swore,
the Children of Israel,
relax they would not,
until their homeland is redeemed.
*

Do you remember, mother?
the time I slept in my cradle,
And be thy singing with me
I listened to it coming from your lips.

Under my son's cradle,
a young goat is now standing.
The young goat will trade goods,
and my son will learn Torah.

In almonds and pomegranates
The young goat will trade.
Clever books
my son will write.

[Column 269]

The author Shmuel Yaakov Imber

In my ears, they are still ringing
The tones of your singing,
In my ears, they are still humming
the melodies of your love.

The almonds and pomegranates
the baby goats have eaten.
Even the clever books
Worn out from old age.

Oh, the time has passed so fast,
I growl like a lion,
I became a man
And the baby goat became a billy goat.

Shmuel Yaakov Imber, a cousin of the poet of "HaTiqva" [Naphtali Hertz Imber] and the son of the author Shmarya Imber was born in 1889. He was a poet, translator, and journalist. He absorbed from Polish, German, and Ukrainian literature. He was a modernist who looked for contacts with the literature of other cultures throughout the world. He acquired a wide education and developed refined humor and sentiment. He was a fierce polemicist. He was a pioneer of modern Yiddish poetry in Galitsia. His first collection of poems was published under the title "Vos ikh zing un zog" ["What I sing and say"]. He authored the poem "Esterkeh" and the travel book about his trip to Eretz Israel "Ain Yidisheh Land" ["In Jewish land"]. He perished in Zloczow's ghetto in 1942.

The field wouldn't say anything to me anymore

The field wouldn't say anything to me anymore,
The forest would not sing again,
the songs it used to sing
to a young yearning heart.

[Column 270]

The distance wouldn't say anything to me anymore
nor would the allure of the sky edges,
I would not recognize the stars,
Your handwriting, oh G-d.

Am I really so close,
Oh G-d to your eternal tranquility,
that I can't anymore see your wonders,
becoming absorbed in them like You?

The most tragic figure among Zloczow's poets was Moshe Leyb Halpern, born in January 1866 and died in New York in August 1932. He never found repose. The big metropolis of New York, with its noise and toughness – alienated him. He struggled to survive and did not find any friends or allies.

Tempestuous with a strong imagination, Halpern searched, in his delicate poems, an outlet for his poetic soul. He tended to embrace the sublime but was arrested within the cruel framework of a cynical reality, which destroys the person with his dreams and aspirations toward good and beautiful.

Moshe Leyb's were lyrical, often sarcastic, and sometimes full of mischievous humor. Some poems were melancholic, naturalist, and slight as slightest could be. Some others are filled with an expectation for a miracle, saturated by tenderness, like an old melody. He had everything in his poetry.

["My Restlessness is Like a Wolf's"]

Translated by Kathryn Hellerstein

I am not what I want, I am not what you think,
I am the magician and I'm the magic trick.

…

I am the fiddle, the drum, and the bass

Of three old musicians who play in the street.
I am the children's dance, and by moonlight
I am the fool longing to enter the blue land.

…

Now I am a candle lit for a dead soul,

…

Now I am the sentiment—the sadness in a glance
That longed for me a century in advance.

…

Now I am the night that commands me to grow tired,
The thick night fog, the quiet evening song.

[Column 271]

[Yosef Kita'ee – The Religion Teacher in Uniform]

["Our Garden"]

Translated by Kathryn Hellerstein

What a garden, where the tree is
Bare but for its seven leaves!
It appears to be amazed:
"Who has set me in this place?"

What a garden, what a garden -
It takes a magnifying glass
Just to see a little grass.
Can this be our garden, then,

Just as is, in the light of dawn?
Sure, it's our garden. What else?

...

What a bird – quick to forget
All the fledglings in its nest.
Doesn't carry food along,
Doesn't sing their morning song.
What a bird, oh, what a bird –
Doesn't lift a single wing,
Or try to fly, or anything.
Can this be our own bird, then,
Just as is, in the light of dawn?
Sure, it's our bird. What else!

He is the Jewel [1]

["Gingeli" - the original name of the poem]

Translated by Kathryn Hellerstein

Oh, Gingeli, my bleeding heart,
Who is the guy who dreams in snow
And drags his feet like a pair of logs
In the middle of the street at night?

He is that jewel Moyshe-Leyb,
Who will freeze someday
While he fantasizes flowers,
Blossoms in the spring;
He will lie in the snow
And not stir anymore,
And, in his dreams, he will
Stroll through cornfields.

Moyshe Leyb, that jewel, dreams
The watchman sings tri-li-li,
The hobo answers with a sneeze,
The puppy yaps,
The kitten meows.

Oh, Gingeli, my bleeding heart,
Who crawls back and forth in the snow,
And thinks he's by a fireplace
In the middle of the street at night?

He is that jewel Moyshe-Leyb,
Who is too lazy to think.
He freezes in the snow and sees
A palace, closed in every wing;
The palace is guarded by sentries
And he himself is the king,
And all his years pass by
Like the sun in the evening.

[Columns 273-274]

Moyshe-Leyb, that jewel, longs,
The watchman sings tri-li-li,
The hobo answers with a sneeze,
The puppy yaps,
The kitten meows.

Oh, Gingeli, my bleeding heart,
Who curls threefold on himself
And hops in the streetlamp light
In the middle of the street at night?

He is that jewel Moyshe-Leyb,
Who stops in the snow to dance
So his feet won't freeze
Completely in his trance.
He sees snowflakes on his sleeve
Like blossoms in sunlight,
And girls with hair let loose
Adorned with fire-wreaths.

Moyshe-Leyb, that jewel, dances,
The watchman sings tri-li-li,
The hobo answers with a sneeze,
The puppy yaps,
The kitten meows.

"The Street Drummer"

Translated by Kathryn Hellerstein

Free and happy, the bird sings.
Trembling on their throne sit kings.
I don't think it's wise to tremble.
I sing like a bird, and nimble
As the wind,
I dance blindly and I spin

Through the streets. I'm sick, old, gray,
Who cares?
For a copper penny
I will play –
Drum until the drum explodes!
Beat upon cymbals!
Round and round I whirl and spin.
Jin, jin, boom-boom-boom.
Boom boom Jin!

Translator's Note:

1. The word "Takhshit" translates literally as "jewel". However, the word is also used cynically to describe a troublemaker and a mischievous child

[Columns 275-276]

The Synagogues and Praying Houses

by David Imber

Translated by Moshe Kutten

A. The Big Synagogue

Zloczow people were known to love and be knowledgeable about cantorship and singing. They used to say that even the "*Shtenders*" (those who used to stand behind the seats), were knowledgeable in cantorship. The Big Synagogue was old. According to tradition, it was built under the sponsorship of King Jan Sobieski.

An enormous stone was fixed in the middle of the ceiling. According to a legend, the builders could not lift the stone from the ground and put it in its place. That legend stated that one of the *Lamed Vav Tzadikim* (36 righteous ones) who possessed great power lifted it and fixed it in his place. The following day, the man died. He received great respect at his funeral as he risked his life and sacrificed himself for the holiness of the synagogue and its glory.

The first cantor of the Big Synagogue, who lived about a hundred years ago, was R' Neteh Schorr A" H [may peace be upon him]. He was pious and prayed with enormous enthusiasm.

He died on Yom Kippur, at the synagogue, in the middle of his singing of the Yom Kippur's prayer. He received a heart attack out of his enthusiasm. He kneeled down and died on the spot.

After him, R' Avraham Trakhtenberg A" H accepted the position of a cantor. He served for several years. Later on, he immigrated to the USA. He acquired many admirers, among them, R' Menly, who was rich and loved the cantor tremendously. R' Menly said that if he would not be able to listen to the cantor during his life, he wished that the cantor would pray "*El Maleh Rakhamim*" [literally - "Merciful G-d" - a prayer sang at funerals] after his death. Years later, after R' Menlhy had passed away, the cantor came to Zloczow before his trip to the USA to say goodbye to his friends. The cantor's followers told him about R' Menly's wish. He accepted their request and prayed "*El Maleh Rakhamim*" after R' Menly.

My mother was endowed with a pleasant voice and good hearing. She remembered many of cantor Trakhtenberg's melodies and musical compositions and used to sing them often.

After Trakhtenberg, R' Shmuel Vinman A" H served as a cantor for several decades. He did not have a strong voice but was a great composer and a talented chorus conductor. Years later, many of his assistants became great cantors. One of them, who sang as an "alto", later accepted a position as a cantor in Ternopil.

At the start of the First World War, Sh. Vinman moved to Vienna, and he died there. In his absence, a chorus was organized under the management of R' Tzvi Shapira. The "First Tenor" was Lipa Schwager A" H. He served as the secretary of "Agudat Yisrael Youths" organization. He wanted to immigrate to Eretz Israel. However, he did not fulfill his wish. He was endowed with a strong tenor voice and was able to "overtake" the entire chorus. Mr. Yaakov Katz (who is now serving as the deputy mayor of Haifa, Israel) sang as the chorus's "Second Tenor". The chorus "alto" was the author of these lines. Zenville or Zvulun Zaltz sang as the "Second Alto" (the latter is currently in Israel and works in the post office). Moshe Vingas - the grandson of R' Mikhel Glazer A" H, who recently made Aliya, also participated in the chorus. Shmuel Schwartz (may G-d avenge his blood), the son of the great scholar R' Yaakov Schwartz A" H, took part in the management of the chorus for a while. Natan Zaltz, may he live long, also participated in the chorus (he now serves as the manager of one of the post office's branches in Tel Aviv). The following people also served in the chorus (among others): Y. Lerner, Wolf Zindwarm, and Wolf Schwager.

After R' Shmuel Vinman, R' Leib Tzvek A"H served as the cantor. He composed melodies for "*Mizmor Shir LeKhanukat HaBait*" attributed to King David ["Temple Dedication Song", Psalms 30,], and the song "*HaNerot Halalu*" ["These Candles", a prayer sang after the lighting of the menorah on Hannukah]. Musicians in Zloczow used to sing the songs.

There were also some "passerby cantors", who stayed in Zloczow for a few weeks and sometimes months at a time. They prayed at the Big Synagogue and often gave concerts conducted in large halls. Among them, cantor David Katzman (currently in Canada) was at the head of the list. He was endowed with a lyrical and delicate tenor and exceptional character. When he prayed at the Big Synagogue, the synagogue filled up with people, including the two women sections. Jews from the various classes and circles in the city stood by the windows and doors to listen to him. When Katzman arrived, the whole city became festive like during a holiday. In all other synagogues, they hurried to finish the praying session to reach the Big Synagogue in time for the Musaf ["Additional Prayer"] to listen to Katzman praying "*Yakum Purkan*" ["May Salvation Arise"], "*Av HaRakhamim*" ["Merciful Father"], and "*Kedushat Keter*". ["Kedushah"- Holy prayer - "They will give you a crown"]. When Dr. Hirshhorn, prominent public and Zionist activist with a pleasant personality, passed away, Katzman came to the city especially to sing the prayer "*El Maleh Rakhamim*" and Psalms songs.

The Cantor Mann, a singer in the Polish opera in Lviv, also visited Zloczow. I recall that the two cantors, Mann and Katzman, appeared at a concert – a cantorial duet, in the large hall "Ulam Ha'Klaim" ["The Curtains' Hall"].

[Columns 277-278]

The Central Synagogue in Zloczow

One of the songs they sang in the concert was the famous Yiddish song *"Vas vet zein, az Mashiakh vet kumen"* ["What will happen when the messiah comes"].

B. Jewish Folklore in the Synagogues, on holidays, Shabbat *Shuvah*, and Shabbat *HaGadol*

During Shabbats, the rabbis used to preach a sermon before the crowd. The sermons were given in the afternoon.

They used to divide the sermon into two parts. The first portion was a *Pilpul* [keen argumentation and debate] and halakha [discussion about Jewish law and jurist prudence] for the interest of the learners and the scholars. For that portion of the sermon, the rabbi would publish a *"marei mekomot"* – [bibliography and references] for the *sugiya* [a passage of Talmud devoted to discussing a specific issue] in the Talmud or the Rambam writings.

Then the rabbi continued with the second part. He discussed the weekly Torah portion and the Haftarah [weekly reading from the Prophets]. The rabbi gave the listeners a mellifluent feeling by mixing a lecture, legend, and moral, seasoned with parables and humor.

During my time, the following rabbis divided that task among themselves:

Rabbi R' Shmuel Shapira, preached in the Big Beit *HaMidrash*, where he prayed. After he passed away, his son, Rabbi Ben Tzion Shamira, may G-d avenge his blood, gave the sermons.

Rabbi R' Mendil Miller z"l was sometimes preaching at the Big Synagogue. Rabbi R' Israel Landau z"l was the principal preacher there. The latter prayed and preached at *"Kloiz* Stratyn". After they passed away, Rabbi R' Khaim Yosef Ailenberg, the rabbinical judge from Kosiv who accepted the same position in Zloczow, may G-d avenge his blood, preached at the Big Synagogue.

On 20 Tamuz, the remembrance day for Theodor Herzl, the remembrance day for Max Nordau [6 Shvat], and later on, the remembrance days after the passing of Nakhum Sokolov and Dr. Khaim Arlozorov z"l, people gathered at the Big Synagogue for a memorial ceremony. Every prominent figure of the local Zionist movement attended the memorial ceremony. Zionist youth movements' members, grouped according to their individual affiliation adorned by their various badges, also flocked to the memorial. The organizers usually invited a speaker from the Zionist movement's headquarter in Lviv, such as Dr. Meir Guyer, Dr. Leon Reikh, or Dr. Fishel Rotenshtreikh. They were tasked with describing the journey and activities of the deceased leader. Before the speech, the speaker was introduced by a local Zionist activist such as Dr. Werpel or the activist of the labor Zionist movement, Dr. Henrikh Teichman, may G-d avenge his blood. The memorial would begin with the prayer "*Av Ha'Rakhamim*" ["Merciful Father"] and ended with the prayer "*El Maleh Rakhamim*" ["Merciful G-d"].

C. The people who served in the Synagogue.

R' Itzik David Shapira A"H served as a cantor and a caretaker in the Big Synagogue. He once used to be a Sofer Satam [a person who writes Torah scrolls, tefillin, mezuzahs, and scrolls] and therefore was nicknamed R' Itzik David Sofer. When the cantor was missing, R' Itzik also served as the prayer leader. He also dealt with all the duties associated with that role (going to weddings and other festive occasions and praying "El Maleh Rakhamim", at the synagogue, during funereal. During wedding ceremonies, he would sing the prayer: "*Mi adir al hakol...*" ["He who is mighty above all beings…may he bless the bridegroom? and the bride"]. R' Itzik David was once a follower of Chortkiv Hasidim. However, when he became a cantor-caretaker, he stopped traveling to Chortkiv. His son, Hershel Shapira, may G-d avenge his blood, knew all the melodies and musical compositions of Cantor Viman. He managed the chorus.

Two others sang zemirot [a group of praises that may be recited daily during Jewish morning services]:

The first was a very old and short man [the name is not mentioned]. The other was R' Khaim Yoel. He later served as the caretaker of the Big Synagogue.

Two primary *gabbai's* [administrators - assistants to a rabbi] served in my time. The first was already old when I knew him, the city watchmaker, R' Yekhiel Blumenblatt.

[Column 279]

Beit HaMidrah "Stratyn Kloiz"

The second gabbai, R' Khaim Perlmutter, was a carpenter, and an owner of a furniture store. The third gabbai was R' Elkana Fogelfenger, who did not have children. He devoted himself to public activism. He worked in fish retail.

He was a philanthropist. His wife was also active in all of the city's charitable organizations, such as the nursing home, orphanage, and the Jewish hospital. When they constructed the new building for the "Talmud Torah" [Jewish elementary school], R' Elkana contributed 1000 bricks for the building.

The "*Ba'al Kri'ah*" [the person who reads the Torah at the synagogue] at the Big Synagogue for many years was R' Moshe Margaliot. He served as the morning prayer leader during "The Ten Days of Repentance". R' Moshe who was a grain trader, was an activist for charity and excelled in hospitality. During Friday nights, he prayed Minkha [prayer before sunset] in "Zidichov kloiz". Usually, he led the prayer. He made sure to arrange accommodations for every guest (who came from other places) and the poor. He never went home without a guest. When he could not find any, he would go to another synagogue to search for one. After my grand uncle, R' Yehoshua Shleifer A" H, who used to read the Torah in "Kloiz Zidichov", had passed away, R' Moshe moved to "Kloiz Zidichov" and became the Torah reader there. R' Moshe educated his three sons to be Torah scholars. The young one, Shimon Yaakov, may G-d avenge his blood" was my friend.

D. The people who prayed at the Synagogue

R' Moshe Koifman liked to pass in front of the ark, and show off his cantor skills. He was a fan of the cantors and liked to argue about who was the better cantor.

R' Yeshaia Tenenbaum, a Jew with a warm heart, an activist, and one of the managers of the "*Folkskikh*"[public soup kitchen], was also a fan of music and cantorship.

[Column 280]

The "Folkskikh" played a crucial role, distributing two to three hundred meals a day for the poor. That institution played a critical role, particularly after World War I when the middle classes were Impoverished and pauperized.

Other unique figures who prayed at the synagogue included:

R' Yankel Steinbrukh, loved to argue about various subjects
R' Yekutiel Dreksler was the only scriber in the city
R' Avremale Hochman was known for his butter and cheeses
R' Leizer Bressler, the tinsmith who was blessed with many children
R' Yaakov Nagler
R' Lipa Bukhbinder
R' Daniel Zoyerhoif was among the Haredi craftsmen who was a public activist. He also prayed at the synagogue of the organization "Yad Kharutzim".

E. The small synagogues

Two small synagogues existed in the corridor of the large synagogue. One had its windows directed toward the river, and the other had windows directed toward the street. People who did not want to pray at the large synagogue, for various reasons, prayed in the first one. They prayed there in two minyans: the first at 6 a.m. and the second at 8:30 a.m.

Artisans and owners of large wagons prayed in the second one. Wagon owners traveled to Lviv and other places to bring products. They prayed early at dawn so that they could leave earlier. The two synagogues employed scholars who taught Torah during the evenings and on Shabbats in the summer – "Pirkei Avot" [Literally – "Chapters of the Fathers" - a compilation of the ethical teachings and maxims from Rabbinic Jewish tradition]. They also employed a person who read the Torah during Shabbat and led the service.

F. The folklore in the second small synagogue and the *Melaveh Malka* meal

In the small synagogue, which had its windows directed toward the street, it was customary to arrange for a big "Melaveh Malkah" [Literally – "Escorting the Queen -Shabbat"] meal, on Saturday nights. Many guests and the poor attended. Prominent house owners were invited to attend. The preparation for the "Melaveh Malka" meal began as early as mid-week. People were asked to contribute khallahs, fish, borscht, and potatoes. The gabbai's and a few helpers served the food. After the meal, they used to sing melodies for Shabbat. The singers were from among the house owners and other guests. An old scholar, R' Yehuda Tzvi Fisher, A" H, served as a *maggid* [preacher] in that synagogue.

———

[Columns 281-282]

The Big Temple (*Beit HaMidrash*)

by David Imber

Translated by Moshe Kutten

The Orphanage

The phrase: "A house where people educated about the Torah and praying", was written on the gate of the Big Beit HaMidrash. It was indeed an institution where the students were educated on Torah and Praying. Certainly, youths learned their lessons about the Talmud, "Ein Yaakov" and "Midrash Rabah". My grandfather, R' Yaakov Yehoshua a"h [may he rest in peace], was a Torah scholar who allocated time to teach Torah there. He was the grandson of the mighty genius, Gaon R' Yehoshua, author of the book "Pnei Yehoshua" (about the Talmud). His wife, grandmother Leah, was charitable and hospitable. She once hosted *Tzadik* R' Israel from Ruzhin z'tz"l, who stopped in Zloczow on the way to Lviv to consult with physicians. My second grandfather, the Torah scholar R' Khaim Imber a"h, studied Mishnah chapters by heart when he became blind. It was said about R' Imber that he joined the Emperor's army during the war and became his advocate.

Some of the people who prayed in the Big Beit Hamidrash were: Moshe Pundak a"h, from the remnants of the old generation, who liked to get involved and raise his opinion on public matters. His son, Rabbi Sender Pundak, was one of those who continuously participated in the chorus. Rabbi Gaon Shmuel Shapira z"l, the head of the rabbinical court in our city. After he passed away, his son, Rabbi Bentzion Shapira (may G-d avenge his blood), who also prayed at the Big Beit Hamidrash, took his place. One of the preachers at the religious lessons was Rabbi Bentzion Kaplan a"h, a dear Jew who possessed a strong voice. He passed in front of the ark during the Days of Awe. He served as both a cantor and a caretaker.

Rabbi Bentzion's two sons participated in the chorus mentioned above. The older one possessed a strong "Tenor" voice. R' Shlomo Tenenbaum served as "*Ba'al Kri'ah*" [The person who reads the Torah]. He came from Brody, which was the original location for many "*Ba'alei Kri'ah*". He was the son-in-law of Rabbi Yaakov Aharonfriz. His wife was called Roiz Mundles, probably named after her mother. He was the owner of a second-hand clothes store called "Tendeit". Rabbi Shmuel Shapira was previously a follower of Zhydachiv's Hasidim, who used to travel to the second Admor, Rabbi Yitzkhak Aizik z'tz"l. After the second Admor passed away he traveled to Chortkiv, to the first Admor, *Tzadik*, Rabbi David Moshe Zetzikle. R' Shlomo prayed enthusiastically in the style of Zhydachive's Hasidim until his last days.

The people who prayed at the "*Beit HaMidrash*"

Rabbi Khanokh Henikh Tzimend was an activist and philanthropist. He supported several institutions, particularly religious organizations, such as "Talmud Torah" and "Orakh Le'Khaim" yeshiva. He was one of the active contributors to the yeshiva who contributed several thousand bricks for the new building of the "Talmud Torah".

R' David Shvig, the owner of a flour mill, was a community public affairs activist. His wife, Heg Shvig, was a clever woman who was a charity activist. They managed to make Aliya to Eretz Israel and bought several houses in Jerusalem. They left a family in Jerusalem.

Rabbi Pinkhas Segal was a Torah scholar and clever man. He was a level-headed man and a public affairs activist. He served as a committee member of the "Agudat Israel" party for many years and one of its consultants whose opinion was valued.

Rabbi Israel Fishel was a dear and honest person. He participated in and supported all public matters, not for attracting attention to himself.

R' Moshe Preger and his son Yitzkhak Preger, a Torah scholar, gave Torah lessons in his free time.

The Small "*Beit Hamidrash*"
(Das Kleineh Beit Midrashil)

In the corridor of the Big "Beit HaMidrash", was a smaller Beit Midrash. The people who prayed there were the owners of shops or people with other occupations. They employed a preacher to teach religious lessons. The lessons were about the weekly Torah portions and commentaries, Mishnah chapters, "Ein Yaakov", and Talmud interpretation. During my time, the preacher was Rabbi Israel Birger, may G-d avenge his blood. He was an outstanding Torah scholar, my teacher, and my mentor. A native of Przemysl, he was the son-in-law of Rabbi Yitzkhak Shteltzberg a"h, a Belz Hasid who prayed in Zhydachiv Kloyz. Rabbi Yitzkhak was the owner of a chocolate factory.

I will expand on my depiction of Rabbi Israel later, as he was the one who taught us the basis of learning.

The gabbai [synagogue administrator] was for many years, Rabbi Nakhum Horwitz, who devoted himself entirely to his role. He was an accountant in his profession. After the death of Rabbi Nakhum Horwitz, Rabbi Getzil Marvitzer, a dear man, may G-d avenge his blood, who owned a paint shop, became the *gabbai*. His son, Moshe, whom I went to school with, immigrated to the US when he was still a youth.

The people who prayed in the Small "*Beit HaMidrash*"

Rabbi Moshe Tenenbaum a"h, was a grain merchant. He was trusted and honest. His "word of honor" could always be trusted. He never went back on his word.

[Columns 283-284]

He was a dear man, pure and charitable. He left a daughter who was staying in an institution. He also left a large family, most of whom are in the USA. His brother, Rabbi Israel Tenenbaum, a"h, and his daughter – the wife of Mr. Kahana lived in Israel.

Rabbi Shmuel Veledniger a"h, called Shmuel the "Americaner" [the American] because he once visited the USA, was a very clever Jew. He served as a "mediator" of quarrels between people who did not want to go to court or the rabbinical court. He was involved in public affairs, issues concerning a selection of a rabbi, and other issues of interest to the public.

Rabbi Shlomo Weintraub a"h, was the owner of groats. He had a pleasant personality and was agreeable to people and the heavens.

Zhydachiv *Kloyz*[1]

The Zhydachiv Kloyz was the oldest synagogue in Zloczow. At the location of the Kloyz, there was once a much older Kloyz, which was later on, renovated and rebuilt. Even during our days, the rebuilt Kloyz was quite old itself. Evidence for that can be found in the responsa by the head of the rabbinical court in Zloczow - [Gaon Rabbi Yoel Ashkenazi (1810 – 1883)] - "From Rabbi Yoel (R"Y) Ashkenazi". In that responsa there is an answer by Rabbi Ashkenazi containing the following introduction: "That was how I have sermonized when the Kloyz was rebuilt".

The entire Hasidic aristocracy prayed once in the Zhydachiv Kloyz. The prominent among Zhydachiv Hasidim knew Rabbi Tzvi Hirsh z'tz"l, the first rabbi from Zhydachiv and the author of "Ateret Tzvi" [a commentary on the Zohar], and were also the followers of the second rabbi -Rabbi Yitzkhak Aizik z'tz"l. Among the prominent Zhydachiv Hasidim who prayed in that Kloyz was Gaon Rabbi Yeshaia Rosenberg who was a rabbinical judge in our city. He had a pleasant voice and knew Hasidic music well. He led the service during the Days of Awe. Later on, Hasidim, followers of other Hasidic dynasties prayed in the Kloyz, including Hasidim of Ruzhyn, Chortkiv, Husiatyn, Sadigura, and Boyan. At that time, remnants of the Zhydachiv Hasidim, such as Rabbi David Lvov, prayed at the Kloyz. After World War I, when many of the towns around Zloczow (such as Bialokomin) were in ruins, Jewish refugees from these towns settled in Zloczow. They were People with a mentality different from that of the oldtimers. Belz Hasidim also joined the Kloyz. That was an extremely rare event in our place until that time.

My deceased father, Meir Imber a"h, was one of the great Chortkiv Hasidim. He was a scholar and a public activist, particularly in the area of Torah teaching. R' Meir was the founder of the yeshiva "Orakh LaKhaim" ["Way of Life"]. Later on, he was one of the founders of "Agudat Israel" [party]. He had a pleasant voice and used to lead prayers, on some occasions, but not regularly, even during the "Days of Awe".

The regular "*Ba'al Tefilah*" [a cantor for whom cantorship is not his profession], was R' Elkanah Billig a"h, who was once one of the assistants of R' Yeshaya Ze'ev z"L. His praying style was almost a complete replica of Meir Imber's style. R' Elkanah was "*Ba'al Musaf*" [leader of the Musaf prayer, which is recited after the morning prayers on Shabbat, holidays, and the beginning of each month].

The brother-in-law of R' Elkanah, R' "little" Fishel (der Kleine Fishel), was "*Ba'al Shakahrit*" [leader of the morning prayer].

R' Elkanah Bilig's father was called "big" Fishel. R' "big" Fishel a"h, was one of the first Husiatyn Hasidim followers of the elder Admor R' Mordekhai Shraga Feibish z'tz'k"l [of blessed and saintly (pious) memory]. The latter was the son of the "Rabbi of all the people in the diaspora" Admor R' Israel [Friedman] of Ruzhyn z'tz'k"l [also known as "the holy one from Ruzhyn"]. When I was a small child, I was fortunate to know R' 'big" Fishel. His seat at the Zhydavich Kloyz was on the west side, near the window close to the door, rather than the [the more respecable] "east" side. He prayed enthusiastically without raising his voice. His face was glowing, like after getting out of a steamy mikveh [ritual public bath], and his eyes were tearing throughout the prayer. He prayed with his entire being, without moving any part of his body. His naturalness and simplicity were endless. He was named after his father, R' Fishel Bilker a"h, who died while his mother, Mrs. Miryam Elki a"h, was pregnant with him.

After the death of R' Elkana and his brother-in-law R' Fishel, the "Musaf" prayers were led regularly by the grandson of the Rabbis from Zhydachiv and Belz, R' Yehoshua Heshil Labin, may G-d avenge his blood. He was a Torah scholar, pleasant and sociable. He had a pleasant voice and prayed in the style of the Zhydachov [Hasidim], mixed somewhat with the style of the Belz [Hasidim]. The prayer "An'im Zmirot" ["Song of Glory"] at the end of the "Musaf" was sung exclusively in Belz's style.

"Ba'al Shakharit" during the "Days of Awe" was my great uncle, R' Yehoshua Schleifer a"h, the son-in-law of my grandfather, R' Yaakov Yoshia, and a native of Brody. He was *"Ba'al Kri'ah"* [Reader] of the Torah in Zhydachiv Kloyz for more than thirty years. He was a Torah scholar, a warm-hearted Jew. Despite being burdened by many children (mostly girls), and a shaky economic situation, he gathered bread and hallahs every week to distribute to needy families. He used to accompany the charity rounds to lend money to others. As I recall, he used to contribute the fee ("Megila Gelt") he received for reading the [Purim] Megila to others, as it was customary then. Most of his daughters live in Israel. One of them resides in the USA.

My uncle (my mother's brother), R' Elyakim Friedman, may G-d avenge his blood, led the Shakharit prayer after the death of R' Yehoshua Schleifer.

[Columns 285-286]

He was a good-hearted man. He set down the entire day adorned with a tallit and tefillin and studied.

The righteous R' Pinkhas Kanner, one of the prominent Chortkiv Hasidim, may G-d avenge his blood was a native of Buchach. He was the son-in-law of R' Fishel Reiz a"h. R' Pinkhas was honest and pious. He devoted his entire life to the Torah, work, and praying. He gave his heart and soul to fulfilling "light" and "severe" commandments.

It was told about him that during the days of the Nazi Dictator, may his name be erased, R' Pinkhas stayed in a bunker and could have survived. However, he went out once to find a "Minyan". He dressed up in peasant clothing but wore a flat cap and was recognized and captured.

R' Moshe Margaliot became *"Ba'al Kri'ah"* of the Torah after the death of R' Yehoshua Schleifer.

My mother's father, R' Khaim Tzvi Friedman a"h, was the reader of the order of the *"Teki'ot"* [shofar sounds] on Rosh Ha'Shana. He was a native of Mikolinitz (near Ternopil) and a descendent of an educated family. I recall that his brother, Feivel Friedman a"h, was a high-ranked official of the court in Lviv. The entire family was enlightened. R' Khaim Tzvi was caught up in Hasidism, which attracted followers in many Jewish social circles. R' Khaim Tzvi's grandfather, R' Heshil a"h, settled at the end of his life, in Zloczow, near his son, and died there. The mother of my grandfather, Mrs. Keilah a"h, was highly educated. She knew French and was one of the admirers of the author and historian, Voltaire. R' Khaim Tzvi was one of the most prominent Husiatyn Hasidim, and their uncrowned leader. He used to travel to the first Husiatyn's Admor. He was a friend and Hasidic colleague of R' "big" Fishel. R' Khaim Tzvi was a pious man who worshiped G-d with joy. He was a good-hearted man who brought joy to people. When he visited somebody who was in sorrow, the whole house would be filled with joy.

I would like to add a few words about his passing:

About an hour before his passing, all the Hasidim, particularly the Husiatyn Hasidim, gathered at his house. R' Mikhel Glazer, who later became the Hasidic leader joined as well. They prayed "Minkah" [Afternoon prayer] in a minyan. My grandfather prayed in his bed despite being close to death. They heard him pronouncing every word of the prayer "Shmonah Esrei" [the central prayer in each of the daily services, recited silently while standing]. When he reached the words "Ha'El Ha'Kadosh" ["The Holy G-d"], he breathed his last. The phrase: "Brought joy to G-d and people" is etched on his gravestone.

After his death, R' Mikhel Glazer a"h became the reader of the order of the *"Tekiot"* in Rosh HaShanah. R' Mikhel was a great Torah scholar. He once studied under the Gaon R' Shalom Mordekhai HaKohen Schwadron z"l, the author of "Maharsham Responsa". R' Mikhel was one of the great Husiatyn Hasidim. He was involved in public affairs. At one time he served as a member of the committee of the "Agudat Israel" party in the city. He was among those who were authorized to deal with the nomination of the head of the rabbinical court. That issue of the nomination was a controversial issue that resulted in divisions. Divisions occurred not only between the Zionists and "HaMizrakhi" [religious Zionists party] or between "Agudat Israel" [ultra-orthodox party] and the unaffiliated Haredim but also within the camps of "Agudat Israel" and the unaffiliated Haredim themselves. That affair should be described somewhere but this is not to place to expand on it.

"*Ba'al Tokeh'a*" [the person who blows the shofar] was, for many years, R' Shmuel Parnas. He was a humble man and made a living from his hard work. His wife Bluma a"h, used to bake bread. Her bread was homey and tasted good. She made a name for herself with her bread. Many jokes were composed over that. One of the jokes was about the meaning of the phrase - "He suspends the earth over nothing" [Job 26:7]. The sages expanded and said that the whole world exists due to… and in the city we used to say due to the eating of Bluma's ("di bekerin" – [the baker"]) bread. R' Shmuel educated his sons on the Torah and good deeds.

His son, R' Ptakhia, may G-d avenge his blood, was a watchmaker in his profession. He was a pious Jew who followed the commandments meticulously. In particular, he followed the command associated with the commentary by the sages about the phrase "This is my God, and I will praise him, my father's God, and I will glorify him" [Book of Exodus 15:2]. [To glorify G-d] he purchased a beautiful tallit adorned with a silver fringe, elegant Tefilin, wide sash, and more. The clowns of the Kloyz called him "der rabbi" ["the rabbi"]. He was the son-in-law of R' "big" Fishel Billig mentioned above.

The son-in-law of R' Shmuel Parnas was a business person, Torah scholar, and educated. He woke up early in the morning to study. He studied and prayed in the Stratyn Kloyz. He was an accountant and worked in the bank of R' Tzvi Hirsch Zeiden.

The *Kloyz* library and the "Tikun Sfarim" ["Books Fixing"] organization

A very large library existed in Kloyz Zhydachiv. It contains books such as the Babylonian and Jerusalem Talmud's. It also contained commentaries of the Talmud, starting from books by the "*Rishonim*" [rabbis who worked between the 11th and 15th centuries] - like the RASHB"A [Rabbi Solomon son of Abraham son of Aderet], and RITV"A [Rabbi Yom Tov ben Avraham Assevilli] and ending with books by the "*Akhronim*" [rabbis who worked in the 16th century and on], like TZALAKH [Rabbi Yekhezkel Landau - author of "Nodah B'Yehuda], and [Rabbi Yaakov Yehoshua Falk the author of] Pnei Yehoshua. It contained books of Poskim [rabbinical legal scholars], such as the RAMBAM [Rabbi Moshe Ben Maimon], [Rabbi Yaakov ben Asher, the author of] Arba'ah Turim, and [Rabbi Joseph ben Ephraim Karo, author of] "Shulkhan Arukh". The library also contained responsa's from the "*Rishonim*" such as the MAHARA"M [Rabbi Meir ben Barukh Rotehnburg], Berabi [Rabbi Yosi ben Rabbi Yehuda], and others, as well as from the "*Akhronim*", such as [Rabbi Yekhezkel Landau, author of] "Nodah B'Yehudah" and "Kamah v'Tnina", [Rabbi Moshe Sofer (Shreiber), author of] Khata"m [acronym of the book's name in Hebrew - "Khidushei Torat Moshe"] Sofer, and more. There was also a section for theoretical and practical Hasidism and Kabalah literature in the library. Books starting with the RAMAK [Moses ben Jacob Cordovero], HaAR"I [Rabbi Yitzkhak ben Shlomo Luria Ashkenazi], R' Khaim Vital, [Rabbi Yaakov Yosef HaKohen of Pollonye, author of the book] "Toldot Yaakov Yosef", [Rabbi Elimelech Weisblum of Lizhensk, author of the book] "Noam Elimelekh", Rabbi Levi Yitzkhak Levi Derbarmdiger, author of the book] "Kedushat Levi", and more.

The association "Tikun Sfarion" ["Books' Repair"] handled the purchasing of the books from the students of the Kloyz. The association also repaired and bound the old books.

Translator's Note:

1. Kloyz - From YIVO Encyclopedia of Jews in Eastern Europe
   (https:--yivoencyclopedia.org-article.aspx-kloyz)

   "The Yiddish term *kloyz* (pl., *kloyzn*) is apparently derived from the Latin claustrum or clausum, which refers to a building or closed complex of structures connected to a monastery. The term first appeared in Ashkenazic culture in the sixteenth century and referred to a house where scholars assembled—a place of study intended for mature, adult male scholars. By the second half of the seventeenth century, there were *kloyzn* in many centers of both Western and Eastern Europe. The term had by then gradually come to refer to a private house of study, existing separately from the institutions of the community and financed by a patron or a wealthy family. A *kloyz* of this kind was generally headed by a prominent scholar appointed by the founder, and was frequented by selected scholars…"

[Columns 287-288]

Cantorship Among Zloczow's People

by David Imber

Translated by Moshe Kutten

A.

It is difficult for me to assess the depth of Zloczow people's knowledge of cantorship as I consider myself almost a layman in these matters. However, it should be said that Zloczow people were enthusiastic fans of cantroship. One example, out of many, serves as proof for that: The famous cantor, Trakhtenberg, lived in Zloczow more than 60 years ago. He and his chorus would astound their audiences, particularly those who considered themselves as "knowledgeable" about cantorship. It was customary, in many Jewish towns and cities, that cantors "would take a vacation" and travel around, between Passover and "Atzeret" [Shavuot holiday], and between "Atzeret" and the month of Elul [before the Jewish high holidays]. The small Jewish communities could not afford to pay their cantors a satisfactory during the summer months. The cantors covered their deficits by appearing in synagogues outside of their locality. In addition, cantors could gain the fame that way. Also, G-d's willing, a cantor could find a better place somewhere else.

Such an event occurred in Zloczow when its famous cantor went on a tour in other cities around the country. "He won the favor of everyone" [Book of Esther 2:15] in the town of Przemys, and he also liked the city particularly since the people there offered to pay him twice the salary he was receiving in Zloczow, so he stayed there. The "Days of Awe" were approaching, and Zloczow remained without a cantor. The cantor's admirers were distraught and refused to be consoled. The fact that the cantor broke a verbal contract was not very important. Their main worry was how to find a new cantor? What community, big or small, would be willing to give up their cantor during the high season? People in the city who considered themselves "Knowledgable" about cantroship, were the most unhappy. They wondered how could "their" Trakhtenberg do something like that to them. In the end, they decided to act in an original way. The cantor's family was placed under siege. Shifts of guards were placed to prevent the cantor's wife and children from leaving town. A brisk exchange of urgent letters followed and, in the end, a compromise was achieved: Cantor Trakhtenberg and his singers would come to Zloczow for several Shabbats, and the city was satisfied with that. They let the family go. The final farewell was difficult for both sides.

There was a person in the city who refused to be consoled. The "compromise" did not satisfy him. That person was the iron merchant, R' Menli. With tearing eyes, he said that if heavens would not let him listen to the singing and praying of cantor Trakhtenberg during his life, he wished that the cantor would sing "El Maleh Rakhamim" after his death so that he would be able to rest in peace in his grave.

Several years later, R' Menli died without hearing the pleasant voice of his beloved cantor again. Cantor Trakhtenberg did not stay long in Przemys – America attracted him. However, before leaving on his trip, he wished to silence his conscience. The news about the will of his loyal admirer reached him, and it continued to bother him. So, he and the chorus arrived in Zloczow to wish farewell to the city by praying on Shabbat. On Friday morning, the cantor and his chorus, accompanied by half of the city Jewish population, visited the grave of R' Menli. Their prayer shook the gravestone of the dead in the cemetery, and the crowd rejoiced with excitement.

B.

As discussed, Zloczow people were uniquely enthusiastic fans of cantorship. There wasn't anybody in the city who was willing to admit not being an expert about cantorship. It could not have been proven, however, just the fact that everybody considered themselves an expert, and the fact that the city had that reputation, sufficed as proof. Another conclusive evidence was provided by R' Leizer, the famous cantor of Zloczow, who acquired a name for himself and was later invited to serve as a cantor at the big synagogue in Krakow. He also praised the Zloczow people for their knowledge of cantorship.

[Columns 289-290]

To eliminate any doubt among the doubtful and unbelievers, and to reassure the "experts", people used to say that in, Zloczow, the pray lecterns were the most "knowledgable" about cantorship. In this context, a story was told about the famous cantor, R' Yerukham [Blindman] "Hakatan" ["The Small One" - known as such due to his small stature]. He arrived in Zloczow once to euphonize the Shabbat prayer. The organizers assumed that a crowd of people from other synagogues would come to listen to the visiting cantor, so they emptied the Big Synagogue of its numerous lecterns. However, as it may happen to any cantor, R' Yerukham did not shine at that time. Perhaps the reason was that Zloczow people had exaggerated expectations. In short, it was a great disappointment. People who considered themselves "knowledgeable" had a hard time explaining the reason for that failure and could not bear the "defeat". The courageous ones approached the cantor and asked: "What went wrong with one of the greatest cantors in the world?" According to the story, R' Yerukham responded: "It is said that in Zloczow, the lanterns are the ones who are the most knowledgeable about cantorship. In my appearance, the lanterns were taken out. So, there was a lack of knowledge in the audience.

A similar mishap happened to the famous cantor, R' Zeidel Rovner. He also experienced a failure in Zloczow. However, during his appearance, the lecterns were not taken out of the synagogue, so the people could not decide who should be blamed for the failure.

****

[Columns 291-292]

In the Music Hall of Zloczow's Righteous People

by Geshuri

Translated by Moshe Kutten

Rabbi Yekhiel Mikhel, The *Maggid* from Zloczow

Rabbi Yekhiel Mikhel "entered the Hasidic orchard" [got involved in the occult], as a Hasid, and became a Maggid [preacher], having a fire in his soul he felt that there was still time left until "the end of time". That polymath appreciated music and became a composer without having his name associated with his creations. Besides being a moral and spiritual movement (within Ashkenazi Judaism), Hasidism was also a movement that promoted *Niggunim* and *Zmirot* [traditional and religious melodies and songs]. The Hasidic violins introduced the most beautiful tones of soul music, engulfing the listeners with heavenly blessings. When it comes to the Hasidic songs, we could use the verse [1 Kings 4:32]: "And he spoke three thousand proverbs, and his songs were a thousand and five" since the number of the Hasidic melodies was large. During the first generation of Hasidism, when the movement took its first steps on an unpaved road full of obstacles, R' Mikhel emerged as unique and distinctive among the students of the Besh"t [Ba'al Shem Tov, Rabbi Israel ben Eliezer]. His influences were notable in the history of Hasidism and even more in the dawn of Hasidic music. He was one of the Hasidic first players and composers.

R' Mikhel was a man with vigor. The BESHT respected him tremendously. The BESHT said that "he was given a tiny soul from heaven, as small as anyone can get in his generation, and he elevated it to the level of the soul of the holy Tannai sage Rabbi Shimon Ben Yokhai". R' Mikhel did not author any books. We only know little about his views and opinions from the books written by his sons and his numerous students. We also know things which passed orally from one generation to the other by the elderly.

His father, Rabbi Yitzkhak from Drohobych, was one of the intimate friends of the BESHT. After investigating the essence of Hasidism, he sent his elder son, R' Mikhel to the BESHT. R' Mikhel became the most renowned student of the BESHT. Despite serving in various locations as a *Maggid,* he was named the '*Maggid* of Zloczow, a city in Eastern Galitsia, situated near the Wallachia region of Romania. That area served as the source for the first Hasidic niggunim [melodies]. One of its premier types is called "Wallachian Niggunim". Despite being named the *Maggid* of Zloczow, R' Mikhel spent most of his life in the city of Yampil [Yampol], where he served as a *maggid* for the Hasidism movement and where he excelled in Hasidic music.

His title was the *Maggid* from Zloczow. However, based on his knowledge, he should have gained higher positions. According to Hasidic fables, the BESHT pleaded with R' Mikhel to accept a rabbinical position in one of the Jewish communities, but he refused to do it. The BESHT scolded him for that and said: "If you do not listen to my plea, you will lose your world – this one and the next". However, R' Mikhel did not relent. The BESHT told him joyfully later on: "You are blessed by G-d, and your choice is also blessed. I was only trying you out, to see what was truly in your heart".

R' Mikhel did not want to name the melodies under his name, and they were called the "Niggunim of the BESHT".

R' Mikhel was one of the righteous men, the Creator endowed generously from all of His noble and beautiful, good and pleasant treasures. He was blessed with a euphonious voice and a musical talent. Thanks to his talent he became one of the best emissaries for spreading Hasidism and one of the principal assistants of the BESHT, as much as he was the emissary for spreading the first Hasidic melodies.

R' Mikhel traveled, like the rest of the Hasidic emissaries from place to place, preaching and sermonizing about morality and bringing the listeners close to him from the pulpit of the synagogues and Batei HaMidrash. He was an excellent speaker who captured the listener with a pleasant song before his speech.

He was modest and ran away from any publicity. However, Hasidism placed him on the stage and knew how to utilize his talents. Hasidism promoted devoutness to G-d, enthusiasm during work and prayer, and joy in life. Most of the virtues of singing and playing music brought joy. The BESHT found a virgin land in music, and Rabbi Mikhel helped him in that.

Chabad Hasidim, including the groups in Israel, still sing today a niggun attributed to R' Mikhel. Rabbi Shneur Zalman of Liadi [The first Rebbe of Chabad], also received melodies from R' Mikhel.

As mentioned, R' Mikhel was influenced by Wallachian music, which was close to his heart. He knew that music intimately as a result of his continuous contact with it. Wallachian music expresses sadness and longing in part, but also life and joy.

The BESHT was also influenced by Wallachian music, as he spent his youth in the Carpathian Mountains.

[Columns 293-294]

It seemed that he was the one who decided which Wallachian melodies could be brought into the secret world of Hasidism. Based upon the decision of his rabbi, Rabbi Mikhel composed piuts [melodies] for Shabbats and holidays. The use of Wallachian tunes fitted the goal of the renewal of Jewish music and its revival. Only later on, the Wallachian effect weakened, and the original source, emanating from the prayers, strengthened. Among the *piut's* (melodies) attributed to R' Mikhel are "Maoz Tzur" [Hannukah *piut* - "Strong Rock (of my Salvation)"] and "Berakh Dodi" (A Passover song) ["make haste my beloved," Song of Songs 8:14].

Chabad Hasidim still sing, until today, with awe of exaltation, a niggun that R' Mikhel used to sing for the BESHT. The BESHT called it "*Hit'orerut Rakhamim*" ["Evoking Mercy"] because that was what he felt while listening to it. Chabad *tzadikim* [righteous] attribute power to the niggun, and sing it on important occasions.

[Columns 295-296]

The Orphanage, Hospital, and Nursing Home

Translated by Moshe Kutten

The Orphanage

The orphanage was established before World War I. The Jewish community, which amounted then to about 7000 Jews out of a total population of 18,000, took on itself a divine obligation: to support, to the best of its ability, the poorest of the poor, which constituted a large percentage of the Jewish population. About 20 boys and girls under the age of 16, were educated at the orphanage. Youths older than 16, were sent to work as apprentices with various artisans. The contacts with the former students were never severed and the graduates came back often to visit the institution after graduation. According to the agreement, the graduates worked as apprentices for about three to four years, and later they would settle down as independent.

Mrs. Belter headed the institution and devoted all of her time and effort to it. She left for London in 1916, where her son lived. However, she never forgot about the orphanage. After a stay of about two years, she collected money and clothing for the institution and returned to Zloczow. She immediately invited an eminent educator, who took care of the students and elevated the level of the institution to a great level. Mrs. Belter was deeply loved. She managed to instill the need for supporting the orphanage, in the hearts of the residents.

It is interesting to note that the orphanage existed all these years without any government or municipal support. Except for the perpetual contributions, Mrs. Belter would solicit contributions for the orphanage in every festive occasion such as circumcision, bar-mitzva, or a wedding.

Mrs. Belter passed away in 1935, a few years before the Germans' invasion, at the age of 63. A large crowd of Zloczow residents participated in her funeral to pay her their last respect.

Engineer Berl took over when Mrs. Betler passed away. Together with the educator, the wife of physician Dr. Rozenbaum, he invested all of his effort to maintain the orphanage. The engineer worked tirelessly until the eruption of World War II when he was transferred to Russia. When he returned to Warsaw after the war, he established a active committee that helped Zloczow's survivors. About 150 Jews survived the Holocaust. Most of them survived due to the assistance of residents of Zloczow.

Some people agreed to host the students when they reached 16 years old. Mrs. Kreger, the sister-in-law of Frida Kreger, took a boy and a girl to her home until they learned a profession. The girl later moved to Lviv for further studies, where she learned to build lampshades. Later on, she married and established a family.

Engineer Berl made Aliya and continued his work in Israel as an engineer. He passed away in Israel.

The Municipal Jewish Hospital

In addition to the orphanage, there was also the Municipal Jewish hospital. The hospital had about 14 beds. Dr. Hertznik, Dr. Reikhert, and other physicians managed the hospital. All of the physicians worked there voluntarily.

The building of the Nursing Home named after Barukh

[Columns 297-299]

Summer camp for the orphanage students

The hospital relied on contributions to supplement its public municipal budget for its survival. The hospital was one of the best hospitals in the area and therefore served not only the poor. Unfortunately, all of the physicians that worked at the hospital perished in the Holocaust.

The Nursing Home

The Nursing Home was located near the hospital. It consists of 4 rooms, two for men and two for women. The municipality helped in supporting that institution. Most of the residents in the nursing home were from among the poor of Zloczow, and some were people who did not have children. There were 18 beds in the nursing home.

And finally, we should also mention the **Soup Kitchen**. The soup kitchen was headed by Mr. Tenenbaum, a merchant and a public activist who devoted himself entirely to that institution. The Soup Kitchen also relied on contributions, which consisted of money and food (mainly meat and bakery items). Mrs. Frida Kreger often took care of supplying all sorts of products to the Soup Kitchen. Some of the needy would come and take the dishes home. Some would eat in the kitchen.

Dr. Heshif's wife, Mrs. Heshif, came to the kitchen every Friday night to oversee the festive meal. The meals began with lighting the candles and concluded with Shabbat Singing.

In the summer, Mrs. Heshif used to manage the transfer of children and adults to neighboring villages of Zetzila and Zhalkovi and ensured to supply all of their needs.

Summer camp at the building of the orphanage

[Columns 299-300]

The Zionist Movement in Zloczow

by Dr. Yosef Shatkai

Translated by Moshe Kutten

I spent the vacations I received from high school in Lviv with my family in Zloczow. My parents moved to Zloczow because of their business – leasing and building paper mills and sawmills. During my visits, I came to know the studying youth. We found the situation wide open for Zionist activities. These were the years of Zionist mysticism.

If we compare the strength of the Zionist movements between Brody and Zloczow, Brody would come on top. I knew the Zionist movement in Brody well. The Zionist movement in Brody was well organized. It was headed by public figures, famous merchants, respected house owners, and famed Hebrew teachers. In Zloczow, only a small group of house owners were members of the Zionist movement. Among them, Rabbi Avraham Yaakov Kigel, an owner of properties and an enlightened person, Yitzkhak Buchacher, a merchant and a contractor, Tzvi Rosenboim, an owner of a store and an agent for the wines from Baron Rothchild's cellars, Yaakov Reis, a clerk in the large fabric store of Leon Offer, Bentzion Lehrer, Zeev Rosen, and others.

However, most of Zloczow's Jews were indifferent to the Zionist movement. There were a few Jews, here and there, who were attracted to the Zionist idea. However, they hid their views from the extreme assimilators within the community. Many Jews received various licenses from the authorities. A whisper in the authorities' ear could have caused them to lose their livelihood.

I recall a fascinating meeting with the chairman of the community's steering committee, Yosef Guld. We decided to hold a memorial service for Herzl on 20th Tamuz. The most appropriate place to hold the memorial was the large synagogue. We turned to the gabbai, Mr. Yekhiel Blumenblat, and asked to receive the keys. However, he had probably already received an instruction from the chairman of the community steering committee not to hand over the key for any reason. He, therefore, refused and referred us to Yosef Guld. We met with Mr. Guld. He immediately began to give us a lecture and preach to us about morality. He claimed that we were distorting the views of the great leader and dealing with "ghetto-like politics". After all of that, we did find a way to get the key to the synagogue. The memorial was held with a large crowd in attendance.

As discussed, the professional intelligentsia people were all radical assimilators or people who were indifferent to their Jewishness. Among the Jewish physicians Dr. Guld, the son-in-law of Yosef Guld, was a radical assimilator. He was elected as the representative to the Austrian parliament in Vienna. He also served as the chairman of the Zloczow municipal management team. He was elected by the majority of the Jewish votes. However, he renounced his Jewishness and served in the parliament as a Polish citizen. He even refused to circumcise his sons. However, in this matter, the older Guld had the final say, as he feared the religious Jews who would not have allowed him to continue in his position as the chairman of the community steering committee. Other assimilators included Dr. Mitelman, a lawyer and the vice-chairman of the community steering committee, Dr. Hesel, and others.

The Zionist Youth

[Columns 301-302]

A group of the organization "Ha'Noar Ha'Tzioni" ["The Zionist Youth"], 1938

The Zionist movement brought about a change in the values. A new generation grew out of the young Jewish intelligentsia. The large organization of "Bar Kokhba" was established. Its activists began to organize the Zionist operation with a fresh style and vigor.

The youth that studied in high school was organized by counselors. Let us mention some of the names of the students: Yekutiel Shuster, the brothers Zeltkis, Yaakov Vigil, Bentzion Shtriker and his brother Herzl Shtriker, Moshe Schorr, Khanan Deutsch, Shmuel Shirtz and Shmuel Epstn.

The first Hebrew school, "Safah Brurah" ["Clear Language"] was established. Its first teacher was Naftali Zigel. Indeed, there was a Hebrew teacher before him, Mr. Broida – a Russian native. However, he taught private lessons according to the [old fashion] style of "Limud Metukan" [Enhanced study or Enhanced Kheder"], which was customed in Russia at that time. Trips to neighboring cities, such as Sasiv and Holohory [Gologory], were organized. These trips were accompanied by lectures about Zionism. There were also special clubs for starting students. Dr. Khaim Zelkai, who made Aliya to Eretz Israel, was among these youths. In Israel, he became the editor of the medical journal of the physician union, but he passed away in the middle of his career.

There were families in Zloczow for whom Zionism was the center of their lives. Among them, the family of Rabbi Yitzkhak "Beniber" Schwadron. He was a pious Jew who dreamt all his life to build a perfume factory in Israel. He owned several large businesses, including the firm "Binovka", which was very well known throughout Galitsia and Austria. Despite his profitable businesses in Zloczow, he was keen on building a factory in Eretz Israel. He had the secret of spicing liquor, which made it very tasteful. He sent his son, Avraham Schwadron, to study chemical engineering at a university in Vienna so that he could, one day, manage a factory in Israel. However, World War II broke, Rabbi Schwadron passed away, so the whole idea was never implemented.

In 1914, during my trip to Eretz Israel, I met with Rabi Yitzkhak Schwadron and he told me about his plans. My father, Rabbi David Schweig z"l, dreamt about Eretz Israel his entire life. My grandfather was fortunate. He decided one day, to abandon all of his businesses. He followed up on his decision and made Aliya to Jerusalem, bought a property, and lived his last years in Eretz Israel, with my mother.

In Zloczow, Zionism began to strike roots among the house owners and craftsmen. Dr. Aidelberg and Dr. Groskopf, both of them Zionists, were elected to the community committee. From among the young lawyers, Dr. Tzvi Hirschhorn who was an outstanding speaker excelled in attracting people to the movement. The city residents loved him because of his philanthropic attributes. He first demanded more of himself before he did from others. Hebrew-speaking clubs were formed. Dr. Vepel and Dr. Simkha Bumim Feldman participated in these clubs. The wife of Dr. Hirschhorn (nee Tratkover), participated in the Hebrew-speaking clubs. I devoted a great deal of time to lectures and debates in these clubs.

[Columns 303-304]

"Tzeirei Tzion" ["Zion Youths"] in Zloczow

by Khaim Reiser

Translated by Moshe Kutten

Zloczow, like the rest of the cities and towns, was a city of contrasts. There were exceedingly wealthy and wrenched poor and luxury homes and slums. There was a wide variety of people: 'Amkhu" [the masses], the intelligentsia class, National-Zionists circles, and a cult of assimilators and their followers. An assimilating Jew, Dr. Guld, who was Zloczow's representative to the Austrian parliament, became the mayor later on. Obviously, he was an instrument by the city's Polish minority. He was not interested in Jewish affairs at all. However, the intelligentsia did not sit idle, so the popularity of assimilation gradually declined, and slowly, the influence of the liberal and Zionist public figures grew more and more.

The route of the Jewish students was not wrapped in roses. The high schools that attracted many Jewish youths were at the hands of Polish teachers, and they created an antisemitic atmosphere. In all sorts of ways, legal and illegal, they placed obstacles in front of the Jewish students. A heavy partition was erected between us and the Christian students. There was almost no direct contact between us and them. We were not allowed access to their clubs or sports teams. However, one must say that the loss of the relationship was our gain. The main objective of the Christians was to see us abandon our own interests, self-deny our identity, and join their camps. However, the segregation, oppression, and antisemitic approach resulted in a completely opposite result. Their maltreatment hurt us deeply. Therefore, we got outraged with them. The assimilation surge was halted. It was replaced by the sense of national identity, which strengthened from one day to another and conquered our hearts. Under the distress brought about by the venom-soaked atmosphere, the need for greater unity developed. Except for an exceptional few, we considered ourselves as one big family with a common interest. As a result of the natural national instinct, we began to feel that the Polish language, taught in school and used in our daily life, was not our language. We began to feel and understand that their poets were not our poets, and their aspirations for independence were not our aspirations. The Jewish students' body, began to look for a new direction and means for escaping the choking of the daily reality. The answer to our quest was found quickly – we had to go back to our sources, to our people. We had to revive our own language, culture, and literature. We had to familiarize ourselves with our own history and with the creations of our geniuses and poets.

I was stopped one day, in school, by the senior students, Schweig and Leider. They whispered in my ear that they wanted to meet with me at the old "vall" [wall ?] to assign a crucial mission to me. I was curious about that small conversation in the school corridor, so I waited anxiously for our meeting. The two presented themselves as the leaders of a secret student association called "Tzeirei Tzion" ["Zion Youths"]. They stated that the organization held member meetings at the Broida Hebrew School.

The Committee for the Child Welfare in the Winter

[Columns 305-306]

A Senior Group of Zloczow's Pioneers

The association was organized by age groups. During meetings on Sunday, we studied the Jewish history and geography of Eretz Israel. Lectures about the pamphlet "Auto-Emancipation" byPinsker, and the book "Rome and Jerusalem" by Moshe Hess were held in the meetings. There were also lectures about Zionism, in general, and about Herzl, Nordau, and others. At times, we read articles from the magazine "Moria", the journal of "Tzeirei Tzion" association in Lviv.

I took on myself enthusiastically the mission to organize the students of my age group. I succeeded in organizing three groups in a relatively short time.

A new world was opened for us. We waited impatiently the whole week for meetings on Sunday. The fact that our meetings were illegal, and held in secret, for the fear that we would be expelled from school, added to our enthusiasm. We felt like "heroes" - uplifted and courageous.

We often organized, obviously confidentially, trips to the countryside for scouts' training. Dr. Shuster, who excelled in organizing youth groups, and Dr. Toperman, one of the high school teachers, an enthusiastic Zionist, and devotee of the youth, assisted us and served as counselors on these trips.

Our association with the Zionist movement and the interest of Eretz Israel received a real boost toward the end of 1913 when Dr. Avraham Schwadron began to be interested in the life of the youths in our town. Schwadron (who was called Avraham Sharon in Eretz Israel), was an enthusiastic Zionist, like his father, R' Yitzkhak Binover. He visited Eretz Israel and was full of enthusiasm and admiration for the way of life of the first groups from the "Ha'Shomer" ["The Guard"] and other movements. Schwadron, who grew up under the German education system, did not know Polish. He describes his impressions from Eretz Israel in vivacious Yiddish. In his weekly discussions, Schwadron spoke a great deal about the exalted ideas of the settlers and the enthusiasm of the workers. He expanded on "Kvutzat" Degania. His talks were very pleasing and heartwarming. Indeed, while sitting on our benches listening to the talks, most of us dreamt about Aliya and imagined ourselves becoming workers in Eretz Israel.

Schwadron has an enormous influence over the youths. We admired him, the way people admire an exceedingly noble figure, although his approach to Zionism was aggressive and "cruel" - he demanded from us an actual fulfillment, in heart and soul and in deeds.

The clouds darkened in the European sky. the horizon for European Jews seemed even darker. As was always the case, Jews served as a seismograph for the future of the rest of the world. Being close to the Russian borders, World War I, which broke in the summer of 1914, brought fear to Zloczow's Jews. We knew everything about Ukrainian Jewry. The pogroms of 1905 – 1906, the Beilis trial in 1913, the antisemitic wave with its origin at the center of the Tzar regime, and the bloody hands of Khmelnytskyi's descendants all cast horrific fear in our hearts. There was, therefore, no wonder that after the shock of the declaration of war, many Jews began to escape [west] from the city and finda residence in other cities far from the border. Some ran away as far as the capital – Vienna. However, after several days of wandering around, the escapes found themselves displaced and without a roof above their heads. They began to think about going back to Zloczow and placing their trust in the Guardian of Israel not to abandon them in their time of distress.

The best of the youths in the city of Zloczow enlisted in the King's army.

[Columns 307-308]

Even young fathers enlisted under the Austrian flag. The peace and quiet ended for our people.

Trouble descended in a flash. The Russian invasion became a bitter reality. Not that many days elapsed before our people savored life under the Russian whip.

In 1916, when the Russians were defeated in Eastern Galitsia, they relied instead on the devil's ploy, namely, the expulsion of the residents from towns located near the border. Zloczow was the only exception. The city "won" the right to host the people who were expelled, under the guard of Kozaks, from its neighboring towns. I would never forget the horrific picture that was uncovered as a result of that expulsion. The refugee camp looked like the famous Hirshberg's painting – "Exile".

Zloczow Jews showed their poor brothers an unprecedented attitude of pity and affinity. There wasn't a single resident, even the poorest of the poor, who did not host a refugee family, or two, in their house. Indeed, Jewish solidarity was revealed in all of its power and glory.

Except for fear of pogroms and forced labor kidnapping, Zloczow's Jews suffered neither economically nor physically during the entire invasion. However, we mentally felt the suffering daily and hourly. All of the Jewish schools were closed and public and cultural life came to a halt. The Jewish youth was left on its own without educators and counselors.

When the Russians left the city, life began to return to normal. Many of the refugees started to come back from Vienna and other places. The Jewish schools were reopened. An urgent need to re-energize and reorganize the youth, and enrich its life with content, was developed. Volunteers from among the youths, who previously acquired experience in the youth movement, came forward and volunteered to replace the older counselors who were fighting on the front. The volunteers organized to revive the student youth movement – "Tzeirei Tzion". Among the activists were Manis Epstein, Kalman Schweig, Betzweig, Yaaov Zaltz, L. Yager, Lunis, and Yekhezkel Aidelberg. A small change was established in the action plan – girls were accepted to the association. Hebrew evening lessons were organized. Parties and festivals were held for various occasions, and traditional and national holidays were celebrated.

Gradually and slowly, the Polish language was shoved aside and the Yiddish language took its place. Another historical correction was made – in the spirit of democracy, youths who were not studying were also accepted into our ranks.

The members who came back from Vienna were not happy with the expansion scheme. They demanded a revision according to the new trends prevalent in Western Europe. The executive committee of "Tzeirei Tzion", which was transferred at the beginning of World War I from Lviv to Vienna, decided upon a new program for the movement. They combined some of the principles of the International Scout Movement and other youth movements with the ideals of the "HaShomer" movement [literally – "The Guard", a Jewish defense organization] in Eretz Israel. With time, a new concept was developed [unification of 'HaShomer" and "Tzeirei Tzion" principles]. That concept was realized with the establishment of "Ha'Shomer HaTzair" [The Young Guard]. They mainly attracted the young section of the youth, which belonged to the studying youth of "Tzeirei Tzion". With the return of Dov Ofer, a student with consciousness and vigor, who was one of the activists of "HaShomer HaTzair" in Vienna, the adaptation to the new program was accelerated. Dov Ofer, a member of a wealthy assimilated family, did not initially possess any interest or affinity toward Jewish interests. In Vienna, he went through a transformation when he exposed the ideals of the "HaShomer". Soon, he became one of the most active operatives of the national movement. When he returned to Zloczow, Ofer devoted himself enthusiastically to the "HaShomer HaTzair" activity. The leadership of "Tzeirei Tzion" finally agreed to the idea of the merger [with HaShomer] after a campaign of explanations and lengthy debates. A delegation went to Lviv to get informed about the new program. Later on, Yssaskhar Reiz, the leader of the "HaShomer HaTzair" in Lviv, was invited to come to Zloczow to assist in the transformation. The unification plan and the new program were approved by the crowded assembly gathered for that purpose.

The renewed organization began with its activities based on experience gathered in the past. The members formed into small groups for study and discussions. The evening lessons were held in good spirits and intensely. Instead of learning grammar, the members began to converse in Hebrew. Instead of studying poetry, the members started to sing songs from Eretz Israel. Nature trips were held from time to time.

Over time, new terrains for activities were opened for the youths, mainly for the benefit of "Keren Kayemet Le'Israel" [JNF – "Jewish National Fund"]. Some of the leaders of the Zionist movement came to Zloczow at the beginning of 1917. Dr. Meiblum, who served as the JNF representative in Zloczow and its environs before the war, returned to Zloczow. Under him, all activities for the benefit of the JNF were reorganized.

When World War I ended, transportation to and from Vienna was disrupted. As a result, our operations were also affected.

[Columns 309-310]

Our situation also worsened due to the eruption of the civil war between the Poles and the Ukrainians. Both sides considered the Jews as scapegoats. Oppressions, robberies, and pogroms became daily occurrences. Our main concern was to preserve the JNF funds, as every penny was sacred and dedicated to the redemption of the homeland. As a person in charge of the funds of JNF in Zloczow, I was burdened by the heavy responsibility. I could not relax until I gathered all of the money, hid it in a clay jar, and buried it in the cellar until the rage would pass. When the storm subsided, dangers diminished, and the road condition returned to normal, I hurried up and transferred the money to the headquarter. Dr. Hausner, the JNF president in Vienna, became emotional and was astonished to find out from G. Orgal, a member of the JNF in our city, about how I managed to save the money.

I would not tell a lie or falsely boast by claiming that there were not that many locations, which were as dedicated to the JNF as the JNF committee in Zloczow. The reputation of the dedication and loyalty of our JNF committee reached America. The following fact would serve as proof for that: When our *landsleit* in America began to send money to their needy relatives during the years 1920 – 1921, they could not find a more honest and loyal address than the JNF agent in our town. As a result of the trust that Zloczow's Jews and the *landsleit* abroad placed in the office of the JNF in town, revenues grew from one day to another.

Our national holidays played an essential role in the activities of the youth movement. Hannukah balls acquired a name for themselves in the city and its surrounding. It warms my heart when I think of the first Hannukah ball in 1917. That was the first time that a public ball was opened with a speech in Hebrew. We had a distinguished guest, Dr. Hirschhorn, who spoke in Polish, as was customary during those days. He spoke about the Balfour Declaration, which was announced when General Allenby stood with his army at the gates of Jerusalem. "And here, the promise is going to be fulfilled", said Dr. Hirschhorn, "and your children shall return to their own border" [Jeramiah 31:16]. At the end of the enthusiastic speech, some of our members stood up and swore, right there and there, to follow the commandment "to make Aliya to Eretz Israel and to build it" [Isaiah 14:1].

The Big War was still raging and nobody knew how and when it would end. The warring sides, the Russians and Austrians, were, once again, situated not that far away from us. However, we got used to that, and life continued, more or less, along a normal route (if one could call life at a time of war – "normal").

In the meantime, the February Revolution broke. Kranski, who became the prime minister of the new interim government, promised equal rights to the Jews. The news about the revolution and the hopes for the Jews arrived in Zloczow too. A large public gathering was held in the city in honor of the return of the Zionist activist Dr. Katz. The distinguished guest described, optimistically, the freedom that was awarded to Russian Jewry. He particularly emphasized the bright future envisioned for Eretz Israel, brought by the immigration of the Russian Jews awaken from their desperation. However, that joy did not last long. With the October Revolution and the take-over by the Bolsheviks, the bitter reality set in and disappointed us. The numerous Russian Jewish population contingency was in shackles again, rotted in its hopelessness.

I must emphasize that the new winds of change that began blowing with the changes and transformations of the Russian regimes did not affect the Jewish youth in Zloczow. Our city's youth were not swept away by any new doctrine and remained loyal to the Zionist ideal. They were ready, at any time, to give a hand in building a new homeland in our renewing land.

In 1918, the popularity and strength of the Austrian government diminished. The Germans and the Austrians came out of the war, beaten and torn. As a result, bad times were approaching for Zloczow Jews and the rest of our brothers throughout Galitsia.

Due to the Austrian defeat, a civil war between the Poles and the Ukrainians erupted. We, the Jews, found ourselves caught between two warring sides. The irony of fate was that the Jews, one of the three minorities in the country, found themselves in that dangerous situation between the two rival minorities.

In the beginning, when the Western Ukrainian Republic was formed in eastern Galitsia, the Ukrainians thought, probably justifiably, that they would need support from the Jews, both inwardly and outwardly. As a result, they promised national and cultural autonomy to the Jews. Dr. Hirschhorn, the admired and courageous fighter for Jewish rights, did not ascribe great importance to that promise, which seemed to be just a temporary wish that they may not be able to fulfill. It was clear that when riots broke by the Ukrainian population, we would not be able the rely on the Ukrainian soldiers to save us. Therefore, Dr. Hirschhorn turned to the interim government with a request to allow us to organize and establish self-defense. We should give credit to the interim government that understood our issue and allowed for the formation of the self-defense force.

[Column 311]

R' Mordekhai Broda – The Hebrew Teacher

Obviously, we relied on the youth that began to return from their military service. These Jewish soldiers and officers, who experienced the war on the battlefields and military hospitals, were fortunate to come back healthy and well, but have not totally healed mentally. The city's Jews hanged their hopes in them as saviors and defenders at a time of trouble.

The famous Zionist Dr. Shwager, an officer in the Austrian army, was nominated as the head of the self-defense force. The organizers were those intelligent and well-trained soldiers and officers who excelled in their service to the Austrian military: They did not serve empty-handed. The self-defense soldiers were equipped, on behalf of the interim government, with proper and efficient weapons. The Jews in Zloczow acquired a real sense of security then. How full of wonder and enthusiasm was their response upon seeing the self-defense companies marching freely in the city's streets.

That state of peace and relative calm existed during the winter months until the change came abruptly. The Ukrainians were losing their civil wars and then recovered. When they joined forces with the oppressing soldiers of the murderer Petliura, their attitude toward the Jewish population changed, and they eliminated the self-defense force. Zloczow Jews became unprotected against any attack.

The economic situation of the Jews worsened from one day to another. The young generation was facing a dark future. Everybody searched for a new way, as in Pslams 121:1-2: "From where will my help come". One thing was very clear and obvious – assimilation became totally bankrupt. The solution to the Jewish problem sprouted out on its own – revival in Eretz Israel, built by Jewish hands. That was the only way left, without any alternative. The time has come to immediately begin with preparation activities – preparation for the body and soul.

[Column 312]

There was no shortage in Zloczow of assertive people with initiative and leadership skills. When the last of the assimilators realized that their game was over, and since their circles had never connected with the masses, they showed the integrity of intelligent people and vacated their distinguished positions, willingly or unwillingly. And so, national Zionist leaders had been appointed the lead the Jewish public.

Soon, a youth center was established. The center became a home for the youths who were eager to learn, study and understand. Evening lessons were re-opened, and a series of lectures and celebrations, devoted to public information sessions and debates, were held. Everything was organized with tremendous enthusiasm and energy.

The driving force in the "Center" was Morkekhai Imber. Together with him, the following people were active enthusiastically and dedicatedly: Ozer Shmirer, Yeshaia Reis, A. Holtz, Khaim Betman, Moshe Kleinman, Mordekhai Bukhbinder, Avraham Mass (today, Dr. Mass, an instructor at the Hebrew University in Jerusalem), and Kalman Schweig (later on, Dr. Schweig, assistant to Dr. Rupin). The following women were active: Sara Nagler, P. Tauber, Rivka Vianchlayer, Mrs. Yosefsberg, and Mrs. Liderkhever. The latter was an assimilator for whom Jewish affairs were far from her mind. With the big disappointment that her ideology suffered, she joined the group of youth leaders expressing her wish to contribute her energy, skills, and education for the benefit of the new movement.

At that time, the "Center" was not affiliated with any party. The principles established by Ekhad Ha'Am, the leaders of [the organization he had established] "Bnei Moshe", and other spiritual leaders served as the basis for the "Center's" program. Several youth clubs and movements blended together. A single basic and general objective unified them all: national revival and the building of Eretz Israel.

In actuality, the "Center" became like a "university for the masses". Lectures, lessons, and discussions based on a predetermined program were held there daily. A whole year of multi-facets activities, extensive *"Hakhshara"* [preparations for Aliya to Eretz Israel], and promotion of national affairs had passed. The "Center's" management decided that the time had come to deviate from the general and neutral frameworks and become a political party with a national political character, similar to the national organization ["Bond"?] in Russia. That led to the establishment of a strong youth union [a faction within "Tzeirei Tzion"] called "The Popular Faction of Tzeirei Tzion".

[Columns 313-314]

Some of the leaders of the new faction were under the influence of "HaPoel HaTzair" ["The Young Worker", a non-Marxist labor-affiliated Zionist party] in Eretz Israel. It was only natural that they led the new youth union according to the program and the needs of the party of "HaPoel HaTzair" in Eretz Israel. From that point on, all of the discussions and debates revolved around the essence of the party, which was based on the direction and methods of A. D. Gordon.

During the Civil War, in 1918 – 1919, Zloczow was disconnected from the outside world. For the Jews in the city, it was like living on a remote island. To strengthen the residents' spirit and generate hope for better days, the General Zionists [Zionists not affiliated with the labor movement or religious Zionism], also energized and acted to revive their Zionist union. The leaders of the General Zionists were Dr. Hirschhorn, Dr. Groskopf, Dr. Feldman, Dr. G. Katz, Dr. Meiblum, Dr.s M. and P. Gruber, Dr. Shwager, Moshe Schorr, and later on also Dr. Werpel and Dr. Shwager. The academic Jews also organized a separate club. "Poalei Tzion" which was extremely active during the years before World War I, was not very active during the Civil War and was reorganized only in 1920 under the leadership of Dr. Reuven Schwager and Yosef Shweig. The religious Zionists – "HaMizrakhi" and Tzeirei Ha'Mizraki" remained active and continued to manage their clubs and organizations according to their ideology, and reaped the fruits of their efforts.

During the Civil War, the General Zionists in Zloczow published a Jewish weekly magazine. The editors of the magazine were Moshe Schorr, Simkha Bunim Feldman, and Yitzkhak Negelberg. The intelligentsia among the Zionists was involved in the publication of the magazine. The magazine included news from throughout the country and abroad. It also contained notes and articles about Eretz Israel and other Jewish issues. It contained local news and the public happenings in the city. During the dark days of the Civil War, that magazine managed to bring light and a sense of civility into the life of Zloczow Jews' homes.

One of the brightest moments during those difficult days was the establishment of the Jewish elementary school. It was obviously established under the agreement by the interim Ukrainian government. Obviously, the Zionist leaders were the founders and the driving force behind this institution. Some of these leaders served as teachers there, like Dr. M. Gruber, Moshe Schorr, Yitzkhak Negelberg, Zlatkis, Delkha Friedman, and the author of this article. The purpose of that school was to provide Zloczow's Jewish students general education. A pure national Jewish spirit prevailed within the walls of that school. Yiddish and Hebrew were taught extensively in the school. The enthusiasm of the students and the joy of their parents were considerable.

However, that joy did not last long. Unfortunately, when the Poles won over the Ukrainians, the school was brutally closed, and the teachers and the students were expelled. I would never forget the cries of the children when they witnessed a Polish policeman hanging a sealed lock on their class door and threatening them that anybody who dares to touch the lock or break the seal would be arrested. My heart was torn when I had to say an emotional goodbye to my young students.

We were consoled by the fact that the school closure decree did not expand to the rest of our public cultural institutions. During those difficult days, when bread and food were in short supply, there was no shortage of spiritual nourishment. While it was not possible for us, for technical or other reasons, to be active during the week, we conducted lessons and lectures in the gathering hall every Saturday evening.

There was no shortage of activities and artistic shows. We were able to bring the film "The life of Dr. Herzl" with the help of the JNF. We rented the "Sokol" hall for seven days and screened the movie every evening in front of a capacity-filled hall. Crowds came in droves to watch it. Encouraged by the success of the movie, we brought, a short while later, the famed Opera singer, Avraham Zneoda (who acted and sang in the opera house in Petrograd). The "Sokol" hall was filled up again with a crowd that enjoyed listening to famous arias and folk songs. All of the revenues from the movie and the singing balls were dedicated to the JNF.

Our city played a significant role in literature. Besides the poet and writer, N. H. Imber, author of "HaTikva", several other Yiddish poets came out of Zloczow during the 1920s. Among them Elazar Bernstien and Moshe Pichinik. These two poets, who made a name for themselves outside of the city, established a literary "Shtiebel" [A little house of praying and learning]. Groups of youth would gather there sometime for lectures about Yiddish literature. They would also play and recite Yiddish poems. Moshe Pichinik would lend books from his extensive library to whoever asked.

[Columns 315-316]

The other "local" poet, Elazar Bernstein, had the talents of acting and reciting. From time to time, he would recite monologues from Peretz, Shalom Aleichem, and others.

Indeed, there were quite a few people with artistic talent among Zloczow's people. Even during the darkest time, some of our academics established a drama club and played from works by Pinski, Hirshbin, and others. Shmuel Shwartz and Keilah Bloishtein excelled. We would not exaggerate by claiming that these two could handily serve as role models for professional actors.

The activists among Zloczow's Jews did not limit themselves to artistic creativity and the development of spiritual values. They found themselves obligated to develop and nourish physical power. There was almost no access for Jews to the Polish sports club. The few Jews who managed to join did not feel at home due to the racist discrimination and an attitude of contempt toward them. The Jewish youths created their own sports club. The sports associations that had existed before the war were revived – and they did not disappoint. During the 1920s, the Jewish athletes constituted a substantial and respectable regiment, and even the elders who were just passive spectators enjoyed the success of the sports team.

From sports associations to other associations that dealt with various aspects of daily life. The craftsmen association "Yad Kharutzim", represented the interests of the Jewish workers. Most of the members of "Yad Kharutzim" were orthodox Jews, and the home of the association also served as a prayer and learning house. The members prayed there three times a day during holidays and Saturdays, as well as during weekdays. On Saturday nights, they gathered to listen to lectures about general and Jewish topics. The lecturers were mostly local. These lectures contributed substantially to the elevation of the cultural level of the masses.

An association, called "Agudat Israel", was originally established to fight a "holy war" against modernization and to shield against the "destructive" influence of the enlightened on the Jewish public in general, and in particular the youth. However, even the activity of that association contributed to the improvement and nourishment of public life.

Zloczow Jews suffered as a result of regime changes, upheavals, and revolutions. They continuously feared new rulers, coming and going, and the violent soldiers of the rival armies, particularly during the days of Petliura. However, the Jews suffered the most at the hands of the Polish "Haller'chik's". These were the hooligans of the Polish Salvation Army ["Blue Army"] who enlisted in America [and France] to help save the reviving Poland, which was fighting for its independence. The anti-Semite soldiers were recruited by General Haller. However, instead of fighting in the front against their enemies, they showed their heroism by brutalizing the Jews. They kidnapped young people, deceptively claiming that they were needed for forced labor, and as part of that kidnapping, they cut their beards with one purpose to humiliate and disgrace the human spirit of the Jew. The Poles who were just yesterday oppressed and enslaved turned a blind eye to the elementary duty of awarding the right of freedom to all citizens, including minorities. That was the state of mind throughout the revived Polish nation.

Echoes of that state of mind arrived in our city, Zloczow, in spirit and practice. The horizon for the Jews became darker from one day to another. Jews were in an awful and unbearable situation. Everybody was wondering where help would come from. The answer seemed to be – immigration. The two major logical destinations were America and Eretz Israel. The body was attracted to the "Golden Land", the soul was longing for our ancestors" land. However, in either place, the roads were blocked. The obstacles to reaching Eretz Israel were particularly hurtful. The British issued the Balfour Declaration. However, since receiving the mandate over Eretz Israel, they turned their back on the Jews, trying to appease the Arabs. They tried all sorts of ways to back up from their promise. The main mean by which they wanted to achieve that was by limiting immigration. They conspired to lock the gates completely. The USA, which, at other times, absorbed thousands and tens of thousands of refugees, got to the point that they thought that there were too many refugees being admitted. The USA came out with all sorts of means to reduce and limit immigration. The new immigration laws hurt the Jews the most. For the Germans, who were the former USA's enemies, America's gates were opened. However, a quota was placed on the number of prosecuted and survivors.

With all of that, the spirit of Zloczow's Jews remained high, and they did not lose all hope. The youth activists did whatever they could to increase the number of people who made Aliya to Eretz Israel. The first group of pioneers was organized by the "HaShomer HaHatzair:" Among the lucky few was nobody else but Dov Ofer. However, he was killed a short while later by Arab rioters. The tragic death of Dov Ofer made a difficult impression on our youth in Zloczow. However, instead of sitting down quietly to grieve and give up, they rallied more eagerly and swore not to relax until everybody gets to go to our country., our homeland, to build, guard, enrich, and revive, for us and for the next generations.

[Columns 317-318]

Obviously, the members of "Tzeirei Tzion" were imbued with the spirit of "Fulfilling Zionism" [making Aliya]. The organization "HeKhalutz" ["The Pioneer"] was founded. Its main objective was "*Hakhshara*" [Preparations for Aliya to Eretz Israel]. A piece of land was leased to train members in working the land. Members then tried to make Aliya. A few certificates for the first group of "Tzeirei Tzion" were obtained following a prolonged effort and vigorous lobbying.

The influence of "Tzeirei Tzion" on the public and cultural life of Zloczow's Jews was significant. Some members excelled in their productive work. They acquired a name for themselves as organizers and counselors. No wonder, therefore, that they were elected as representatives to the Zionist conference in Lviv. Indeed, their appearance left a big impression at that conference. Mordekhai Imber particularly excelled, and echoes of his speech, in which he demanded special attention to the Aliya of the youths, reached the media. Zloczow also participated in the establishment of the "Union of Tzeirei Tzion". Representatives from Zloczow participated in the first conference of that union.

A district committee to coordinate the Zionist activities in the surrounding cities and towns was established in Zloczow. The heads of the district leadership team were Dr. Werpel, Dr. Hirschhorn, and H. Reizer.

The action plan of the district committee was extensive and broad. However, when the secretary had to travel around the district, he had to do it at his own cost or travel by foot. Once, when he walked for several hours to Jezierzany to attend a JNF ball. After the ball, the members set aside some money from the ball's revenues, which were sizeable, for a trip back on a horse and cart…

The author of these lines was often going around in the corridors of the court to ambush Dr. Werpel, who was a lawyer, to discuss matters associated with the committee with him. We spent the short breaks between the trial, in one of the corners, to discuss matters related to the JNF, culture, certificates, etc. …

The life of the youth in Zloczow before the Holocaust was beautiful and full of interest and importance. We do not purport that our city was exceptional over the rest of the cities in Eastern Galitsia. Nevertheless, its role in that colossal project of winning over the hearts of the youths and masses was substantive.

Let these pages serve as a testimony and a memorial candle for all of those people who were vigilant and who were ready to serve the needs of their nation and homeland.

[Columns 319-320]

"Ha'Shomer Ha'Tzair", 40 Years Ago

by Shlomo Bar-Am

Translated by Moshe Kutten

It was during World War I, in 1917. Despite being the third year of that cruel war and even with the front located not that far away from our city, life progressed as "normal". The schools were opened and the youth was alert and active.

The youth movement of "Tzeirei Tzion" ["Zion Youths"] was active then. It consisted of tens of youths, particularly students of the local high schools. The aim of "Tzeirie Tzion" union was to improve the moral and physical attributes of its youths. It strived to educate its members to act decisively, courageously, and honestly fitting Jewish youth. There were several ways to achieve that aspiration:

1. Teaching of the Hebrew language
2. Teaching of the history of Zionism
3. Teaching Jewish history
4. Teaching knowledge about Eretz Israel
5. Lecturing about Yiddish literature
6. Organizing balls on national holidays
7. Conduction sing-along sessions
8. Collecting contributions for the Jewish National Fund (JNF)

The movement "HaShomer" ["The Guard"], which wanted to imitate the "HaShomer" movement in Eretz Israel, was also active in Galitsia, even before the war.

Upon the take-over of Galitsia by the Russians, some of the residents escaped west. Some of the escapees reached as far west as Vienna. In Vienna, discussions about the unification of the two movements into a new organization called "HaShomer HaTzair" ["The Young Guard"] took place. (We should mention here, that the head of the "HaShomer" movement in Vienna was the Lawyer, Dr. A. Veshitz, a native of Zloczow).

The purpose of the unification was to combine the good of the two movements and educate healthy and skilled youths for life, based on human and national foundations.

[Among other influences], the "HaShomer HaTzair"] movement was influenced by the German youth movement. However, it was more practical and aspired to escape to Eretz Israel, rather than just to the surrounding forests.

When Galitsia was freed from the Russian occupation, the refugee families began to return to their homes. Among the returnees was the Ofer family, which was one of the wealthiest in our city. Dov Ofer, who was one of the family youths, was a member of the unified movement "HaShomer HaTzair". He was already hooked on the Zionist ideal. When he returned to Zloczow at the end of 1917, he was 16 years old. He had an average height, broad shoulders, red hair, and a face full of freckles. He gathered boys and girls of his age and established the core of the new movement. Since he excelled in organization skills, he widened the movement's charter by adding training for physical work [*hakhshara*] as a preparation for making and Aliya to Eretz Israel and the fulfillment of the Aliya ideal.

בדרך ביל"ו

The "HaShomer HaTzair" Named after the "BIL"U" Movement

[Columns 321-322]

הנופש

A Group of "HaShomer HaTzair" Counselors

When I look back, after 40 years, I have to admit that Dov Ofer was the one who initiated the idea of Aliya and also influenced many who did not belong to his movement.

In the summer of 1920, the first group of youths made Aliya and Dov among them. However, he did not live long in Eretz Israel, as he was shot by an Arab murderer.

Going back to the establishment of the "HaShomer HaTzair" in Zloczow": The first group called "Nesher" ["Eagle"] included boys and girls aged 12 – 18 from different circles in town. They spent their time in discussions, learning the Hebrew language, and going on trips to areas around Zloczow.

Toward the end of 1918, when the regime was passed to the Ukrainians, the activity in the movement continued regularly. During the winter of 1919, the older groups began to do physical work. They even worked in wood sawing. What a revolution in the city!

The money collected was destined for members with limited means who wished to make Aliya to Eretz Israel.

In the Spring of 1919, a piece of land outside of the city was purchased. We converted that piece of land into a vegetable garden. During the summer of the same year, the older members went to work in agriculture at one of the farms of a Jewish farm owner.

In the meantime, the movement expanded and contained about 10 [100?] boys and girls. Some of them realized their dream, made Aliya to Eretz Israel, and thus survived the Holocaust.

As for myself, I made Aliya in 1920, and my physical connection to the city was severed. However, I still have a spiritual tie to the city, where I was educated on pioneering and fulfillment, and the memories.

[Columns 323-324]

"Gordonia" Youth Movement

by Y. Zendberg

Translated by Moshe Kutten

Among the ebullient youth movements, which played a leading role in the way of life in Zloczow, was the "Gordonia" movement, founded and nourished by a few members in 1928.

Most of these members perished in the Holocaust, and their memory would stay with us forever. I will mention here the most active ones:

Dr. Tzvi Teichman – participated in the movement foundation conference in Prague. He was influenced by A. D. Gordon and Khaim Arlozorov. When he returned, he dedicated himself to the education of the youth and the [Hit'akhdut – Union] party in our city.

Feibush Bernholz – was a man of the people, a noble soul, innocent, with wide horizons. He dedicated his best efforts to the consolidation of the "Gordonia" movement and its organization.

Feivel Reizer - received a traditional education. He had a deep knowledge about the happenings among the people, the Zionist movement, and the socialist movement. He was entrenched in Jewish folklore.

A group of boys, formally members of the "HaShomer HaTzair" joined "Gordonia" during its initial steps. "HaShomer Hatzair" underwent a severe spiritual crisis at that time. After the first generation of its founders made Aliya to Eretz Israel ("The Third Aliya"), the movement remained defenseless against the influence of the invading Communism, which penetrated the branches of the "HaShomer Hatzair" and conquered the hearts of the youth.

However, [the part of] the same youth, for whom the Zionist spirit was imbued in its heart, did not accept that influence and looked for [other] ways to fulfill its aspirations. They left "HaShomer HaTzair" and joined "Gordonia" with heart and soul and youthful warmth. They saw it as the perfect blend of socialism and popular Zionism.

That group of Zloczow's youth, who organized itself in "Gordonia" with the active assistance of the members mentioned above, set themselves a goal to recruit youths from among the masses and high school students, unify them, and cast them in the same mold.

The "Gordonia" movement educated the youth for pioneering, simplicity, and Aliya to Eretz Israel. It educated me for life in a kibbutz and the values of A. D. Gordon. In addition, the members took an active role in the work of funds and in the Jewish public life. Our group of youths had 12 members:

[At publication time] the following members live in Israel: Tzvi Ox, M. Hochman, Y. Zendberg, L. Pasternak, A. Zimand. Levintah who was one of the first to make Aliya in 1931), P. Zilbershitz and Feivel Strassler z"l also made Aliya. The following members perished in the Holocaust: Z. Katz z"l, Y. Mesher z"l, Khoben z"l, B. Tzukerdel z"l, L. Reizer z"l, and Y. Strassler z"l.

Among the prominent members who joined the movement a year later, I would like to mention Mordekhai Porat (Preis), who resides in Kibutz Mishmar HaSharon, Israel, his brother, M. Preis z"l, who perished in the Holocaust, and L. Katz. The latter was a youth with extraordinary skills and broad education, whom the movement expected great things of him.

The life that combined work and education in the movement branch was not easy.

A Group of the "HeKhalutz" members

[Columns 325-326]

The movement often suffered from the lack of a club to operate in and shortage of funds. Educational programs were sometimes held outside during rainy and cold days.

An amiable comradery atmosphere was developed over time. The meetings at the place called "Kempa" in Zloczow and the frequent trips to Zezula forests added character and joy to the meetings.

I would like to mention two families in particular, who provided a place for the movement for a symbolic fee: The family of Borideh, the baker, and the Mesher family. The latter provided the branch, during a very difficult period, a spacious club. That family was immersed in Zionism values and understood the importance of unifying the youth in the movement and its education.

The movement grew and developed, and Zloczow became the location of the district headquarter of "Gordonia". Members of the branch established branches in the area, such as in Sasiv, Olesko, Bilyi Kamin, Lopatyn, Ulashnitze [?], Belshkov [?], Pomoryany, and others.

Mrs. Mina Member, an activist from New York, visiting the school in Lakhish province

[Columns 327-328]

"HaMizrakhi Union"

by Barukh Imber

Translated by Moshe Kutten

It is undeniable that the Zionism idea penetrated the "Batei Midrash" [religious schools] and synagogues thanks to the "HaMizrakhi" movement. It was only natural that Jews who prayed, mornings and evenings, for "Shivat Tzion" ["Returning to Zion"] would bring with them the Zionism ideal, and spread the idea of actual redemption. The leaders of "HaMiztrakhi" undertook it upon themselves, during the movement's initial steps, to participate in carrying the burden of the Zionist activities. Following them, the members engaged by fulfilling the actual Zionist commandments. They participated in the activities of the Zionists' funds and the Jewish Colonial Trust, as well as making Aliya themselves. Their effort in spreading the Zionist idea was not an easy one. Cooperating with the Zionist movements, most of which were secular, made it more difficult

"HaMizrkahi" Youths in Zloczow

A Gathering of "HaMizrkahi" Youths in Zloczow

[Columns 329-330]

for them to fight against the zealous Hasidism, which resisted Zionism and fought against it with all of their available means. It was up to the "HaMizrkahi" movement to prove to the masses that Zionism was not standing against the Messiah, a belief that the people felt strongly about. They brought it up in every publicity speech, every sermon at the synagogue, and every public appearance in front of the masses. They had to base their assertion on phrases from the Torah or the writings of the sages. Without these references, there was no chance for their claims to be accepted by the listeners. That publicity campaign was conducted steadily, stubbornly, and tirelessly, out of devotion and endless love for the Zionist idea, through self–sacrifice and not to receive a bounty. The movement activists became convinced that they should aim at bringing redemption as close as possible. They were determined not to let the masses "fall into a deep sleep". "Wake up Israel. The time has come for your enslavement! to end". That call emanated from the hearts of the visionaries who saw the future. That call, during those days, brought us to the "*atkhalta d'geula*" – the beginning of redemption in our time. We have to keep in our hearts the memory of these activists, who lay the foundations for Israel's revival, and who did not live to see Israel being built. May G–d avenge their blood.

———————

[Columns 331-332]

The Trail Blazes of the *Haredi* Movement
(Memory Chapters about Zloczow)

by Member of the Knesset Y. Katz

Translated by Moshe Kutten

The idea of an organization under a single union was supported by prominent Jews headed by the *Admor* [prominent Hasidic rabbi] Magor z'tz"l and Rabbi Khaim Ozer z'tz"l. An awakening among the Haredi [Ultra -Orthodox] Jews resulted in the establishment of the organization "Agudat Shlomei Emunei Yisrael" ["Union of Faithful Jewry"]. The movement spread and grew throughout Poland and the Lithuanian areas annexed by Poland.

No such organization took place in Galitsia. There, people were conservative. They did not appreciate the advantage associated with the unification of the Haredi ranks – "every person to his own olive-grove and vineyard". However, some prominent people tried to follow the Polish organization of [Haredi] Aguda [union], which was announced in the Katowice Conference in 5672 (1912).

A conference was also held in Lviv. Some prominent leaders and visionaries stood out among the conference's spirited activists, organizers, and speakers. Among them were people like Rabbi Yitzkhak Teomim z"l, and Rabbi Meir Shapira z"l, the 22-year-old rabbi of Galina. They and other inspiring rabbis rose up to unite the ultra-orthodox Judaism and Hasidism. In the meantime, the [First World] war broke, and the activities ceased for various reasons. The *Admors* from the house of Rizhin, headed by R' Ysrael'nyu from Chertkiv [Chortkov] z'tz"l. R' Yisrael'nyu was among the people who conceived the idea of unification. Unfortunately, he resided in Vienna, which was separated, after the war, from Galitsia (which was previously part of the Austrian Empire).

Cities and towns that suffered horribly during the war as the front lines passed in their surroundings encountered many hardships in trying to maintain their educational institutions. [unification would have helped in that].

Only during the first election to the Polish Sejm in 5682 (1922), the idea of a single union was revived. At that election, the union movement was incorporated as part of a larger party. As a result, a substantial number of the Agugah's representatives (among them, the great rabbis - Rabbi Aharon Levin, may G-d avenge his blood, and Rabbi Meir Shapira) were elected. Only then the Ultra-Orthodox in Galitsia were awakened into action. The Agudah movement established its center in Lviv, and branches began to spread throughout the country, with sections for adults and youths. They also incorporated the "Poalei [workers of] Agudat Israel", jointly or through separate organizations.

The movement encountered some obstacles since influential and prominent *Admors*, did not subscribe to the idea of unification and stood aside or even resisted…

Nevertheless, the movement progressed and took roots, and became a factor in the elections to the communities and municipalities. Weekly journals appeared in Lviv and Przemysl. First-rate literary and activism talents were discovered. The Galitsian Haredi youth was gifted with unique virtues, scholarship and Hasidism, and knowledge about the matters related to Jewish life. The youth became the Haredi intelligentsia and acquired a name for itself and its influence spread throughout Congressional Poland. Over time, a common ground for cooperation was found. Despite having two separate centers in Lviv and Przemysl, they coordinated and managed to attract crowds to the ranks of the Agudah.

Many prominent people took part in the effort: Rabbi R' Yaakov Vitels and Rabbi Moshe Hirschfrung, may G-d avenge his blood. Leaders like the spiritual, thinking, and speech gaon, Rabbi R' Tzvi Hirschhorn, may G-d avenge his life, Dr. Mordekhai Rozner, Dr. Ben-Tzion Pesler, Yosef Shaul Tzuker. Other leaders included Yaakov Halperin, Rabbi R' Shlomo Shikler, Sh. B. Modlinger, David Rosenfeld, Rabbi Reuven Winkler, Rabbi Sh. B. Meizlish, Shalom Hash, Y. M. Moskovitz, may G-d avenge his blood, and R' Elimelekh Shteyer. Other prominent people were the great scholar brothers, Rabbi Moshe Khaim and Rabi Lau, may G-d avenge his life, and Dr. Hillel Zeidman, may he live long. The authors and poets – R' Alter Schnorr, and R' Elimelekh Shtaye; Many other prominent figures and activists, scholars, loyalists, men of letters, logicians, and philosophers. All of these prominent figures contributed to the Galitsian Agudah movement with all of its sections and filled up it with content and grace, thereby led to its entrenched and growth. The idea of an organization under a single union was supported by prominent Jews headed by the *Admor* Magor z'tz"l and Rabbi Khaim Ozer z'tz"l. An awakening among the Haredi [Ultra -Orthodox] Jews resulted in the establishment of the organization "Agudat Shlomei Emunei Yisrael" ["Union of Faithful Jewry"]. The movement spread and grew throughout Poland and the Lithuanian areas annexed by Poland.

* * *

[Columns 333-334]

A group of Poalei [workers of] Agudat Israel Youths

In our city, Zloczow, situated on the main road between Lviv and Ternopil, near Brody, the Haredim awakened only in 1923. The need and the urgency were only recognized following their failure in the election for the community council. Due to the electoral system, which was not proportional, the Haredi party did not receive any electoral mandate and remained with no representation in the council. It was left without any ability to influence an institution, which controlled all religious and community affairs in the city. People learned a lesson and realized that the way to gain ground and save the youth from grazing in foreign pastures was to organize and unify. They began that activity enthusiastically. And a short while later, hundreds of Hasidim joined the organization along with merchants, workers, and youths in the Batei Ha'Midrash. Not long after that, the Agudah movement in Zloczow, which included youths, homeowners, and workers, became an influential factor that aggressively stood guard and fought for future successes. In the next election for the community council, forty-five percent of the party candidates were elected. Representatives for the city council were also elected. Charity and educational institutions were established. The school "Beit Yaakov" was founded following the successful visit by Sara Shnirer and her students. Public gatherings were held, eyes opened, and the ranks strengthened. The number of youths grew and became part of the organized religious camp. They took part in all of the center's organized activities. Funds have been transferred to the "Keren HaYeshuv" [Religious appeal for the redemption of Eretz Israel] and other appeals. Zloczow acquired a name for itself as a citadel of the Agudah. Desolation was replaced by redemption. Earlier, Zloczow was known as a modern and enlightened city, and people did not see any chances for such a successful awakening and organization.

Rabbi R' Tzvi Hirschhorn became famous in Zloczow. There, he gave his first enthralling speech and was discovered as a person with enormous rhetorical talent. He was a regular guest in Zloczow, excited and captivated his listeners, fans, and opponent alike. Zloczow became an Agudah's citadel until its destruction during the Holocaust. Loyal and dedicated activists, from among the prominent city leaders and philanthropes were active in the union. Hasidism, followers of various courts, and Torah scholars found an organization where they could all cooperate. Even Belz Hasidim joined the Agudah movement in Zloczow. Some of them were elected to the community and municipal councils as part of our list. During the election to the Polish Sejm, the Agudah list received numerous votes. The district center of the party was located in Zloczow, and the election publicity, in the district's tens of towns, and cities, was managed from there.

At the head of the movement in our city served many dignities and activists: R' Shaul Ruller and his in-law - Shlomo Ritter, R' Neteh Willig, R' Moshe Zilbershitz, R' M. Tzipper, my deceased father - R' Khaim Katz z"l, the author and educator – R' Benyamin Zusman, R' Sender Shpigel, R' Aharon Ort, R' Henikh Tzimend, R' Michael Glazer, R' Meir Imber and his brother – R' Shalom, R' Elyakim Yeshayahu Katz, R' Uri Shapira, Lipah Shwager, R' Shlomo Floher, Meir and Tzvi Roller [or Roller], Khaim and Lable Gottlieb, Nakhum Ort. Y. Titel, Yitzkhak Karrotchtik (enthusiastic Agudah member), and many other talented youths. All were Torah scholars, knowledgeable and assertive. Most of them perished in the Holocaust. They were among the first victims of the Nazis who annihilated most of the city's Jewish population.

* * *

It is appropriate to devote additional words about the head of the above-mentioned honorable group. He was a leader who devoted himself to the strengthening of the movement and its institutions. His name was R' Shalul Roller [or Ruler?]. He was a fascinating and unforgettable figure. He was calm and restrained, but also a passionate and exciting man when it came to observance of the Torah and religion. He was the owner of several businesses on central streets. He worshiped G-d diligently. He woke up early in the morning, while it was still dark to study his regular Torah lesson, and was also deeply involved in his studies in the afternoons and evenings after his workday. He prayed in the large and crowded synagogue of Stratyn Hasidim.

[Columns 335-336]

A regional gathering of the Poalie [workers] of Agudat Israel in Zloczow

His place at the synagogue was in the corner. He did not get involved in any unrelated conversation, covered his Talith and Tefilin, turned to the wall, and prayed enthusiastically and with purpose. He had a name as a phalarope and as an exceptional host. He supported the Torah and its learners, was a "Mokir Rabanan" ["cherished rabbis"], and visited Admors frequently. His house was open to the needy and oppressed. During holidays, people gathered by his home, and he and his wife their guests warmly. A visitor that happened to stop by the city would always be hosted by R' Shaul Roller. Before making a fundraising trip to the US for the Yeshiva of Lublin scholars, the Rabbi of Lublin z'tz"l came to Zloczow. He stayed at the spacious apartment of R' Shaul Roller for two weeks, while R' Shaul's wife was serving delicacies to the many guests. Even though nice housewares broke and damages to furniture and chandeliers were caused because of the congestion at the house, the hosts always had a smile on their faces. My mentor and teacher, the Gaon- *Tzadik* Rabbi Israel Landau z'tz"l, great-grandson and a grandson of the [author of the book] "Nodah Be'Yehudah" [Rabbi Yekhezkel ben Yehuda HaLevi Landau] settled in Zloczow after World War I. Who did make a spacious apartment of four rooms on the main street available rent-free for him? None other than R' Shaul. He also provided for the Rabbi's upkeep and made an apartment available free for the school "Beit Yaakov", as well as a nice rent-free place for a club and a large hall, big enough to contain a thousand people for gatherings, public bowls, shows by the "Beit Yaakov" school and other Haredi public events. All of that was contributed by R' Shaul Roller willingly and with an open heart. He also contributed large sums for religious-related affairs and the local and national needs of the Agudah. R' Shaul made the first contribution to Rabbi Meir Shapira z'tz"l for the "Yeshiva of Lublin Scholars. Other city philanthropes followed and contributed money to the Yeshiva. The financial success of the fundraising was a surprise and provided enormous momentum for the construction of the Yeshiva building. A sign with the name of the generous contributor, R' Shaul Roller, hanged in the large entrance hall of the building. He appeared at the celebratory opening. He also participated in the selection of the city Rabbi. The Haredi strove to choose a prominent rabbi who excelled in all virtues and skills, and somebody whose reverence eclipsed his wisdom. R' Shaul invested unprecedented efforts, along with others who worry about the city image and its rabbinical dynasty, to prevent an election of a rabbi whose reputation did not fit a Jewish city with a big Haredi and Hasidic population.

R' Shaul participated in the Agudah conferences in Warsaw and Lviv, leaving his extensive businesses behind. He traveled to these gatherings to be close to the affairs, which were decided upon there by the religious leaders and the great *Tzadikim* of Poland and Galitsia. That allowed him to work for the strengthening of the religion and its Torah followers in his city. He did not pay much attention to his rivals from other camps and continued his work toward his own goals while encouraging his followers. Thanks to his efforts, the Haredi tradition flourished in Zloczow, despite the spiritual changes that occurred there during that time. The number of youths who studied in the local Yeshiva "Orakh Le'Khaim" continued to grow. Many others traveled to other cities to study there. The Haredi public was unified and its influence on public and private life was substantial. The lion's share to that success should be attributed to R' Shaul Roller. He was the planner, dynamiter, and financier.

[Columns 337-338]

Even during a slump in his business, he did not abandon the campaign and did not cease helping the needy. He kept watching for everything that needed charity and continued to be loyal to the public needs and the Agudah movement with all of its branches and extensions. Due to his wisdom and knowledge of the written and oral Polish language, he was the one who represented the Jews with the authorities. He defended the interests of the Jewish population, particularly those of the Haredi Jews.

Due to his talents and powers, he became gradually more successful. During the various wars, he suffered greatly from the conquests of the Russians and the Bolsheviks and was forced to leave the city and settle in a safer location. When he returned after the liberations, he became soundly established again. He continued his custom of supporting and contributing generously and getting involved in public affairs loyally a dedicatedly.

Only one of his daughters and her husband survived. They live in Haifa along with his grandchildren.

When we raise memories from those days of storm and turmoil but also days of vision and action within the Haredi Judaism in Poland and Galitsia, the leaders and activists, whom I only mentioned a small part of, R' Shaul deserves of being highlighted and commemorated.

Their images are glowing and shining. When the history of the organized Haredi revival will be written, these images should be etched with golden letters as the trailblazers for the Torah followers and its carriers. The image and acts of R' Shaul Roller would be memorialized with feelings of respect and admiration.

[Columns 339-340]

The Activities Among the Zloczow's Youths

by Leah Raviv

Translated by Moshe Kutten

The year was 1918 – the end of World War I.

During the war years, we lived in Vienna as refugees. We worked in various industries and were not given the opportunities to study or meet other youths. We were totally disconnected from what was happening in the Jewish world.

There was exhaustion from the physical effort. While we experienced limited absorption of the Viennese culture of those days, we did not participate in any Jewish folklore activities.

When the war ended, we returned to Zloczow. I was surprised to find the city full of vigilant youths mulling over the Zionist problems and aspire for salvation. Everybody talked about the expression: "Change of Values". The need to change the Jewish people and to give them hope for the future was apparent.

Quickly, I joined a youth movement, and my life seemed to have just begun. What was the concept of being a "pioneer" for us? First of all, it meant changing ourselves. Relieve ourselves from our wants and personal ambitions. It meant becoming available only for the movement and its needs. It meant integrity in whatever we did - in doing agricultural work, learning the language, preparing for life in a commune, and training for building our new land.

There was no room for fear of hardships in the pioneering movement.

We went for "*Hakhshara*" [training in agricultural work as a preparation for making Aliya] in the neighboring villages without proper food and sleeping on haystacks infested with mice. But how great was the joy in our hearts? We worked hard and felt that our work would be useful in preparing ourselves for our life in Eretz Israel.

The boys worked chopping wood for heating. They passed through the streets proudly, carrying their axes on their shoulders. They chopped trees in the cold and snow. We became farmers and felt that our sacrifices were carried out for a better future.

We planned to make Aliya to Eretz Israel, work the land, and eat bread we grew ourselves. We would not eat bread that was grown by gentiles.

In elementary school, I had a great interest in studying history. I read much about the subject and knew it well. It was my bad luck, one day, that when the school superintendent came to visit our school, he liked my answers immensely. After the visit, the teacher entered the class angrily and said to the Polish girls: "Isn't it a shame that "the Jew girl" provided the best answers about our history? And where were you?". Afterward, she turned to me and said: "Since you are so interested in Polish history, you would probably be an outstanding Pole?" I answered innocently: "How could I? I am Jewish". The teacher burst out shouting: "You are going to a Polish School. A Polish teacher teaches you. You are eating Polish bread. How can you not be Polish?"

That exchange agitated the entire class and also my Jewish girlfriends. They claimed that I cause them tremendous damage by my behavior.

A Group of Youths in Zloczow

[Columns 341-342]

"Nesher" ["Eagle"] Group of "HaShomer Hatzair"

I asked myself: "do I really eat Polish bread? After all, my father works. He can always be seen bending over plans and talking to construction workers and other craftsmen. He is building houses in the city. Isn't he working to feed me?"

I was restless since then. Finding the Zionist movement was the solution to my dilemma.

When the Jewish school was later established, the studies there were ours. We studied the history of our own nation and our own language. We prepared ourselves for life in Eretz Israel, the land of the "eternal spring". We marched toward fulfilling the dreams of numerous Jewish generations.

The enthusiasm about Zionism was conveyed to us by our teachers, for whom Zionism was their whole life. They felt that it was their holy duty to pass that enthusiasm to us. The teachers in that Jewish high school were Dr. Schwadron (Avraham Sharon), Moshe Kleinman, Mordekhai Imber, and more.

I would like to highlight the brilliant and unique figure of Dr. Schwadron.

He used to say: "Don't do anything halfway, always complete your work. Free yourself from shallowness. A pioneer should serve as a role model in everything: in his or her life, character, and behavior. The pioneer should erase the words: 'I thought' and 'I did not know' from his or her dictionary. The gentiles always mock us with the phrase: 'Jewish work'. Don't let them mock us with the words: 'pioneer's work'".

A Company of
"HaShomer Hatzair"

[Columns 343-344]

The teacher, Moshe Kleinman, suffered quite a bit from Dr. Schwadron's punctuality. I can still hear Kleinman's pleasant singing. I remember his love for every Hebrew creation, his joyfulness, and his vigor.

I acquired my initial knowledge of the Hebrew language from my teacher Mr. Zigel z"l. He taught a whole generation of people to use and love the Hebrew language. He continued his crucial educational work in our homeland.

In my article, I meant to provide an overview of the richness of our life in Zloczow. I wished to highlight the abundance of ideas, the folklore, and the longing in the youth's hearts toward creative life as a free nation.

The days of the "Third Aliya" arrived. We abandoned our studies; There was no use for matriculation certificates; We were going to build our homeland.

We made Aliya in 1921.

Religion Teacher – Yosef Kuta'ee – In Military Uniform

[Columns 345-346]

A. The Sport Movement in Zloczow[1]

by Dr. E. Boneh (Bauman)

Translated by Moshe Kutten

A. The Sports Associations in Zloczow

Despite having a relatively small population, of fewer than twenty thousand people, Zloczow was blessed with lively and vibrant sports life. There were four sports associations in the city:

The first, "Yenina", contained studying youth and youths who served in one of the three battalions that stayed permanently in the city. Jewish youths were not accepted into that association, although there were no rules against them.

That association excelled in soccer and had the best team among the four associations. Starting in 1928, the team managed to climb up to the top league, and as a result, teams from throughout our district and beyond visited the city. The infantry battalion (Battalion no. 52) made its superior soccer field available for the team. Besides soccer, the association developed the sport of tennis. Two tennis courts were also made available for the association of the infantry battalion. The association enjoyed the support of the wealthy Poles in town. Its members walked around with a feeling of superiority. That resulted in a feeling of arrogance and prestige among some Polish youths, particularly among the Polish "golden generation" who saw themselves as the "elite". That was evident during sports matches held between

"Yenina" and other sports teams in the city. Nonetheless, it was true that the level of sports at that association was much superior to the rest of the associations, particularly in soccer.

The second most important sports association was the Z. K. S. [Zydowski Klub Sportowy – The Jewish Sports Club], where the Jewish youth concentrated. The character of the association was folk-oriented and national. Jewish youth from all classes participated in it. The association kept its national-Jewish nature without hiding it and without feeling inferior. On the contrary. The full name of the association, "The Jewish Sports Club", appeared in all of its advertisements and appearances. The colors of the soccer team uniform were the national colors – blue and white.

The associations consisted of several sports, including soccer, track and field, table tennis, and volleyball. Obviously, the soccer team was at the center of the association. The association wished to elevate the level of its players in order not to fall behind "Yenina".

The soccer team
"Yuchenka Aurora"

[Columns 347-348]

The soccer team Z. K. S. in 1920

A fenced soccer field, equipped with the accessories for track and field and a bowling arcade, was made available to the Z. K. S. association.

The Jewish community in our town was proud of the sports activities of their youth. There were many activists in the associations, despite not playing sports themselves. It would be difficult, in this short article, to mention many names. However, it would be worth mentioning the name of the prominent athlete and the association's activist for many years, Mr. Harry - the owner of the vinegar factory who was the driving force of the association. In his day, he was one of the prominent and outstanding soccer players in our city. He later organized all of the elder players to play, once and a while, in friendly games, particularly on holidays, just to entertain the crowd. For the young players, such competitions were exciting events. For them, it was an opportunity to play and win against players who were once admired soccer "stars".

The third-largest sports association in our town was also Jewish. It was really a spin-off of the Z. K. S. association. It separated from the Z. K.S. and established its own association called "Aurora". According to my own personal memory, the separation resulted from the assimilation tendencies of some of the activists, who could not bring themselves to agree with the overt activities by the mother association as a Jewish organization. With the Polonization process affecting all aspects of life, some of the Jewish activists found it necessary to conceal the association's national uniqueness. It pushed them to separate and establish another organization with a name and uniforms that could not be associated with Jewishness.

The Z. K. S. Viochka
Team in Uniform

[Columns 349-350]

The Soccer Team Z. K. S. Practices on their Pitch

The "Aurora" association concentrated its efforts on soccer, as well as Tennis.

In terms of the level, their team was much weaker than the other two teams. The association did not have a dedicated soccer pitch and had to practice in an open field, which bordered the high-quality field of the Z. K. S. On the other hand, the association excelled in organizing balls, particularly dance balls. Assimilated Jews were obviously invited to these balls. They considered the association as means for strengthening their national assimilation.

The three associations mentioned so far were members of the state's sports union and were subjected to its authority and rules. The fourth sports association was a group of high school students named G. K. S. It only appeared in soccer matches outside of the framework of the state sports union. The team consisted of a mix of Polish and Jewish players, all students of the high school. Its playing level was not consistent since its composition changed from year to year at the end of the school year. However, it did provide the students with the opportunity to practice soccer and contribute individually, later on, to one of the three sports associations in the city.

In the preceding section, I briefly described the character of the sports associations in Zloczow. I will now highlight the important sports events in the city. That would also be brief due to the limited material available in my memory book.

B. Sports Events

One of the most noteworthy events in our city was the soccer match between "Yenina" and Z. K. S. For many years, the two teams belonged to the B league. Each one of them wished to advance to the upper A league. That wish was common among soccer teams anywhere. The match between the two teams carried a "derby-like" character, that is, a match between two local teams, where the will to win was what guided the players rather than the quality of playing. Obviously, hundreds of fans of both teams showed up for the game. Each side was cheered by its own enthusiastic supporters. Besides the "derby-like" atmosphere, the match also carried the aura of a competition between the Jewish and the Polish youths. With that aura, the soccer match attracted most of the population of the city. More than once, a mass brawl erupted among the spectators after the game, particularly when "Yeninina" lost. Sometimes, these brawls overflowed the boundaries of the soccer pitch onto the boardwalk. The players did not participate in these brawls. Among themselves, they maintained good relations, regardless of what association they belonged to.

Another special soccer event took place upon the arrival of famous soccer teams from other cities. The Z. K. S. took care to bring Jewish teams who made a name for themselves. That was how a team from Lviv, which called itself "Hasmonea" (*Hashmonaim*), and the team "HaKo'akh" "The Power"] from Vienna visited the city. Obviously, the hosting of such teams was accompanied by a special festivity. That elevated the enthusiasm about the sport to its peak. "Yenina" association also invited some of the country's best soccer teams.

Besides soccer, our city excelled in the development of other sports.

[Columns 351-352]

Z. K. S. Soccer Team, 1931

One of the most fascinating sports events was the bicycle race from Zloczow to Sasiv. Tens of youths took part in the race, either by organizing it or by riding in the race. We should note that our municipality, headed by Moshinskly and his deputy, the lawyer Meiblum, showed interest in the competition. The city provided the prizes for the youths who won the race.

Table tennis competitions under the auspice of the municipality were held in the elementary school, which was named after Mitskevitz. Jewish youths excelled in that sport. In 1929, two Jewish youths won first and second place. A Polish youth won only third place[2].

The sport of tennis was more developed among the Polish youths that belonged to the "Yenina" association. The reason for that was simple – the sport was very costly, and only a few among the Jewish youth could afford it. However, we did also play a role in that sport. A few youths even participated in competitions organized by the city, when the sports stadium was opened.

During the winter, the most popular sport was ice skating. The two soccer fields, the ones of the Z. K. S. association and that of "Yenina" were flooded by water and were naturally frozen and thus converted to huge surfaces where hundreds of youths skated. When the stadium was opened, it was also used as an ice-skating rink in the winter. A troupe of ice dancers was brought over from Lviv. They performed magnificent dances, accompanied by the orchestra of the 52nd [Polish military] battalion. The ice-skating sport was favored by the students of the high school. More than once, whole classes could be seen going out to ice skate with their gymnastics teacher.

Since our city was surrounded by mountains, of which Vromaky[?] mountains were the best known, we also liked to ski. In a location near the municipal jail, we built a ramp and organized ski jumping competitions. The officers of the military battalions, lodged in the city, were among the best jumpers. However, there were some Jewish youths, although not members of Z. K. S., who were also among the best jumpers.

Another sports area that was quite developed in Zloczow was bowling. The only bowling arcade was located at the Z. K. S. field. Youths from throughout the city, including Polish and Jewish youths, played there. Hundreds of youths, and sometimes even older adults, took part in daily competitions. The records were written on the walls. Upon entering the arcade, one could fill the desire of the youths to beat those records. The fact that the names of the record holders were written on the wooden boards, served as an incentive to encourage the players to play harder and break the records.

Indeed, there were numerous and diversified types of sports in our town, and the sports life was buoyant and full of excitement. Not all sports embodied many participants, but there wasn't any type of sport that was not supported by the city. Horse riding and equestrian competitions were also held in the city.

[Columns 353-354]

Z.T.G. Team in 1934

Volleyball was another sport developed, particularly by the Z. K. S. association. The sport attracted some of the older athletes who had to retire from soccer due to their age.

Benefit balls were often held by various associations. They attracted not only the athletes but also substantial parts of the population, including public leaders.

However, these tens and hundreds of Jewish youths, my childhood friends, are not with us anymore. They perished, along with our other people, by the Natis beasts. May these lines serve as a memorial for their pure souls.

Author's Notes:

1. The goal of this article was to put down some impressions about the sports life in our city, as it was preserved in my memory. The content of these notes relates to my personal experience and obviously cannot be a comprehensive description of all of the sports affairs and events. The writer of the article made Aliya in 1932 when he was a young man of 20. Until then, he participated in most types of sports available in Zloczow at the time. He also participated in various sports events that took place in the city.
2. That event was full of tension since the mayor himself, Moshinsky, was personally interested that his relative, Gorsky, would win first place. However, my brother, Motl Bauman z"l, came in front of him, capturing second place. Oskar Shalit, may he live long, won first place. Gorsky only won third place after he hardly beat me.

[Columns 355-356]

The Jewish School in Zloczow

by Prof. Hirsch

Translated by Moshe Kutten

I would try to refresh my memory about two Jewish historical topics - education and self-defense. They became a single topic later on. The youths who studied Hebrew because of their Jewish national orientation became the defenders of the community during the Ukrainian period. They also became the pioneers of the "HaShomer" [" The Guard"] movement.

The first stage was the Jewish school. As was customary in Galitsia, Jewish schools were founded in various cities and towns, wherever the Jewish population existed. Zloczow was not an exception. The local Jewish school was called "Safa Brura" ["Clear Language"]. It did not replace the state school but served as an alternative to the old traditional "kheder". Children went to the Jewish school in the afternoons, mainly to study Hebrew. But they also went to widen their Jewish cultural and national knowledge. Two teachers served as the pillars of the school. The first, Brodeh, was a Jew who escaped from Russia. He arrived in Zloczow in about 1908 and began to teach the Hebrew language. The second was Naftali Zigel, who later made Aliya and continued to teach in Haifa. He passed away about four years ago. Initially, there was a hidden t competition between the two teachers. However, later on, they decided to cooperate and manage the local Jewish school together. Their commendable activity was enormously successful. The Jewish community was relatively enlightened and educated. Therefore, it deemed it its duty to support the school and send its children there.

The second stage began with the break of World War I. The activities among the Jews did not cease. On the contrary, it expanded. When the "HaShomer" movement was established, the members were obliged to study Hebrew. The school grew and improved. An additional teacher began to work there – the journalist Moshe Kleinman. He was an educated and broad-minded person. He stayed with the school until about 1920 and taught high-level courses. The leaders of the "HaShomer" movement improved their knowledge vastly by studying with him. During that period, the Hebrew language was taught at the Ukrainian state's high schools. The Bible and Hebrew teacher in these schools was

Dr. Simkha Bunim Feldman. He was a fascinating figure. He was a religious Jew and a lawyer by his trade. When the Ukrainian Republic ceased to exist, Dr. Feldman became a regular teacher in one of the local high schools.

As mentioned above, the Jewish school played an important role in Jewish self-defense during the Ukrainian regime. In 1918, a self-defense force was organized by the students of the high schools. That was very beneficial for the defenders and the community. The defenders received training in the use of weapons while the community gained an effective defense force. That force proved effective during the several attempts by the surrounding farmers to rob and murder Jews. The self-defense served as a deterrent against attacks,

[Columns 357-358]

as the mob knew that they would encounter quite a substantial resistance. The military training brought about another consequence. The latest news confirmed that the front was not too far and that the Poles and Communists were approaching fast. As a result, many young men deemed it their duty to volunteer for the army.

As a side note, when the Poles took over the area, a fairly large group of "HaShomer" members went to actual "*hakhshara*" [agricultural training program in preparation for making Aliya]. The program lasted for two months, during the entire summer.

[Columns 359-360]

The Teaching of Hebrew in Zloczow

by Naftali Zigel

Translated by Moshe Kutten

Forward

The screen that separates me from those old days thickened over the many years that passed and accumulated dust, rust, and plenty of molds. Peeking into these past days requires turning away from my daily life and current life problems and isolating myself without any barriers with that city – Zloczow, which I knew and in which I resided for two years.

The task of writing the things down was exceedingly hard because it required the shedding of reality, removal of barriers, and relying totally on memory (except for a few meager notes).

Please forgive me, the reader, if I just draw a few lines, describe only some parts that may not be the most prominent, and leave vast space for your imagination.

A. How I was Accepted a Position of a Teacher in Zloczow

One day, while residing in Pidhaytsi [Podhaitza] and working as a teacher in the Jewish school, I received a letter from Zloczow in these words:

"Dear honorable Mr. Naftali Zigel,

Dr. Elazar Rokach[1] brought to our attention that his honor is a master teacher and a respectable educator. Since we are about to establish a local Jewish school, we are looking for a suitable teacher who is well-versed in religion and subscribes to the spirit of the Jewish national revival and renewal of its language. We are honored to invite your honor to invite you to visit us on Tuesday, the first day of Passover's "Khol HaMoed" [regular weekdays of the holiday]. That would allow us to know your honor and for your honor to know us. If agreeable, we would negotiate the term of the matter before us.

With our blessing of a national revival,

Members of the school "Safa Brura",
And founders of the Jewish school in Zloczow

Mordekhai Gevandter
Tzvi Rosenboim

I lived in Pidhaytsi for three years. During that time, I managed to plow deep furrows, and my efforts bear fruits. The sound of the Hebrew language could be heard in the streets. I was spoken to by the youths and even many of the adults. With the establishment of the school, these adults resurrected the language they were taught during their own childhood. Should I leave the city where I acquired so many friends and a good name for myself?

However, there was another concern to consider. In recent times the members of the school committee became philanthropic and accepted students for free without securing new sources of revenue. When they found out, one day, that the deficit exceeded 700 Krones, the committee decided to fire one teacher. The chairman of the teachers union in Galtisia and Bukovina, Soferman[2], who was aware of the situation, contacted me and suggested that I accept a position in Rohatyn. [The teacher,] Kabitner [Naftal Yaakov?] proposed that I take the offer at Hvizdet [Gwozhdzhiets]. I received telegraphic invitations from both of these towns. An emissary from Horodenka also arrived. I submitted the committee my resignation. The rumor about me leaving the city spread quickly. People began to talk about closing down the school. During their meeting, the committee decided not to accept my resignation. I was in a quandary. How could I refuse the invitation from Zloczow? I went to Zloczow on "Khol HaMoed" of Passover.

The city was much larger than Pidhaytsi and closer to Lviv, not far from my parents' home. The people who interviewed me made an excellent impression on me. The head of the "Safa Brura" ["Clear Language"] school committee, the lawyer Dr. Yaakov Groskopf, was an old-time Zionist, a devotee of Hebrew, pleasant, a gentle soul that evoked respect and appreciation. A similar impression was made by the rest of the committee's members: Dr. David Werpel, Dr. Sh. B. Feldman, the brothers (both Dr.'s) Schwager, Yosef Riss, Hersh Rosenboim, Lerrer, and Mordekhai Gevandter. Even the salary offered to me was much more generous than the one I earned in Pidhaytsi. All that pleased me and I could not refuse their offer.

I was relatively young and I felt that a heavy burden was placed on my shoulders. Just as a coincidence, two of my articles were published in the same month, in the journal "HaMitzpeh" ["The Observatory"] issued in Krakow. One of the articles was a research-oriented paper about the "Pilegesh B'Giv'a" ["Concubine In Givah", Judges 19-21]. The other article was a criticism of school books. These articles and the recommendation by Dr. Elazar Rokakh raised my value in their eyes. The association of ["Khovevei" Tzion" [Those who are] Lovers of Zion] hung the journals where my articles were published, thereby promoting my name among the people who were interested in the school. I agreed to accept the offer, and we were ready to sign the contract. Before signing, Dr. Feldman suggested that I grow e beard. He said that they would add 20 Guldens to my monthly salary. That was a very tempting amount! However, I responded that I knew some teachers from the teacher's association and that I could provide him with their names. He retreated immediately and stated that it was not a condition for my employment, just a suggestion…

[Columns 361 - 362]

A Group of Hebrew Teachers

Despite being tall, I considered myself a youth and could not see myself growing a beard…

My goodbye in Pidhaytsi was very hard on my students, the parents, and not the least on myself. Many accompanied me to the train station. I continued to receive longing letters from my students for months…

B. The School During the First Year

The registration for the school was a new kind of event for most of the city's residents, which yielded about sixty students. The school committee rented the ground floor of the slaughterer, Betman Bekhov's, new house. There were two classes on one side, an office and a room for me on the other. During the first year, I was the principal and the only teacher. There were classes for children aged six and seven, a class for eighteen years old, and special classes for the youths and the students of the Polish high school. Everybody was a beginner. I taught four hours a day but felt exhausted and the end of the day. During the first three months, I had to teach without books by talking all the time.

There was no shortage of difficulties. I discussed my new method of teaching the language with the parents. I told them that we teach speaking and writing first, and only then do we proceed to teach reading and studying from books. But they insisted that we study according to traditional methods - prayers blesses and Torah… I could not choose any other way except for enforcing my approach by working hard work and then demonstrating the results.

Toward the end of the school year, I prepared a Hebrew show with a diversified program that included singing, recitation, and plays. Dr. Feldman and his wife helped me with the singing parts by playing the piano they had in their house. The first scene captivated the audience. It generated a huge and enthusiastic response. Six- and seven-year-old children stood in a row along the entire length of the stage, each dressed up as an artisan: A tailor standing by a sowing machine holding a thread and needle, a shoemaker holding a hammer and a tar wire, standing at his desk supporting an awl, a shoemaker's and a last for a shoe and a sandal, a blacksmith holding a sledgehammer standing at his anvil, and a baker holding a dough-trough kneading dough. Every child sang his song while pointing at his tools. In the end, they sang in a chorus:

We are all artisans, making an honest living,

Rejoicing with our portion [Patriarchs 4:1], we would experience no scarcity

Woe to the lazy they are miserable.

With thunderous applause, the children were called out three times to repeat their song. I have forgotten the rest of the details about that show. I only recall one thing:

[Columns 363 - 364]

Students in the Jewish School

According to the published program, I was supposed to bring the show to its end by giving a speech in Hebrew. I was extremely tired and anxious from the exhausting preparation work during the last few days and the work behind the stage. However, when I appeared on the stage I was accepted with roaring applause and cheers that lasted for about 10 minutes. After my speech, they carried me on their hands to the hall (literally).

There was excitement in the city and the success of the children in their show was the subject of talks in the stores, butcher shops, market, and synagogue for weeks. A long article about the show was published in the journal "Tageblatt" [the Jewish Daily News]. That served as useful propaganda for the registration for the new school year.

Author's Notes:

1. Elazar Rokeakh, an author and activist, from the main and one of the main speakers in "Khibat Tzion" movement. He was active in both Eretz Israel and the diaspora. He was the uncle of the former mayor of Tel-Aviv, Israel Rokakh.
2. Refael Soferman (1789 – 1956), was a teacher, author, and education activist in Eretz Israel and the diaspora.

[Columns 371-372]

The Theatrical Clubs in Zloczow

by Herman Mass

Translated by Moshe Kutten

Four drama clubs operated in Zloczow at different times. I will try to describe these clubs, although the passing of time had erased the details from my memory.

The first drama club was established by the Bund and was active during the years 1921 – 1927. Its manager was the magister Victor Gdoldig. They showed various plays among them: "HaDybbuk", "Got fun Nekumeh"[" A Vengeful God"], and "Der Zinger fun Zeineh Leiden" ["Singing about your Own Sufferings]. The director was Mr. Gdoldig. Most often, he also played the main characters. We also should mention the promoter, Zalman Shapira, and the actors, Moshe Zisman, Leib Gruber, and his sister.

The second drama club was founded by "Poalei Tzion" ["Workers of Zion"] and was active during the years 1927 – 1933. The manager was Yaakov Hokhberg. He was known as a person who loved folklore and as a talented director. He used to appear as a singer and actor and was the driving force of the troupe. When the club founded by the Bund declined, some of its actors moved to the drama club of "Poalei Tzion". The following are the names of the actors that I remember: Kessler, my brother Avraham Mass, Lifshitz, Ester Ushpis, Halperin, and the writer of these lines.

I still remember the success of the show "Der Toiter Mensh" ["The Dead Man"] by Shalom Ash. The barber Leider did the makeup, and artist Froikeh Nakhumovitz z"l, worked on the theater set. The latter was killed in the forests of Zloczow, along with the other victims of the Nazis.

The third drama club was named after Sh. Anski. It was managed by Dr. Rubin and Buni Greenbaum. The club was quite advanced. Buni Greenbaum was the driving force in that club. He served as the director and an artist. He even wrote some of the texts for the plays. The club hired the best actors in the city. Membership in that club was considered a privilege. The following plays were shown: "BaLailah BaShuk HaYashan" ["At Night in the Old Market"], "Hagibur BeKvalim" ["The Hero Tied with Ropes" - a short version of Les Misérables by Victor Hugo], "Der vos Krigt di Petsh]?]", "Di Ziben Ghungeneh", and more. The members of the troupe included: Gedalia Bressler, Mendik Rosenbaum, Zigah Schutz, Kubah Schnapp, and the young woman Reiss. Anski's shows always filled the theater since their acting and direction levels were superior to the other theaters in the city (including the Polish and Ukrainians). Since the troupe showed plays in Yiddish, the youths, who formally knew only Polish, acquired Yiddish and thereby got closer to the Jewish culture.

Members of the Sports Organization in Zloczow

The fourth drama club was named after Menedleh Mokher Sfarim". The troupe was active during the late 1930s. That club held reading evenings and thus disseminated the creations of the Jewish authors. The manager of that club was the younger brother of Buni Greenbaum. The following people were active in the troupe, Yekhezkel Wagman Steller Tzimmer, Klara Zaltz, Henis, Efraim Rosen, Shlomo Meir, Khana Ruten, Avraham Kimmel, and the writer of these lines.

In addition to the drama clubs, the excellent chorus conducted by Mr. Zindwarm was known in Zloczow.

We need to note that Zloczow had an enthusiastic theater-going crowd. The city attracted many theater troupes, including the "Vilna Troupe", Sigmund Turkov, Idah Kaminska, Dzigan and Schumacher, The Warsaw's Theater, and more.

The Jewish youth contributed tremendously to the development of the culture and art in Zloczow. However, the cruel war annihilated the best of the youths. May their memory be blessed.

[Columns 377-378]

Chapter D

Personalities and People
in Zloczow

Translated by Moshe Kutten

[Columns 379-380]

[Blank]

[Columns 381-382]

The *Maggid* from Zloczow

by Moshe Leiter

A person familiar with the *Tzadikim's* books and is knowledgeable about Hasidic literature, would not recognize the name - Rabbi Yekhiel Mikhel. However, if you say R' Mikhel'i Zlotsover, or "The *Maggid* from Zloczow [Zlotsov]", he would immediately know that this is about the famous Rabbi, admired by tens of thousands of Hassidim, and people of action, for many generations now. However, Rabbi Mikhel'i was not born in Zloczow and did not die there either. He was born in Brody in 5486 (1726) and died in Yampol on Shabbat, 25 Elul 5546, (1786).

Yet, he is named after the city of Zloczow because it was where he rose and ascended, lived, and disseminated Hassidism. In Zloczow he acquired a large group of Hassidim and admirers and brought up Hasidic disciples, Torah greats, and famous *Tzadikim*. His mentor and teacher, R' Dov-Ber the *Maggid* from Mezritch, wondered about that and asked: "Why was he so fortunate to merit so many Hasidic followers?".

Gaons-Tzadikim were also among his Hassidic students and disciples such as:

– The Kabbalist *Gaon* [Torah Genius scholar] R' Yitzkhak Isaac HaCohen, ABD [Head of Rabbinical Court] of Korets community, the author of the book "Brit Kehunat Olam" ["Covenant of Perpetual Priesthood"];

– R' Khaim, ABD Chi°inãu - Chernivtsi, [Kishinev – Czernovitz], the author of the book "Be'er Mayim Khaim" ["Refreshing Water Well"] about the Torah, "Sidduro Shel Shabbat" ["The *Siddur* of Shabbat"], "Sha'ar HaTfila" ["The Prayer Gate"], and "Eretz HaKhaim" ["The Land of the Living"];

– Rabbi Meshulam Feibush HaLevi from Zbarazh, the author of the book "Derekh Emet" ["The Path of the Truth"], a friend of the *Gaon* Rabbi Tzvi Kara [spelled Karu in the article], ABD of Buczacz and the author the responsum book "Netah Sha'ashuim" ["Plantation of Pleasures"]. Both were the disciples of Rabbi Moshe-Tzvi Heller HaLevi, the author of the book "Gaon Tzvi" about the Mishnah order "Kodashim" ["Sanctities"], as well as the responsum book "Gaon Tvi";

– The famous *Tzadik*, Rabbi Mordekhai, *Gaon* ABD Nishchiz;

– The *Gaon* Rabbi Yisaskhar Ber ABD Zloczow, the author of "Bat Eini" ["The Apple of my Eye"] about the Mishnah, and the book "Mevaser Tzedek" ["Heralding Justice"];

– The son-in-law of Rabbi Yisaskhar Ber from Zloczow, the *Gaon-Tzadik* Rabbi Avraham-Khaim, who ascended to the rabbinical position in Zloczow, after his father-in-law, Rabbi Yisaskhar Ber, made Aliya to Eretz Israel, was also among the disciples-students of Rabbi Mikhel of Zloczow;

– The holy Rabbi Aharon Leib from Peremyshliany. He was the father of Rabbi Meir'el from Peremyshliany, who was famous for his holiness and cleverness;

Rabbi Mikhel's salient mentor rabbi was the *Gaon* Rabbi R' Shmuel Shmelke of Nikolsburg. His first wife was the daughter of R' Shmuel Shmelke's brother, Rabbi Pinkhas HaLevi Horowitz, ABD Frankfurt.

Rabbi Mikhel's famous five *Tzadiks* sons were also obviously among his students. They were not named after the city of Zloczow but after the names of the towns where they lived and disseminated their father's wisdom. They were Rabbi Yosef of Yampol, Rabbi Yitzkhak from Radyvyliv, Rabbi Velvel'e Zbarazer, Rabbi Moshe of Zvohil, and Rabbi Mordekhai of Kremenetz.

Rabbi Mikhel'i had one daughter. He married her to Rabbi David HaLevi, a *Maggid Meisharim* ["Preacher of Righteousness"] in the town of Stepan, who was from among the students of the BESHT.

Rabbi Mikhel'i was the son of the "*Mokhiakh*" [the "rebuker"] Rabbi Yitzkhak'l from Drohobitz, about whom the BESHT said that "his holy work elevated him to the level of [tannaitic sage] Rabbi Shimon Ben Yokhai". Rabbi Yitzkhak was the son of Yosef "Ish Emet" ["Man of Truth"], the son of the holy Rabbi Moshe from Svirzh, near Lviv, who was killed "on *Kiddush Hashem*" [as a martyr; The latter was the grandson of the Gaon Rabbi Yitzkhak Khayut, a Providentza [Prostìjov?], Hassid, and ABD of Prague-Krakow.

Rabbi Mikhel'i was considered the leader of the Hassidim and their admired spokesman. Therefore, Rabbi Yekhezkel Landau, ABD Prague, the author of the book "Nodah BiYehuda" [Known in Judah" – the name is based on Psalms 76:2] and "Dagul MeRevava" ["Preeminent among Ten Thousand" – the name is based on Song of Songs 5:10], the leader of the "*Mitnagdim*" [People and Rabbis who opposed Hassidim], aimed his critical arrows against him. *Gaon* Rabbi Pinkhas Horowitz, the authors of the books "HaMikneh" and "Hafla'a"[Literally – "Turning into a Miracle"], ABD of Frankfurt turned to the *Gaon* Rabbi Tabl'i from Leszno [Lissa] to write to *Gaon* Rabbi Yosef from Poznan to ask his father-in-law, *Gaon* Rabbi Landau, not to harass Rabbi Mikhel'i, since his brother, Rabbi Shmuel Shmelke, ABD Nikolsburg testified about Rabbi Mikhel'i "that all of his work was in honor of G-d".

People who want to avenge Rabbi Mikhel'i's insult by claiming that Rabbi Yekhezkel Landau, the author of "Nodah BiYehuda", opposed Rabbi Mikhel'i because the latter encroached upon his territory by settling in Yampol, are mistaken. The fact is that when Rabbi Yekhiel Mikhel settled in Yampol, Rabbi Yekhezkel Landau, who served as the ABD in Prague, was already known as the greatest rabbinical judge of his generation, and was famous among the Halakha and logic scholars. He opposed R' Mikhel only because he considered him the leader and the spokesman of the Hassidim.

[Columns 383-384]

Students in the "Yeshiva" named after the Maggid R' Mikhel

We should also note that Gaon Rabbi Yekhezkel was nominated to the position of ABD Prague in 5515 (1755), while Rabbi Mikhel'i from Zloczow died in Yampol in 5546 (1786). That means that R' Mikhel arrived in Yampol at an old age.

Since he was considered the head of Hasidism, his followers in Brody could not find a better location for the book "Toldot Ya'akov Yosef" [The History of Ya'akov Yosef"], other than the house of Rabbi Mikhel'i from Zloczow. That book, authored by the Gaon Rabbi Yaakov Yosef, contains the main principles of BESHT Hassidism.

The following story, told by Rabbi Elimelekh from Liznesk, serves as proof of how great and holy the Hassidim viewed Rabbi Mikhel'i. Rabbi Elimelekh said that he aspired to see Rabbi Mikhel'i from Zloczow in person in his youth. When he heard that Rabbi Mikhel was visiting Krakow, he traveled to that city and met somebody there. Rabbi Elimelekh asked that person why the city seemed to be in the mood of Yom Kippur. The person responded that the town people gathered in the synagogue to listen to Rabbi Mikhel's enthusiastic sermon. In his sermon, the Rabbi called the residents to come back to worship G-d in good faith. To hurry them up, he described the sin of every person in the audience. The whole audience burst into tears. When Rabbi Elimelekh heard the story, he began to fear that his own "sins" would be publicized, so he decided to return home without meeting the Rabbi.

Rabbi Mikhel'i from Zloczow was a pioneer of the Hassidic movement. However, like his great father, Rabbi Yitzkhak from Drohobitz, he was not initially attracted to Rabbi Israel BESHT. Moreover, his father kept his distance from the BESHT and bore a grudge against him since the latter used amulets. However, Rabbi Yitzkhak once visited the BESHT's court, and the latter convinced Rabbi Yitzkhak that he also opposed amulets. However, since that custom was so entrenched from the days of the Talmud, it was difficult to uproot it. Nevertheless, the BESHT stated that he was not using the names of the holy people in his amulets but only wrote his name and the names of his parents on the amulets. Rabbi Yitzkhak was satisfied with that explanation, and he became a good friend of the BESHT. They became close friends who admired each other.

Rabbi Mikhel'i followed the old paved road, which had nothing on it but Torah and G-d fearing. A person who unwillingly almost desecrated the Sabbath came to Rabbi Mikhel'i to relay to him his heartful worry about his sin. Rabbi Mikhel'i responded that the only remedy for that serious sin was to seclude himself and abstain from the pleasures in this world. The person who sinned regretted it with the whole of his heart. But he was weak and could not physically follow the Rabbi's severe judgment. When that person heard that the BESHT happened to stop by the adjacent city, he hurried and traveled to see him. He told the BESHT that despite his strong will to follow Rabbi Mikhel'i's instructions, he could not possibly do so, as he was weak and ailing. The BESHT comforted him and ordered him to provide the synagogue with a litra [unit of weight about 12.5 Oz] of candles and his sin would be forgiven. When that person visited the BESHT the second time, the latter asked him to hand over an invitation for Rabbi Mikhel'i to come and stay with him in the following Shabbat. Rabbi Mikhel'i received the invitation and traveled to Lviv to spend the Shabbat with the BESHT. He had some difficulties finding his way in the dark and was late to arrive. The BESHT waited for him with his Kiddush cap in his hand. When Rabbi Mikhel'i finally arrived the BESHT welcomed him with a greeting of peace and with a complaint that the Rabbi did not notice the sadness and heartbreak of that sinner. At that moment, Rabbi Mikhel'i realized that possible for a Jewish person to lose his way in the dark on Shabbat eve. Rabbi' Mikhel'i became a BESHT follower since then.

[Columns 385-386]

Yet, Rabbi Mikhel's remained faithful to his strict way of keeping the sanctity of the Shabbat. So much so that he claimed that a Jew might desecrate the sanctity of Shabbat with excessive speech. Thus, when Rabbi Khaim, the author of "Be'er Mayim Khaim" ["A Well of Fresh Water"], visited him, he asked him to provide proof, from the written literature, that excessive speech may cause a desecration of the sabbath. Rabbi Khaim responded that in the Book of Leviticus, [VaYikra 19:30] it says: "…and you shall observe My Sabbaths…". And what is the G-d's Sabbath? – ceasing from work. And what is G-d work? - speaking, as it was said: "By the word of the Lord the heavens were made…" [Psalms 33:6], and also "The world was created with ten divine utterances" [Mishnah, Avot 5:1]. One could therefore conclude that people that excessive speech should be avoided on the holy day of Shabbat. Herewith, the views of the author of "Be'er Mayim Khaim" and his spiritual outlook matched those of his mentor. It was appropriate for him to bring to light his hidden wisdom to his mentor.

Rabbi Mikhel'i warned not to shame a fellow man even if he was a known evil person. He followed Rabbi Shimon Bar of Yokhai, who said: "One needs to be careful not to shame anybody".

Rabbi Mikhel'i practiced what he was preaching. When he addressed his congregation with words of reprimand, he would raise his face toward the heavens and say: "Master of the Universe, it is evident and known to you, that they are worthy and deserving. The only reason I admonish them with words of heaven is to honor of your great name, and so that they would serve you commandments with awe and compassion".

That custom was anchored in Shimon Bar Yokhai's teachings: "Don't investigate a camel or a pig, investigate a lamb".

When the BESHT decided to try to convince Rabbi Mikhel'i to accept a rabbinical position, the latter insisted courageously: "Even if I lose the two worlds - this one and the next, I would not accept the position as a Rabbi". with hat refusal (adressed to his teacher and mentor) Rabbi Mikhel followed the Tannai Rabbi Shimon Bar Youkhai who said: "brikh rakhmanah Delinah khakim Midon" ["Blessed he who is relieved me of the duty to judge"].

Rabbi Mikhel'i was mindful of two things. He testified: "I had never set down at a heater to warm up as warmth should come from within". He also said: "I had never bowed my head to a bowl of food since the head symbolizes spiritualism and considered the source of thinking. The head should not bow to worldliness and materialism".

[Columns 387-388]

"Love of Israel"
by the *Maggid's* Sons

by Avitov

Translated by Moshe Kutten

The fire broke out and quarrels erupted among the Jews, between the Hasidim and Mitnagdim [people who opposed Hasidism]. The fire is burning and even the cedars [in Judaism - a symbol of strength and might] caught fire. There is no extinguishing. Every resolute combatant defeats his rivals. In Lemberg [now - Lviv], the Mitnagdim have the upper hand. A decree was issued, with the approval of the authorities, that Hasidic rebbes, can only stay 24 hours in the city. Beyond 24 hours, the rebbes would be expelled.

One day, the two Admors brothers, R' Velvele of Zbariz [Zbarazh], and R' Yitzkhakle of Radziwill, the sons of R' Mikhel [The *Maggid*] from Zolochiv [Zlotzov], had to stay in Lviv for more than 24 hours for various reasons. On Shabbat, as customary among the Hasidim, hundreds of admirers crowded the tables, to enjoy seeing the glamourous face of their rebbes and to listen to their Torah talks.

As known, the flame of "Love of Israel" burned within him. He considered every Jew a *Tzadik* [righteous]. He would greet everyone he met with the words: "Well Tzdikle, how are you?"

Suddenly, a policeman appeared, on behalf of the authorities, requesting to see the rebbes' papers (to further aggravate the situation, he was a Jewish convert). The policemen ignored all requests and lobbied to prevent the desecration of the Sabbath. R' Velvele sighed from the bottom of his heart and complied with the policeman's request. However, R' Yitskhakle was very careful not the desecrate G-d and Shabbat. R' Velvele intervened and said: "My dear brother, please comply with the demand by the policeman and do not cause grief to the *Tzadikle* Gunter" (the name of the policeman of Jewish descent). R' Yitskhakle raged and answered: "Your modesty does not have any bound, which aggravates me. Do you consider this evil man a *Tzadik*?". R' Velvele responded: "Could I correct an explicit Mishna's saying that 'Your people are all Tzidikim'? That means that a Jew, even if he sinned, he is still a Jew. After all, this Gunter is a Jew". R' Yitzkhakle relented and complied with the policeman's request. After witnessing R' Velvele's doing, the policeman changed his ways and became observant. From that point on, no day passed without him visiting R' Velvele until the end of his life. People talked about him that he became a martyr who died in purity and holiness.

[Columns 389-390]

Rabbi Yissaskhar-Ber

by Geshuri

Translated by Moshe Kutten

There is no doubt that Rabbi Yissaskhar-Ber from Zolochiv was a descendant of dynastic lineage. He was the son of Rabbi Liebush "Geza Tzvi" and the grandson of Rabbi Naftali from Frankfurt, author of "Smikhat Khakhamim" ["Certification for Sages"]. In his personality, he blended scholarship and Hassidism. The published books he wrote are typical Hassidic books, like the rest of the books by *Tzadikim* of his generation. In his books, he is revealed as a Torah's great. He also corresponded with other prominent scholars. Yet, there is a big difference between him and

Rabbi Yekhiel Mikhel, the *Maggid* from Zolochiv, who lived one generation ahead of him! Rabbi Mikhel was eminently famous in Hasidism and scholarship. He was also known as a composer and disseminator of *Nigunim* [melodies]. Rabbi Yissaskhar-Ber, on the other hand, did not make a name for himself. The lack of fame can be attributed to his modesty. His books were only published after his death and were known only within a limited circle.

He was hardly mentioned in the Hasidic literature, and the Hassidic historians passed over him in silence. But Rabbi Yissaskhar-Ber was the Rabbi and *Maggid* of Shink [Sianky ?] Hassidim and met the Hassidic greats of his generation. Despite being removed from the Hassidic melodies in his upbringing, he was not indifferent toward Hassidic *Nigunim*. In his generation, the *Nigun* [music, singing] was allowed and neither the "*Mitnagdin*" nor the enlightened considered it an oddity.

Rabbi Yissaskhar-Ber made Aliya to Eretz Israel at the end of his life. However, he did not live much longer there and died (on 7 Av, 5570 [1810]). In Zolochiv, his son-in-law, Rabbi Avraham-Khaim, the author of "Orakh LaKhaim"["Way of Life"], took his place.

As mentioned above, the two books by Rabbi Yissaskhar-Ber were printed and published after his death. "Bat Eini" ["The Apple of My Eye"] includes innovatory and casuistry commentaries of the Mishnah. His other book, "Mevaser Tzedek" ["Heralding Justice"] contains some of his sermons and discussions about the Torah. Both books were first published in Lviv in 5610 [1849/50]. A second edition of the book "Bat Eini" was published in Lviv in 5639 [1879. The Hebrew date in the article is erroneous]. His son, who brought the books to print, testified that he made an extensive effort to collect the author's phrases from his students.

The author's descendants, who put a lot of effort into collecting the material, did not bother to lengthen their introductions and add details about the author's life. That is why we do not have the exact date of his birth and the date of his Aliya to Eretz Israel. Many other details are also missing.

We do learn some details from the notes of approbation at the front of the books.

Rabbi Ze'ev Wolf, Av Beit Din [ABD - head of rabbinical court], and Chief Rabbi of Dubno testified that he knew about Rabbi Yissaskhar's glorious wisdom. He wrote about him: "The *Gaon* Rabbi, famous for his knowledge of the Torah, and his fear of sinning, who taught Torah in a few communities. When his eyesight dimmed in his old age, he embellished his legacy by authoring this delightful book with innovations on rules, and astonishingly alluring wise and articulated sermons".

The second note of approbation was written by Rabbi Shmuel Henipalkon. He wrote: "Deceased Gaon Rabbi and famous Hassid Yissaskhar-Ber, who was the ABD in Zolochiv, went to the holy land at the end of his life. He studied the Torah all of his life. He had a heart of a lion and was G-d fearing since his childhood". The book was also adorned by a note of approbation by the rabbinical judges of Dubno.

All the notes of approbation were received at the time of publication and provided to ensure the copyrights of Rabbi Yissakhar-Ber's decedents-publishers for ten years.

In the introduction to "Mevaser Tzedek", the author's son-in-law, writes that while he was studying with Rabbi Yissaskhar-Ber, and listening to his Torah gems every Shabbat (The author was a "*Maggid* Meisharim" ["Preacher of Righteousness"]), he thought about writing them down and later publish them. He asked his father-in-law's permission to do so. He began writing things down, but life's worries prevented him from continuing, so he only managed to save a drop from the ocean.

When the time for Rabbi Yissaskhar-Ber Aliya approached, he said that it would be better to wait [with publishing the book] until he sends new Torah sayings. Unfortunately for his admirers, he did not live long in the holy land, and the publishers only received a little.

The son-in-law also acknowledges his good friend, Rabbi Khaim Ze'ev Wolf from Zolochive, who helped him in writing the book. The author's son, R' Yehuda Leibush, and grandson, R' Efraim Fishel, also helped in writing the book.

The book "Mevaser Tzedek" was published in a large format and contains 44 pages using Rashi's letters. The style follows the phrase:" Fine goods in small parcels". The book contains innovative interpretations of the Torah.

What was Rabbi Yissaskhar-Ber's opinion about the *Nigun* [singing and music]?

[Columns 391-392]

There was no reason for Rabbi Yissaskhar-Ber to expand on *Nigun* in his book "Bat Eini". That book contains only new interpretations of the Torah and responsa about some Talmud tractates.

However, in the book "Mevaser Tzedek", the author could not have avoided discussing it. Most of the Hassidic authors about the Torah tried to state an opinion about the Torah statement about songs and singing. R' Yissaskhar-Ber found a way to fulfill his Hassidic obligation toward Nigun. He chose the opposite way to other Hassidic authors, who found it necessary to elevate Nigun and praise it. Rabbi Yissaskhar-Ber used it only symbolically. He used Nigun allegorically by taking it out of its musical interpretation and placing it in a different meaning. He used that method three or four times in the book to evade a direct explanation and thus "extricate himself out from danger".

For example, most of the Hassidic authors did not avoid talking about the verses that begin with the words - "Az Yashir" ["Then sang"]. These words appear several times in the Torah [in three places]. One of these is in the chapter about the Exodus from Egypt – at the beginning of "The Song of the Sea", [Shemot 15]. Another place is in the "The Song of the Well" [Bamidbar, Numbers 21:17]. Rabbi Yissaskhar skipped over "The Song of the Sea" altogether. When he discusses the "Song of the Well", he explains the Hebrew word Shira [singing] as it is used in the verse - "I see him but not now, I behold him but not near…" [the Book of Numbers 24:17]. So he considers Shira as a kind of "fore-seeing" [In Hebrew the word "behold" has the same root as the word "Shira" – "singing"].

[Columns 393-394]

Rabbi Israel Landau
(Chapters of Impressions and Appreciation)

by Ya'akov Katz

Translated by Moshe Kutten

The noble and shining image of my teacher and rabbi- Gaon Rabbi Israel Landau ZTZ"L, is standing in front of me in its full glory whenever I invoke the memory of the people of my city, Zloczow, and its scholars, leaders, activists, and the masses. He was etched in my heart and memory throughout my life until his death on 23 Elul 5689 [28 September 1929]. He died after a long illness that confined him to his bed. We, his students and admirers, were sitting by his bed until dawn and kept shifts at his bed to support and serve him.

I came to know Rabbi Landau, ZTZ"L after he came to settle in our city after a prolonged period of wandering and suffering as a refugee in Budapest. He was exiled there when the war broke out in his native Brody. Despite being born in Brody, he resided in Kyiv from the day of his marriage. He was considered there one of the most talented students-scholars. He and his family were hosted by his father-in-law. He occupied himself with studying Torah and G-d's work without worrying about making a living. His friends said that he lived in a palace-like house. The house was wide open to guests, dignitaries, and student scholars, who came to visit him and entertain themselves with quibbles about halakhic instructions and friendly discussions about world affairs. He was respected in the big synagogue of Kyiv, where prominent rabbis prayed. Among them, Rabbi Hillel Zlatopolsky Z"L. They honored him because of his lineage and his fascinating personality. I have heard about that period of Rabbi Landau's life from his friend Gaon Rabbi Levi Grossman, may he live long and good life, one of the prominent Tel Aviv rabbis who served as the chief rabbi in Kyiv until his Aliya to Eretz Israel. When Rabbi Landau ZTZ"L came to Zloczow, he was impoverished, as his assets remained in Russia. Hassidim and the people of action recognized his skills and appointed him as a rabbi and rabbinical judge in our city, a position he held until he passed away. The mourning of his death ran deep. Prominent rabbis from the city and its surroundings came to eulogize him. The day of his funereal was etched in my memory. Wide circles of people participated. The shops closed and wailing and eulogies spoke about the wondrous and righteous Gaon Rabbi who passed away. In the eulogy by Gaon Rabbi Shlomo Shikler, may G-d avenge his blood, the rabbi of Holohory (before he was elected as the rabbi of Kalush), invoked weeping and wailings. Rabbi Shikler's eulogy was particularly memorable.

Rabbi Shikler was one of the first students of the MHR" M Shapira ZTz"L. The latter adopted Rabbi Shikler as his dear son, as he recognized him as a great talent, eloquent, and a prodigy in the Torah and knowledge. He was also a skillful author (he was the editor of the Haredi monthly magazine "HaNetzakh" ["Eternity"], which was published in Lviv]. He shook his listeners with his eulogy of Rabbi Landau, one of the most prominent and noble rabbis. Rabbi Shikler mentioned that he knew Rabbi Landau to work on authoring books. His books were never published, except one. That book was "Nefesh Khaya" ["Living Soul"] about the Megila Tractate, which he dedicated in memory of his daughter, who was blessed with many attributes and knowledge. She passed away in her youth.

He immortalized his daughter in his book of considerable quality and quantity, which is named after her [Khaya]. He originated from a family of "Mitnagdim" [people who opposed Hasidism]. He was the son of Rabbi Yehuda Landau Z"L, one of Brody's most prominent people. He was the grandson of the famous Gaon, Rabbi Eleazar Landau ZTZ"L, the chief rabbi of the city, annotator of the Mishnah, named "Yad HaMelekh"["King's Hand"], and author of Halakha and Aggadah books. He was also the great-grandson of [Yekhezkel ben Yehuda HaLevi Landau] the author "Nodah BiYehuda". However, Rabbi Israel Landau ZTZ"L and his brother Gaon Rabbi Elazar, the author of "Yad Elazar" ["The Hand of Elazar"] approached the Stratin Hassidim. Brody served as the Statin Hassidim's strong citadel. Stratin Hasidim excelled in learning and were known for their highly vocal and fervent praying, following the style of the *Admor* Rabbi Uri of Sterlisk and his student Admor Rabbi Yehuda Tzvi of Stratin.

During the First World War, Rabbi Israel landau escaped the oppression in Galitsia to Budapest, where many of the war refugees concentrated. He was attracted to the city since his teacher and rabbi, the Admor Rabbi Avraham Langner] ZTZ"L from Stratin-Knihinicha settled there. The Admor established his court in that city and acquired a name of an exemplary *Tzadik*.

[Columns 395-396]

Rabbi Israel Landau ZTZ"L was very close to the Admor ZTZ"L and became more and more enthusiastic about Startin Hassidism. When the Admor from Startin-Knihinicha passed away, Rabbi Israel ZTZ"L was orphaned. When the front moved away from Eastern Galitsia, moving back became possible. He chose Zloczow as his new place. The philanthrope, R' Shaul Roller, provided Rabbi Landau a rent-free spacious apartment and added an allowance for his living expenses until he was nominated as the community rabbi. Many people gathered around him. They were all impressed with his vast knowledge of the Torah. His pleasant and noble manners earned him an honorable and admirable status. He prayed in the synagogue of the Stratin Hassidim, where many people prayed. During the "days of awe", other holidays, and special Shabbats, he "passed before the ark", in the attractive style of Stratin Hassidim (a style that excites the heart). What a fervently and devoutly prayer leader he was! When he reached his climax, it seemed like he rose above the floor along with his heart and soul. He roared and impelled when he delivered his sermons in the central synagogue and the *kloiz* where he prayed. The content was filled with Torah talk, Halakha innovations, and flashes of teaching and thought – all based on the Torah. He was deeply knowledgeable about the Mishnah, the Halakha's *Poskim* [Jewish law rabbinical scholars] *Rishonim* [the first], and *Akharonim* [the latest]). There was no secret hidden from him. He delved into the Hassidic literature and said things that pleased the ear and the soul. He loved the Hassidic community, and during the holiday of Simkhat Torah, he would join the circle and dance, holding the Torah scroll tight to his body. People were fascinated by the joy emanating from his pure soul. He was an educated person and knew German, French, and Russian. He was informed about classic literature and could cite long chapters by heart from the literature, philosophy, and poetry works.

All of that knowledge did not affect him, and he remained loyal to the freshwater wells of the Torah and rabbinical work. He was polite, well-mannered, and respected everybody, including non-religious people. He eulogized the Jewish secular leader, Dr. Hirschhorn, who devoted his life to serving our townspeople. Dr. Hirschhorn devoted his effort, particularly to the Ukrainian refugees, and risked his life to save Jews during pogroms and riots. Dr. Landau was not affected by what zealot Haredim said about that eulogy, since he valued self-sacrificing to save others, even if it was done by a secular person. His appearance left a deep impression because he knew to adjust every word and every sentence according to the event and the various crowds who might have been different from him in their lifestyle and views.

He was always elegant and tidy. People looked at him with respect and dignity when he walked on the street. Many, who were fascinated by his explanations, flocked to his regular lesson - "*Daf Yomi*" ["the page of the day"], which he conducted for homeowners and the youth. He also had several outstanding students who learned a lesson or two about pilpul about the Torah, Mishnah, and *Poskim*. When he became older, he lost his sight. I witnessed how he accurately cited entire Mishnah's tractates with commentaries by heart. He practically knew the entire six books of the Mishnah by heart. He would surprise everybody by adding innovative Torah commentaries during lessons of the Gemarah, *Tosafot* [commentaries on the Talmud], or of "Orakh Khaim" [first volume of Shulkahn Arukh – "Way of Life"] on Shabbat, Passover, and Hannukah laws.

I was fortunate to observe him during his daily routine. I saw him waking up to worship G-d. He accepted everything with love, with no complaints, even during his illness and weakness. He settled for less, despite being used to wealth and luxury during his past good days. He was strict about the proper arrangement of the utensils, plates, and glasses on his table. Everything sparkled like in the days he sat at rich people's tables. I witnessed that great G-d worshipping man, go to sleep. In his communion for "*Kri'at Shema*", thinking back on his day and repenting sincerely, he was wholly fervid and glowing by the flame of holiness.

I was impressed, not once, by the Torah's innovative commentaries. His writing was clear, vivacious and stylish, clean, deep, and full of happiness which brought up literary gems. He wrote commentaries for the entire Mishnah. He authored the Halakha innovations and commentaries and was also known as the author of responsas. He also authored many booklets about the bible. He provided food to the poor, particularly to needy students, who came to him and ate at his table. He dispensed money from his wages to support them and urged others to help them. He had one son, Dr. Yehuda Landau, the son-in-law of the famous charitable wealthy Rabbi Shmelki Rokeakh Z"L, the owner of the Bertshitz estate near Belz. That son was a scholar and Haredi. The first *Hakhshara* [a training Camp for people who plan to make Aliya] of the Aguda party [religious Zionist party] in 5883 [1922/23] (The founder of the group and its head was R' Ze'ev Zohar). Dr. Yehuda Landau's elder daughter was married to R' M. Kevkov, a scholar from Minsk, who was exiled from his city upon the Bolsheviks' conquest and settled in Lviv. The second daughter, who was learned and noble, was married to Isaac, the young son of the old Gaon Rabbi Avraham-Menakhem Steinberg. They all perished in the Holocaust along with their children and including the old *Rebbetzin* [rabbi's wife]. May their memory live forever.

———————

[Columns 397-398]

Rabbi Shalom Mordechai Hillel HaCohen Schwadron

by Moshe Leiter

Translated by Moshe Kutten

R' Shalom Mordekhai is known in the rabbinic world by the name of his responsa book - "Maharsha"m".

He did not serve as the Av Beit Din [ABD - head of the rabbinical court] in Zloczow but he was born in the city on 27 Nisan 5595 [26 April 1835] to his father, R' Moshe [Schwadron] HaCohen, and mother, Ester Gitl. He was named after his grandfather from Berezany.

R' Moshe Schwadron resided in the village of Benyon near Zloczow. He owned there a whiskey distillery. He enjoyed two worlds: The world of the Torah and wealth. He completed reading the Mishnah six times and had innovations in the Torah, Pilpul [casuistry], and Halakhah. His elder son printed and attached them under the name "Zikhron Moshe" ["Moshe's Memory"] to his book "Da'at Torah" ["The View of the Torah"] about [the book] "Yoreh De'ah" ["He Will Give Instruction" - by Rabbi Jacob ben Asher - a compilation of Halakha].

R' Moshe used to donate Ma'aser [a tenth] of his profits. He handed the money to the famed charity Gabbais of his generation, the known *Tzadik* Rabbi Meir'l of Przemysl, and *Tzadik* Rabbi Shlomo of Ozeryany, for distribution among the poor and needy scholars.

He was blessed with seven sons. The elder, Shalom Mordekhai, showed signs of a rare talent as early as six years old. He was diligent in his studies, and his father made sure he was taught by distinguished melameds. At first, he studied with the city's rabbinical judge Rabbi R' Yeshaya Zeev Baumgarten. He later learned from Gaon *Tzadik* Rabbi Yoel Ashkenazi ABD in Zloczow.

He told me that, in his youth, he studied 16 pages of the Gemarah daily, besides his lessons in Iyun [deep study], Rambam, and "Shulkhan Arukh".

When Shalom Mordekhai was a young child, one of the melameds, a secret enlightened person, wished to teach him Hebrew grammar. He gave him the book "Talmud Lashon Avar" ["Study of Past Language"] by Ben Zeev. That enlightened person gave him the book, on the condition that he would not tell his father… Two weeks later, R' Moshe Schwadron traveled to see Rabbi *Tzadik* Meir'l and took his son, Shalom Mordekhai, with him. The *Tzadik* Rabbi told him: "Do not set foot on their paths, for their feet run to evil, and make haste to shed blood" [Proverbs 1:15-16]. He repeated the verse loudly several times. When the *Tzadik* gained his composure, he told Shalom Mordekhai: "Do not study things that your father does not approve of. Ask your father, and he will tell you if that study is permitted. Don't listen to others as they aim to divert you from being righteous. Follow the path of your ancestors, excel in your studies, rise and become a leader in our nation, and live a long life. Remember my words, and you will succeed".

When Rabbi Meir'l Z"L greeted him farewell, he again warned Shalom Mordekhai:" My son, please remember not to listen to any person and read any book without the approval from your father. It is necessary because there are people who chase after you to divert you from the right and good path".

His Hasid father listened to the warning and ordered his son to tell him anything that happened without hiding anything. The child told his father about the enlightened melamed who enticed him to study grammar from Ben Zeev's book. He also told his father that the melamed requested not to tell his father about it. When his father, R' Moshe, found out, he understood the warning of his Rabbi R' Meir'l Z"L and ordered his son to burn the book. He warned his son not to have any more contact with that enlightened melamed.

Shalom Mordekhai obeyed the instruction, devoted himself to his studies, and became a Torah scholar. However, he initially detested being a rabbi and preferred to be a merchant in forest woods and linen.

When they offered him the rabbinical position after the death of R' Yoelish ZTz"L [May the memory of the *Tzadik* be blessed], R' Shalom Mordekhai refused. His excuse was that a person who is talked to in the first person was not worthy of becoming a rabbi. That person would not be able to impose authority, nor would he be able to motivate the members of his community as much as a rabbi who came from another city.

In the summer, when the days were long, he used to sit alone in the synagogue and study undisturbed.

He insisted on not becoming a rabbi until he reached the age of 32. Only then, in 1867, after losing his wealth, he accepted the offer to become a rabbi in Potok-Zloty. The town was legally owned by the Admo"r Rabbi David Moshe Z"L from Chortkiv.

Despite not spending any time at the court of the Admo"r *Tzadik* from Chortkiv, the latter requested that the people of Potik elect him as the city's rabbi.

He resided in Potik-Zloty for five years and continued with his studies there until he acquired a name for himself throughout the entire country. A short while later, he was offered to serve as the rabbi in Yazlovets. He served there for about seven years and never stopped studying. One day, one of the city's distinguished homeowners came to him to talk. The Maharsha"m explained to him, very politely, that he did not have the time to talk idly. He added that if he had time for friendly discussions, he would not be the rabbi in the city of Yazlovets.

[Columns 399-400]

Rabbi Shalom Mordekhai Schwadron

From Yazlovets, he was called to serve as the ABD in the city of Buchach, a community known for its learned leaders and famous great rabbis, scholars, and authors.

Despite being a city of "*Mitnagdim*" [people who oppose Hasidism], they elected him since they appreciated his greatness in the Torah and righteousness.

From Buchach, he was invited to serve as the ABD in Berezany, known for its *Gaons* rabbis. There were three candidates for that rabbinical position: Maharsha"m, Rabbi Ya'akov Weidenfeld, the Gaon ABD of Grzymalow [Hormilov], and Gaon ABD Gorodenka [Horodenka], Rabbi Moshe Teomim, the author of the books "Meshiv Davar" ["Answering"] and "Uriyan Tlithai" ["The Three Parts of the Torah"]. The Mahatrsha"m was elected out of that trio of *Gaons*.

Old *Gaons* recognized him as the leading upcoming *Posek* [literally a "decider" – an authorized Halakhic legal scholar] when he was still young. He was praised by *Gaon* Maharsha"k of Brody and also by Lviv's Rabbi Gaon Yosef Shaul Nathanson. The latter testified about the Maharsha"m's exceptional proficiency and rare teaching ability. *Gaon* Maharsha"k summed it up with the following words: "I do not see anybody else in this generation who is wiser than him". He chose Maharsha"m as his successor to spread the word of G-d and teach Halakha to the generation's scholars.

Rabbi Avraham [Eliyahu] David Rabinovitz-Teomim, the rabbi of [Yeshiva] Mir in Jerusalem, son-in-law of Gaon HaCohen Kook, the Rabbi of Eretz Israel Z"L, chose Maharsha"m as his rabbi. He urged Maharsha"m to provide him with a recommendation, as his loyal and dedicated student, when Gaon Rabbi Yitzkhakl Elkhanan Spector, *ABD* of Kaunas [Kovno], passed away.

There was a consensus about our great Rabbi Maharsha"m as the last deciding *Posek* because he astounded all of his generation's scholars with his brilliant proficiency in all of the Torah's hidden treasures and with his genius ability to issue halachic decisions decidedly with any hesitation or doubt. His wisdom and clarity of thinking helped him to make rulings firmly based on the Babylonian and Jerusalem Talmuds, *Safrah* [Midrashic interpretation of the Bible], Tosaftah [collection of traditions from the *Tannaim*, not included in a Mishnah], and the books of the *Rishonim* [the first *Poskim*]. In addition, he was exceptionally proficient in the books by the *Akhronim* [the last *Poskim*]. There was no secret concealed from him. He thought that one can always find innovative interoperation of the Torah worth reading. That is where he drew his great strength from, to rule *Kokha Dehitra*[1].

He was blessed with a penetrating vision to see fruits scattered around in the orchards of the *Rishonim* that were overlooked and passed over by the great scholars. He uncovered the covered treasures and piled them up on the tables of the great rabbis.

At times, he based a permit on one of the *Rishonim*, which was overlooked by the *Akhronim*. If any of them would have known about the work by the *Rishonim*, they would not be so strict about that rule or another.

In his book "Mishpat Shalom" ["Judgement by Shalom"] about "Khoshen Mishpat"[2], he allocated a special section to partnerships, intermediaries, negotiations, deception, nullification of agreements due to non-conformity, and community laws. In any areas lucking in "Shulkhan Arukh", he conducted in-depth research looking for solutions in all the responsa books and *Poskim* – from the first of the *Rishonim* to the last of the *Akhronim*. He conducted thorough research into problems that "were complicated enough to glorify any mystery not mentioned in Shulkhan Arukh".

He drew attention to himself and his book by the old Gaons of his generation, the generation of knowledge, for a reason. The old Gaon Rabbi Yosef Ba'abad, the author of "Minkhat Kinukh" ["Offering of Education"], said about him:" The wisdom of that "Tzorba D'Rabanan" [a sharp young rabbi], is greater than ours". In his *Haskama* ["consent"] to the book, Rabbi Yosef Shaul Nathanson, wrote: "We are blessed from heavens to receive these new writings".

His books "Da'at Torah" [literally- "The Opinion of the Torah"] and "Gilui Da'at" ["Revealing of Knowledge"] about "Yoreh De'ah" and his rulings were accepted in all corners of the Jewish diaspora as a complete doctrine. However, in his humility, he expressed his view: "I called the book "Revealing of Knowledge" because that is the only thing it meant to do. A teacher should not rely on my book as a replacement for the original book just because I made it easier to read it. I wrote my book so that if one likes my explanations, he should then read the original book". The Maharsha"m added: "I did not make it easy to understand [the original book], because of my exalted spirit but because the Torah aims to save our people [effort and] money".

[Columns 401-402]

"Despite his sincere humility (he considered humility as the essence of the house of G-d"), he had, at first, some adversaries from among some of his generation's greats. The adversaries were led by a *Gaon*, who sharply criticized Mararsham's *Kokha Dehitra* approach. In his response, instead of humility, our great Rabbi showed his greatness. He protected the validity of his view, which he considered the opinion of the Torah. He responded to that greatest opponent:" How did you find the courage in your mind to arrogantly intervene in a place already established by the greatest ancestors?" His opponent rabbi fell to silence and thanked him. He also thanked the instructions in Maharsha'm's book, "Da'at Torah, which became the norm for Halakha teachers.

When I was younger, I heard from a scholar student who studied with our great *Gaon* Rabbi's opponent. The scholar told me that a complicated problem was once presented to that Gaon and his legal court. The *Gaon* went into his office and took out the book, "Da'at Torah". He reviewed it alone, returned to the court hall, and issued a judgment as instructed by the book. It was an admission of how great is the force of truth in Maharsha"m's book.

In the six-volume responsa, we see not only a brilliant fundamental proficiency in all the hidden treasures of the Torah but also a logical profundity and distilled quality of the sources and definitions. A holy and genius spirit, rare and amazing, is hovering over the pages of his book. The author carries us on his shoulders like a swimmer through a whirlpool. He introduces us to the sea of the Talmud and with a self-assured and secure hand, he places us on the seashore, bathed and purified - immersed in the river flowing out of the Garden of Eden.

He used to lecture, with precise clarity, about the most complicated matters. Even in places where the road was already paved [things have been previously clarified], one can find a method in his book. He would find a new path, which no other eye caught sight of. He explains things simply, although he goes in deep and wide until we understand the law thoroughly.

His organized teachings were anchored in both Talmuds [Jerusalem and Babylonian]. He advocated that "a good and correct idea and an honest comment are true in any book if you can find them". Therefore, it is necessary to look for them. That view helped him in finding the required solution for every severe and complicated problem.

There were cases where he reasoned his permit, opposing the prohibitions by others because they overlooked the ruling of one of the *Rishonim* or the other.

When he found that his reasoning was shared by other rabbis, he would announce that as a significant finding. He would say: "On the problem presented here, there were some *Akhronim* who issued a permit, and I am happy that my opinion is the same as theirs".

There were cases where he set aside his own view for a more stringent opinion. In these cases, he would write: "In places where they exercised forbiddance, I would not permit". Even *Kokha Dehitrah* has a limit.

Despite his greatness in the Torah and righteousness, he was timid and good-hearted. When one of the rabbis was unsure about a ruling, he would turn to him to talk about his worries (e.g his divorce was not done properly) the *Gaon* Maharsha"m would hurry up to calm down the panicked rabbi.

In his six-volume responsa, we meet the names of great and famed rabbis, the greatest of the *Akhronim* - planets in Judaism's sky.

He always took heed of the people. He ordered his family not to hold up anybody who came to ask him a question but bring that person to him and even wake him up if needed.

He was particularly passionate about *Agunot*[3] and made an effort not to delay the ruling of those poor women. He wrote the dispensation, in his own handwriting, on the ninth of Av, a day he called "The day of fasting for the destruction of our house of glory".

Noble, honest, and pure-hearted person, who felt other people's misfortune with every ounce of his soul and tried his best to ease the lives of the misfortune and do good for them. His enthusiastic love for the Torah and its scholars, sprouts from every line he wrote. He was a wise and investigative man. He used the results of his investigation to explain his judgments without any difficulty. That is why his rulings were considered and accepted as final judgments.

He was also proficient in the gentile law, proofs of which can be found in his books. We knew that he absorbed rulings by the civil courts with his judicial mind. Hints for that we find in his books in various rulings (e.g. "… in a civil court, the official inquiries about all of the heirs").

He was respected and esteemed by the judges of the district court. The judges in Berezany used to send him complicated judicial cases, which they claimed that there was no wise man who could resolve. Maharsha"m would immediately dive into the depth of the problem and bring the litigants to agree to his ruling. The chief district court judge used to say: "I was working on this complicated case for years with no resolution. I handed this case over to the Rabbi and he found a solution right away".

The chief judge once advised the litigants, one Jewish and the other not, to go and argue their case in front of Maharsha"m. The gentile litigant refused. His excuse was that he could not rely on a rabbi to rule his fate because he suspected that the rabbi would rule in favor of the Jewish litigant. After all, they share a common religion. When the civil judge heard the excuse of the thickheaded gentile

[Columns 403-404]

he was filled with rage and slapped the gentile for being rude, daring to speak evil of the Rabbi, and daring to doubt the honesty and objectivity of the Gaon. He immediately ruled in favor of the Jewish litigant.

Dr. Sh. B. Feldman remembered that he once attended the court of the Maharsha"m when two non-Jewish lawyers argued their cases on behalf of their clients. They came from the state's district court, presented their claims, and accepted his judgment.

While he was a good-hearted and compassionate person, his opinion about the reformers was harsh. He considered them like monkeys imitating the gentiles and thus desecrating the sanctity of Judaism. He defined their worship as paganism and condemned the *SHU"V* [slaughterers and the Kosher inspectors] who served as public activists in their temple. He defended our holy language from those who insulted her by introducing foreign languages into the temple: "Using foreign languages instead of our sacred language is an abomination". He explained his ban on foreign languages by saying:" We need to use our own language so that the people of all nations on earth would know that the spoken and the written Hebrew language is alive. Other world's nations should consider it as the leader of all languages and the first when it comes to anything sacred".

He was also no stranger to natural sciences. He relied on natural sciences in some of his rulings and hinted about his sources offhandedly.

His knowledge of medicine is also hinted at in his book. He regrated that physicians treat religious issues lightly. He often used sources from among the researchers of the Middle Ages.

In addition to all that, he used to count the letters in the bible. His wonderous proficiency in the Book of Books arose astonishment among professional scholars, who devoted much of their time to bible research, some of whom became famous for their knowledge.

I saw with my own eyes that he studied a bible lesson daily. He used to walk by his open bookcases in his court office, holding the book in his hands and studying it.

During the month of Elul, he used to seclude himself, sit down covered with his Tallit, adorned with his Tefillin, and study the occult [Kabbalah], in which he was very knowledgeable.

The Maharsha"m was blessed with physical beauty and majestic appearance and his presence radiated respect and nobility. His wisdom and cleverness were reflected in his beautiful eyes. His attributes included moderation, settled thinking, a clear mind, and tenderness, in addition to his doctrine and righteousness.

At times he came out of his confined world of the Halakha judgment and teaching and jumped into the public activity whirlpool.

In 5664 [1903/4], he called for a gathering of rabbis to put the distribution of funds for Eretz Israel, in order. All the rabbis, Admo"rs and public activists heed his call and came. They accepted his authority, obeyed him, and competed in serving him.

He had a great desire to strengthen and improve religious education. He planned to establish the union of "Yeshurun" for that purpose. He intended to invite Rabbi Dr. Yosef Zeliger HaLevi Z"L, an original scholar and expert educator, to develop a plan for the improvement of Jewish education. However, because of the objection of one influential and famous Admo"r, the Maharsha"m was forced to postpone his plan until a more suitable time. His name was Shalom [peace] and he exercised peaceful ways. He established, on his own, the "Da'at Torah" yeshiva in his city. Many sharp and witty scholars, proficient in many tractates and expert certified teachers, graduated from that yeshiva.

[The following paragraph was seemingly taken from another article, because it describes a period after the establishment of the State of Israel, many years after the death of the Maharsha"m]

He also tried to ensure that the Israeli soldiers were given a vacation during the holidays. Once a military officer resisted and refused to accommodate the rabbi's request. Later on, the officer regretted his refusal and hurried up to ask for forgiveness. He called excitedly: "There is G-d, and the rabbi is his favorite son, whose wish would be accommodated". He became the admirer of the rabbi.

I would not expand on his miracles, since I know that he used to be strict about avoiding being called "*Ba'al Mofet*" ["Miracle Man"] by naive people. He also asked, in his will, not to include any honorary title besides the words "The Fame Rabbi" and the names of the books he authored.

[The following paragraph may have been taken from another article since it seemingly describes a family tree of another family]

He was the great-grandchild of Cabalist Rabbi Tzvi, *Maggid* Meisharim [Preacher of Righteousness] of Hlyniany [Gliniani or Glina], and the author of "Nishmat Tzvi" ["Tzvi's Soul"]. He was the grandson of Rabbi Yitzkhak, *Maggid* Meisharim of Drohobitz, and the father of Rabbi Mikheli of Zloczow. He was a descendant of *Gaon* Rabbi Yitzkhak Khayut, the author of "Api Ravravi" [Also called "Pnei Yitzkhak"] and *Av Beit Din* of Krakow-Prague. He was also the great-grandchild of Rabbi Yosef Karu, author of "Shulkhan Arukh".

For some reason, the number 16 played a role in his life. He studied 16 pages of Gemarah every day. He got married at the age of 16 and died on 16 Shvat 1911 in Berezhany. *Gaon* Rabbi Nathan Levin Z"L came from Risha to eulogize him.

He authored a series of valuable Halakha books that *Poskim* always placed on their desks, ready to use in their rulings.

[Columns 405-406]

The books were mentioned in almost all of *Poskim's* books, and he was praised by them verbally and in writing. His books became the books of choice in teaching and rulings. Gaon [Rabbi Yisrael Meir Kagan author of] "Khafetz Khaim" used to send him any complicated case brought in front of him.

The names of his printed books are:

   a. "Mishpat Shalom" – about "Khoshen Mishpat". Three editions.
   b. "The books of "Sifrei Torah" about slaughtering religious laws. Two editions.
   c. "Gilui Da'at" about Treifa religious laws. 5651 [1891]. Two editions.
   d. Annotations and innovations about "Shulkan Arukh – Orakh Khaim".
   e. Responsa "Darkhei Shalom". 1891. Two editions
   f. "Darkhei Shalom" – rules of the Mishnah and Poskim. Two editions.
   g. Maharsha"m - annotations about the Mishnah 5692 [1931-32].
   h. "Tkhelet Mordekhai" about the Torah.
   i. The booklet of HaDrushim.
   j. The book "Da'at Torah" about "Orakh Khaim". Published in Jerusalem.
   k. Responsa Maharsh"m. Six volumes.
   l. A eulogy of Rabbi Tzvi Rapoport.

He also left many written manuscripts, which were not published during his life. His two sons, Gaon Rabbi Yitzkhak Schwadron in Jerusalem, and Rabbi Tzvi of Bobrka-Lviv divided the inheritance of their Gaon father between the two of them. Among the manuscripts assigned to his son in Jerusalem, three volumes about "Orakh Khaim" have already been published. The three volumes contain comments and commentaries of the Maharsha"m and letters from Jerusalem's great rabbis.

The Gaon Chief Rabbi Yitzkhak A. HaLevi Hertzog ZTZ"L wrote:

"Here is the Gaon and true Hassid, the Rabbi of the Jewish diaspora, the Maharsh"m from Berezhany, may the memory of the *Tzadik* [righteous] and Kadosh [holy man] be blessed. He was accepted as Posek, and his rulings are like the words of the Torah".

Translator Notes:

   1. From Wikipedia: "In its original sense it is a rule of Talmud that teaches how to formulate a disputed case, in such a way that the mind of the permitting party is clarified more clearly due to the perception that the renewal of the permitting is as a greater principle than that of the forbidding.
   2. Khoshen Mishpat is the last volume in Ya'akov ben Asher's "Arba'a Turim" ("Four Columns") and the parallel part in "Shulkhan Arukh" about property and finance laws].
   3. Aguna is a Jewish woman her husband would not grant her a divorce (including cases when the husband has disappeared, either in a war or at sea).

[Columns 407-408]

The Gaon Rabbi Yoel Ashkenazi

by Moshe Leiter

Translated by Jerrold Landau

Edited by Moshe Kutten

We have not been given the birthdate of Rabbi Yoel Ashkenazi, and we are also unable to determine the time of his death.

However, from the approbation of Rabbi Yaakov of Lissa, the author of *Chavat Da'at*, on the book *Torat Adam* by Rabbi Moshe, the father of Rabbi Yoel[a], written on Sunday 5, Adar 5583 [1823], we can estimate the date. The approbation does not mention that the author is the father of his daughter's husband, Rabbi Yoel Ashkenazi. From this, it can be determined that this was before his granddaughter was given as a wife to Rabbi Yoel and before the match was made. We can surmise that Rabbi Yoel Ashkenazi was born around the year 5570 [1810], for it was their custom to arrange matches at the young age of 12 or 13.

The date and year of the death of the Gaon Rabbi Yoel are also not known. However, he was alive in the year 5641 [1881], for he issued a responsa to Gaon Rabbi Yehoshua Heshel Wallerstein, the head of the rabbinical court of Rzeszow.

Rabbi Yoel drew the waters of life from the blessed wellspring of his father, the author of *Torat Adam*. He also served his wife's grandfather, Rabi Yaakov of Lissa, of blessed memory. If he found favor in the eyes of that Gaon, so that he gave him his granddaughter as a well, he evidently regarded him as a source of blessing.

Rabbi Yoel Ashkenazi was accepted as the head of the rabbinical court of Gologory and Chodorow. From there he was called to serve as the rabbi and head of the rabbinical court of Zolochiv.

From his book Responsa of Rabbi Y. Ashkenazi, we see that he engaged in didactics with his two brothers-in-law, the *Gaonim* Rabbi Avraham Teomim, at first the head of the rabbinical court of Zborow, and later the head of the rabbinical court of Buchach, the author of the enlightening book of Responsa *Chesed LeAvraham* on the four sections of the Code of Jewish Law; and with Rabbi Yosef Yoel Deitch, the head of the rabbinical court of Karchynow-Chodorow, the author of the book Responsa *Yad Yosef*.

Similarly, he engaged in deep didactics with his relative, the great Gaon Rabbi Mordechai Zeev Ittinga of Lwow, and with his student, the Gaon, and final decisor Rabbi Shalom Mordechai HaKohen Schwadron of blessed memory.

Rabbi Yoel Ashkenazi was a man of peace, who distanced himself from all traces of dispute. According to his faithful testimony, he "did not get involved in any situation where there is a dispute and argument, for this could lead to numerous obstacles, may the Merciful One save us."

He was especially careful to refrain from intermixing in matters of other communities, lest some unpleasantness for the rabbi of that city ensue from his involvement, and through his expressing his opinion. He held that "one must support a rabbi in one's city so that things are established in the way he determines." If he ever expressed his opinion and responded to a scholar on matters of a community, even if the asker was not a rabbinical leader of the city, it would be such that "they told me, and also with the agreement of the rabbi and head of the rabbinical court of their community that they consulted with me on this matter without entering any suspicion or doubt in their hearts, etc. Therefore, I agreed to hear them out." However, without the agreement of the rabbi of the city, he would not be willing to express his opinion, so as not to give a pretext and a sword to the hands of the rabbi's opponents so that they can work against him.

Even though he was completely filled with pure righteousness, and he forged marriage bonds with the great *Tzaddikim* of his generation, *Admorim*, and people of good deeds, he did not recoil from publicly opposing the rule of the Hassidic rebbes, for he saw in this a factor in the separation of hearts and for fomenting words of dispute within the city.

He publicized his negative, sharp judgment against someone who studied the trade of *shechita* [ritual slaughter] and "was not a fearer of the living G-d, and prepared his sharp implements and his soul for ruin, to damage the livelihoods of the *shochtim* [ritual slaughterers], and he supported some of his family members to the extent that he could, and he caused a decline in the livelihood of the *shochet*, as he acted with a strong hand against the will and without the agreement of the vast majority of the city leaders, and without the knowledge of the teacher [i.e. the rabbi], etc. It is appropriate to scold this man and to forbid that which he slaughters. His slaughtered meat is as pierced [i.e. improperly slaughtered] in accordance with the Torah."[1]

However, after being scolded by a scholar, he somewhat softened his judgment for the sake of peace, and wrote, "It is indeed a good thing to strive for peace, and to save Jewish souls, etc. And in the good path and peace in your tents."

[Columns 409-410]

People of moral learning took pride in their rabbi, who had fine traits. If he sent a letter through a messenger, he would purchase postage stamps and tear them up so that the government would not lose out.

According to the opinion of Rabbi Yoel Ashkenazi, with his knowledge of the Torah, it is forbidden to evade affixing stamps [on letters], and even scholars who are exempt from taxes are obligated in this: "And since he is a scholar, is the king obligated to give him gifts? In this matter, there is no difference between a scholar or a regular person, and all are equal." He added, "Even Maimonides of blessed memory wrote that the law of the land is the law. This is also explained in the name of the Meiri of blessed memory. in *Shita Mekubetzet*[2].

It was his way to honor and recognize those with whom he disputed, and to acknowledge their greatness in Torah. When the Gaon Maharsha'm wished to avenge the honor of his rabbi during his young days and to demand restitution for his embarrassment by contradicting the words of one of the *Gaonim* of his generation who published sharp words of criticism against the Torah novellae of his rabbi, Rabbi Yoel Ashkenazi hastened to calm him down, writing the following: "I have seen in your letter that a complaint is arising in your heart regarding the book of the Gaon of renown. Therefore, you have waved your sword, girded yourself with zealousness, asked my opinion, and requested my response, to enter the battle and to react to this. Behold, the friend of my heart, let it not seem difficult in your eyes, for this is the way of Torah. One builds and another deconstructs, one hardens, and the other breaks down. They grind it very well, and everything is from the forger of many forms so that none is exactly like the other. We have found people such as that among the fathers of old in the Talmud and decisors."

This is what Rabbi Yoel said to calm the spirits and to give his opinion to his great student, who was dedicated to him. Not only did he advise him to refrain from attacking his "disputant" via his pen, but he also gave him handfuls of recognition, and called him "the Gaon of renown."

We learn another thing from his calm words, which demonstrate the opinion of the scholar – he knew how to adorn his words with linguistic ornaments and weave them into fine rhyme, taken from the Bible and built on the statements of our sages of blessed memory, using the Hebrew language in good taste.

Even though it was his way to recognize his disputants and to admit their greatness in wisdom, we also see the strength of his opinion. He never missed an opportunity to reprove and point with his fingers at those who make a breach in fundamentals through which they built their legal verdicts. He cleaved to the dust of their feet, but he never gave up on his opinion in favor of theirs. He would dig for the fundamentals and the truth, and he would not play favorites in judgments even toward those great in Torah.

He was daring, and he did not refrain from opposing the opinion of the Gaon Rabbi Mordechai Zeev Ittinga of Lwow. He wrote to him in his sharp style, including the claim that he would stand by his opinion, and not give in to the great of the greats.

One who searches for his mindset in his clear book will come to the conclusion that he followed after the Gaon the *Noda BiYehuda*[3] with great reverence for his vast amount of Torah and his deep wisdom. If one of the great ones of his generation would come and venture to demonstrate some crack in the sanctuary of the Torah of the *Noda BiYehuda*, and disagree with him – Rabbi Yoel Ashkenazi of blessed memory would gird himself with his Torah, and hasten with his strong logic to prove the veracity of the Torah of the great decisor and mighty Gaon, and, in good taste and understanding, contradict the objection of the objector.

When the Gaon, the author of the *Ketzot Hachoshen*, sought to slight the Noda BiYehuda, Rabbi Ashkenazi of blessed memory did not recoil from setting out against him with his weapons, the weapons of Torah. He wrote, "According to my modest intellect, scanty understanding, and short wisdom, his holy words are too lofty for me, and I am amazed that they are not correct in my eyes. Even though the disputant is a rabbi and a sage, the truth will show its path, that the words of the Noda BiYehuda of blessed memory are as solid as a mirror, and the judgment is a judgment of truth; all his words are just and correct, G-d is with him, and the *halacha* is according to him. The concerns of the Ketzot Hachoshen of blessed memory have no basis."

Again, his words are set against the Gaon Ketzot Hachoshen with the intention of defending the Gaon the Noda BiYehuda: "According to my simple knowledge, the net was cast for naught, the bow and arrow is for a void, he cast arrows without substance, to fell a sublime city, set up like a wall, and what am I – like a small fly against the great lion. However, it is Torah, and I must study it, to justify the *Tzadik* in his fundamentals. The words of the Noda BiYehuda are constructed on the foundations of intelligence and truth."

However, when the Gaon Rabbi Yekutiel Asher Zalman Enzil wanted to deal in his glosses with such matters regarding his rabbi, the Gaon Ketzot Hachoshen, even with his great merit in being a veteran student of the Ketzot, who never moved from his presence; and he was the one who edited and arranged for publication the writings of his rabbi the Gaon, something not done by his sons or sons-in-law; for he was the choices of the students of the Gaon the Ketzot – the Gaon Rabbi Yoel set out to contradict the logic of his glosses and to uphold the words of the Gaon, the author of *Avnei Miluim*, and wrote as follows: "I have seen there the words of the rabbi who wrote the glosses, Rabbi Enzil of blessed memory, and even though he was my acquaintance, and I knew him previously as a scholar with a straight intellect – but he made a great error, and did not understand the wisdom of his rabbi."

Not only did he disagree with the Ketzot in order to support the words of the Noda BiYehuda, but he also wrote the following about the Gaon the Chatam Sofer: "Further, I have seen with regard to the Chatam Sofer words that were not correct in my eyes." Indeed: "I have seen in this some error that emanated from the ruler, the Chatam Sofer of blessed memory."

[Columns 411-412]

Because of his love of truth, he became involved in a dispute that he hated. We have written that he was not content with the deeds of the *Tzadikim* whose way was to send a *shochet* to the city in which they were powerful and in which they had many people who were of their ilk. This caused disputes, schisms, and arguments within Jewish communities. He stated what he had witnessed:

In the city of Zolochiv, the Hassidim of Rabbi Avrahamche of blessed memory of Strettin complained about the *shochet* of the city. Rabbi Avrahamche sent a *shochet* who was of his ilk. Rabbi Yoel the rabbi of the city, banned the slaughtered meat of that *shochet*, who had come to encroach on the *shochet* of the city. What did the Hassidim of Strettin in the city of Zolochiv do? They traveled to nearby Brody and related their suspicions to the Gaon Rabbi Shlomo Kluger, the *Maggid* of Brody. The Gaon, the *halachic* decisor of Brody, banned the slaughtered meat of the *shochet* of the city of Zolochiv. However, the Gaon, the head of the rabbinical court, did not heed the ban on Rabbi Shlomo Kluger of blessed memory, and he permitted it. The Gaon Rabbi Yoel was known as a *Gaon* and *Tzadik* to the people of his city, whose entire striving was for pure truth. A typical theme for his spiritual countenance, full of both childlike simplicity and unmovable strength of heart, can be seen from the following fact: Once, two wealthy people came to him for adjudication regarding a large sum of money, and they brought two arbitrators-solicitors with them. One of the arbitrators-solicitors was the preacher of Lwow, Dr. Lowenstein, the father of Dr. Nathan Lowenstein, a deputy of the Austrian parliament[4]. He, whose power was with his mouth, dared to speak before this pure rabbi, Rabbi Yoel Ashkenazi, who served as an" adjutant" – not as an arbitrator to his commander. This was like the rabbi of the state living in the capital city in contrast with a rabbi of a small city… In his simplicity, Rabbi Yoel Ashkenazi reacted to the brazenness and arrogance of that preacher: "Have respect! I am the Platz Kommandant [local commander] here," that is, I am the rabbi of the city. He continued and told him, "I am not afraid of you, despite your good connections with the government rabbis. I can forgo the rabbinate and my position, and go to my in-law in Ilsk… And I will not pervert the judgment, and will not favor you in the case."

He did not favor *Tzadikm* and *Amorim* of influence, and he would not show favoritism to the strongman preacher. He was straightforward with his G-d.

It is worthwhile to note another characteristic of the spiritual countenance of that upright *Tzadik*, who was illuminated with a special hue of the light of the Torah. This is about his pleasant use of the Hebrew language, and his style full of ancient grace and moistened with the morning dew. During the Middle Ages, the Torah giants would decorate their words on matters of *halacha* and law with rhyming verses full of poetry. They would even do so when they were expressing their views on legal decisions. That great man of Torah and benevolence did the same thing. Not only this, but he would include with his sharp pen lines of simple but pleasant verses in almost every responsa, as "I desired to walk with him, and I drew near to fulfill his request, therefore I did not slacken"[5]. Further, "I directed my eye to all his doors, and his great splendor, that he inscribed with his letters." Or "Your shadow is pleasant, your fruits are sweet, and you dove into mighty, deep waters."

Even with respect to a serious question regarding purity and impurity, he found appropriate words to express his opinion in verse, even though his mind and his heart were focusing on the essence of the law and *halacha* at that time.

These lines are pleasant, for the beauty of poetry sparkles from them, as he inserted them between the *halachic* exchanges with the young *Gaon*, the final decisor, the rabbi the Maharsha'm of blessed memory, who wrote about him with fatherly love with words of friendship and appreciation. He expressed his love for him with charming words of the verse. He described him with a crown of the verse: "To the man who is a scribe, quick in his work, a friend of G-d, and a friend of my soul and heart. May he ascend in holiness, may he go up and up on the route, full of praise."

Just as Rabbi Chanina the son of Chama, the rabbi of Rabbi Yochanan, merited to see his great student preach in the *Beis Midrash* of Rabi Banai in Zippori [Sepphoris], he also merited to see the star of his veteran student rise in the skies of the rabbinate and illuminate with bright light and was also not jealous of his great student[6].

Rabbi Yoel left behind many Torah novellae that we did not merit to see published. His son, Rabbi Yosel, may the memory of the holy be blessed, continued in the rabbinate of Zolochiv. He later made *aliya* to the Land of Israel, died, and was buried in honor in Safed. Rabbi Yoel left behind other sons and sons-in-law who were great in Toran and in the rabbinate.

Author's Notes:

a. Rabbi Yoel Ashkenazi's father made *aliya* to the Land of Israel and was accepted as the rabbi and head of the rabbinical court in the holy city of Safed. In the Land of Israel, he published his books *Torat Adam* [The Torah of a Person], and "Didactics on Discussions and Ideas of the entire Talmud." The *Gaonim* Rabbi Yaakov of Lissa, the author of *Chavat Da'at*; and Rabbi Yaakov Ornstein, the Gaon, and head of the rabbinical court of Lwow, the author of the book *Yeshuat Yaakov* gave approbations for the book that Rabbi Moshe David wrote in Tultshava. The approbation of the author of *Chavat Da'at* is interesting, in that his modesty is expressed: "And even though I know in my soul that my worth is small, etc. and furthermore, this person has no need of me." He described him as "The Gaon of renown, our Rabbi Moshe David, may his light shine."

The Gaon Rabbi Yaakov Ornstein wrote, "And I have seen that he is fitting to teach the sons of Judea the bow [translator: an obscure reference for something of significance, based on II Samuel 1:18], and to open for them the gates of halacha in a clear path, so they will not stumble in them, with clear didactics, to delve deep into the *halachot*, to understand the learning of the holy ones, the source of wisdom, and the proper path in which dwell the light and wit of the words of the sages." The aforementioned book was written in the Diaspora, as is shown in the aforementioned approbation, and published in Jerusalem in the year 5605 [1845]. He wrote another book on Torah when already in Safed, in the year 5610 [1850] with approbations from the great Sephardic sages Rabbi Chaim Nissim Abulafia, and Binyamin Mordechai Navon. It was published in that same Jerusalem publishing house by the printer Rabbi Yisrael Bek in the year 5613 [1853]. The book is called *Be'er Sheva*.

Translator's Footnotes:

1. These words of reproof are written in rhyme, in a highly poetic fashion. I was unable to do justice to all the idioms with this translation.
2. See https://en.wikipedia.org/wiki/Bezalel_Ashkenazi/.
3. Rabbi Yechezkel Landau of Prague.
4. See https://www.encyclopedia.com/religion/encyclopedias-almanacs-transcripts-and-maps/loewenstein-von-opoka-nathan
5. The Hebrew here and in the following quote has a rhythm and rhyme which could not be captured in translation.
6. This story is noted here, with its Talmudic references: https://en.wikipedia.org/wiki/Hanina_bar_Hama.

[Columns 413-414]   *

Gaon Rabbi Shraga Feivel Rohatyn

by B. Tzverdling

Translated by Moshe Kutten

Rabbi Shraga Feivel Rohatyn was appointed after the death of Rabbi Yoel Ashkenazi in 5642 [1882]. Rabbi Shraga possessed unique attributes. On one side, he was a *Gaon* of the Torah, and on the other side, he acquired a general secular education. He was observant of religion with all of its rules and details. He was also involved with people. His manners all flowed in complete harmony. He was a native of Lviv, a student of Rabbi Avner, a known scholar in Lviv, and Rabbi Yitzkhak Ettinger. He received his confirmation from the *Gaons* at a young age and acquired a name for himself as a Torah great. When he served as a rabbi, he was studiously studying Torah and secular subjects. He successfully passed the matriculation examinations from Zloczow's high school in 1893. Rabbi Shraga conducted research about the Ramba"m and received a philosophy doctorate degree.

He was exceptionally good-looking and his majestic appearance brought about respect from anybody who saw him. Rabbi Shraga taught a daily lesson in *Gemarah*, Rashi commentary, and *Tosafot* (annotations to the *Talmud*). Every youth tried to become his student. I was fortunate to be his student, and I learned good portions of the Torah from him. He was proficient in the six books of the *Mishnah* and *Poskim* [Jewish law adjudicative literature] and could easily cite the location and the name of the author of any article in the *Gemarah*. He was proficient in the literature of the Middle Ages and the research literature. He was a wise man in daily matters and knew how to advise on every complicated issue. Rabbi Shraga gave sermons at the big synagogue and in the *Beit HaMidrash* on *Shabbat Shuva* [The Shabbat during the "Days of Awe"] and *Shabbat HaGadol* [The Shabbat before Passover].

He would open his sermon with an *Aggadah* [a general topic for a sage's article that does not deal with Jewish law]. He would stop upon reaching the middle of the *Aggadah* and would provide a comprehensive, sharp, and spicy argumentation about the subject matter. In the end, he would return to the *Aggadah* at a greater length. During *Shabbat Shuva*, the *Aggadah* portion contained content about morals, and during the Shabbat HaGadol, just an *Aggadah* about daily matters. At the end of the *Aggadah*, he would teach halakha laws. On the approach of the holidays, Rabbi Shraga would publish a list of references. It was a list that specified the locations in the *Mishnah*, Babel or Jerusalem *Talmuds*, *Tosafot*, Ramba"m, etc..., on which the sermon and the argumentation portion would be based. A list of references would be posted in most synagogues and Batei Midrash. Rabbi Shraga would send the list to the homes of prominent scholars, such as R' Ya'akov Shwartz Z"L, Rabbi Khaim Mikhel Izen Z"L, and others, to their homes. Receiving the list at home was considered an honor. By doing that, anybody who wanted to prepare themselves for the sermon could do it. The scholar students would sound their commentaries after the sermon. A debate ensued, the type of which could only be heard in previous generations. The student scholars presented their poser and the Rabbi answered, and then Rabbi Shraga presented a poser, and they answered. One thing connected to another, and the argumentation lasted for hours.

Rabbi Rohatyn authored a book by the name "Mishpat Mekhokek" ["Legislature"]. Rabbis from far and near places dispatched questions to him since he became known for his proficiency and sharpness. His torrential style has also promoted questions. He was eloquent, and his lecture was pleasant and fluent, when he spoke about the Torah, delivered a rabbinic sermon, or delivered a speech in Polish. His talks were agreeable to his listeners and captured their hearts. He was wise to adjust and direct his talk based on the type of listeners.

In 1901, the authorities issued a tender to build barracks for the military. Rabbi Rohatyn Z"L was among the people who submitted bids. He became known as a general contractor since then and managed to acquire a fortune. Rabbi Shraga was both a prominent figure and a Torah great.

He led the rabbinate in our city for fifteen years before he left. His admirers and fans asked him to return, and he agreed to return without pay. When he returned to our city in 1907, he accomplished great projects: He built a large public bath and improved the Torah school. Rabbi Shraga took an active role in public affairs and served as a member of the municipal council. Despite his failing health, his friends, admirers, and students hoped for bigger deeds. However, his death came early. He passed away on 15 Adar 5671 (1911). The Gaon Rabbi Avraham Mendel Steinberg Z"L eulogized him using heartfelt words. He left three sons and two daughters. Among his sons, R' Naftali Rohatyn excelled. The deceased Rabbi wanted him to become a rabbi. However, R' Naftali turned to banking and was appointed as the manager of the "Deposition Bank" in Ivano-Frankivsk [Stanislav, Stanislawow]. With the break of the First World war, he moved to Vienna and in 1945 made aliya to Eretz Israel. He lived in Haifa with her daughter Miriam. He passed away on 6 Iyar, 5710 [1950].

Rabbi Shraga Feivel Rohatyn was appointed after the death of Rabbi Yoel Ashkenazi in 5642 [1882]. Rabbi Shraga possessed unique attributes. On one side, he was a Gaon of the Torah, and on the other side, he acquired a general secular education. He was observant of religion with all of its rules and details. He was also involved with people. His manners all flowed in complete harmony. He was a native of Lviv, a student of Rabbi Avner, a known scholar in Lviv, and Rabbi Yitzkhak Ettinger. He received his confirmation from the Gaons at a young age and acquired a name for himself as a Torah great. When he served as a rabbi, he was studiously studying Torah and secular subjects. He successfully passed the matriculation examinations from Zloczow's high school in 1893. Rabbi Shraga conducted research about the Ramba"m and received a philosophy doctorate degree.

He was exceptionally good-looking and his majestic appearance brought about respect from anybody who saw him. Rabbi Shraga taught a daily lesson in *Gemarah*, Rashi commentary, and *Tosafot* (annotations to the *Talmud*). Every youth tried to become his student. I was fortunate to be his student, and I learned good portions of the Torah from him. He was proficient in the six books of the *Mishnah* and *Poskim* [Jewish law adjudicative literature] and could easily indicate the location and the name of the author of any article in the *Gemarah*. He was proficient in the literature of the Middle Ages and the research literature. He was a wise man in daily matters and knew how to advise on every complicated issue. Rabbi Shraga gave sermons at the big synagogue and in the Beit HaMidrash on Shabbat Shuva [The Shabbat during the "Days of Awe"] and Shabbat HaGadol [The Shabbat before Passover].

He would open his sermon with an *Aggadah* [a general topic for a sage's article that does not deal with Jewish law]. He would stop upon reaching the middle of the *Aggadah* and would provide a comprehensive, sharp, and spicy argumentation about the subject matter. In the end, he would return to the *Aggadah* at a greater length. During *Shabbat Shuva*, the *Aggadah* portion contained content about morals, and during the *Shabbat HaGadol*, just an *Aggadah* about daily matters. At the end of the Aggadah, he would teach halakha laws. On the approach of the holidays, Rabbi Shraga would publish a list of references. It was a list that specified the locations in the Mishnah, Babel or Jerusalem *Talmuds*, *Tosafot*, Ramba"m, etc…, on which the sermon and the argumentation portion would be based. A list of references would be posted in most synagogues and Batei Midrash. Rabbi Shraga would send the list to the homes of prominent scholars, such as R' Ya'akov Shwartz Z"L, Rabbi Khaim Mikhel Izen Z"l, and others, to their homes. Receiving the list at home was considered an honor. By doing that, anybody who wanted to prepare themselves for the sermon could do it. The scholar students would sound their commentaries after the sermon. A debate ensued, the type of which could only be heard in previous generations. The student scholars presented their poser and the Rabbi answered, and then Rabbi Shraga presented a poser, and they answered. One thing connected to another, and the argumentation lasted for hours.

Rabbi Rohatyn authored a book by the name "Mishpat Mekhokek" ["Legislature"]. Rabbis from far and near places dispatched questions to him since he became known for his proficiency and sharpness. His torrential style has also promoted questions. He was eloquent, and his lecture was pleasant and fluent, when he spoke about the Torah, delivered a rabbinic sermon, or delivered a speech in Polish. His talks were agreeable to his listeners and captured their hearts. He was wise to adjust and direct his talk based on the type of listeners.

In 1901, the authorities issued a tender to build barracks for the military. Rabbi Rohatyn Z"L was among the people who submitted bids. He became known as a general contractor since then and managed to acquire a fortune. Rabbi Shraga was both a prominent figure and a Torah great.

He led the rabbinate in our city for fifteen years before he left. His admirers and fans asked him to return, and he agreed to return without pay. When he returned to our city in 1907, he accomplished great projects: He built a large public bath and improved the Torah school. Rabbi Shraga took an active role in public affairs and served as a member of the municipal council. Despite his failing health, his friends, admirers, and students hoped for bigger deeds. However, his death came early. He passed away on 15 Adar 5671 (1911). The Gaon Rabbi Avraham Mendel Steinberg Z"L eulogized him using heartfelt words. He left three sons and two daughters. Among his sons, R' Naftali Rohatyn excelled. The deceased Rabbi wanted him to become a rabbi. However, R' Naftali turned to banking and was appointed as the manager of the "Deposition Bank" in Ivano-Frankivsk [Stanislav, Stanislawow]. With the break of the First World war, he moved to Vienna and in 1945 made aliya to Eretz Israel. He lived in Haifa with her daughter Miriam. He passed away on 6 Iyar, 5710 [1950].

———

[Columns 415-417]

Rabbi Shraga Feivel Rohatyn

by Moshe Leiter

Translated by Moshe Kutten

They were three prodigies of the same age. All three were borne to wealthy and prominent Torah scholars. All three were natives of cities where the sun of the Torah shone brightly. These prominent Torah greats served as the city rabbis, whose reputation preceded them throughout the diaspora. Those rabbis served as an example and urged the trio to emulate their diligence in learning, resemble them, and be like them. As far as we know, they achieved that.

The three were Rabbi Gedalia Schmelkes, Rabbi Nathan Levin, and Rabbi Shraga Feivel Rohatyn.

It is not me who placed them on the same level. The tremendous Gaon, Rabbi Yitzkhak Shmelkes, and Av Beit Din [ABD – head of rabbinical court] of the Lviv community was the one who put them on the same level.[1]

Rabbi Shraga Feivel Rohatyn was born in 5618 [1858] in Lviv to his wealthy Torah scholar father, R' Leizer Rohatyn. His father tried to provide him with knowledgeable teachers to develop his superior talents. When he grew up a bit, he studied with Gaon Rabbi Yitzkhak Ettinger in Lviv. At the young age of 16, the Gaon Rabbi ordained him to teach and judge. After that, he was conferred and ordained by Gaons Rabbi Tzvi Orenstein and Rabbi Schmelkes.

In 5643 [1882/83] he was elected to serve as ABD in Zloczow. He left the small town of Narayov, known to host prominent rabbis, and came to sit on the rabbinate throne in Zloczow. Two scholars served as judges in his court.

In Zloczow, the district city, he came in contact not only with the biggest merchants but also with the government officials, and he also talked to the Austrian military commanders in his city. He concluded that acquiring knowledge of general sciences and foreign languages was needed to represent the Jewish congregation. It took him a short time to study and pass the high school matriculation tests. That opened the doors of the college in Lviv for him. It was said about him that he translated the book "Moreh Nevokhim" ["The Guide for the Perplexed"] by the Ramba"m]. According to Mr. Mordekhai Deutsch, he only authored a research paper about the Ramba"m as a requirement for a doctor of philosophy degree. However, we do not know whether he received the degree.

He corresponded with Dr. Rabbi Moshe Gidman, the Chief Rabbi of Vienna, Dr. Tzvi H. Miller, a professor at Vienna University, and Rabbi Shlomo Buber from Lviv, about matters related to Judaica. He also corresponded with Torah greats, such as Gaon Rabbi Yitzkhak Shmelkes, about the *Halakha* and argumentations about the written and oral Torah.

He did not publish anything about Khokmat Israel [Jewish Sciences]. However, he published a high-quality book about the complicated issue of reasoning mentioned in article no. 23 of "Khoshen Mishpat". In that book, he had shown his great strength in logical sharpness. He went deep into that complicated issue, managed to clarify it with his analytical talent, and placed his assumptions and conclusions on solid foundations.

His generations greats appreciated his strength in argumentations about the Torah, his radiant personality, and his kindness. He one set in a high court together with the Gaons Poskim [legal scholars who determine the position of *Halakha*], Teacher and Rabbi R' Mordekhai HaCohen Schwadron, ABD Berzhan and Rabbi Moshe Teomim, ABD of Horodenka, author of the responsa's, "Oryan Telitai", ["The Three Parts of the Bible"], and "Meshiv Moshe" ["Moshe Answers"]. These two generation's greats raised the chair of Rabbi Rohatyn above theirs and placed it between them. Gaon Maharsha"m [Schwadron] set on his right, and Mahara"m Teomim on his left, to honor him in front of the people. Like his friends, Rabbi Gedalia Shmelkes and Rabbi Nathan Levin Z"L, he was blessed with physical beauty and a noble gaze. His wisdom and cleverness were reflected in his eyes and his curly sidelocks adorned his temples like clusters of grapes.

He was the only rabbi in the country who served without getting paid. He was not only a Torah scholar, philosopher, and wise but also a visionary and full of youthful energy. He became a construction contractor who built the barracks for the Austrian military. He was the architect and engineer for the walls he had constructed and also the only manager and accountant for all of his branching business, without any help from anybody. In doing so, he amassed a fortune, in addition to what he inherited from his wealthy father.

He was both wealthy and a Torah great, which provoked jealousy from his opponents.

[Column 417]

Rabbi Shraga Rohatyn

In 5661 [1901], a conflict erupted between Rabbi Shraga and some of the city's influential Hasidim, who wrapped their jealousy in a cover of G-d-fearing multi-colored excuses. They explained their complaint against Rabbi Shraga with the claim that a Jewish rabbi should not dirty his hands by managing the ledgers of his businesses and should not balance up his accounts by working with the military accountants. He should deal with the "disputes between Abbey and Raba" [two great Babylonian rabbis] and leave the construction contracting of military forts to professional construction contractors.

[Column 418]

They also thought that it was a sin to read a scientific book, which was improper for a G-d-fearing rabbi to do so. He left Zloczow in the same year [other sources state that it happened in 1905].

In 5667 [1907] the people in Zloczow decided to call their great rabbi to come back and sit on the rabbinate throne, which was still vacant, and he agreed. They showed him a great honor on his return to the city. They welcomed him joyfully and showed their joy publicly since they realized that they would not be able to find anybody like him. They appreciated his Torah wisdom and his kind and delicate manners. Even most of his former opponents reconciled or almost reconciled with his return.

However, in 5670 [1910], his weak body was tired of carrying the heavy burden he loaded on his shoulders. He fell under his load and passed away.

A bright star collected back his splendor. He was given a great eulogy. *Gaon* Rabbi Avraham Mendel Steinberg, *ABD* of Brody, author of the responsa "Makhazeh Avraham" ["Avraham's Vision"], came from Brody to eulogize him. He was buried in a mausoleum near the grave of the *Gaon Tzadik* Rabbi Avraham Khaim, the author of the book "Orakh LeKhaim" ["Way of Life"], who served as the city's rabbi in the past. For his memorial on the 30th day, the city leaders invited his friend, Rabbi Gedalia Shmelkis of Przemysl, to eulogize him. He opened with a biblical verse [taken from the lament of David eulogizing Saul and Jonathan, 2 Shmuel 1:17-18]. The verse was previously used by Rabbi Yosef Saul Nathanson, the Rabbi of Lviv, in his eulogy of *Gaon* Rabbi Tzvi Khayut Z"L: "The beauty of Israel is slain upon thy high places: how are the mighty fallen!"

Author's Note:

1. In his book "Beit Yitzkhak" ["The Home of Yitzkhak"]

[Columns 419-420]

The Departure of Rabbi Rohatyn from Zloczow

by Yaakov Meizlish

Translated by Moshe Kutten

A.

I remember the beginning of that event from my childhood days like a fading echo from afar. I also witnessed the end of the event, like other readers of this article.

The predecessor of R' Shraga Feivel Rohatyn was Rabbi Yoel Ashkenazi, a great scholar, and pious and virtuous man. His successor was a completely different person. R' Faivel Rohatyn was born to a wealthy family. He was not snobby, but his appearance and demeanor radiated a front of a distinguished rabbinical personality. He was known as a prodigy and a scholar student, having a quick and sharp apprehension and wonderous memory. He was an outstanding speaker also in Polish and German. At his time, he was justifiably considered a learned person. His blond beard and tall fur hat granted him a majestic appearance, allowing him to go in front of government ministers and nobles. However, he was not a "Hassid". That made him unlikeable to the Hassidim. His great wisdom, level of genuineness, and wealth helped him in securing the rabbinic position. However, that was like "a fly in an ointment". His opposition to Hassidism and his wealth caused him troubles later on.

During those days, the Austrian government began constructing barracks and forts in Galitsia. Rabbi Rohatyn showed interest in the tenders and submitted a bid to the authorities in Vienna. Surprisingly, his bid won. When he succeeded in the construction project around Zloczow, he won additional contracts in other locations. He became very wealthy very quickly. That provided a weapon in the hands of his opponents to criticize the Rabbi more vigorously. They claimed that his duty was to be engaged in the Torah and not in construction. And so, the great controversy was revealed, and Zloczow experienced the taste of a deep divide. Although such occurrences did occur in other Jewish communities, the memory of that controversy caused sorrow and pain to every Jewish resident in Zloczow. The quarrel between the two camps was managed by two "headquarters" operating in the "rear". The Rabbi's supporters from among the "enlightened" and homeowners were supposedly humble. They did not realize their views through melee acts. The fighters came from among the masses- those who were scrappy and "trigger-happy". The fighters on the side of the Hassidim were the youths from the Kloizes.

I must say that Zloczow was also blessed with a different kind of Hassidim. These Hassidim did not let their pure spiritual world be spoiled by provocative actions. I came to know those Hassidim closely. My grandfather used to take me to their parties when I was a child. The home of Shmuel Itzik [Yitzkhak] Imber served as a gathering place for those pure-soul people, particularly on holidays like Simkhat Torah or any other holidays or vacations. Chortkiv Hassidim were the majority of those groups. The Husiatyn and Sadigura Hassidim were also proud to be part of that distinguished lineage. Almost none of these signs of condescension or jealousy were apparent among that crowd, signs that were prevalent in the other groups. As mentioned, the center of activity for peace-loving Hassidim was the home of Sh. Y. Imber. His wife, Mrs. Gitla (if my memory serves me right), used to serve "kugel" and other Shabbat delicacies. The guests used to bring their wine. They would start to discuss Torah subjects and stories about *Tzadikim* with the first sip. Then they began to sing, softly at first, and later, enthusiastically, up to a trance, and finished with a "dance". The celebrants would feel like on "cloud seven". Not once, particularly during the holiday of Simkhat Torah, did somebody from the opposite side, would run in, in a trance-like state, and declare that he is taking himself out of his circle, and delivering himself to our circle. That would warm the hearts. To promote "love, friendship, and comradeship", they would proceed to pour themselves another cup and, with a tempestuous dance, would storm out and encircle the kloiz like the "Hakafot" in Simkhat Torah.

The euphoria of the holidays did not last long. Immediately following the holiday, when life returned to the mundane six-day week of toil, the group would scatter - every man to his camp and each person to his flag...

[Columns 421-422]

B.

Rabbi Rohatyn was forced to leave Zloczow because of the dispute. At first, none of the sides dared to think about a new rabbi for the city. However, over time when the flames of the controversy died down, everybody recognized that the temporary arrangement of two judges, the representatives of the two feuding sides, was not a good alternative. A city with a large Jewish community can not operate without a spiritual leader for long. A pious crowd can not function without a city rabbi. In a short time, the issue of the city rabbi became the central issue on the agenda. All sorts of candidates from different circles began to flock to the city. They came from the most zealous among the zealots to the progressive and enlightened. It included highly educated people who were known in Jewish circles internationally and within the state's political system. The latter, who sought the support of the Zionists because of their significant influence in the city's affairs, considered themselves worthy of approval by the authorities. Some of these candidates became later prominent people of action in the education field of Eretz Israel.

Every candidate had to appear three times in front of the Zloczow public. Each candidate had to deliver three sermons. One of these sermons had to be filled with Halakha argumentations – in front of the city's scholars. Another one was supposed to be about morals and manners. It was to be delivered in front of "Amkha" [simple people of the Jewish masses]. The last one was like a political "speech" on daily affairs to prove that the candidate was abreast in current affairs and would be able to deal with the authorities, as the community's leader. Delivering these three sermons was not an easy task. It was not inconceivable that one R' Yankel Shwartz would jump in the middle of a sermon and prove to the candidate that the "poser" or argumentation he presented as his own was "acquired" from another source. A goad of that kind or another was lurking for every candidate. Scholars and sharp-minded candidates would linger in the city for days and weeks so that they could knock on the doors of the community leaders and influential people to attract them to their side. However, the efforts of all of the candidates were in vain. Zloczow people simply tried to find a person like Rabbi Rohatyn. None of the candidates could fill the shoes of Rabbi Shraga Feivel Rohatyn. Things got to the point that the number of people who opposed Rabbi Rohatyn began to shrink more and more. People concluded, one bright day, that they needed to bring Rabbi Rohatyn back to the rabbinical throne. Nobody knew who was the first person to express that idea, however, when the idea was born, it received positive reactions very quickly. The old admirers of Rabbi Rohatyn rejoiced. The neutral people expressed some doubts, and the old opponents listened and kept quiet.

A voice came out to say: Zloczow decided to ask Rabbi Shraga Feivel Rohatyn to return.

Not that many days passed before a distinguished delegation went out to Lviv, to let Rabbi Rohatyn know about the city's decision. However, the delegation encountered an absolute refusal. People did not give up. It meant simply that a new official community delegation must be sent on behalf of the community's committee. However, that delegation also returned empty-handed. That resulted in a short pause in that matter. However, the city recovered very quickly and began to deal with it with a renewed and increased effort. The Rabbi's admirers proposed that the correct and best way to proceed is to hold an election. Meaning that the community would legally elect Rabbi Rohatyn. The election was held ceremonially, according to faith and law, in public and Rabbi Rohatyn was elected unanimously.

A new official delegation went to Lviv on behalf of the community committee, to announce the election results to Rabbi Rohatyn, and invite him to come back to Zloczow to serve as the city's rabbi. Moved by the announcement, the Rabbi thanked the delegation for the honor that was bestowed on him, however, he stated that unfortunately, he would not be able to accept the offer, as he was old and frail, and his wife became very sick (controversy hurt her tremendously, and she was yet to recover from it).

That was a convincing and depressing reason. There was probably no solution. The delegation said farewell to the rabbi with a heavy heart and returned to Zloczow. Little by little, the names of other candidates began to be raised. With that, the fear of negative occurrences resulting from renewed controversy and disputes increased. And there, at a big public gathering to discuss the issue of the rabbinical position, somebody from the crowd brought up a "practical" proposal – to try again to convince Rabbi Rohatyn using an "impressive moral power". He proposed that the "entire city" would travel to Lviv to lay out their strong request before the Rabbi. The proposal was accepted by the crowd and with enormous enthusiasm, it was decided to execute it.

[Columns 423-424]

A train full of the entire community traveled to Lviv on Sunday. Nobody was missing. Every one of the travelers considered themselves the official delegate of Zloczow's community.

The peaceful and quiet street where Rabbi Rohatyn resided, was suddenly blackened by a huge crowd. Jews from all the classes and circles, dressed in colorful attire, stood at the door of the Rabbi's house. A small delegation entered the house and delivered the wish of the crowd. They added that the congregation was determined not to leave until the Rabbi agreed to their request.

Surprised and astonished by what he heard and saw, the Rabbi could not refuse any longer and gave up.

Only very seldom a rabbi was welcomed so enthusiastically and festively as the way Rabbi Rohatyn was received when he came back to serve again as the Rabbi of Zloczow.

Gates of honor were erected at the train station, the entrance to the city, and the synagogue, with signs carrying the blessing "welcome in peace". All the stores were closed. Work ceased. They all came out as one to welcome the Rabbi. The agile ones came early to the train station, and crowds lined up on the side of the roads where the parade was supposed to pass. The moment the Rabbi's entourage was seen from afar, the musical band began to play, and the cantor and his singers sounded the song of Hallel [praise]. The Rabbi's admirers untied the horses but could not pull the wagon because of the overcrowding. Many non-Jews in the crowd wished to be honored by the honor bestowed on the Rabbi.

At the synagogue, the Rabbi gave a sermon about the day's event. His talk dealt with the values of peace, tranquility, and friendship. He preached about following the Torah and about good deeds. He also talked about the revival of the Hebrew language and the rebirth of Eretz Israel.

Rabbi Rohatyn was later the true spiritual leader of the city. There was no affair in the life of the Jewish community that was not carried out under the influence and inspiration of that praised Rabbi,

After he passed away, Zloczow remained without a leader for many years because the community could not find a person who could replace Rabbi Rohatyn.

[Columns 425-426]

Rabbi Shmuel Shapira and his Family

by [Israel][1] Shapira

Translated by Moshe Kutten

Rabbi R' Shmuel Shapira ZTz"L, was born in 5615 [1855] to his father, Rabbi *Tzadik* R' Avraham Kahim Z"L, a friend of Gaon Rabbi Shmelkes ZTz"L. He left many handwritten manuscripts and died at the young age of 37.

Rabbi Shmuel was the grandson[2] of the author of "Brit Avraham" ["Avraham's Covenant"] about the Torah and "Be'er Mayim Khaim" ["Fresh Water Well"], about the Passover *Haggada.* On his mother's side, Rabbi Shmuel was the grandson of Rabbi Shmuel Wilner[3], who was a student of the BESH"T. The famous Rabbi Shmuel Wilner, *Av Beit Din* [ABD – head of the rabbinical court] of Helitch, was Rabbi Shmuel's uncle.

He was a great Torah scholar in the revealed and occult. There was no *sugia* [a Talmudic conversation and argumentation] in the Mishnah that he did not write about, keenly and in-depth, like one of his generation's great scholars. Rabbi Shmuel used to write his comments on the margins of the [Holy] AR" I's books, and the books of "Zohar. The rabbi from Olesko once visited him, as was customary among the *Admors* [Great Hassidic Rebbe] to visit a city rabbi for a *Kiddush* after the Shabbat prayer. During the *Kiddush*, the rabbi from Olesko held the Siddur of the AR"I and saw the comments written by my father on the margins. He liked the comments and asked his elder son to copy them for him.

Rabbi Shapira was one of the Hassidim of R' Yitzkhak Izik from Zhydachiv. When he visited the *Admor* R' David Moshe from Chortkiv ZTz"L, during the *Kiddush* of Shabbat, he witnessed the intensity of the *Admor*'s emotion. After the *Kiddush* he said: "I will settle here, at the *Admor*'s court, because I want to experience it". He became one of the *Admor*'s unequivocal Hassidim until the end of his life.

At a young age, he married *Rabbanit* Malka Khaya, the daughter of Rabbi R' Arye Leibush Wilner, *ABD* of Helitch. He became a rabbi at the age of 18 while serving his father-in-law. He served there as a rabbi until he reached the age of 27 when he accepted an offer from Dobromyl to serve there as a rabbinical judge and teacher of religion. It has been said that the leaders of the neighboring city Noishtat [?], who respected him as a great man and activist, offered him to become their rabbi. He probably agreed, but the people at Dobromyl did not want him to leave and invited him to a meeting and advisement by *Admor* R' Moshe David from Chortkiv ZTz"L. After listening to the arguments of both sides, the *Admor* advised him to stay at his position in Dobromyl, as he appreciated Dobromyl people's pleas. He served the city for fifteen years until he was accepted as the Rabbi and *ABD* of Zloczow.

His house served as the meeting place for the scholars. Scholar students and other Jews came to hear Torah from him. Many were very fond of him, and came to visit him every holiday and Shabbat for the third meal.

During that meal, the excitement grew, and after the *Zmirot* [singing], he used to sermon about the weekly portion and other occult and revealed Torah topics. He inherited the enthusiasm and excitement from his great *Admor* Rabbi R' Izik from Zhydachiv ZTz"L, who made a deep impression on him. He used to hold the prayers and orders according to the style of Zhydichiv Hassidim.

His first wife died at a young age. He had four sons with her. His second wife was *Rabbanit* Fridah Roza, the daughter of *Admor* and mentor Rabbi Meir Shapira of Zbarazh Z"L. The latter was the grandson [son of the son] of the *Maggid* of Zaliztsi, Rabbi Yosef Moshe.

My father Z"L died at the age of 72, on the seventh night of Passover 5688 [1928]. May his soul be bound in the bundle of life. The manuscripts of my father were lost in the Holocaust.

The Sons of Rabbi Shapira Z"L

The oldest son, Rabbi R' Ben-Tzion Shapira, Rabbi and *ABD* of Zloczow, was born in 1900 and was nominated at a young age to the rabbi and *ABD* of the town of Lysiec, near Ivano-Frankivsk [Stanislawow]. He was later nominated as the successor of his father in Zloczow. He was educated and a scholar. He inherited his studiousness and his enthusiasm for learning the Torah from his great father. He had connections with people considered important by the state authorities, and he used his connections for my benefit. I planned to emigrate to Eretz Israel but was found fit and qualified to serve in the Polish military. As a result of my brothers' effort, I was released for that duty and I made *aliya* to Eretz Israel. My brother's letters were filled with longings to Eretz Israel. He was murdered on 8 Tamuz 5701 (July 3, 1941).

Eyewitnesses told the following testimony about his death (from the book of Shlomo Meir, "Der Untergang von Zlotzov" ["The Downfall of Zloczow"]):

[Columns 427-428]

"When they brought the group containing Rabbi Ben-Tzion, his brothers and their families, additional Hassidim, and many activists to the killing location, they began to pray enthusiastically. Their emotion and excitement grew from one moment to another until the prayer turned into an intense and powerful singing. It was so powerful that even the murderers were startled until they recouped and began to shoot at the people. One by one, those heroes fell. The ones who remained standing, continued with their singing and enthusiasm, which weakened from one minute to another until the last of the martyrs fell, and the singing ceased".

The second son, Rabbi Ya'akov Shapira, *ABD* of Tovste [Toist] near Hrymailiv [Rimlov] possessed outstanding attributes, was educated, and was a great speaker. He wrote poems and essays and left fascinating written manuscripts. He was endowed with a pleasant voice and served as a cantor. In his later years, he organized a religious pioneering movement in his city. Many registered for agricultural settlement in Eretz Israel. In one of his letters, he wrote:" Although I reside far away from our holy land, I am tied to the Israeli lives, and to everything that happens there, with my heart and soul". However [the Second World] War put an end to his aspirations. He was mortally wounded, and people considered him dead. However, he later recovered from his wounds and was led to be exterminated on Thursday, 8 Tamuz 5701 [3 July 1941], along with the rest of his brothers. May G-d avenge their blood.

The third brother, Rabbi David Moshe (1906 – 1941), was a great Torah scholar. He was one of the *Maggids* of the *Daf Yomi* [daily page] at the youth movement of "Agudat Israel" [*Haredi* movement and party] in our city. Even his "small talks" were those of a scholar. He always found a fitting verse, a witty and fitting phrase, which was like "fine goods in small parcels". The city leaders nominated him to be a rabbinical judge and *Posek*. He married the daughter of *Admor* R' Khaim Grinberg from Hlyniany [Glinah], the sister of the poet A. Tz. Grinberg. His wife, Rachel, was likable and beloved, educated and knowledgeable. Her letters were soaked with sorrow and pain about the need to live her life in the bitter diaspora. She wrote:" Precisely those who yearn, in their heart and soul, for the coveted Land of Israel do not get to fulfill their dream". She was murdered, while still young and full of life and energy, along with her husband the rabbi, and their children.

The fifth brother, R' Yisaskhar Dov Shapira, hated being a rabbi. He loved working for a living and worked as a merchant. He made great efforts to make aliya to Eretz Israel. He became the son-in-law of Berish Weiser from Zloczow. He was murdered in Belzec. The exact date is unknown.

The fifth brother R' Elkana Shapira, my parents' youngest son, served as a slaughterer and [Kosher] inspector in the city of Svirzh during the latest years [before WWII]. His letters were filled with longing for Eretz Israel. He emphasized that he considered himself a tourist who stopped [in the diaspora] for the night. He experienced many hardships, but the words "Eretz Israel" sweetened his bitter life in the diaspora. He went to a *Hakhshara* [training course for pioneers who planned to make aliya] and was active in the [Haredi Zionist organization and party] "Poalei Agudat Israel" ["Agudat Yisrael Workers"]. He was unsuccessful in reaching his coveted homeland and was cruelly murdered. May G-d avenge his blood.

The fate of the siblings, children of R' Shmuel ZTz"L from his first wife, was not different from that of my brothers, except for the elder brother who passed away in 1926 in Lviv while his father was still alive. He was granted a permit to teach from Rabbi Mordekhai HaCohen Schwadron *ABD* Berezhany. They wanted to nominate him to be the rabbi but he refused as he did not want to use the rabbinical position as a means of making a living. He became a merchant. He died at a young age. Two of his sons survived the war and now reside in Israel.

The second son of R' Shmuel from his first wife was R' Avraham Khaim *ABD* Obertyn, near Kolomyia. He was a scholar and left many manuscripts. His sons were also *Haredi* and scholars. The son of Rabbi Reuven Babad *ABD* Pidvolochysk [Podvolotzisk] , was his son-son-in-law. Rabbi R' Avraham Khaim was led along with his family to the killing town of Belzec and they were all annihilated there.

The daughter [of R' Shmuel Shapira], Yenta Buber, wife of R' Yitzkhak Buber from Hlyniany [Glinah], perished with her entire family in Belzec.

Many other members of my family, which was branched and contained hundreds of people, disappeared and perished in that manner. I was orphaned and the only one left.

Translator's Footnotes:

1. Since all of his brothers are mentioned, the author of this article must be Israel Shapira.
2. The author attributes the books to Rabbi Avraham, Khaim HeLevi Shapira, who was Rabbi Shmuel's father, rather than the grandfather.
3. That seems to be an error. The name should be Rabbi Uri Wilner. (Rabbi Shmuel Wilner was his uncle).

[Columns 429-430]

Gaon R' Yekhiel Mikhel Leiter

by Moshe Leiter

Translated by Moshe Kutten

R' Yekhiel Mikel did not serve as a rabbi in the city of Zloczow. He resided there temporarily during the years of the First World War. He became friendly with the residents, and they became fond of him.

After the war, the city of Dunaiv [Dunyov], near Zloczow, was in ruins. Its residents were scattered throughout the world. Most of them reached New York and organized themselves as an association. They remembered their beloved rabbi and urged their leaders to call for an assembly. It was unanimously decided to invite their former rabbi to come to them and serve as their Av Beit Din [*ABD* - head of rabbinical court]. The association sent him money to cover the travel expenses, rented him an apartment, and bought new furniture and kitchen tools. He accepted the offer and arrived in New York. All of Chortkiv, Husiatyn, and Sadigora Hassidim also concentrated around him.

The leaders of the synagogue "Makhzikei HaDat" ["Keepers of Religion"], of Zloczow's natives in New York, also set their eyes on him. They called for an assembly of their members, which elected him to also serve as the *ABD* of the Husiatyn-Sadigora synagogue.

He served as the rabbi of Zloczow's people in New York for about 12 years until his death. After his death, the people of the Dunaiv association and Sadigura Hassidim, natives of Zloczow, argued about the location of his grave since both associations wished to bury him in their cemetery.

When I came from Vienna to New York to erect a gravestone on his grave, R' Nakhman Billig was on his deathbed. I visited him, accompanied by the Hassidim R' Mikheli Imber and his brother-in-law, R' Yitzkhak M. Shapira. He was happy to see me, the son of his beloved rabbi. R' Nakhman Billig fell sick and never recovered after my father's death, as he was very attached to him.

My father-teacher was orphaned when he was four or five years old. His father, the *Gaon* Rabbi Shalom Leiter, a rabbi in the city of Bobrka, accompanied his elder son, *Gaon* Rabbi Dov Leiter Z"L, to the town of Zbelov, where he was nominated to serve as a rabbi and *ABD*. Rabbi Shalom caught a cold and died there. My father Z"L grew up in the home of his elder brother in Zbelov.

My father's elder brother, whom *Gaon* Rabbi Yitzkhak Shmelkes wondered about his sharp wisdom and quick apprehension, was my father's teacher and mentor. My father-teacher also possessed a sound sense of criticism, the ability to ask questions, and a great problem-solving ability. Some of his wonderous innovations aroused the astonishment of his elder brother and other students. They tried to reject his innovations and annul them so that he would not be too proud of his success. However, my father-teacher Z"L was convinced that he had the truth is on his side. He wrote about his innovations-argumentations to the Torah greats of his generation, like the *Gaon* Maharsha"m, the author of "Oryan Telitai", *Gaon* Rabbi Pinkhas Burstein *ABD* Siret [Seret], and others. These Torah greats were amazed by my father's brilliant Torah innovations and sided with him. He stood with the Torah greats during his youth and demonstrated his powerful sharpness and knowledge. When he was only 17 years old, he published his book "Mazkeret A'hava" ["A Souvenir of Love"]. The book was about the Mishnah's *sugiyot* [subjects for a study], and my father reserved space for the answers by Judaism's greats in it.

Rabbi Maharsha"m, praised him, not in his presence:" "The rabbi from Dunaiv is wise and a scholar".

When he was twenty years old, he visited the *Gaon*, Rabbi Ya'akov Yottes in Lviv, the author of the books - responsa "O'halei Ya'akov" and "Mikra'ei Kodesh". The Gaon conducted argumentations with him on various subject matters and was impressed by his common sense, his knowledge of the Torah, and his tremendous sharpness. The *Gaon* ordained him to be a rabbinic judge and *Posek* [decisor] with [the customary rabbinic ordination] phrase: "*yoreh yoreh* [permission to rule on ritual matters) and *yadin yadin* [permission to serve as rabbinic judge]. The *Gaon* Yottes testified about him: "Rabbi Leiter is very knowledgeable about our Holy Torah and knows how to conduct argumentations with a tremendous sharpness".

At that time, R' Leiter was supported by his father-in-law where name preceded him. The two local rabbis disagreed about the ordination. They agreed that the young rabbi would select a court consisting of three famous and established rabbis, which would decide on the argument between them. They agreed in advance to accept that court's decision. Both rabbis accepted the selection by RI" M Leiter and approved the following rabbis to serve in the court: *Gaon* R' Shalom Lilienfeld *ABD* Pidhaitsi [Podhaitsa], *Gaon* Schorr, *ABD* [head of a rabbinical court] Monasterzyska, and as the third rabbi they approved the selection of the old *Gaon* Vittles from Bobrka [Boiberik]. The three rabbis lodged at the home of the young rabbi, my father-teacher Z"L, and consulted with him about every detail since they appreciated his wisdom and sincerity.

He chose these three *Gaons* wisely, since each one of the rabbis excelled in a different area, and shone a light on it during the court hearings. The rabbi from Monasterzyska was proficient in the four parts of "Shulkahn Arukh", particularly in "Khoshen Mishpat". R' Shalom Lilienfeld was proficient in the *Tosafot* [Middle Ages' commentaries on the Talmud] and knew how to use its logical arguments wonderfully. The third rabbi, old Rabbi [Khaim] Simkha Lilienfeld, was proficient in the Sha"s [The six books of the Mishnah]. When they argued the case, every member of the threesome showed their strength by using their own weapons and fighting like war heroes about their opinions.

[Columns 431-432]

I mentioned that story, which I heard from my father-teacher, for the benefit of future generations. Future descendants would be able to learn about what is hidden behind the images of the rabbis in the distanced and the not-so-distanced time.

After his ordination by the three wise men, he sat down for another five years and studied diligently. In the meantime, the leaders of the Dunaiv congregation offered him the position of rabbi in their community. On his way there, he stopped by the Gaon Maharsha"m Z"L in Berezhany. He asked the Gaon to study him and provide him with a permit to rule on ritual matters and serve as a rabbinic judge. He began with argumentations about halakha-based rulings. The Gaon Maharsha"m asked, and the young rabbi answered successfully. His answers were short but thorough. They kept going until the waggoneer came in and hurried R' Yekhiel to go on his way, given the lateness of the hour. The Maharsha"m realized that my father was in a hurry to leave and pointed at a youth who sat across from them:" This young man is a decent student scholar. He has been studying and residing in my house for about a year now, and I have yet to fulfill a similar request for him. Your honor came to me only for a few hours, and in a hurry to leave. At the same time, you desire to receive a permit to judge and serve as a rabbi?" A smile was raised on Maharsha"m face, and he added:" I guess I would fulfill your request". He sat down and wrote him a certificate of ordination as a rabbi and a permit to judge, filled with praises and sincere words of appreciation:" I know the man and his words. He has been argumenting and negotiating [Torah and Halakha] for some years. I have talked to him about issues of halakha-based judgment and found him fit. I am thereby awarding him the [rabbinic ordination] permit 'Yoreh, Yadin, Yadin'. The rabbinic crown suits him well". Maharsha"m blessed him the Priestly Blessing [Book of Numbers 6:22-27] and accompanied him to the door with love.

In his town, Rabbi Yekhiel Mikhel gathered several young men around him and taught them Gemara and Poskim for free. He also shared with them his studies and perusals until they became proficient in the Torah and became rabbis or just great Torah scholars.

His name proceeded him as a great Torah scholar and as a person blessed with wisdom and knowledge of the Talmud. Rabbinical judges from other cities came to see him. Rabbis from neighboring and far away cities invited him to argue complicated cases since they knew about his great Torah talent.

During the First World War, when he could go from Zloczow to Vienna, his public activity talents were discovered. He became a public rabbinic activist and a speaker since he tuned to any affair related to Judaism and his people.

When hunger struck during the war, affecting the Jews, and the days of Passover were approaching, the rabbis of Galitsia-Bukovina, who resided in Vienna at the time, gathered to discuss the issue of permitting legumes as Kosher for Passover.

The following Gaons-rabbis signed on the permit: Rabbi Shteinberg, ABD Brody, Rabbi Meir Erik, ABD Tarnov, Rabbi Yosef Engel, ABD Krakow, Rabbi Yerukham, ABD Staryi Sambir [Old Sambor], Rabbi Yekhiel Mikel Leiter, ABD Dunaiv, and Rabbi Bentzion Katz, ABD Borshchiv-Chernivtsi [Burshchov-Tsherovich], since they have been ordained as the heads of the rabbis, and as certified Poskim [rabbinic deciders].

Although there were hundreds of rabbis in Vienna at the time, he was elected as the rabbi at the Haredi synagogue "Makhzikei HaDat". Most of its members were Galitsia natives who settled in Vienna many years before the [First] World War. The members of the synagogue were very fond of him because of his distinguished manners and knowledge of the Torah.

When the Haredi associations gathered for a conference in Vienna, the rabbinic association in the city elected Rabbi Yekhiel Mikhel Leiter Z"L as its representative and special delegate to the conference.[a]

When the Gaon Rabbi Meir annulled the marital status of an Agunah [a woman whose husband is missing or refusing to divorce her], he stated that he had one condition:" Only if the Gaon Rabbi Yekhiel Mikhel Leiter, ABD Dunaiv, who negotiated that matter, would allow me to annul the marriage".

In 5692 [1931/32], my father-teacher Z"L sent me his manuscripts for me to organize and publish. When I managed to publish his two-volume responsa "Darkhei Shalom" ["Peaceful Ways"], I sent the book to New York. My father wished so much to see his work in all of its glory, but unfortunately, he passed away before receiving the book. I was not able to cheer up his soul.

His two ordained sons, Rabbi Nathan Neteh Z"L, the editor of the Torah collection in Vienna, "Raboteinu SheBagolah" ["Our Sages in the Diaspora"], and the prodigy, Rabbi Yehoshua Heshel Z"L, the rabbi of the Bronx synagogue in New York, died when he was still alive. My brother, Rabbi Yehoshua, passed away just about ten weeks before the death of my father-teacher Z"L. My father could not overcome this last sorrow.

My father-teacher was born in the city of Bobrka in 5624 [1864] and died on Shabbat during the Minkha prayer, 22 Shvat 5693 [18 February 1933].

Author's Note:

a.   A discussion about changing the name of "Agudat Israel", was held at that conference. Rabbi RI" M Leiter objected and said:" It is appropriate that the association be called "Agudat Ya'akov" [Ya'akov Association] since Rabbi Ya'akov Rosenheim was its initiator, founder, and spiritual leader. However, G-d's angel has already said:" Your name will no longer be Ya'akov but Israel [Genesis 32:28]". So, the name has been already changed, and should not be changed again". The gathered people liked the reason presented by the Rabbi, and the name of the association remained without a change.

———

[Columns 433-434]

Rabbi Khaim Moshe Zilbershitz

by Ben-Tzion Tzverdling

Translated by Moshe Kutten

On Thursday, 8 Adar I (2.11.1954), on the 30th day of the passing of Rabbi Khaim Moshe Zilbershitz, a memorial service was held in "Ateret Tzvi" synagogue. As one of his students, I eulogized him with the following words:

A sacred duty is imposed on me to eulogize Rabbi Khaim Moshe Zilbershitz.

I had the great privilege to be one of his students and studied Torah taught by him. Rabbi Khaim was a warm-hearted man and attracted his students to love and admire him. His teaching was pleasant like the trickling fresh water from a pure spring.

There isn't any study which is as difficult than the study of the Babylonian Talmud. However, Rabbi Khaim Z"L eased the study. By his teaching, even a person of average skills could understand most of the Sugiyot [A topic for an argumentation] of the Sha" s [The six books of the Mishnah] .

He educated us and showed us the right and straight path to follow.

The love of Zion, and the settlement of Eretz Israel, were precious ideals for him at the time. He loved Israel's Torah, Israel's language, and Eretz Israel. He thought that we would be purified in the melting pot of our land.

My Rabbi Z"L was a scholar, as he was described by the famous Gaon, Rabbi Shraga Feivel Rohatyn Z"L.

R' Khaim Moshe Zilbershitz

[Columns 435-436]

My Rabbi Z' L published many articles in the magazine "Makhzikei HaDat", which appeared in Lviv (Galitsia). He also devoted a substantial portion of his time to the publishing of his books "Mishna Brura" ["Clear Mishnah"], and "Khemdat Israel" ["Israel's Delight"]. His pure heart and honest measures rise and sprout from every word laid down by his pen.

He was modest and shied away from honor. His simple modesty was real, natural, and pure.

He educated his children in the way of the Torah. They knew to respect and honor their father Z"L during his life and promptly kept the commandment of "horning thy father".

With the passing of my Rabbi, his family and students suffered a great loss. A sigh of pain is coming out from the bottom of my heart.

The crown of our heads fell. May his memory be blessed and name etched on the board of Israel greats. May his soul be bound up in the bond of ethereal life.

[Columns 437-438]

Writer and Educator R' Binyamin Zusman

by Ya'akov Katz

Translated by Moshe Kutten

When we raise the memory of those who perished- those holy and pure slain people, who were choked to death and burned as martyrs during the horrible Holocaust, our heart is filled with tremor and reverence. We see revered and shining images of those who served their people and the Torah. They were annihilated by murderers who did not have any pity for our dearest people – men, women, and children.

We remember the Torah greats, *Tzadikim*, rabbis and their students, and the vivacious and rooty masses, whose entire lives were pure. We remember them silently with pain. Parents and teachers, young and old, live in our memory and are etched in our hearts. They would not be removed from us, and their name will continue to live for eternity.

* * *

Among the prominent and shining figures, I see the image of R' Benyamin Zusman, may G-d avenge his blood. A talented author and distinguished educator who was born in Zloczow. The dammed Nazis murdered him during the Holocaust when he resided in Krakow. He moved there from his native city to serve as the principal of the Haredi school "Yesodei Torah".

I remember the man and his work from when I was a student at the Yeshiva and *Talmud Torah* [religious elementary school] "Orakh LaKhaim" in Zloczow.

We were boys who devoted days and nights to our studies within the walls of that modest building, which served as an inn for Torah studies. The Yeshiva was acclaimed for its high-level education held under the management of my rabbi and teacher, Rabbi R' Khaim Zilbershitz Z"L. He was a guardian and the great patron of the Torah and knowledge and an educator par excellence. He was the author of the books "Mishnei Brura" about the Mishnah tractates "Brakhot" and "Shabbat", for studies in Torah schools and additional books and pamphlets on original Jewish philosophy.

Students who were educated in that Yeshiva were superior in their level of education. They began in the first grade up to the Yesevia higher-level classes. They studied Gemarah, Rash" I commentaries, and *Tosafot*, "Yoreh Da'at", "Orakh LaKhaim", "Khoshen Mishpat" including "Ketzot", and other commentaries.

The *Talmud Torah* school, "Orakh LaKhaim" [A Way of Life], was named after R' Avraham Khaim ABD Zloczow ZTz"L [the author of the book by that name]. The number of its students continued to grow, particularly after the First World War, when the refugees who escaped to faraway places due to the nearby front, began to return.

R' Khaim Zilbershitz Z"L, was a modest man, knowledgeable and profound thinker, radiated his gleaming personality. He was always looking for ways to widen his knowledge in all areas of studies, including the bible, morality books, research, and grammar. The *Gaon* Mahara"m Shapira, who was the rabbi of the town of Galina, near Zloczow, visited the Yeshiva and *Talmud Torah* "Orakh LaKhaim", from time to time. He tested the upper class students and conducted lessons. He was always impressed by the high levels of studies and expressed his wonderment from the top students. He was not satisfied with the flimsy building, but the inner beauty and the exalted content that filled the house more than compensated for the scanty exterior.

* * *

One of the teachers in the school was R' Benyamin Zusman, may G-d avenge his blood. He was a tall and graceful young man who commanded respect in his appearance and teaching. His father was a glazier. The father was a pious, innocent, and honest man, but clever and witty. He made a living by the labor of his own hand. He devoted all of his energy and might to the education of his sons, among whom R' Benyamin was one of the best.

He distinguished himself from a young age, by his skills and diligence. He studied with teachers and rabbis, attended a Yeshiva in Galitsia, and was a frequent visitor to the city rabbi, from whom he drew wisdom and knowledge. He did not stop sharpening his knowledge even during the [First World] War. When he was discharged from the Austrian army, he was immediately accepted as a school teacher of the Talmud, the Bible, and the Hebrew language and its grammar. I will never forget the spiritual delight he bestowed on us in his bible lessons, even when we studied with the principal in the upper class.

I will never forget the lessons about Isaiah and Jeremiah, the colorful pictures he painted for us from different points of view, and the enthusiasm and vision he instilled in us. These lessons were etched in the hearts and souls of the survivors in Israel and throughout the world.

[Columns 439-440]

We also remember his Hebrew teaching. With his original and polished style, he uncovered the beauty of the language and its delights.

As the class educator, he devoted himself to conferring from all the good hidden in his soul and mind.

He had pleasant manners and was a sociable, conversational, cordial, and captivating storyteller, all of his being projected with respect and glamour.

He was loved by all, big and small, homeowners and Hassidim, old and young. They all envied his innocent father for his successful son, with those unique characteristics and skills.

With the Haredi organization in Poland and Galitsia and the establishment of the unified organization of Agudat Israel, Agugdat Israel Youths, and the Workers of Agudat Israel in Zloczow, he integrated himself into that union and assumed the role of the secretary of the organization in our city, with all of its offshoots.

He contributed from his beautiful soul and pleasant manners and shaped the course of events through his personality. He advocated extremism for the sake of extremism. The idea charmed and attracted him. He loved the idea of the religious Aliya movement and was particularly devoted to education, which he considered his life's mission.

He was blessed with an agile Yiddish and Hebrew pen. His talent was unprecedented. He enriched the Haredi magazine that appeared in Poland and Galitsia with thoughtful and brilliant ideas. His articles were published in the Aguda's newspapers, as well as in the general daily newspapers.

He possessed a subtle sense of humor and wrote many humorous essays, which made an impression and attracted attention. His poems filled the textbooks of "Beit Ya'akov" and Talmud Torah. He published numerous articles in the monthly magazine "Beit Ya'akov", edited by R' Eliezer Gershon Friedenson from Lodz, may G-d avenge his blood. He also filled the pages of the Journals "Digleinu" ["Our Flag"], "Yiddeshe Arbaiter Shtimeh" ["Jewish Workers' Voice"], and "Das Yiddishe Tagblat" ["The Yiddish Daily"]. He was an easy writer, and only a few were like him. His style was polished and folksy in both languages.

My first writing contributions, in my youth, passed through his critique. He educated and guided me, corrected and edited, and taught me the secret of style and analysis.

I felt like his student even when I became an activist, particularly on my way to the newspaper and magazines.

His soul was tied to mine, even when he left our city to manage the "Yesodei Torah" [school] in Krakow. I corresponded with him there, and later, after I made Aliya to Eretz Israel, he continued to correspond.

He also continued his loving ties with his cousin R' Kh. Zilbershitz Z"L, who settled in Haifa and lived there for several years.

R' Kh. Zilbershitz was imbued with the love of Zion. He brought up, in his pamphlets "Khemdat Israel" ["The delight of Israel"], jewels about sermonizing and the idea of united and organized Torah-based Judaism, building and creating in the lovely land.

He died in Israel, old and full of years. He lived to see Israel's independence. He was happy, despite his sorrow about the spiritual and religious decline. He saw divine Providence in all the events and was among the greatest patriots of the state. He believed that upon the "return of the sons to their homeland" - they would also "return to the rock whence they were hewn".

As for R' Benyamin Zusman, he remained in Krakow, where he lived as the principal of Haredi schools, where he invested all of his energy and strength. He was recognized as a distinguished educator. His name preceded him in Krakow and its surroundings. He was respected because of his ideas and knowledge, and depth of thought in the educational field.

He was diligent and worked wonders until his last day and was not afraid of tyrants and oppressors. He continued to teach his students in hiding.

His daughter Feiga, may G-d avenge her blood, was educated at the "Beit Ya'akov" seminary in Krakow. She was conspicuous in her extraordinary skills. She worked as a teacher.

R' Benyamin and his entire family were annihilated in the Holocaust. Only one son, who lives in the U.S.A, survived.

R' Benyamin Zusman perished in the fire and gas chambers and along with the other millions. However, his exalted energetic, and active personality, his contributions to educational and Haredi literature, and his devotion to the entire nation and the pious Jews are etched on the memorial board.

[Columns 442-443]

Assortment of Personalities in Zloczow

by Yekhiel Imber

Translated by Moshe Kutten

R' Shlomo Meites – was one of the figures that aroused respect and affection. He was a pious Jew and a loyal follower of G-d. He would not miss fulfilling a commandment when he encountered an opportunity to do so. Furthermore, he looked for these opportunities. Shabbat was very dear to him. He would hurry up and prepare for it early. Later on Friday, he would go around the city and hurry up the shopkeepers to close. Helping the poor, Hakhnasat Kalah [helping poor brides get married], "Kemkha DePaskha" [a charity to help the poor before Passover] were close to his heart. When it came to charity, he was always the first to volunteer. More than anything else, he kept the commandment of hospitality. He was the one who helped the poor who happened to arrive in the city. He positioned himself at the entrance door of the synagogue at the end of the service. He did not leave until he verified that all the poor visitors would be divided among the congregation regulars and guaranteed a proper Shabbat meal. When some visitors could not be accommodated by other worshipers, he would host them all himself and share his Shabbat meal with them. He was not a wealthy man. He hardly made a living and had often supplemented his income by being a "melamed. Despite being poor, he was always in a good mood. Those who have not witnessed him during the "Hakafot of "Simkhat Torah", [encircling the synagogue with the Torah], with his euphoria and devoutness, which filled his whole being, have not seen supreme happiness in his life.

R' Shalom Shlomo Meites – was a refined young Torah learner and a scholar. He was blessed with a pleasant voice. He charmed the congregation of the Stratyn kloiz, where he used to pray, singing Zmirot [Hymns] during the holidays and on Shabbat during the "Three Meals". When he sang, an uplifted atmosphere prevailed over all present. He sang while the worshipers were sitting around a long table, over a small piece of bread, the tail of herring, and a shot glass of schnapps (leftovers from a yahrzeit of one of the worshipers). His singing was like a medical potion for the bones, dry from the daily struggles. The worshipers drew consolation from his singing, and as a token of appreciation, they expressed exceptional affection for him. May his memory be blessed.

Lawyer Dr. David Werpel – was one of the distinguished Zionists in Zloczow. He served as the chairman of the United Israel Appeal committee. He was always diligently and persistently active and was mobilizing others. Thanks to him, the number of contributors reached its peak and included most of the city's Jewish population. He also invested a tremendous effort in instilling the Jewish youth with the Hebrew language. The Zionist movement was dear to his heart. He was the only one among the General [Non-aligned] Zionists who attended (and follow the progress tentatively) the conference of the [Zionist youth organization] "HeKhaluz" ["The Pioneer"] Movement [associated with the labor movement] when it was held in Zloczow. He always stepped forward to help the people making Aliya to Eretz Israel when they encountered difficulties imposed by the Polish authorities. His help was also substantial and recognized in other Zionist, municipal, social, and public matters. Among the city Zionists, he was the only one who traveled to Eretz Israel to tour it. He even bought an estate so that he would be able to make Aliya and settle in Eretz Israel in the future. He did not live to achieve that. His son, the only survivor of the family, inherited the estate.

Lawyer, Dr. Zygmund Meiblum – He was a man of action, not of speech. As such, he mastered enormous influence at the *Histadrut* [Zionist Organization]. When a polemic debate erupted about a particular matter, and it seemed that there was no solution, he would be the one who would come up with a reasonable compromise, as he was a person who had been blessed with a practical and logical sense. Nobody could resist his rationale and reasoning. He was the one responsible for the authorities in all matters related to the Zionist Organization. He was responsible for ensuring that the Zionist Organization conformed to the rules (e.g. announcing a gathering, balls, or shows). He served as a member of the municipality. His defense of the interests of the Jews of the city Jews was noble, productive, and admirable. His role as the chairman of the Judenrat during the Nazi regime was the most delicate in his life. It was so because of a great responsibility that was loaded on his shoulders. His anguish and torments in fulfilling that unfortunate role were enormous. He was tormented until the moment he paid with his life to save the lives of other Jews. May G-d avenge his blood.

Avraham Auerbach – was the son of an iron materials merchant and assisted his father's work. However, during his free time, in the evenings, Saturdays, and holidays, he devoted his time to the [Zionist] movement. Avraham was a member of "Hit'akhdut Tzeirei Tzion" [Youths of Zion Union] and one of its leading spokesmen. He shared his spiritual energy with his friends during each gathering and meeting.

Faibish Bernholz – was one of the leading activists of the "Hit'akhdut Tzeirei Tzion" [Youths of Zion Union]. He possessed a robust national spirit and a deep proletarian orientation. In that movement, he found the perfect merge of national aspiration and socialistic views. He influenced his friends and attracted many other people.

[Columns 443-444]

Shmuel Meisels – was a senior member of the "Hit'akhdut Tzeirei Tzion". He was moderate and amiable. He was fully devoted to Zionist activism, particularly to the "Keren Kayement Le'Israel" [JNF], for which he volunteered his services as a treasurer. He devoted a lot of effort and time to that activity.

Ze'ev Zidenworm – was a member of the young age group of "Hit'akhdut Tzeirei Tzion". He was endowed with musical talent and had a pleasant voice. He organized choruses and conducted one during public appearances. He entrained the Jewish public by selecting popular Jewish songs.

Dr. Tzvi Rosenboim – was one of the most enthusiastic fans of the national revival idea. Although he was not among the main speakers and speech givers, he served as the principal propagandist during the weekdays. He spread the Zionist idea, mornings and evenings, at the *Beit Hamidrash* [Synagogue and learning house] and on the streets. Any place he happened to pass by and see two or three Jews standing and talking, he would join and direct the discussion toward Zionism and making Aliya. He did not miss any opportunity to meet Zionist leaders such as Herzl, Weitzman, Sokolov, and Ussishkin. He listened to their speeches and heard from them firsthand about the revival idea. He was fully captivated by his wish to make Aliya and always dreamt about fulfilling his dream. When it came to a choice between attending his business and a Zionist gathering, the latter came first. He was also a member of the Jewish school committee, and all of his five children – one son and four daughters, got their education in that school. Great was his joy when one of his daughters, Ester, was fortunate to fulfill his dream to make Aliya to Eretz Israel. She was also the only survivor in the entire family. She built a home in Israel – the home of Ester and Yekhiel Imber. However, he did not live to accomplish his dream. He died in 1934.

The Lawyer, Dr. Gustav Katz – was a popular captivating, and persuasive speaker. With his unique soft voice, he mourned the fate of his people and begged his audiences to pay attention to his reasoning. His words came from his heart and entered the heart of his listeners. While his Yiddish vocabulary was limited and interspersed with words from the Polish language, it was rich in content and full of emotion and tenderness. That was how he managed to subdue the resistance of those who belonged to camps hostile to the Zionist movement.

Nathan Rekht – received a traditional [religious] education but was "captured" by the Enlightenment and Zionist movements, which went against his father's wishes. Even when he was still a learner at the *Beit HaMidrash*, he brought with him "external" literature, such as Hato'eh BeDarkhei Ha'Khaim" ["The Wanderer in the Paths of Life"], by Smolenskin, and "A'havat Tzion" ["Love of Zion"] and "Ashmat Shomron" ["Guilt of Samaria"] by Mapu. He would then drop the books on the laps of his friends at *Beit HaMidrash*. He left his home in 1921 and made Aliya. He was the first pioneer who did so from our city. The news about his tragic death spread quickly and sadden deeply to everybody who held the idea of making Aliya dear to their hearts.

Yaakov Vilig – was one of the prominent figures at the General Zionists Union and the youngest among its leaders. He was tall and sturdy, with a fierce and assertive character. He disdained routine and mundane acts and the bragging about them, rather than acting practically and purposefully. He staunchly insisted on boldness and making Aliya. In his speech, he was sullen like a river that cast out rocks. However, his style was not agreeable to other leaders, who preferred the methods of pleasantness and persuasion. Years later, when he assumed the leadership position, he vigorously began to organize the Zionist activities, assaulting all of the goals at once: the community, school, sports association, hospital, etc. However, he devoted most of his effort to activities related to Eretz Israel. At that time, the [non-affiliated] Zionists were split between General and Progressive Zionists. Yaakov Vilig was the leader of the progressive Zionists. His attitude toward the [Zionist] movement was exceedingly warm. Every pioneer, regardless of party affiliation, received moral and financial assistance. Yaakov considered pioneering in the act of making Aliya the pinnacle of Zionist activity in the diaspora. Despite being aware of the prevailing problems faced by the Jewish public in the city and the entire country, the Hebrew culture was the area that was dear to his heart, and there wasn't any major Hebrew book that was not available in his library. Those books were not for decoration but reading. The club of the "Ha'Ivria" [The Hebrew] organization was his creation, and he invested money, effort, and love to maintain it.

Dr. Yosef Guld – was an excellent physician who was respectable by the [Jewish] city residents. However, when he decided to turn to politics as the representative of the assimilators, most of the [Jewish] residents in the city abandoned him. Nevertheless, he was easily elected to the position of mayor. He won with the votes of the assimilators and the Haredim [ultra-orthodox] and through the support of the Poles. He was also elected as the head of the Jewish community and as the representative in the Austrian parliament. When somebody else won the parliament seat, he abandoned his public involvement completely but continued his adherence to the assimilation movement. However, the spread and crystallization of the Zionist movement after World War I undermined his views. He then began to retreat in the face of reality. In the end, amid the surging wave of Aliya, when financial means were needed, he expressed his willingness to participate by adding his "public standing" to the fundraising effort. He agreed to head the committee for aiding the pioneers, provided that the meetings would be held at the community house rather than a conspicuous Zionist club,

[Columns 445-446]

The author, Shmaria Imber

because he feared the devil's eye. Guld's new views were a source of encouragement and satisfaction for the leaders of the Zionist movement and its activists.

Dr. Henrikh Tikhman – was the only son in a progressive family who received a purely secular education. He completed his studies in Vienna, where the national movement captured his heart. He returned to his native town as an enthusiastic and dedicated Zionist. He joined the "Zion Youth Movement" and became its leader. He was liked by all because of his modest conduct, gentle manners, and unwavering honesty. During the [Nazi] conquest, he was a member of the community committee. When the Nazis demanded that the committee complies with the "Jewish Quota", he bravely announced that the committee would not provide the Nazis with any names. He paid with his life for his bravery. He was shot on the spot.

Feivel Reizer – was a member of the "Zion Youth Union." He joined the "HeKhalutz" ["The Pioneer"] movement in 1923. However, his desire for life in Eretz Israel conflicted with the feeling that he could not withstand the harsh working conditions in Eretz Israel. That feeling was a result of his refined sense of criticism toward others and particularly toward himself. He feared that he would become a burden on society instead of helping to build the homeland. That feeling repressed his will and delayed his Aliya. He did not even consider doing non-physical work in Eretz Israel as he regarded that as parasitic work. In addition, he felt a responsibility toward his mother and his young brothers. He was, therefore, forced to continue his work as a clerk in the diaspora. He regretted his fate throughout his entire life. However, possibilities for a wide range of activities opened up for him when he joined the community steering committee as a secretary. In that role, he found a reward for his "parasitism". He perished in the Holocaust.

Shmaria Imber – [Anan author who] made Aliya to Eretz Israel as a tourist, outwitting the British mandatorily authorities. He tried to work in construction in Tel-Aviv but was forced to move to Jerusalem, where he hoped to find better opportunities. Only after his family followed him to Eretz Israel, Shmaria established a source for a minimal livelihood. He was fortunate to see all of his four children making Aliya and establishing families in Israel.

Berish Glazer – left his wife and children in Zloczow and emigrated to Eretz Israel without any means to support himself. He began to work as a carpenter without having any previous training. However, he was fortunate to have supporters who were prominent in the community. He got a job in public and national institutions, so it was easier for him to make a living. He managed to bring his family to Eretz Israel and establish a sound and stable home.

Judge Diver – was a fascinating figure who could have absorbed the Zionist spirit, which was prevalent even among assimilated families. When I once left the house of Dr. Guld, the chairman of the committee to aid the pioneers, he stopped and said: "I desire to have my daughter learn Hebrew, and I would like you to teach her for an hour, every day. I would pay you any fee you would request". Unfortunately, I had to reject that offer as I was too busy. I regretted that decision for a long time. I could have probably saved a Jewish soul from being assimilated among the gentiles. Perhaps, Judge Diver meant to bring his daughter closer to her people…

[Columns 447-448]

Eliezer Bernstein – was a peculiar character in his manners, appearance, and way of life. His hair reached his shoulder, like a writer's or an artist's. He lived as a bachelor for many years, away from his mother's home. He wrote songs and poems. When he came back from the U.S., where he worked as a printing worker (where he lost a few fingers in his left hand there), he continued with the same way of life. He used his limited knowledge of the English language to make a living by teaching lessons to individuals and groups. His apartment, or more accurately, his room, served as a meeting place for youth who had a propensity for writing. Some of them acquired fame as Yiddish authors. He married, eventually, a young woman from Wrotslav [Wroclaw] who fell in love with him from afar through a narration of him.

Rabbi R' Eliezer Wagschal (R' Leizer) – resided in a modest house with a square yard in the middle of it. The house had five rooms, two of which were devoted to praying. The large one was for men and the small one for women. A significant number of homes, owned by homeowners and their families, surrounded the house. These families provided Rabbi Eliezer with income. Many Jews, particularly women, who needed encouragement or "G-d's help" turned to him to pray for them. The Rabbi always found words of encouragement and comfort, and people who left him felt calmer and more assured that they would find salvation.

Rabbi R' Barukh (R' Barukh'l) – resided in a modest house built by his students down the Zlotsovska River. The location was prone to floods. During the tide, the house was unsuited for habitation. The Rabbi was "like a tree planted by streams of water" [Psalms 1:3] since the river split into two branches near the house. One of them led into the flour mill which was driven by the water. There was a derelict bridge, where people passed to get to the heart of the Jewish area where "Beit Midarishes" ["houses of learning in synagogues) and "kloizes" [a place of study for scholars] were located. When the river flooded, after heavy rains or after the snowmelt, the wooden dams, which were patched over and over every year, broke. The roaring and the tumulted water deviated from the channel designated for them by people and breached their boundaries as their turbulent nature pleased, licking with their tongue the rickety foundations of the clay houses. The flooding water caused devastation for the residents of that area. However, during the rest of the year, the Jews also knew how to enjoy the river. Firstly, the merchants raised their fish at the river in boxes built especially for that purpose. Since Rabbi Barukh blessed the fish, they followed the commandment: "be fruitful and multiply and replenish the earth" [Genesis 1:28], or in this case, the water. Secondly, During the "days of awe" – the holy days of Rosh Hashanah, the Jews would go down to the river to fulfill the commandment of "Tashlikh" ["Thou should cast (Tashlikh in Hebrew), all of your sins into the depth of the sea" – Mikha 7:19]. Thirdly, the laundry women would bring their whites to the river to wash them. The homeowners would save the expenses of paying the water carriers who drew water from the well and distributed them to the homes.

Rabbi Barukh himself was not wealthy. His heart was with heaven. He concentrated on the next world. However, those who saw him at the 1912 (or 1913) wedding of his daughter, which everyone - old and young, attended, realized that righteous and honest people could be rewarded even in this world. The Jews opened their heart and their pockets and gave him gifts generously.

In his modesty, Rabbi Barukh his pure spirit over all of those who asked for his help. For the despondent people, the Rabbi served as a source of comfort and encouragement.

Rabbi R' Yisrael Landau – When Rabbi Rohatyn passed away, the rabbinical position in Zloczow became vacant as there was no acting rabbi. The controversy that prevailed during the reign of Rabbi Rohatyn did not subside from the public arena [see article page 419] after his death. The leaders of the community and its activists were divided. The followers of various rabbis from different dynasties were also feuding. There were plenty of prominent candidates, but none were acceptable to all the factions, and confusion and embarrassment prevailed. Even the candidacy of Rabbi Shapira of Hlynjany [Gliniany], who later became a rabbi in Piotrkow [Pioterkov], the head of 'Agudat Yisrael", and a representative in the Polish Sejm, was rejected by the people in power, despite his deep knowledge, his solid expertise, and exceptional skills. The damage caused to the prestige and good-name city by that rejection was enormous and was considered a desecration of the honor of the Torah. The two rabbinical judges - R' Shmuel Shapira and R' Mendel Miller, who served as assistants to Rabbi Rohatyn in matters related to Jewish law, could not be appointed to the position of a rabbi. The first was because he was too stringent in daily affairs and the other was because of his flexibility in matters related to Jewish law.

As it happened, R' Yisrael Landau arrived at Zloczow and chose the Startyn *Kloiz* as his place of prayer. He was an ingenious and honest man, pious and very knowledgeable about the Torah. He had a majestic appearance and aroused respect with his manners. The Stratyn Hasidim chose him as their rabbi. They hoped that other "*Beit Midrashes*" and "*Kloizes*" would follow suit. But that did not materialize. Only a small number of people followed him. However, more than he served as a rabbi, he became the center around which people gather and under whose light they would warm up on Shabbat and holidays. Some wealthy people among the rabbi's followers and Hasidism covered the expenses of his home and family needs.

The midwife Tzirel (Tzirel Di Babi) – was not just a midwife. She was much more than that. During those days, mothers did not give birth at the hospital. Tzirel served as the physician for the baby and the mother. Tzirel could have boasted that she helped deliver the entire Jewish population of Zloczow. She did not only help deliver the babies but also kept them in good health. She took care of the baby and the mother long after the birth. She watched over the

[Columns 449-450]

health of the mother. She taught the mother how to take care of the baby, and how to diaper and wash the baby. Prominent people who captured important public positions were like children to her, and she would address them using the first-person pronoun – "You". She kept watching over the baby for at least thirty days after the birth and would pay surprise visits beyond that if she suspected that anything was wrong. We could say about her what had been said about Khava [Eve]: "The mother of all the living."

[Columns 451-452]

A Few Words about Writers and Poets in Zloczow

by B. Tzverdling

Translated by Moshe Kutten

During the enlightened period, the city of Zloczow has also been blessed with some intriguing figures deserving of appreciation.

1) Naftali Hertz Imber (1856 – 1909) - was a Jewish poet who was born in Zloczow. After wandering around through several cities in his homeland he moved to Romania and then to other countries. During 1882 – 1887, Imber settled in Eretz Israel, and later on, he moved to England, where he won great respect. He was close to [Israel] Zangwill. From England, Imber immigrated to the USA and died in New York. He was the author of "Ha'Tikva", the national anthem of Israel.

The first collection book of his poems, "Barkai" ["The Morning Star"], was published in Jerusalem in 1886. Another collection of his writings was published in Tel Aviv in 1929, on the fiftieth anniversary of the poem - "Ha'Tikva". Yet another collection of his poems was published in 5706 (1945/46) [According to Israel National Library (INL) it should be 5711 or 1950].

When he made Aliya to Eretz Israel, he immediately felt the new national momentum. His poem "Rishon Le'Tzion" [literally - "First to Zion"], was a cheer to the work and toil burst from a rejoiced heart that was witnessing the national "salvation and transformation". Here is a section from his poem:

> How the times have changed
> Like wheels going and coming...
> Stomp, stomp on the grapes in the vat
> The wineries are filled with their juice...

He did not become acclimated in Eretz Israel, as the diaspora gnawed away at his roots with no cure. The poetry about the work and toil in the homeland was silenced in the diaspora. His bones were later brought over to Israel.

2) Shmuel Yaakov Imber - born in 1889 in Zloczow. He was the son of Shmaryahu - the brother of Naftali Hertz Imber. He was a Yiddish poet. He published several collections of his poems (one of them about his impressions of Eretz Israel). The influence of the best German and Polish poetry is apparent in his poetry. He edited several journals and fought against the "Collective Modernism" in the Yiddish literature. He published literary research about Oskar Wilde.

3) Israel Yehuda Teller - born in December 1839 [According to INL, he was born in December 1835 and died in 1921].

4) Tzvi Eliezer Teller, born in 18 July 1840.

They were both born in Zloczow and were among the Enlightened Movement pioneers in our city.

Israel Yehuda Teller was a grammarian and linguist. He published poems in newspapers and literary supplements. He published them all in a special collection - "Hegion Lev" ["Logic of the Heart"] in 5673 [1912/13. according to INL - 5663 or 1902/3]. The rest of his publications included: "Otzar Balum" ["Overflowing Treasure"], Jaffa, 5682 [1921/22. 5680 or 1919/20 according to INL], "Binah Be'Toldot Avoteinu" ["Wisdom in the History of our Ancestors", Jaffa, 5676 (1915/16)], and "Ben Oni" ["Son of My Strength"], Jaffa, 5672 [1911/12/5674 (1913/14) according to INL], in memory of his son, Yehuda, who was a teacher in Rekhovot and died at the age of 24.

Tzvi Eliezer Teller translated to Hebrew the play "The Jews" by Lessing. The translation was published in Vienna in 5641 [1880/81]. He also wrote the biography of the preacher from Lviv, Bernhard Löwenstein - "Shem Olam" ["Everlasting Name"] (Krakow, 5649 [1888/9]). As an author, Tzvi Teller was a typical enlightened person, who considered literature as a mean for preaching and teaching.

5) Moshe Leib Halperin - was a Yiddish poet who was born in Zloczow in 1886. He died in New York in 1934. He was one of the best Yiddish poets.

6) David Shretznel - was born in Zloczow in 1897. He published a collection of poems by the name of "Oisen Hartzen" ["From the Heart", Psalms 31:13].

7) Moshe Pitznik" - was born in 1895 in Zloczow and published a weekly there by the name of "Folks Blat" ["Folklore Paper"]. He was interested in folklore. He translated to Yiddish Homer's Odyssey with commentaries. He also published two novels in old Yiddish: "Rav Kalman Ani" [The Poor Rabbi Kalman"], and "Moshe Kabtzan" ["Moshe the Beggar"]. The novels dealt with topics from the Enlightened period.

8) Yaakov Mestel - was born in Zloczow in 1894. He completed his studies in the teachers' college in Lviv and became a teacher. In 1918, he immigrated to the US and was accepted to the theater of Morris Schwartz. He authored the poem "Shir Milkhama" '["A War song"].

[Columns 453-454]

Naftali Hertz Imber,
the Poet of "Ha'tikqva"

by Yaakov Meizlish

Translated by Moshe Kutten

The life of the poet, essay writer, and author of "HaTikva", Naftali Hertz Imber, a native of Zloczow, was filled with oddities and contradictions. A lot was written about Imber and his work. Some of the things were real and some were speculations and the fruit of the imagination. However, there are many things in the life of Imber authentic and fascinating, which were never published. Anecdotes told about his childhood and youth in his native town of Zloczow are particularly compelling. Such tales are particularly intriguing when they are told by people of his generation and age.

The news about the Turkish-Russian war in the second half of the 19th century attracted the interest of the Jews for several reasons: The first was political. There were many Jews who possessed vigilant and ebullient political awareness. The second was that any political change resulting from war could affect the Jews, directly or indirectly. Sometimes for good and some other times badly. In any case, the interest in the happenings in that war was considerable. News from the front would not arrive on the same day, like in our time. They usually took days, weeks, and even months to be disseminated. People got their information from news and reviews published in weekly and monthly magazines after many transfigurations. However, that in itself did not detract from their value. On the contrary, People treated appreciated that kind of information and news better than the information or rumors circling around on the same day.

A person who was a fan of the Hebrew language and literature found out that the eight-year-old child, Naftali Hertz, was writing many poems. That person embraced the child and persuaded him to write his poems about the state of the warring troops on both sides. Many years later, that person often revealed how that young child succeeded to depict the events poetically, with incredible clarity using coherent and fluent language.

There was once a case when the whole city panicked because of the youth Naftali Hertz. A gendarme appeared one day in the market square, where all the Jewish trading stores and shops were located, and asked to see a man named N. H. Imber. Seeing the gendarme cast fear and panic over the entire city, including the non-Jews. Some brave people responded to the gendarme. They claimed that, as far as they knew, there was no person in town named N. H. Imber. The gendarme ignored what the Jews told him and insisted that the wanted man be brought up to see him. They repeateddly say that, although there are several people whose name is Imber, there is nobody, in that large family, with the initials N. H. They told him that there was a person by that name once, but he passed away fifteen years ago. The gendarme weighed these explanations and was inclined to believe the Jews. He returned to the district bureau and reported the results of his investigation. The bureau official told the district minister, but the minister did not accept it. He called the gendarme and yelled at him angrily that it was not possible that the person does not live in the city. The gendarme went back to the market square and burst into the first shop owned by a person by the name of Imber. He told him forcefully that all the people named Imber would be arrested if the person is not found within two hours.

The Imber family members cried and swore that there is no N. H. Imber among them. However, when the gendarme insisted and repeated his demand, fear descended over the entire city. "A cruel decree, blood libel", people pleaded. When everything looked hopeless, one of the Imbres came out with an idea: "Let us go to the birth record office and check in the records if there was a person by that name". The gendarme agreed. The two went to the office – followed by the entire city. They conducted a thorough investigation until they found the name of Naftali Hertz Imber. However, that person was a nine-year-old child. The gendarmes, who eagerly wanted to end the whole matter peacefully, said: "Fine, bring me that baby". The child's parents shuddered: "Who knows what they are plotting against the child?" They were afraid that the child pulled off one of his pranks, and the authorities would have them and the child pay for it. They found him after a thorough search, immersed in playing with his friends. His father gave him a piece of his mind as an advance.

[Column 455]

Naftali Hertz Imber

When the people gathered in the big magnificently furnished hall of the city hall, they anticipated that the whole community would be condemned by the high court. They had already visualized a whole list of sins and crimes that would be hurled at them. They already physically experienced the hardship of the sentence. They did not have the time to contemplate much before everybody was led to another lounge, seven-time more beautiful than the first one. The gendarme took the youth and presented him to a big entourage. The mayor stepped forward toward the boy, bowed, and read aloud from a document, praises in German. He then shook the boy's hand ceremonially and repeated verbally the praises sent to him by His Majesty the Emperor.

Neither the boy nor his parents grasped what the ceremony was all about. When the matter became clear, everybody breathed a sigh of relief.

Naftali Hertz Imber wrote a poem and dedicated it to Emperor Franz Joseph (that was the now-famous poem "Austria" or "Beit Tefilati ["My House of Prayer"], which was dedicated to the Austria-Prussia War. Imber received a prize for that poem). Upon receiving it, the court minister gave the poem to the Hebrew poet Meir Halevi Letteris, who translated it to German.

The emperor sent the little poet a greeting card with a prize. That prize helped the poet, later on, to reach the city of Brody, which served as the spiritual center for the Jewish enlightened in Galitsia. From Brody, Imber went to Lviv where he stayed for a short while. In his travels, he reached Vienna, Romania, the Balkan countries, and Istanbul. He finally arrived in Eretz Israel, a place he was longing from the time of his youth. It was during these wanderings that he wrote the poem "HaTikva".

[Column 456]

Naftali Hertz Imber was an eccentric and bohemian person almost throughout his entire life.

To end the article, I would like to review some of the additional anecdotes, that were talked about him.

During his life in America, he was known as a poet and author of articles in different Hebrew, Yiddish, and English magazines. He wrote papers and also essential research articles on religion, philosophy, and Kabbalah matters. A magazine article was once returned to him, and the editor reasoned the rejection by claiming that it would not be of interest to the readers. Imber was deeply hurt and left the magazine editorial office in protest. A week later, the magazine received a telegram from a distanced city that Naftali Hertz Imber passed away. The editor, who was shocked to hear the news, published a lengthy article in which he eulogized the great poet and essayer who passed away before his time. He listed his praises, one by one, and even translated some of the poems and published them in the same magazine issue. Several days later, Imber appeared at the editorial office holding the eulogy issue. He confronted the magazine editor and proclaimed: "Here is standing, in front of you, the poet and essayer, whom you so -highly praised, and the one whose latest article you had rejected".

Naftali Hertz Imber's childhood took place during a time of strife between parents and their children. The youths were attracted by the enlightened movement, which revolved around the revival of the Hebrew language and its literature. "Shomrei HaKhomot" ["Watchmen of the Walls" – religious conservatives) considered that movement a breach in the fence of the Jewish tradition and religion. They did everything they could to stop the fire from spreading and swallowing the Jewish home to its foundation. Things reached the point that they even considered the studying of the bible unfavorably. They considered it as the elegance of language and the trilling of speech and writing. They also despised the teaching of Hebrew grammar and proper pronunciations claiming that the main objective in praying was about the intention or meaning and not the language.

In that vein, a story was told about Naftali Hertz. One Friday evening, when the family sat at the table, and the head of the family was about to begin the Kiddush [blessing over the wine], they found out that Naftali Hertz was missing. They looked for him in all the rooms and corners of the house. They even went outside, called his name, and looked for him. The boy was nowhere to be found. The father controlled his anger and sadness and pore the wine. When he was just about to begin the citing the "Kiddush", the "takhshit" [literally – jewel, but used to sarcastically call a young prankster] appeared holding a rooster in his hand. When he saw that "Kiddush" was about to begin, he hurried up and placed the rooster on the table. The frightened bird spread its wings and began to wiggle and run around. It snuffed the candles, spilled over the wine, and flew outside through the open window. The family members were terrified and astonished at the same time. However, they restrained themselves as it was forbidden to shout on Shabbat. The father poured the wine again, blessed over the wine in the dark, washed his hands, and everybody sat down to eat the Shabbat meal like a grieving family. The only thing the father did was order the boy to go to sleep without eating.

[Columns 457-458]

The following day, when the father calmed down a bit, he asked his young child why he brought the rooster home.

"To bless over the wine", answered the child.

"To bless over the wine?" wondered the father, "does a rooster know how to say "Kiddush?"

"And you?" answered Naftali Hertz with a childish hutzpah. "You too do not know how to do it properly, but you do it nevertheless" …

That was the child's way to protest against his father, who did not pronounce the Hebrew language correctly.

The poet was born on Shabbat Hanukkah, 5617 (1856), and passed away on Simkhat Torah, 5670 (1909).

———

[Columns 459-460]

Dov Ofer, The Pioneer from Zloczow

by Levi Ofer

Translated by Moshe Kutten

I remember well the image of my brother Dov, who was murdered in Israel forty-two years ago, as he went on a movement's mission. He was only twenty-two years old. According to eyewitnesses, three Bedouins robbers attempted to take off his shiny boots, but Dov preferred death over surrendering to the foreigners on his land, which absorbed his blood. That was at the start of the Third Aliya. The words "Dov Ofer, murdered 1 Elul 5680 [15 August 1920]" are etched on his gravestone in Kvutzat [small communal settlement] Kineret.

Dov was an unusually developed child. His talents spread over many different areas. He was often asked, what he wanted to become when he grew up. He answered: "Israel's King". He was then only four years old. When he was nine years old, he solved complicated mathematical questions. When he was ten years old, he could recite, by heart, an 80-page long poetry book. He was also interested in music and art. His teachers said they could talk to him like an adult. His teachers envisaged a bright future for him.

He joined the Zionist movement while a student in a Polish high school in Vienna, Austria's capital. He became one of the pillars of the "HaShomer HaTza'ir" ["The Young Guard"] movement. His articles in the magazines left a great impression.

Our family returned to Zloczow at the end of the First World War. Dov started the work on establishing a branch of the youth movement immediately after we moved. After a short period, the "HaShomer Hatza'ir's" battalion in our city was one of the largest and the best organized in Eastern Poland. The heads of other youth movements admired Dov as a great young leader.

Dov devoted most of his time to the movement, but at the same time, he did not neglect his education. His library, which occupied a whole room in our apartment, was well-known in our city. It contained old and modern Hebrew literature, classical and philosophical literature, many exact-and nature-sciences books, and books about Zionism and Eretz Israel written in foreign languages. He mastered five European languages and pure Hebrew at the age of sixteen.

Prominent figures such as Dr. Avraham Sharon. Dr. Werpel, Dr. Kalman Shweig, and many others came to meet him for valuable discussions.

Dov passed the matriculation exams with honors in 1918. Despite his parents' objections, he decided not to continue with higher education. Instead, he went with a group of friends to an agricultural *Hakhshara* [a training camp for people preparing to make Aliya]. Dov returned home after spending a year and a half at the farm of Rabbi Dr. Rapoport. When he returned, he spent all of his time in the "HeKhalutz" ["The Pioneer"] movement, for which he was elected as one of its representatives in Poland.

These were the days of revolutions. The Austrian empire disintegrated. The Poles and the Ukrainians fought against each other to rule Eastern Galitsia, and the Bolshevik Revolution took place at a far distance. Regimes changed hands often, and in the villages, the Ukrainians revolted and broke into our city from time to time, robbing and looting. The Zionist Union established a self-defense organization. The local authorities supported the organization and allocated 120 rifles and a machine gun for it. Indian officers took it upon themselves to train and prepare the members. Dov Ofer headed the organization. He was only 18 years old at the time.

We were four brothers and one sister at home. Dove was four years older than me, but it seemed that he was at least ten years or more, older. We always stood before him trembling with respect. My father was very proud of his older son, although he tried to hide it somewhat. Dove used to argue with my mother about various problems, as she was an educated, book lover, and a devout believer. Her heart told her that Dov would leave one day and never return. She tried her best to stop his Aliya and delay his departure. She also tried to convince him. All of her efforts were in vain. Eretz Israel pulled him. It was his life goal, and he devoted all of his dreams and life to it.

One day, my mother asked Dov: "What would you do if I lay on the threshold and would not let you go?" His answer was: "I would skip over you". That was the answer of a son whose love for his mother and his homeland was strong.

Dov made Aliya in 1920 with a group of members and younger trainees. He did not sound very encouraged in his first letters, but he came to terms with his reality.

It would be difficult to describe the living conditions of those pioneers of the "Work-Brigade", who constructed the road between Tzemakh [a road junction at the southern tip of the Sea of Galilee] and Tiberia. For some of the Brigade's members, it was difficult to withstand the harsh conditions. However, when they looked at the inner piece exhibited by Dov and his devotion, the sufferings became a bit more bearable until singing erupted. He captured their respect and appreciation in a short period, but fate was cruel to him and put an end to his life, a short and glorious life, full of purpose and doing. Undoubtfully, Dov was destined for great and sublime things.

[Columns 461-462]

I found out about Dov's death from a letter sent by Milek Golan. I was shocked by that letter. Fifteen years later, when I made Aliya, I returned it to the sender. In his letter, Milek described the circumstances around the tragedy.

Dov was summonsed one evening to an urgent meeting. The way to the meeting location in Tzemakh led through hills descending into a wadi, not far from where the Kibbutz Degania Bet is today. He left with two other members. All three held firearms.

One member told me that she asked Dov to postpone his trip until the following day, as dark had already descended. Dov responded that people were waiting for him and that the issue was important and urgent.

The group was attacked by Arab murderers above Kvutzat Kineret. Dov's two friends retreated immediately, leaving him alone. The murderers ordered him to take off his boots. He took out his gun, facing three rifles. His naked body was found the following day, following a horrific night.

My father found out about the disaster a short time before Milek Golan's letter. He kept it a secret, and so did I. However, my father could not recover from that tragedy. He faded from one day to another and finally succumbed to the pain. My father passed away, taking his secret with him.

The horrible news reached my mother. It is hard the describe the effect of that news on her. It was a sad and dark period.

Later on, my mother devoted all of her time to pray. Every Friday, the day she received the horrible news., she fasted, placing Dov's picture in front of her. She had three basic questions: Was it really necessary to go during the night? Would Dov leave his friends the way they left him? Why did you leave home, my son? When I parted from my mother, I promised to bring her to Eretz Israel so that she could be buried near her dear son. I was not able to fulfill my promise. Khana Ofer was murdered by the Ukrainian Hjdmaks [kozak hooligans]. I can see my mother with Hitler's thugs accompanying her from both sides, bringing her to the gallows. According to the rumors, she did not reach it. They killed her with iron bars in the city's main street.

My mother held a Psalms Book murmuring: "My dear Dov, my older son, our souls will unite now".

[Columns 463-464]

Dr. Avraham Sharon

By M. Deutsch

Translated by Moshe Kutten

Dr. Avraham Sharon (Schwadron), was born in the village of Binov, near Zloczow (Eastern Galitsia), in 1889. He was one of the sons of Rabbi Moshe Schwadron, or R' Moshe Binover, as he was called in Zloczow. Schwadron family attained greatness and prominence in the Torah. Rabbi Moshe would often walk from Binov to Zloczow, a distance of a few kilometers, to ask City Rabbi Yoel Ashkenazi about a Rashi's commentary he did not understand. Rabbi Moshe had a son who became a Luminary of the Exile – *Gaon* [genius] Rabbi Shalom Mordekhai HaCohen, a rabbi in Berezany, Eastern Galitsia. He was one of the Torah greats of his time, and rabbis in all corners of the diaspora turn to him with their questions. His answers were short, and he always cited the source for his response. All of that without sophistication and argumentation. He was considered a great scholar, and all of the generation's greats marveled at his proficiency and memory. Dr. Avraham Schwadron was a student of his uncle, the Gaon from Berezany. He was known as a child prodigy, and the family was convinced that he would become the spiritual heir to his Gaon uncle. The Rabbis considered him a Rabbi and a teacher when he was fifteen years old. The father of Dr. Sharon, Rabbi Yitzkhak Schwadron, was a learned Jew and a talented merchant. He managed all the businesses of his family. Since he often traveled to Vienna for his business, he heard about Dr. Herzl and "his" Jewish State. He met Herzl, and also served as a representative to the Zionist Congress. His son, Dr. Avraham Sharon, aimed to be a Rabbi Gaon. However, Herzl said that the Jewish nation does not have a future in the diaspora, and Jews should return to Eretz Israel. Therefore, Dr. Avraham Sharon gave up on his plan to become a rabbi and moved to Vienna. He passed the entrance examinations, was accepted to the university, and continued his studies there. In the meantime, the first World War erupted and he was recruited to the Austrian army. He refused to become an officer. His rank was corporal. He returned to Zloczow at the end of the War. His father was not alive then, and the son managed the businesses together with his sister's son, Engineer Nusbaum. However, his heart was with Eretz Israel. When the "Keren Geula" ["Redemption Fund"] was announced, following the "Balfour Declaration".

[Columns 465-466]

About the Image of Avraham Sharon

by B. Tzverdling

Translated by Moshe Kutten

Avraham Sharon Z"L was born in 1883 [according to other sources, he was born in 1878] in Zloczow, Eastern Galitsia. He was the son of an owner of a liquor distillery who was a descendant of a famous rabbinical family. The spirit of enlightenment prevailed in his home. His father, R' Itzikel Schwadron Z"L, was a prominent sociable figure and an enthusiastic Zionist who participated in all [Zionist] congresses.

Avraham Sharon Z"L was a publicist and a collector of autographs and portraits of prominent people.

Early in his childhood, He was known as a prodigy who sharpened his brain by studying Mishnah and Poskim. However, he was not content with that. He also studied chemistry at Vienna University and received a degree of doctor in philosophy.

At the end of the First World War, he changed his surname to Sharon. That constituted a turning point in his life. He fought against the quarrels among the various parties and the splintering tendencies on the left and right. He stood out in his uncompromising position toward the Arab minority in the country. He called them "tomorrow's enemies" and demanded their expulsion from Israel.

He made Aliya after the First World War. He continued publishing essays and pamphlets, some of which were gathered in his book "Mishnei Evrei HaSha'ah" ["From the Two Sides of the Hour"]. His publishing activities continued, in various venues, until close to his death. He researched and acquired signatures and portraits of prominent religious, cultural, and scientific figures. Later on, he donated his collection, which included about 11,000 letters and autographs, to Jerusalem University. He always struggled to make a living and was content with very little. He detested life in the diaspora and wished to educate the nation about a new spirit. He aspired to straighten the crookedness in the heart and brain and create order, regime, and framework.

He struck roots in Eretz Israel and remained loyal to the nation until his last day.

He passed away on the eve. of Simkhat Torah 5718 [1957] in Jerusalem at the age of 74. His death was caused by a car accident he was involved in a few weeks earlier. May his memory be blessed.

————

[Columns 467-468]

Dr. Tzvi Hirshhorn

by Shulamit Ofer

Translated by Moshe Kutten

The noble image of Dr. Tzvi Hirshhorn is standing before me, despite the many years that passed: tall and handsome with a sizable forelock and a smile on his lips. An exemplary Jew and Zionist who was ready to help the needy.

His home was a home of an enlightened, where Hebrew was spoken and the Jewish tradition directed the way of life and education of the three children.

More than anything else he captured the hearts with his willingness to help his people. Indeed, they needed his help during those antisemitic days. Nobody who turned to him for help ended up out disappointed. He always provided a handout, help, advice, encouragement, and fondness. The Christians recognized the greatness of his soul too and respected him. He had connections with authorities, and he used them to help any person in trouble.

That was a period of regime changes between the Poles, Ukrainians, and Bolsheviks. There was a great deal of hatred among them and a lot of blood was shed. They had a common denominator – anti-Sedentism, murdering Jews, and robbing their property. Our city suffered tremendously from all of these evils.

I recall a calamity that befell our home during one of thepogrom nights. Our father was sick, so we, then the children and our mother, hid in a hideout. The militia entered the house to arrest our father. When they did not find him, they took our mother, a single woman among many city residents. We remained dumbfounded, without parents and a robbed house.

There were rumors that the authorities would transfer the prisoners to Ukraine. We searched for a solution with very little hope. Help came from an unexpected source – Dr. Hirshhorn. He lobbied the authorities, endangering his freedom and life to help the prisoners. First of all, he asked to free the woman and mother to small children. He also visited our mother in jail and delivered the first words of encouragement since she was taken from her home. He said: "They will not take you away from here. You will return home in two days". Indeed, mother returned home. She and we never forgot what Dr. Hirshhorn did for us.

Dr. Hirshhorn died a short time after the war, still relatively young and in the middle of his dignified and benevolent way.

[Columns 469-470]

My Husband, Dr. Hirshhorn

by Mrs. Hirshhorn

Translated by Moshe Kutten

As one of the leaders, my husband was very active in Zionist and Jewish public affairs devoting all his heart to these activities. He participated in many gatherings where he delivered speeches explaining the Zionist ideology. He was also a member of various committees aiming at improving the Jewish cultural life in the city. As an example, he devoted himself to establishing a Hebrew school and worked hard to find a proper venue for it, which until then wandered from one apartment to another. He was one of the most loyal assistants to Mrs. Belter, under the initiative of whom, the orphanage was established. The poor economic situation of the Jews following the First World War was well known. Many people left the city and immigrated to America. My husband headed the welfare committee established in the city. He devotedly and dedicatedly tried to distribute the fund fairly. His goal was to use the money constructively. The responsibility weighed on him. I remember the worries he had about the money before the arrival of the Bolsheviks in 1920. We both looked for hideouts in our apartment to hide the treasure.

We divided the cash under the darkness of the night. We hid it under the window panes, behind the stoves, and in the door frames. We both feared for the fate of the money and our own fate if the Bolsheviks find out about our "misdeed".

When The Bolsheviks approached Zolochiv, a dire fear fell on the Jewish population, particularly on the upper layer. The city's honorable people hid and did not dare come out. However, caution did not help anybody. Many got arrested and their fate was never known. My husband was one of the few who walked around free. Without fear he tried to help his fellow citizens. His luck smiled upon him unexpectedly. In one of the high-ranked Russian officers, he recognized his childhood friend, whom he went with to the elementary school in Yezerna. Life separated them. That friend wandered around overtime to Russia, became a Bolshevik, and reached a high rank in the army. Both joyed when they met again after so many years.

They toyed with memory of their childhood and the friendship that tied them up once. With these feelings, the officer was willing to help my husband in his lobbying to help the Jews. Indeed, many of the prisoners were set free thanks to the officer's intervention, among them Mrs. Ofer. She did not forget that help. After the tragic death of my husband, she stood by me with advice and deeds, like a good and loyal mother.

The short invasion by the Bolsheviks, the spiritual and economic turbulence that followed, antisemitism, which increased in Poland more and more, lack of security, and other factors influenced my husband to mentally and practically prepare for making Aliya to Eretz Israel. Since he knew that he would not be able to work as a lawyer in Eretz Israel, he searched for ways to secure means that would allow him to make a living there. To accomplish that goal, he widened his practice, which was one of the best in the city, and accepted Dr. Shternshus as a partner. He began to prepare daring plans, based on which he hoped to secure those means. He paid a down payment on a piece of land in Bat-Yam, two weeks before his death, as the first step toward his Aliya.

However, everything was in vain when his life was cut tragically short.

[Columns 471-472]

Dr. Yosef Shatkai
(1904 – 1961)

by B. Tzverdling

Translated by Moshe Kutten

Dr. Yosef Shatkai (Shweig) was born in Ternopil. His parents moved from there to Zloczow, where he studied in high school and received his matriculation certificate. He was one of the founders of the monthly magazine "Snunit" ["Swallow" in Hebrew], published in Lviv. He was an enthusiastic Zionist from his youth. When he studied in college in Vianna, he became a member of the Zionist association "Kadima" ["Forward"]. During his work as an optometrist in Lodz (Poland), he held various positions in Zionist organizations. He first visited Eretz Israel in 1914. He visited Eretz Israel every year since then and sometimes twice a year, and n 1942, he made Aliya to Eretz Israel. He continued his activities in the medical fields, education, and Zionist publicity more vigorously and with more dedication. He was a member of "Kupat Kholim's [health maintenance organization of the labor union] steering committee, head of the "Beilinson" Hospital, and one of the founders of the Israeli branch of the OSE [an international Jewish physicians' organization – active as a humanitarian organization]. His assistance and advisement also contributed to the absorption of immigrants and teaching the youth productive occupations. He was active until his last day.

Dr. Shatkai died on 23 Iyar 5722 [27 May 1962]. May his memory be blessed.

———————

[Columns 473-474]

Eliyahu Schorr, the Painter from Zloczow
(1904 – 1961)

by Kh. Finkelstein

Translated by Moshe Kutten

Eliyahu Schorr studied art in Warsaw and Paris, and his place of residence and cradle of his work was New York. However, the "Kheder", "Kloiz", crooked alleys, men covered by the shtreimels, women, delightful boys and girls, smiles, and sorrow, were always in front of his eyes. He also always had the domestic fowls that Jews had in their yards in front of his eyes, and he immortalize them in his paintings. His artistic eyes and diligent hands adequately reconstructed the joy and the sorrow [in the Jewish shtetl].

The work of Eliyahu Schorr was like a message – the glamour and the splendor of Poland Jewry, as reflected by his city – Zloczow.

In his eyes, that city served as an example and symbol, and he considered its Jews as the essence, blood, and guts of Judaism.

Eliyahu learned to hold a painter's brush from his father, a pious sign painter. Later on, during his studies in Warsaw, he received a scholarship from the Polish government to further his studies in France and Italy.

Eliyahu was a vivid multi-facet figure. He rejected dogmatic piousness, but his creation was influenced by religion, with which he dazzled the world.

Everybody praised his work, but he did not have an easy and pleasant life. He was the only one who revolted against the modernistic approach to wipe out any memory of the Jewish tradition from art. Schorr did not abandon his principles and remained loyal to himself, despite the adverse effects on his economic state.

He did not deviate from the artistic truth, which drove him as a person, Jew, and artist. He did not betray Zloczow either. He believed with every ounce of his being that a Jewish artist must be nourished from his roots. He believed that the destiny of any Jewish artist is to immortalize the "Ancient Treasure" for the benefit of future generations and to draw his or her artistic vision from the "Eternal Well" (as he expressed himself in one of his articles). He aimed at building a bridge between Zloczow of the past and the reality of the modern Jew in the present.

During his creation years in America, he painted an infinite number of pictures and formed many religious tools and ritual articles. His torn soul wished to discover new forms and ideas. He worked feverishly as if he felt that the time was short and the work was plentiful. He sacrificed his eyes, brain, and nerves on the altar of creation.

His decorations of the bible and the modern Yiddish literature and English translations from Yiddish – are masterpieces of decoration art.

He worked on decorations for the "Hagadah" and left sketches and drawings but did not manage to publish them.

Acquiring fame did not come easy for Eliyahu Schorr. He struggled for years the gain recognition for his work and creations. In the end, he lived to see that museums and collectors had to wait a year or two, and sometimes even longer, to receive their orders.

He considered his work – like worship. He knew how to breathe life into any raw material he handled. His creations are a delight for the eyes, a source of joy, and attractive. They invoke the feeling that they have been created by a godly creator.

As a flawless artist, he did not solicit help from anybody, except his wife, Resha. She served as a loyal companion from the time they studied together at the Warsaw art academy. [During their marriage] she gave birth to two talented daughters.

Resha was a painter in her own standing. In America, she made a name for herself as Resha Ein (short for her maiden name – Einstein). However, she preferred to live under the shadow of her husband as if she wanted not to overshadow his fame. Many of their acquaintants in America did not even know that she was a painter until her exhibition opened in New York. After the death of her husband, she began to create in metal. Although her style of work and execution was different, the influence of the man she spent her life with is apparent.

The wealth of Eliyahu Schorr's work is astonishing. Pieces of jewelry and ritual articles created by him can be found in the [Modern] Art Museum in New York, the Jewish Museum, large synagogues in America, and private collections in America, Europe, and Israel.

He designed and created crowns for Torah scrolls, urns, perfume bottles, boxes for Etrog's, dreidels, noisemakers [for Purim], and Hannukah menorahs. Passover plates. Lamps, candle holders, *Kiddush* cups, knives for cutting the challah, and covers for *makhzorim* [Jewish prayer books]. He particularly liked to decorate mezuzahs in red, blue, and golden colors. Nobody before him elevated the mezuzahs to such a high artistic level as Eliyahu Schorr.

His jewelry attests to a high artistic vision and every product was an artistic masterpiece. He used to cast birds on top of his signature and thereby, imitated the Middle Ages authors, who painted tiny animals or birds under the last line of the manuscript.

The synagogue in Zloczow served as a never-ending source of inspiration for his creations. He painted on the Holy Ark, the *Parokhet* (the ark curtain), the Bimah [raised platform with the Torah reading desk], and the walls. The synagogue was crowded with praying for people on Shabbat and holidays (like Yom Kippur, Simkhat Torah, and Purim).

[Columns 475-476]

A picture from Zloczow of the painter Schorr

In his eulogy, Professor Avraham Heschel said among other things: "Eliyahu Schorr was a Jewish artist who knew the essence of Judaism: How to hold a Torah scroll, how to hold a Lulav [a closed frond of the date palm tree. It is one of the Four Species used during the Jewish holiday of Sukkot], how to tie *Tefillin*, and put on a *Talit*".

Eliyahu Schorr painted the devoutness and enthusiasm of a G-d-fearing Jew and the quiver he experiences when the ark is opened. He painted the rich man at the synagogue' eastern wall and the suffering of *"Amkha"* [Common people].

Various figures are revealed in his paintings: the rabbi, butcher, matchmaker, musicians playing on their instruments, *kloiz* students, comedians wearing their flat caps holding Purim flags, haggling, cart owners pulling their merchandise, A Jew leading his horse to the water, a melamed teaching Torah to his students, Jews in a succah, a groom and bride under the canopy, and Zloczow's Jews walking around on Shabbat after their afternoon nap, encountering a cat jumping at them.

There are no dogs in Schorr's pictures since Zloczow's Jews did not like dogs.

Eliyahu Schorr's paintings shine with humor, filled with tenderness and beauty with not a drop of mockery.

As aforesaid, Eliyahu Schorr's art spans many fields – graphic art, decorative art, design, painting, and toward the end of his life – sculpturing.

His creations depict other than just Jewish subjects. He also expressed in his work the inanimate and the blooming. In his sculptures, he conveyed the expressionistic abstract.

His design and technical implementation, such as a Torah scroll crown or a Hannukah menorah, were as good as any creation on a canvas.

[Columns 477-478]

The impression of their creator was imprinted on all of his creations.

Every piece of paper or a wood board served clay in the potter's hands. One of his miniatures describes a typical Galitsian boy wearing a round cap on his head, under which his black and curling locks are revealed. His fiery eyes, watching in awe and fear ahead to the future. Another miniature portrays the synagogue: brilliant light around, the sun rays dancing around joyfully and festively, descending over the Torah scroll and the praying people.

He never walked around idle. Paper and pencil accompanied him everywhere. He sketched tirelessly and always collected material for his work.

Eliyahu was not only an artist but also a family man for whom his wife and daughters, Meomi and Mira'le, were the essence of his life. It was them who encouraged him to create and overcome agitation and doubts, common to all artists. He always spent his time, after the workday, with his family, listening to music or reading in English, French, German, Polish, or Yiddish.

The Schorr family was known for its hospitality. The home was open to anybody, and Eliyahu used to immerse himself in long arguments with his guests filled with flowery language, proverbs, and rhetoric.

Despite knowing and mastering many languages, Yiddish was his favorite.

Everybody was fascinated by Schorr's house. The paintings and antics on the walls, the tables and shelves, and the pleasant manners of the hosts created an exceptional atmosphere.

However, his life was cut short. The wife and daughters were orphaned, and the artist's hands ceased to create forever.

In the modern period, new, different, and strange styles pop up in art. These styles change form, pass, and disappear while still young. For these passing styles, tradition does not have any meaning.

Schorr's merit comes from his art rigidity and disapproval of the conventions of short-lived artistic styles for all their upheavals. He disregarded and stayed away from the global trends of progress, which he found the blighted and lucking soul. Against these trends, he possessed a Jewish soul, which gushed out like a perennial spring in all of his creations. His subjects were drilled and rose from the "Eternal Well", and were imbued with Jewish content and spirit, while the framework, conception, style, and technical knowledge were always fresh and flowing.

About 12 years ago [12 only years before the publishing year of the Yizkor book – 1967], the *"Lamed Vav Tzadikim"* served as a subject for a holy ark's door made of silver. The *Tzadikim* depicted a semi-abstractive way, a style that is being developed now.

In the future, when no trace would remain from the modern experiments and the art's false prophets, the creations of Eliyahu Schorr will provide a momentous eternal testimony, in memory of the wonderous Zloczow native.

[Columns 479-480]

Dr. Khaim Zalkai (Leider)

by B. Zalkai

Translated by Moshe Kutten

Dr. Khaim Zalkai Z"L was born on 21 December 1896, in Zloczow, to a large family. He received his first education in the *Kheder* of a tuberculosis patient. Later on, he studied at the Jewish school, "Safah Brura" ["Clear Language"], of Rabbi Rohatyn Z"L. After completing four classes of the elementary school, he was admitted to the state gymnasium in Zloczow. From a young age, he was forced to tutor other students to continue his studies.

When he graduated from the seventh class of the gymnasium in 1914, he was recruited to the Austrian army upon the breakout of the [First World] War]. He passed through all of the service's "Seven Departments of Hell" on the front.

In 1915, he passed the state matriculation exams with honors, and in 1918, he was accepted to the university in Lviv, where he was forced to make a living by tutoring. Thanks to an application, written in flowery Hebrew, which he submitted to the management of the [Jewish] Academic House in Lviv, he received a room there, sharing it with another student. He was attracted by the medical profession, and possessed the required attributes for that, as he understood the human soul and how to access it.

On 22 January 1925, he graduated, with high honors, from his studies at Lviv University, earning a medical doctorate. In a very short time, he acquired a name for himself in his native city of Zloczow as a physician and a man of conscience.

He was a dedicated Zionist from his youth and was depressed by the need to reside in the diaspora among the gentiles. His will to make Aliya was strong. He dared to give up on the comfortable physician life – residing among his people in the diaspora and exchanging them with a life of poverty and distress.

Dr. Zalkai made Aliya in 1934. The first years were a period of suffering and scarcity since the state of the physicians at that time was poor. He served as a teacher for a while since he was a linguist with a witty style and an excellent educator for teaching the Hebrew language. A few years later, he was accepted as a physician in Kibbutz Giv'at Khaim, where he had a difficult time. The individualist Zalkai was not a good fit as a man and physician in a communal setting.

In 1937, he accepted the position of secretary of the physicians' organization of "Kupat Kholim" [the health maintenance organization of the labor movement]. He worked there until his last day.

In 1956, he originated the publication of a bulletin of Kupat Kholim's physicians, "HaRofeh BaMosad" ["The Physician in an Institution"]. He devoted all of his energy to that magazine, where he could set free to his witty pen. Zalkai's fight for improvements in the physicians' working conditions bore fruit but he did not live to witness that.

He dreamt all his life about issuing a memorial book for Zloczow. He did not live to see his dream materialize either.

May his memory be blessed.

————

[Columns 481-482]

To the Image of Mrs. Kreger

by E. Davidsen

Translated by Moshe Kutten

Mrs. Frida Kreger, approaching 80, is still showing undiminished rigor. When she raised the memory of Zloczow, which does not exist anymore, it seems that she is young again. She was in Vienna, the Austrian capital, at the break of the First War World. After two years of wandering around, she succeeded in reaching her native town – Zloczow. She often "got stuck" on the way, after she was forcefully pulled out, along with other civilians, from a train destined to transport soldiers to the front. When she returned to Zloczow, she found everything destroyed to the ground and began to build her life anew. Thanks to her immense energy, she succeeded to reestablish herself and was active in extenuating the suffering of the residents who were left with nothing and needed support.

She continued with her effort until the breakout of the Second War World when the communists loaded many onto rickety train carts and transported them to Siberia. Among them, there were many Poles whose fate remains unknown. Her husband, R' Nakhum Kreger, was one of the few who survived after endless tortures and interrogations by the communists.

Shae made Aliya to Eretz Israel with her husband in 1937, with a certificate sent to her by her son-in-law, Mr. Davidsen. Her husband passed away two years later, as he was feeble from the suffering in Stalin's Russia.

[Column 483]

Shalom Mendel & his Wife,
and Grandmother Meita Tennenbaum

by Mrs. Kh. Laks

Translated by Moshe Kutten

R' Shalom Mendel was loved and admired by all, secular and religious alike because he also understood people whose views were different from his. He acquired friends from the intellectual circles since he had a common language, was a good listener, and gave wise advice. He was a scholar, an agreeable person, full of humor, and a dedicated friend, who was always ready to help others as much as he could afford and even beyond.

He fought hard to make a living and feed his large family but was not always successful. His wife was always helpful and assisted in making ends meet. When R' Shalom Mendel had the opportunity to better his situation and become a slaughterer, he had to give it up because he was soft-hearted and kind. That happened after the death of slaughterer Gedalyahu. The community offered him to be tested and become a slaughterer. He studied day and night to prepare. However, when he took the exam, he was disqualified since he could not bring himself to slaughter a chicken. His hands trembled, and he felt sick. He went home joyful and announced, to his wife's disappointment, who expected relief, that he would not have to slaughter living animals.

Despite the difficulties, he was content with what he had. He never complained to people, and certainly not to G-d, to whom he was dedicated in his heart and soul and had total faith in him.

From right to left: R' Shalom Mendel, R' Baumgarten, and Rabbi
Hollander

[Column 484]

Gita Mendel Z"L

Gita Mendel Z"L was Shalom Mendel's wife. She was a simple and quiet woman who had her hands filled with her household chores and making a living. As the wife of a scholar student, she had to manage a small store to earn a living for her big family.

She was an exemplary Jewish mother, dedicated and loyal, for whom the well-being of the children and husband was her first and foremost worry. She was content with very little and indeed did not have much. She was content with the difficult situation without any complaints or jealousy about the success of others.

I recall what she told me after she lost her eight-year-old daughter when the neighbors came to console her: "May earth be shut for other small children, so no other Jewish woman would experience the suffering that I have endured".

Grandmother Meita Tennenbaum Z"L

There is one fact, which has no precedent, that can attest to the greatness of grandmother Meita's soul and generosity: After the death of her daughter, the first wife of Shlomo Meites, she remained in his home, welcomed his second wife with open arms, and became like a mother to her. Grandmother Meita continued to help the family by supplementing their income with money she received from her dairy. She also helped take care of the household chores.

People thought that Meita was Shlomo Meites' mother. The truth is that she was his mother-in-law, and he was named after her. It was very rare for a man to be named after his mother-in-law.

In addition to managing the dairy, she found time to fulfill the commandment of visiting the sick. Since she was poor, she would collect many things from rich people and bring them to the sick. She often visited the fame philanthrope, Mrs. Ofer, and never left empty-handed.

———

[Columns 485-486]

Memories about Personalities in the City

by Yehoshua Sherletzki

Translated by Moshe Kutten

When I remember Zloczow, I think that every one of its Jews, poor and wealthy, or those who pretended to make a good living (these people were the majority), was up to their neck in their day-to-day struggles and efforts. However, everyone tried their best to hide their everyday worries and not display them in public (many did it for business reasons…)

Relatively to other places, the city had many educated people and people who held free professions. Some of them did not complete their high school education but studied there for several years. Others acquired their education in other ways. That had an effect on the customs, manners, and appearance of Zloczow's Jews.

However, the intelligentsia was not necessarily wealthy. On the contrary, the educated people lived modestly and scantly. Some were "real paupers". But they all knew how to maintain a respectable appearance. They also contributed, from their meager income to the public needs.

In Zloczow, the intelligentsia was rooted in the national spirit in the broadest sense of the word. It was not defined by speaking Polish, as was customary in other small towns. The intelligentsia was proud to speak Yiddish, the language of the masses. In addition to the Zionist newspaper, which was published in Polish in Warsaw, they read Warsaw's Yiddish and Hebrew newspaper "Haynt" ["Today"].

Almost everybody was a Zionist "volunteer" without any aloofness, arrogance, or competition. People were loyal to the national revival idea. Their standing was apparent outwardly and meant dedication and zealous devotion inwardly.

Trembling and with a feeling of sorrow, which would accompany me until my last day, I mention the name of my dear friend, Yaakov Warlig. I can still see him running around the corridors of the local "magistrate" ["City Hall"], followed by an old Jewish woman, on whom the "evil municipal officials" imposed an unbearable heavy tax or another harsh decree. He would make her bitter argument before the authority officials, using his refined Polish and articulated and fiery speech, while supporting the claim with his astute and shiny eyes.

He always wore a serious expression on his face. He used to joke and even throw a stinging remark, with his sharp tongue, at anybody who talked to him. However, his expression and manners would quickly change when the topic of discussion changed to "his favorite subjects", namely a Zionist-National topic or a topic related to the "eternal" troubles of old Jewish women.

Another role model that grew, and rose to greatness within the ethical and spiritual atmosphere of Jewish Zloczow, was Dr. Avraham Sharon. All his life, he loved Zionism, the Hebrew language, and his autographs collection. Toward the end of his life, he became a zealous and eccentric figure. He was an oddity among the conciliatory and indifferent Jerusalem academists.

Another Zionist idealist was Dr. David Werpel. He was a prominent jurist, a pleasant person who loved Hebrew and the bible. He used to wake up his only son, very early at dawn, to teach him several chapters from the bible.

Although Zloczow suffered from a cold climate, it served as a greenhouse for that sort of zealous people.

They were some people among commoners that should also be mentioned. For example, a Jew named Beltzer. He was an old man, a remnant of the enlightened generation. He was loyal to his point of view until his last day. Yet, he was one of the people who visited the synagogue regularly and probably did not miss any of the public Minkha [afternoon] or Maariv [evening] prayers. However, he would always rage about and mock the Hasidim. When we met, he used to "grant me the privilege" of listening to some of his fables and phrases and would proudly take credit for his "creativity". He did not consider me a person who was worried much about the "next world" or a person who followed commandments zealously. However, he found it necessary to "empower" me so that my intellectual side would not be harmed.

There was another person there by the name of Tzukerkendel. He was a commoner who was one of the wealthiest people in the city, although I am not really sure that he was actually rich. He dressed very simply, wearing heavy peasant boots. He wore them on the cold days of the winter and the hot days of the summer. If I am not mistaken, he was a construction contractor. He was clever, diligent, and innovative.

[Columns 487-488]

He once had a clever idea, to improve transportation in the state. He immediately wrote a detailed memorandum about his idea to the transportation minister in Warsaw. A short while later, the district governor received a letter in which he was requested to urgently summon Mr. Tzukerkendel to the capital about an urgent matter. Mr. Tzukerkendel was honorably invited by the district governor. Then governor surveyed him from head to toe, and his eyes grew dim.

"Do you expect to appear before the minister in Warsaw in these boots?" Asked the governor. He immediately put the wheels in motion. A shoemaker and a tailor were called in and ordered to supply Mr. Tzukerkendel, with elegant shoes and clothing.

The minister accepted Mr. Tzukerkendel in his office and discussed his proposal with him (Mr. Tzukerkendel was a well-spoken man who could explain himself cleverly and logically). Later on, the man returned to his home in Zloczow. However, nobody ever saw him in his elegant suit again. That was representative of the simple people in Zloczow.

There was another Jewish person in Zloczow by the name of Tzukerkendel – Wilhelm Tzuketrkendel who was one of the most known figures in Polish publishing history. He founded and managed a publishing house that owned numerous publishing rights. The publishing house was active throughout Poland, but it was headquartered in Zloczow.

The city was also the birthplace of some of the Torah greats, poets, educated scholars, artists, and others.

Located on the border, or close to it, between the Russian and the Austrian empires, Zloczow Jews embodied the ardor, innocence of faith, and inner joy of the Hasidism in the east, and the delicate taste, pleasant manners, and refined culture of Vienna in the west.

A Jewish community sprouted and grew, between these two poles, an ancient and rooted in folklore, soaked with the tradition of its ancestors, although there were only a few Haredim in the city. The Jews were loyal to the ideal of national revival, although most people, particularly the youths, were educated in Polish schools and other foreign school systems.

I remember well the time I spent as an educator in Zloczow. I will keep in my heart the grace and dignity that emanated from the youth when I stood among them, teaching an ancient with "strange" grammar and "impossible" writing. Not once, I felt powerless against a living, fluid, and flexible [foreign] language that attracted and conquered a momentum-filled culture. [We had to fight against] a language that had an answer for every question, sweeping everything, rising and ascending in its assertive, seductive, and overwhelming approach.

It was the youth's great love, which encouraged me in my modest and multi-experiences fight.

Only some of that youths were fortunate to reach the shores of our homeland. It is with awe and reverence that I write these pale recollections in holy memory of all who perished. We should never forget them...

[Columns 489-490]

In memory of Mordekhai Baumgarten Z"L

by Member of the Knesset, Y. Katz

Translated by Moshe Kutten

R' Mordekhi (Markus) Baumgarten Z"L was a distinguished and noble figure. He was the husband of the praised activist, Mrs. Sabina Baumgarten, may she set apart for long life, who heads the organization of Zolochiv's natives ["Zloczower Relief Verband of America"].

The life of Mordekhai Baumgarten Z"L was cut short when he was only 52, in the prime of his vitality and vigor. With his personality, he represented the deep-rootedfolksy Jew. Despite being immersed in his businesses in the big metropolis of New York, he did not abandon his father's tradition linked with all his heart and soul to his native country's people.

He was blessed with virtuous attributes and prerequisite qualifications. He was imbued with an unlimited love of Israel, wise and clever, diligent and modest. He excelled in his affection for Eretz Israel from his youth. The national revival in the homeland of his ancestors was an inseparable part of his being and his life's vision.

He established himself economically under his own initiative and with the help of his distinguished wife and managed many affiliated businesses. He was known for his honesty, skills, and exemplary generosity. As an activist in Zionist and social institutions, he always volunteered for any activity that benefited the public. He contributed substantial sums to various Israeli fundraisings. He also took it upon himself to solicit contributions, despite being busy with his private and family affairs. He did not spare any effort to help others and along with his wife, contributed tremendously to the Zloczow landsmen organization in Israel.

He grew up in his distinguished parents' home, who rooted in him the commitment to tradition and Judaism. During the years of the First World War and beyond, and later on in Columbia, he kept the lifestyle that he absorbed in his youth and continued to adhere to his father's heritage. When he settled in the USA, he continued with his exemplary behavior. He was liked by all of his acquaintances and loved ones. He acquired many friends, and his home was always open. He was always ready to help the fallen or needy.

The distinguished deceased headed the Zloczow's "Makhzikei HaDat"["supporters and promoters of the religion"] organization which is famous for its activities and unique character. The organization had the grace of our city resting on it. In the synagogue where he regularly prayed, he was considered one of the individuals of virtue and one of the leading philanthropists. He was known as a person of wisdom and reason who helped many.

When the state of Israel was established, he followed it intensely and with interest after the development of Israel's independence. He fulfilled his longing to see the homeland with his own eyes when he visited Israel with his wife. He toured the country through its length and breadth and was elated to see the wonderful creation with his own eyes. He was particularly pleased to see that his donations to the various Israeli fundraising efforts were utilized wisely and efficiently.

May the man have remembered for his good deeds. May his name be remembered forever. May his memory be blessed.

[Column 491]

R' Shmuel Tenenbaum

by Mina Mamber

Translated by Moshe Kutten

My father, R' Shmuel Tenenbaum, known by his nickname R' Shmuel Mershlek[?]. was a known figure in Zloczow and the neighboring towns as a scholar, immersed in the Torah and observant. He had a patriarchic image adorning a sizable neat and tidy beard. He devoted his free time to studying the Torah and writing. He wrote poems and articles for a Lviv newspaper, and his writings were at a high level. He was respected and admired by people from all classes, and despite strictly adhering to the Torah's commandment, he was far from religious zealotry. My uncle, Shlomi Meites, said about him: "It is a pity that R' Shmuel who is so knowledgeable of the Torah and he is an Apikores". Many people stopped by to consult with him because he had a sharp and profound mind. The rabbi of Zloczow, Rabbi Rohatyn, and the rabbinical judge, R' Mendeleh, often came to consult with him about an awkward.

He has been sought-after at weddings because he instilled a joyful atmosphere with his jokes and life-filled sayings. Despite hating unclean circumstances, he always hosted guests for Shabbat. The guests were miserable and wore tattered clothes. When he was asked why he brought such guests home, he said that those people were hungry and that other homeowners refused to host them.

He was always ready to help others, as he had an understanding and warm heart. Once the neighbor, tailor Israel, became sick with typhus. A guard was positioned by the house, but my father sneaked in and took care of him. When other neighbors scolded him, he responded:" Could we just abandon the man to take care of himself?"

R' Shmuel also used to teach, but he chose only talented students. At the synagogue, he often served as "*Ba'al Tefilah*" [cantor, leading the prayer]. His voice was pleasant, and it was considered a great honor if he agreed to pray the "Musaf" ["additional service"] on "Yom Kippur" in the big synagogue.

[Column 492]

He also worked as a real estate agent to make a living. A merchant from Ternopil wished once to purchase a house in Zloczow. My father traveled to Ternopil, received a large sum of money, and came back to Zloczow to close to deal. During the transfer of the house, going over the deed books, my father noticed a flaw, which could have thwarted the buyer. He canceled the deal immediately. When the merchant appeared and wanted to pay him for the effort, my father refused to receive any payment.

My mother, a righteous and quiet woman, accepted everything in a good spirit. She did not make his life difficult, as she was gentle-minded and understood him well. She helped the needy as much as she could. Very often, she did not eat, claiming she was not hungry. Later on, people found out that she gave her meals to a poor person who came to her house. She was a Jewish woman and a mother in the full sense of the word. Her devotion to the children and her husband was exemplary.

***The gravestone on
Shmuel Tenenbaum's grave***

[Columns 493-494]

Memories from my Father's Home

by Leah Raviv

Translated by Moshe Kutten

I loved my city, Zloczow, with its small red-roof houses and narrow streets.

The smell of the lilac, and the green of the chestnut trees, flowering in the spring, accompanied that memory.

We lived in the city, in a crowded but unified Jewish settlement.

In my childhood, my father told me stories about the heroism of our ancestors, and I dreamt about giving my life to our people.

We studied with the non-Jews in the Polish school, but how different was our world from theirs.

My father's home, the home of the Yosefsbergs, was like the other Jewish homes, where our generation was imbued with the fondness of Judaism in its heart and soul.

In the big and long dining room, a large table was placed, enabling many guests to sit down comfortably and be served a meal.

The phrase: "If I forget you, O Jerusalem, let my right hand forget her cunning" [Psalms 137:5] was written in big letters above the door.

My big brother, Dr. Yehoshua Yosefsberg (who lived later on in Petach Tikva), was like a container into which maximum Torah and secular studies were pushed.

Melamed, Rabbi Meir Kapon, was a regular in our house like a family member. His Torah teaching was conveyed to us day and night. My brother learned secular subjects from the teachers of the state high school who prepared him for the external matriculation exams for a hefty wage. That was done because it was unimaginable for him to sit down in school with the gentile students.

When my brother passed the matriculation exams (our father was already dead by then), the high school principal summoned my mother and told her: "Your son is destined to be the Mendelssohn of his generation". Despite being busy with his studies, my brother took care of pigeons, bees, and alike, which were considered a waste of time at that time.

As a physician, he respected human life and fulfilled his dream of loving the fauna and the Torah.

My older sister, Shnetzia, was 13 years old when Father chose a groom for her, the son of an *Admor*. To get engaged to a Haredi boy was considered a tragedy for the girl who possessed modern views. However, she did not want to resist Father's will and cause him sorrow. When Father died, Mother told Shnetzia: "My dear daughter, you are free to do as you wish. Nobody is forcing you to marry that boy, who was chosen for you by Father". Shnetzia did not respond. She married the *Admor's* son, and they were happily married. They had good sons and grandchildren.

The traditional spirit and keeping the laws of tradition, were supreme laws in our home. When Father died on the Seder night, none of the Seder customs and holidays were changed. My brother led the Seder instead of Father, and we sang the same Nigun as we did every year. Only Mother cried and wiped out her tears quietly.

Our mother had an important role in our education. Her many stories about our ancestors and the *Tzadikim* who gave their lives in acts of heroism were etched in my memory.

I allow myself to bring here her description of the death of our grandfather, Rabbi Yehoshua Wolf Z"L, who was a rabbinical judge in the city of Zloczow. This is what my mother said:

"I was in a delivery bed when people came to call me. I knew that Saba [grandfather] was sick, so, despite my weakness, I ran to him. I saw Saba lying in bed, surrounded by the elders of the community. Saba said to Savta [grandmother]: Go fetch me a clean shirt". Savta brought him a clean shirt that had a patch sewn on it by her. Saba, who never paid attention to a patch before, said: "I would not wear that shirt now, as I am about to stand before G-d. Savta brought him another shirt. Saba then called the members of his community and shook the hand of one after the other. He then said "*Vidui*" [confession], and at the end of the prayer, his soul departed".

In 1914, during the First World War, we left Zloczow as war refugees and moved the Vienna, Austria's capital. We found many values in the big world, however, the seed of the love for our nation, sewn in our souls during our childhood, brought us to Eretz Israel.

[Columns 495-496]

In Memory of Dr. Eizen Mozes

by Rabbi David Eizen

Translated by Moshe Kutten

A quarter of a century passed since the Nazis and their collaborators, the Ukrainians, murdered my brother, Dr. Mozes Eizen Z"L. According to the rumors of those days, his head was chopped off with an ax.

In his youth, he used to read to my mother about the pogroms that took place during Petliura's reign. He himself was murdered in a pogrom.

Since the exact day of the murder is unknown, we are in perpetual mourning, even though we did not pray "*Kadish*" and did not sit "*Shiv'ah*". He was not buried according to the Jewish laws, and his burial place is unknown. He was our "*Moshe Rabeinu*".

Only a Jew could have excelled in so much humanity and kindness. He was liked by Jews and non-Jews alike.

He was born in 1898 and received a secular and religious education. He made his mark on our family and was the main breadwinner during the years after the break of the First World War. In 1916 he was recruited to the Austrian army, where he reached the rank of a lieutenant. The returning soldiers said that during the battle on the Italian border he allocated time for the Jewish soldiers for the Ma'ariv and Minkha prayers.

When returned to Zloczow after the war he became an active member of the "Bar Kokhba" group, a Zionist academic organization. During the Polish-Ukrainian riots in 1919, he was a member of the Jewish self-defense force.

When Poland experienced an economic crisis and a wave of antisemitism, he spent several years as a teacher in the "Yavne" school, first in Wloclawek and later in Stolin. It was a school affiliated with the "HaMizrakhi" [Religious

Zionist movement], under the management of Moshe Shorer Z"L. When he returned from Stolin, he decided to complete his law school studies, which he had to stop due to the need to support a family with nine children.

He studied day and night (under candlelight), and under conditions of hunger. He had a slice of bread in his pocket and the law book in his hand. These were his material and spiritual food for several years. He finally received his law doctorate in 1930.

During his short life, he was an active Zionist and participated in fundraising for the JNF and the Foundation Fund. His dream was Israel. However, the [British] White Paper [Policy], and family connections put an end to his dream.

Our older brother, who introduced us to the worlds of culture and religion, did not get himself a grave. May these few words serve as an eternal memorial for him. May his soul be bound in the bundle of the living. Amen.

The youngest among Eizen's children was Malka. She married Moshe Greenspan. The year she gave her soul up for the sanctification of G-d is unknown. Likewise, the year when her husband and daughter were murdered is unknown. They lived in Lviv, and Malka was purity in its incarnation.

A third of our family was annihilated, as was the third of our nation.

May G-d avenge their blood!

————

[Columns 497-498]

Modest Light

by Dov Sadan

Translated by Moshe Kutten

(In memory of Rivka Bar'am nee Yeger)

A.

During the days of our distanced childhood, the days of innocent calm, which did not foresee the coming of the thunders, it was not a prevalent event in our area, under the shadow of the Habsburg regime, that youth from among those who dreamt about Zion, would rise up and fulfilled his dream. Perhaps one young man from the city or two from the district would be infected by the Second Aliya bug, touched by the wave that had arrived from beyond the border, and swept away by it. A young man, but not a young woman. Not that the second Aliya had a shortage of young Galitsia native women. On the contrary, we are obliged to mention the few young women who rose up and made Aliya during those days, with a veil of wonder and affection spread over them. Case and point: our city native, Sara Brakha, who went along with Khaim Tzimmerman, the native of Berestechko, the neighboring town; Another Zloczow native, Linah Andoman, who went along with Yehoshua Aker; Lviv native, Dvora Shpinner, who went with Yehoshua Feldman (R' Binyamin); A native of another town, Sara Brant, who went with Yaa'akov Tahun; A native of another town, Dinah Reitzis, who went with Eliezer-Meir Lifshitz; A native of Snyatyn, Leah Rosenkrantz, who went with Yosef Zelinger; and many others. The common thread among them was that they all built a home in Eretz Israel. Some built their home in the Galilee region, some in the coastal plain, and some in Jerusalem. Those homes made that small [Second] Aliya, a reality.

If the chronicles of those women would have been written down, it would span a long scroll. Thes chronicles were based on heroism, which embodied the force of being uprooted from one environment and planted in another. The energy of creating a new environment was a life-changing process that burdened mainly the woman – the housewife and the mother of the sons. Even if it was not explicitly stated in that scroll that a certain woman went with that certain man, it is true that, in most cases, women went with their men. However, the bold decision about making Aliya and the courage to make Aliya should be attributed to the women.

During the calm days of our childhood, it was rare in our area for a single woman to dare and make Aliya on her own, as was the case across the border in Lithuania and Belarus. Even if there was one unusual woman, the exceptionality was just proof of the usual.

Unlike our childhood, the calm was disturbed during our youth and we were exasperated, even more than the youths across the border, one generation before us. The young women from our area became the driving force behind the revival of the Aliya process and perhaps even its foundation. World war I was one of the factors that encouraged the renewed process. Not less excruciating were the uprooting and wanderings. Then came the two revolutions - the one amid the war and the one just after it. These factors and the innocent teaching of the youth movement gave rise to an enormous youth wave. In a storm, it carried the young man with his power and the young woman with her brightness, all the way to the shores of our land.

B.

Like a sketch of a thought or a memory revealing itself when drawn, the idea that the circle of life of the wives of our youth was nearing its end revealed itself at the sight of the silent and mourning crowd that stood around the coffin of Rivka nee Yeger.

Rivkah was among the first pioneers of that [Third] Aliya. Unfortunately, she died prematurely, a year ago, at the end of her fiftieth year. Like many of the people who walked behind her coffin last year, she made that life-changing decision about making Aliya during the same period of a year and a half, between the tail end of World War I and the start of the Third Aliya. During that same period, the Jewish communities in Eastern Galitsia lived like lonely brigades of poverty and isolation. During those days of the Ukrainian Republic, the Zionists became the rulers in the Jewish Street. While the adults, who still deceived themselves with the idea of autonomy, found the Jewish Street to be a strait within a strait, the youths, the real innocent children, naïvely managed to create a whole world for themselves within that strait. The "Local", as the meeting hall of the branch of the "HaShomer HaTzair" movement, was called, was not only a refuge from the present. It also, in its essence, served as a refuge into the future. The "Local" also served as a place for gaining strength. For the Zionist adults, the Local" was like the verse "Let the young men now arise for a contest before us" [Shmuel 2 2:14. In Hebrew - an expression of contempt for inexperienced people trying to engage in matters they do not understand]. In time, they were surprised to find out that the game that the young ones were playing was not like their own old game – namely, the local activities such as the school - "Safa Brurah" ["Clear Language"], stamps of the JNF, or its collection box, the "Betsalel" exhibition, the reading of the....

[Columns 499-500]

The youth acted according to the expression: "The fool takes the matter seriously." The young pioneers wandered to Vienna and Bratislava [Pressburg]. There, they were tormented until they boarded the ships that sailed toward Eretz Israel. In short, they went [fulfilling their dream], and more importantly, the young women went.

Whatever was accomplished at the "Local" of my city [Brody], during that same period of a year and a half, was also was accomplished at the "Local" of the neighboring city of Zloczow. However, in Zloczow, some additional factors resulted in more vigorous activity, the echoes about which reached our city. A Jewish weekly newspaper was founded in Zloczow. A Jewish high school was also established there. And more importantly, pioneering activities were also carried out there by people who were not that young. The master of the doings and the head of the doers was Dr. Schwadron. He nominated himself as the school caretaker and served as a role model for people who followed their talk by actual deeds. He also taught other people how to distinguish between informed Zionism and zealous Zionism. His essays, which helped in sharpening that line of distinction, also shaped the spirit and decisiveness of the young generation. He and people like him left their significant or minor marks on the character of the young men and women. These youths applied their Zionist theory in practice, not only decisively and thoroughly but also simplistically and modestly. That simplicity and modesty were evident in that group of pioneers from Zloczow, and it is still is evident today in most of its individuals. It was more apparent in its women – the daughters of Israel, for whom the traditional calm of their ancestors was swallowed by the storm of their revival.

Rivka Yeger was a member of that group of joyful youths who disembarked from the ship Karniyola at the harbor of Haifa during the heat of the [Hebrew] month of Tamuz. Like then, she embodied that incredible character of a daughter of Israel during the thirty-four years until her death. Her journey began in kibbutz Bait Gan, in the lower Galilee [Today part of the Moshava Yavniel]. It continued with the group of Zloczow pioneers [50 people out of that group joined Kibbutz Upper Beitania. The rest joined the Shomria Work Battalion, which constructed the road between Haifa and Jeda (today - the town of Ramat Yishai)]. That group preserved the idyllic atmosphere. The views in the group were not necessarily suffragist, although people were careful not to offend women. Rivka was not ashamed to work in the kitchen, preparing meals or patching clothing, like her mother and grandmother before her. A brief description of her character during those days, an image of a soft and brave young woman, was provided in the compilation "Kehilateinu" ["Our Community" - a journal first published by the Work Battalion in Upper Beitania, 1921- 22], and more broadly in the book by Yehuda Ya'ari - "Ke'Or Yahel" ["Like an Illuminating Light"].

Insomuch as one could wonder about the connection between Rivka's concealed simplicity and the asserted pride of the dozen extra-ordinary pioneers (who described themselves as sitting on an eagles' nest), one could not question why did Rivka rise, along with some of her friends, and left the group for kibbutz Makhanaim. That departure happened following some misfortunes and difficulties: the head of the Zloczow group, Dov Ofer, was killed by Arabs. The group also experienced some unemployment. That led to internal adversities (resulting in a "selection"- forcing people to leave like a sieve that selects only the best). Rivka, in her self-explained, left as a protest against the "selection", as she considered it a game people played with the lives of other people. With the same self-explained simplicity, she rejoined the group upon its subsequent expansion when the first kibbutzim of the "HaShomer Hatzair" movement were formed. She was with the group throughout all of its wanderings: starting with the road construction (on the fifth kilometer) through the establishment of the kibbutzim - Nahalal, Gevah, and Beit Alpha (participated as a member). Through all of these wanderings, her soul and body fought a disease, overcoming and surrendering alternately. The swamp fever that she dragged with her from Bet Gan weakened her body. However, she was forced to return to the diaspora and spend six years there against her will. Her longing for our land was eating her from the inside. It was more than she was willing to admit outright, but it was evident through the voraciousness of her interest in any news coming from Eretz Israel. The whiteness of the snow surrounded the city of Zloczow. I recall a trip with her to the center of her city. The truncated spoken words between us, carried away by the chilled breath, were like a scorching heatwave descending on [kibbutz] Ein Kharod in Jezreel Valley. Even the consolation of being able to plant a piece of Israel in the diaspora – she conducted fruitful educational work in Lodz (after completing studies as a kindergarten teacher in Vienna), did not satisfy her. She continued her fight, which only ended with her return to Israel. Loyal to her longing, she first tried to settle in a kibbutz. She returned to Beit Alpha. Later on, she moved to Jerusalem and worked as a kindergarten teacher at the school established by Dvorah Kallen. At that school, she was able to show her unique virtues by dedicating her soul to the children and soaking them in an atmosphere of clarity and kindness. From that period, which we spent together, I recall the mornings, which she brightened by the freshness of a folk song. I also remember the Shabbat evenings, which she sweetened with delicacies of [Shabbat] "Three Meals".

In that connection, I still remember the amusing affair about a search after a spice, which ended at an "alchemist" store in Meah Shearim". Rivka was a person who induced an incredible calm around her, which embodied more of a subdued mental turmoil than spiritual cool. At the end of her wanderings, she moved to Haifa, built her own house, and raised her children. The house was shrouded by the brightness and warmth of her grace. However, even in Haifa, she was drawn to the village, and she traveled to kibbutzim Beit Alpha and Ramat Yokhanan, and in her latest years, to kibbutz Dorot in the Negev, any time she could. Those who have not seen her during her travels have not witnessed a human being absorbing the beauty of natural scenery - a human being with a soul which was tangled between the vigor spirit and the wearied body.

[Columns 501-502]

Somewhere around [kibbutz] Alonim, she leaned against a tree trunk, tired, and her body was like a light butterfly absorbing the allure of the entire world.

The people who stood by her casket in a semicircle about a year ago formed a kaleidoscopic crowd. They came from different corners: a farmer and a cropper, a shepherd and a herdsman, an activist and a manager, an official and a teacher. They were all unified by the same feeling - that it was their sister in front of them. She was the essence and a reminder of their childhood. In their thoughts, they probably passed in front of their eyes their encounter with her. Every meeting with her felt like a budding holiday sprouting in the soil of the mundane daily life. At fifty, she was as vigor as a 20-years-old. Her tall and vulnerable stature and the warm brown eyes, which sufferings and disease could not dim, emanating a modest light, virtuous and benevolent light of wisdom that comes from the heart. That was the image of a Daughter of Israel embodied by the verse from King Solomon's song - "The mandrakes have given off fragrance, and over our door is every choice fruit, both new and old, that I have stored up for you, my lover". [Song of Songs, 7:14].

(Published in "Dvar HaPoelet" ["Female Worker Word"], January 1955)

[Columns 503-504]

Yankaleh Baumgarten

by Shlomo Altman

Translated by Moshe Kutten

In the gallery rich with folksy characters called "*Amkha*[1] people of Zloczow", the image of Yaakov Yitzkhak Baumgarten Z"L, who was called by the people Yankaleh Baumgarten, would capture an honorable position.

He was born in Zloczow in 1878 and had a difficult childhood. He received his traditional education in a "*Kheder*", finished elementary school, and continued his studies on his own.

He was forced to acquire a profession from a young age, making copper candlesticks. He worked 12 – 14 hours a day of grueling work, with his master yelling and abusing him. As a result, he developed a mental and physical resistance to any exploitation and injustice.

He started his workday early at dawn and finished it in the late hours of the night. According to stories he used to tell in later years, his employer's wife used to move the clock hands backward to elongate the workday. Despite all of that, he managed to "steal" a few priceless minutes to read a book without his employers noticing him.

In 1904, after the "Big Fire" when he was already an excellent professional, he married and moved with his wife to Chernivtsi [Tschernovitz], where he worked until 1911. Later on, he immigrated to the "Golden State" and settled in New York.

He walked the path of honesty and justice and helped others, all his life. He remembered that the needy ate at his grandfather's and father's homes, and never left hungry, even if his parents had to save the last slice of bread for their guests. He remembered that and continued in their tradition.

Yankaleh Baumgarten was known for his good deeds. He could not tolerate any abuse or injustice. We have already mentioned that he acquired that in his youth. He undoubtfully also inherited that from his grandfather. who was nicknamed "Elimelekh *Sheigetz*[2]" (in a positive sense!) due to his defense of the weak and the deprived.

During the First World War, Ya'akov Baumgarten was among the founders of the association of Zloczow's natives in New York - "Makhizikei HaDat" ["The Keepers of Religion"]. He devoted a lot of energy to that organization and donated substantially to help Zloczow's Jews. He helped Jews all his life, particularly people from his native city.

In 1919 he returned to Poland and lost all of his money in a failed business. He was forced to return to the USA to start the beginning.

In 1938 he became sick with paralysis and fought hard to overcome his illness.

He did not live any property when he died, except his good name, which deserves to be inscribed in gold letters.

His son Harry and daughters Sabina and Anna remained faithful to ancestral tradition and they continue in a public activity like their father Z"L.

Translator's Notes:

1. The every-man, everyday people, the folk (as opposed to the elite).
2. The term Sheigetz in Yiddish is used for a non-Jewish boy or young man. It is usually used disparagingly but sometimes as a compliment for a non-conforming Jew.

———

[Columns 505-506]

Dr. Yaakov Yehoshua Yosefsberg

by Mordekhai Deutsch

Translated by Moshe Kutten

Dr. Yehoshua Yosefsberg was born in Zloczow in 1892. He was the grandchild of R' Fishel Reis on his mother's side. Fishel was a descendant of the Gaon [R' Yaakov Yehoshua Falk, author of] "Pnei Yehoshua", who served as a rabbi in Zloczow and Lviv. R' Falk published books about the Shas [Six books of the Mishna] and Poskim [legal scholars].

The father of Dr. Yosefsberg, R' Zeev, was a "Talmid Khakham" [scholar student] and a prodigy. He was ordained as a rabbi at the age of 18. He educated children in the spirit of the Torah and Zionism and dreamt about making Aliya to Eretz Israel. He did not live to fulfill his dream and died at the young age of 43.

The death of the father left the family without a guide and educator, and the burden fell on the elder son, Dr. Yehoshua Yosefsberg, who helped his mother to educate his brothers and sisters.

Dr. Yosefsberg graduated from the Zloczow's high school as an extern since he refused to go to school on Shabbat and study the manners of the gentiles. Along with his secular studies, he acquired knowledge of the Torah from selected Melameds in the city. When the First World war erupted, the family wandered to Vienna. Dr. Yosefsberg was recruited there to the Austrian army and was wounded on the Italian front. At the end of the war, he registered at Vienna University, where he completed medical school. He then returned to Zloczow with his family.

Following his upbringing and his father's dream, he decided to make Aliya. He arrived in Eretz Israel, in 1925, as a physician and a pioneer. In his heart, he carried the love of the homeland and the hatred for the diaspora.

Dr. Yosefsberg worked as a physician for "Kupan Kholim" [HMO of the labor movement], in the Galilee and [Jezreel] Vallee. Riding on his horse, he endangered his life by visiting the area's Kibbutzim and Moshavim. He was known to all the settlers as a figure bringing help, comfort, and medical assistance to the sick. He performed his work tirelessly, with love, in all hours of the day and night.

In 1935 he settled in Petakh Tikva. The Galilee and Jezreel Valley's settlers were sorry to see him leaving and even sent a petition to "Kupat Kholim" to bring back their beloved physician. In Petakh Tikva, he endeared himself to all patients and worked there until his last day.

He died in May 1961 and was eulogized by many.

Dr. Yosefsberg served as the chairman of the Zloczow landsman association in Israel. Like in other roles, he did not know what half-work was. His devotion and dedication to the job were exemplary.

He once invited me to his home to talk about publishing the memorial book of Zloczow. He was exceedingly interested that the immortalization of the city would be accomplished quickly. Our discussion was held after he recovered somewhat from his illness. A few more friends came to visit him that evening. He was kind to everybody. He was interested in their health and was even ready to examine me because he said that "it has been some time since I last examined you". Who would have thought that it would be his last day? I was astonished when his son called me the following morning to tell me about his father's passing.

Dr. Yosefsberg was an exemplary father and husband. He was also an exemplary son to his widowed mother, whose life was very hard. He treated her kindly and emanated his spirit over the entire family.

He reserved a special love for Israel's capital – Jerusalem, and the Western Wall. When the idea arose, before the establishment of the State of Israel, to purchase plots of lands near the Western Wall, he was among the first people who requested to participate and even sign on banknotes at the JNF. Sadly, the idea did not come to fruition.

Dr. Yosefsberg had an additional special love for music. He played several instruments in his youth, and when he matured, he began to collect classical music and opera records. He knew every musical work by heart and used to listen to his records often.

The house of Dr. Yosefsberg in Petakh Tikva was a meeting place for scholars, music lovers, and friends from all walks of life.

With his death, we lost a good friend and a beloved landsman. Zloczow natives, pained by his death, will remember Dr. Yosefsberg and his work for a long time.

[Columns 507-508]

Dr. Kalman Shweig

by Leah Raviv

Translated by Moshe Kutten

Dr. Kalman Shweig was known and dear to any agriculturalist in the Galilee and [Jezreel] Valley. He used to visit their fields and vegetable gardens as a friend and teacher. Everybody used to gather around him and present questions such as:" How to exterminate this pest? Or "How to take care of that species?"

His head was adorned with a silver forelock for years, although he was only 60 years old when he died. His body was bent somewhat, his eyes surveying the area around him and ears tuned to listen to any questions directed at him.

His answers were encouraging and compassionate, delivered with a confident and calm voice. They showed how immense his knowledge and scientific understanding was and how close he was to the flora world.

Dr. Kalman Shweig was born in Zloczow in 1900 to a large and tradition-keeping family. When he was young, he stood out in his talents and his craving for knowledge. He fell sick in his childhood with a disease that caused a partial disability. However, his disability did not detract from his vigor, diligence, and learning ability. In later years, it did not detract from his ability to teach others.

He studied at the Ukrainian high school (when the Ukrainians ruled the city) and later at the Polish high school. He passed the matriculation exam in Zloczow in 1918.

After graduating, he was admitted to the Vianna University, where he received a doctorate in natural sciences. In parallel, he also completed studies in the English and French languages. His studies years were filled with Zionist activities. For these activities, he trained in the seminary of Rabbi Khis[?].

After completing his studies in Vienna, he served as a teacher in the Jewish gymnasium in Pinsk for several years and later in Mukcebo [Munkatch], Hungary. In 1929, he fulfilled his dream of making Aliya to Eretz Israel.

He married Nekhama [Nusya] Yosefsberg from Zloczow.

In Eretz Israel, he first worked in an agricultural school in Mikveh Israel. In 1932, he was accepted as an entomology researcher, by the [British] Mandate government, at the experimental station in Jerusalem. He was later transferred to become the manager of the experimental station in Akko.

In his work, he won the respect of his supervisors and students. He divided his time between the research work at the lab and self-observing of the plant life in Eretz Israel.

He wrote books about pests and their eradication. He published articles in agricultural journals in Israel and abroad. He also worked as a biology instructor in the Technion [Israel Institute of Technology] in Haifa.

During the War of Independence, The Haganah stooped an Arab car near his home that carried weapons. That car and its content exploded. Dr. Shweig and one of his two sons were injured, and their house was demolished. After two months of unimaginable suffering, he returned to his work.

With the establishment of the State of Israel, he became the manager of the ministry of agriculture's entomology institute. He served in that role until he died in 1958. He lived to receive, in person, the Haifa municipality's Ruppin award for his book on chemicals for the eradication of pests. The [Ruppin] Academic Agricultural College established an institute for entomology studies named after him.

His colleagues noted his culture, knowledge, and his modest and noble demeanor. May his memory be blessed.

[Columns 509-510]

Trifles from the City of Our Youth

by Dr. Eliezer Boneh (Bauman)

Translated by Moshe Kutten

The experiences of our childhood, even the tiny ones, are etched in our hearts. We bring them up here willingly since we cannot fully evaluate the present, and the future is obscure and incomprehensible.

Although 35 years after I had left my city, these experiences became blurred somewhat, they could still portray our youth (nurtured by our loving and devoted parents).

Some of my friends paved their path in life for themselves even before the Holocaust. These lines would certainly arouse longlining in them. However, others among my friends perished in the Holocaust - murdered by the Nazi human beasts. May their memory be blessed.

A. How I Met One Graceful Girl

The building of the state elementary school in Zloczow, named after [the Polish poet] Adam Mickiewicz, was divided into two wings – one for the boys and one for the girls. The school set a goal for itself to encourage social activities among the students. One of those activities was a cooperative managed by students and supervised by a teacher.

In that cooperative, students could purchase school supplies, sweets, and alike. I was chosen, along with a Christian friend, to sell pretzels at the girls' wing. And so, we stood there daily during lunch break, holding the fresh pretzels basket. Our role was enjoyable and evoked a feeling of superiority in us since the boys were usually forbidden to enter the girls' wing. We should note here that we were only 12 years old at that time.

Admittedly, most girls brought their lunches from home, and only the wealthy among them needed to purchase our pretzels. These girls knew how to show off their richness by walking along the corridor while eating their pretzel during the entire lunch break.

During one of the days of May 1925, we stood there as usual, at the girls' wing, when a graceful girl approached me. Her heartwarming smile revealed two dimples. Her brown eyes shined like two diamonds, and her dark blond hair fell down her shoulders in waves. She took a pretzel from the basket and took a bite of it with her white teeth.

Suddenly, she became pale. It turned out that she forgot her money at home and could not pay for the pretzel. My Polish friend, who was in charge of accepting the payment, began to scold and insult her. He alleged that all she wanted to do was to show off and pretend to be wealthy in front of her friends, despite not having a penny in her pocket. The girl looked down, and when she raised her head again, I saw tears in her eyes. I could not bear her humiliation. I also felt close to her, attracted by her grace and innocence. I took out the required amount and told her that she could pay me back the next day.

The "noble act" made a deep impression on her, and she rewarded me with a smile of admiration and gratitude. She did not wait for the next day and appeared in our house in the afternoon, accompanied by her mother. She thanked me again.

Since that day, we had exchanged childish admiration glimpses, which turned into a friendship. When we finally studied in the same class at the state high school in Zloczow, our friendship deepened to such an extent that every boy knew that she was not "available".

Some of the older high school students certainly tried to "steal" her from me since her grace, character, and noble manners attracted many. However, our "romance" lasted until I reached 18, despite the ups and downs in our relationships, mainly "quarrel games" due to jealousy.

In 1930, I left Zloczow to study abroad. Two years later, I left my studies at the university, and under the influence of students from Eretz Israel, I made Aliya. My connections with age group friends in Zloczow loosened, and a while later severed altogether. I received only echoes about the beauty and success of that graceful girl of my youth.

About a year before the eruption of the Second World War, I received a letter from her, when I had already struck roots in Eretz Israel, experiencing its life rhythms intensively. In that letter, she described her situation and predicted a dark future for the youth of Zloczow. She also wrote that she wanted to change her way of life and make Aliya to Eretz Israel. I encouraged her to do so. However, her doubts and indecision may have lasted too long. The war broke, and the Nazis conquered Zloczow. Among the young people who paid with their life was that graceful young woman. Her name was Ginia Blum.

[Columns 511-512]

Many of my friends would have escaped the Holocaust if they would have taken the path leading to Eretz Israel one hour earlier.

However, in our youth - the period of rejoicing and happiness, with no material concerns about material survival, who could have predicted the future?

B. The Convert Teacher

The high school in Zloczow was a Polish state school, and only a few Jewish students attended it. Although there was no official and open discrimination, a Jewish student admitted to that school could consider it a substantial achievement.

There was another high school in our city – a private Ukrainian institution. However, Jews did not study there since the level of study was low and because the teaching language was Ukrainian (and not Polish).

A new literature teacher with a typical Jewish surname arrived one day at the school. We found out quickly that the teacher was a convert who changed his religion for career reasons.

We should note that Jewish teachers were a rare occurrence in that school, except for the Jewish religious teacher. At that time, conversion to Christianity was a widespread phenomenon among Jewish teachers looking for a position at the high school. However, not all the converts intentionally antagonized the Jewish students like that literature teacher.

The Jewish students attended the Polish high school on all Shabbats and Jewish holidays, except for Rosh HaShana and Yom Kippur. And there, that teacher chose Rosh HaShana, from all other days, to lecture about Homer's epic poem Iliad. Straight after the eight Jewish students had returned to school from the holiday break, he began testing them about the poem.

His first victim was Ginia Blum. The teacher gave her a failing grade and wrote it down in his notebook. She accepted the verdict silently. However, when I realized that the teacher was not going by an alphabet order of the class students but tested only the Jewish students who were absent due to the holiday, I stood up and explained the reason for our absence. I asked for a delay of two days to prepare for the test. The teacher answered that he was not interested in Jewish holidays and demanded that I answer the question. I repeated my explanation one more time, and so did the teacher. I blabbed innocently, without any intention to insult, that teacher used to be Jewish and that he was aware of the significance of Rosh HaShana. The teacher was filled with rage and anger and sent me to the principal claiming that I was insolent.

The principal listened to the versions of the teacher and mine and ruled that I should spend eight hours of detention in school during Sunday (our day off). The punishment did not frighten me since I had already accumulated many detention hours ("Kertzer"). If I had been in Zloczow today, I would still have to complete these hours.

Yet, I was still enraged that Ginia Blum received a failing grade since she was an excellent student, and the humiliation in front of the other students hurt her. I found it to be my duty to teach that teacher a lesson.

As noted, my actions stemmed from romantic and personal reasons. However, the national spirit also played an unconscious role.

As early as the same day, I organized a few students from among my very best friends. Among that group, Olesh Mroz and Stephen Melgoshovitz were Christians, while Lunek, Linsker, Oskar, Shalit, and I were Jewish.

Although we were not all from the same class, the one thing that unified us all was the antipathy we felt toward that teacher, who showered us with failing grades.

We hid in the ally where that convert resided, equipped with a large sack. When the teacher approached, Olesh emerged from his hideout and threw the sack on top of the teacher's head. It was raining a short while earlier, and the water was still standing. The teacher panicked and fell in the mud. We threw at him rotten tomatoes, prepared in advance for that purpose. We then ran away from there.

The story would have never been discovered if not for Mroz. He boasted about it to his girlfriend, our classmate Irenka Gvendzinka. She was a beautiful girl but exceedingly talkative. She even used to talk about the card games of her father, the vice "Starosta" [District Administrator], and about the amounts of money he lost.

The five of us were ordered to appear in front of the principal in short order. We named the principal "Bidko" ["the poor guy"] because he had to solve the problems of all the students sent to him. He was a kind and pleasant person but stringent.

We denied any involvement and brought Lunek Rott, who testified that we spent the evening in his house developing pictures. The principal ordered to bring Irenka to him. However, she has been "worked on" by her boyfriend, Olesh Mroz, and denied everything.

[Columns 513-514]

We held a meeting on of the benches located at the "Kempa" [a park on top of a hill in Zloczow] to celebrate the event. In that meeting, the four girlfriends awarded Irenka with kisses for her "courage". Needless to say, that we escaped any punishment.

However, the story about the convert had a curious continuation. During the Second World War, a part of the Polish army, under the command of General Anders, arrived at Eretz Israel on their way to England, where a Polish government in exile was forming.

One day I met that convert teacher on a bus in Haifa. When I called his name, he asked me where I knew him. When I told him that I was his student in high school, he opened his heart. He told me about his hardships and suffering. He did not hide his conversion to Christianity but explained that he would fight for Poland in England. Nevertheless, he expressed his regret that he could not stay in Eretz Israel, a place he heard a lot about during his childhood.

During the bus trip, I reminded him about his treatment of the Jewish students and disclosed the identity of those who had attacked him. He pretended not to remember that e event but mumbled something about making mistakes while he was young. He said that he would have chosen another path if he could go back 35 years. I did not feel sorry for him because converted people who intentionally antagonize people of their old religion are probably incurable.

C. A Brawl Between the Poles and the Ukrainians

Three sleds tied to each other and pulled by two horses, adorned by various ornaments, went out on a traditional sled ride [Kulig in Polish] on New Year's Eve. 1928. As customary, the girls who participated in that trip took care of the food, and the boys brought blankets and musical instruments.

The girls in the group were Ceska Shotz, Etka Czyzer, Ginia Blum and Esterka Reis. The boys included Salek Parness, Lunek Linsker, Oskar Shalit, and myself. We went on our way, joyful and happy. Each boy sat behind his girlfriend. The waggoneer was a Ukrainian from the neighboring village of Sasiv. We progressed toward the Zamek [Polish for the castle] when our waggoneer suddenly stopped the horses. A group of about 12 brawling people appeared in front of us. Two Ukrainian students lie down on the ground while a group of Poles was kicking them.

The Poles Staszek Paulo and Zboczek Pshebislavski appeared to be the leaders of the group. There was a lot of commotion, and the screams of the beaten students reverberated throughout the entire area, which was not populated.

We quickly realized that the background for that brawl was the hatred that existed between the Poles and the Ukrainians. Our first concern was to ensure the safety of the girls. We left the sleds and backed away from the main road toward the nearby trees to find shelter. Our waggoneer untied the horses and ran along with one of the brawling Ukrainians toward the Poles. The horses raved and kicked the Poles, who ended up on the ground a few minutes later. All the Ukrainians ran away along with our waggoneer and his horses.

We waited a while until a complete silence descended. We came out of our hideout and turned toward the sleds. Since we were on the top of the hill, we could have easily slid down, almost to the center of the city. However, we could not realize our plan because the Poles recovered, approached our sleds, and intended to brawl with us. They thought that we sent the waggoneer and the horses toward them.

The Poles intended to repay us for the humiliation they endured at the hand of the Ukrainians. However, we avoided using any force because of the worry about the safety of the girls. The Poles knew that we were not scared. They knew us well and learned to appreciate our ability to defend ourselves.

I approached Zboczek Pshebislavski and told him to collect his friend and leave us alone. I had encountered that Pole often, on the soccer pitch, as a player for the Z. K. S. team. He played for our rivals "Yanina" team. Since we were both known as aggressive players, we reached an "understanding" of each other. Although he was a few years older than me, the sides seemed even as we had Salek Parness with us. He was tall and athletic and could block any attack.

We explained to the Poles that the waggoneer was a Ukrainian, and he ran to help his people without our knowledge. As proof, we claimed that we remained without horses. The Poles were convinced but refused to move away. In the end, Ceska intervened. Staszek Paulo was her neighbor, and his parents maintained good relations with her parents. She spoke to him softly. Paulo was known to be a thug but confronted with the charm of the pretty girl, he lost his audacity. In the end, the Poles left, and we prepared to return to the city.

Suddenly, we heard the galloping of the horses and the ringing of the bells. Our waggoneer returned. It turned out that he stood on a hill and waited for the Poles to leave. He did not want to lose the fee we promised to pay him for the trip. We were happy to see him back, as our adventure ended peacefully. When the horses responded to the whipping and began to move, we continued our trip toward Zboriv during that eventful New Year's Eve.

During the entire rest of the trip, the waggoneer did not stop explaining why he was quick to help the Ukrainian youths. At the time, we did not appreciate his reasoning since we concentrated on our enjoyment of the trip.

[Columns 515-516]

On the following day, we found out that the Poles recognized the waggoneer, who used to transport passengers from Zloczow to the train station, about 2 – 3 kilometers from the city center. They waited for him outside of his stable and attacked him and beat him to the pulp. He was collected by passersby and brought over to the hospital, where he stayed for many weeks.

When he recovered, I met him on his wagon and approached to console him. However, he did not need consolation. Although he did not specifically say so, it was apparent that he did not regret helping his allies. On the contrary, he seemed delighted.

That waggoneer endeared himself to me that day. I learned from him a chapter about solidarity with him, despite the risk for himself. That lesson stood in front of my eyes in later years, before we achieved our national independence when fights between Jews and Arabs were quite frequent.

Indeed, memories from our childhood and youth are rooted deep in ones' heart. Even decades later, they evoke many associations, although our way of life has changed from one end to another.

————

[Columns 517-518]

The Jews and the Municipal Authorities in Zloczow

by Dr. Altman

Translated by Moshe Kutten

During the days of the Austro-Hungary regime of Eastern Galitsia, Jews could serve as mayors since they were considered loyal to the empire.

A Jewish mayor served in Zloczow at the end of the First World War when the empire fell. The mayor was Dr. Yosef Guld, a successful physician and a descendant of a family of estate owners. He belonged to the assimilating intelligentsia. Even when he was elected to the Austrian parliament, he benefitted from the support of the national democratic party of the Polish population. He was a member of that party, even before Poland became independent.

Dr. Guld was respected and popular among the people since he was agile and because he took care of people regardless of their race or religion.

However, despite being an assimilator and far from the Jewish faith, he maintained relations with the famous Rabbi from Sasiv, R' Shlomo z'tz"l. He traveled to the Rabbi often and loved to talk to him.

Dr. Guld was our family physician. I recall that many years after he ceased to serve as mayor, he confessed to me that he realized, too late, that assimilation was not a solution to the Jewish problem. He also conceded that he was rescued from a total disconnect from Judaism only because of his relationship with the Rabbi of Sasiv.

That served as a consolation for him in his old age. He told me about a question he once asked the Rabbi from Sasiv, a question that showed him as a person with a good sense of humor.

One day, he passed by the Rabbi's house and decided to enter. Since the Rabbi was in good spirits, he asked him: "Why are Jews allowed to eat chickens, geese, and cows, but pigs are forbidden? While a chicken provides only eggs and meat and a cow only milk and meat, the pig provides meat, fat, skin, and guts to make strings, and even the hoofs could be used to make glue. Hence, the pig is much more useful than any of the other animals. Why are Jews forbidden to eat it?"

The Rabbi did not hesitate and replied: "Other animals provide while they are still alive, while the pig provides whatever it provides, only after its death."

Dr. Guld, the assimilating physician and famous mayor, passed away in 1940 in Lviv during the Soviet regime, poor and forgotten by the Poles and Jews alike. Nobody remembered his days of fame.

With the consolidation of the regime, after Poland had won its independence in 1918, the situation of the Jews worsened. After that time, it was very unusual for a Jew to serve as a mayor. However, due to the organization of the

Jewish nationals, many Jews managed to reach high-rank positions of deputy mayors or members of municipal councils.

In Eastern Galitsia, Jews constituted a substantial portion of the population. Also, the Poles supported Jewish candidates over the Ukrainians because of the Poles' struggle against the Ukrainians. In consequence, The Jews reached high-rank positions.

Dr. Meiblum served as the deputy mayor in Zloczow under Mayor Dr. Moszynski [or Moszcenski], about whom we should devote a few words.

Dr. Moszynski was a descendant of the noble family of the Knight Von[?] Moszynski. He began his career as a prosecutor in the civil service.

When he left that position, he settled in Zloczow and worked as a lawyer. He acquired a name of a skilled and clever jurist and endeared himself to the entire population, Jews and gentiles alike. He too liked the Jews, and he used to say that he preferred one clever Jew over ten stupid Poles. He did not hide his affection for the Jews, the poor, and the common masses. His partner was Jewish, Jewish interns worked for him, and most of his office workers were Jewish.

When I settled in Zloczow in 1925, Dr. Moszynski had already served three terms as a mayor. Since he was a brilliant speech-giver and a very active public figure in Zloczow, he succeeded in being elected as a representative to the Polish national assembly.

Very quickly, he became a central figure in the district of Ternopil, which Zloczow was part of. He was able even to remove the district governor when disagreements arose between them. The central regime had to support Dr. Moszynski because the city population supported him.

[Columns 519-520]

As mentioned, the deputy mayor was Dr. Meiblum. The deputy served as the right-hand man of the mayor and provided ideas for the city's improvement. His initiatives led to the enlargement of the power station, the construction of a beautiful stadium, and the establishment of industrial plants. Together, they made efforts to improve the roads, maintain the sports facilities, and cleanliness of the city (which was considered exceptionally clean).

Dr. Moszynski worked in complete harmony with the rest of the members of the municipal council. The [Jewish] members included Dr. Schutz, Yaakov Vilig, Yosi Tzimmer, Dr. Gruber, Dr. Prager, Khanokh Tzimmend, Monish Margalit, R' Shaul Ruler, A. Ort, Mensberg, and others. The Zionist block was always on top and contributed greatly to the development of crafts, industry, and education in the city.

In 1936 – 1937, the Moszynski – Meiblum coalition collapsed. The reason for the collapse was the disagreements between Dr. Moszynski and the district administrator, Plakhta.

The background for the disagreements was the new winds that began to blow in the political arena after the death of Pilsudski. His heirs began to drive the Jews out of high-rank positions. Poles who were supporters of the Jews suffered too. In the following election to the Sejm, Dr. Moszynski failed to preserve his seat in the parliament.

Among those who subverted against Dr. Moszynski was the priest Lagosh. He deceitfully took advantage of the disagreements between Dr. Moszynski and the district administrator. During the second half of the 1930s, he succeeded in attracting some elected Jews by promising them positions (including deputy mayor) in his municipal administration.

As a result, the rival of Dr. Moszynski, officer Bzhezinski was elected. His deputy was Dr. Hilery Tzverdling (the heir of the famous Tzukerkendel publisher and bookstore).

Following the take-over of Zloczow by the Soviets, Dr. Moszynski escaped to Lviv and secured, after a great effort, a position as a doorman for a small Polish theater. After World War II, Dr. Moszynski married the widow of the former district administrator, Mrs. Pshibislavski, who was known to be his good and intimate friend for decades.

After her death, he survived with the help of an allowance he received from her son in Katowice.

Dr. Moszynski's deputy, Dr. Meiblum, died as a martyr, during the liquidation of the ghetto, on 2 April 1943.

The Market with its Stalls

[Columns 521-522]

The Zionist Movement in Galitsia and Zloczow

by B. Tzverdling

Translated by Moshe Kutten

In 1858, the [Zionist] association "Khokhma Ve'Haskala" ["Wisdom and Education"] was founded in Zloczow. It did not last long due to resistance by zealous Hasidim,

Another Zionist association was founded in 1885 by Itamar Idelberg and Aharon Rapaport. They established a Hebrew library with a reading room containing Hebrew Journals. The objective of the association was to disseminate the knowledge of the Hebrew language. Over time that association ceased to exist.

In 1894, a gathering took place, headed by Dr. Aharonfreiz and Dr. Yehoshua Tahun. Mr. Moshe Aharon Neiger, the father of the fame Zionist activist R' Khaim Neiger, served in the steering committee established at that gathering.

Mr. Moshe Aharon Neiger was a pious Jew but educated, who dedicated himself to the Zionist movement. Thanks to him, the association "Degel Yeshurun" ["Flag of Yeshurun" – Yeshurun is a poetic name for the Jewish people], unified the best of the Haredi Jews in Zloczow. It included people like Yitzkhak Schwadron (the father of Dr. Avraham Sharon), Shmaria Imber (the brother of the poet Naftali Hertz Imber) - a teacher at the school named after Baron Hirsch, who educated the youth in the national-Zionist spirit, and Igel Barash. The association "Degel Yeshurun" managed to survive despite the resistance by the extremist Haredim.

During the Sukkot holiday of 5655 [1894], "Degel Yeshurun" held the first Zionist ball, in which the author Reuven Asher Broides, Yitzkhak Schwadron, and Khaim Neiger gave speeches.

One of the initial activities of the Zionists was the fight against the school founded by Baron Hirsch, which intentionally neglected the teaching of the Hebrew language. Rabbi Shraga Faivel Rohatyn, Shrued Garfunkel, and Tzukerkendel left the school committee in protest.

In the second election for the community leadership, in 1901, the Zionists managed to prevail over the assimilators and win in the election with four Zionists candidates: Dr. Itamar Idelberg, Fabius Leiter, the president of "A'havat Tzion" ["Love of Zion"] organization, Avraham Igel, and Shmuel Lev.

The years 1903 – 1904 were a turning point in political life in Austria and particularly in Galitsia. On the agenda was the issue of awarding the right to vote (for the Austrian parliament in Vienna and the Sejm in Galitsia) to all citizens. As a result, the Zionist movement was forced to clarify its political position.

In 1903, the Zionist movement began to spread more and more. The local political trends brought closer even circles, which previously did not show interest in Eretz Israel or exhibited any Jewish historical national orientation.

When in 1905, when Dr. Emil Bik, who served as the parliament representative from the district of Brody-Zloczow, suddenly died, the Zionist party decided to advance the candidacy of Adolf Shtand. That was how it discovered, to its surprise, that Zionism had taken roots in the hearts of the Jewish masses.

The initial [Zionist] election rallies, held in the largest halls in Zloczow, attracted large crowds and the speakers received enthusiastic applause. The Jewish leaders, who until then considered the Zionists as a gang of reckless youths, were caught off-guard in their political routines, and they began to worry about their seats.

The local authorities recognized that concern and began to impose a series of administrative restrictions according to the famous Galitsian method (like prohibiting renting the large halls for election rallies).

The assimilators chose a candidate who received the approval of the Poles and the authorities – Dr. Yosef Guld. He was a physician in Zloczow and a formal mayor and announced himself as a national-Polish candidate. The entire state apparatus was made available to him, including the means for coercion.

The support of a national Jewish representative from Chernivtsi [Tzernovitz], Dr. Benno Straukher, in the middle of the stormy campaign to the candidacy of Adolf Shtand, should be recognized. Although he was not a Zionist and his nationality was not based on any historical orientation, he was a good-hearted Jew with national dignity. These traits helped him conquer the hearts of the Jewish masses in Chernivtsi against the powerful who leaned on their wealth and social standing.

Dr. Benno Straukher considered the Zionist movement as a widely popular movement, and agreed to travel to Brody and Zloczow to support the candidacy of Adolf Shtand.

[Columns 523-524]

The Zionists took advantage of the popularity of Dr. Benno Straukher, advertised his visit, and secured a large hall for a rally. A large crowd went to greet him at the train station and accompany him to the hotel. However, when they reached the hotel, they found the doors locked with two gendarmes and a government official standing in front. They notified the crowd that the municipal sanitary committee hotel closed the hotel. They stated that the closure was because of the hotel owner's daughter, who resided on the upper floor with her family. They claimed that she fell sick with the flu, and there was a risk of transmission.

This scoundrel act by the authorities invoked anger in the crowd who wished to break into the hotel by force. Most of the anger was directed at Dr. Guld, who utilized such acts to prevent his rivals from succeeding in the election.

It was Rabbi R' Shraga Faivel Rohatyn who saved the day. The Rabbi, who was a wealthy man, notified the Zionist party that he would make his spacious apartment available for the guests. The offer was accepted with great joy, as it solved the lodging problem and symbolized a moral victory.

In actuality, there was another development resulting from that offer. Rabbi Rohatyn z"l won the hearts of the crowd and the party, which until then did not consider him a friend. The rally with Dr. Straukher ended in unprecedented success.

After the rally, the crowd lifted Dr. Straukher and carried him on their shoulders in a festive parade that ended at the house of Rabbi Rohatyn.

A [Zionist] convention was held in Lviv on 15 November 1903, headed by Dr. Pordes. Dr. Groskopf (from Zloczow) was elected as the president, and P. Kornegrin (from Ternopil) was elected as his vice. In that convention, they mainly debated about the political position of the Zionists in Galitsia and the Uganda proposal.

In 1905, when the seat occupied previously by Dr. Bik became available, a parliament representation special election for of the curia [district] of Brody – Zloczow was held. It was an opportunity for the Zionist Union to realize its political standing with the Jewish masses.

Dr. Braude was nominated as the campaign manager and Shtand as the candidate the party candidate. That was the first time that the Zionists could demonstrate their political power. The announcement itself about the Zionist candidate generated tremendous enthusiasm among the Jewish population.

The assimilators nominated the Jewish national-Polish figure, Dr. Yosef Guld as their candidate. The latter was elected as the representative to the parliament, but only with the help of forgeries and fraud.

Zloczow's Zionists - Dr. Zilberstein, and Heinrich Reitzes were elected in a secondary election in 1907. In the municipal elections of 1912, the Zionists secured three seats: Dr. Idelbergh, Dr. Groskopf, and Dr. Lansberg. Dr. H. Hirschhorn and Yitzkhak Schwadron were elected as representatives to the eleventh [1913 Zionist] Congress.

In 1911, the Zionist commercial assistances in Zloczow formed a club called "Bnei Tzion" ["Sons of Zion"]. In 1913, the "Hamizrakhi" chapter and a Union of Zionist Women were founded in Zloczow.

As mentioned, Dr. Yosef Guld won the parliament representation election. However, the election campaign served as proof that neither the assimilators nor the government circles could ignore the power of the Zionist movement.

In the meantime, winds of change began to blow as the general election for the Austrian parliament approached. That election was based on a new constitution, in which the curia-method was eliminated.

Instead, all the state citizens were awarded equal voting rights.

That political change thrilled the various parties, and all of them embarked on a feverish campaign work to consolidate their powers.

The Jews, with the Zionists included, sprung into organizational action. Since the Zionist party was young, preparing for its first major campaign, it had to make a fresh start in developing its political platform.

The [Zionist organizations] of the three Galician districts united and formed a national union. A national Galitsian committee was elected. Three people were given full authority to manage the campaign: Adolf Shtand, Gershon Tzipper, and Dr. Brodai.

The election in the Brody-Zloczow district was among the most successful. Adolf Shtand was elected with an overwhelming majority in the first round.

It would be a sin not to mention the essential role that the [Yiddish] newspaper – the "Togblatt" ["Daily Newspaper"] played in that election. The newspaper, published in Lviv, was the only newspaper that was read in every Jewish home, regardless of the orientation, from the Belz Hasidim to the assimilators. The "Togblatt" was the mouthpiece of the Zionist Union. The editor Moshe Gleinman and his chief assistant Meir Hertoner worked miracles for the campaign.

And that was how the bootlicking assimilators suffered a callosal blow while the Zionist movement was on its way to prominence.

[Columns 525-526]

Artisans and Workers in Zloczow

by Shlomo Bar-Am

Translated by Moshe Kutten

Most of the residents in Zloczow worked in commerce or business brokerage. However, some owned or worked in industrial plants (such as leather-making and vinegar production). Other workshops belonged to independent artisans.

Zloczow municipality had jurisdiction over about 70 villages that surrounded it. That resulted in good conditions for the development of workshops and artisan shops. These workshops addressed the needs of the entire Jewish and non-Jewish populations. According to my estimate, 20% of the Jews in Zloczow Jews worked in crafts, and their influence was substantial. There were also public figures who made sure to establish an umbrella organization for all the artisans – "Yad Kharutzim" ["Diligent Hand"]. The building of "Yad Kharutzim" also served as a synagogue, which unified its members spiritually.

The name itself is evidence of the skill of those artisans, and it is appropriate to raise a memorial for them.

A. Kilned Brick Producers

In 1903, a kerosene lamp fell in one of the houses, and the entire city burnt. The damages from that fire were so enormous that people began to count the days before and after "the big fire". It also affected the economy of the city. After the fire, A vigorous construction boom began, which required professionals in many construction-related fields. The capital for building the new homes became available through long-term and low-interest state mortgages.

To rebuild a city safe from any future fires, they ceased building houses from wood and began using bricks. On the southeastern side of the city, they found suitable materials for producing bricks. Jewish entrepreneurs such as Leib Fishman, Buchacher, and others arose quickly, and they established an industry of kilned brick. The area was named "Tziglana" [Tzigle = a brick in Yiddish]. Over time it became a location for trips, games, and meetings for youths. Several tens were employed in producing kilned bricks, and the industry attained substantial achievements.

B. Carpenters

Jewish craftsmen rose to fill the demand for carpenters at the newly constructed home. The established carpentry shop for producing lintels for the doors and windows. At the beginning of the 20th century, all of the carpentry work was done by hand. Almost all of the construction carpentry profession was at the hands of Jewish craftsmen. The famous carpentry shops were those of Velvel Akerman and David Kaleb (Mazor). We also should mention the carpenter Yaakov Rekht, who was also active in public affairs (during the municipal and the Austrian parliament elections). Other carpenters belonged to the Mistler and Shulder families, who also produced furniture. Some carpenters found a good living by doing repairs. Among them, we should mention Wolf Bernos.

C. Locksmiths and Tinsmiths

The locksmith workshops produced railings for terraces and staircases and also steel shutters for the stores. The better-known locksmith workshops were of Hoffman and Reuven the "Schlosser" [Locksmith in Yiddish]. The son of the latter also worked as a locksmith. Also known were the locksmiths from Daniel Zaurhof's family, whose workshop was located near the "Kempa" [park]. Most of the workshops of Zloczow's locksmiths and ironworkers were built around a large yard. The sounds of hammers poundings on the large anvils could be heard from far away.

To prevent fires the roofs were covered with tin sheets. The tinsmith industry developed as a result and branched into other needs in the house. That profession was held exclusively by Jews. They even worked in monasteries and churches. Eaves and gutters of various shapes and galvanized roof sheets were produced by artisans in the workshops.

There was also a demand for milk jugs, cooking pots, samovars, water barrels, and pails. The tinsmiths had a significant influence within the organization "Yad Kharutuzim". Some of them, like the families of Negler and Tzipper, were the leading activists of the organization. Other tinsmiths in the city were Steinhaur, Bressler, and Gruber.

D. Glaziers and Painters

To complete the discussion about crafts related to construction, we should also mention glazing and painting. Almost all of the famous glazers in our city belonged to one family – the Imber family.

[Columns 527-528]

There were also importers of glass, such as the families of Schorr and Fishel. They supplied glass to all the villages around Zloczow.

The painting was also at the hands of the Jews. They performed all painting work in Zloczow houses and the surrounding villages. The known painters were Teichman, Zusman, Shulder, Zilbershitz, Pepper, and others.

E. Eggs Sorting and Packaging

As mentioned, Zloczow was located in a large agricultural area. One of the occupations held by Jews was related to chicken growing. A few Jewish families owned egg warehouses. These families were also engaged in sorting, packaging, and marketing eggs. The following families excelled in that occupation: Mansberg, Tenenbaum, Nusan, Teibeh, Kirshen, Shmeterling, Meir, Bozes, and others. They used to purchase enormous amounts of eggs from the neighboring farmers and market some to Germany. Surpluses were stored in lime water. Every egg was tested under a flashlight to check for any defects. Egg-sorting methods were not developed in those days, and the packaging method was quite primitive. However, professional know-how was required, and the Jews were very successful in that field.

F. Bakeries

Another occupation developed by Zloczow's Jews was baking. The owners of the bakeries in the city were: Peres, Bauman, Kaczik, Ettinger, Faivil "the Baker", and others. These bakeries employed many Jewish workers. The occupation was not mechanized, and everything was done by hand. However, the products were of high quality. All sorts of bread, rolls, and other baking products were produced in these bakeries.

The cakes were exceptionally very well known. They were baked by women who made a name for themselves. Among them were Bluma 'di Bakrin" ["the baker"], Krintzki, Dvora Schorr, and Khaya-Sara Masher, the wife of Shimale the waggoner.

They obviously baked *matzot* in Zloczow. They would make the oven Kosher for Passover, immediately after Purim, or built special ovens for that. The work progressed day and night. *Matzot* were supplied not only to Zloczow's Jews but to the entire rural area. The baked *matzot were* of various shapes: square, round, and *Matza Shmura*. Many Jews made a living in that occupation.

G. Meat, Fish, and Milk

The supply of meat for the Jewish population came from the slaughtering of chickens and cows. The slaughterers were: Gedalia, Nakhtzi, and Yankle. They ensured that the slaughtering followed the Kosher rules. The meat was sold by Jewish butchers, among them the families: Ox, Wiederhorn, Schwadron, and others. Other workers that were employed in these butcher shops included purgers, skinners, and delivering people.

There were no fish in the Zlotzovska – the small stream that flew in our city. They were brought from great distances, from lakes and rivers. They were stored in wooden barrels in the river, not far from the road that led to Brody. The families of Shustak and Krug worked in that occupation which required substantial oversight, sorting, and marketing the fish.

We should also mention the milk distributors in our city, most of which were women. Ester-Golda, Shibi, Spodek, Shpetz, and others could be seen loaded with milk jugs in the morning, hurrying up to distribute the priceless liquid. Years later, the milk distribution was done by the farmers themselves, and the occupation disappeared.

H. Tailoring and Shoemaking

Another craft held by Zloczow's Jews was tailoring. Some tailors produced new clothing from measures, and others worked in mending and alterations. Some tailors sew suits from journal patterns, and others specialized in women's clothing. Among the distinguished tailors was Zalman Lifshitz. Everybody marveled at his ability to tailor clothes that fit the body measurements. Other tailors were Nadel, Tzvikle, Tabak, and Shpringrol. The distinguished seamstresses were: Yiti, Bintzi, Rozhi, and Pepper.

Except for suits and dresses, the tailors also made undergarments. Etil "di Schvetzkeh" ["the perspiring"], was the one who made the new brides, their undergarments.

Shoemaking was also a common occupation in our city. Avigdor "di Shuster" ["the Shoemaker"], Moshe Fein, and Hekht, sew, repaired, and sold shoes. They were all outstanding craftsmen. There were also some shoe stores for which shoes were imported from larger cities. However, their owners were shopkeepers rather than craftsmen.

I. Barbers and Watchmakers

Some barbers considered themselves "physician assistants" because they laid cupping glasses and leeches, and extracted teeth.

[Columns 529-530]

Some barbers were called "der Rofeh" ["the Doctor"], such as the brothers Lercher, Meginzi, and others. Known barbers in our city were Leider, Fergangk, and Lubek.

Yekhiel Blumenthal worked in watchmaking and Jewelry. He bent over the complicated mechanism of watches until he reached old age. He was also responsible for the clock on the church tower. The families of Weis, Kromkhel, Mesher, and others also worked as watchmakers-Jewelers. There were many jewelry stores in the city, selling all sorts of watches. One could see the watchmakers doing their work through the display windows, with a watchmaker's magnifying glass stuck in their eye.

J. Turnery, Printing, Cobbling

Wood and metal turnery was one of the occupations in Zloczow. The turnery workshop of Hersch Mesher produced pestles, hammers, candlesticks, weights, and the like. The man was a true professional, and he left the workshop for his son, who modernized it and introduced machinery. After them, Avrumtzi Avend continued in that profession. He was known by his nickname "der Leichter Macher" ["the lighter maker"], but he also produced weights and exported them outside of Zloczow.

The wood turnery belonged to the family Dreksler. They produced creative work despite the primitive machines.

A few printing houses existed in Zloczow. The most famous one (known outside of Zloczow) was the printing house of the Tzukerkendel. They printed textbooks and science books. There was also an advanced printing house that belonged to the Landsberg family and a smaller one of the Zaltz family.

The cobbler shops were concentrated on "Cobblers Street". Jewish artisans worked there to produce various accessories such as saddles, harnesses, and the like. Many Jewish artisans worked in cobbling, including the Akselrod, Pfau, and other families. The customers of the cobbling shops were the owners of the carriages and wagons, who were numerous in Zloczow.

K. Conclusion

I have not mentioned all of the craftsmen and workers of our city because the list is long, and the number of occupations is vast.

For example, I did not mention the bookbinders (the most prominent was Bukhbinder, whose name pointed to his occupation). I also did not mention the water carriers: Yosa'le "der Vassertreiger" ["water carrier" in Yiddish], Barukh "Behemeh" ["the animal" in Yiddish], Hershel'leh Mattes, and Henili Fauker. They were all figures that the entire city knew. I did not mention the midwife, nicknamed "di bobeh", ["grandmother"], who helped in the birthing of generations of children. I also did not mention the gravestone engravers who performed their work with reverence.

There was a city, and its name was Zloczow. Thousands of artisans and workers lived and worked there. These lines, which I devoted to the various occupations, serve as an eternal memorial for them.

———————

[Columns 531-532]

Some Quality Characteristics of My Teacher R' Israel Mashir Z"L

by B. Tzverdling

Translated by Moshe Kutten

In 1905, the parents' committee in our city headed by Shmuel Weldinger, Mendel Weintraub, Nathan Negelberg, Mordekhai Semel-Tzverdling (my father Z"L), Israel Wolfshoit, and Moshe Auerbach, established a General Kheder [Kheder with general studies], under the management of our enlightened R' Israel Mashir Z"L.

The Kheder was situated in the house of Lemel Mestil. Hundreds of students studied in it.

R' Israel Mashir taught Bible, Hebrew, grammar, and Jewish history.

He was an extraordinary figure. A Torah scholar with general and secular education. He was observant of religion in all of its minute details and was involved with people. Seemingly these were contradictions, but they all blended and fitted him.

He understood the value of Jewish education and continuously acted to maintain it. He emanated his image onto his many students, some are in Israel, and others are abroad. Every one of these students is grateful for the privilege of being his student because he was not only a teacher, but also an advisor, and source of encouragement love, help, and guidance.

He had a majestic appearance. His long beard cascaded down, and his eyes shone with the glow of youth and the wisdom of the aged.

He was flushed with profound ideas, and his goal was to tie the souls of his students to the Book of Books.

R' Mashir taught us that the bible is a treasure of souls, solaces, and memories. He also taught that hundreds of generations sacrificed their lives for every letter in it.

We will remember R' Israel Mashir, and we will continue on his path.

———

[Column 533]

In memory of Malka Akselrod

by Khana Laks

Translated by Moshe Kutten

Malka Axelrod

[Column 534]

Malka Axelrod, daughter of Meitah, was known for her charity and enthusiastic assistance to the needy.

She and her family left Zloczow on their way to America a few years before the First World War. In America, she became an institution of one person. She provided support and aid to all Zloczow natives. She also helped her city natives from afar.

She was not wealthy. She became a widower at a young age and had to grow six children. Despite that, people can tell legends about her willingness to help others.

Malka Akselrod used to visit and collect donations from wealthy families and distribute the money among those who needed it while taking their steps in a new land. Alas to those who remained in Zloczow.

May her memory be blessed.

[Columns 535-536]

Yehuda Zilbershitz

by Member of Knesset, Yaakov Katz

Translated by Moshe Kutten

The organization of Zloczow's natives was very active thanks to the donations of our city natives in the US.

That "relief" assistance encompassed all charity and philanthropy activities, which the needy benefited from, particularly the new immigrants – the Holocaust survivors.

The founders of the organization included: Yehuda Zilbershitz (Aviel) Z"L, Dr. Reuven Shwager Z"L, Yekhiel Imber Z"L, Dr. Yosefsberg, and the members of the committee.

Yehuda Zilbershitz was the life of the organization. He personally took care of anybody who appealed to the organization.

He did not rest and did not stay quiet and continuously urged the heads of the "Relief" people in the USA and Zloczow landsmen in Eretz Israel to volunteer for substantiative deeds.

Yehuda Zilbershitz excelled in his kind and charitable heart and in his agility. He was horrified by the poor state of the Holocaust survivors, the remnants of the Zloczow people, who arrived in Eretz Israel, naked and destitute. However, he did not neglect the affairs of Zloczow natives who were already in Eretz Israel for some time.

He took care of the affairs of the needy, arranged loans, and saved them from distress.

Everybody found an attentive ear by him because he performed his role readily and with great diligence.

He would tirelessly go from one person to another, travel between the needy and the committee, present the appeals, and propose ways to address the needs of the poor.

He did not only maintain relations with our brothers and sisters in the US but also succeeded in persuading them to visit Eretz Israel and witness the situation with their own eyes.

As a native of Zloczow, he felt a deep mental impulse to help people in need.

Yehuda Zilbershitz made Aliya to Eretz Israel in the 1920s because of his enormous affection for Zion. He suffered from malaria in Eretz Israel and was forced to return to Zloczow for health reasons. However, he could not stay in Zloczow for long. Despite enjoying a stable social and economic status, because he was the son-in-law of R' Elkanah and the son of R' Khaim Moshe Zilbershitz, he abandoned all of that. Along with his wife Malka (may she have a long and good life) and his two daughters and son, he made Aliya again.

He worked in jobs, which overtasked him, but he did not let the difficulties overwhelm him.

He absorbed much of the spirit of Zionism he was imbued with, from his father - the Torah scholar, author, and great educator, R' Khaim Moshe Z"L. For his part, Yehuda Zilbershitz conferred that spirit to his children.

With time he reached a state of rest and security. He educated his children to live a life of work and fulfillment and also succeeded to establish a business with his wife in Tel Aviv.

He was still young and full of vigor and dedicated to Zloczow's immigrants when he fell sick and became bedridden, from which he had never gotten up.

He left a significant inheritance – the organization of Zloczow's natives to which he devoted a good part of his heart.

May his good deeds serve as an eternal gravestone in his grave, and may his memory be blessed!

[Page 537]

My Memories of Zloczow

by Shlomo Buchacher

Translated by Gloria Berkenstat Freund

The *shtetele* [small town] Zloczow will forever
Remain in my memory
There where I spent
My most beautiful childhood years.

I also will never forget
The small house of pasted lime
Where I lived
Happy and content with my mother.

It is impossible to describe
Her devotion
She would have gone
Through fire and water for me.

She did not close her eyes
The entire night
When I was sick
Or felt bad.

She sat the entire time
Bent over my bed
Did not take from me
Her tear-filled eyes.

Her words still
Ring in my ears;
I should have your pain
My dear, dear child.

Fate wanted
To separate me from my home

Cast me to Russia
Thousands of miles away.

[Page 538]

I lived there
In poverty and in need
Through entire weeks
I did not see a piece of bread.

And, after hearing
Cruel news from my home
My bed was
The cold, naked ground.

Life was so ugly
Death was preferable
Only the small spark of hope
Kept me on my feet.

That perhaps I would
Travel home to my mother
And with her as before
Again be happy together.

I consoled myself
Did not want to believe
In the dreadful news
Written in the newspapers.

It was impossible
That people could
Burn alive
Innocent children.

Bury them alive?
This must be a lie
Because the entire world
Would not have been silent about it.

———————

[Columns 539-540]

Memorial Service for Zloczow's Martyrs

by B. Tzverdling

Translated by Moshe Kutten

Dear friends who gathered here today!

The committee of Zloczow landsmen tasked me to eulogize the martyrs of our city, may G-d avenge their blood.

It is impossible to evaluate, with a clear mind, what the Nazis did to the Jews.

From a psychological and educational point of view, we should not overdo the unwrapping of the scroll of the Holocaust, lest the despair and desperation would haunt the mental powers of our nation. The extent of the slaughter and the lack of restrains in executing it – cannot withstand any scientific scrutiny and stand counter to common sense. The cruelty organized by a meticulous bureaucracy, the feeble resistance by the prosecuted, and the unwillingness of the western powers to intervene on their behalf combined into a horrible tragedy.

If we ask, what is the difference between that Holocaust and other holocausts that befallen our nation, the answer would be - the coolness by which the order to murder masses of people was issued. In that sense, there is no precedence to Hitler's period in the history of the world.

During the war criminals' trials in Nirenberg, Judge Robert Jackson said: "There is no precedent in history, for a crime, which was executed against so many victims, with such a calculated cruelty".

Zloczow was among the cities and towns, which were totally destroyed, uprooted from the earth. That was a glamorous city, famous for its glory, that produced Torah scholars and distinguished people of wisdom and talent. We stand today, hunched over and gloomy, on the ruins of the city and the graves of its people, old and young. We, the remnants who survived the inferno, stand here with our eyes tearing over our dear ones, who gave their lives as martyrs for the sanctification of G-d.

We gathered here today on the anniversary of the ghetto liquidation and mourn and pain over the memory of parents, brothers and sisters, and teachers.

Our loss is enormous, but we are determined to erect an eternal memorial to the Zloczow community in a memorial book in which we will tell future generations what the evil oppressor did to our people.

May their souls be bound up in the souls of the living, and may their memory live for eternity.

Yizkor Pages

Transcribed by Linda Richman

Family name	First name(s)
ALTMAN	Josef Nehamia
ALTMAN	Rachel
ALTMAN	Peshi
ALTMAN	Szraga Feiwish
ALTMAN	Reizel
ALTMAN	Miriam
ALTMAN	Ita
ALTMAN	Frida
APFELBAUM	Szlomo
APFELBAUM	Mordhai
APFELBAUM	Beile
APFELBAUM	Bracha
AMER	Wolf
AMER	Leah
AMER	Shmuel
AWERBACH	Abraham
AWERBACH	Shalom
AWERBACH	Libe
AMBUS	And family
AKSELROD	Wolf
AKSELROD	Malka
AKSELROD	Azriel
AKSELROD	Benjamin, Dr.
ABEND	Awraham
ABEND	Sheindel
ABEND	Joel

BAUMAN	Moshe
BAUMAN	Haje Ita
BAUMAN	Motyl
BAUMAN	Syma
BATISZ	Ester
BATISZ	Israel
BATISZ	Gitel
BATISZ	Chaim
BATISZ	Shlomo
BATISZ	Clara
BATISZ	Sara
BATISZ	Michal
BATISZ	Gedalia
BATISZ	Szancie
BATISZ	Awraham
BATISZ	Fajwel
BATISZ	Basia
BATISZ	Dawid
BARDACH	Israel Wolf
BARDACH	Reisel
BARDACH	Klara
BARDACH	Chaim
BARDACH	Zalman Eliezer
BARDACH	Herman
BARDACH	Jakob
BRANDES	Izydor
BRANDES	Beti
BRANDES	Josef
BRANDES	Rywka
BRANDES	Jeshayahu
BRANDES	Chana

BUTERMAN	Dawid
BUTERMAN	Ester
BUTERMAN	Lewy
BUTERMAN	Berl
BUTERMAN	Benjamin
BUTERMAN	Hirsh
BUTERMAN	Jakob
BAUMGARTEN	Markus
BAUMGARTEN	Hersh
BAUMGARTEN	Sali
BAUMGARTEN	Jakob
BAUMGARTEN	Meilech
BRUCK	Ester Chaje
BRUCK	Meir Leib
BILLIG	Anna
BILLIG	Awraham
BILLIG	Feiga
BILLIG	Nachman
BARER	Nachman
BARER	Chaja
BYSTRYCKI	N.
BOKSER	M.
BUCZACIER	Izchak
BUCZACIER	Zamach
BUCZACIER	(Bar Am) Rywka
BLUM	Ginia
BLAUSTEIN	Natan
BLAUSTEIN	Batie
BLAUSTEIN	Ahron
BROJDE	Aleksander
BROJDE	Pnina

BROJDE	Henia
BROJDE	Mina
BROJDE	Mordehai
BERNHOLZ	Feiwash
COHEN	Gita
COHEN	Miriam
CHODAK	Dawid
CHODAK	Nachman
CHUTINER	Lisa
CHUTINER	Moshe
CHUTINER	Keile
CHUTINER	Liebe
CHARY	Salo
CHARY	Paulina
CZYZER	Etka
DRETEL	Joel
DRETEL	Amalia
DRETEL	Mina
DIAMAND	Zelig
DIAMAND	Wolf
DIAMAND	Taube
DISTENFELD	Feige
DISTENFELD	Israel
DISTENFELD	Taube
DUBOWY	Moshe
DUBOWY	Clara
DUBOWY	Ita
DAWIDSOHN	Izhak Arya
DAWIDSOHN	Sara
DAWIDSOHN	Tola
DEUTSCH	Gitel

DOLLNER	Ahron
DOLLNER	Melech
DAUBER	Wolf
EICHENSTEIN	Ratse
EICHENSTEIN	Jitzhak
EICHENSTEIN	Alta
EISEN	Zwi Hirsh
EISEN	Riwka
EISEN	Dr. Moshe
EISEN	Giza
EISEN	Riwkale
EISEN	Chaja
EISEN	Malka
ERBSEN	Michal
ERBSEN	Jakob
ERBSEN	Basha
EPSTEIN	Dr. Shmuel
EPSTEIN	Dr. Mundyk
EIDELBERG	Malka
EIDELBERG	Josef
EIDELBERG	Rosa
EIDELBERG	Beno
EIGER	Baruch
EIGER	Azriel
ETTINGER	Chana
ETTINGER	Witel
ETTINGER	Clara
ETTINGER	Sane
ETTINGER	Zipora
ETTINGER	Rachel
ETTINGER	Jente

ETTINGER	Israel
ETTINGER	Jehoshua
ETTINGER	Riba
EHRENPREIS	Nathan
EHRENPREIS	Herman
FRENKEL	Jehuda
FRENKEL	Dwojre
FRENKEL	Ruven
FRENKEL	Mordash
FRENKEL	Henoch
FRENKEL	Moshe
FRENKEL	Chana
FRENKEL	Daniel
FRENKEL	Elka
FRENKEL	Roza
FRENKEL	Riwka
FRIEDMAN	Chana
FRIEDMAN	Klarcia
FRIEDMAN	Dorcia
FRIEDMAN	Giza
FRIEDMAN	Herman
FILLER	Rachel
FILLER	Jakob Pinchas
FEURING	Leib
FEURING	Heshi
FEURING	Ester
FREIMAN	Avniel
FREIMAN	Philip
FREIMAN	Jehoshua
FREIMAN	Wilo
FURGANG	Zeev

FISCHEL	Sprinze
FISCHEL	Israel
FENSTER	Izhak
FENSTER	Sara
FENSTER	Regina
FENSTER	Mina
FRIED	Zlata
FRIED	Jakob
FISHER	Abraham
FISHER	Chana
FISHER	Molly
GRUBER	Isaak Leib
GRUBER	Samuel
GRUBER	Leiza
GRUBER	Shmuel
GRUBER	Chana
GRUBER	Izhak Mordehai
GRUBER	Hirsh
GRUBER	Jakob
GRUBER	Zwi
GRUBER	Nachman
GRUBER	Roza
GRUBER	Meier
GRUBER	Dr. and family
GRUBER	Fani
GRUBER	Bunie
GRUBER	Funia
GRUBER	Lea Miriam
GERBEL	Leizer
GENZER	Jona
GENZER	Helena

GRUMEL	Ida
GELLER	Jakob
GELLES	Rose
GELLES	Samuel
GOLDBLATT	Rachela
GOLDBLATT	Daniel
GRINSHPAN	Malka
GRINSHPAN	Moshe
GRINSHPAN	Rivkele
GROSKOPF	Berish
GROSKOPF	Chancze
GROSKOPF	Feige
GROSKOPF	Moshe
GROSKOPF	Aron
GROSKOPF	Shalom
GROSKOPF	Jerucham
GROSKOPF	Josef
GROSKOPF	Frida
GLEICHER	Nachum
GLEICHER	Feige
GLEICHER	Meier
GLEICHER	Abysh
GLEICHER	Jakob
GLEICHER	Ester
GOLDBLAT	Rachel
GOLDENBERG	Brane
GOLDENBERG	Emil
GOLDENBERG	Berta
GOLDSTEIN	Manek
GOLDSTEIN	Regina
GOLDSTEIN	Jakob

GOLDSTEIN	Lonck
GOLDSTEIN	Peshy
GOLDSTEIN	Edzio
GOTTWORT	Erna
GOTTWORT	Lusio
GOTTWORT	Regina
GOTTWORT	Henryk
GLANZ	Leizer
GLANZ	Tania
GLANZ	Artur
GOTTESMAN	Israel
HALPERN	Rachel
HALPERN	Naftali
HALPERN	Moshe
HALPERN	Pepi
HALPERN	Josef
HELIN	Wolf
HELIN	Nusia
HELIN	Asher
HOCHMAN	Awraham
HOCHMAN	Shifrah
HOCHMAN	Ahron
HOCHMAN	Shlomo
HOCHMAN	Fani
HOROWITZ	Chaim
HOROWITZ	Brane
HOROWITZ	Ira
HOROWITZ	Itamar
HOROWITZ	Shlomo
HOROWITZ	Chaja
HOROWITZ	Zwi Hersh

HOROWITZ	Brunie
HOROWITZ	Ryvkaly
HOROWITZ	Julius
HOROWITZ	Nachum
HOROWITZ	Klara
HOROWITZ	Feige
HOROWITZ	Samuel
HOCHBERG	David
HOLLÄNDER	Joshe
HOLLÄNDER	Frime
HOLLÄNDER	Chaje
HOLLÄNDER	Ronia
HOLLÄNDER	Shmuel
HELLER	Jona
HELLER	Paula
HUNGER	Mina
HUNGER	Aron Leib
HUNGER	Sheindel
HUNGER	Hirsh
HUNGER	Moshe
HUNGER	Zalel
HUNGER	Mordhai
HUNGER	Mendel
HUNGER	Miriam
HENIS	Awraham
HENIS	Syma
HENIS	Dr. Adela
HENIS	Jakob
HENIS	Zelina
HENIS	Jehuda
HENIS	Ester

HENIS	Shoshana
HUBEL	Chana
HUBEL	Meier
HUBEL	Lola
HUBEL	Klara
HOFFMAN	Mindel
HOFMAN	Awraham
HOFMAN	Beile
HOFMAN	Leibysh
HOFMAN	Rachel
HOFMAN	Regina
HERMAN	Bernard
HERMAN	Dudek
HERMAN	Klara
HERMAN	Amalia
HERMAN	Michael
HERMAN	Giza
IMBER	Shalom
IMBER	Sara
IMBER	Shoshana
IMBER	Towa
JULEK	Dr. Marek
JEKES	Sheindel
JEKES	Israel
JUNG	Josef
JUNG	Shoshana
JUNG	Mali
JÄGER	Chana
JÄGER	Moshe Eisik
KAPHAN	Jeshaiahu
KAPHAN	Miriam

KAPHAN	Eliezer
KAPHAN	Leibis
KAPHAN	Nusia
KAPHAN	Shmuel
KAPHAN	Zwi
KATZ	Laura
KATZ	Klara
KATZ	Israel
KATZ	Gedalia
KATZ	Reisie
KATZ	Welwel
KATZ	Jehuda
KATZ	Pesach Zwi
KATZ	Perl
KATZ	Benjamin
KATZ	Zahava
KATZ	Sara
KATZ	Chaje
KATZ	Israel
KATZ	Awraham
KATZ	Izhak
KATZ	Sofia
KATZ	Arye
KATZ	Leib
KATZ	Brane
KATZ	Eliakim Jeshaya
KATZ	Michal Jehiel
KATZ	Scheindel
KATZ	Adam
KAHANE	Moshe
KAHANE	Zalman

KAHANE	Chana
KAHANE	Cyla
KACZEK	Wolf
KACZEK	Dzivnck
KACZEK	Markus
KRIEG	Berish
KRIEG	Shiesel
KRIEG	Michel
KRIEG	Lea
KRIEG	Jakob
KRIEG	Ester
KORNFELD	Psachie
KALAFE	Zeev
KLEID	Shymon
KANER	Pinchas
KANER	Sara
KUPPER	Rachel
KIRSCHEN	Herzel
KIRSCHEN	Beile
KIRSCHEN	Shmuel
KIRSCHEN	Mendel
KIRSCHEN	Chana
KIESSEL	Dwora
KIESSEL	Jehiel
KLUG	Sara
KLUG	Elles
KITAJ	Josef
KITAJ	Laura
KITAJ	Dzinka
KITAJ	Ignacy
KITAJ	Isaac

KITAJ	Cyla
KITAJ	Adam
KITAJ	Oskar
KITAJ	Helena
KITAJ	Zygmund
KITAJ	Olek
KORSH	Isidor
LEBER	Jehuda
LEBER	Lea
LEBER	Chawa
LEBER	Shlomo
LEWINTER	Emanuel
LEWINTER	Riba
LEWINTER	Zwi
LEWINTER	Zelig
LEWINTER	Chana
LAUFER	Shlomo
LIFSHITZ	Berish
LIFSHITZ	Leib
LIFSHITZ	Helen
LIFSHITZ	Rachel
LIFSHITZ	Zalman
LIFSHITZ	Iser
LIFSHITZ	Hirsh
LIFSHITZ	Ester
LIFSHITZ	Lipshe
LIFSHITZ	Meier
LIFSHITZ	Joel
LIFSHITZ	Zelig
LIFSHITZ	Beile
LIFSHITZ	Jeti

LIFSHITZ	Dawid
LERCHER	Dwojre
LERCHER	Jitzhak
LERCHER	Chaim Shmuel
LERCHER	Lipe
LANG	Hencze
LANG	Pinchas
LAUER	Bezalel
LAUER	Sara
LAUER	William
MANDEL	Shlomo Maltes
MANDEL	Shalom
MANDEL	Jakob
MANDEL	Gitel
MANDEL	Etel
MANDEL	Josef
MANDEL	Regina
MANDEL	Jente
MANDEL	Dow
MANDEL	Chaje
MANDEL	Shmuel-Josef
MASS	Jakob
MÜNZ	Psachie
MÜNZ	Herman
MEIER	Liepe
MEIER	Frieda
MEIER	Shlomo
MEIER	Rojse
MEIER	Nachum
MEIER	Miriam
MEIER	Ester

MEIER	Izhak
MEIER	Faiwish
MEIER	Natan
MEISELS	Samuel
MEISELS	Neche
MEISELS	Doncia
MESHER	Chaje Sara
MINDLIN	Taube
MARKUS	Wolf
MAJBLUM	Dr. Zygmund
MEIBLUM	Henek
MEIBLUM	Flora
MORBERG	Jehuda
MORBERG	Bluma
MORBERG	Natan
MORBERG	Moshe
MORBERG	Mina
MARDER	Wiktor
MARDER	Moshe
MARDER	Chawa
MANSBERG	Jehuda
MANSBERG	Henia
MANSBERG	Edgar
MANSBERG	Helena
MANSBERG	Gusla
MANSBERG	Asher
MANSBERG	Ina
MANSBERG	Klara
MANSBERG	Joel
MANSBERG	Rywka
MANSBERG	Regina

NAGLER	Jakob
NAGLER	Cyla
NAGLER	Dr. Mina
NAGLER	Frieda
NAGLER	Elies Hersh
OPER	Anna
OPER	Professor Jakob
OPER	Lea
OPER	Leon
OPER	Lilit
OPER	Dow
OEHIL	Arnold
PFAU	Chanania
PFAU	Berl
PFAU	Taube
PFAU	Genia
PFAU	Ordi
PFAU	Salka
PINKAS	Frieda
PINKAS	Chaim
PINKAS	Rosa
PRESSTADT	Aron
PASTERNAK	Regina
PFEFERSTEIN	Hersh
PFEFERSTEIN	Regina
PUNDYK	Mechel
PUNDYK	Hudie
PUNDYK	Josef
PREIS	Ida
PREIS	Natan
PREIS	Shalom

PREIS	Meier
PREIS	Zosla
PREIS	Moshe
PREIS	Ester-Malka
PECZENIK	Riwka
PECZENIK	Pepka
PECZENIK	Saul
PECZENIK	Munio
PECZENIK	Pepe
PECZENIK	Moshe Leib
PARNESS	Sheindel
PARNESS	Aron
PARNESS	Jetta
PARNESS	Psachie
PARNESS	Jakob
PARNESS	Frieda
PARNESS	Bluma
PARNESS	Salek
PARNESS	Hasia
PULWER	Rachel
PULWER	Wolf
PRESSMAN	Jakob
PILSNER	Azriel
PILSNER	Ester
PRÄGER	Izhak
PRÄGER	Towa
PRÄGER	Moshe
PRÄGER	Zlate
PRÄGER	Efraim
PRÄGER	Emila
PRÄGER	Zipora

PRÄGER	Regina
POLAK	Jakob
POLAK	Adela
PODOSHYN	Herman
PERSINER	Brayne
PASTERNAK	Shlomo
PASTERNAK	Josef
PASTERNAK	Beile
PASTERNAK	Chaim
PASTERNAK	Miriam
ROSEN	Wolf
ROSEN	Fani
ROSEN	Gete
ROSEN	Jakob-Jehuda
ROSEN	Brajne
ROSEN	Wawe
ROSEN	Feiga
ROSEN	Israel
ROSEN	Meilich
ROSEN	Sabina
ROSEN	Maks
ROSEN	Gitel
ROSEN	Roza
ROSEN	Pepi
ROSEN	Josefina
ROSEN	Irena
ROSEN	Awraham
ROSEN	Lote
ROSEN	Bela
ROSEN	Jakob-Leib
ROSENMAN	Rina

REICHENSTEIN	Simcha
REICHENSTEIN	Chawa
ROTSTEIN	Ronia
ROTSTEIN	Tamar
ROTSTEIN	Maks
ROTE	Philip
ROTE	Enstina
ROTE	Dr. Josef
ROTE	Gerta
ROTE	Janek
ROTE	Isidor
ROTE	Betka
ROSENBERG	Wolf
ROSENBERG	Isak
ROSENBAUM	Jehuda
RECHT	Jakob
RECHT	Klara
RECHT	Leon
RECHT	Israel
RECHT	Anna
RECHT	Mania
REIS	Moshe
REIS	Beile
REIS	Jakob
REIS	Israel
REIS	Elkona
REIS	Joshe
REIS	Janek
REIS	Pepka
REIS	Esterka
REISER	Izhak

REISER	Elka
REISER	Rywka
REISER	Awraham
REISER	Shalom
REISER	Feivel-Shraga
REISER	Chana
REISER	Beile
REISER	Ruti
REISER	Ester
REISER	Shalom
REISER	Eliezer
RINGEL	Isack
SMAL-ZWERDLING	Mordhai
SMAL-ZWERDLING	Eidel
SMAL	Pepci
SALITER	Moshe
SALITER	Erna
SALITER	Josef
SALITER	Herman
SALITER	Sheno
SALITER	Leo
SAFRAN	Simcha
SAFRAN	Shava
SAFRAN	Hilel
SOBEL	Herman
SHMETERLING	Shlomo
STERN	Helena
STERN	Shimon
SCHWADRON	Chana
SCHWADRON	Pesach
SHUSTER	Chaim Leib

SHUSTER	Gitel
SHUSTER	Rosa
SHUSTER	Benjamin
SHUSTER	Klara
SHUSTER	Hersh
SHUSTER	Mina
SHALIT	Dr. Racha
SHALIT	Dawid Meier
SHALIT	Awraham Pinchas
SHALIT	Chana
SHALIT	Moshe
SHALIT	Dawid
SHALIT	Jite
SHWAGER	Fishel
SHWAGER	Matel
SHWAGER	Jakob
SHWAGER	Shalom
SHWAGER	Rachel
SHWEIG	Benjamin Dawid
SHWEIG	Ester Brane
SHWEIG	Dr. Josef
SHWEIG	Hala
SHWEIG	Bernard Dov
SHNEE	Maks
SHNEE	Chaje
SHAPIRA	Eisig Manes
SHAPIRA	Jenty
SHAPIRA	Baruch
SHAPIRA	Bince
SHAPIRA	Jechiel
SHAPIRA	Chana

SHAPIRA	Chaja
SHAPIRA	Chaim
SHAPIRA	Moshe
SHAPIRA	Efraim
SHAPIRA	Chawa
SHAPIRA	Chaim Meier
SHAPIRA	Lea
SHAPIRA	Pinchas Fishel
SHAPIRA	Izyk-Leib
SHAPIRA	Rachel
SILBERSHITZ	Josef
SILBERSHITZ	Jizhak
SILBERSHITZ	Srul
SHNITZER	Helen
SIVERSTEIN	Nachum
SCHOR	Israel
SCHOR	Mila
SCHOR	Giza
STOLZENBERG	Emil
STOLZENBERG	Zeev
STOLZENBERG	Jakob
STOLZENBERG	Chana
STOLZENBERG	Lola
SPITZER	Roza
SPITZER	Arye
SPITZER	Chana
SHULDER	Dr. Israel
SHULDER	Izhak
SHULDER	Mordehai
SHMOTEF	Meir
SHMOTEF	Bela

SHMOTEF	Henryk
SHREIBER	Anshel
SHREIBER	Liebe
STRASSLER	Israel
STRASSLER	Elka
STRASSLER	Josef
STRASSLER	Pinka
SHOTZ	Moshe
SHOTZ	Rosa
SHOTZ	Ceska
SHOTZ	Mordehai
SHOTZ	Mina
SHAHAL	Dawid
SHAHAL	Dena
SILBER	Zwi Hirsh
SILBER	Ruven
SALTZ	Nachum
SALTZ	Izhak
SALTZ	Herman
SALTZ	Jehuda
SALTZ	Peshle
SALTZ	Berish
SALTZ	Mechel
SALTZ	Chaja
SALTZ	Perl
SALTZ	Rutz
SALTZ	Daniel
SELDEN	Lea
SELDEN	Moshe
SELDEN	Oziash
SEIDENWURM	Moshe

SEIDENWURM	Miriam
SEIDENWURM	Mechel
SEIDENWURM	Shaje
SEIDENWURM	Rachel
SHNEIDER	Chaim
SZPIKULITZER	Chaim
TENENBAUM	Junio
TENENBAUM	Jakob
TENENBAUM	Mordhai Aron
TENENBAUM	Samuel
TENENBAUM	Henoch
TENENBAUM	Taube
TENENBAUM	Maite
TENENBAUM	Sarah
TENENBAUM	Isaak
TENENBAUM	Shaja
TENENBAUM	Pessil
TENENBAUM	Moses
TENENBAUM	Bina
TENENBAUM	Chaim Mechel
TENENBAUM	Randa
TENENBAUM	Dina
TENENBAUM	Nechamia
TENENBAUM	Miriam
TENENBAUM	Zwi
TENENBAUM	Golda
TENENBAUM	Sheindel
TENENBAUM	Leib
TENENBAUM	Lea
TENENBAUM	Awraham
TENENBAUM	Fruma

TENENBAUM	Pepe
TENENBAUM	Chaim
TENENBAUM	Mosha
TENENBAUM	Ruven
TENENBAUM	Iser
TENENBAUM	Oskar
TENENBAUM	Chaje
TENENBAUM	Fishel
TAHLER	Elka
TAUBER	Jehuda
TAUBER	Keile
TAUBER	Ester
TAUBER	Pepi
TAUBER	Miriam
TURKELLAUB	Shraga
TENEN	Mordhai
TENEN	Zunia
TENEN	Rachel
TERK	Mordhai
TERK	Sabina
TERK	Zalman
TAHLER	Mina
TAHLER	Bernard
TAHLER	Jitka
TEICHMAN	Dr. Heinrich
TEICHMAN	Sarah
TEICHMAN	Dr. Wolf
TISHMINITZER	Bluma
TISHMINITZER	Mordhai
TISHMINITZER	Kopot
TISHMINITZER	Chaja

WOLFZOHN	Israel
WOLFZOHN	Reisal
WOLFZOHN	Sarah
WEIGLER	Malcia
WEINTRAUB	Syma
WEINTRAUB	Dawid
WEINTRAUB	Chaje
WILLIG	Wolf
WILLIG	Frieda
WILLIG	Jakob
WELFISH	Nisan
WELFISH	Leon
WELFISH	Genia
WELFISH	Nachman
WELFISH	Pepi
WELFISH	Frieda
WELFISH	Rivka
WAGNER	Genia
WACHTEL	Taube
WINTER	Jona
WIEDERHORN	Shmuel
WEILGOSZ	Moshe
WEILGOSZ	Perl
WEILGOSZ	Aron
WEILGOSZ	Gershon
WEILGOSZ	Shoshana
WEILGOSZ	Frieda
WEILGOSZ	Feige
WEILGOSZ	Jehuda
WEILGOSZ	Chaja
WEILGOSZ	Josef

WITLER	Mordehai
WITLER	Golda
WITLER	Jehuda
WUGMAN	Monisz
WUGMAN	Taube
WUGMAN	Josef
WUGMAN	Regina
WUGMAN	David Moshe
WEIS	Zeev
WEIS	Frieda-Basia
WEIS	Hersh-Zwi
WEIS	Ruth
WEIS	Mania
ZWERDLING	Chana
ZWERDLING	Mendel
ZUCHARKANDEL	Zwi
ZUCHARKANDEL	Benjamin
ZUCHARKANDEL	Ahron
ZIMAND	Feige
ZIMAND	Baruch
ZIMAND	Jehezkiel
ZIMAND	Meite
ZIMAND	Reise
ZIMAND	Gitel
ZUNKER	Shlomo
ZUNKER	Chawa
ZIMMER	Josef
ZIMMER	Ela
ZIMMER	Stela
ZLATKES	Dr. Motle
ZLATKES	Berta

ZIPER	Awraham
ZIPER	Chawa
ZITZDEMER	Perl
ZITZDEMER	Nechama
ZITZDEMER	Awraham

ENGLISH SECTION

[Column 11 - English] [Column 13 - Hebrew]

Introduction

By Dr. Eliezer Boneh

This book describes the life of the people of Zloczew, the foundation of the town until after the tragedy. Life during the two World Wars has been particularly emphasized, for it was during these decades that Jewish life reached its summit.

Suddenly, at the outbreak of World War II, life stopped and one of the centres of the Diaspora was not more.

Zloczew lies in the southeastern part of Poland which is called Little Poland. A piece of land which, under the Austro-Hungarian Empire, was called Galicia. An agricultural level country partly covered with forests.

The natural borders of the town were in the south, the hills of Vorniaky; in the north the Zloczowka river and in the west and east, the town came together with neighbourhood villages.

Four wooden bridges crossed the river and a railroad, about 2km from town, connected the place in the west with Lwow and in the southeast with Tarnopol. A railroad-branch led northward to the city of Brody. Three paved roads also connected Zloczew with these cities.

The town of Zloczew was surrounded by many villages: Vorniaky, Polorky, Bianiov, Zazola, Jalochoviczy, Chicic, Lacka and a chain of small towns: Bialokamin, Busk, Sasov, Olesko and Goligory.

[Column 12]

Zloczew was a part of the Tarnopol region. In it central institutions could be found which served the whole region: The Governor's offices; the Tribunal Court, Land Registry, Post, hospital and colleges. Since the town was near the frontier, two regiments were stationed there.

Corresponding with the municipal and governmental foundations, there were also Jewish ones which served the Jewish inhabitants: the Communal Committee, rabbis, judges, hospitals, synagogues, schools and social relief.

The town was known for its cleanliness and beautiful appearance. The houses were mostly of bricks and only in the suburbs could wood or clay houses be seen.

The Lwow-Tarnopol road crossed the town and from it a branch led to Brody.

Where the road branched there was the market with its wooden huts, the centre of all retail dealings. This was a "Green Market" where on the second day of the week, cattle trade took place.

A promenade built on the ruins of a Middle Age wall divided the town. Another part of the wall became a beautiful garden gathering place of Jewish Youth. There, one could see the younger ones playing and singing Hebrew songs while the older ones discussed daily problems.

Compliments of Mr.& Mrs.ASH

[Column 13]

The town folk prospered and so did the Jews, especially when Zloczew became a town (for it was not always so).

At the outbreak of World War II the total number of the population was 16,000. The Jews formed the majority (9000) and the Poles and Ukrainians completed the number.

The Zloczewer Jews occupied themselves with all the branches of trade and workmanship. Of course, those of free professions could also be found. Villagers from afar and nearby and the small-town merchants sold their products in Zloczew. As to the Zloczewer merchants, they assorted and packed the products and sold them in Poland and abroad. A big part of the agricultural products found its way to the factories and was used as raw material.

Robinson's meat was world-famous; Ritter's and Shweig mills were well known; Polasiok's leather goods were of the best quality and so was Zimand and Lynwand's sawmill production. And last but not least, Schwadron's Brewery supplied the need of the whole of Poland.

That was Zloczew's situation between both World Wars.

And yet, the youngsters who thought about their future and that of their nation found no place in the town and decided to immigrate to Israel. There were those, of course, who chose other countries across the sea, mainly the United States.

Those who remained in town at the outbreak of the war were mostly killed. Only a few survivors were able to join their brothers in Israel or in other countries.

[Column 14]

The immortalization of Zloczew is no longer an idea and has not been so for many years. The Central Committee of Zloczew has seen to it. They helped to create this book and to present it to the survivors. The book appears about 25 years after the outbreak of World War II; a war that inflicted a terrible tragedy upon our people and struck our town in the cruellest of ways.

The chapters of this book tell about the cruel deeds of the human beasts who acquired power over Zloczew and its inhabitants. The place where we were born and grew up was small and beautiful. Perhaps one of the most beautiful in Easter Galicia.

It was blessed with spiritual giants, poets, rabbis, writers, artists, devoted social workers, youth movements, schools, relief foundations, synagogues and houses of study.

This book tells all of this in order to erect an immortal monument on the mass grave of our brothers.

The town of Zloczew is no more. The fountains of life are dry. The spiritual and physical treasures are gone. The busing energy of the youngsters, blessed with talent and deeds, is silenced; cut down is the grandeur of the Zloczewer Jew.

But the memory will live forever. It will remain in the book of Poland's Jewry – in the history of our nation – in the renewed achievement of our people on the soil of their independent country – in the hearts of the Zloczew folk, dispersed in countries of the world.

In their hour of death, our sacred brothers have commanded us to live. So we the living do our best to immortalize the dead.

The Committee together with the Zloczew townsfolk in the United States has toiled and brought the book to its end.

[Column 15]

The Committee feels no gratification at the thought of the hard work invested in this undertaking. The Committee saw it as a sacred duty and hoped that the town and its good people would not be forgotten.

We thank deeply Mr. Benzion Zwerdling, President of the Committee; Mr. J. Katz, M.K.O; Dr. Altman; Mr. M. Deutsch; Dr. E. Yosefberg and M.J. Imber of blessed memory and many others. The Committee thanks our countrymen in the United States:

[Column 16]

Mrs. S. Baumgarten; Mr. H. Baumgarten; Mrs. M. Memberg and all those who have contributed and made others contribute in order to enable the publication of this book. The committee also thanks the Editors and Publisher of the book for their devoted and good work.

Dr. Eliezer Boneh (Bauman)
Chairman of the Committee in Israel

Zloczower Relief Verband of America

A story of compassion translated into deeds

(*Compliments of Zloczower Ladies organization*)

This is the last chapter of a glorious story. This is the last link between the new world and a world that is no more; a world of noble spiritual values, famous for learning and moral heights which was monstrously annihilated.

This last chapter should not be forgotten. This last link should not be destroyed by the passing of time. We should remember the chapter and preserve the link for the sacred memory of our forebears and for our brothers and sisters – the martyrs – and for the sake of our children and grandchildren.

Let them know and tell their children and be proud of it. May they learn and apply the true moral of this story in their own lives and deeds.

We cannot comprehend in our thoughts all of the 6 million Jews who perished at the hands of the German murderers; this crime and this tragedy, both the most horrible in al recorded history, are beyond the comprehension of the human spirit. But we can and should think of our own brethren and the city from which we came from.

For this is the place from which we and our forefathers came. This is the ground where our roots were set. These personal ties should be passed on to our children who never set foot there but still may know and learn and translate the tradition in their own lives and deeds.

There were high standards and moral values in the city like Zloczew which should not perish with their bearers. There was real piety and learning and reverence for learning. Bread might be scarce but not books.

[Column 17]

There was true compassion and mercy and charity in Zloczow. There were spontaneous good deeds there and spiritual earnestness. Life was hard but the light of faith gave the Jews strength and endurance.

Now there is no Zloczow anymore. No Jewish Zloczow, our own community where our roots grew. Our kinsmen, our brothers and sisters, our friends and countrymen were all, with their wives and children, wiped out by ruthless assassins. The old synagogues and houses of learning, where our ancestors worshipped God for countless generations, the Orphans' Asylum, the Old Age Home – all these were destroyed. Even the cemeteries, the old one which we helped to put in order and the new one for which we contributed have been entirely erased by the Polish neighbours.

Thus Zloczow, our Jewish Zloczow which is no more, remains only in our memory. Let us, therefore, bear in mind the ties we maintained with the "Old Home" as long as it existed; our ties of brotherly compassion and love.

This report tells us of a number of men and women who came to this country from the city of Zloczow in Galicia to escape misery. Now we know that it was in order to escape massacre. They struggled hard for a living. They had their worries and troubles but they never forgot the kin and friends and countrymen they left behind. They remembered them especially in time of distress.

[Column 18]

Such a time arrived in 1914 at the outbreak of World War I. On August 1, 1914 the war began and on August 3rd, Zloczow had already been invaded by the advancing Russian army since Zloczow is not far from the old Austro-Russian frontier.

The fate of Jews in a city like Zloczow as in any place in Galicia was never a very happy one. Even in quiet times, a great number of the Jewish population, in fact the majority, suffered want and many were poor; and we should remember that their needs were very modest. But war came no matter whose war it was. The Jews were the first and most afflicted victims, and when peace came, whoever was the victor, the Jews lost the war as well as the peace.

This is what happened to the Jews of Zloczow. This was a community of about 10,000 people. Most of them were small storekeepers. There was a class of artisans and many poor people. The majority struggled hard to extract a meagre living from whatever their occupation was.

Most of the Jews of Zloczow were Orthodox but there were also progressive people mostly of the free professions: lawyers, doctors, etc. The Zionist idea took root among many at the beginning of the century and the Zionist Movement became stronger with the years.

Compliments of the Children of Azriel & Malke Axelrod

[Column 19]

Zloczow prided itself on its famous Rabbis and Talmudic scholars and also on the Hassidic rabbis of the 18th century. There were many houses of worship, but the main synagogue was a very imposing building. The synagogues and Hassidic so-called "Klausen" were the centres not only of religious activities but of the whole community life.

This was the situation when World War I broke out. Then the population was suddenly and completely cut-off from the rest of the country by the invading Russian army. Though the Russians occupied only a small portion of Galicia, those who lived there were cut-off from the rest of the world.

The income of the Jewish population, which was never high, shrank to very small proportions. Poverty afflicted large numbers of people. The attitude of the Russian military authorities toward the Jews made their lot even worse. Persecutions and chicanery were the new rulers' rule. In spite of the cutting-off of communications with the outside world, word reached America of the plight of the Jews in occupied Galicia. As to Zloczow, a number of Jews managed to escape from the city before the Russian Invasion. They now lived as refugees, mostly in Vienna, the capital of Austria, but also scattered in Bohemia and Hungary.

It was they who notified the countrymen in New York of the plight of the Jews in occupied Zloczow and also of their own hard lot as refugees without any means of existence.

When these reports reached New York, a number of countrymen from ZLoczow decided to come to the rescue of their countrymen in the old "Country". In the emergency, they acted quickly.

[Column 20]

On October 18, 1814 the first meeting was called and a motion was passed to found a Zloczow Relief Verband. This institution was constituted by the delegates of the following societies:

1. Erste Zloczower Kranken Unterstutzung Verein (Society for support of the sick).
2. Chevra Mahazikei Hadat Anshei Zoczow.
3. M. Lunenfeld Zloczower Lodge.
4. Independent Zloczower Young Men's Progressive Society 382, Workmen's Circle.
5. Zloczower Brith Sholom Lodge.

On January 28, 1915 the relief was formally organized and the following officers were elected. Isadore Friedman, President. Joseph Silberschutz, Treasurer. David Hochberg, Secretary.

Bern acted as secretary at the first meeting and $124 was collected.

The Relief Verband was quite active from the beginning. Its main work consisted of raising funds. For this purpose, no way was left unused. Package parties, mass meetings, balls, theatre benefits, appeals on various occasions as for example: the Slyyum Hasefer in Mahazikei Hadat were arranged.

The Zloczow Countrymen in New York, later also in Philadelphia and in other cities, were most responsive to the need of their brethren in distress.

From the beginning, the main worry of the leadership of the Relief was how to reach the needy Zloczower overseas. No efforts were spared but to no avail. Zloczow itself remained hermetically closed.

Compliments of Augusta Axelrod

[Column 21]

The officers of the Relief did not give up. At the end of three months, a contact was established with the refugees from Zloczow in Vienna. On March 25, 1915 the printed report of the Relief notes, first financial assistance was furnished to Zloczower refugees in Vienna, Austria. From then on, financial assistance was given to Zloczower refugees stranded in various parts of Austria, Czechoslovakia, Hungary, Italy and to Zloczower prisoners in Russia.

The report contains an interesting item. On October 2, 1915 a Young Folks' Auxiliary was organized. This shows that the Zloczower in New York not only mobilized everyone for the rescue work, even their young people, but they endeavoured to teach their children the moral lessons taught by their fathers; the qualities of compassion and mercy and the duties to help and give. This lesson was not forgotten. The children of the Zloczower learned to help and give not only for their kin in Zloczow but for every worthy cause everywhere.

The activities of the Relief increased during the war years with the ever-increasing needs of the supported refugees.

After a year of strenuous efforts, the Relief managed to establish contact with Zloczow itself. On February 18, 1916 we read in the Report of the Relief work: "First relief money forwarded directly to Zloczow".

This was quite an achievement. The direct assistance to Zloczow stimulated the Relief to even greater efforts. Mass meetings, package parties, etc. were organized for the purpose of fund raising.

[Column 22]

These activities however came to an abrupt end on April 14, 1917 with the entrance of the United States into the World War.

This was, however, only a temporary suspension. As soon as the Wart came to an end and the Armistice was signed on November 11, 1918 the relief resumed its activities with even greater devotion. Funds were raised not only through meetings and functions but also through house canvassing. Representatives of the Relief visited the members at their homes to collect funds.

From 1919 on, closer contact was established between the Relief and Zloczow. When Dr. Samuel Margoshes, editor of the Day visited Easter Galicia, the Relief used the occasion to send $500 to Zloczow through him.

From then on, Zloczowers from New York frequently visited Zloczow and on every occasion, the visitor who travelled at his own expense was nominated a delegate of the Relief and various sums were forwarded through him. In the Report of the Relief, this left for Zloczow and Relief funds to be distributed were entrusted to him. (*sentence is often repeated: "Mr. X".)*

During the post-war years and in general between the two World Wars, a number of delegates performed an important task during their visits to the old country.

They stayed in Zloczow for a time and besides distributing the Relief funds, made approaches to the Polish authorities (in 1920 to the Slavic Occupation) on behalf of the Jewish Population, obtaining important concessions for the benefit of the community. They also performed other tasks which were of great help to the Jewish population.

[Column 23]

Meeting of the Ladies' Auxiliary of Zloczow in New York

[Column 24]

During the twenty years between the two World Wars, these visitor delegates were the keepers of the sacred ties between the Zloczower in the Old and New Worlds.

Compliments of Zloczower Relief in N.Y.

*****

[Column 25]

A short history of the Zloczower, N.Y. City Branch 382 of the Workmen's circle

By Sol Katz

In New York City in 1910, a group of twenty-five young men broke away from the Zloczower Young Men's Society and applied to the general office of the Workmen's Circle for a charter. They all passed the medical examinations and the new Zloczower Branch 382 was launched. The charter members were: H. Bettinger, Jacob Chartan, Harry Circus, Morris Circus, Isidore Goldstein, Tobia Goldstein, Louis Green, Morris Green, Max Gruber, Aaron Mestel, Max Pasternak, Harry Patchen, Isidore Pauker, Nathan Roth, Bernard Schorr, Sam Schorr, J. Sobel, Sam Steinbauer, Lippy Tannenbaum, Max Tannenbaum, Harry Unterlag, Willy Weiss, Sam Wittman, Harry Zwerdling and Louis Zwerdling. This original group soon started a campaign for an enlarged membership and quickly managed to enrol over one hundred members. From 1916 to 1919, during which time I served as secretary, we had a membership of over 150 enthusiastic and active people.

The history of the Zloczower Branch actually has two main phases. The early years of the branch's existence were dominated by the Bundist from Russia and Poland who, in large numbers, staffed the Education department of the Workmen's Circle and were bitter enemies of Zionism and Poale Zionism.

[Column 26]

The various branches of the Workmen's Circle received their instructions and ideological direction from this department. The majority of the members of Branch 382 had received their ideological education in Zloczow as members of the Jewish Social Democratic Party. This party in Galicia had been influenced by the Bundist who had fled from Russia into Austria soon after 1905.

The main premise of the Bundist was that the Jewish workers did not need Palestine or Israel or any Jewish homeland. They believed that Jewish workers could build a successful semi-autonomous Jewish life in Europe. The **Vorwaerts** acted as the Bundist' mouth-piece and made repeated attacks on Zionism. These same anti-Zionist feelings were expressed at many union meetings and lectures dominated by the Bundist.

[Column 27]

The spokesmen of Zionism were constantly ridiculed and maligned. When I served as secretary of the Branch, it was part of my job to read the appeals for aid which came to us from all organizations. Requests from Poale Zionist groups were always received with a stony silence. For me, this was a great and painful embarrassment.

The Bundist' dream of semi-autonomy soon exploded with finality. Hitler and Stalin wrote the final chapters in the story of the Jewish Bundist ideal. Those who escaped Hitler found no better fate in Russia where the Bund leaders were murdered mercilessly and where the party was declared illegal.

The destruction of the Bundist ideology had a sobering effect on the Jewish labor leaders in America. The Workmen's Circle began to enter a new phase of thinking. And soon, the Histadrut began to receive substantial help from the newly pro-Zionist Workmen's Circle.

[Column 28]

Today, after fifty years of existence, the Branch is known as the Zloczower Branch 382. This union took place about fifteen years ago and was due to a shrinkage of membership in both branches, partly due to the drying up of immigration after World War I. Our membership is now made of older people with an average age of over 60 years.

At our Fiftieth Jubilee dinner held in February of this year, only a few of the old members attended. Amongst them were: David Hochberg, Izzy Goldstein, A. Wasserman, I. Weiss, J. Pepper, B. Silber, Mr & Mrs H. Kaplan, A. Hoffman and myself.

We are still active in taking care of those of our members who need assistance and in helping Jewish organizations to carry on their good work. And, every now and then, we feel a touch of nostalgia when we tell our children and grandchildren what Jewish life was like, many, many years ago in Zloczow.

Group of workers from Zloczow in New York
Compliments of Harry Baumgarten

[Column 29 - English] [Column 153 - Hebrew]

Haunting Memories

By Dr. S. Altman

In eternal memory of my dear parents, sisters and brother

In Zloczow, Jewish life pulsated and grew steadily. Despite its comparatively small population, this town played an important part in shaping the Jewish community of Eastern Poland. Its memory is dear to all those who were born there and equally to those, like myself, who came to settle.

Each survivor who miraculously escaped the hell of the Holocaust has the sacred duty of recording every detail known to him of the many crimes committed against Zloczow Jewry by expert Nazi murderers with the aid of Ukrainian hooligans.

We must fulfil this sacred duty and unwritten testament of those who, helpless, defenceless, with the "Shema Israel" on their lips, made a last request of those who might survive; that they should tell the world of their unspeakable suffering and tragic martyrdom. It was their last wish that like those wrecked at sea who leave their message in bottles floating, no man knows whither, we should tell uribi et orbi what befell them in order that humanity in general and Jewry in particular should never forget.

Accordingly, I have set out to give an objective account of the terrible events that befell against the back ground of my own experiences during this period of Hell on Earth.

[Column 30]

Recording this terrible tragedy brings back the saddest and the most painful memories. They emerge up from every cranny of my soul. These memories I cannot suppress. They haunt me by day and by night. One memory chases the other chaotically and it is only with great effort that I can give even a fraction of that unending and inhuman suffering.

Humiliated, degraded, beaten, tortured, starved, they were finally murdered by the cruel Nazi beasts with systematic relentlessness of a satanic robot which implemented the destruction to the last detail.

Neither riches nor fame, neither wisdom, common sense nor intellect gave any chance of survival. The 20th Moloch, in the heart of "civilized" Europe, pitilessly swallowed its hopeless victims. There was not a single ray of hope and there was no help. The world looked on with indifference, observing that dance of death as though it were bewitched.

1. Before the Storm

[Column 31]

The whole Jewish population of Eastern Poland was transfixed with terror on 22nd June, 1941 when the trembling voice of Mr. Molotov, then Prime Minister of the U.S.S.R. was heard announcing that Hitler, the ally of yesterday, had abruptly broken the "treaty of friendship" between the two countries and, without formally declaring war, had ordered his armies to cross the frontiers so recently established between them. Those who did not believe Stalin's propaganda about the Soviet military might knew that Russia at first had little chance to offer successful resistance against the well-equipped and highly disciplined German armies. The danger of immediate invasion was particularly great in those parts of Poland like the eastern provinces, where the local population was largely hostile to the Russians.

The Soviet troops retreated in panic unable to meet this sudden planned attack. The situation grew rapidly worse. Three factors accelerated the deterioration:

1. The desertion of a number of trapped Soviet army units (Wlassow):
2. The guerrilla warfare of the Ukrainian nationalists who harassed the retreating Soviet troops;
3. Above all, the incessant German air raids which literally mowed down the Russians, paralyzing the movements of the retreating army by bombing the main roads and bridges and made re-grouping and escape impossible.

By the third day of the war, the Russian officials in charge of the local administration had quietly left for the East with their families. Before their flight they urged their local colleagues and officials to remain at their posts until victory.

Not only the Russians but also the Jews were anxious to escape the looming menace of the German invasion but the Jews had neither the opportunity nor the possibility of running away. Only a handful, a small number of unencumbered families managed to escape to Russia. These were mostly communist in their leanings and sympathies.

[Column 32]

At dawn, within ten days of the outbreak of the war, on July 1, the first German patrol entered Zloczow after an intensive air raid. The Jewish population were hidden in cellars and improvised air-raid shelters and awaited developments in dread. The local and neighbouring Ukrainians began to pour into town to welcome the Germans. They covered the buildings with swastikas and their national yellow-blue flags. Representatives of the Ukrainian intelligentsia flocked into the streets and demonstrated in support of the conquerors. They all pinned notices on their lapels reading: "Ukrainian – speaks German and gives information". These offers of "information" cost the Jews dearly.

Within 24 hours, hordes of villagers began looting Jewish property. Rumours of rapes of Jewish women and the cruel beating of men began to spread. Very soon, there were corpses lying in the centre of town. Among the first to be identified were those of 2 feeble-minded brothers nicknamed: "Jopaks" whom the Germans had killed on the spot.

Warned by rumours and by clandestine radio and press reports of what the Nazi were capable of doing, I suggested to the male members of my family (i.e. my father-in-law Markus Shnapp and my two brothers-in-law Kuba and

Mundyk) that we should flee together to an acquaintance of mine, a certain Mr. Olejnik, half Pole and half Ukrainian, who lived in a little house on the outskirts of Zloczow. My father-in-aw, an invalid of World War I and my brother-in-law opposed my suggestion insisting that they had nothing to fear. I therefore took my younger brother-in-law with me and we went to Olejnik whose little cottage stood at the end of the Ujejski Road near the military barracks on Jablonowskich. Our host gave us a room and told us that He would be away the whole day and would only return at night to sleep. He warned us to beware of his neighbours and advised us to keep out of their sight. After about three hours my brother-in-law grew bored and restless and decided to return home against my advice. I resolved to remain where I was. Suddenly, a terrific noise was heard that was caused by the arrival of a company of S.S. troops. It soon became clear that this was part of a special murder squad. Peeping cautiously through the window, I saw a German patrol approaching the house next door. At the same time, I heard voices shouting "Are there Jews or Russians here?" (sind hier Juden oder Russen?). One of the soldiers started beating up a man standing on the doorstep, taking him to be a Jew. Seeing this, I decided to leave my unsafe shelter. As I left the house I fell straight into the arms of another S.S. patrol which was already belabouring one victim, Dr. Opperer.

Compliments of Mr. & Mrs. Patchen

[Column 33]

Dr. Opperer[1] and I were driven to the barracks where some sixty Jews were herded in the yard. None of us knew why we were there. We were all sure that we were going to be shot. At the height of the tension, a sergeant-major ordered us to clean up the barracks' yard and the road leading to it. We all breathed a sigh of relief. The spectre of death which only a moment before had been hovering over us, now vanished and hope was restored. How vain was this hope and how short lived!

After a few of us were given tools, we were led to Jablonowsky Street and ordered to fill the pot holes in the road. Work started with shouting, beating and kicking. Those without tools – and they were the Majority – had to collect earth and stones with their bare hands and carry them in their coats to the pot holes. The work had to be carried out at a rate that no human being could possibly keep up with just a pair of bare hands.

[Column 34]

A wild scene followed. I was one of the lucky few who had received a spade. Who would have believed that this seemingly insignificant fact would save my life and that of Dr. Opperer? With my spade, I doubled and trebled my capacities in order to shovel the maximum amount of earth for those without tools at my side. Streams of sweat blinded me, my heart threatened to burst but I could not relax for a moment. On the contrary, I had to work faster and faster shovelling earth for those beside me for they were being mercilessly spurred on and beaten. The sergeant-major who stood nearby watched this scene with unconcerned satisfaction. When he left us, he remarked cynically: "Work makes one happy and paves the way to eternity" (arbeit macht Freude and ebnet den Weg zur Ewigkeit).

Dr. Opperer who worked near me could not keep up with this monstrous pace because of a recent illness. A soldier who had meanwhile replaced the sergeant-major gave vent to his brutality and tormented Dr. Opperer because he was so slow. He beat him with the butt of his gun and kicked him several times with his hobnailed boots until the poor man reeled and collapsed. The soldier would have killed him had not the sergeant-major returned unexpectedly and sent him back to the barracks. Without a moment's hesitation, I approached the sergeant-major and explained that Dr. Opperer had been a major in the Austrian army and had received the highest distinctions. As such, I appealed to him to let the poor man go home and allow me to do his work for him.

[Column 35]

On hearing my request, the sergeant-major asked me how I came to have such a good command of German. I told him I had studied at a German school in Bielsko (a town not far from the German border) and had a school friend who looked very much like him. Carl Jenkner was his name. To this he answered: It's a pity you are a Jew. You Jews are dirty people. In Beuthen you committed atrocities on the Germans. You cut off their noses and ears and put out their eyes. We have to the Jews differently; a few slaps and kicks at the most and afterwards – tra-ta-ta with the machine gun!"

I plucked up a little courage and told him that his information about the Jews was ill-founded. Compared with other nations, I said, there are few sadists and murderers among Jews. But, he assured me with great conviction, that what he told me was the very truth, for he had been briefed about it in his S.S. officer training course.

After a moment, he turned to Dr. Opperer and me saying: "off with you and quickly! It is going to be hot here today" (meaning that a day of bloodshed was ahead).

Not only did he allow us to leave but he conducted us to the end of the lane in order to prevent molestation by other soldiers. I brought Dr. Opperer, who could hardly walk, to the home of his relatives and quickly returned to my old shelter, distressed and downhearted. This depressing experience, the sight of humiliation, bestiality and brutal violence, shocked me to the very depths of my being. But it was only a trifle to what was to come later on.

I fell into a state of torpor and at last sleep overcame me. But not for long. After a brief nap I was suddenly awakened by the rattling of a machine gun nearby.

[Column 36]

It was 8 in the evening. Then, just as suddenly, the shooting stopped. Half an hour later, Olejnik returned and told me that on his way home he had stopped at his neighbour near the barracks and saw a group of Jews being machine-gunned while at work.[2] That was where I too had worked that morning. I suddenly realized how close to death I had been. Yes, Providence had saved me from certain death that day.

The next day I spent in anguish because of the further bad news my landlord had brought - the uncovering of a mass grave in the Sobieski Citadel causing a great tension in town. The grave was said to be that of Ukrainians murdered by the Soviets. What followed soon confirmed our worst fears.

2. Mass Slaughter

Simultaneously with the planning of the military campaign against the U.S.S.R. in march 1941, a secret understanding to form four units of "S.S.-Einsatzgruppen" was reached between the R.S.H.A. (Reichs-Sicherheitshauptampt)[3] and the O.K.W. (Oberkommando der Wehrmacht). The moment any military action was to begin, the four main German armies were to be joined by one of these four S.S.-Einsatzgruppen whose task.

Compliments of the Children of Jacob & Sali Baumgarten

[Column 37]

was mass extermination of unwanted elements especially the Jews. The units were recruited mostly among thieves, bad characters, criminals and degenerates who were specially trained for their brutal assignment.

Einsatzgruppe "C" was sent with Dr. Rash at its head to Eastern Poland. One of its units under S.S. Hauptsturmführer Schultze[4] entered Zloczow and occupied the barracks on Jablonowskich Street.

As mentioned earlier, the Ukrainians had ambushed the retreating Russians and directed the German Air Force from secret radio-stations to the Russian points of concentration. In order to prevent these activities and in retaliation for this treason, the Soviets jailed a number of Ukrainian intelligentsia who were kept as hostages in the ancient Sobieski Citadel. Before their retreat, the N.K.V.D. had these hostages murdered and buried in the courtyard in a mass grave. On Wednesday 2nd July, these graves were found by the Ukrainians and they boiled with anger. In the meantime they had formed a temporary Executive Committee which in due course was to become the nucleus of the local

Ukrainian Government. The members of this committee were: Antoniak, Dr. Gilewicz, Oleskiewicz Symczyszyn, Mrs. Wanio, Dr. Jojko, etc.

The Executive of this Committee went to the Citadel and identified the murdered victims, included Dr. Grosskopf and his brother-in-law Gruber. They had been arrested by the Russian N.K.V.D. before the outbreak of the German-Soviet war. The first spontaneous reaction of the Ukrainians was to turn their fury on the Jews who were now regarded as Soviet sympathizers. They called a mass meeting at which they accused the Jews of murdering the hostages. After inciting the mob to revenge, they sent a delegation to Hauptsturmführer Schultze of the S.S. Kommand to ask for formal permission to launch a pogrom against the Jews. Schultze happened to live in the house of a Ukrainian clerk named Lewitski in Kolejowa Street. His daughter, whose Polish husband was in a German prison, became Schultze's mistress. During a walk near their house where the cemetery lay, she drew his attention to the Mausoleum erected in 1918 in memory of Poles who had been murdered by Ukrainians. The mausoleum, she alleged, commemorated the murder of Ukrainian patriots by Jews.

[Column 38]

The day of revenge was set for July 3, 1941. The Ukrainian mob was given a free hand. The descendants of Chmielnicki and Petlura proved worthy of their Nazi patrons. Crowds armed with axes, hatchets, shovels, iron bars, hammers and fire-arms simultaneously stormed all the Jewish streets and houses, dragging their occupants into the streets. The pogrom began from pre-selected places like "Targowica", the old market square, the Lwowska Street and the courtyard of Lippa Mehr (Klonowicza Street) but the main centre of operations was the Citadel. Hordes of Ukrainians and S.S. men swooped down upon their defenceless victims with whatever they had in their hands. The Jews could not even hide. Those who tried to escape were forced back by new waves of attackers. Ukrainian neighbours with whom only the day before there had been friendly or business relations were now relentless enemies. They lured Jews into their homes only to hand them over to the savage mob. When the wave of terror eventually died down, people were found drowned in latrines and sewage holes, some with heads chopped off. A number of scoundrels had caught Rabbi Ellenberg, tied him to a motorcycle with a rope and dragged him up the street. The Rabbi, with his tongue hanging out, had to keep up with the motorcycle to the delight and wild laughter of the street urchins. As the motorcycle gathered momentum, the venerable old man fell from exhaustion and his body was dragged along, mutilated and unrecognizable.

[Column 39]

In another part of the town, a number of Jews were forced to exhume the Ukrainian corpses from the grave, wash them, carry them out of the yard and arrange them in rows. Many, women and children among them, could not go through with this terrible ordeal and fainted in with the horror and stench. They were mercilessly beaten and killed on the spot. Meantime, others were brought and ordered to jump into the now empty graves where they were machine-gunned by the S.S. men. Without bothering whether the victims were alive or dead, they were covered with new people and the procedure was repeated. The screams of the wounded and those buried alive rose to heaven but none heeded them. On that day Jewish blood flowed like a river.

The perfidy of the Ukrainians may be illustrated by a single incident. Among those driven to the Citadel were Joseph Zimmer and Dr. Moses Eisen. A Ukrainian acquaintance of theirs pulled them out of the mob and sent them home. He asked them to fetch strong ropes which he said he needed badly. Trusting their "acquaintance" these fine men returned with ropes instead of hiding away! They were politely thanked in the presence of the spectators and hanged with the ropes they had brought.

Among those driven to the Citadel was my father-in-law Schnap, my younger brother-in-law Mundek, soon followed by my older brother-in-law Kuba and Wilo Freimann. Kuba barely had a glimpse of the mutilated bodies of his father and brother when he was ordered to jump into the grave. He and Wilo had the presence of mind, rare in such situations, to thrust themselves in deep among the corpses around them and escaped with slight wounds. A few others escaped in the same manner namely: Dr. Sternschuss, S. Wiederhorn, M. Laufer and Abraham Rosen.

[Column 40]

The massacre went on from morning till late that afternoon. Piles of corpses lay everywhere in the yard and by the mass grave. Nobody interrupted the mob in its diabolical work. Then suddenly something like a miracle happened. A strong wind swept the town. Dark and heavy clouds suddenly covered the blue July sky, followed by heavy rain.

The heavens seemed to weep with the bereaved mothers, widows and orphaned children as though joining them in their great sorrow. Amid the thunder and lightning, the storm grew and the rain turned into a cloudburst. The murderers were forced to disperse and the slaughter ceased. The gang tried to resume their slaughter after the rain had stopped but an unexpected development frustrated them. A big military unit headed by a General arrived in town. At the sight of the bodies, the General ordered the slaughter to be stopped. S.S. Hauptsturmführer Schultze, head of the "Death Platoon" objected at first but eventually had to obey. The Ukrainians, of course, did not like this turn of events and sent a delegation to the General to persuade him to change his order. They were so sure they would get the order withdrawn that they did not allow the fresh graves in the Citadel to be covered or the scattered corpses in the yard to be collected. But their hopes of liquidating the entire Jewish population at one stroke were disappointing for neither the General nor the District Commander acceded to their demand.

Compliments of N. Diamond

[Column 41]

Meanwhile, night fell. As I have already said, a few people who covered themselves with dead bodies escaped death from the bullets and hand grenades but the danger of being buried alive still loomed. The downpour was their salvation. Under cover of night they began to crawl out from under the dead. There was only one – Laufer – who did not succeed in escaping. As he tried to rise from the pile of corpses, he found that the arms of a corpse in rigor mortis had caught his leg so tightly that he could not extricate himself. His companions trued to help him but the sound of approaching footsteps frightened then and forced them to leave him to his fate.

While death was stalking the town, I was hidden in the house of Olejnik, awaiting my host and news about the situation. At three in the afternoon he returned, completely transformed. He told me abruptly that I could not remain in his home. Seeing the yellow-blue ribbon on his coat, I understood his mood and did not try to plead with him. In order to get rid of me as soon as possible, he did not tell me the news of the slaughter at the Citadel or the situation in town. As I was about to leave, a downpour began again. Taking not notice of it, I walked to my own home safely through the deserted streets. As my mother-in-law and wife were telling me of the abduction of my father-in-law and my younger brother-in-law, they noticed an S.S. man approaching the house. I quickly ran down the staircase and hid near the entrance to the cellar. From there I heard the soldier yelling for Kuba and me to come out of hiding. Obtaining no response, he threatened to shoot my wife and my mother-in-law. We learnt afterwards that our concierge[5] (a Ukrainian woman) had told the German thatonly my father-in-law and my younger brother-in-law had been taken away. Luckily, an officer seeking living quarters, arrived at that moment and ordered the .S. man to leave the women in peace otherwise he certainly would have shot them.

[Column 42]

In the cellar I found young Brummer, the son of the only musician in town who had managed to escape the slaughter in Lipa Mehr's yard. We stayed in this hiding place for three days until things quietened down. Here and there isolated cases of violence, robbery or murder continued but the main action had stopped. What finally put an end to the wild orgy of the Ukrainian hoodlums and the S.S. hangmen was the promulgation of the District Commander's Order forbidding violence to civilians, irrespective of creed or nationality.

Among the local Ukrainians who distinguished themselves in their ferocity were Pawliszyn and the chimney sweeper, Serba. These two scoundrels prided themselves on having broken a score of Jewish heads. The only Pole who took part in the slaughter was young Terlecki, a butcher's son. Many German officers watched the pogrom with calm cynicism, clicking their cameras all the time. A few months later, I happened to come across some of these photographs in an illustrated German weekly. One of them depicted a scene at the Citadel with women weeping over a pile of corpses. Among these, I definitely recognized Lusia Freimann, the daughter of Shyjo and Dziunka Kitaj. The scene bore the caption: "Ukrainian women mourning their husbands who were murdered by Jews".

[Column 43]

The first pogrom accounted for 2,500 victims, and marked the beginning of the end of Zloczow Jewry. There was an uncanny deathlike silence in the town. The survivors fled, hiding wherever they could. Every Jewish home was a house of mourning. Thus fell the curtain on the first act of the tragedy.

When order returned to the town, I left my hiding place and took the job of clearing the demolished Petesh Pharmacy near the Greek-Orthodox Church, management of which was temporarily assigned to Mr. Salitr by the Military authorities.

3. The Proclamation of the Ukrainian Republic

The Ukrainians, having satisfied their lust for blood in the pogrom and exultant at the quick victories of the Nazi, now set out to establish their long-cherished dream of an independent Ukrainian State. They naively believed that in return for their small help, mainly in murdering Jews, Hitler would favour their ambitions. At the order of their leaders in Lwow and with the personal assistance of Bandera, a Cossack chief, a group of Ukrainians in Zloczow proclaimed the Independent Ukrainian Republic. The declaration was made in the Church Square in the presence of the Orthodox clergy and a large crowd of spectators. I was watching the parade from the pharmacy where I was working and noticed, with satisfaction, the faces of the Germans ridiculing the whole affair. Two officers entered the pharmacy and one said to the other: "This is all shit" (das is alles Scheisse).

Meantime, the Ukrainians began to organize the local administration appointing a mayor and a municipal body. On 14th July the newly elected mayor (a local district teacher) issued an order for all male Jews to gather in the market square. Nobody responded, everyone suspecting some trick behind it. When the sheriff came to know that his schoolmate, Dr. Zlatkes was still alive, he called on him to persuade the Jews to leave their hiding places and clean up the town, assuring him that no wrong would be done to anybody. Dr. Zlatkes declared that he had no influence on the members of the Jewish community. Only when the order was given by the military commanded coupled with an assurance that any act of violence would be punished by death, was it obeyed.

[Column 44]

The next morning, a number of people appeared in the market square. The Ukrainian sheriff announced that all male Jews above the age of 14 were liable for forced labor and that all Jews from the age of 12 upwards, regardless of sex, were to wear white bands with the blue Star of David on their right arms. The order, signed by the Military Commander, was worded as follows:

As from today, members of the Jewish population above the age of 12 have to wear a white band with the blue Star of David on the right arm as a distinguishing sign.

1. A Jew is a descendant of three generations known to be Jewish.
2. A Jew is a person born of mixed marriage, two of whose grandparents were Jewish.
3. A person who is a registered member of a Jewish community.
4. A person who is married to a Jew or about to marry one.

Jews found not wearing this armband will be severely punished. This order does not apply to foreigners.

Signed.
Commander of the Town of Zloczow.

Compliments of Elie & Gertie Baumgarten

[Column 45]

This announcement was printed in three languages: German, Ukrainian and Polish and displayed prominently on the walls of the town. Compulsory labor and hunger even more forced the people into the open. Labor recruitment was not yet regulated and the Ukrainian militia and the German soldiers hunted for recruits separately. This resulted in chaos. The biggest concern of the Jews was the absence of an organized food supply. The men who worked for the German received a little food or a loaf of bread. Those who still had cash or valuable could exchange them for food. But the great majority of the Jews had nothing and were facing starvation.

This situation was suddenly relieved by help from an unexpected quarter. At the head of the Food Supply Department of the German Administration was a certain Engineer Hahn of Olshanice, an acquaintance of Dr. Schotz whom he came to know through Dr. Zlatkes. As soon as this man learnt of the grave food situation of the Jews he promised that upon receiving a detailed list of the Jewish population, he would issue a single emergency ration of flour, groats, peas and sugar from the supplies left by the Russians and without waiting for permission from higher German authorities. Dr. Schotz and Dr. Zlatkes undertook to prepare a list of the Jews. On this occasion, they decided to prepare a list of those murdered in the pogrom. The two went from door-to-door. Tears, despair and misery met them wherever they came. They almost broke down under the burden they had imposed upon themselves but they had to go on. They toiled at their task for two weeks. To meet the needs of those who could not wait, they organized an illegal Relief Committee. In response to their appeal, a number of people offered to collect whatever food they could obtain. In spite of the general misery, people deprived themselves of their last morsel of food in order to share it with those who had nothing. Most active on that committee were the late S. Safran, Jacob Willig, Buskier, Hesio Feuring and others. I offered my cooperation but it lasted for only a day as I fell ill with a gall attack. Several ladies cooked big pots of soup and tea in their homes. These were carried to the hungry. Of the ladies, the most active were the wives of Dr. Henryk Teichmann, Dr. Gärber, Dr. Schotz and Buskier.

[Column 46]

After two weeks of nerve-racking toil, Dr. Schotz and Dr. Zlatkes established the dead at 2,500 including a number of women. On receiving the list, Eng. Hahn kept his promise and allotted a quota of food. He also promised that when a general rationing system would be introduced, the Jews would be given special "Jewish ration cards" (Judenrationen). The Jewish rations were near starvation amounts which were distributed through elected representatives recognized by the Germans.

Notwithstanding the self-appointed Ukrainian Administration, the real administration remained in the hands of the German Town commander. He took up his quarters in the house of Moses Zuckerkandel, whom he ordered to be at his beck and call. On the first day the Commander called Zuckerkandel and, reading from a list, probably supplied by the Ukrainians, he asked him to bring Dr. Mayblum, Dr. Schotz and Dr. Dyver to his office. These, he said, were to be considered as representatives of the Jewish population.

When they arrived, he peremptorily told them that the Jews no longer had any rights but only duties according to the strict letter of the regulations issued by the Germans. The slightest disobedience or opposition by fellow Jews would be considered as sabotage for they, - the three representatives, as well as hundreds of other Jews, would be shot immediately. Seeing the reluctance on their faces, the commander shouted: "refusal to accept the duties just imposed on you will be considered a first act of disobedience, the consequences of which you know". Finally he announced that Mr. Zuckerkandel would act as the go-between and with the order "quick – march" (abmarschieren!) he terminated the meeting. In this way the so-called "Jewish self-government" was born. The "chosen" men did not realize what unhappy surprises were in store for them.

[Column 47]

The first office of the forcibly established Representative Jewish Committee was the premises of the "EzratIsrael" Synagogue at Mickiewicza Street.

The parallel existence of the Ukrainian Administration and the German Military Government caused great hardship to the Jews particularly in the recruitment of forced labor. But this state of affairs did not last long. In about three weeks, following the arrival of the new District Commander (Kreishauptmann) appointed by Governor Frank, the German civil administration took over from the Ukrainians. This was a heavy blow to the Ukrainians. Stripped of their short-lived power and reduced to a status where they were denied the right of decision, they were forced to play a secondary part as assistants to the Nazi executioners.

The ousting of the Ukrainian Administration brought about a deep rift between the Germans and the Ukrainians. The Ukrainians were in a state of fury but they were helpless. Nevertheless, there remained one thing which they could share with the Nazi – their blind hatred toward the Jews.

The District Commander (Kreishauptmann) whose jurisdiction extended to the neighbouring towns of Brody, Przemyslany and their surroundings were followed by several German administrative officials.

[Column 48]

The new District Commander, an official by the name of Mann, lost no time in summoning M. Zuckerkandel and Dr. Mayblum to his office. In a short speech similar to that of the Town Commander, he ordered them to form a larger representation of the Jewish Community within three days. This Committee would be held responsible for all the activities of the Jews in town as well as in the neighbouring districts. He warned that according to German law a Jew was not allowed under any circumstances to approach the German authorities except through their officially recognized representatives. This appointment of the new Committee marked the beginning of a tragic chapter in the history of the town…the chapter of the JUDENRAT.

It is not easy to approach this subject without a certain amount of prejudice and animosity to which many writers have succumbed. This is particularly true of those who did not themselves live under the Nazi occupation and did not experience those terrible times at first hand. I personally am far from defending the Judenrat as a whole. But on the other hand, my conscience does not permit me, as one who has gone through that hell on earth, to accuse or condemn all the unfortunate members of that "Institution" who were drawn against their will into its accursed circle and from which there was no way out save suicide.

It is well known that in occupied Poland the task of representing the Jewish population was forced on the intelligentsia and mainly on prominent Zionist leaders. Yet, it would therefore be absurd to accept the suggestion of those writers, generally with communist leanings, who claim that the Jewish intelligentsia, headed by Zionist leaders, betrayed their own people and collaborated with the Nazi. It is true that in those abnormal and inhuman conditions, a few individuals devoid of strong character and national self-respect occasionally succeeded in obtaining key positions as "Machers" (functionaries) by cooperating with the Nazi. These individuals without scruples and with only their personal gain in view, did in many ways exploit members of their own defenceless community. But those isolated cases do not justify the criticism of all Judenrat members. I can declare, and all survivors of that period will testify, that from the moment they entered the Judenrat until their tragic death, Dr. Mayblum, Dr. Schotz and Dr. Praeger did not soil their hands or conscience with any unworthy deed. On the contrary, they bore their sorrowful burden with a sense of great responsibility to the bitter end and more often than not, were the prime target for German brutality.

Compliments of Mr & Mrs Drettel

[Column 49]

4. The Judenrat

As already stated, Dr. Mayblum was given three days to form a Judenrat. In spite of seeming privileges likes exemption from forced labor, very few Jews were willing to serve on it. Dr. Zlatkes succeeded in escaping it because of illness. Dr. Schotz, broken in body and soul after those two weeks of door-to-door registration of the Jewish community, also tried to withdraw. But even with a doctor's certificate, he did not succeed. Faced by the argument that the food problem was a matter of life and death for the community and that he could help a great deal through his one-time colleague, Engineer Hahn who was the only member of the Ukrainian Administration left in office, he finally gave in. After difficult negotiation, Dr. Mayblum succeeded in forming a committee represented by the following: 1. Dr. Mayblum, chairman; 2) Bernstein; 3) Dr. Dyner; 4) Dr. M. Gruber; 5) Jakier; 6) Dr. Rubin; 7) Dr. Schotz; 8) Ojzer Schmierer; 9) Dr. Gärber; 10) Dr. Hreczanik; 11) Dr. Glanz and 12) Dr. Praeger.

[Column 50]

M. Zuckerkandel remained the connecting link between the Judenrat and the Kreishauptstmann.

The Judenrat required a big apparatus to carry out all the manifold tasks imposed on it. It had to supply the German administration with every possible demand: - apartments, furniture and forced labor at the shortest notice. In addition, it had to meet the most pressing needs of the Jewish population.

The various departments of the Judenrat were: - 1. Secretariat. 2. Finance. 3. Labor. 4. Food supply. 5. Health and Hospitals. 6. Social welfare. 7. Housing. 8. Stores of the Judenrat. 9. Postal service. 10. Accounts. 11. Provision and buying.

An auxiliary institution, a so-called Jewish militia, was created under the formal leadership of Dr. Landesberg, but was, in reality, headed by his deputy – one Henek Steinwurzel, a former employee of the Bacon Factory. The members of the militia were mostly recruited from newcomers to the town, refugees from Western Galicia, etc., who aided the Judenrat. Among those little known newcomers were a few bad characters and rogues who managed to sneak into places of authority. In course of time, three persons succeeded in becoming entirely independent of the Judenrat:

[Column 51]

Mr. Zuckerkandel who was in charge of the "Geschäftsstelle" – a liaison office for Jewish affairs under the jurisdiction of the head of the Gestapo in Tarnopol.

1.   Dr. Glanz who was in charge of the "Judeneinsatz" under the German labor department (Arbeitsampt). 3) Lonek Zwerdling who became a confidant and the right-hand man of Obersturmführer SS Warzok, the commandant of the Forced labor camp (Zwangsarbeitslager) in Lackie and who later became Hauptsturmführer as a reward for his efficiency in liquidating Jews.

After the shock of the pogrom and the stormy transitional period of the Ukrainian and Military governments, the establishment of a German Civil administration seemed to bring a more or less normal life back for the Jews as well as the rest of the population. The Jews grew accustomed to the blue Star of David badge, long curfews, reduced food-rations[6], and the forced labor of the men. A number of people found permanent occupation in various German offices, military and civilian. Women sought domestic service which gave them a little income and an additional morsel of food. But the main problem of supplying people for urgent day-to-day work remained unsolved. In order to avoid daily "hunts", which often ended tragically, the Judenrat undertook to supply the Germans with any required number of working hands at short notice. But how to get those hands?

[Column 52]

In spite of its undertakings and appeals, no volunteers came forward. Dr. Glanz, who was in charge of labor, ordered hunts by the Jewish militia but this only aggravated the already tormented community without producing the desired results.

At the suggestion of Dr. Schotz and Dr. Praeger, it was decided to pay 10 zloty in cash and a loaf of bread to everyone who would volunteer for work. Then the hungry people started to report to work, not so much for money as for the bread. Dr. Schotz and Dr. Zlatkes had to exercise great pressure (with the help of an expensive present) in order to obtain an additional amount of bread for this purpose from engineer Hahn. At long last, the hunts and their deplorable results were stopped.

5. "Ransom of Souls" – Financial Tribute

This seeming calm lasted only a short time and was abruptly broken by a new blow – this time financial. A ransom, or contribution, was demanded of the Jews. At the end of August, 1941, Dr. Mayblum and Mr. Zuckerkandel were summoned to the Kreishauptmann's office. A high official in S.A. uniform – one Matthaus – received them and told that in all German-occupied territories a ransom was to be levied on the Jews as being mainly responsible for the outbreak of World War II. The population of Zloczow had to contribute, in the course of 14 days, a ransom of two million marks which amounted to four million rubbles (then still in circulation) otherwise, 100 Jews would be shot. A great panic ensued in the community for, in the meantime, rumours spread from Lwow that several hundred hostages had been shot there even though the ransom was paid in full.

Compliments of the children of Hersh Baumgarten

[Column 53]

These rumours helped to make the community realize the gravity of the situation and those who had means readily came forward to offer their contribution. In the face of the new threat, the Judenrat formed an "Assessing Committee" which met with a ready response and remarkable solidarity. Within an hour the entire sum was collected in cash and kind – jewels, silver, gold and anything of value. At the same time, this deep sense of responsibility tended to magnify the tendency for self-deception among the community who believed, for quite a long time, that they could buy life with money. Luckily, no hostages were taken in Zloczow as they were in other places thanks to the fact that the wife of the Kreishauptmann and Matthaus, the official involved, were handsomely bribed. Moreover, the original ransom was reduced by half.

From the late Mr. Frenkel and the accountant Nadel, who were members of the Assessing Committee, I learnt confidentially that a considerable part of the ransom money remained with the Judenrat and was used as a reserve fund for current expenses. Two facts confirmed this information afterwards:

1. For some time the Judenrat did not collect any fresh taxes or dues;
2. The Judenrat staff did not requisition things needed for installing German families, as was the practice in all other Polish occupied towns, but bought them from those who were willing to sell their remaining belongings.

After the shock and alarm caused by the "ransom" subsided, people breathed with relief. There had been no killings. Only money was exacted.

The Judenrat then moved from the "Ezrat Israel" Synagogue to the house of Mr. Pundyk at Ormianska Street and set up proper, separate departments for its various administrative functions. This became necessary for internal reasons – the need of keeping a card-index for housing and food rations – as well as external – to keep pace with the multiplying offices of the German administration, each of which adversely affected the Jews when it was established.

[Column 54]

After the Kreishauptmann arrived, other departments were set up. I list them here because each of them directly or indirectly was instrumental in persecuting the Jewish population beginning with financial exactions and ending with final destruction.

1. The Gestapo – headed by SS Officer Ludwig – which was directly under the Gestapo in Tarnopol.
2. The regional "Kripo" (Kriminal Polizei – criminal police) under Commander Zigmunt and his deputy, Zinke. The rest of the Kripo staff consisted of Polish detectives, the biggest rogue of all being one Ebert.
3. District Gendarmerie under Captain Schwartz and his deputy Fueg.

4.   Housing Department.
5.   Arbeitsamt (Labor Office) with the Judeneinsatz under its direct jurisdiction.
6.   Treuhandverwaltung under Krämer.
7.   Finanzamt (Finance Department) run mainly by the Ukrainians.

The Judenrat was ordered to establish and furnish these new offices from A to Z. On the face of it, it looked as if the Judenrat, the representative body of the Jews, with all its administrative apparatus, had some authority.

[Column 55]

In reality, it was no more than a blind tool in the hands of the Germans. Every German, civilian or military, no matter what his rank, as well as any Ukrainian Militiaman, could walk into its offices at all times and at will. They treated all the Jews there with contempt, including Dr. Mayblum, the Head of the Judenrat and the Commander of the Jewish Militia, regarding them like worms on which they could trample whenever they felt like it. No wonder that the Jews blindly did whatever was asked of them, being in permanent danger of ill-treatment and death. Unfortunately, such visits were daily occurrences, prompted by endless demands and accompanied by blows and beatings. It was clear that the slightest refusal of any demand could bring about tragic consequences since the shooting or killing of a Jew was not considered a crime and was therefore not punished. It was in such an atmosphere that the "chosen ones", the so-called "Protektionskinder" (the Privileged) lived and worked. The worst to suffer were Dr. Mayblum and Dr. Schotz.

I no longer remember the exact date but one day at the end of October 1941, an unknown officer accompanied by a young Jewish stranger rushed into the Judenrat office with a club in his hand. On the threshold he met Dr. Schotz. Without a word he hit him a few times in the face and over the head with the whip he was carrying. Afterwards he enquired who the Chairman was and when Dr. Mayblum introduced himself, he ordered the boy to hit him. Seeing the boy hesitate, he snatched the stick from him and began to beat Dr. Mayblum until it broke and Dr. Mayblum fell to the ground bleeding. The SS officer immediately yelled: "Aufstehen und aufmerksam zuhören" (get up and listen attentively). All present in the room including the staggering Dr. Mayblum stood up in order to hear the following speech: "I, SS Obersturmführer Warzok have been appointed by the SS Police Commander in Lemberg as Commander of the Forced labor camp in Lackie. In this camp, which you damned dirty Jews will consider a Paradise[7], five hundred Jews have to appear for work. I hold you responsible for arranging and equipping this camp with everything needed for it. Woe to your co-religionists if my orders are not carried out to the last letter. You have been far too well-off so far. Now you are going to learn what SS means. Tomorrow morning at 9 o'clock we meet here again". And with that, he left banging the door with all his might.

[Column 56]

Terror, consternation and panic spread not only through the Judenrat but among the whole Jewish population and passed like wildfire in the town. The next day, in a state of utter despair, Dr. Mayblum appeared in the Judenrat with a bandaged head. With him came his colleagues Dr. Dyver and Dr. Schotz fully aware of the grave consequences facing them and the whole community. They appeared against the wish of their families. At 9 o'clock sharp, Warzok and two SS-men drove up to the offices of the Judenrat. When he saw only the three men awaiting him, he ordered his men to take them into the car and to drive off with them. Soon afterwards, M. Zuckerkandel showed up. He rushed to the Commander and begged him to intervene on behalf of the leaders who had been carried off. The Commander, after some hesitation (he did not want to interfere with the SS), telephoned to the Lackie camp and was told that the abducted men would be returned within a few hours. After five hours, they returned to the anxious community, not to mention their desperate families. They said that they were taken to work unloading trucks in the Lackie Convent. There they pledged to send on time, whenever Warzok made the demand, a number of craftsmen and laborers to convert the stables, formerly used by a mounted Soviet Division, into living quarters for the inmates of the Lager (camp).

Compliments of Sol Druck

[Column 57]

As luck would have it, I was the first to be sent there.

Now let me record a few events which, though personal in character, are closely connected with the story.

A few days after the pogrom, I fell ill with a gall attack which ended in jaundice. More serious than my illness was the horrifying fact that in the prevailing conditions, every German or Ukrainian in German uniform was authorized to kill, on the spot, any Jew who was too weak to work. Luckily, I managed to remain in bed unnoticed for a few days. After the fever had left me yellow and on shaking legs, I went to the Judenrat to ask for employment or at least a work certificate. On the way I met an acquaintance, a Pole, the owner of the Jasinski bakery, who expressed his sympathy on the death of my father and brother-in-law. In the course of our talk, he mentioned that in his house lived a German District Officer, a "Volksdeutscher" by the name of De Mare Himpel[8] who was looking for somebody with a good command of German, Polish and Ukrainian for the Ettinger bakery which was under Ukrainian management. He offered to recommend me if I were interested – and I was taken on the very same day. My duty was to keep a check on supply of flour and the quantity of bread sent out. He drew my attention to the fact that in that bakery the bread for the Jews would also be baked but only during the day shift. He asked me to keep a watchful eye on the Ukrainian personnel and the foreman who might misappropriate the ration allotted to the Jews. This concern and decency astonished me greatly. Who would guess that in a man, who had the appearance and the name of a Polish nobleman, a warm Jewish heart was beating?

[Column 58]

After having been given that job, I received a permanent working licence (Arbeitsausweis) and a loaf of bread in payment. Difficulties and troubles were not lacking, particularly with the Ukrainian workers. Later on a few Jewish bakers were also taken on and this made things easier. But the Devil did not sleep! The moment Warzok appeared on the scene events took a different turn and I was personally destined to go through all the circles of hell.

6. Lackie – the Forced Labor Camp

Within a few days of Obersturmführer Warzok's first visit to the Judenrat, he demanded that a number of craftsmen and workers be sent to Lackie and prepare the barracks for the planned camp. In order to mobilize the force, the Judenrat offered each volunteer a double salary and an additional food ration which attracted more people than necessary. Dr. Rubin, a member of the Judenrat who spoke a very good German, was assigned to accompany this group.

As this assignment was not a very attractive one, he tried to evade it by shamming illness. On hearing this, Dr. Mayblum, who happened to be in my bakery together with Dr. Schotz, asked me to help him and replace Dr. Rubin as a translator. At first I flatly refused, but after his insistent appeal on my sense of solidarity and our long-standing association, I had worked a few years in his office as an articled clerk when I was a young lawyer, I acceded to his request.

[Column 59]

The next morning I set out for Lackie with a group of 18 people. In the Convent yard a SS Sergeant-Major received us. We were made to stand and wait in military formation for Warzok for about half an hour. When he saw the group he gave a sneering look promptly followed by a speech. Pointing to the huge iron gate of the Convent he said: "Here on this gate will be hanged all those Jews who won't work well. They will hang there until they are replaced by the next group". He then began to drill us in real German style. We had to run along the big yard, sit and drop every few steps, get up, run and drop again. While we were at this exercise, Warzok and his companions kept on shooting their pistols off behind our backs for fun and in order to mortify us, at which they certainly succeeded. Each of us expected a bullet in his back at any minute. After half an hour of this macabre drill, he asked us to stand in line. I was singled out from the group and ordered: "Fall and roll!" (nieder und rollen!). I threw myself on the ground and rolled in that large courtyard full of puddles. When I fell into a pool of dung and lifted my head in an effort to avoid the stinking mess, Warzok followed me and pressed my head into the mud with his boot saying: "The nose in the filth!" (die nase muss in Dreck sein!). As my face was pressed against a stone, I broke a couple of teeth and began to choke with the dung filling my mouth. I thought that my last hour had come when suddenly my oppressor let go. He was summoned by an SS man to an urgent telephone call from Lwow. The sergeant who had first received us came up to me and asked me to get up and return to the Judenrat with an urgent order for window panes, nails and coffee beans[9]. Bleeding and unwashed, I left the camp and staggered to the road. A passing farmer's cart picked me up and brought me to town, straight to the offices of the Judenrat. The people there were shocked when they saw me. I said I had fallen from the cart and broken my teeth and told the truth only to Dr. Mayblum, Head of the Judenrat, as I had to ask him to send the above-mentioned order to the camp.

[Column 60]

The shock of this experience and my worry about those left in Lackie brought on a second gall attack. Fortunately, as I learnt later on, Warzok calmed down and the group of workers who had accompanied me were given a detailed plan of work and sent back home unharmed that evening. For two weeks they travelled to the camp every day and returned home unmolested. It looked as if Warzok had needed a victim for his cruel whims and his scape-goad had been I who, in all innocence, had stepped into the tiger's den to oblige Mr. Mayblum. Of that whole group, called "pioneers", only two remained alive: Nathan Pasternak and I. Pasternak lives in Israel today at Acre.

From then on, events at the Lackie camp, which left an indelible mark on the fate of the Jewish community of Zloczow and its surroundings, followed each other in quick succession.

Compliments of Anna Berkowitz

[Column 61]

Warzok had decided to take up his residence in Zloczow. The Judenrat, of course, had to provide him with an apartment. Neither effort nor money was spared to satisfy this brute. The task was given to L. Zwerdling who, in every possible way, and mainly with presents at the expense of the Judenrat, had managed to become Warzok's protégé and right-hand man. This "friendship" in due course not only aggravated the Judenrat but also the whole community. In fact, it became the darkest page in the history of the community under the occupation.

In the meantime, the Lackie stables provided with window panes and bare bedsteads became the camp centre for 500 Jews abducted from Lwow. The occupants were caught in the streets, loaded like cattle and dumped into the stables. They were mostly poor people who had no means of bribing their captors. They told us they had been promised by their Judenrat that they would be ransomed after four weeks. This promise, which with the best will in the world was impossible to fulfil, remained a vain hope.

Similar "forced labour camps" which in the course of time were to become "liquidation camps" were set up in a line along the bigger towns starting from Lwow via Zloczow, Tarnopol, Podwoloczyska and right into Russia. The line was called the "DG 4" route. In the Zloczow district alone, seven camps were erected: - Lackie, Kurowice, Jaktorow, Pluhow, Sassow, Zarwanica and Kozaki.

Private German organizations together with the so-called "Organisation Todt" were commissioned to keep the roads in constant repair for the enormously heavy traffic of the German war machine. The "labor camps" had to supply cheap labor. Such captive concentrations of Jews in the course of time enabled the Nazi to carry out their brutal liquidation of our people, gradually and systematically.

[Column 62]

Besides the exclusively Jewish camps, there were camps set up for unwanted elements of non-Jewish origin. These were also under a barbarous regime and handled by inhuman methods. Fritz Saukel, the Reich's commissioner for labor, was largely responsible for these camps. Yet, no matter how badly the non-Jewish slaves were treated, their conditions were idyllic compared with those of the Jews.

Warzok was actually only the commandant of the Lackie camp but as this was the biggest in the district and he himself had the highest rank among the camp commandants, all the camps subsequently came under his supervision.

Each one of these camp commandants seem to have been selected from a gallery of degenerates. They were trained in the same school of sadism and torture and practiced their skill ruthlessly on their victims over whom they exercised unlimited power. They cynically called the camp inmates their "charges" and supplemented the generally brutal SS manual of rules with their own specific methods of degradation. They inflicted untold suffering upon their victims.

In the other camps in the Zloczow district, excepting Kozaki where people were mostly employed in casual jobs and coal mining, the Jews worked in quarries, road-mending and stone-breaking. The work carried out under such inhuman conditions and with such a poor diet that people fell dead like flies. The commandants were not at all worried at the rapid loss of working hands for the Jewish population in the surrounding area was a steady reservoir of manpower. With regular transports arriving from Lwow, Brody, etc., Warzok had no immediate need to organize "hunts" in Zloczow. In return for this consideration, the Jews of Zloczow were charged with the upkeep of the camps and had to provide presents and bribes to humour the most extravagant whims of the camp commandants. At the end of November 1941, Warzok informed Dr. Mayblum in a moment of weakness, after receiving an expensive riding horse from the Judenrat, that he would allow the Jews of Zloczow to send a delegation of three men to Lwow to bring parcels of food and clothes to the inmates of the camp.

[Column 63]

As Jews were not allowed to venture out of their town limits under penalty of death, Warzok agreed to furnish travel permits to the delegates and to give them a big truck for the purpose. A journey in the then prevailing conditions was not free from mortal danger, even with a travelling permit, and therefore, nobody wanted to undertake it.

Let me explain here why I volunteered to go to Lwow in spite of the danger involved. Since the outbreak of the German-Russian War, I had not heard a word from my family, my parents, brother and five sisters. I only knew that they had moved from Przemyslany to Lwow where they had hoped to be safer from the Russian purges and mass evacuations to Siberia. When I heard about Warzok's proposal, I began to consider it seriously and came to the conclusion that this was perhaps the last opportunity I would have to see my family. I therefore volunteered for the trip against the violent opposition of my wife and friends. The fact that Dr. W. Teichman and Dr. Oscar Kitay had also volunteered in the meantime, likewise for family considerations, strengthened me in my decision. With the greatest of difficulty we got a ride to Lwow in an open truck loaded with potatoes from the Ukrainian Cooperative "Sojush". Drenched, almost frozen and only half-alive, we reached our destination. To my great joy, I found all my family alive[10]. But what a terrible state they were in! They were emaciated from the starvation diet of thin soup and a morsel of bread per day. What little foodstuff I brought with me was a priceless treasure. After the meeting, I went to the Lwow Judenrat to meet my colleagues.

[Column 64]

The news of our arrival spread like wildfire. Crowds began to fill the office of the Judenrat; mostly wives and children who came to enquire about their dear ones. The scene was heart-breaking. We had to lie to them in order not to deprive them of hope in a situation which was hopeless. Weeping with them, we asked them to prepare their letters and parcels and bring them to the Judenrat office at the Starotandetna Street near the old synagogue.

From there, I went to the main Judenrat centre at n°12 Bernstein Street. The place looked like a beehive with people milling around in the rooms and corridors. These unfortunate petitioners came to seek advice about the latest order of Dr. Lash, the district governor of Eastern Galicia, who had decided to establish a separate Jewish district, the so-called Jüdischer Wohnbezirk.

With much difficulty, I managed to reach the chairman, Dr. Rotfeld, a one-time member of the Executive of the Zionist Organization whom I had met before the war. I informed him of the terrible plight of the 500 Jews from Lwow who were shut up in the Lackie stables and stressed that without the help of their own Judenrat, these people would perish. I assured them that our Judenrat was trying to help them wherever it could but that they were breaking down under the burden of their own responsibilities.

Compliments of Gershon & Yettica Geller

[Column 65]

Dr. Rotfeld declared that he too was helpless as Lwow was also surrounded with labor camps which his Judenrat had to support. He also told me that in one of them, Sokolniki, the situation was desperate. In spite of this gloomy picture I insisted on asking for help from Lwow. The town, I said, still had a big and fairly well-to-do Jewish community and its members had to be helped, the more so as they had been promised that they would be ransomed.

After prolonged negotiations, the Lwow Judenrat agreed to send a considerable sum of money for bribing Warzok in order to ease the situation of the 500 Jewish hostages under his charge. I asked Dr. Rotfeld to delegate his own representative to Lackie but he said that he had full confidence in Dr. Mayblum.

At that moment Dr. Kitay arrived. I gave him a short report on my negotiations with Dr. Rotfeld. After consulting his staff, Dr. Rotfeld decided to include the following item for Warzok: 1) a gold Schaffhausen watch; 2) a man's fur coat; 3) a gold signed with a precious stone. These were to be handed to us before our departure.

[Column 66]

On our way to the place where the parcels were to be collected, Dr. Kitay told me he had heard that apart from the Judenrat, another organization, a "Jewish Relief Committee" (Jüdische Soziale Selbsthilfe) was functioning in Lwow. It had been established by the famous advocate, Dr. Leib Landau and its task was to help the poor and lonely. In 1939, Dr. Landau was held up for a few days in Zloczow while trying to escape eastwards before the German invasion. During those few days, I came to know him as I was one of the people who had to look after him. Dr. Kitay and I decided to visit him and obtain some information about his work. He recognized me and received us very warmly. He explained to us that he had organized the Relief Committee with the consent of the German authorities and that many such Committees were already in existence in the General Government. Part of the necessary funds came from the Judenrat and the rest were contributed by the few remaining Jews of means. In strict secrecy, he told us that he hoped to get some money from the American Joint Distribution Committee through the Polish underground organization in Warsaw. He also promised solemnly that if this hope materialized, he would repay Zloczow for the care and generous help given to the camp inmates from Lwow.

Ruins of the "Yad Harutsim Synagogue in the Holocaust

[Column 67]

Satisfied with this interview, we went to the office at Starotandetna Street where Dr. Teichman was already waiting for us, preparing a list of the parcels. Meantime, we were called back to Dr. Landau who rightly suggested that parcels for those who had no families should also be provided. He was ready to assign a certain amount for that purpose. The rest was to be given by the Judenrat. To our great surprise, we met with indifference and coldness from some of the members (Teichholz and Seidenfrau) but Dr. Rotfeld decided in favour.

[Column 68]

As we were about to take leave from Dr. Rotfeld, we were summoned to the office of the Jewish Militia where an urgent telephone message had been received from Warzok demanding that the parents of a youth who had escaped while on the way to the Judenrat, escorted by a Ukrainian militia man, be sent to Lackie. Soon after, a telephone call from the Judenrat informed us that Warzok was infuriated at the escape of the boy and had had three camp inmates hanged. In order to punish the Jews of the town as well, he suspected they had aided and hidden the boy, he sent SS men to "hunt" and 150 people including two sons of Dr. Mayblum were caught and sent to Lackie. Dr. Schotz warned us not to stop in Lackie with the parcels but to come straight back to Zloczow.

In the meantime, the parents of the escapee arrived at the Judenrat and the militia commandant insisted on sending them to Lackie. This would have meant sheer murder. We all knew what would await them there. After much thinking and discussion, we prevailed on Dr. Rotfeld and Dr. Landau to telephone Warzok and assure him that the boy had no family left in Lwow. In this way the unfortunate old couple were saved from certain torture and death.

Discovery of common grave of victims of the Holocaust

Compliments of the Bruck brothers

[Column 69]

After three days a 5-ton truck, driven by a Pole from Zloczow whom I knew, came to take us home. Heart-broken, I took leave of my family. I was never to see them again. I set out with my colleagues on our return journey. Bribed with a present, the driver agreed to take us straight to the Judenrat. There we were awaited in spite of the late hour. We gave our report to Dr. Mayblum and handed him the presents for the German. The problem then arose as to who should give the presents to Warzok? To the general regret, Lonek Zwerdling was delegated for this mission. He was the least suitable person and exploited the occasion to gain personal favours from the Nazi.

Luckily the fugitive boy returned to the camp. He swore that he had not tried to run away. His escort, feeling cold, had stopped at a farmer's hut, got drunk and told him to go wherever he liked. He intended to return to the camp but not knowing the district, he lost his way. It took him a long time before he finally found the camp. Of course, the death of three people did not worry Warzok. But, after accepting the presents, he magnanimously released some of the "hunted" people, cynically pointing out that the presents were all intended for a man and nobody had trouble to remember that he was married.

7. Life in the Labor Camp

The term "life" is scarcely suitable for that agonizing existence of slow starvation, super-human manual labor and torture of which even the Middle Ages would have been ashamed. I shall not go into details. In all the camps, the SS employed the same barbaric methods which are known to everybody by now. I shall therefore restrict myself to describing some of the practices peculiar to the commandants of Lackie and Jaktorow.

[Column 70]

The camp commandants had mapped out fixed territories for their "hunting" expeditions. After each expedition, the victims were brought to the camp, searched, deprived of all valuables and subjected to a fateful selective process. The young and healthy that were thought capable of doing the hard labor expected of them were spared. The rejected ones were herded into the yard and promptly shot before all eyes.

In the Jaktorow camp near Przemyslany, the commandant Grzymek sat on a balcony with his mistress and fired at his selected victims with telescopic guns. In that camp, a recurrent punishment practiced in winter, was to keep a victim in a barrel of water until he froze. I know of a case in which Grzymek, in an attack of rage, put one of his erstwhile protégés into a pot of boiling water to be cooked alive. I gave evidence of this horrible crime at Grzymek's trial in Warszawa in 1948.

In Lackie, every newcomer went through an "initiation ceremony" of 25 lashes intended to serve as a warning against misbehaviour. During the flogging, the victim had to repeat: "order must be kept" (ordnung muss sein). The "lightest punishment" was 50-100 lashes which often ended in death depending on the weakness of the victim or the viciousness of the lashing. The favourite punishment of Warzok and his successor Salzborn was the so-called "Anbinden" – 'tying-up'. A "mild" form was to tie the victim's arms and legs to a pole for a few hours. The severest form was to tie the victim with his head downwards which always resulted in death. The baker Schleicher died in this way, hung by order of Zalzborn.

[Column 71]

It is impossible to recount the atrocities committed on unfortunate people who after ten to twelve hours of the hardest work, subsisting on meagre food-rations, were subject to the whims of their tormentors. In the evening and on their bare planks, Warzok would come into the barracks with his "entourage" to check on cleanliness. Those whose feet were found to be a little bit dirty were dragged out of bed and flogged on the soles of their feet until the blood spurted. The victims were sometimes ordered to run from end-to-end of the yard, sometimes over live charcoal especially strewn for the purpose. Such an ordeal led to the death of Victor Marder of Brody, a distant relation of mine who died of festering wounds that turned into gangrene.

The commandants, the SS gatekeepers and their Ukrainian assistants, tried to find new ways in torturing their victims and the harvest of death was abundant. Unfortunately, there were a few Jewish kapo- sadists who also tortured their fellow inmates. In Lackie there was one such individual brought from Brody, nicknamed "Leibele Gonef" – I cannot recall his real name – who was assigned by the SS guards for flogging. According to them, he did the job better than they themselves could. Besides being a sadist, this Leibele was an informer and a real terror in the camp. In the middle of 1942, he fell ill with typhoid and was sent to hospital. He did not recover.

[Column 72]

Early in 1942, there was a sudden improvement in the Lackie labor camp. This turn for the better was certainly not motivated by humanitarian considerations. The reasons were more probably the following:

1. The awaited rapid victory of the "Blitzkrieg" did not come off. The extended front lines and the enormous losses suffered by the Germans demanded more working hands in the rear and a larger war machine. The longer routes over which the supplies were moved

Ghetto victims on their last
journey
<u>Compliments of Mrs & Mrs Charles Fisher</u>

[Column 73]

Had to be kept under constant repair and the camp commandants had to provide more and more forced labor for this purpose.

2. As the war dragged on, more and more SS men from the guards and the police force, the so-called Waffen-SS, began to realize that the rapid liquidation of the camp inmates would bring them nearer to the prospect of being despatched to the frontline which they wanted to avoid at all costs.

3. Both Grzymek and Warzok quickly realized the prospect that awaited them. They saw that the continued existence of the camps was an assurance of their own safety. By keeping the Jews alive they had the added incentive of battening on their wealth. Every "hunt" brought in a few rich individuals who still had some valuable tucked away with which to buy freedom and life, even though it was only for a short time. Through their go-betweens, the Nazi initiated a lucrative business – a trade in souls – on a large scale.

This temporary improvement was felt in the behaviour of the whole camp personnel. Apart for some isolated, whimsical outbursts of cruelty, they showed a more reasonable approach to the inmates.

First of all, food and clothe parcels might be received regularly by the inmates.

Secondly, sick rooms were established in the camps with doctors and medicines supplied, of course, by the Judenrat.

Thirdly, the Jewish hospital in Zloczow was designated a District Camp Hospital.

Fourthly, by order of Warzok, smaller camps and workshops ("Nebenlager") were set up in towns and affiliated to the main Lackie labor camp.

Fifthly, the camp secretariat, the so-called "Schreibstube" and the main food-store were transferred to the town. Its secretary was a Jew from Lwow, one Bischel, and the store-keeper was Weirauch, the son-in-law of Tauber. The store-keeper of the Jaktorow camp, whose stores were also located in Zloczow on Pocztowa Street, was Kusik Landesberg.

[Column 74]

These little innovations, though insignificant, were immediately sensed by the Jewish community – always alert to its desperate plight – and a ray of hope entered the hearts of the optimists. Unfortunately, they did not have to wait long to realize that the Germans were only using delay tactics.

8. The Relief Committee

Life in town dragged on with sad monotony. It was an existence of slow starvation under the shadow of sinister camps. Misery and hunger visited practically every home and the need to send help to the camp inmates called for an urgent relief organization. Accordingly, a Relief Committee similar to the one in Lwow was created. It was called: "Jüdisches Committee für Sociale Selbsthilfe" and the office-bearers were as follows: chairman Dr. Katz; deputy-chairman Dr. Kitaj of Krakow; members: Jacob Willig, Bursztyn (a refugee writer from Warsaw), Buskier, S. Safran, Hesio Feuring and J.Z. Imber(Buskier, Feuring and Imber afterwards worked in the Jewish Hospital). I was co-opted to the Committee later after I had come in closer contact with Mr. Mayer. Our task was enormous – our means negligible. A very important and vital department in this Committee was the one which dealt with the supply of parcels to the camps. Here, credit should be given to Mrs. Dzialoszynska (née Kitay). The collection and distribution of food and clothing, apart from the efforts of the Judenrat in this field, was very hard and often dangerous. Partly legally, partly illegally, parcels were smuggled into the camps and distributed among those who had nobody to care for them or help them. Those active in this charitable work and who often risked their lives were Buskier and the late Leon Blaustein of Brody. Blaustein survived the war and in 1964, died in Kfar Vitkin, Israel.

[Column 75]

The initial donation to the fund was received from the Judenrat, the second from Dr. Landau, the head of the Lwow Relief Committee but the main income came by collection from the community and voluntary donations by individuals. Resources were very limited and the efforts of all the committee members were not enough to overcome the main difficulty of procuring food supplies. At a critical moment when it seemed that the Committee had reached a hopeless deadlock, unexpected aid descended from Heaven in the person of Mr. Joseph Meyer[11] the new head of the Food and Agriculture department in the District Office.

The arrival of this remarkable man, endowed as he was with the highest humanitarian principles at a time when we were engulfed by an ocean of hatred, violence and murder, was like a powerful light breaking through the dark clouds in which our existence was shrouded. To illustrate his character, I shall recall a few incidents:

[Column 76]

At the end of 1941, District commander Mann, acting on orders from his head office in Lwow, dismissed engineer Hahn, the last Ukrainian employee who represented the Ukrainian authority as director of the Food Department. He was replaced in his key position by a German. This transfer took about fourteen days to accomplish. As was to be foreseen, it was the Jews who suffered, for distribution of food to them was temporarily stopped. This worried Dr. Schotz very much for he was responsible for the food supply and also because some kind of normal relationship had already been established with engineer Hahn. When the new German official took over, he paid an unexpected visit to the bakery I was attached to for bakeries were also under his control. As I was the only one who knew German, it fell to my lot to talk with him. With my heart in my mouth I gave him a detailed report on the bakery and my position there.

After our short conversation during which he questioned me thoroughly and understood that I was a Jew, he ordered me to follow him to his car and drive away with him. I cannot find the words to describe the fear and despair which I felt at that moment. I felt like a person condemned to death and led to execution. Afraid to ask questions, I did not know where I was being taken. When we arrived at Kopernika Street and stopped near Lutsak's house, he asked me to enter his flat with him. It consisted of one scantily furnished room. Then he introduced himself, offered me a chair and explained that he was a newcomer and not acquainted with the place or its conditions. He said he was quite helpless, particularly as regards the setting up of his flat. I ventured to answer that he should turn to the Judenrat.

To this suggestion he angrily retorted that he did not want anything gratis from the Jews like the other Germans. At that moment he said all he needed was a quilt as he had been freezing at night.

Compliments of Yeckes brothers

[Column 77]

In the course of our talk, he enquired about my profession and on hearing that I was a lawyer, he asked me about the Jewish intelligentsia. Seeing my reluctance to answer this question, he asked me to tell him the truth as it also interested him to know who had staged the pogrom in the town: "Sagen Si emir bitte die Wahrheit, ausserdem interessiert es mich wer hier den Judenpogrom organisiert und ausgeführt hat! Das haben ohne Zweifel unsere SS-Banditen gemacht". He said he was sure that the SS bandits had done it. Dumbfounded and afraid of some trap behind his outburst, I stood silent.

Not getting a reply, he said: "You needn't be afraid of me. I am a staunch Catholic and a German patriot and therefore an inexorable opponent of the criminal Nazi regime.

[Column 78]

"The mad Fuhrer and his criminal followers who have caused this war and all its unheard – of horrors, have brought the greatest misfortune not only on Germany but on all humanity. In spite of these striking initial victories, I am sure that we shall lose the war because the whole world is against us. My country and my people will pay dearly for this crime – for which no penalty is high enough. I have come here from Radom where the Jews know me and of my convictions. Tell your unfortunate co-religionists that I shall do my utmost to help them". At that, he glanced at his watch, which stood at 12, locked the door and turned on the radio. I heard the voice of the B.B.C. – "Here is London calling!" I should mention here that Jews were forbidden to listen to the radio under penalty of death.

Blood rushed to my head and my heart seemed to be near bursting when I heard about the enormous losses of the German armies on the Eastern front because of the frost and snowdrifts. I did not know whether it was a dream or reality. I could not restrain the tears that rolled down my cheeks. Mr. Mayer came closer to me, tried to calm me and embraced me. From that moment we became friends. This friendship was all the more precious because it was extended through my person to the whole community at a time when a Jew was treated worse than the lowest beast on earth.

Common grave of Zloczow Jews, 1943

[Column 79]

Mr. Meyer asked me to visit him daily (if possible, of course) as he felt very lonely and in need of someone to talk to and confide in. I left him in a state of semi-consciousness as I could not believe that what had happened had really taken place. Perhaps it was a hallucination of my exhausted brain?

On the way home I met Jacob Willig, whom I hugged with happiness, unable to utter a word. Willig took me into the house of Dr. Schotz nearby where Dr. Kitaj also was present. After I had recovered a bit, I told them about Meyer and the English radio announcement. Dr. Mayblum, Dr. Schotz and Dr. Kitaj naturally concluded that we should immediately approach this new friend of the Jews for help in our grave food situation. But there was no need to do so. The next day Meyer himself summoned me through his driver and informed me that while examining the documents he had discovered that the Ukrainians had, on their own initiative, diminished the food ration legally allotted to the Jews. For instance, the weekly ration of bread had been reduced from 1,000 to 700 grams; the jam ration from 100 to 50 grs and against the 200grs of white flour, nothing was allotted.

The first thing Meyer did was to give the Jews the full rations due to them. He then began to investigate what had happened to the misappropriated rations. Seeing that the full quota allotted was below the bare minimum, he advised the Judenrat to double the number of manual workers in the monthly census returns. Manual workers, it may be mentioned, were entitled to a double food ration. But I do not wish to repeat here the details which Mr. Meyer himself mentions elsewhere in this book. I shall restrict myself to a few typical incidents which he has refrained from touching upon.

[Column 80]

Since the German occupation, meat was beyond reach for Jews. Mr. Meyer suggested that he could find a way of allotting a weekly ration of bones and scraps to manual workers from the German slaughter house. Under the excuse of sending those scraps, Arjeh Steinman, the one-time director of the Bacon Factory who was now employed at the slaughterhouse, added some extra bits and pieces which made it possible to open a little meat shop in Pundyk's house. He also managed to earmark a few scraps for the Jewish Hospital which carried a special tag: "Allgemeines Krankenhaus" (General Hospital).

Though all these tricks, coupled with Meyer's friendly efforts, helped a little, they could not bring much relief. The bulk of the Jewish population was starving. Dr. Schotz and Dr. Mayblum insisted that I should try and persuade Mr. Meyer to provide some additional provisions to enable us to open a kitchen to feed the very poor and solitary. Opening a kitchen on the part of the Jews was a suggestion almost bordering on madness! Where would we get such articles as potatoes, groats, fat, etc – things which Jews had no right to procure and would not even dream of asking for?

With a heavy heart, I went to Meyer fully aware of the risk in which the suggestion involved a good and noble man who had already done far more for us than his official duty warranted. But in view of our helplessness, I plucked up courage and told him that this help was the only way out that we could see from our tragic food situation. In his face I could see the intense inner struggle going on within him. At last his innate goodness and nobility prevailed. What was duty on my part – to ask for help – was an act of courage and heroic self-sacrifice on his. The allotments for this kitchen were written out for certain imaginary, non-existent institutions and military units. We had to be very careful in receiving these supplies since most of the stores were in the hands of Ukrainians who would have been only too willing to disclose forgeries or similar misdemeanours to the Gestapo where Jews were concerned.

Compliments of Chava Hoffman

[Column 81]

With the help of the husband of Eve Tinter, the Jewish accountant in the "Soyus", the Cooperative on the Podwojcie, we bribed the manager of the Food Stores, a Ukrainian named Pietryk who hated the Germans even more than the Jews for not having ranted independence to the Ukrainians. After that, things worked out smoothly.

Thanks to Meyer the kitchen provided about 200 people with a warm meal which consisted of soup and potatoes or a cereal. Those who could afford it paid half a zloty for a meal. They very poor, of course, received it free of charge.

To round off the picture of Meyer's nobility of character, I shall recall another action of his which, were it not for the tragic situation it reveals, would sound like a good farce.

The fat problem in every war is difficult. During the German occupation, the fat shortage was so serious that the strictest control was imposed on this vital article of food. Very bit was sent to the front. As the feast of Passover drew near, the food situation worsened. Not only was there no fat but even the promised potato ration – the Bezugsschein – remained a paper promise. The farmers did not deliver the quota demanded by the German authorities and the stores were empty. Nevertheless, our friend Meyer found ways and means of helping us. He sent out special groups of gendarmes to collect produce from the farmers and ten tons of potatoes arrived at the Kitchen stores. More difficult, however, was the problem of the fat. Here the noble Meyer conceived an extraordinary plan.

[Column 82]

[Column 83]

The "Soyus" Cooperative had stored up a few hundred litres of crude vegetable oil. Meyer staged a real farce to get it for the Jews. He drove up one day to the Cooperative and, pretending to have come to take stock of all the food supplies, went around sniffing and searching in every corner. When he came to the place where the oil was stored, he yelled out that something rotten was lying there. The storekeeper explained that it was crude vegetable oil for the Germans. Asking to be shown the stuff, Meyer indignantly berated the storekeeper: "Is this what you keep for us Germans? Do you want to poison us? Out with it! Throw it away to the Jews! (*Das soll für uns Deutsche bestimmt sein? Ihr wollt uns vergiften! Heraus damit! Gibt es den Juden!*).

According to our pre-arranged plan, I went to the"Soyus" Cooperative soon after under the excuse of having to settle an urgent matter. The store-keeper, it seemed, was only too happy to see me. He asked me to relieve him as quickly as possible of that "stinking" oil and take it away. This of course I gladly did! Thanks to the cunning trick of Mr. Meyer, the community had oil that Passover.

9. The Final Solution of the Jewish problem

The gloom of German occupation covered Europe like a shroud. People choked and war against England, America and Russia was declared by Goebbels as a holy war against Jewish capitalism and communism. Roosevelt, Stalin and Churchill were nothing more than servants of International Jewry. The Jews brought about the war and therefore they had to be mercilessly destroyed. Such was the theme of Nazi propaganda.

[Column 84]

One would have thought that the great losses suffered by the Germans would tend to reduce the preoccupation of the Nazi with the Jewish problem. But the opposite was the case. Having grown accustomed to quick victories at the beginning of the war, the first great defeat which they suffered near Moscow served to intensify their murderous rage against the Jews. Thus the "Eindlössung", the Final Solution of the Jewish People seems to have crystallized in the brains of Hitler and Himmler when the tide of war began to turn against them.

One 20ᵗʰ January, 1942, in the "Interpol" building at Swansee, a secret conference of the SS, SD, RSHA and the Gestapo took place. Here, it eventually transpired, the tragic fate of our people was sealed. At this meeting, it was decided that all the Jews of Europe should gradually be sent to their death in special death camps. The proposal was made by Reinhard Heydrich and promptly confirmed by Hitler and Himmler.

The first step in this move was the isolation of the Jews in separate districts from which they were to be deported to hermetically sealed ghettoes. The details of this plan were entrusted to Office IV of the RSHA whose head was SS-Gruppenführer H. Müller. Within his office was a special Jewish Department IV B under the command of Adolf Eichmann.

The next step was the methodical construction of the Death Camps to carry out the liquidation. Death Camps were erected at the following places in Poland:

Oswiencim
Chelmno near Lodz
Treblinka on the Bug
Sobibor near Lublin

Compliments of Rabbi David Eisen

[Column 85]

Maydanek, near Lublin
Belzec near Lwow

Simultaneously with the plan for the physical liquidation of the Jews, a detailed plan for the plundering of victims was drawn up. This operation was designated "Aktion Reinhardt".

The satanic plan was to be carried out gradually because of strong opposition from certain quarters in the Government who insisted that for economic as well as strategic reasons the final liquidation should be postponed until after victory. With the increasing needs of the war fronts, the Jews, these quarters argued, could be very useful. The liquidation should therefore be limited in the first instance to "anti-social" and unproductive elements. This milder proposal, though opposed by the top leaders, served to lull public opinion abroad and also to deter the Jews from organized opposition. The Germans declared hypocritically: "urbi et orbi": - "Only productive work gives on the right to live".

[Column 86]

*****

Footnotes:

1. Dr. Opperer perished in 1943 while sorting old ammunition in a German military outpost. A grenade dropped from his hand, exploded and tore him to pieces
2. Among the dead he recognized Salitr, the owner of the main bookshop. Chary Schimmelmann the pharmacist. Frosh and many others
3. R.S.H.A. –Reichssicherheitshauptampt – the Security Bureau of the German Reich which consisted of: 1) Sicherheitspolizei, security police – SIPO: 2) Security Service (Sicherheitsdienst) – SD. 3) Criminal Police – Kriminal Polizei (KRIPO). 4) Secret Government Police – Geheime Staatspolizei GESTAPO. At the head was R. Heydrich and, after his death, Müller (known as Gestapo Müller)
4. The authenticity of this name, given by one of the Ukrainians, cannot be guaranteed
5. The same woman informed the Gestapo later that we had hidden valuables and clothes as well as money from the sale of our house and we nearly paid for it with our lives
6. The Ukrainian officials on their own tried at all cost to reduce the starvation level of the food rations for the Jews whenever they could do so
7. Unfortunately, his prophecy came true. The moment the Ghetto was liquidated and Zloczow became "judenrein" (free of Jews), the few survivors who crawled out of bunkers and holes tried at all costs and for big sums of money to get into that Inferno of a camp, for those who worked there still had the right to live
8. This so-called Volksdeutsche 'i.e. Pole of German origin) was a disguised Jew from Lwow, a member of the well-known family Gimpel who were the owners of the Jewish Theatre in Lwow. After the war, he lived for a few years in Lodz and later immigrated to the United States
9. Coffee beans were scarce and the article most sought by the Germans
10. I persuaded my family to return to Przemyslany at all costs. They did. But unfortunately, it did not help them. They all perished in the massacre of December, 1942, except my younger sister who was killed later in the Janowski camp
11. Mr Joseph Meyer, a native of Bavaria and a devout Catholic, at present resides in München-Moosach, Seydlitzplatz 17. As a man of high principles who believes in and practices the precept of love one's neighbor, he showed great sympathy for persecuted Jews and became a true friend of Israel and its people. During the war, he was a sworn enemy of the Nazi regime and its practices which he bravely opposed, often endangering his life. After the war, he helped to bring many Nazi criminals to trial and is one of the founders of the Jewish-Christian Friendship Committee in Munich. Two articles of his appear in this book.

[Column 86]

10. The Workshops and Employment in Forced Labor Camps

In order to give this new propaganda slogan, the appearance of truth, the Germans began to set up work outposts where only

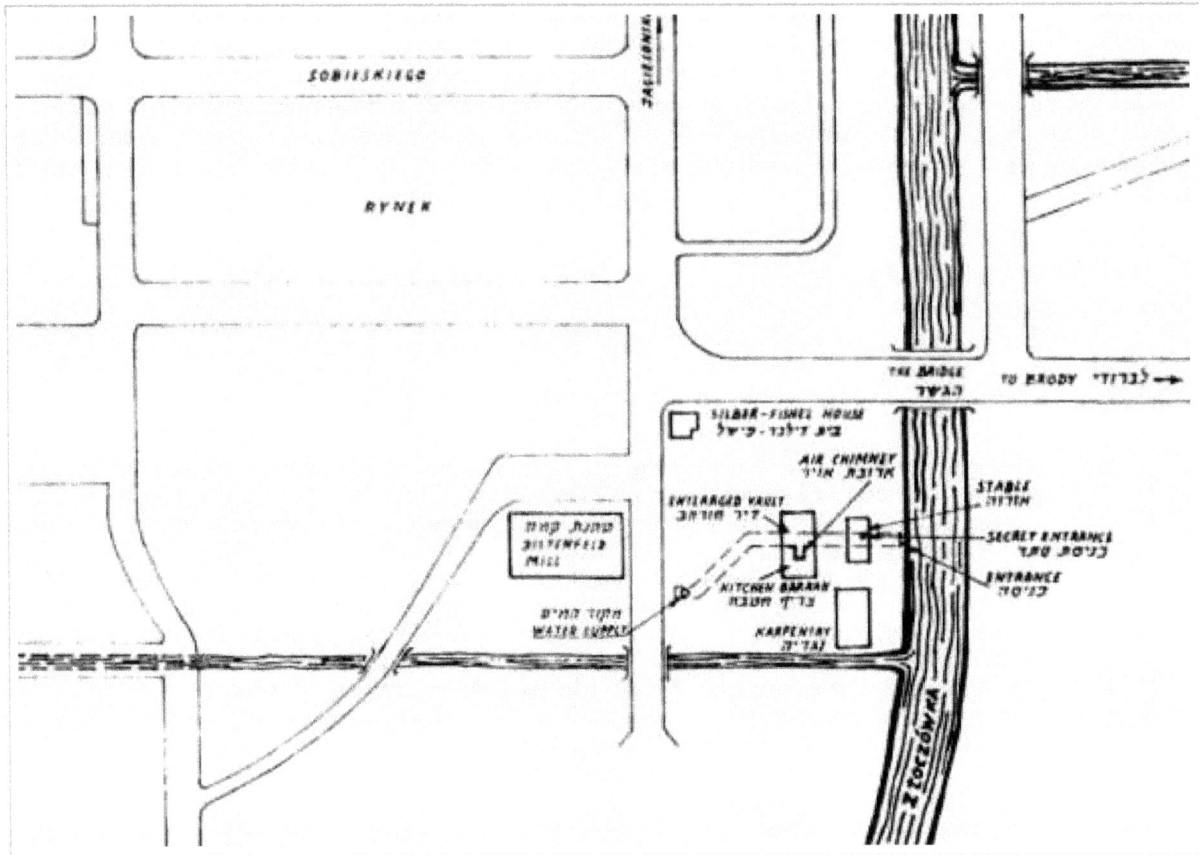

Wiklicky bunker plan

[Column 87]

Jews were employed. These were big private firms, the S.S. or military institutions. The Jewish community and its leaders fell readily into this trap not sensing what was behind it. A race for work began and even more for work-certificates (the so-called "Arbeitsausweis"), which, bought at a high price, gave their owners a doubtful security for an even more doubtful length of time. Because of the demand, prices varied according to the category of the work and the financial capacity of the buyers. In order to make all this appear more credible, employment cards were classified according to the importance of the place of work: -

1. A certificate with the letter "W" (Wehrmacht – German Defence Forces);
2. A certificate with the letter "WV" (wirtschaftlich verwendbar – useful for economy);
3. A certificate with the letter "A" (Arbeiter – worker).
4. A certificate with the letter "H" (Haushalt – housework for working wives).

Every owner of an Ausweis had the corresponding letter market on his armband. By order of the SS Camp Commandants began to set up new, smaller camps called Nebenlager around the original mother camps. Warzok, who was very business-like (he was a business agent by profession), was one of the first to organize a number of small workshops in Zloczow which were affiliated to the main camp workshops as the name indicates: ("Zwangsarbeitslager Lackie, Nebenstelle Zloczow Lagerkwerkstätte"). The main workshops were in the house of Engineer Alda at Lwowksa Street opposite the Jewish Hospital. The Ettinger bakery, in which I was working, was also requisitioned for a workshop in which Jews were to replace Ukrainians. The camp workers wore yellow armbands and had special certificates with the letter "L" (Lager Juden).

[Column 88]

At the time of the hectic search for life-preserving "Ausweise", Israel Strassler, the owner of a little sweet factory in his house at Rynek, asked me to have Mr. Meyer use his influence with the Food Department to take over his factory which would then supply its entire output to the "Deutsches Lebensmittle-Geschäft", the only German grocery in town. Strassler and his sons rightly calculated that if their suggestion were accepted, the workshop would become a place of employment and a haven of safety for a few Jewish families under the protective wings of Mr. Meyer. This proposition seemed sound and also appealed to me personally, for an event had taken place in the bakery a few days earlier which nearly cost me my life.

One night-shift, an offence was committed at the Bakery. Usually only Ukrainians worked at the Bakery during the night-shift but that night, the Jewish baker Schleicher was temporarily replacing the Ukrainian baker. The next morning SS officer Salzborn, the deputy of Warzok, dropped in at the Bakery and took away the Ukrainian Bakery Manager, Schleicher and myself to the Lackie camp. The manager was decent enough to point out that I was absolutely innocent as I was employed only during the day. The full weight of the accusation thereafter fell upon the unfortunate Schleicher who was promptly suspended from the legs, head down, until death ended his slow agony. I escaped with a few lashes.

Mr. Meyer readily agreed to the Strassler proposal and in addition entrusted us with the job of producing a mixture of cooked potatoes for the bread[12] so as to give our enterprise more validity and an appearance of greater usefulness to the local German Food Administration.

Compliments of I. Horowitz

[Column 89]

This little factory, which was affiliated soon after to the camp workshops, became an island of rescue, and an asylum for a few families who eventually survived the extermination.

11. Gestapo in Sight

A new and threatening shadow fell on our town the moment a Gestapo branch, whose district head office was in Tarnopol, was established. This institution was the dread of the whole population including the Germans themselves. Its tentacles reached out to every sphere of life, particularly Jewish life.

From the first moment the Judenrat tried to make some kind of contact with the head of the local Gestapo, one Ludwig and later on with his counterpart in Tarnopol, Müller. This task was undertaken by Zuckerkandel who went to Tarnopol for the purpose. Thanks to the intervention of Fleischer, a member of the Tarnopol Judenrat and with the help of some expensive presents, Zuckerkandel succeeded in reaching Müller himself. Zuckerkandel returned with an order to form an intermediary body ("Geschäfts- stele") between the Judenrat and the Gestapo as in Tarnopol. This task was again entrusted to Zuckerkandel with Dr. S. Kahane as his secretary.

[Column 90]

The first step taken was to provide sufficient funds for this office. These were collected from all the "Judenräte" in the district. Soon after, Müller 'graced' our town with several visits which extracted truckloads of gifts, not to speak of the jewels and precious stones that Zuckerkandel personally took to him to Tarnopol. It should be mentioned here that Zuckerkandel's intervention usually met with success, though only in small and unimportant matters.

The first victims of the Gestapo were Dr. Ambus and Mr. Aryeh Steinman, the former director of the Bacon Factory. One day they were suddenly arrested and taken away to Tarnopol. At the requests of their wives, Zuckerkandel was sent to intervene on their behalf but Müller told him that it was too late as he had already ordered them to be shot.

Besides the Gestapo, there was another authority, the "Kripo" (Kriminalpolizei) which inflicted much suffering on the Jews. One Polish detective – Ebert was particularly obnoxious. This rogue used to lie in wait for the Jews, secretly leaving the Jewish quarter – which was forbidden under penalty of death – in order to buy some food from the farmers. He pounced on these Jews ruthlessly and arrested them, only agreeing to let them free for a ransom which his partner, a Jewish militiaman, would fetch from their families.

[Column 91]

The "Gendarmerie" under Commandant Schwarz, was kept busy watching for Jews who dared leave their ghetto. Caught by the gendarmes, they would pay with their lives, as freedom of movement was limited even in the town itself, not to speak of outside its borders and inter-urban movement was strictly forbidden to Jews and punished with death. Is it any wonder that the Jewish communities were completely sealed off from one another and had no information as to what was going on? Sometimes nebulous gossip leaked through, spread by Ukrainians or Poles. Its credibility was usually doubted.

12. The First Alarm

[Column 92]

The first alarm pierced the hermetically sealed walls of our town because of a tragic accident. In the spring of 1942, Herman Friedman, the representative of the Okocim Breweries who remained in his position under a Ukrainian manager and travelled with him on business to Lwow, was arrested by the Gestapo on his arrival there. As the Beer Warehouses were under the control of the Food Department, Friedman's daughter, Lusia and married to Hessel (who now lives in Warsaw) came running to me for help – for Meyer's intervention. Meyer tried to use his influence and declared that he himself had sent Friedman to Lwow on behalf of his department. His effort was of no avail as Friedman had already been put to death. (It seems that American dollars had been found on him). But Meyer's visit to the Gestapo was not in vain. On that occasion he came to know that in Lwow and neighbouring towns, some action was due to take place against so-called unproductive elements (Aussiedlungs-Aktion). On his return, and assured of the strictest secrecy as to the source and person from whom he had obtain this information, he asked me to warn the Judenrat, which I, of course, immediately did.

Compliments of Herman Fruhman

[Column 93]

The Judenrat, like all civic bodies, usually contained two opposite groups: one of pessimists who had no illusions as to the tragic fate awaiting the Jews; the other of optimists who believed that every difficulty could be overcome with bribes and gifts. The optimists were sceptical as to the authenticity, arguing that if it were true, Zuckerkandel would know about it. Their naivety and blindness went so far that Dr. Gruber scolded me for spreading defeatism and panic instead of encouraging the people.

The Judenrat decided to send Zuckerkandel immediately to Tarnopol to see how the wind was blowing. He returned with the reassuring news that, as far as could be seen, nothing threatened Zloczow.

In spite of this good news, tension and fear were felt in the Jewish streets. Everybody tried frantically to get some "Ausweis" or other. Trade was brisk not only in real certificates but also in forged ones. All sorts of cheats and crooks exploited the situation. There even arrived a "specialist" from Lwow on forging documents and passports in Aryan names.

Others, more careful and practical, did not trust all these papers and began to build secret hiding places and well-camouflaged shelters. I myself was taken into confidence by four parties who decided to erect such shelters: (1) Strassler; (2) Furgang; (3) Munesh Margulies and (4) Barash at the carpentry.

13. The Beginning of the End

The Nazi began to carry out their plan of annihilation by instalments. After other towns, the turn of Zloczow came too.

[Column 94]

In the middle of August 1942, Zuckerkandel was suddenly summoned to the Gestapo in Tarnopol. There, Sturmbannführer Müller told him that the Judenrat was called upon to supply 3,000 people who fell into the category of "unproductive". He, of course, used the well-known propaganda trick that the removal of the unproductive elements was for the good of the community, as their elimination would ease the unbearable food and housing situation. At the same time, he added a warning that in case the Judenrat refused to comply with the order he would stage a "wild action" on his own in which he would take everybody he could lay hands on. Zuckerkandel returned with Fleischer, the go-between of the Judenrat and the Gestapo in Tarnopol, who was supposed to help him to convince the Zloczow Judenrat to carry out Müller's order. Fleischer stated at our Judenrat meeting that the Tarnopol Judenrat had made a compromise approved by the Rabbinate. (This statement was false).

Frantic, dramatic consultations began. They were secret. There were single votes for the compromise but the majority were against it as nobody wanted to burden his conscience with such a crime. Fleischer returned to Tarnopol without a definite answer and had to report to Müller that the Zloczow Judenrat was about to take a final decision and that it would take some time to compile the list of the victims.

In spite of the well-guarded secrecy of the deliberations, the news of the Gestapo demands spread like lightning. I cannot find adequate words to describe the panic and terror that seized the community. Though a mortal blow had been expected for some time, nobody knew how or when it would fall. There had been no warning of it and now here it was! The sly Nazi bandits had even kept wagons in readiness for the tragic load.

Compliments of Dr. & Mrs. Sol Jollek

[Column 95]

Late in the night of 27-28 August, Zuckerkandel was called to the local Gestapo at Podwojcie. He was accompanied by two Jewish militia men. (One of them was Landau). Müller was waiting for him. When asked for the list of the victims, Zuckerkandel, afraid to disclose that the Judenrat had refused to draw it up, stated that it was not ready yet. Müller yelled: "…You swine! I shall show you what the Gestapo is like".

Meantime, one of the militia men who accompanied Zuckerkandel noticed a number of big trucks with dimmed lights at a distance near the brick factory (Cegielnia) on the Tarnopol highway. He deducted, or perhaps sensed instinctively that those trucks had been brought by the Gestapo for carrying away their victims.

Not waiting for Zuckerkandel, the militia men ran back to town and informed everyone they met about their misgivings and fear. This warning travelled like wildfire! People did not wait for any confirmation of the news but began to hide wherever they could – in shelters, cellars, garrets, lifts and holes. Some just barricaded themselves in their flats. I left my family in Furgang's shelter at Lwowska Street and myself, remained with the Strasslers.

It will never be known whether Müller told Zuckerkandel about the impending action on the following day. Zuckerkandel vehemently denied that Müller had said anything about the action. He claimed that he only received an order to appear at the Judenrat building at 7a.m. the following day, together with all the members of the Judenrat and the militia men.

On August 28th, in accordance with Müller's order, Zuckerkandel with a few members of the Judenrat and most of the militia men, reported punctually. At 7 o'clock, Müller drove up to the Judenrat building, followed by a long line of trucks manned by "Rollkomando", SS and Ukrainian militia men. At the same time, a detachment of local gendarmes arrived on the scene. On seeing that only a few members of the Judenrat were present, Müller ordered Zuckerkandel to bring the rest with the help of the Jewish militia. This he did. Only Dr. Schotz was missing. Guessing what was in store for the Jews, he had hidden himself together with his family in the house of his Polish neighbour, Soltynski.

[Column 96]

From the moment of his arrival, Müller was struck by the extraordinary quiet and complete inactivity in the Jewish quarter which was like a house of the dead. Asked about the reason for this lifelessness, Zuckerkandel stammered and gave lame excuses. Müller, suspecting that the Judenrat had warned the people, was enraged and roared like a wild beast: "– You cursed dogs; you shall pay for this dearly!"

Just then an SS Officer entered the room and declared that all the Jewish houses were locked and that nobody had responded to the call of his men to open them. Müller, now furious, ordered the Judenrat (with the exception of Dr. Mayblum who was ill at that time) and the Jewish militia to go out into the streets, each with an axe in hand. He divided his men into small groups, each led by a member of the Judenrat and a few militia men. At the point of the SS men's bayonets and under incessant beating by the butts of their rifles, these unhappy people were compelled to lead the way to Jewish homes, to break open the doors and to expose their terrorized occupants to the savage brutalities of the Nazi attackers. Old and young, sick and invalid, were forced out of their flats, cellars, nooks and corners by enraged beasts in human guise. The children's cries mingled with the wailing of the women and the moans of the beaten men. Above all was heard the wild yell of the Nazi: "Los, los – schnell! (out, out – quickly!). The turmoil was accompanied by ceaseless bursts of gunfire as Müller had ordered his men to shoot anyone who tried to escape. Once again the streets of Zloczow were strewn with the dead. It is impossible to delineate these blood-curdling scenes. Only two remain in my memory which I saw with my own eyes together with Wilo Freiman of Strasslers.

Compliments of Mr & Mrs Lewinter-Grinseid

[Column 97]

The late Marcus Smal who lived next door to the Strasslers was a corpulent man but owing to prolonged starvation, he became terribly bloated. Pursued to Ormianska Street with whips and blows, he could hardly keep pace and Müller ordered him to be shot. His order was promptly executed by a gendarme named Hirsakorn. The corpse was left for three days in the yard of a relative who buried him after the "action" had stopped.

The other incident also took place Ormianska Street, near the Judenrat. Müller ordered all the sick in the new Jewish Hospital to be taken away. Among them was a teacher, Samuel Schwarz who had gangrene in his foot. He asked the SS man to release him or shoot him as he had been an officer in the Austrian army during World War I. The SS man, himself an Austrian, wanted to let him free but Müller, who happened to be nearby, had the Jewish patient mercilessly shot.

The "action" lasted two days. The "hunted" were driven to a collecting point in the old Market Square, and from there, were sent to the railway station where they had to wait for a goods train. At the station, and later in the carriages, scenes from the inferno were enacted. The people were entirely without food but worse than the hunger was the thirst in the terrific heat of August. The Ukrainian hyenas, taking advantage of the suffering of the Jews, sold bottles of water for 100zl (about 2 dollars) each. The Ukrainian militia on guard exceed their SS colleagues in brutality and ruthlessness. Some German guards tried to help the unfortunate people. When their superiors were not watching, they fetched a bucket of water or even a little bread for the hungry children. The Ukrainians in such cases called the attention of the SS men, to prevent such little mercies.

Compliments of the children of Berl Cornfeld

[Column 98]

When the cattle train finally arrived, people were loaded like animals: 100 and more to each wagon. People choked from the heat and lack of space. Müller moved constantly between the town and the railway station, personally supervising the loading of the "goods". Eye-witnesses told us that the officer in charge, wanting to put an end to this terrible work, submitted to Müller a bigger list than he had actually loaded. To be on the safe side, he supplemented the number with the bodies of those who had been killed earlier so that the wagons were crowded with the living and the dead.

During the loading, Warzok appeared at the station to take back a few of the inmates of the camp but without their wives and children. Among others he tried to take back, Mann – the brother of Mrs. Sternchuss – but he was not allowed to have his wife Noemi, née Spanier, join him and he voluntarily returned to the train.

On 30th August, in the afternoon, the "death" train left in the direction of Lwow-Belzec. In spite of strong guards and sealed locks, some people who probably smuggled some tools with them, managed to break the doors during the journey and jumped out of the running train. Ninety-nine per cent of such escapees were fatal. Most of the desperate escapees found death under the wheels of the running train. Very few indeed succeeded in saving their lives and survived the war. One of them is Mrs. Irena Poplawska, née Rozka Lerner, and her seven year old son Jurek, who now lives in Haifa.

[Column 99]

Having completed his murderous task which costs about 2,500 lives, Müller levied a tribute of 200,000 Zloty on the Judenrat to cover the cost of the "action".

Later, we learnt from Mrs. Poplawska and some Polish railwaymen, including the train driver that the train had been sent to the liquidation camp in Belzec.

After the "action" the "Rollkommando" units vanished. Once again mortification, silence and mourning enveloped Zloczow. People slowly began coming to enquire about the fate of their dear ones who had been carried off. Some preferred to go on deluding themselves and would not believe the bitter truth.

The uneasiness of the people found an outlet in quarrels and heated arguments in the Judenrat. Once I heard Dr. Glanz accusing Dr. Mayblum and insulting Dr. Schotz, calling the latter a coward because he had hidden himself during the "action". They nearly came to blows. Dr. Schotz said that he had done no harm to anyone by his absence and there was nothing to prevent anyone else from doing the same. Some of the people condemned those members of the Judenrat who took part in the action. But, the vast majority did realise the extenuating circumstances which accompanied this tragic event – and that one had no right to condemn a person who acted under brutal compulsion and whose only alternative was suicide.

After this "amputation" of the community, the Nazi, following their consistent line of deceit, tried to persuade the Jewish leaders that now that the deportation of the unproductive elements had been completed, normal and peaceful conditions would return. Unfortunately, there were still some naïve people who believed them.

[Column 100]

Not long after the deportation, I visited Mr. Meyer and told him all about that "hunt". Shocked to the depth of their hearts, he and his wife wept and wrung their hand in helpless despair and Mr. Meyer cried: "For God's sake, why do you go to slaughter like defenceless sheep?" But he immediately corrected himself, apologized for his words and said: "The German people and other nations are also helpless in the face of this Godless brood. Be on your guard and don't believe the treacherous assurances of these murderers. They will certainly go ahead with their devilish game".

His prediction was fulfilled only too soon. Fundamental changes in the administration dealing with the Jewish population were introduced soon after. In spite of the reservations and protests of some high German dignitaries as well as a few generals * the whole Jewish community was transferred to the care of the Gestapo and the SS. The so-called: "Work-centres" were closed down and from now on, only Gestapo representatives might decide whether a certain workshop was to continue to operate and how many Jews were to be employed in it. A new order appeared annulling all "Ausweise" – work certificates – unless they were re-confirmed and signed by the district Gestapo official. Zuckerkandel was assigned to deal with this matter.

The Judenrat called on all holders of the "Ausweise" to hand in these life-giving, priceless documents – passports to life commonly and ironically called: "Hoshanah Rabah Quitlach" (Mighty Salvation Slips) in orderto have them renewed by the Tarnopol Gestapo. Fees had to be charged for this transaction as it was impossible to go to Müller without a handsome gift. This order did not apply to camp inmates or workshop workers as they had already been long under SS rule.

* * *

Compliments of Samuel & Rose Gelles

[Column 101]

Zuckerkandel returned from Tarnopol in triumph since he had succeeded in having all the certificates he took with him confirmed as valid.

After that, tension and terror subsided for some time – about 2 months – and relative calm seemed to prevail.

In the middle of September,1942 I was suddenly summoned to Mr. Meyer. On my arrival I found an elegant and handsome officer who introduced himself to me as Capitan Pollinger * from the military town command. Noticing my reserve in the presence of the stranger, Mr. Meyer explained that he was an ardent anti-Nazi and absolutely trustworthy. They told me that only after a severe inner struggle did they decide, in spite of the serious risk they ran, to inform me of the terrible news they had received from the higher Nazi authorities in Lwow; the strictly-kept secret of the imminent and final liquidation of all the Jews. They did not yet have details or the exact date when this was to take place but it would be carried out gradually in the very near future. They had arrived at a conclusion which they suggested to me – that single individuals might perhaps escape their doom by hiding among non-Jews or in some safe hideouts. The only alternative hope lay in a quick victory by the Allies which did not seem to be very near.

****

His messenger was Mr. Joseph Batish – at present resident in Detroit, U.S.A. whom I placed in Meyer's home as a domestic servant and who served as our liaison.

[Column 102]

They permitted me to share this distressing news with some of my associates who could be trusted. I passed this "death sentence" on to Dr. Mayblum without, of course, mentioning the names of those who had given me this strictly guarded secret. Dr. Mayblum received the job-like biddings with sad resignation saying that only a miracle could save the Jews. At the next Judenrat meeting he tried to break the news very gently, camouflaging it among other matters under discussion. But those present were not all prepared to believe this hopeless truth and called the others pessimists and panic-stricken cowards who saw everything in black colours.

14. The Second Action

Only a few days after my talk with Meyer and Pollinger, Batish came again to me with the shocking news that the Gestapo had arrested Meyer and transferred him to Lwow. This was the greatest blow that could have befallen us and particularly me. I awaited arrest at any moment. To get some details about Meyer's arrest, I secretly went to his desperate wife who thought that her husband had been arrested because of his friendly attitude toward the Jews and also because of the anti-Nazi convictions which he openly expressed in the presence of his colleagues, some of whom must have denounced him.

After three days of fear and suspense, Mr. Meyer returned and sent for me at once. When I came I found him exhausted, dirty and unshaven. He told me that he had been kept in the Gestapo jail at Lwow for the reasons which his wife had correctly guessed. Thanks to his administrative abilities and perhaps even more, thanks to the intervention of some high-ranking personalities, he succeeded in escaping from the Gestapo clutches. He assured me that he did not intend to change his friendly attitude toward the Jews but more caution would be necessary.

[Column 103]

After our consultation with Meyer and Pollinger *, Mr. Meyer advised us to keep watchmen at night on the outskirts of town in order not to be surprised by sudden 'surprise' actions. He also promised to keep in touch with us and immediately pass on any information he would get about suspicious movements. It was not easy to place guards at important points of traffic but a way was eventually found. It was done partly by the personnel of the Jewish hospital at the end of the Lwowska Street and the workers at Weintraub's flour mill kept constant watch on the highway leading to Tarnopol.

At the end of October, Mr. Meyer informed us that Pollinger had received news about orders for preparedness given by the higher authorities to all local police, gendarmerie and even units of the military town command.

This might have no connection with the feared action, as such orders had sometimes been given in the past under the pretext of approaching partisans; but in any case, we intensified our watchfulness.

On the night of November 1, 1942, somebody from the Jewish hospital (if I remember rightly it was Hesio Feuering) brought news of a column of military trucks drawn up nearby. Without waiting for any confirmation of this news, the Jews began to hide. People ran crazily from place to place to find a shelter. Everyone thought that others had a better one than their own.

****

At that meeting I came to know that the town commandant, a major whose name has escaped me, was aware of the activities of Meyer and Pollinger.

[Column 104]

This time the blow came from Lwow. On November 1, 1942, a special representative of the SS, Police Führer SS Völke descended on the town at the head of a destruction squad called: "Vernichtungs-Kommando". This time there were no negotiations, no bargaining with the Judenrat. The hangman, experienced in manhunts, set about his work with great efficiency.

This time, people were dragged out of homes and shelters with greater bestiality and cruelty than ever. It was said that in this action the Lotyshe who took part exceeded all previous executioners in bestiality. They pulled babies out of their cradles before the eyes of their mothers and smashed their heads against the walls.

Again, about 2000 victims went to the slaughter. At the end of the action and in order to crown it with success, Vöbke himself selected a number of Jewish militia men, including the commandant – Dziunek Landesberg – and ordered them to be added to the transport. He wished to do the same with the members of the Judenrat but here he met with opposition from Warzok who telephoned the Police-Führer in Lwow and convinced him that as long as there were still Jews in town and some labor camps in the district, the Judenrat was indispensable. Vöbke gave in only after the order was confirmed from Lwow. As was done after the first 'Action', the Judenrat was called upon to pay a big tribute to cover the expenses of the transport which was loaded as the first one had been and followed the same route – Belzec.

In this, as in the previous action, the scene of events were the streets near and around the Judenrat, particularly theOrmianska Street, the Green Market and the railway station. Vöbke and his "aides" displayed a murderous zest for killing and soon the Jewish streets were littered with corpses. The old and the children, weakened by prolonged hunger were frequently shot on the way to the collecting-point as they could not run fast enough for their oppressors who used their whips generously and mercilessly.

Compliments of Rose Kissel

[Column 105]

Vöbke himself shot an old woman, Mrs. Sharer, in the street opposite our workshop. Inside the Jewish hospital, he also killed a number of patients who seemed to him unfit for transportation.

On December 1942, Vöbke staged a similar "action" in Przemyslany.

15. The Closing of the Ghetto – Hunger and Epidemics

After the second action, the noose on Zloczow Jewry was gradually tightened. At the end of November 1942, the order to seal the ghetto off completely was carried out.

A few weeks earlier, buildings and walls of the main street had been covered with big posters * showing a life-size Jew with a thick beard and side locks, an enormous hooked nose, dirty, tattered and covered with lice with a text that read as follows: "The Jews are the carriers of typhoid". (It was the infamous cartoon from "The Sturmer").

The area allotted for the ghetto consisted barely of a few streets, already overcrowded at the beginning of the German occupation which now concentrated the Jewish population in a "Judenviertel" (Jewish Quarter). The ghetto, reduced to a minimum, was enclosed with barbed wire and put under the guard of the Ukrainian militia. It had only two outlets – one in the corner of Mickiewicza Street and Poczlova and the second, at Sokola Street, to link it with the rest of the town. Anybody who dared leave the ghetto without a special permit was liable to be shot on the spot.

****

*Vöbke had carried out an action in Lwow on August 10th in which some 50,000 victims were destroyed.

[Column 106]

Into this hermetically sealed and greatly diminished area were forced 7500 souls – what remained of the Jewish population of Zlozcow and the surrounding townships after two actions. The overcrowding was simply unbearable. In every flat, several families were huddled, 10-15 persons in one room. It sounds unbelievable but people had no place to lay their heads and took turns in snatching a little sleep. The lack of space and of elementary hygienic conditions (soap was a luxury beyond dreams), coupled with widespread hunger, swiftly led to devastating consequences. An epidemic broke out and took a heavy toll on lives.

In these terrible conditions, the situation became very serious, indeed beyond control in spite of the superhuman efforts of the Jewish doctors and the sanitary personnel. The Judenrat spared neither effort nor money in this struggle for life, but in vain. It seemed as though the forces of darkness had joined together to bring the catastrophe nearer and nearer. There was no home without sick or dead. One misfortune after the other befell the worn-out people. And at this point, the German authorities ordered that the Jewish Hospital should be placed at the disposal of the District camp commander. Dr. Hreczanik, then director of the hospital, was asked to remove all the sick that did not belong to the camp without delay. The Judenrat swiftly organized a temporary hospital in the ghetto at Scharer's house in Chodkiewicza Street, but this could not function satisfactorily because of lack of such basic requirements as medicine and linen, which could not be had for gold.

[Column 107]

In addition, news came of the outbreak of typhoid in the Lackie camp. Everything led us to believe that there was no hope and that the terrible fate of the camp lay before us.

The camp commandants were ordered to liquidate the camp in case of a severe epidemic and to burn everything including the sick and healthy alike. In any case, they were only Jews, of course;

At this moment, one of the camp doctors, Dr. Salomon Yollek who now lives in the United States, 156 Jackson Ave., New York, proved a real guardian angel. Thanks to his presence of mind, courage and heroism which bordered on madness under the prevailing circumstances, a great catastrophe was averted.

In order to give a clear picture of the situation, I have to return to the initial stages of the Lackie camp.

The first doctor of the camp was Dr. Silber, a refugee from western Poland who, with all his goodwill and the best of intentions, could not cope with the prevailing difficulties. During his term of office, the sick room of the camp hardly functioned. The sick and the injured in work accidents (there were many in the quarries) did not come there for treatment as they feared to be shot, in accordance with Nazi practice. After Dr. Silber's death (he contracted typhoid in the camp) Warzok requested the Judenrat to appoint a new doctor immediately. Here, a difficulty arose. Nobody wanted to take such a post which exposed the holder to the permanent danger of death at the hands of some Nazi brute. After various negotiations and a long search for a doctor without any family, the Judenrat required Dr. Yollek to take this position. Though Dr. Yollek had a wife and child and, had the right to refuse the job which was equal to walking into the lion's jaws, he volunteered for it readily as he felt it is duty and mission to help his fellow Jew. In spite of his family's strong protest, he stuck to his decision.

[Column 108]

Before going to the Lackie camp he first demanded that the Judenrat should supply him with medicine and equipment which would enable him to work efficiently. With the help of Dr. Hollenderski, he set out to organize a proper dispensary which would meet the urgent needs of the camp inmates.

He worked with such devotion, zeal and dignified authority that even the Nazi brutes, including Warzok, could not help but admire him.

First of all, the practice of shooting the sick stopped. Dr. Yollek succeeded in transferring some patients to the hospital in Zloczow from where they freed themselves completely from the camp. When things settled down and it seemed that in this field at least conditions had improved and had become routine, a terrific epidemic of typhoid erupted in the Lackie camp. It began during Warzok's absence while he was on leave. The sick-room was full to overflowing and Dr. Yollek was under terrific pressure. What's more, he realized that the position might soon become tragic and without a second thought, he decided to save the camp no matter what befell.

The deputy commandant, SS Salzborn had made all preparations to carry out standing orders for such cases, namely – to burn the camp. He waited only for Warzok's return. He had already sent notice to the Judenrat to bring a few barrels of kerosene for the purpose. Dr. Yollek arrived with this cart and told the members of the Judenrat the situation and what was about to happen. He assured them at the same time, that he was ready to fight to the bitter end, but under the sole condition of receiving support and help, particularly with medicines. He had worked out a plan for convincing Warzok that the epidemic was not typhoid but the flu and chicken-pox. After receiving a promise of unconditional support from the Judenrat, he went back to Lackie where, in the meantime, Warzok had returned. Much courage was needed to put such a proposal to the Nazi hangman who could have shot him at will on the spot. Dr. Hollenderski (Dr. Yollek's colleague) offered to be the first to face Warzok and report on the latest events in the camp. He volunteered to bear the brunt of this encounter with Warzok in order to spare Dr. Yollek, but the latter refused and risking his head, went to Warzok who had already been informed about everything by his subordinates

****

Compliments of Max Gruber.

[Column 109]

Warzok, as was to be expected, was infuriated and received Dr. Yollek with insults and curses. He declared his intention of burning the whole camp including the sick and the healthy, with the addition of the doctors and some of the Judenrat members. But Dr. Yollek, never losing his nerves, insisted convincingly that it was all a false alarm. He guaranteed by his own head that this was only a severe influenza which could easily be overcome with a little effort and good-will. Dr. Yollek knew well that there was no use in appealing to Warzok's humanitarian feelings for he had none, and decided, therefore, to strike a different note in order to save the camp from being turned to ashes. He tried to stress that during Warzok's absence, his subordinates had lost their heads because they lacked his own experience and resolution.

Warzok, as a practical and shrewd businessman, calculated that the destruction of the camp would lead to the loss of a high and lucrative office and expose him to the danger of being sent to the front, as had already happened to many other camp commandants. He, therefore, gradually softened and allowed himself to be persuaded by Dr. Yollek's arguments until he finally gave up the idea of burning the camp. To be on the safe side, he requested Dr. Yollek to produce a written statement, signed by two doctors, that the epidemic was not typhoid. Moreover, he ordered Dr. Yollek to have all the sick appear in the square for a roll-call. It was a great 'test' and an unbelievable sight: the victims of typhoid, shivering with high fever, barefoot and in underclothes, formed in rows – the stronger ones in front, of course. Warzok, at a safe distance, stood in front of them and shouted: "what is wrong with you?" (Was ist los mit euch?) To which he received a collecting answer: "Nothing serious, Herr Hauptsturmführer". Warzok was only too keen not to prolong this macabre spectacle, and ordered the sick to be sent to the hospital in Zloczow *

[Column 110]

So the first part of the battle was won by Dr. Yollek but there was still a long way to go. First of all, Dr. Yollek had to suppress the epidemic and prevent it from spreading. This was a life or death struggle. In the end, life triumphed. But was it life? Or an adjourned death sentence?

The next step was to obtain medicines and disinfectants and in sufficient quantities. For that, the Judenrat did its utmost but with poor results as it was next to impossible to secure medical stores for Jews. Here the Jewish pharmacist, Berish Lifschütz, Kaczek and Salitra proved a great help. As employees in pharmacies, they had access to medicines which they supplied legally or

*Dr. Hreczanik received from the director of the Municipal Hospital, Dr. Martynowicz, a fine and noble Pole, 100 beds to enlarge the Jewish hospital.

[Column 111]

Illegally, sometimes even stealing them in order to relieve the community. But all this was far from enough. Here too our guardian angel, Mr. Meyer, saved us as he had done so many times already *.

Dr. Yollek, for his part, toiled day and night to the verge of collapse. It was a fight against bitter odds. He had to bring medical help to people in the ghetto as well as the camp. He himself had to do all the disinfection and take steps to keep the epidemic from spreading among the weary and the starved. After his work in the camp, he would go from house-to-house, in the ghetto. Often, touched by the misery there, he would not only forego his fee but would leave some medicine or a little money to buy bread for starving children. He was loved and adored by everyone and well deserved the name of: "The Angel of the Ghetto". Dr. Yollek's activities in that sorrowful period have indeed printed his name in letters of gold in the history of Zloczow Jewry.

16. The Epidemic Subsides

Yet, were it not for Mr. Meyer, all these individual efforts as well as those of Dr. Martynowicz and the Jewish doctors, would not have brought the epidemic under control. Medicines could not be obtained only in exchange for alcohol which, being a rare and precious commodity during a war was absolutely out of the reach of the Jews. No money could buy it.

Details of this effort of Mr. Meyer and his intervention are given elsewhere in this narrative.

[Column 112]

In this hopeless situation, an unexpected event occurred. Warzok had given his magnanimous permission to transfer the sick from the camp to the hospital and now wished to safeguard himself against possible informers, so he made frantic efforts to please his superiors. He did it in two ways: One, the most acceptable, was by sending valuable presents to high SS officers, these being jewels supplied, of course, by the Judenrat, who also had to supply an expensive car for Warzok himself. To please all who might be concerned, he had the idea of sending drinks and gifts for wounded SS men to one of the military hospitals. He decided on a home-made Eiercognac (egg-brandy) and began seeking an expert in making this speciality. He ordered Zuckerkandel to find one and also turned to me, thinking that I might have a recipe from my late father-in-law. He then approached Mr. Meyer for several hundred litres of alcohol, sugar and eggs, all needed for the preparation of this commodity, and this gave our good friend Meyer an opportunity of diverting some of the precious alcohol to the Jewish hospital. In this round-about way, the spirit destined for the egg cognac turned into medicines for the sick and helped to suppress the epidemic, which by then, had taken a toll of several hundred victims. Paradoxically as it sounds, the survivors envied those who had died and were decently buried; and in the Jewish quarter a new saying was coined: "Today W or Y died a luxurious death".

Yet, even this luxury was not to last long for very soon, the dead were given no respite either. By order of the Nazi authorities, Jewish cemeteries were devastated. The marble tombstones were sent to Germany while ordinary stones were broken up by the Jewish slave laborers for use in roadmaking. By accident or miracle, the barbarians did not disturb the tomb mausoleum of the revered and saintly Rabbi Mechele of Zloczow.

****

Compliments of Donia Mir.

[Column 113]

17. In Search of Rescue.

The shattering defeat of the German armies on all fronts during the years 1942-43 – Stalingrad in Russia and the defeat of Rommel's Africa Corps – together with the heavy bombardment of German cities did not in the least slow down the crimes of Hitler and his helpers. On the contrary, it led to the speeding up of their mad destruction, murder and loot as the idea crystallized in their sick minds that the fear of revenge for the atrocities perpetrated would prevent the Germans from capitulating. Needless to say, the first and main object of this fury and hatred remained the Jews. "The Final Solution" entered its last stages. The "Holy Task" begun by Heydrich was taken over by Ernst Kaltenbrunner who tried to outdo his predecessor in brutality.

Although the victorious offensive of the Allies raised some faint hopes in the hearts of the doomed, the slow progress made salvation look like a remote dream that was far from realisation. People began to think in different terms. Time was against them and they tried to find some immediate, practical ways of survival, a last straw to grasp at.

First of all, fair and tall people with "good looks" whose features could not be classified as Semitic began to make us of these attributes and tried to prove their "Aryan" origin with false birth, baptismal or marriage certificates. Again, there began a flourishing trade in these Christian certificates. This was carried on by Poles, some genuinely wishing to help, some heartless crooks who demanded exorbitant prices for a scrap of paper. There were many priests who provided Jews with original birth certificates in the names of persons long dead. The quest for an Aryan document was only the first step. The next acquisition had to be a so-called "Kennkarte" – a German identity card, the possession of which enabled one to find a "protector" who would arrange to transfer the "new-hatched Aryan" to a distant town where he was unknown and could hope to move about unsuspected. The larger the town, the safer. Yet, on the other hand, the more difficult it was to find food and accommodation. These "lucky Aryans" did not have an easy time. Very few of them survived their initial success. Many were recognized by Poles and Ukrainians; the dregs of society called "Schmalzowniks" *, who blackmailed their victims and extorted their last penny only to hand them over in the end to the Gestapo. A very few managed to escape these informers by changing their addresses quickly enough.

[Column 114]

The more common and simpler way of hiding was, of course, to find a shelter, called a "bunker". People who still had a little money or some valuables left and knew a reliable Pole or Ukrainian, tried to persuade him to build a little hideout. To find an acquaintance willing to engage in such an enterprise was more than difficult and to survive in such a bunker was a veritable miracle. Hiding or feeding a Jew was forbidden under penalty of death and who would risk one's life to save a Jew? The German even promised cash prizes and the property of the person denounced to those who handed over hiding Jews. In light of these circumstances, deep gratitude and great credit should be given to those noble Christians who, no matter what their motives may have been, took it upon themselves to hide Jews and persevered till the end. Not only the survivors, but the whole Jewish people are indebted to those heroes, to those great-hearted, individuals, many of them Germans like Mr. Meyer who risked their lives to help their down-trodden, outlawed and hunted fellow-beings. The warmth of their hearts, their nobility and mercy nourished within us a tiny flicker of faith that evil would not ultimately triumph.

****

Schmalzownik meant an informer against Jews under the Nazi occupation.

[Column 115]

It is interesting to note that most of those saviours belonged to the Polish upper class, to the intelligentsia and the peasant proletariat. This middle class was absolutely indifferent.

There were many cases of criminal luring of victims into a bunker and then handing them over to the Nazi after having deprived them of all of their belongings and sometimes even killing them. Money was not a decisive factor in finding safety. The opposite was often the case; many perished because of it, falling victims to human greed. In this way died: a) Dr. Sane Kahane with all his family (eight persons handed over to the Germans by a peasant who hid them for money); b- the dentist Zwerdling and his wife, killed by the bailiff of the village Kozaki; and many others.

Children were frequently renounced by desperate parents who, in the face of total destruction, tried to save at least one of their children. Using entreaties, presents and promises of rewards, they implored Polish families to "adopt" a girl. Those willing were afraid of their neighbors who immediately sensed such a feminine addition in a family. There was also a great difficulty in such a change-over which called for the prolonged training of the children who had to learn prayers, go to church, absolutely deny their Jewish origins, etc. A great number of such unfortunate children were caught by the Germans thanks to informers. I know of a few cases of survival. A number of children entrusted to convents were baptized and remained as Christians. I also know of a man, Kruth, who found refuge in the house of the Rev. Dzieduszycki and embraced the Catholic faith together with his whole family.

[Column 116]

I wish to stress here that in Zloczow as elsewhere, there were many courageous and reckless people who had been brooding over the idea of obtaining arms and fighting their way to the forest. They dreamt of facing the mortal enemy and selling their lives dearly. But this remained mostly an unfulfilled dream in the face of terrific odds. This is not the place to engage in polemics or to defend those accused of cowardice because they allowed themselves to be led like sheep to the slaughter. To those hero-critics who never came anywhere near the horrors of neither war nor Hitler's hell for the Jews, I can only say that they are using empty arguments which are not worth answering. If the Jews of Europe had the slightest possibility of organizing themselves for self-defence – which is the first reaction of everything living creature, human or animal – the Nazi Moloch would not have claimed six million Jewish victims and our history would be full of the deeds of heroes whose names would belong to eternity.

A single glance at the geographical and ethnic conditions of Eastern Poland explains the tragic helplessness of the Jews there.

As in all occupied countries and at all times, there was a fighting underground under the German occupation. Its success depended not only on the bravery of its members but also on the flow of supplies – of arms and food. The success of guerrillas depends largely on the friendly milieu in which they move and on the cooperation of the local population. Eastern Poland, which the Nazi in their cunning chose as the "Cemetery of European Jewry", was the most suitable place for this because of its favourable conditions. In those parts of the country inhabited only by Poles, the leftist underground helped to supply the Jewish fighters with arms.

****

Compliments of Chana Grubstein

[Column 117]

The rightist Polish underground organization, the so-called N.S.Z. (National Armed Forces), openly helped the Germans in mopping up and wiping out Jewish fighters and murdering Jews wherever they could. In Eastern Galicia, predominantly inhabited by Ukrainians who from the outset of the war were the most ardent collaborators of the Nazi, any Jewish underground was absolutely doomed. The loitering bands of Banderists and Wlassovists – aspirants to an Independent Ukrainian State – fought the Poles but even more the Jews whom they mercilessly liquidated.

To support my statements, I shall give a few incidents known to me:

1. A group of people from my district, who hid in the Ciemierzyuce forest shortly before the liberation, were killed by the N.S.Z.
2. Friends of mine, Dr. Shulim Teichberg and his wife, both doctors, hid in a forest where they fell into the hands of Ukrainian band. For some time, they worked for them day and night as doctors. When they were no longer needed, the bandits killed them brutally, cutting off their heads.

3. The same fate befell my own cousin, Cesia Schotz and her husband, Dr. Mayblum in the forests near Tarnopol. Dr. Davidson, who was with them, miraculously escaped.

4. Josio Strassler and his wife preferred the forests to the bunker. They perished with all their family in the same way.

Such cases numbered hundreds and thousands. Only a handful of Jews, disguised as Poles, survived among the Polish guerrilla fighters.

The rural population was mostly Ukrainian. At its best it was passive and did not help the Jews hiding in the forests. More often than not, they handed them over to the German executioners.

[Column 118]

Understanding and insight into the specific conditions prevailing in Poland are needed. Any charge of cowardice is a vicious slander and an insult to the sacred memory of those who died the death of martyrs.

18. Strassler's Bunker.

Our camp-workshop at Strassler's was an exclusive outpost inside the Ghetto. There work went on at a very swift pace in producing the potato ad-mixture for bread and the egg cognac for Warzok. We worked feverishly, in constant tension and fear of Warzok, master of our lives, who threatened us with the most savage punishments should anything go wrong or any poison be found in the liquor.

Realizing that such a luxury as egg cognac might attract certain German officials, he forbade us to admit anybody into the workshop. This beneficial isolation was a boon. It enabled us to start working on a long-conceived plan to build a shelter which could offer safety during an action and perhaps help us to survive the war.

The initiators of this quite elaborate plan were the three Strassler brothers, Wilo Freiman and I. After again examining the plan and the possibilities of carrying it out, we set out to work, each of us with his own individual hopes and prospects. All the men and several women took part.

In the later stages of the work, after the liquidation of the Zloczow ghetto, two professional craftsmen joined our crew. These were Steinhauer and Rosen, who came to us from another outpost and were to play a sad part later in the tragic death of Wilo Freiman in the bunker.

[Column 119]

It is worth while giving a few details about this bunker which was a unique construction used for a unique propose to live in hiding under the surface of the earth. Thanks to it, twenty four people escaped the jaws of certain death and lived to see the liberation.

The building was planned to be executed in three stages:

1. Walling up the entrance to several cellars and at the same time opening another, a well-concealed one.
2. Digging a tunnel leading to an artesian well which would provide water and air.
3. A). Digging big niches on both sides of the tunnel which would serve as sleeping quarters;
4. Connecting the tunnel with the sewers which would provide the only escape route in case of need;
5. Camouflaging and fortifying all openings leading to and from the bunker.

Strassler's house which was centrally situated in the Market Square and only 100 meters from the well had many spacious cellars and was well suited to our plan.

Having decided on the place, our next problem was to secure the necessary building materials and tools as well as suitable professionals who would be reliable enough to carry out the work in absolute secrecy and under strict precautions.

First the cellars were walled up by Shyo Freiman, Wilo's brother. In one of the ground-floor storerooms above a walled-up cellar, an opening was then made in the corner to serve as a new entrance. In order to camouflage it, a big iron frame was constructed with a normal oven attached which could easily slide away. In an emergency, this entrance could be used and bolted from the inside with strong hooks.

After this beginning, the next step was to dig a hundred-meter long tunnel, two metres in diameter. This was a gigantic task for the disposal of such enormous amounts of earth was a formidable difficulty. The tunnel was dug in the form of a horizontal shaft and the earth was pushed into the sealed-off cellars.

[Column 120]

At the beginning, work progressed very slowly and clumsily because of misunderstanding between the participants and financial obstacles. These were gradually overcome thanks largely to the will and energy of Wilo Freiman who knew how to inspire others with his courage and enthusiasm. The building was finished in time as scheduled.

19. The Liquidation of the Ghetto.

The ghettoes were slowly perishing. The Jews were behind walls and barbed wire under guard day and night, writhing in agony and despair. Although they knew what was to come, they waited for a miracle, clinging to the slightest ray of hope.

Conditions in Zloczow were not different from any other place. The five cold winter months after the last 'action' were terrible and there was no day without some sad event.

People, or rather shadows of people, lost their heads in their daily struggle to get a little bread and fuel for their freezing children who were swollen with hunger.

Risking their lives for a little food, they would leave the ghetto to search for it, only to be caught by the lurking Ukrainian police and handed over to the "Kripo" who shot them mercilessly on the spot.

Another calamity was the frequent visits of various German officials, either on duty or in their own private capacities, who raided Jewish homes for fun. For some time, poster reading "Beware, Typhoid here!" kept those visitors away, but after a while, this warning ceased to work. Particularly dreaded were the visits of the infamous gendarmes Mury, Hirsakorn, Zwillinger and Radke, who often used to drop into Jewish homes to torture people, mostly women and children. One day, these four creatures while drunk, broke into a flat, attracted by the moans of a woman – a certain Mrs. Gutfreund – and a child's whimpering. They found a woman that was ill, unconscious and with high fever. They stripped her naked and poured buckets of cold water over her, yelling as they roared with laughter that this shower would bring her fever down. They did the same to another woman, Mrs. Speiser.

****

Compliments of J. Müntl.

[Column 121]

Besides these individual tragedies, there were cases of a more general character which nearly brought disaster on the whole community.

One morning, a red flag appeared on the roof of the synagogue * - obviously an act of provocation by some unknown mischief maker. The Gestapo promptly arrested the executive of the Judenrat and a number of people residing in the neighbourhood. Mr. Treiber, the German using the premises, courageously explained and proved that the roof could be reached only by a person in possession of the keys which were in the hands of the exclusively Ukrainian personnel. Next day, one of them disappeared with the keys. Suspicion was diverted from the Jews and the incident ended without any loss of Jewish life.

Soon after, another incident happened which might also have had tragic consequences. A young boy, Siunio Freimann, Shyyo's son, left the ghetto and joined a group of shady partisans who, as rumours had it, were ordinary bandits. One night, an armed gang raided the homes of the Judenrat members and robbed them of cash and valuables and threatened to kill them if they reported it to the German authorities. The Gestapo came to know from another source and the Gestapo chief arrested the Judenrat accusing them of paying voluntary contributions to partisans and encouraging them to attack German outposts; proof of this being the participation of a local Jew in the raid. Zuckerkandel's intervention at the Gestapo Head Office in Tarnopol, supported as usual with an expensive present for its chief, put an end to this affair.

****

The synagogue was used as a warehouse by a German industrialist.

[Column 122]

Another shock was caused by a so-called "parcel affair" in the Lackie camp. As mentioned before, the Relief Committee sent food parcels to the inmates regardless of the parcels sent to them by their families. Once, the late Leon Blaustein brought a batch of parcels from both sources to the camp. In Warzok's absences, his deputy Salzborn examined the parcels very carefully and found a small kitchen or pocket knife in one of the parcels. He immediately ordered the addressee to be shot and Blaustein to be detained in the camp after a severe flogging. He also threatened the Judenrat with reprisals for smuggling arms into the camp. This time, Zuckerkandel succeeded in pacifying Warzok and the matter was dropped.

These and similar events were the only distractions of the miserable Jewish existence until the day of the final destruction.

A few lucky "divers" managed to dive into nowhere and find shelter with Polish friends or left for the unknown with Aryan papers. The unlucky remainders pinned their hopes on the increasing victories of the Allies on the war fronts.

One of the signs indicating the impending catastrophe was the extensive digging of ditches by Russian prisoners of war near the village of Jelechowice. When the news of the mysterious diggings was brought by peasants to the town, people, still optimists, thought that they were army trenches and thus a good omen of the approaching Front and subsequent deliverance. Very soon, they were to find that those supposed trenches were their own future graves.

[Column 123]

At about midnight on April 1, 1943, the ghetto plunged into complete darkness was surrounded by a double cordon of special murder units called "Mordscommando" brought from Lwow and Tarnopol for that purpose. They were followed by auxiliary "gendarmerie", military police, "Orpo" and the Ukrainian militia of the entire district. The head of this large-scale slaughter was Hauptsturmführer Engels, a deputy for Jewish affairs in the S.S. Police, under General Katzman, Warzok, Lex *, Ludwig and Füg, all of the same rank, assisted Engels in his task.

Early that morning, leading ferocious and specially trained dogs, the murderers entered the ghetto and swiftly advanced through all streets simultaneously. Breaking into houses, they dragged everyone out and drove them forcibly to the "traditional" meeting place – the Green Market. This time the first to be brought were the members of the Judenrat and the Jewish Militia with their families. These were ordered to line up and place whatever money and valuables they had in baskets prepared for the purpose. Engels came up to the Judenrat members who stood in a row under the walls of Nussen's house and asked Dr. Mayblum to sign a statement that the ghetto had been liquidated because of an epidemic of typhoid. When he refused, the infuriated Engels began to be-labor him and finished him off on the spot. The same happened to Dr. Schotz and Jakier who also refused to sign. Then Engels unleashed his fury on a standing woman nearby who carried a baby in her arms. He seized the baby by its little feet and smashed its head against the wall. The unhappy mother, mad with shock and sorrow threw herself at Engels but was killed with a shot by Ludwig.

****

Lex, deputy of the head of the gestapo in Tarnopol, was identified by an officer of the Israel Investigating Police at Landsberg. In April 1965, he was sentenced to 15 years imprisonment by an Austrian court.

[Column 124]

Meantime, more and more victims were brought. In the rainy and snowy weather of that April day, hundreds of people stood cold and wet, numbed and bewildered. No screams or cries were heard in this desperate crowd, resigned to their fate – only the whimpering of small children hugging their mothers. Everyone felt that their end had come. When the market was full and the three chiefs of the "Action" – Engels, Warzok and Ludwig – inspected the lines, a few bold optimists: Brown, Weinstock and Salitre, still hoping for salvation at the last moment, stepped out of line to plead for mercy. Brown, the dentist asked Warzok to spare him because of his devoted service which he was ready to continue. Warzok lashed him in the face with his whip shouting: "you cursed Jew; you won't touch German teeth anymore!" Salitre, the pharmacist reminded Ludwig that he had been an officer in World War I. Ludwig did not answer but released his Alsatian dog which bit him through the throat. The same happened to Munek Weinstock.

Many of the camp and workshop inmates who still had a lease of life came to the ghetto that tragic night and were also rounded up. A few were saved, without their families, by one decent German businessman – Shweiger by name – who courageously insisted on having his Jewish workers back in his firm and pulled them out one by one from the death row promising them to save their families later. Of course his promise remained unfulfilled but the eight people whom he rescued survived the occupation. The late Bunio Rosen did not take advantage of this chance of survival as he refused to part with his wife and baby and perished with the others. Shweiger also intervened with Warzok and Ludwig and saved a few more people. One was Josio Tauber who, in the confusion, dragged two non-inmates with him. The Nazi refused to save Tauber's wife who served in Warzok's house as a servant.

****

Compliments of The Greenwalds.

[Column 125]

20. Jelechowice – A New Jewish Cemetery.

This time the murderers did not bother to send their victims to a distant spot like Belzec. The Jelechowice woods, a place for Sunday outings and picnics, were destined to be their last resting place.

Military trucks drove up to the Market and each loaded up 40-50 people. Under strong guard, the ghetto dwellers made their last journey straight to their mass-graves in Jelechowice. Naked men, women and children were pushed into the ditches and machine-gunned. One transport followed the other; dead, half-dead and wounded filled the graves, layer by layer. Blood spurted and stained Nazi uniforms and faces, but Nazi heart and hands did not tremble nor stop their hellish work. The massacre went on for two days claiming some 6,000 souls. The hopeless agony and three-year old struggle of the Zloczow Ghetto came to an end in Jelechowice.

Two women escaped this slaughter by running into the woods under the hail of bullets. One – Leah Frankel – was hidden by peasants. The second, a young girl named Czortkower, disappeared without a trace.

[Column 126]

The truck hearses brought their loads to their destination and returned to the camp workshops with the clothes of the slaughtered which were first carefully searched by SS men for sewn-in valuables and were then passed on to be sorted by the inmates who often recognized the clothes of their near ones.

To hide their crimes, the Nazi covered and levelled the mass graves and ordered the neighbouring villages to plant trees over them. But this disguise did not succeed. According to reports from the peasants, the earth, soaked in blood, fermented and moved and rose in unyielding mounds for over six months.

21. The Last Manhunts.

While the ghetto was gradually perishing, the few Jews left in the labor camps were helpless and heartbroken onlookers. Some deserted to their families in the ghetto to join them in their death-march. Many committed suicide in despair. A very few let their comrades persuade them not to take this desperate step.

After the two days of slaughter, the Murder Commando left Zloczow entrusting the mopping up to the local gendarmerie and the German Auxiliary Police, the ORPO. The new Kreishauptmann Dr. Wendt, Captain Schwarz and Captain Füg took great pains to execute their task with real German precision. I wish to emphasize here that the Commandant of the ORPO, Lieutenant Oberst, flatly refused to participate in the liquidation of the ghetto. He was arrested and immediately sent to the Front*

****

Of the fate of Oberst in Gotha, Thuringia, I came to know later from my correspondence with Mr. Meyer. This case should be used in the trials against Müller and other Nazi who claim that disobedience would have cost them their lives.

[Column 127]

For a couple of weeks there was an additional hunt for people who had managed to find a shelter of sorts. Some, forced by hunger, came out of their hiding places, others were detected by the trained dogs of the gendarmes. The notorious Hirsakorn loitered day and night in the dead town.

All the actions took place under our very eyes as our workshop, unlike the others, was not outside the ghetto but in its very heart near the Green Market. Under strict orders, our gates were shut and locked and had a big, protective sign-post marked "camp workshop". More than about ourselves, we were concerned for our dear ones who were with us but had no right to live after the liquidation of the ghetto. We placed the old people, the children and adults who had no 'camp certificates' in the bunker. There were the aged mothers of Freiman and Lonek Zwerdling, old Strassler and his wife, my wife and son, Rozka Lerner and son, Josio Strassler's wife with a new-born baby and a few others. Our situation grew more precarious each day. After the liquidation of the ghetto, some escapee knocked at our gates almost every night. Some even came crawling over the rooftops. What were we to do? On the one hand it was dangerous to take in these unfortunate wrecks; on the other, refusal meant pushing them straight into the arms of death.

In spite of the danger, we decided to take them in and keep them in the bunker with our families. A few survivors had good hiding places of their own but they visited us at night for food and news. Fed and provided with whatever we could spare, they then returned to the nearby forest in Woroniaki.

The nightly visits and contacts were possible because our outpost was guarded by a Jewish Militia man, Ephraim Prager. We felt that this favourable state of affairs would not last long. The change came very soon and from an unexpected source.

[Column 128]

Hirsakorn, that human hyena in the form of a gendarme who was constantly hanging around in the deserted ghetto, found a woman named Leider. He promised to let her live in exchange for information about hiding Jews. We do not know whether she knew about our bunker or whether there were rumours or whether sheer chance brought Hirsakorn to us.

On the evening of the 12th April, Hirsakorn accompanied by the woman and his Alsatian dog which was trained in sniffing out humans, broke into our workshop and called on us to hand over immediately the persons illegally hidden by us. On hearing our denial of this accusation, he ordered us to face the wall and set out on his search, luckily beginning with the upper floor. While we stood shocked at this sudden dangerous turn of our situation, Wilo Freiman reminded me that according to the rules, access to our workshop required the permission of the camp commandant, Warzok, in this case. In a split second, we decided to act and ran to Warzok as though our very lives were at stake; the dog might detect the bunker at any minute, smelling the people there. We knew that Warzok was at a party given for the personnel of the German firm "Radebeule". On arriving there breathless, we asked Dr. Glanz's brother-in-law, who was serving, to let us in to see Warzok. Dead scared of the Nazi, he would not listen to our appeal. Luckily Warzok heard our argument and his name being mentioned and came to the door in the company of his mistress. Standing to attention, I reported Hirsakorn's intrusion. Warzok, probably wishing to show off before his lady, telephoned the Gendarme commandant and requested him to recall the gendarme. He also rang up his own staff asking one of the officers to take a few SS men, go to the place and expel Hirsakorn. He told us to go back and promised to follow soon. Covered with cold sweat for fear of arriving too late, we reached "home". Hirsakorn had not yet reached the cellars. Almost at the same time, a car drove up to our gates with Warzok's people. A little while later, Warzok himself arrived.

****

Compliments of Mr & Mrs Morris Nagler.

[Column 129]

When he saw the gendarme and his dog, Warzok, furious and most probably tipsy, disregarded our presence, lashed at Hirsakorn with his whip and without listening to his explanations, ordered him to clear out. Then he turned to us and said: "woe to you if there is anybody here besides the legitimate crew!" Then he left hurriedly with his men, issuing a new order that besides the Jewish militia man, a Ukrainian militia man should be placed on guard. What a relief this miraculous end was! This was the first time I saw a flicker of humanity in Warzok. We were all convinced that he knew quite well that we had hidden for he asked where Old Mother Strassler was and left without waiting for an answer.

The indescribable slaughter can be imagined by the effect it had on one of the professionally-trained Nazi murderers as illustrated by the following event.

One day, the above-mentioned Gendarme Muri knocked at the gates of our workshop. When he was told that admission to our outpost was strictly forbidden except with a special permit from the camp commandant, he begged and begged to be admitted and given a drink which he needed very much. Seeing him pale and in a queer state, we did not wish to irritate him but opened the door. After drinking, Muri covered his face with his hands and cried hysterically: "I can't bear it any longer! I have enough of this slaughter and mass-blood bath! What do they want of us these superiors of ours the Kreishauptmann and Captain Fueg?"

****

Compliments of J. Halpern

[Column 130]

We were greatly relieved when he left us. We were not surprised to hear later that Muri had had a severe nervous breakdown and had been transferred.

The new Ukrainian guard kept troublesome intruders like Hirsakorn and Muri away but at the same time, he made it hard for us to keep in contact with the bunker. We had to use all kinds of ruses and tricks to get him away from the chimneys and openings which were our life-lines. In the remotest room we treated him to the best food and drink, often until he was drunk.

The happy end of this first intrusion made us unhappy and concerned our future as to other possible informers and the Gestapo itself. We decided to act quickly in every possible was so as to safeguard our position. First, we tried to get some camp certificates the holders of which could leave the bunker. Others, who had relatives in some still existing ghettoes begged to be sent there or to some hiding places they had known about before the liquidation, but had not had time to use. With money and effort which we did not spare, we finally found a reliable Polish driver, Tadeusz Skorny* who risked his life to save them.

One night, Skorny, who was an employee of a big German building firm, drove up with his big truck, took all those concerned and brought them to safely to their destination. We later came to know that he did it for purely humanitarian reasons as most of the money we gave him as a reward for his dangerous enterprise was used to bribe the German guard.

*Mr. Skorny at present lives in Cracow, Poland with his Jewish wife who is the daughter of my acquaintance, Fechter of Przemyslany.

[Column 131]

For some time we kept the two aged and ailing mothers, W. Freiman and L. Zwerdling in a little cell in barrels covered with potatoes. Later on their sons transferred them to the Jewish hospital where they found a merciful death by poison and were saved from the savage brutality of the SS men. Josio Strassler and his wife decided on a similar merciful death for their new-born baby. The incessant crying of the infant, who was hopelessly ill with a double pneumonia, was a continuous threat to us all. A dose of morphine put it to sleep forever. Rozka Lerner's son Jurek was kept alone in the garret during the day and only at night was he taken to the room by his mother. The little boy of Nacio Feigenbaum, who was Warzok's driver, was hidden all day long in a box.

22. The Unsuccessful Revolt.

After the liquidation of the ghetto, only the handful of Jews employed in workshops and other German outposts remained alive. They were, of course, assured of their right to live and even survive the war, provided they worked hard and did not attempt any sabotage or opposition. Nobody believed these assurances. Whoever could, attempted to escape. Before the sealing of the ghetto, single youths and small groups tried to flee to the forests with arms. One of them, as I mentioned before, was Shyo Freimann who first joined a band of gangsters but soon left them and together with the painter, Nachumowicz, a camp worker, formed a group of some 30 people who were equipped with small arms and determined to fight in the forests. As they had no contact with any serious guerrilla force and no means of existence except looting raids on the local population, they did not have the slightest chance of success. They lived in two bunkers. One of them was accidentally discovered by a passing peasant whom they spared although Freimann advised that they should kill him so as to escape betrayal. Though the peasant swore by God that he was a friend of the Jews, he soon set the Germans on their track. They were all caught and shot by an expedition of the SS and the gendarmes. The second bunker with more people was deeper in the forest where the "brave" Germans did not venture. Instead, Warzok who headed that expedition, left sheets of paper on the trees calling on Nachumowicz to return to the camp and promising him safety. Nachumowicz responded to the call and returned to the workshop. Warzok kept his promise. When the time finally came to liquidate the camps too, Nachumowicz was sent with others to the Janowski Camp to find his death there. The other Jewish "partisans" were brutally murdered by various ravaging bands.

[Column 132]

Of a more serious character was an uprising planned by two engineers; Hillel Safran and Bialystocki, a refugee from Warsaw, both employees of the German road-building firm 'Radebeule'. They planned to organize a big resistance group of young people who would fight to the last man. They tried to contact the Polish guerrilla in order to get arms from them and fight side-by-side with them but most Polish guerrilla were rightists and did not want to have Jews so they organized themselves separately under a five-man leadership with the two engineers at their head. The first step was to secure arms which could then be obtained in two ways: either by a lot of money or by stealing.

A certain amount of arms were bought from a reliable Pole at a very high price. The bulk had to be smuggled in very risky and dangerous ways. A few, who were working in the one-time arsenal of the artillery,

****

Compliments of Fabian Lauer.

[Column 133]

Sorting out old arms and ammunition left by the Russians, were drawn into the conspiracy and ordered to steal suitable arms, hand grenades in particular. These stores of arms, useless to the Germans, were not rigidly guarded. The stolen articles were taken out and buried in the nearest forest. Now the most difficult part was to bring the precious consignment to its destination.

There was nobody bold enough to do it so Engineer Hillel Safran volunteered. As a trusted worker of 'Radebeule' which was situated behind the cemetery not far from the place where the arms were concealed, he managed to transfer some arms each day in his briefcase among papers and documents and deposited them in affixed place – the worker's cloakroom in one of the firm's blocks. Thus, while preparing his escape, he carried out this most dangerous duty, day in and day out.

Meantime, the wiping out of the Nachumowicz group discouraged and disheartened many of the conspirators so Safran and Bialostocki decided to hasten the flight. According to all preparations and careful calculations, success seemed to be assured but things took a very different turn.

In spite of the secrecy and precaution, there had been somebody spying on the planners who betrayed the five leaders on the eve of their enterprise. The informer was a boy from Lwow, the converted offspring of mixed marriage named Lewandowski. The five leaders were arrested and kept in the building of the Kripo which tried beating and inhuman torture in order to extract the names of their associates and the hiding place of the arms. Not one of the five betrayed their comrades. There were rumours that help was organized for them and escape offered but the Police quarters were so centrally situated – on the "Stare Waly" – that success was out of the question.

[Column 134]

Zuckerkandel took up the matter and pleaded with Ludwig, the Gestapo head. But he was just fooling himself and those concerned as the doomed men best served the Germans as an intimidating example. They were all shot publicly in the Green Market Square.

From the balcony of our workshop we saw the late Hillel Safran, dignified in his calm, being led to the place of execution. When he was thrust against the wall by an SS, he threw himself on him trying to wrest the gun from him. But the Ukrainian militia man fired and he fell shouting: "death to the Nazi murderers".

Such was the sad end of a heroic attempt on the part of Zloczow youth. Blessed be their memory!

23. The Changing of the Guard.

In spite of the victorious advance of the Soviet armies which were coming nearer and nearer, our nervous tension grew steadily together with our fear of the impending speed-up in the liquidation of the Jewish remnants. We felt that death was nearer than the dawn of liberation. The will to survive seemed stronger in us than ever before.

In spite of difficulties and squabbles, the work of improving our bunker made great progress. Nevertheless, I decided to leave and seek my own way to safety. I could, of course, count on my good friend Mr. Meyer, but as luck had it, a new source of help arrived unexpectedly as a reward for saving one worker, Wladyslaw Kulpa from being exiled to Siberia during the Russian occupation in 1940. In May 1943, this man – a small farmer in Jelechowice – came to me and told me that he had moved into a house at the end of the village. The previous owner of that house had been a Jewish innkeeper who had built himself a strong and well camouflaged shelter. Now he offered it to me and my family instead of giving it to someone else for a big sum of money. He mentioned incidentally that he knew about my friendship with Mr. Meyer who could assist him in obtaining a liquor licence for which he had already applied, as well as food supplies for his business. Though I had other plans, I promised to consider his proposal and give him an answer within a few days. And meantime, the course of events forced my decision.

[Column 135]

Rumour had it that Warzok was about to be transferred to the Janowski camp in Lwow; his successor was to be the Jaktorow commandant who had liquidated the Lwow ghetto and elsewhere in the vicinity; a notorious murderer of exceptional brutality named Grzymek. Soon, Warzok confirmed this news as he took him around from outpost-to-outpost, inspecting the "live inventory" of the Jews. A few days later, Nacio Feigenbaum, Warzok's driver, brought me a letter from my youngest cousin in the Janowski camp warning me about Grzymek's arrival which would certainly bring about our annihilation and asking me to send her poison.

To begin with, Grzymek played a careful game. He did not appear often in the camp. Most of his time, according to the Jewish driver he brought with him from Lwow, was spent visiting the neighbouring camps and at home with his mistress Hildebrand and the bottle. But this simulated calm of his frightened us and did not augur any good. Whoever had any workable plan decided to implement it immediately.

In spite of the accepted practice of families to live or to die together, I decided, guided by instinct rather than reason, to separate from my family in the hope that, with a little luck, one of us might remain alive. My first efforts were to arrange matters for my wife whose persistent cough, due to a chronic bronchitis, made it impossible to keep her in a shelter. She looked very Aryan* being tall and blond, so I obtained an original certificate of baptism for her and decided to send her to some distant town. This risky and dangerous undertaking went off safely thanks to some lucky coincidences and, of course, the help of our guardian angel, Mr. Meyer.

[Column 136]

Wilo Freimann who was one of the initiators of our bunker became dissatisfied with the constant friction among the people and also wished to leave our shelter. He persuaded me to accept the offer of Kulpa whom he believed to be honest and sincere. To make absolutely sure about it, he went to Jelechowice on bicycle one night and came back enthusiastic about the isolated situation of the cottage at the edge of the forest and other conditions. We immediately took Mr. Meyer into our confidence. Without delay, he granted a licence to Kulpa promising him a steady flow of foodstuff, cigarettes, alcohol and above all a pair of horses and asking him in return to keep us safely and protect us like the apple of his eye. I promised Kulpa one of our houses in Zloczow** in case we survived.

On an appointed night, our new protector took my brother-in-law Kuba and my son Mark, Wilo (whom Kulpa agreed to take against a small payment) and I were to follow later.

****

My wife describes her experiences in a separate article entitled: "Aryan documents".

**I could not keep this promise because Zloczow belongs now to Russia; but I am in constant touch with Kulpa and aid him in a modest way in gratitude for what he did for us.*

****

Compliments of Mr & Mrs Ygmund Schotz

[Column 137]

Unexpectedly, one of my Polish clients appeared at the same time. This was Mr. Jakubowsky who brought news that the Polish underground in the Zloczow district would accept in their ranks a few reliable Jews who were willing to fight. Wilo and I were, of course, only too willing to avail ourselves of this opportunity and awaited further developments. In great secrecy, Jakubowsky disclosed the name of the Polish leader, Kalecinski, the same man with whom the deceased H. Safran had negotiated. In the meantime, should the situation in our outpost become threatening and unsafe, Jakubowsky offered to shelter us in his home on Konowicza Street. For that, he expected generous payment. Unfortunately, this plan fell through, like Safran's first one.

24. The Last of the Slaughter.

At the end of June 1943, we learnt that the smaller camps around Lwow had been completely liquidated. Some of the inmates were shot on the spot; others were transferred to the Janowski camp. What this meant was plain to us. Our turn had come. People became desperate and sleepless even after a hard day's labor, wishing to be on guard. There was not a night when somebody did not disappear.

At the end of June, Grzymek ordered the inmates of all camp outposts except our own and Ettinger's bakery to sleep in the barracks. This order was a clear indication of what was coming. The murderers wanted to have their victims all in one place. This order and a warning from Meyer meant that we must move; but I still had a few things to do. I had to finish trying to save my sister and supply our bunker – Strassler's bunker – with food. The problem of food supplies which had engaged us most seriously when we first decided to build an independent, self-sufficient place of safety, became even more urgent now. Although some individuals tried with their own meagre resources to secure some provisions, this was far from enough to last for months on end. I, therefore, took Mr. Meyer into my confidence. In spite of my decision not to remain there, he allotted a sizeable quantity of imperishable products which could be stored away: sugar, flour, groats, macaroni, etc. These articles, rationed out very sparingly, lasted for a few months. When they came to an end and starvation and death loomed, Mrs. Irena Poplawska (Rozka Lerner) crept out of the bunker and obtained fresh stock at exorbitant prices, of course, from a peasant that she knew and who had agreed to supply them till Liberation. Thus she saved herself, her little son and all the occupants of the bunker from certain death.

[Column 138]

In the middle of July, I made my final decision to leave. I went to Mr. Meyer who took me to Jakubowsky's where I had to await the final outcome of our negotiations with the Polish underground. I sat there on knives, not on pins. Every minute seemed a year. I crouched in a hole specially scooped for me under the floor of the pantry over which stood a case with a sliding bottom. At night, I slept in the pantry.

On the night of 23rd July, a loud noise of machine-guns was heard. Jakubowsky thought it was an attack of the underground forces on the town. How wrong he was became clear in the morning. It was the epilogue to the three-year old tragedy of Zloczow Jews. Gendarmes, SS men and the Ukrainian militia had surrounded the barracks and driven the Jews into the yard where a hail of bullets awaited them. People jumped out of windows armed with chairs, tables, stools and whatever they could find. With their bare hands they fought their last, hopeless battle against the machine-guns of the murderers. Jews from other outposts were brought to the barracks and the last death march set out to the Jaktorow camp where the last massacre was staged. Simultaneously, all the inmates in the remaining outposts near and around Zloczow were being slaughtered. The labor camp had turned into death camps. Jewish life was over. The towns and townships were Judenrein and dead. All that remained were devastated streets, cemeteries and mass-graves, soaked with innocent blood crying out to Heaven in a terrifying silence.

[Column 139]

25. Human Rats.

Human rats – that is the only description for the survivors who, after the total liquidation of the ghettoes, had no more right to existence on the face of the earth. They continued their sub-human lives under sub-human conditions, namely like rats, in caves, holes, bunkers, graves and sewers. Very few were lucky enough to flee to a nearby forest and join a partisan group. The agony and suffering of these wrecks (I was one of them), beggar description. We were hunted day and night and methodically and scrupulously annihilated. The vociferous Goebbels splashed headlines in all the German newspapers and shouted on the radio that by 1944, a Jew would be a rarity to be found only in museums.

In spite, or perhaps because of this diabolical drive against us, we clung to life. The urge to hold out was stronger than ever. All of us without exception were hiding in terrible places, deprived not only of the basic necessities of life – hygiene and medical care, but even without sufficient air to breathe! Our hope to live and see the liberation was nurtured by news of the constant victories of the Allies and the rapid approach of the Soviet armies. Unfortunately, not all who escaped the slaughter lived to see the dawn of liberation. Some were spied out and murdered on the threshold of it. The Kreishauptman of Zloczow, Dr. Wendt and his deputy captain Fueg as well as the gendarmerie commandant Schwartz were particularly devoted to this task of hunting down every Jewish soul.

[Column 140]

My mind returns to the two incidents which took place in August 1943 while I was staying with Jakubowsky in Klonowicza Street. About 100 meters from my shelter there were two hiding places. One was built in the cellar of the house of a Ukrainian named Dubno who ran the shop of Mr. Merwitzer. For 1000 dollars per person, he hid the entire family of Merwitzer and a few others. The fact that Dubno was buying large quantities of food aroused suspicion and drew the attention of informers to the place which was not adequately camouflaged. It was also rumoured that Dubno pocketed all the money, abandoned his Polish wife and moved to Lwow where he betrayed his "paying guests".

The second incident frustrated my plan of joining the partisans with the help of Jakubowsky. It involved a bunker set up in the garret of an outhouse next to the well-known printing press of Zuckerkandel. This shelter had been well built by Wladek Bialobrzeski, a Pole who had formerly been employed in Landesberg's printing press. He did his very best to save a few of his colleagues and their families. If I am not mistaken, the following were hidden there: 1) Kusik Landesberg with his wife, née Freundlich; 2) Nunek Nass with his family; 3) Oyzer Segal; 4) Kreminitzer.

Compliments of J. Lifshitz

[Column 141]

Wladek risked his life and took care of these people with great devotion.

When the hideout at Dubno's was discovered by Cap.Fueg, he ordered all the Jews to be shot save one. The exception was Mr. Sobel, an employee of the Bacon Factory who was promised his life and that he would be sent to Janowska camp in Lwow in return for information about Jews in hiding. This trick had often been used by the Nazi who, of course, never fulfilled their promise.

Sobel led them on to the Zuckerkandel bunker. Here things took a completely different turn from Dubno's hiding place. The murderers met with stiff resistance from the group who, seeing the hopelessness of their situation, decided to fight to the last breath. Armed with pistols, they defended themselves with skill and bravery. Kusik Landesberg succeeded in shooting the gendarme Radke who was notorious in the ghetto for his brutality.

The fight last two days. The gendarmes summoned an army unit to help them. There could be no doubt about the tragic outcome but nobody fell alive into the hands of the Nazi brutes. All this went on next door to Jakubowski's flat where the soldiers dropped in for a drink and I could hear them talking.

Under the cover of darkness, two men succeeded in escaping over the roof-tops. One of them was Kreminitzer who is now living in the U.S.A. The second survivor was Oyser Segal who lives in Israel. Wladek Bialobrzeski and Dubno's wife were arrested. I do not know what became of them. Sobel was shot for the services he rendered and never saw the Janowska camp.

Jakubowski, frightened to death by the events next door, decided not to hide me any longer. I had to seek an alternative place. Luckily I had a choice between Mr. Meyer or Kulpa in Jelechowice where my son and brother-in-law had already been for some time. As I had 'Aryan' documents provided for me by Mr. Meyer in the name of Bialecki, I could 'dive' into the 'Aryan' side of the country and 'get lost' in one of the big towns there. I preferred Kulpa's bunker.

[Column 142]

I do not intent to describe in all its horror this period of our life which lasted several months. Nor shall I mention here my daring adventure of leaving Kulpa's bunker on one occasion in order to save my poor sister from the Janowska camp and my eventful return. I shall only recall a few dramatic and near fateful moments but first, let us have a glimpse of our dwelling.

The bunker at Kulpa's was a hole dug under the larder and large enough for us to lay or sit. The entrance led from the kitchen. It was the size of a human head and served as the only source of fresh air for the three of us. It was as dark as a grave. Only at night, after closing the hole which meant blocking the air, did we sometimes dare to keep a small light burning for a few hours to enable us to read a bit. We spent our days talking in whispers about memories of our once human past. In those eleven months of 'cave-dwelling' we came out into the open only twice and had a wash about that number of times.

One of our anxious moments was when gendarmes unexpectedly appeared in the village to search for Jews. Of course, they visited our farm too but luckily without dogs who would have certainly detected us. We sat trembling with fear as we heard their voices above our heads and heard them say: "surely there must be Jews here?" At that Kulpa led them to the pigsty and pointing to the pigs said in bad German: "These are my Jews". They were treated to some liquor and refreshments and quickly left.

[Column 143]

Another nerve-wrecking experience was when a SS Waffen unit was stationed at Kulpa's farm for 10 days. Afraid to provoke the slightest suspicion, our protector did not contact us all that time. We had to starve and, what was worse, live in constant dread as we heard the Germans talking and walking above our heads.

We had our worst moment just before the liberation when the front halted for some time about ten kilometres or so from our village. The military authorities conscripted all men up to the age of 60, Poles and Ukrainians alike for urgent work. As Kulpa ignored the order, he was arrested to be court-martialed for his disobedience. His pregnant wife remained alone with three young children in their lonely cottage at the edge of the village. As she was afraid of the Germans and even more afraid of the Ukrainians who attacked the Poles wherever possible, she decided to return to her parents in a neighbouring village. She gave us two alternatives: 1) remain alone in our shelter with food for seven days; 2) leave for the forest.

We were in great despair as the countryside was full of Germans, soldiers and SS men but we were saved thanks to our patron's younger brother, Tadeus Kulpa who was employed by Mr. Meyer. He had been initiated into our existence and acted as a liaison between Mr. Meyer and ourselves. When he heard of his sister-in-law's plans, he threatened to shoot her if she abandoned us to our fate. To keep her spirits up, he offered to take care of her and the children until the return of his brother. I advised her to go to the commandant and beg him to release her husband because of her condition. She succeeded and brought him back home.

[Column 144]

Apart from these constant dangers, I worried all the time about my wife who was hiding in Warsaw and of whose fate I knew nothing about all this time.

26. The Liberation.

As the battle-front drew nearer, our tension and nervousness increased. Day-by-day strong formations of the Soviet Air Force relentlessly bombed the German positions near and around us. The deafening detonations of bombs were sweet music to our ears though they threatened our lives too. We knew no fear! In spite of our exhaustion, we eagerly awaited Liberation.

And at last, the great moment arrived! At dawn on 13th July, 1944, the first Soviet patrol showed up. Three very young Russian soldiers – young boys. We crawled out of our shelter. Blinded by the daylight and the tears in our eyes, unable to utter a word, we embraced and kissed those first harbingers of our freedom who stared at us like ghosts, for like ghosts we looked!

Our first reaction of happiness was followed by complete physical and spiritual collapse. We were no longer human beings but human wrecks on the verge of death. The three of us had shrunk to less than half our normal weight. My son Mark and I were unable to use our legs – disused for nearly a year in the shelter. We had to walk on crutches for several months.

In spite of the battles still raging, the few survivors began to emerge from their holes. The happiness of reunion was marred by deep sadness and mourning. How shocking was the balance! Of 14,000 Jews in the ZLoczow district, a handful of about six score remained. All had left the town save for two men – Vordernach and Schorr – a musician from Sassow.

Compliments of David Spitzer.

[Column 145]

Zloczow is still on the map as a Ukrainian-Russian town called 'Zolocziv' but Jewish Zloczow no longer exists. It lives only as a symbol in the hearts of our generation, former citizens of Zloczow who are now dispersed all over the world. Slowly this symbol is also fading away. The new generation knows little or nothing about the hometown of their parents and it is a tragedy.

May this volume remain as an everlasting memorial to a once flourishing Jewish community which was wiped out together with so many others in our century – the century of the greatest Holocaust in Jewish history.

After liberation, I remained until 1945 in Zloczow where I worked in the administration of army barracks. There I came across one of the participants of the 1941 pogrom on the Citadel, the notorious chimneysweeper Serba – a mass murderer who openly boasted of having killed ten Jews during the occupation by breaking their heads with a French key. I reported immediately on his activities to the prosecutor who started an investigation which was unfortunately shelved by the most powerful N.K.G.B. where Serba was employed.

In 1946, while I was a government servant of the Polish Republic, on one of my official sojourns in Warsaw, I met in the street near the railway station, a former Kripo detective in Zloczow, Volksdeutsche Ebert – the most dreaded Nazi in the ghetto. I had him arrested and he was sentenced to 15 years imprisonment in spite of the efforts of his influential brother who lost his position and was thrown out of the Party.

During an official tour in Wroclaw district in 1947, in the town of Sycow, a client announced himself requesting my assistance in some business matter. As I had been previously informed by a Zloczow Pole about a Ukrainian criminal hiding in Silesia under the disguise and name of a Pole, I was on the look-out for him and recognized him in my client; it was Pawliszyn, an accomplice of Serba who ravaged the ghetto during the pogroms. I took up the matter with the legal authorities, gave evidence in court myself and recommended a number of other reliable witnesses. The criminal was sentenced to death by the court in Wroclaw.

[Column 146]

In the same year, I was also a crown witness in the trial of SS Grzymek, the liquidator of the ghettoes and camps in Lwow and Zloczow. His trial created an international sensation as he confessed his participation in the sham attack of Poles staged of course by the Nazi in 1939 on the German Radio station in Bytom.

Selected SS men, disguised as Polish soldiers, attacked the Radio station and murdered the whole crew. This provocation was supposed to have been one of the immediate reasons for the outbreak of World War.

Grzymek was sentenced to death and executed.

As soon as I settled in Israel, I made contact with Mr. Friedman, the Director of the Historic Institute investigating Nazi crimes. I gave him all particulars known to me about Hauptsturmführer Warzok and his assistants.

In 1960 and 1961, I was interrogated as a witness by the Investigation Department of Tel-Aviv Police and the District Court in Haifa in connection with the Gestapo head in Tarnopol who had organized the first "action" in Zloczow – Herman Muller – arrested in Germany and sentenced for life in a court in Stuttgart.

****

(note: the author's account will be published separately).

Footnotes:

12. In accordance with the orders of the authorities, 25% of cooked, peeled potatoes were added to bread baked for the Jews and 10% of cooked, peeled potatoes for the non-Jewish population. The Germans received pure bread.
13. These facts are contained in reports to be found in the archives of the IWO in New York which are cited in Dr. Friedman's book: "The destruction of Lwow Jewry"
14. These facts are contained in reports to be found in the archives of the IWO in New York which are cited in Dr. Friedman's book: "The destruction of Lwow Jewry"

[Column 147]

In Memory of Dr. Moses Eisen

by Rabbi David Eisen

It is close to a quarter of a century, 1941, since my brother Dr. Moses Eisen, of blessed memory, was murdered by the Nazi and Ukrainian hordes. According to reports circulating at the time, he was beheaded with an axe.

"Remember what the German Amalekite has done to You". We shall never forget. For countless times we visualize this execution. In his adolescent years, he used to read to my mother, of blessed memory, about the pogroms in the Ukraine during the Petlura terror. The exact date of his execution is not known. Therefore, we remain mourners unto eternity, without fulfilling the ritual prescriptions of the Shiv'a and Kaddish. He was not buried according to Jewish law and we do not know his burial place until this day. He was our Moishe Rabeinu.

Only a leading son of Israel could have possessed so much humility and kindness structured into his personality. He was the favourite of the Jewish and non-Jewish community. Born in 1898, he received a religious Jewish education and a classical secular education. He stamped his personality upon our family whose main supporter he was in the years following World War I. In 1916, he was drafted into the Austrian army where he achieved the rank of lieutenant. Stories were told by returning soldiers that on the Italian front in World War I, he allowed the Jewish soldiers time for Minhah and Maariv services.

[Column 148]

After the war he returned to Zloczow where he was an active member of the Bar Kochba group, an academic Zionist organization. At the time of the Polish-Ukrainian riots in 1919, he was a member of the Jewish Selbstschutz.

His goodness was legendary. When Poland suffered from a deep economic crisis and economic anti-Semitism in the early 20's, he spent a few years with distinction as a teacher in the "Yavneh" Mizrahi schools led by Moishe Schorr, of blessed memory, first in the city of Wloclawek and later in Stolin Polesie. When he returned from Stolin he decided to finish the law course which he had interrupted in order to help a family of nine children; and he studied day and night by candle light under conditions of starvation. A piece of bread in his pocket and the legal scripts or books, walking and studying in the direction of the Folwarki was his physical and intellectual food for a number of years. He obtained his doctorate of law in 1930. During the years of his short life he was an active Zionist, attended conferences and participated in collections for Keren Kayemet and Keren Hayesod. His dream was Israel. But the British White paper, family ties and responsibilities were enough to invalidate any ideal. My great brother, who introduced us to the realm of culture and national religious sanctities, does not even have a grave. Let these few words serve as a memorial and monument. May his soul be bound with the living! Amen.

Compliments of The Children of Jacob Mass

[Column 149]

His intellectual partner was my sister Chaje Eisen, married to Hersch Horowitz – murdered in Lwow, year unknown. She graced the city of Zloczow with her deep knowledge of Hebrew and served for a while as a Hebrew teacher under the auspices of the Tarbut schools. She knew the Bible by heart as well as Modern Hebrew poetry. She taught for a few years in Kamien Koszyrski and matriculated with distinction after attending a Polish gymnasium in Lwow for only two years. She was the expression of our intellectual and spiritual potential. While attending school she had to support herself but nothing kept her back from achieving her academic and teaching goals to such an extent that she won the accolades of the highest educational authorities. In 1939, she became a mother until the Satanic German murderers liquidated a family of three persons.

Compliments of Sadie Suchman

[Column 150]

The youngest of the three children named Eisen was Malka, married to Moishe Greenspan. The year of her Kiddush Hashem is unknown as is that of her husband and daughter. They lived in Lwow. Malka symbolized innocence in its noblest sense. She suffered from the earliest years owing to economic stresses and craved to be united with the family, without effect. One third of our family was destroyed, the heart and soul of the family paralleling one-third of our nation.

May the Lord avenge them!

*****

[Column 151]

Beyond the Wall
(Aryan Documents)

by Mrs. N. Altman

The meaning of these words seems so innocent that one could suppose that those who succeeded in escaping beyond the wall – entered Paradise.

So, I would like to tell briefly my experiences in order to prove that life was Hell on Earth!

After all the horrors of the ghetto and the three "actions" in which my father, mother and younger brother were taken from me, everybody tried to persuade me to use my "Aryan look" and move to one of the larger cities in Poland.

In the beginning, I lacked courage and could not accept the idea of tearing myself away from my family. But my husband insisted saying that his plan of separation might grant us the possibility of salvation.

Such an argument; if not all the family, at least somebody might be saved, was terrible and cruel. The thought alone that I should leave behind my only son, husband and brother and go toward the unknown, drove me mad.

But in the end and because of my bad health, I gave in. My coughing attacks became worse and worse in moments of excitement so that our bunker was in danger of being detected.

[Column 152]

After many attempts, my husband succeeded in obtaining original birth and baptism certificates in the name of Maria Rubiczenska.

We consulted with our guardian angel, Mr. Joseph Meyer and it was decided that I would be employed as a housekeeper by an anti-Nazi but high-ranking clerk in Lwow.

I consoled myself with the thought that at least I wouldn't be far from my family and could get in touch with them through Mr. Meyer.

To my great sorrow, fate decided otherwise.

Due to an informer, the clerk who had already employed a young Jewess as a seamstress not only refused to accept me but was forced to send away the first one.

We had to abandon our plan or seek another opportunity.

It was in Mr. Meyer's office that my husband met a young Pole by the name of Kazyk. This young man said that he was ready to take someone, especially a woman, to the "other side".

Since Hitler's satanic plan was yet unknown, my husband did not regard the offer seriously.

In May 1943, after the failure of the Lwow plan, my husband met the young Pole once more. The later was still ready to help someone with a "good look". K. knew me and without hesitation agreed to take me. It was light-mindedness to rely upon a stranger but I did it in a state of mind that I could not describe nowadays.

Compliments of Sheindel Spitzer

[Column 153]

After a dramatic departure, frightened and crushed, I was driven to Warsaw. I later found out that K was a member of the Underground. He brought me to a village near Warsaw, to a family of workers.

I stayed there for only a month. The neighbours started to get interested in me. I was desperate and close to suicide. My guardian K did not appear. I felt like a hunted and wounded animal.

Finally K did arrive. He found a new shelter for me in Warsaw. This time it was with a widow whose daughter-in-law, Betya, was also a member of the Underground.

There I was known as the wife of a Polish officer who had been arrested by the Gestapo. And here, I also did not stay long. The former lodger, also a Jewess, warmed of the widow's son, then temporarily in Lwow: A dangerous hoodlum, a Jew-eater with a special talent for detecting them.

His wife, Betya, also warned me. And not long afterwards, she received a message saying that her husband was back.

As if all this was not enough, I was struck by a new calamity. During a bus-ride, my money and papers were stolen.

In those days, thieves used to take for themselves all valuables and give the documents, especially identity cards, to the police. There was danger that through my false identity, my true one would be found out.

At a loss and desolate, I did not know what to do. My only way out was my friend Lina Ber who lived with her small son in Milnowek where she was brought by her brother in 1942. They had Aryan documents and lived as Poles. I came to them, sick with fear and nervousness and Lina took me in and we lived together until liberation day.

[Column 154]

It was a life of want and need. From time-to-time we got help from the "Joint" but even this was very risky because of the secret agents who lay in wait and delivered the Jews to the police.

Fear was with us day and night. We became dead pale whenever a uniformed German happened to pass by our house and fainted with every knock at the door. At times we thought of leaving Milnowek and returning to Zloczow, to the bunker.

Meeting Ukrainians from Zloczow was especially dangerous. Still, I was lucky. I did meet some acquaintances from Zloczow but they were Poles. Decent people who were happy to see me alive.

One of my late brother's friends, Mondek, was even very happy and warned me against his sister.

My feelings when I went to the police to get a new identity card are indescribable. I had to have one for without an identity card it was forbidden to move in the streets. And staying at home was equally impossible because it drew the neighbour's attention.

The daily hunt for people never stopped and informers never rested. They squeezed their victims mercilessly and then delivered them into the hand of the Gestapo.

Weak in body and soul, I awaited the day of liberation. It seemed so near!

The Soviet offence began and at the same time, the Warsaw revolt. In vain. The Russians conquered Praga and stopped on the eastern bank of the Vistula.

The Germans crushed the revolt in fire and blood and the inhabitants of Warsaw ran away. Milnowek was filled with refugees among them a few Jewish survivors. Fear and hunger became stronger. Men and women were caught and sent to labor camps in Germany.

[Column 155]

I was also caught and brought to a camp in Prushkov. Due to the kindness of a Polish doctor, I was not sent to Germany. Our situation became worse from day-to-day but at last, the day of liberation came.

The Red Army conquered Warsaw. We were free. Free, but hot happy for I was deeply worried about my family.

[Column 156]

In March, 1945, hungry and beaten, I started on my way home. After three weeks of wandering, I was caught by the Russians together with a group of Ukrainians and accused of spying. They did not want to believe that I was a Jewess on her way home!

Miraculously, I was not deported to Siberia.

At last, I arrived in Zloczow, or rather – the cemetery of Zloczow. Among the few survivors, I found my family and after two years of separation, we were united again.

We all looked like skeletons.

The Leah Opel Women's Organisation

Compliments of Minah Mamber

[Column 157]

Between the Millstones

by Joseph Meyer, Munich

Fate did not treat me badly but not well either when it sent me to Zloczow in Galicia toward the end of 1941. When I say 'not well', the reason is because as a consequence of my service in charge of market organization, my duties in connection with provision of foodstuffs caused me to undergo experiences which have left an ineradicable impression on my soul.

Soon after my arrival in Zloczow, I learnt from Polish quarters that in July 1941 and shortly after the occupation of the town, no less than 2500 Jews had been killed in the Zloczow castle. I wished to convince myself of this and accordingly visited the fortress one day. It served as a prison and there were 300 Russian prisoners there. The sergeant-major on duty showed me the little hillocks under the wall which covered the mass graves. But, when I asked him the reason for this mass murder, he informed me that the Russians had done it.

[Column 158]

This information did not satisfy me. I felt doubtful and wanted to know more definitely about it. Dr. Altmann was the first who gave me clear information. I came to know him at the beginning of 1942 as a member of the Zloczow Committee for Social Self-Help and immediately recognized that he was a very reliable person who could be fully believed. When I declared myself to him as being an opponent of Hitlerism and told him that I had already found ways and means of helping both the Polish and Jewish population in my former post at Opatow and Radom, Dr. Altmann began to have confidence in me. When I asked him to inform his unfortunate brethren and sisters that as far as it was possible for me to help them without endangering myself, I would gladly do so, we became friends.

So it was natural that Dr. Altmann frequently became my guest in secret. Among other things, he naturally came with all kinds of requests for his oppressed co-religionists and I must admit that he often caused me to have considerable conflicts of conscience within myself. After all, I had to fear for myself and my own family if ever the Gestapo or German police were to begin to suspect the additional allocations I made in contravention of the National Socialist laws to Dr. Altmann for the Jews in the ghetto, the neighbouring camps and especially for the patients in the Jewish hospitals and the so-called 'Jewish Folkitche'.

Group of survivors with Joseph Meyer, the Righteous Gentile who helped them

[Column 159]

One case I still remember very well. In the summer of 1942, Dr. Altmann called on me most urgently to see that the Jewish "Self-Help Committee" should receive a large allocation of foodstuff.

Dr. Altmann justified his request in an impressive fashion by showing that there was a state of real starvation among the Jews which was causing the death of many of them including many little children. I cried in despair that I was helpless in this case but Altmann declared, with tears in his eyes, that he himself was aware that it was almost impossible to demand anything of me, yet he was convinced that I would find some way to present, or at least, to ease the dreadful situation. My conscience would not let me resist Altmann's appeal particularly as my knowledge of the diabolical methods used in the Hitlerist extermination system left me no doubt at all about the facts Dr. Altmann gave me. After mature consideration regarding the 'how to do it', I gathered my courage as a responsible citizen and decided to help in accordance with my conscience, in spite of all the dangers.

[Column 160]

I demanded large quantities of potatoes, sugar, millet, groats, etc., all for military units whose names and numbers I had to invent.

On a smaller scale, I often provided additional allocations for Jews in other towns of the Zloczow district such as Prezemyslany and Brody.

It was inevitable that I should be arrested by the Lemberg Gestapo at the beginning of 1943. It is to nothing but my good relations, particularly with the higher Field Command of Lemberg among whom there were many opponents of Hiterlism and particularly of the pogroms against the Jews whom I knew, together with the shortage of persons capable of organizing the market, that I owed my liberation from Lemberg prison after three days.

I would like to mention another case in particular. Early in July 1943, Dr. Altmann informed me that the workers in the camp workshops of the Strassler factory were building a secret bunker underneath the cellars in which about 30 persons could be hidden. At Dr. Altmann's request, I gave a corresponding allocation of non-perishable foodstuffs.

I really hope that by my actions I helped a few of those helpless sufferers to survive that dreadful and gruesome period and to reach the saving shore of life.

In this way, I believe that I have acted in the best way possible for my homeland and for the maintenance of human honour and self-respect in accordance with the commandments of God.

Compliments of E. Stolzenberg

[Column 161]

The Poet of Hatikva

by W. Winchel, N.G.

Fifty years ago, a poet was found unconscious on Forsyth Street in New York's lower East-side and subsequently died in a nearby hospital of starvation and cheap whiskey. He would have been unnoticed in the immigrant-filled bustle of the ghetto but for the fact that he was a writer of songs, songs in Hebrew, one of which was "Hatikva" – (The Hope). Ten thousand people lined the streets at his funeral and followed the hearse through the narrow streets chanting the immortal words of the song that was to become the national anthem of a new country – Israel.

The man's name was Naftali Herz Imber and the strange story of his life was recently told by the composer-conductor Franz Waxman. Mr. Waxman, on a recent conducting tour in Israel, came across the legends and tales of this modern François Villon and recently began to write a song cycle, based on the works of this almost forgotten poet. Even in Israel, the nation that sings his songs and speaks the language in which he wrote, few remembered his name. Waxman relates that Imber lay for 46 years in a simple grave at Long Island's Mount Zion Cemetery with only the words of his anthem engraved on a tablet to commemorate his genius. Four years ago, he was taken in honour back to Israel.

Compliments of Elias & Salomon Mayer

[Column 162]

Imber was born in the city of Zloczow, Galicia which is in the area now a part of Poland and was at that time part of the Austro-Hungarian Empire. He was a brilliant child from a poor, rigidly orthodox family. At the age of 8 he knew more than more 15-year olds and at 10, he was a fully-fledged Talmudist and a student of Cabala – the mystic interpretation of numbers in the Hebrew religion. At 12, he left home and began a roving existence that was to take him half way around the world.

* * *

He wandered down the Danube, stopping from time-to-time with various friends who provided for his formal education until adulthood. While working as a secretary to wealthy men or as a tutor to their children, the 19-year old poet aroused by the hopeless attitude of his people praying in their synagogues for a far-away land from which they had been banished some 2000 years earlier, scrawled 8 irate verses on a piece of paper and entitled them: "Tikvosenu" (Our Hope). The paper joined the others in his pocket.

[Column 163]

He passed through the Russo-Turkish War with the instinct developed as a Jew raised on the Russian border: - stay out of the path of the Cossacks. Wandering into Constantinople, he found work as secretary to a wealthy British couple – the Lawrence Oliphants, who took him to Palestine. He wrote profusely during his years in the country that was to emerge as a nation a half-century later and published his poetry in a volume called "The Morning Star".

* * *

With the death of Mrs. Oliphant, the idyll was over and Imber wandered on, finally arriving in England. He was a misfit because however he tried, he could never lose the philosophy of the Eastern European Jew. Material wealth meant little to him in comparison with spiritual and educational values. When he had money, he gave it away. All he acquired in England was the wrath of Israel Zangwill (who called him a schnorrer) and the trappings of the West; a cane, nationalism and a taste for alcohol. Ever a wanderer, Imber arrived in New York in 1892 in the steerage of a ship.

[Column 164]

Here his disappointment grew as he was given the treatment common to all immigrants of minor news value who do not know how to 'cash in' on their momentary glory. He was hailed by the press as a thinker, poet, and scientist for a day and then left to his own devices. "Tikvosenu" was chanted by Jewish immigrants to a folk tune of uncertain origin; they simply called it: "The Hope" – Hatikvah – and rarely connected it with the gaunt immigrant until he introduced himself. He also learned the N.Y. philosophy that his songs "and a nickel would get him a ride on the trolley".

He began to drink excessively and lived purely by his wits. "A good steak is better than a gilded epitaph" he sighed and turned out new poems. Their datelines: Chicago, St. Louis, Pittsburgh, Philadelphia, marked his meandering trail to the Lower East-side. In a St. Louis hospital, as he was about to be operated on for blood poisoning, he wrote a confession: "I cry like an erring child/ From my father's house driven -/ And Thou, Priest good and mild/ Speak out the word, 'Forgiven'".

Mr. Waxman pointed out that these latest poems were different. Their themes were personal, their sarcasms gentler and their language, English – the last tongue of the six or seven he had learned. On his return, he found a patron – a philanthropist who allowed Imber his strange whims and enjoyed the cavorting of this poetic court jester. It didn't last because Imber spent his entire month's allowance on a glorious 50th birthday party for himself to which he invited the entire Lower East-side. His patron punished him by cutting him off with a dollar a day. He arranged for the dollar to be hidden in a book in the New York Public Library's Jewish Division – the purpose to make Imber come and search for it while forcing intellectual nourishment before he would begin drinking.

Compliments of Lester Pundyk

[Column 165]

He became a comic figure even in his East-side haunts and like a good trouper; Imber played the part of the jester to the hilt. Evenings, on his round of the cafes, the gaunt poet would pay for his liquor in verses improvised on demand, in sardonic humour and paradoxical brilliance until he was carried home.

Often now, he thought of death. "Wine they give me but they would not give me a burial", he bemoaned to an undertaker friend. The friend promised to bury him in exchange for a poem. A contract was drawn up and the verse: "A grave as a cure for sickness" fulfilled Imber's part of the bargain. The pauper made his will. "To the Rabbis I leave what I don't know – it will help them to a longer life. To my enemies, I leave my rheumatism. To the Jewish editors, I leave my broken pen so that they can write slowly and avoid mistakes".

Compliments of Milton & Paula Tenenbaum

[Column 166]

He deteriorated almost hourly but his pockets continued to bulge with scraps of paper. Those who joked about: "his carrying his life's work with him" came close to the truth. The scribblings of Imber's years of decline, published posthumously, contained a wealth of material. In mid-September, 1909, he finished a Hebrew poem on the Hudson-

Fulton celebration and was taken to Mount Moriah Hospital with " a complication of diseases". He remained in the hospital just long enough to write a humorous obituary of himself and "under the charm of the mild autumn weather", as the New York Times reported, - he "left and wandered to all his old time haunts". The next morning he was found unconscious on a street corner and brought back to the hospital. He died at dawn on October 8th, the day of Simchas Torah (The Holiday of the Testament) and a Jewish newspaper ran his obit with the caption: "On this day, all drunkards are sober".

*****

[Column 167]

Zloczow, A City of Poets

by Sol Katz

Most of us know by this time that the man who wrote the words of Hatikvah, the Jewish song of hope, was a Zloczower, Naphtali Herz Imber. While in Israel last summer, I witnessed a Persian Jewish wedding. The Persians sang Hatikvah with gusto but when I asked people around me whether they knew the name of its author, most of them said it was Chaim Nachim Bialik.

Around the years of 1908 and 1910, a number of Zloczower intellectuals came forward with books of poetry in Yiddish. The first one was Samuel J. Imber, a nephew of Naphtali Imber. He named his publication "Wus Ich Zing un Zug" (What I sing and say). This book received a warm reception in the Jewish press and established him as a poet. The Jewish literary magazines of Warsaw and other Jewish centres were open and ready to print his prose and poetry. In 1927, S.J. Imber spent a few months in New York. Here he published an Anthology of Yiddish poetry. It was a heavy volume of 350 pages and contained, among others, poems written and published previously by M.L. Halpern and Jacob Mestel as well as those written by S. Imber himself. The book contained a novel idea. It did not use the Hebrew alphabet; instead, the Roman alphabet was used. The translators tried hard to convey the pathos and beauty of Jewish poetry to the non-Yiddish reader. Although an outstanding scholar and poet, S. Imber never achieved the stature of his uncle.

[Column 168]

Moishe Leib Halpern's writings were published in New York around 1930 under the name of: "The Goldene Pave (The Golden Peacock). He was acclaimed as the "Heinriche Heine of East Broadway". Of Halpern, Imber writes the following in his introduction to the Anthology: "One of the first, M.L. Halpern found himself far from the beaten track. With an unusually bold stroke, he pierced the time-worn sheath of poetical sentimentalism. In his weaker moments, however, he comes back with songs in which strongly pulsates that kind of old poetry which ever remains young and is never ashamed of its sentiments". Although Halpern won recognition as a leader of the young poets and had his works accepted and published in the Yiddish press (which at that time enjoyed a fabulous prosperity); he was in great financial need most of the time.

Compliments of Sol Katz

[Column 169]

Jacob Mestel, another native of Zloczow, published in Lemberg a book of poems entitled: "Ferchulemte Shuen (Twilight Hours) in about 1910. He later became active in Jewish drama. He was the first to stage Ansky's Dybbuk for the theatre in Warsaw and also directed it into a wonderful cinema production. In New York, he was active mostly in the Jewish theatre. His work seemed to follow the path of J.L. Peretz, touching the borders of mysticism and Kabbala.

[Column 170]

There were also some minor poets in Zloczow who succeeded in having their poetry printed. Max Zwerdling started to write while in Gymnasium. Shija Josephsberg was another minor poet to whom I acted as "consultant" and friendly critic.

Zloczow was indeed a town of culture.

Mrs. Minna Mamber in Israel

Compliments of Wife & Children of Nathan Preiss

[Column 171]

The Youth of Zloczow

by David Eisen

The city was known as a Zionist fortress, constantly electing in the national election to the Sejm, proven Zionists whose names were glorified by young and old. The contributions of the Jewish community to Keren Kayemet and Keren Hayesod were considerable in view of the hopeless economic conditions of the members. The Jewish youth was a colourful mosaic of different organizations and Zionist groups, keeping in tune with the organizational structure of Israel. There were dreamers and idealists who left Poland, the homes of their parents, in the early nineteen twenties, to build a new life, a new Jewish nation in the Promised Land. Dov Opper, of blessed memory, the founder of Hashomer Hatzair, immortalized the name of Zloczow by giving his life on the shores of Kinneret for an independent Israel.

In the two decades between 1918-1939, it became clear to every Jewish youngster that the only solution to the Jewish problem was Eretz Israel. Their longing and nostalgia for Israel found its expression within the

[Column 172]

walls of every organization in the form of discussion and song, starting with the Revisionist organization, Betar, Zeirei Agudath Israel, Zeirei Mizrachi, Bnei Akiva, Gordonia, Herzliah, H.A.C., Hechalutz and Zeirei Zion. Each group had its own hachshara preparation for hopeful immigration to Israel. The membership of these groups included also youngsters from neighbouring towns and villages. The frustration and agony of the youth, because of the closed-door policy of Britain, knew no limits. Most of the gymnasium students swore allegiance to one of these organizations. The loyalty and devotion to organizational life reminded one of the lives of the first pioneers in our Holy Land. Hebrew was a prerequisite for intelligent development and growth. The songs and dances which filled the air of the kepa-park cegielnia, the lawn near the first or second (zakret) of the Zloczowka, in the beautiful summer nights were exclusively in Hebrew. Our non-Jewish neighbours enviously observed the behaviour of the youth, finding it hard to explain how Jewish children motivated by ideals of Jewish renaissance, without supervision and direction from official spheres, grew in terms of personality, national pride and stamina.

Compliments of Nathan Recht

[Column 173]

It was enough to go out to the kepa-park and to fill your heart with euphoric joy at the sight of youngsters born in the Diaspora singing in thrilling voices their love for Zion, their readiness to sacrifice their lives for Israel. The leaders of small groups (kvuzoth) were held in high esteem and affection. To this position they qualified by reasons of personality and culture. Their meetings, two or three times a week, were educational along the lines of the Zionist movement, its history and Hebrew culture, etc.

Every meeting ended with songs and hurrah. A deeply moving experience were the hikes, a few miles from the city. This was a whole-day affair. The whole membership participated in affairs of this type. Discussions and games were the highlights of the hike after reaching the point of destination. Males competed for their ideal females, trying to win the heart of the happy girl through debates in discussion, bravery in games and physical prowess. Many emotional unions were thus consummated and in later years, sanctioned by marriage. The religious groups, Zeirei Agudath Israel, met in their headquarters and learned early in the morning the Daf Hayomi. The Zeirei Mizrachi combined in a wonderful synthesis, old and new Jewish culture and tried to impress its members with our rich heritage based on Torah.

[Column 174]

Each member of any group craved for self-realization and the first step toward fulfilment was Hachsharah. The behaviour pattern of the members of different groups, appearance and poise, differed in accordance with their ideological stress and emphasis. You would never find a member of Bnei Akiva without a hat, whereas members of Gordonia & Hashomer Hatzair would parade in their unique style which meant to express freedom from convention and tabooed behaviour. To think that this intelligent mass of youth-humanity was wiped out, murdered in the early spring of their lives, in the midst of hopes and dreams for a re-born Israel, of readiness to die for our Holy Land, equals an atomic destruction of our world that we knew and loved. They didn't live to see the fruits of their hopes. Their lives were mainly spiritual, woven on the canvas of idealism. Physically hungered to death, with the song of Zion on their lips, they have won eternity. We are all partners of this great legacy which they left behind. They were our eyes and heart, the embodiment of our wishes and cravings. We were not there at the time of their execution! We couldn't wipe their tears in their hour of agony. Let us remember them and never forget. Yisgadal Veyiskadash shmei rabo.

NAME INDEX

Pfau, 296, 319

Pfeferstein, 319
Phillipson, 57
Pichinik, 180
Pilsner, 320
Pinkas, 319
Pinnes, 54
Pinnles, 55
Pitznik, 59, 254
Planer, 50
Podoshyn, 321
Polak, 321
Polasiok, 332
Pollinger, 370, 371
Poplawska, 369, 388
Pordes, 292
Postin, 17
Potashnik, 77
Praeger, 347, 348
Prager, 99, 100, 289, 383
Präger, 320, 321
Preger, 161
Preis, 186, 319, 320
Preiss, 401
Pressman, 320
Presstadt, 319
Princess Sapieha, 9, 11
Printz, 140, 143
Pshebislavski, 287
Pulwer, 320
Pundyk, 349, 360, 399
Pundyk, 319

R

Rabinowitz, 47
Radke, 379, 389
Radziwill, 9, 10, 11, 18
Raler, 147
Raller, 142
Rapoport, 45, 50
Rash, 342
Raviv, 193, 275, 282

Recht, 322, 402
Reichard, 106
Reichenstein, 322
Reikh, 158
Reikhert, 169
Reinhardt, 362
Reis, 46, 171, 179, 281, 286, 322

Reiser, 3, 173, 322, 323

Reiss, 208
Reitsis, 80
Reitzis, 277
Reiz, 136, 137, 163, 177

Reizer, 2, 182, 185, 186, 250
Rekhen, 39, 41
Rekht, 62, 144, 249, 294
Retel, 29
Rezen, 139, 144
Riez, 136, 146
Ringel, 323
Riss, 205
Ritter, 52, 191, 332
Rittses, 64
Ritvomatsov, 123

Rohatiner, 97
Rohatyn, 16, 43, 48, 49, 52, 61, 76, 77, 142, 205, 230, 231, 232, 233, 234, 235, 236, 237, 243, 251, 267, 273, 291, 292

Rokakh, 204. 205, 207
Rokeakh, 23, 58, 130, 207, 218

Roller, 64, 191, 192, 193, 217
Ron, 3, 65
Rosen, 78, 98, 171, 209, 321, 343, 378, 381

Rosenbaum, 208, 322

Rosenberg, 43, 46, 136, 162, 322

Rosenboim, 61, 78, 171, 205, 249
Rosenfeld, 190
Rosenkrantz, 277
Rosenman, 321
Rote, 322
Rotehnburg, 164
Rotenberg, 50
Rotenshtreikh, 158
Rotfeld, 354, 355
Roth, 337
Rothchild, 53, 171
Rotstein, 322
Rott, 286
Rozen, 110
Rozenbaum, 104, 168
Rozhi, 295
Rozner, 190
Rubchinska, 118
Rubin, 41, 99, 208, 348, 351
Rubinstein, 45
Ruler, 45, 289, 191

Rupin, 179
Ruten, 144, 209
Rutiner, 121

S

Sadan, 90, 277
Safran, 101, 109, 110, 112, 346, 358, 385, 386, 387
Safran, 323

Yosefberg, 46, 333

Yosefsberg, 76, 84, 137, 179, 275, 281, 282, 283, 299
Yottes, 241

Z

Zalkai, 84, 267
Zaltz, 156, 176, 209, 296
Zalzborn, 356
Zangwill, 54, 399
Zaurhof, 294
Zbarazer, 211
Zborovski, 8, 11

Zeiden, 137, 139, 164
Zeidman, 190
Zeliger, 224
Zelinger, 277
Zelkai, 77, 173
Zeltkis, 172
Zeltz, 77, 143
Zendberg, 185, 186
Zidenworm, 248
Zigel, 48, 172, 196, 203, 204
Zigmunt, 349

Zilbershitz, 186, 191, 243, 244, 245, 247, 294, 299

Zimand, 101, 107, 186, 332
Zimand, 330
Zimmer, 330, 343

Zindwarm, 156, 209
Zinke, 349
Ziper, 331
Zitzdemer, 331
Zlatkes, 99, 330, 345, 346, 347, 348

Zlatkis, 180
Zlatopolsky, 217
Zlotsover, 21, 210
Zlotsovsky, 11
Zneoda, 180
Zolkver, 16
Zoyerhoif, 159
Zucharkandel, 330
Zuckerkandel, 346, 347, 348, 349, 350, 365, 366, 367, 368, 370, 375, 380, 386, 389
Zunker, 330
Zusman, 62, 191, 245, 246, 247, 294
Zvierhoif, 145

Zwerdling, 106, 330, 333, 337, 348, 352, 355, 377, 382, 384, 401

Zwillinger, 105, 379

www.ingramcontent.com/pod-product-compliance
Lightning Source LLC
Chambersburg PA
CBHW082005150426

42814CB00005BA/235